Industrial Locomotives of Durham

Coal, for use at home or abroad, has been the basis of Durham's industrial greatness. Lambton Staithes, Sunderland, with the disused Hetton Staithes beyond, in July 1966, six months before closure.

INDUSTRIAL LOCOMOTIVES of DURHAM

HANDBOOK L

Compiled by Colin E Mountford and   L G Charlton

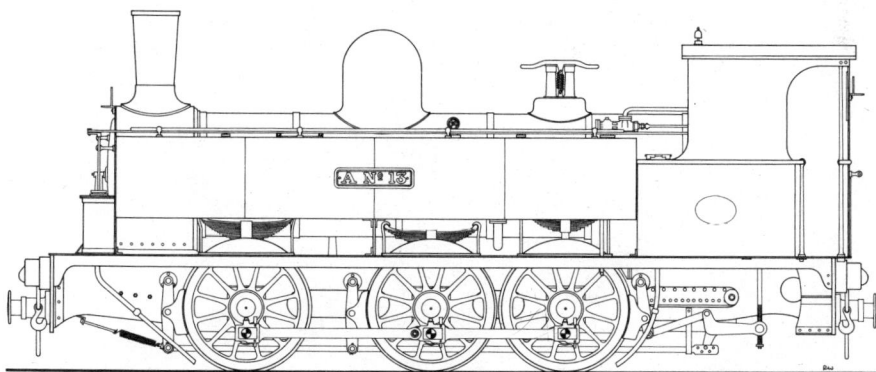

Consett pannier tank A No 13 − drawing by   Roger West

INDUSTRIAL RAILWAY SOCIETY

Published by the INDUSTRIAL RAILWAY SOCIETY
at 4 Adam and Eve Street , Market Harborough , Leicestershire

© INDUSTRIAL RAILWAY SOCIETY 1977

ISBN 0 901096 30 X (hardbound)
ISBN 0 901096 31 8 (softbound)

Printed in Great Britain by AB Printers Ltd , Leicester

Distributed by IRS Publications, 47 Waverley Gardens , London NW10 7EE

CONTENTS

PREFACE

Co. Durham is an area of striking contrasts. Few counties have such a wide variety of mineral wealth, and for most people it will always be associated with heavy industry. Yet Durham has never suffered the endless industrial sprawl of South Yorkshire, nor the barren desolation of some South Wales valleys. In the coastal plain which forms two-thirds of the county, farming continued while colliery villages remained villages; while in the west the Pennine Dales retained their beauty and peace.

Coal gave North-East England its pioneering place in the English Industrial Revolution. In Durham the coalfield lies beneath virtually all of the coastal plain and far out to sea, the numerous seams thicker and closer to the surface in the west, thinner and deeper in the east. Through it run the three rivers of Tyne, Wear and Tees, which provided the early transport so essential to the development of the industry. Moreover, in the early nineteenth century it was found that coal from West Durham made the best coke in the world, while in the east it was excellent for gas production. By 1914 the expansion of the industry was complete, and the county was raising annually over 45 million tons.

This development was linked with the growing iron industry, which was first to be found in west and central Durham because of iron ore deposits in Weardale and around Consett, but after the discovery of the Cleveland ironstone deposits in mid-century, the industry became increasingly centred on Teesside. Not only were massive deposits of coal and iron close at hand; so too were vast quantities of limestone, not only in Weardale but in many other parts of the county. In Weardale this was especially fortunate, for as the lead industry of the upper dales declined its workers became absorbed into the huge quarries carved out of the Great Whin Sill. In turn, these three industries stimulated the growth of both shipbuilding and railway engineering, making Durham one of the most famous industrial areas in the world.

Today Durham presents a very different picture. The coal industry continues; but the west has largely been abandoned, and in the east the future lies only in collieries drawing on under-sea reserves. The iron and steel industry survives, but not without the threat of closures. All locomotive building, both main line and private, has already gone, and although shipbuilding remains, many staithes and docks have closed, leaving trade a good deal less than what it was. Quarrying in the east of the county survives, but in Weardale it is almost extinct. In place of the old heavy industries, Durham has become an area of industrial estates and new towns, struggling with new industries and office blocks to regain the prosperity which has been lost.

In most industrial development in England in the nineteenth century the initiative was taken by local businessmen, who borrowed capital to lease land, set up works or sink mines. In Durham too this holds true after about 1840, especially in the iron and engineering industries. But in the coal industry it was much more common for the landowner to work the coal under his land himself (as it was in parts of the Midlands). This was notably so in the older areas of mining. In the early nineteenth century the Tyne valley was controlled by Lords Ravensworth and Strathmore, while the Wear valley was dominated by the Lambton family (later Earls of Durham) and the Marquis of Londonderry. Only in the south of the county does one find typical entrepreneurs - often Quakers - such as the Pease family.

This pattern had a marked effect on the county's railway development. In other parts of the county coal owners invested money in public railways and then ran their own wagons over the lines to the ports for shipment. In South Durham the Peases were behind the Stockton & Darlington Railway; but in the rest of the county the proprietary interest led to the building of private railways. This was not only to fulfil a need; equally important was a desire to control their activities completely and to reduce costs. This lead was followed by later companies, so that the development of private systems, even if only a few miles long, continued virtually until the turn of the century.

i

The coal owners' initiative provided much of the impetus and money behind locomotive development too; but having done this, the colliery railways veered away significantly from later technological development. Instead of locomotives - or even horses in some places - rope-worked inclines were built all over the county, and developed to a refined standard unknown elsewhere. Even though locomotives were later introduced in many places, a considerable number of inclines were in use in 1900, and a handful still survive, having seen the steam locomotive come and now go.

Because of its historical development, the coal industry continues to be the main operator of industrial locomotives in the county. Besides inclines, it remained faithful to steam locomotives too for many years, but by the beginning of 1976 only one regular steam locomotive working survived - at South Hetton. Elsewhere - the iron works apart - few firms still use rail transport, most having gone over to road haulage. All over the county one can see the abandoned trackbeds of both British Rail and private lines, a desolate reminder of a past age. Yet not quite: for while locomotive working on the surface has rapidly declined, it has expanded underground, not only in coal mining, but also in the growing Weardale fluorspar industry.

Although this book is basically a revised version of the original Pocket Book 'L', published in 1962, it bears little resemblance to it or to the experimental Pocket Book 'F' (North Wales), published in 1968. It was decided at an early stage to exclude the Teesside area from the new edition, not only to keep the planned size of the work within reasonable limits, but also because economically Teesside is more a part of North Yorkshire, or even an independent unit, than part of Co. Durham. The area of the county thus defined has been retained, despite the huge local government re-organisation of 1974, which took the whole of southern Tyneside, Washington and Sunderland into the new county of Tyne & Wear, and Hartlepool into the new County Cleveland, which also includes Teesside and part of North Yorkshire. This edition, however, does include the 1974 merger of the National Coal Board's Northumberland, North Durham and South Durham Areas, which begins a new era in the industry.

On the other hand, this new edition contains a large amount of historical information, much of it previously unpublished, both on the companies and private railways, including their methods of operation. Even a brief examination of this will reveal the extremely complex nature of railway development within the county; so to try to help the reader find his way about more easily, the indexes have been greatly enlarged and many more maps have been included, together with a wide variety of photographs.

Such an expansion is the result of many years of painstaking research. Every company in the county still using locomotives, and many of those whose rail traffic has ceased, willingly made their records available to us. The National Coal Board, with the extensive help of many of its employees, kindly made available not only their own records going back over twenty years, but also the records of constituent companies where these survived. We were fortunate to have access to steam locomotive records in a period of such rapid change, for sadly many of these have since been destroyed, either because diesels or road transport replaced steam or because the works or colliery has now closed. We have also made extensive use of the Durham County Records Office and many local libraries and institutes, as well as the kind use of so much work done by our friends and predecessors. We are sincerely grateful to everyone who has so willingly and patiently helped us, and we hope that in seeing the finished work they will feel it was worthwhile.

Yet not finished: for while we hope that what we have eventually committed to paper is accurate, we are only too aware of the large gaps which remain in our knowledge, and of the further research which awaits attention.

The current locomotive position given in the book was accurate to 1st April 1975, except for the NCB. where the current position was brought up to 31st December 1975.

The history of Co. Durham's industrial railways and locomotives is one of the most complex and varied in the country. We hope that through this new edition others may gain a similar interest and pleasure from its study.

December 1975   Colin E. Mountford
                                                 L. G. Charlton

EXPLANATORY NOTES

GAUGE: The gauge of the railway system is given at the head of the locomotive list.

NUMBER and NAME: A number or name formerly carried is shown in brackets ( ); one unofficially bestowed and used by the staff but never carried by the locomotive is shown within inverted commas " ". A dash indicates that no name or number was carried.

TYPE: In general the Whyte system of classification is used, but when the driving wheels are not connected by outside rods they are shown as 4w, 6w, as the case may be. The following abbreviations are used:

T	Side tank or similar - denotes a tank positioned externally but fastened to the frame, and includes wing tanks.
CT	A tank locomotive fitted with load-lifting apparatus.
PT	Pannier Tank - side tanks not fastened to the frame.
ST	Saddle Tank
WT	Well Tank - tank located between the frames below the level of the boiler.
VB	Vertical-boilered locomotive.
D	Diesel locomotive : unknown transmission system
DE	Diesel locomotive : electric transmission
DH	Diesel locomotive : hydraulic transmission
DM	Diesel locomotive : mechanical transmission
P	Petrol locomotive : unknown transmission
PM	Petrol locomotive : mechanical transmission
BE	Electric locomotive powered by a battery
WE	Electric locomotive supplied by current from overhead wire
F	Fireless steam locomotive
F	in conjunction with DM or DH denotes "flameproofed mines loco"
TW	Tower wagon

CYLINDER POSITION:
  IC   Inside cylinders
  OC   Outside cylinders
  VC   Vertical cylinders
   G   with geared transmission

MAKERS: Abbreviations to denote locomotive builders are listed on page 358.

MAKERS NUMBER and DATE: The first column shows the works number and the second shows the date which appears on the works plate, or the date the loco was built if this was not shown on the plate. N.B. The date given here may be different from the delivery date, especially if the locomotive was delivered early in a new year.

REBUILDING DETAILS: As there are widely-differing views as to what constitutes a "rebuild" of a locomotive, we have tried to include only those which are known to have resulted in a structural change to a locomotive.

SOURCE OF LOCOMOTIVE: "New" indicates that the locomotive was delivered from the makers to the location. A transfer from elsewhere is denoted by a bracketed letter, the full details, including date of arrival, being given in a footnote where the information is known. If the locomotive changed owners but remained at the same location, the full date is given.

DISPOSAL OF LOCOMOTIVE: Similarly, a locomotive transferred to another location is shown by a bracketed number and footnote, the date of departure being given if it is known, and the full date if the locomotive changed hands but remained at the same location. Sales to scrap merchants are not shown unless the context requires it. In other cases the following abbreviations are used:
  Scr   Loco cut up for scrap on the date shown (if known)
  s/s   Loco scrapped or sold : disposal not known

Many sales of locomotives were effected through dealers or contractors, and to avoid repetition abbreviations are used for most of these, details of which are given in the table below. If no location is shown, the loco either went direct to its new owner or else definite information is lacking. If a direct transfer is known to have been effected by a dealer, the words "per" or "via" are used.

GENERAL ABBREVIATIONS

c	circa; i.e., about the time of the date quoted
contr	contractor or contractors
form.	formerly
orig.	originally
prev.	previously
reb.	rebuilt
reg.	the date on which a company was registered
ret.	returned (after loan or hire)

FOOTNOTE ABBREVIATIONS

Adams	A.R.Adams & Son, Pillbank Works, Newport, Mon.
APCM	Associated Portland Cement Manufacturers Ltd
BV	Bolckow, Vaughan & Co Ltd, Middlesbrough, Yorks, N.R.
Bungey	G.W.Bungey Ltd, Hayes, Middlesex
DL	Dorman, Long & Co Ltd, Middlesbrough, Yorks, N.R.
DP	Disposal Point (for opencast coal)
Ellis	James W.Ellis & Co Ltd, Swalwell, Co. Durham
ESC	English Steel Corporation Ltd
Frazer	R.Frazer & Sons Ltd, Hebburn, Co. Durham
Galloways	Galloways Ltd, Manchester
GS	Generating Station
ICI	Imperial Chemical Industries Ltd
MOM	Ministry of Munitions
MOS	Ministry of Supply
Mowlem	John Mowlem & Co Ltd
NCB	National Coal Board
NCBOE	National Coal Board Opencast Executive
Pauling	Pauling & Co Ltd
PP	Pease & Partners Ltd
Pugsley	J.Pugsley & Sons Ltd, Stoke Gifford, Gloucs.
Ridley Shaw	Ridley Shaw & Co Ltd, Middlesbrough, Yorks, N.R.
ROF	Royal Ordnance Factory
SDSI	South Durham Steel & Iron Co Ltd
SLP	Sir Lindsay Parkinson & Co Ltd
SRM	Sir Robert McAlpine & Sons Ltd
TIW	Pease & Partners Ltd, Tees Ironworks, Cargo Fleet, Yorks, N.R.
TJR	Topham, Jones & Railton Ltd
TWW	Thomas W.Ward Ltd
Wake	J.F.Wake & Co Ltd, Darlington, Co. Durham
WD	War Department

In addition to the above, the usual abbreviations for locomotive builders and main line railways are used in footnotes where appropriate.

DATES IN FOOTNOTES: Where it is known, the date of disposal is given with the month and the year. However, when the location merely passed to new owners, the locomotives not moving, the full date (day/month/year) has been given whenever possible.

DOUBTFUL INFORMATION: Information which is known to be uncertain is followed by a question mark (?). In addition, whilst every care has been taken in the compilation of this book, we do not preclude the possibility that some errors may have been missed during proof reading, and would much appreciate these being brought to our attention.

MAPS

        In the first series of maps Co. Durham is divided up on a grid system, as shown on the master grid map. These maps are lettered from A to Z,and the locations on each map are numbered upwards from 1, the combined reference (e.g. A1) being given alongside each location in the text. This series of maps is as follows:

In addition, all the major colliery railway systems are included:

On both series of maps the symbols used are identical; these are shown below

——————————————— North Eastern Railway

++++++++++++ private standard gauge railway

-o-o-o-o-o-o-o-o-o-o- running powers over North Eastern Railway

- - - - - - - - - - - narrow gauge railway

++━━━━━━++++ engine powered incline

++++++++++++ self-acting incline

■ colliery

o mine

🪨 quarry

underground connections and aerial ropeways noted as such

PHOTOGRAPHS

Before about 1950 few people took a photographic interest in Co.Durham's industrial railways and locomotives apart from those who worked on them. Thus photographs from this period available now are usually either copied from originals discovered during research or taken from sets of negatives which have fortunately survived. Since 1950 more photographs have been taken; but with all industrial work certain allowances must be made. Most photographs have to be taken on private property, often on a day previously arranged with the management; thus photographers, few of whom are professionals, are frequently compelled to work quickly and in poor weather conditions to take shots which they often cannot repeat. We are aware that some of the photographs included here are for various reasons poor in quality; but we feel that their exceptional historical interest outweighs their technical defects.

In compiling this collection we have attempted to include every type of locomotive used in the county, including some "freaks"; we have also tried to incorporate examples of the standard locomotives of the main builders, together with locomotives from as many local builders as possible, including firms who built their own. Within this framework we have tried to include locomotives from as wide a range of owners as possible, and in the National Coal Board section to trace locomotive policies since 1947.

We are sincerely grateful to all our friends who have so generously allowed us to draw on their work and collections.

The photographs were taken as follows:

J.Adams : 17, 18; I.S.Carr : 36, 47, 48, 71, 115, 131; F.G.Carrier : 8, 83; D.Charlton : 22, 24; L.G.Charlton : 1, 4, 13, 14, 19, 20, 29, 31, 33, 38, 50, 51, 54, 55, 62, 75, 76, 77, 80, 81, 89, 90, 93, 108, 109, 116, 118, 120, 121, 123, 124, 125, 126, 130; L.G.Charlton's collection : 3, 5, 6, 11, 15, 25, 53, 57, 59, 60, 63, 82, 84, 86, 88, 97, 101, 103, 104, 112; T.D.A.Civil : 100; J.Clewley : 78, 111; K.Coolbear : 67; courtesy North of England Open-Air Museum, Beamish : 30; courtesy N.C.B. : 139, 140; courtesy South Tyneside Libraries : 58, 99; F.Jones : 7, 23, 37, 41, 42, 43, 44, 49, 52, 61, 66, 68, 69, 72, 73, 74, 87, 94, 105, 106, 107; F.Jones' collection : 12, 28, 46, 64, 85, 102; C.J.Kenyon : Frontispiece, 79, 119; C.E.Mountford : 2, 16, 21, 27, 32, 34, 39, 40, 45, 56, 65, 70, 95, 96, 110, 113, 114, 117, 122, 127, 128, 129, 132, 133, 134, 136, 137, 138, 141, 142; C.E.Mountford's collection : 9, 10, 26, 35, 92; B.Roberts : 91; A.E.Tyler : 135; B.Webb : 98; P.Weightman (Stephenson & Hawthorn Loco Trust) : 143, 144.

SECTION 1

GRID MAP and MAPS A to Z

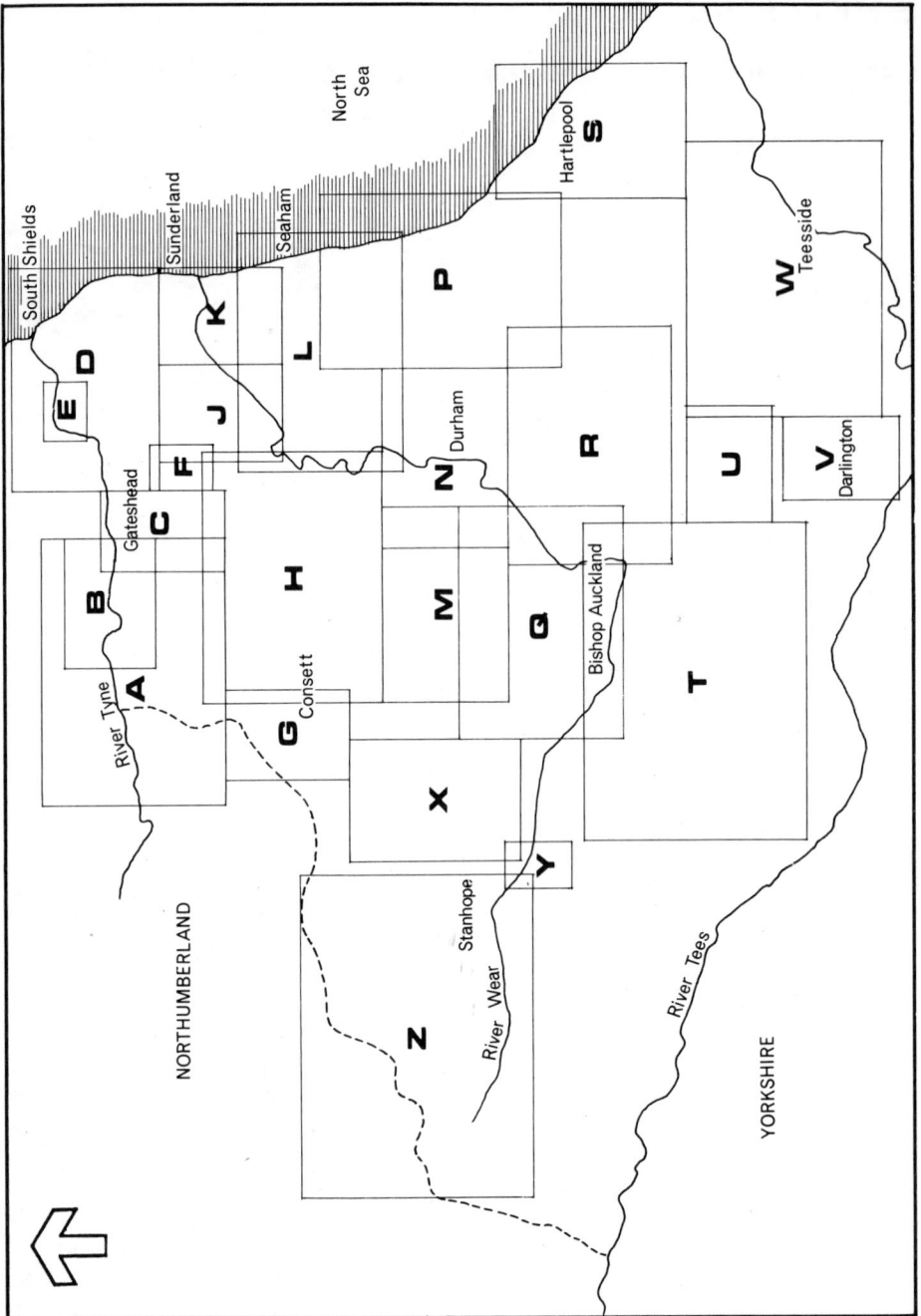

North Sea

South Shields

Sunderland

Seaham

Hartlepool

Teesside

Durham

Darlington

Gateshead

Consett

Bishop Auckland

Stanhope

River Tyne

River Wear

River Tees

NORTHUMBERLAND

YORKSHIRE

A B C D E F G H J K L M N P Q R S T U V W X Y Z

A North West Durham

miles $\frac{1}{2}$ 1 2 3 4

R. Tyne

to Carlisle

Prudhoe

NORTHUMBERLAND

DURHAM COUNTY

to Blackhill

to Newcastle

Ryton

Greenside

Blaydon

Whickham

Swalwell

aerial ropeway

R. Derwent

Chopwell

Chopwell and Garesfield Railway

Whittonstall Railway

underground railway

Tanfield branch

for this area see enlarged detail map B

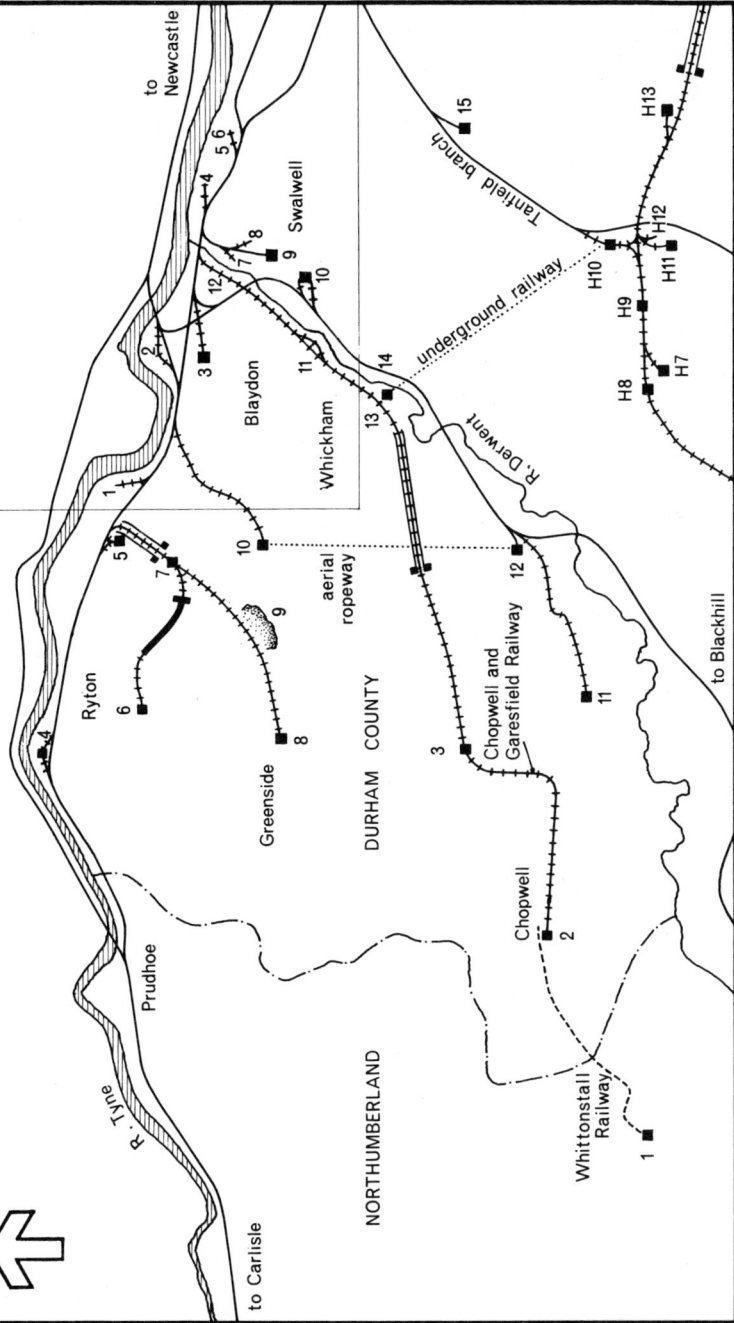

1 2 3 4 5 6 7 8 9 10 11 12 13 14 15

H7 H8 H9 H10 H11 H12 H13

3

B Swalwell and Blaydon

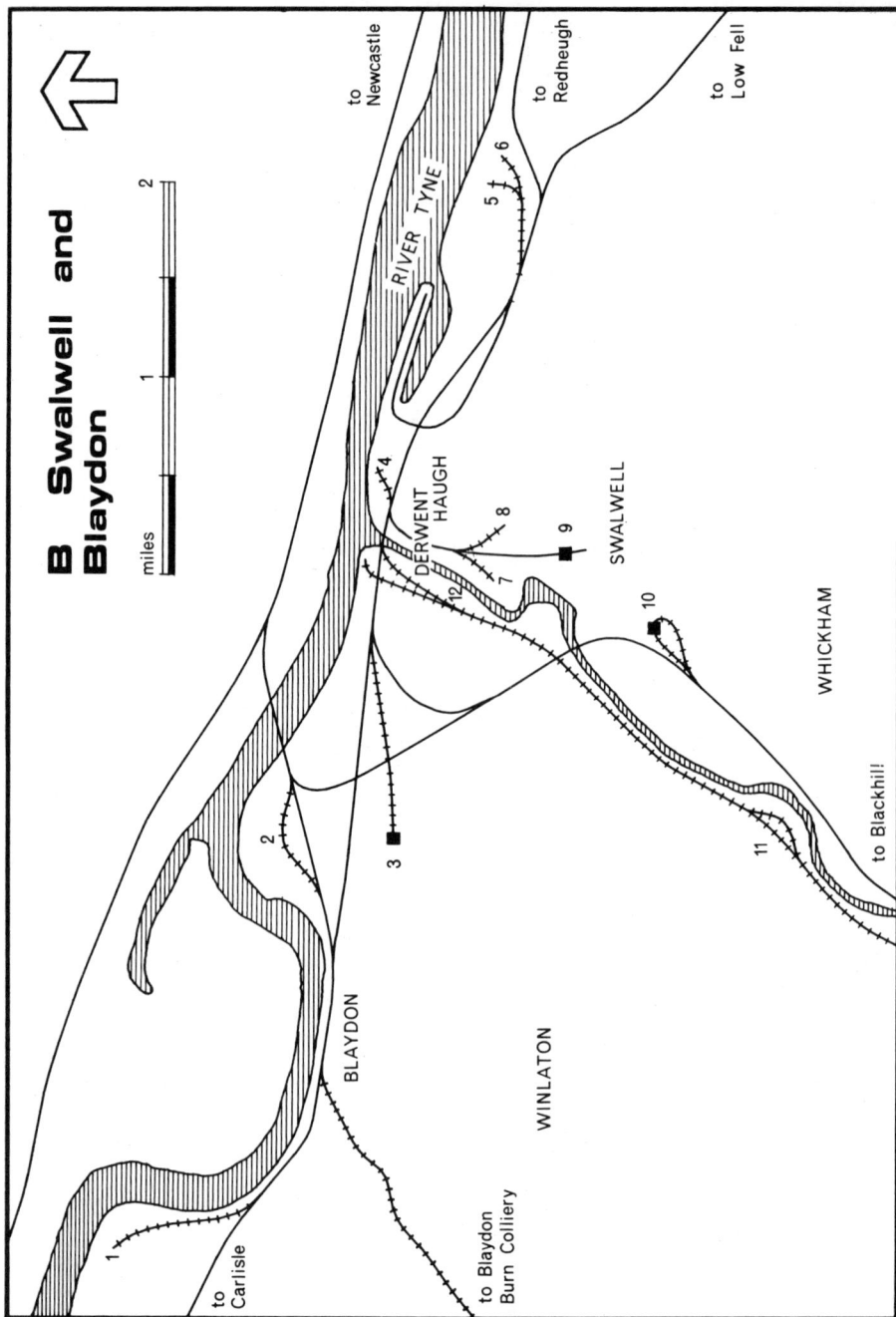

miles

2 1

to Newcastle

to Redheugh

to Low Fell

RIVER TYNE

5 6

4

DERWENT
HAUGH

8

9

SWALWELL

7

12

10

WHICKHAM

2

3

11

BLAYDON

WINLATON

to Carlisle

to Blaydon
Burn Colliery

to Blackhill

1

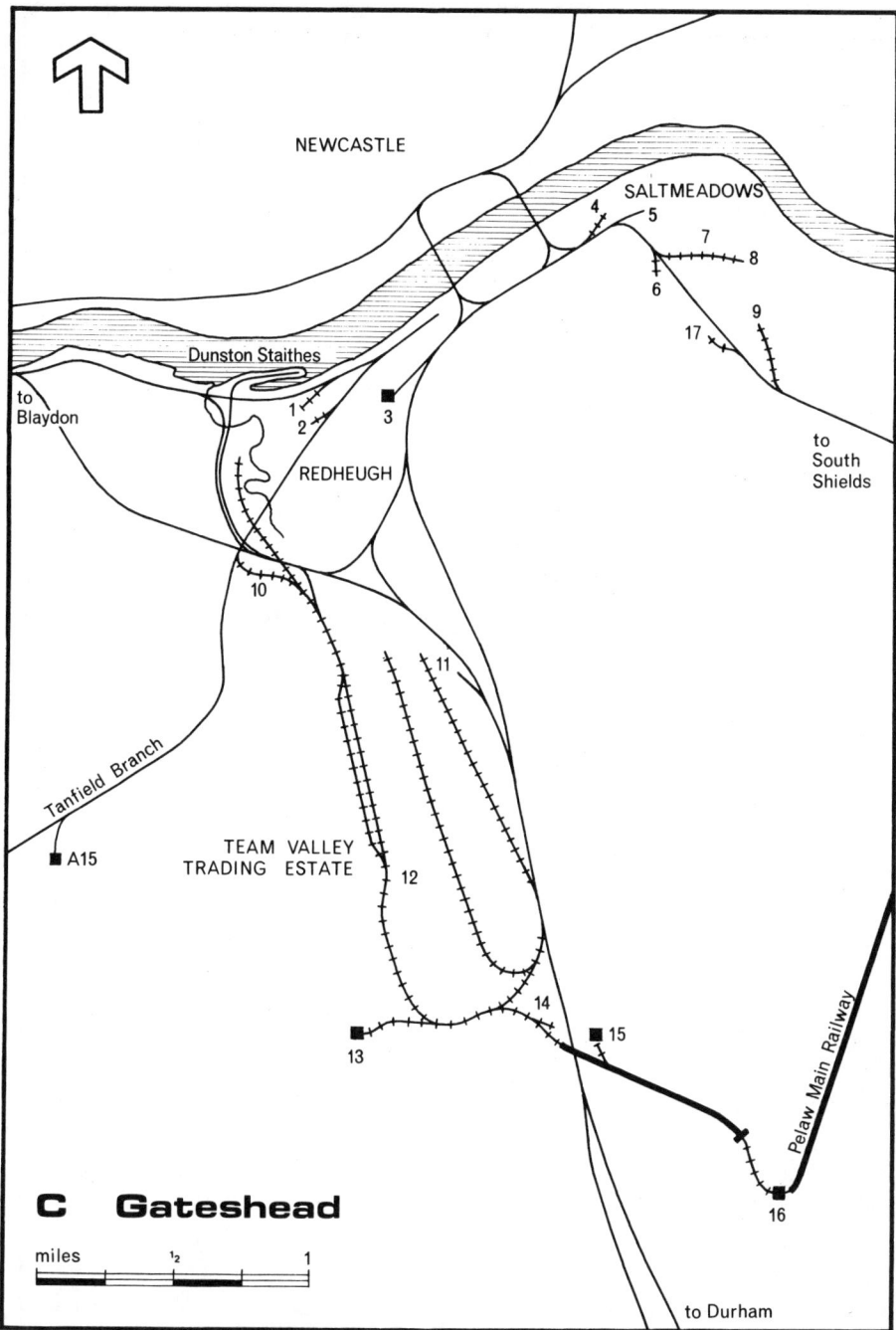

NEWCASTLE

SALTMEADOWS

4
5
7
8
6
17
9

Dunston Staithes

to
Blaydon

1
2
3

REDHEUGH

to
South
Shields

10

11

Tanfield Branch

A15

TEAM VALLEY
TRADING ESTATE

12

13

14

15

16

Pelaw Main Railway

C Gateshead

miles   ½   1

to Durham

D Felling and South Shields

miles

unknown location 16

for this area see enlarged detail map E

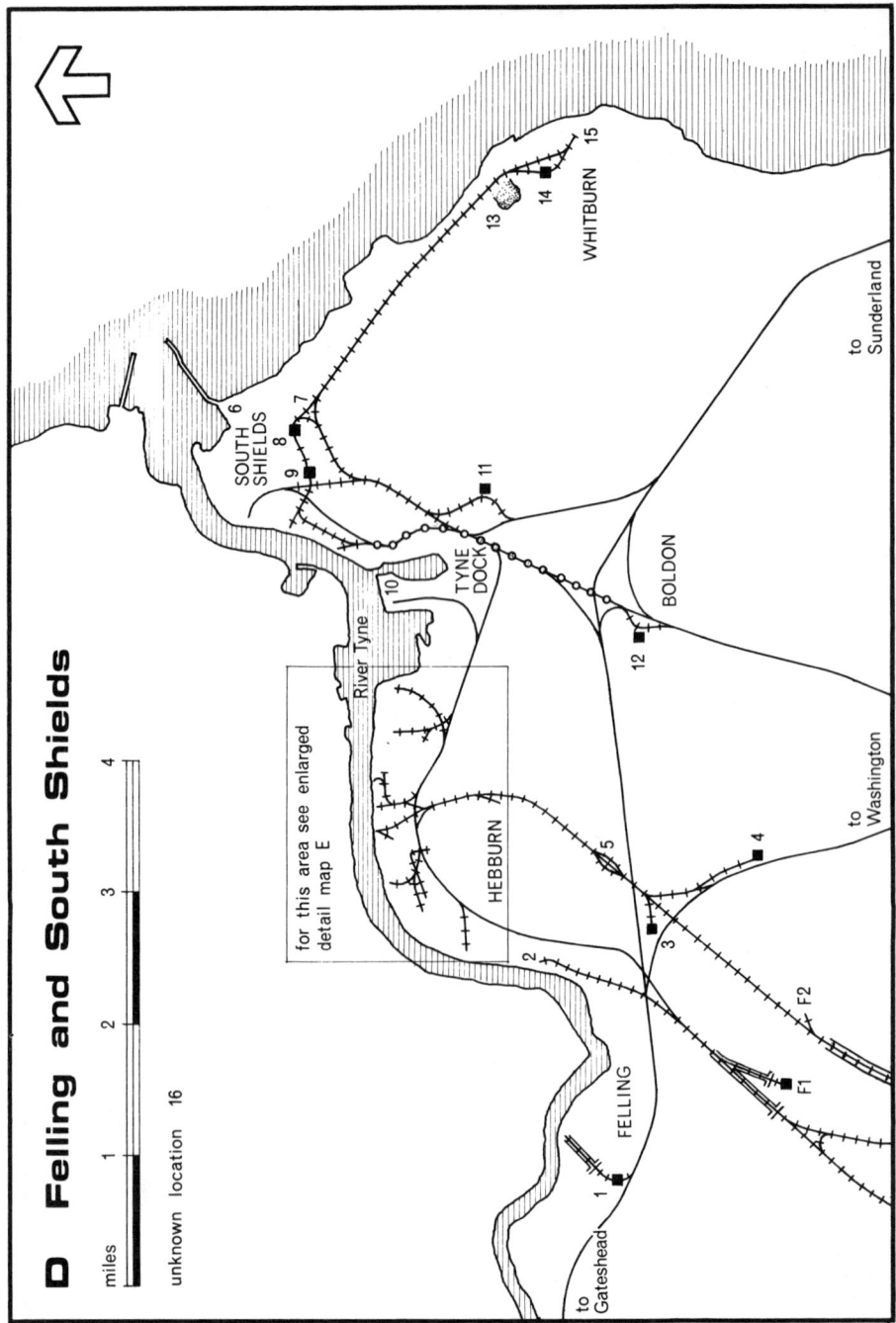

River Tyne

SOUTH SHIELDS

TYNE DOCK

HEBURN

FELLING

WHITBURN

BOLDON

to Gateshead

to Washington

to Sunderland

F1
F2

E Hebburn and Jarrow

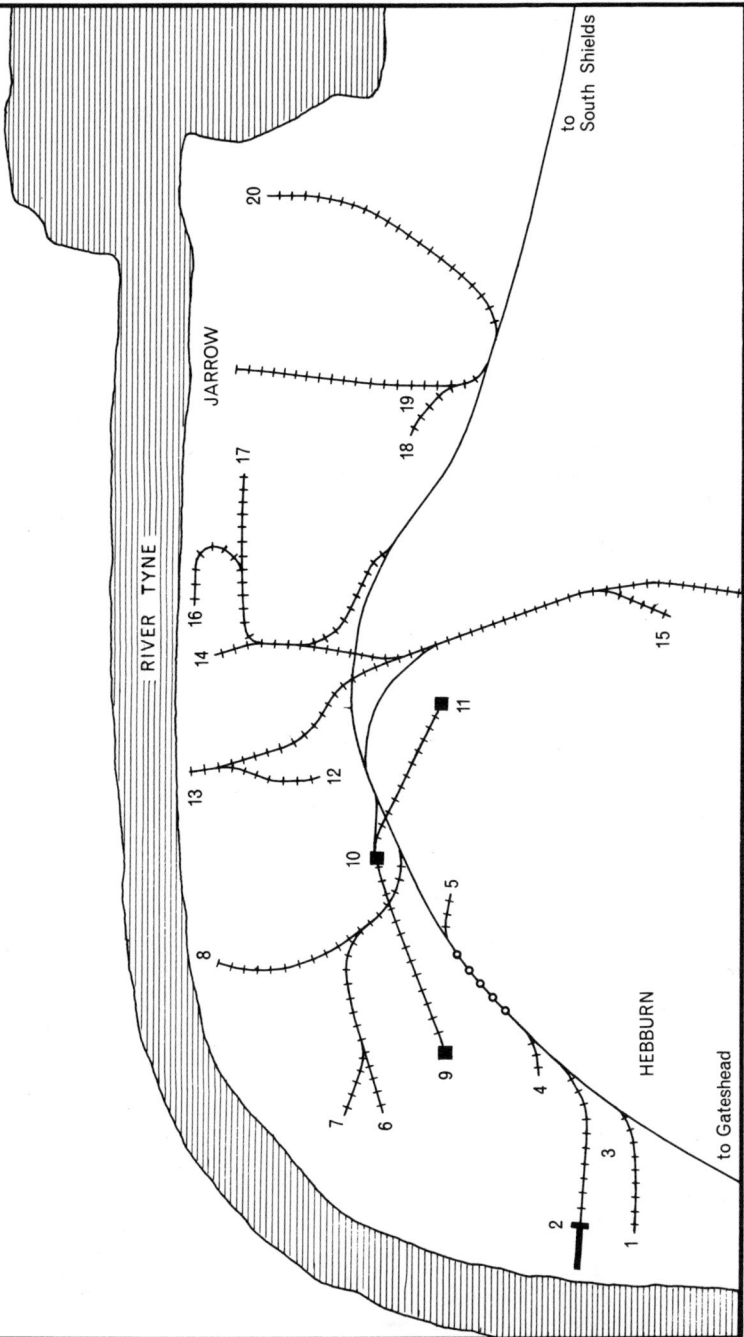

miles

RIVER TYNE

JARROW

HEBBURN

to South Shields

to Gateshead

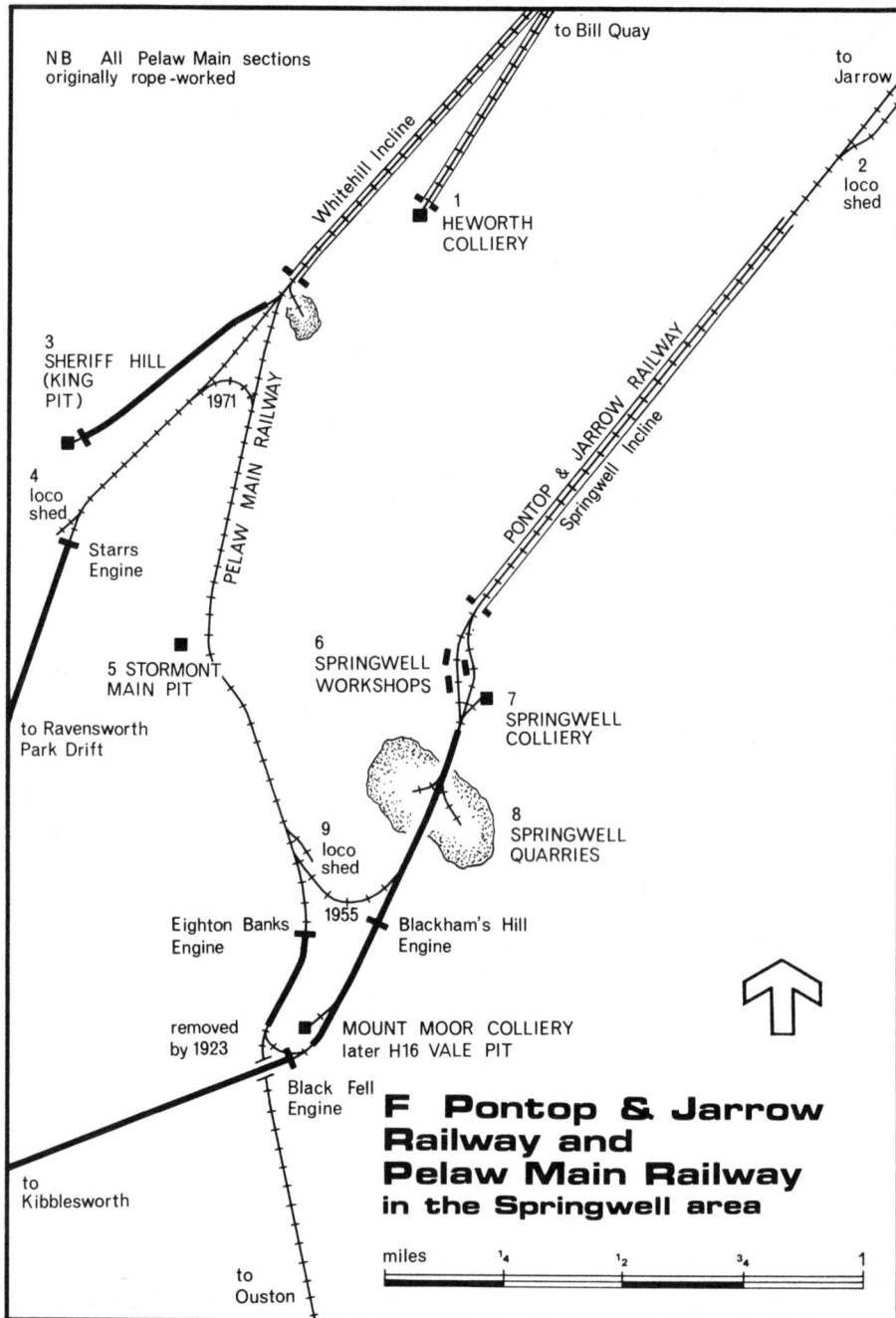

to Bill Quay

to
Jarrow

Whitehill Incline

2
loco
shed

1
HEWORTH
COLLIERY

3
SHERIFF HILL
(KING
PIT)

1971

PONTOP & JARROW RAILWAY

Springwell Incline

PELAW MAIN RAILWAY

4
loco
shed

Starrs
Engine

6
SPRINGWELL
WORKSHOPS

5 STORMONT
MAIN PIT

7
SPRINGWELL
COLLIERY

to Ravensworth
Park Drift

9
loco
shed

8
SPRINGWELL
QUARRIES

1955

Eighton Banks
Engine

Blackham's Hill
Engine

removed
by 1923

MOUNT MOOR COLLIERY
later H16 VALE PIT

Black Fell
Engine

to
Kibblesworth

**F Pontop & Jarrow
Railway and
Pelaw Main Railway**
in the Springwell area

to
Ouston

miles   ¼   ½   ¾   1

G Consett from 1948

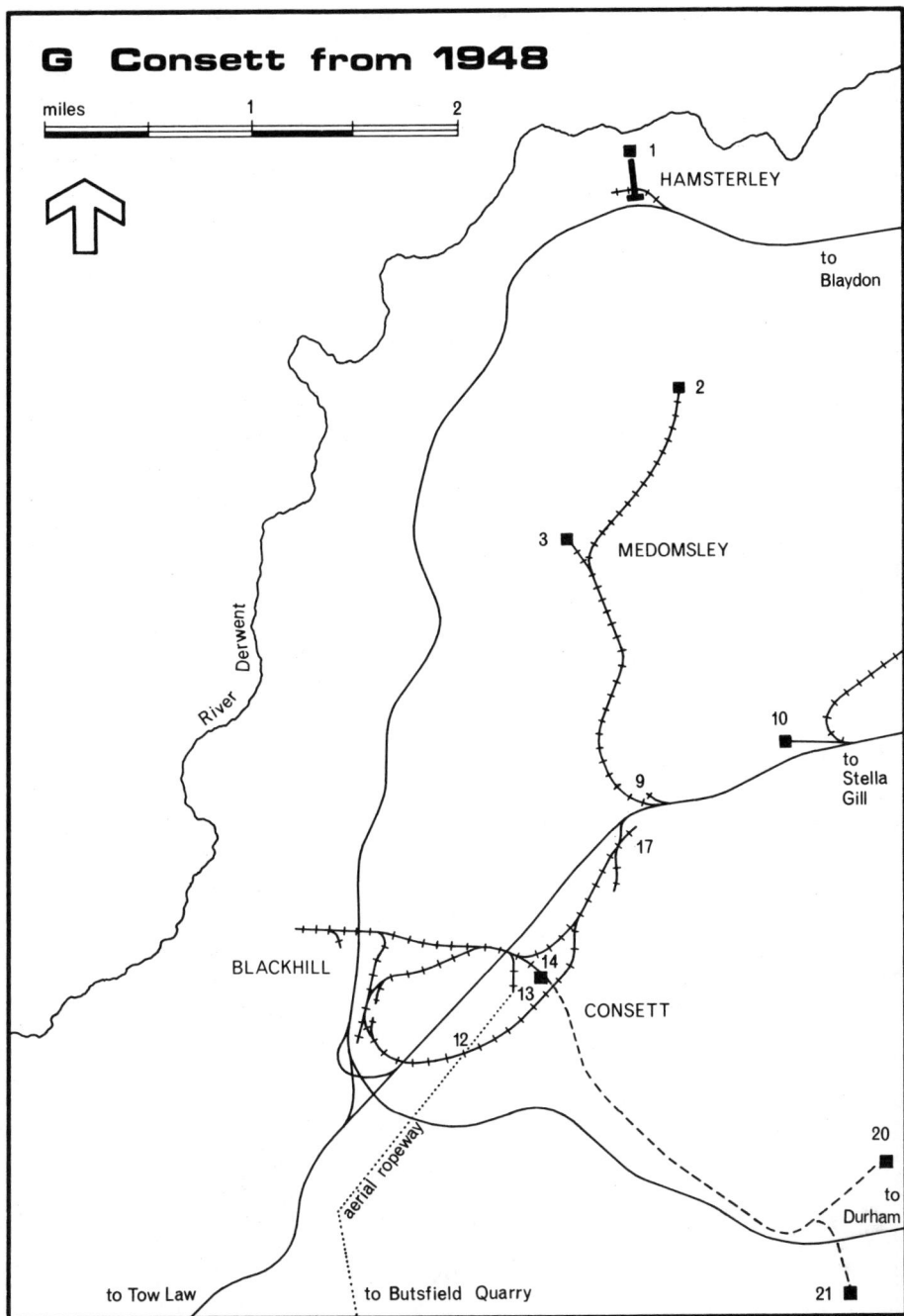

miles

1 2

1 HAMSTERLEY

to
Blaydon

2

3 MEDOMSLEY

River Derwent

10

to
Stella
Gill

9

17

BLACKHILL

14

13

CONSETT

12

20

aerial ropeway

to
Durham

to Tow Law

to Butsfield Quarry

21

9

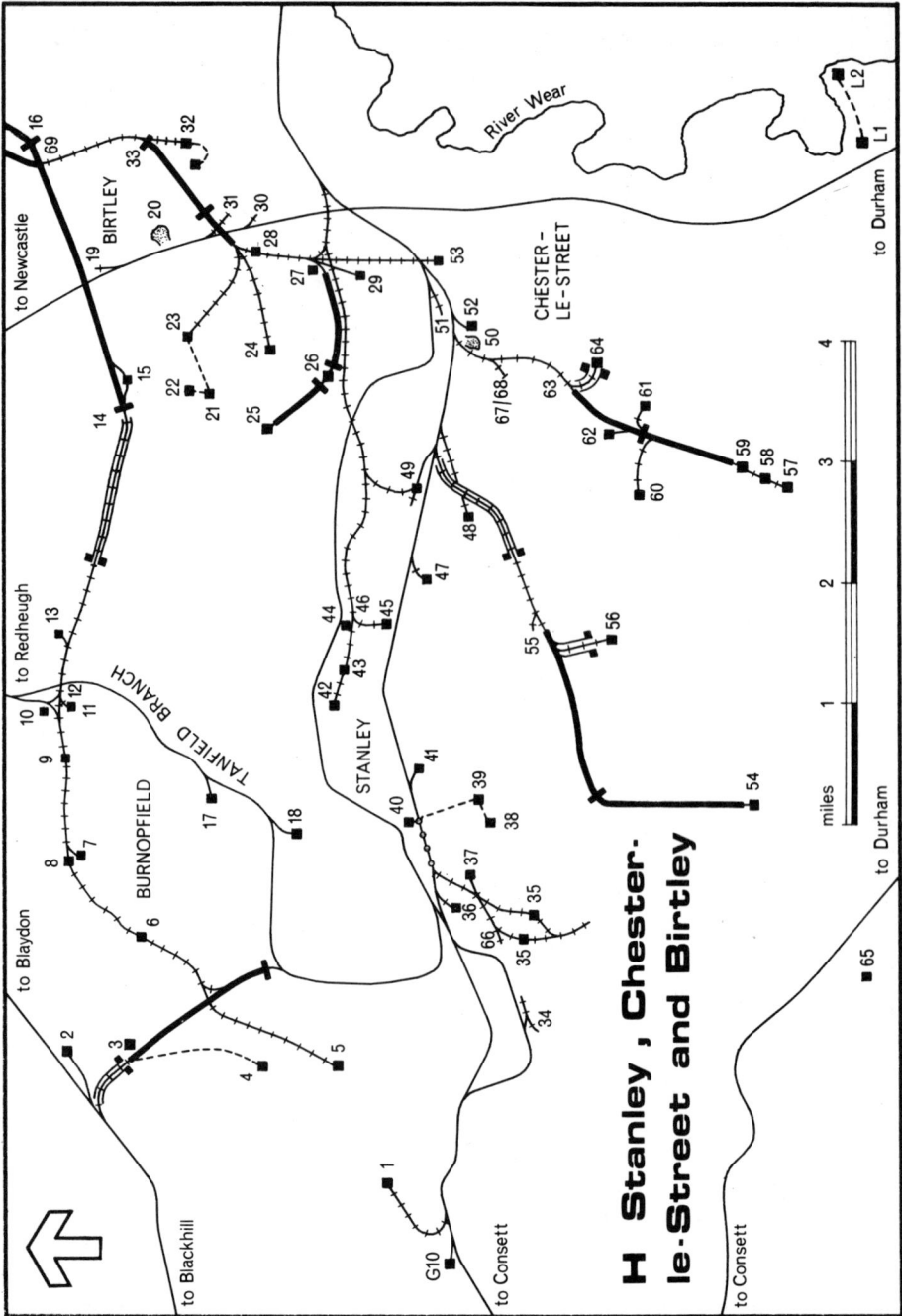

H Stanley, Chester-le-Street and Birtley

J Washington

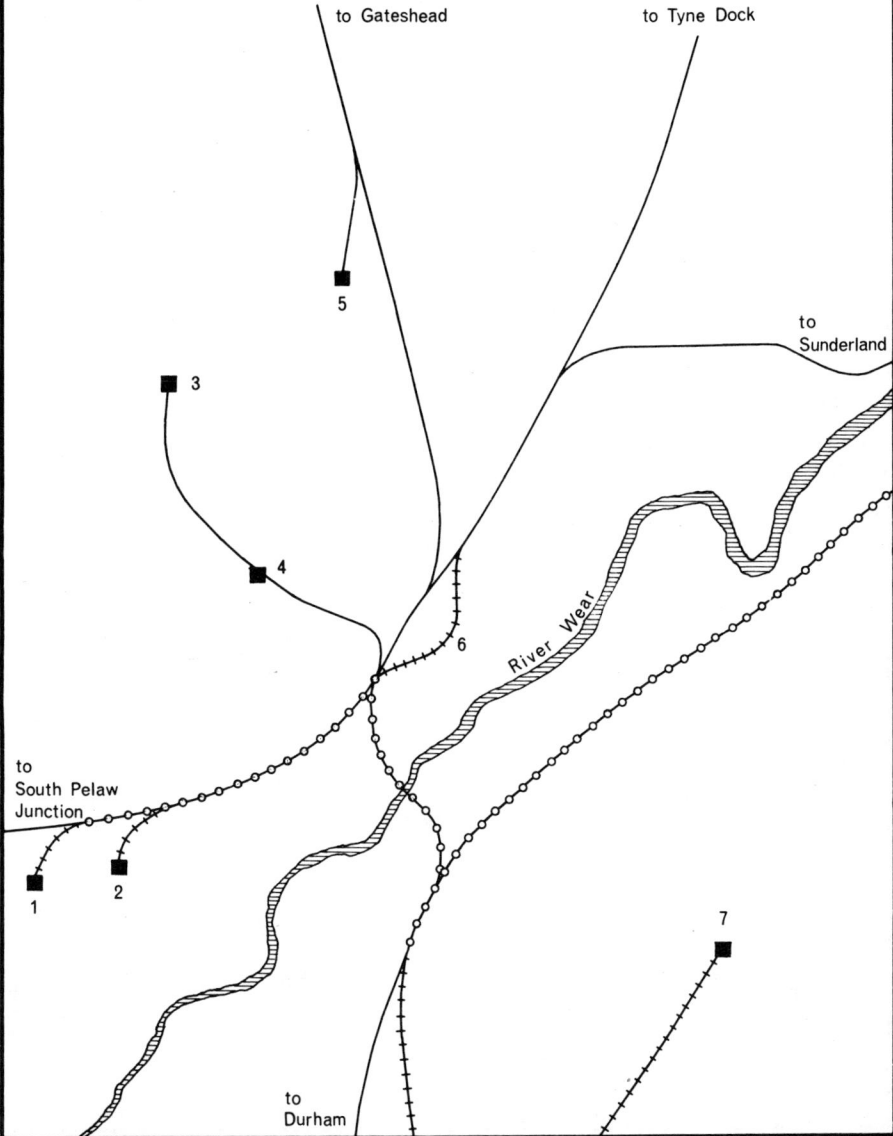

miles

to Gateshead

to Tyne Dock

to Sunderland

River Wear

to South Pelaw Junction

to Durham

1

2

3

4

5

6

7

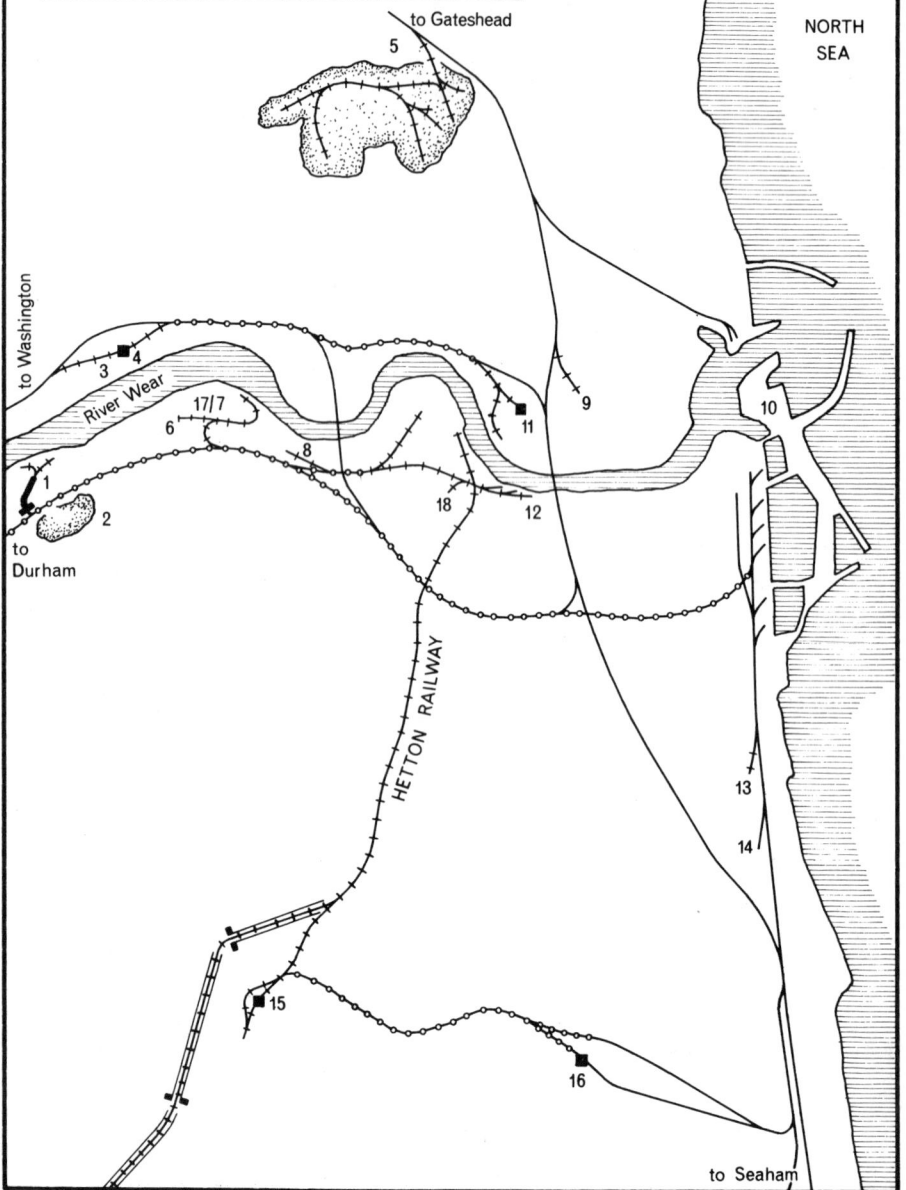

K Sunderland

miles 1 2

to Gateshead

5

NORTH
SEA

to Washington

River Wear

3 4

17/7

6

8

11

9

10

1

2

18

12

to
Durham

HETTON RAILWAY

13

14

15

16

to Seaham

12

L Houghton-le-Spring, Hetton-le-Hole, Seaham Harbour

miles

SEAHAM

to Sunderland

to Hartlepool

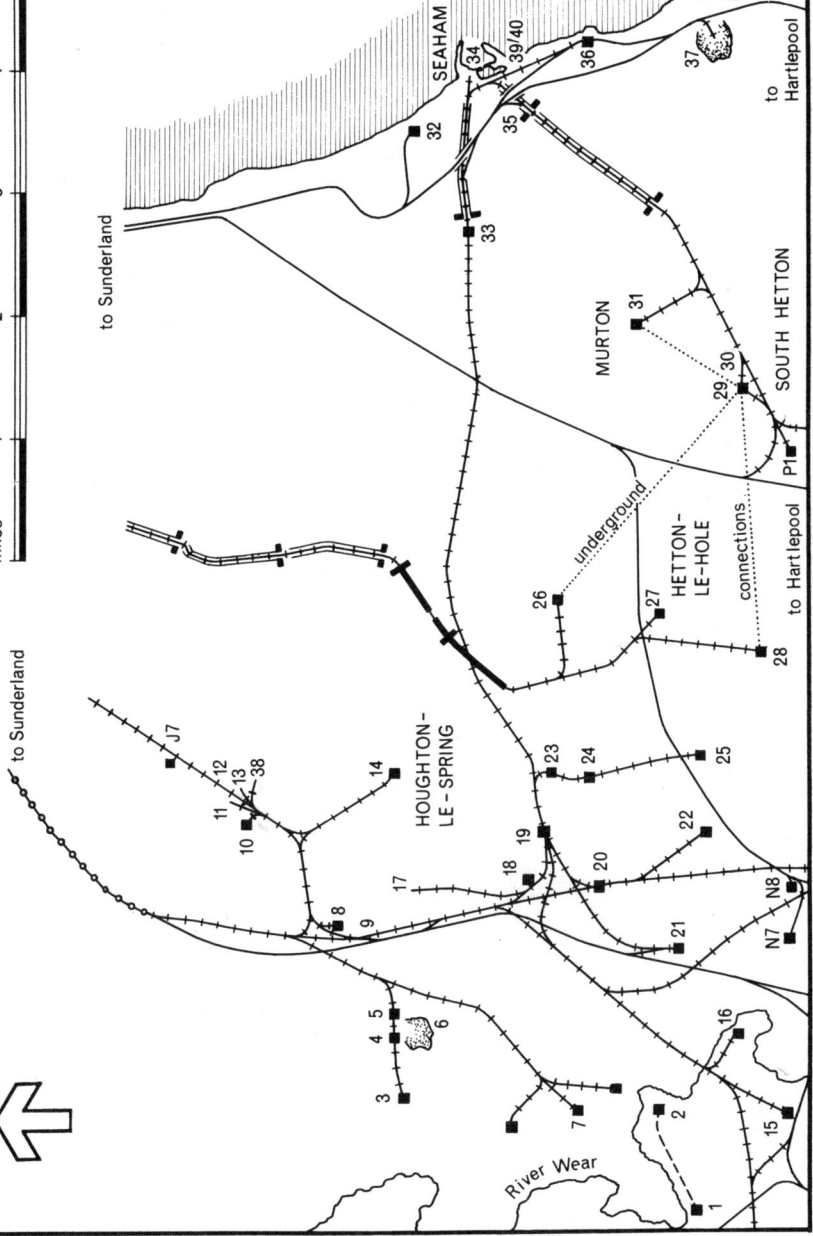

MURTON

SOUTH HETTON

to Hartlepool

HETTON-LE-HOLE

underground

connections

HOUGHTON-LE-SPRING

to Sunderland

River Wear

13

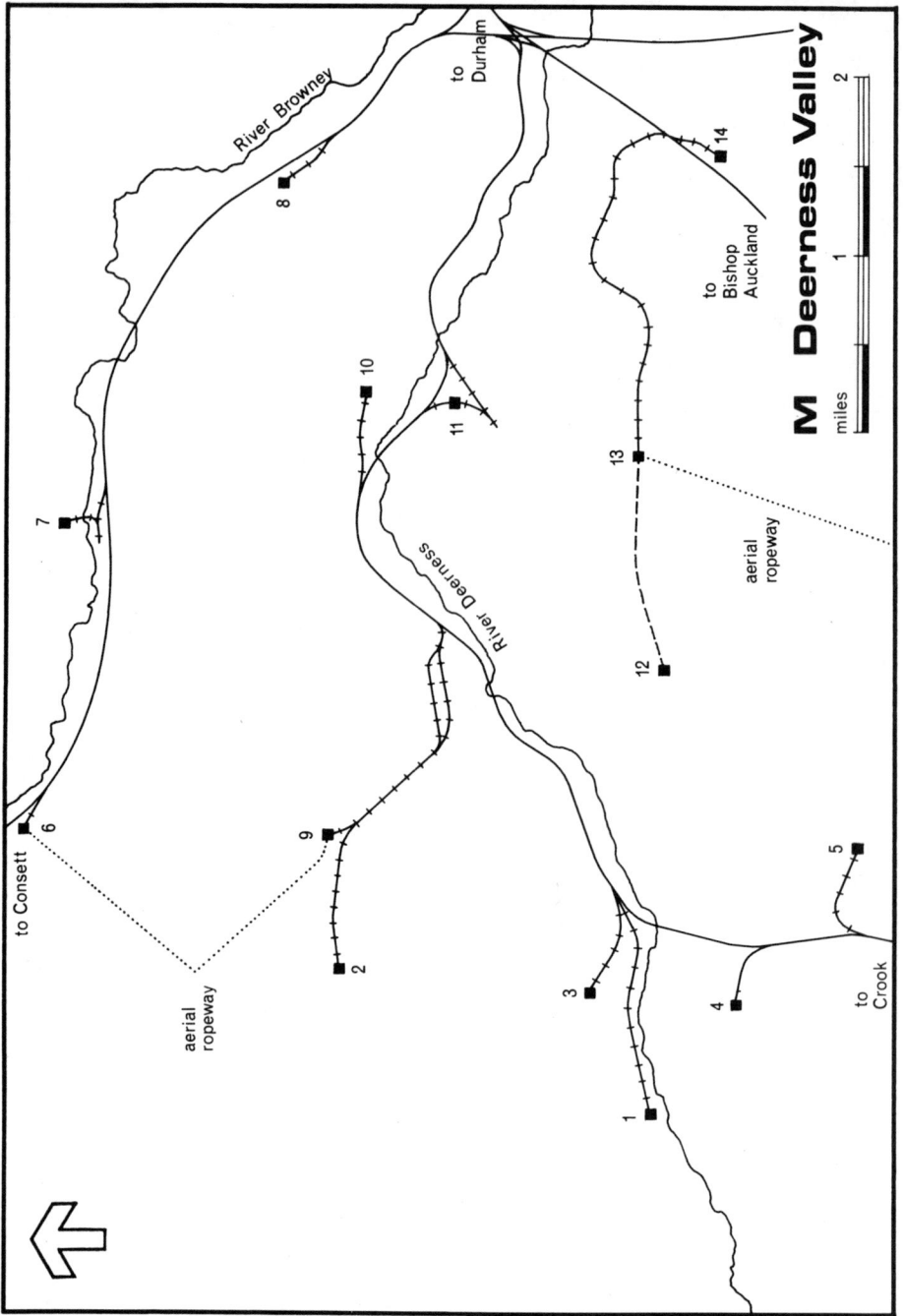

M Deerness Valley

River Browney

River Deerness

to Durham

to Bishop Auckland

to Consett

to Crook

aerial ropeway

aerial ropeway

miles

1

2

14

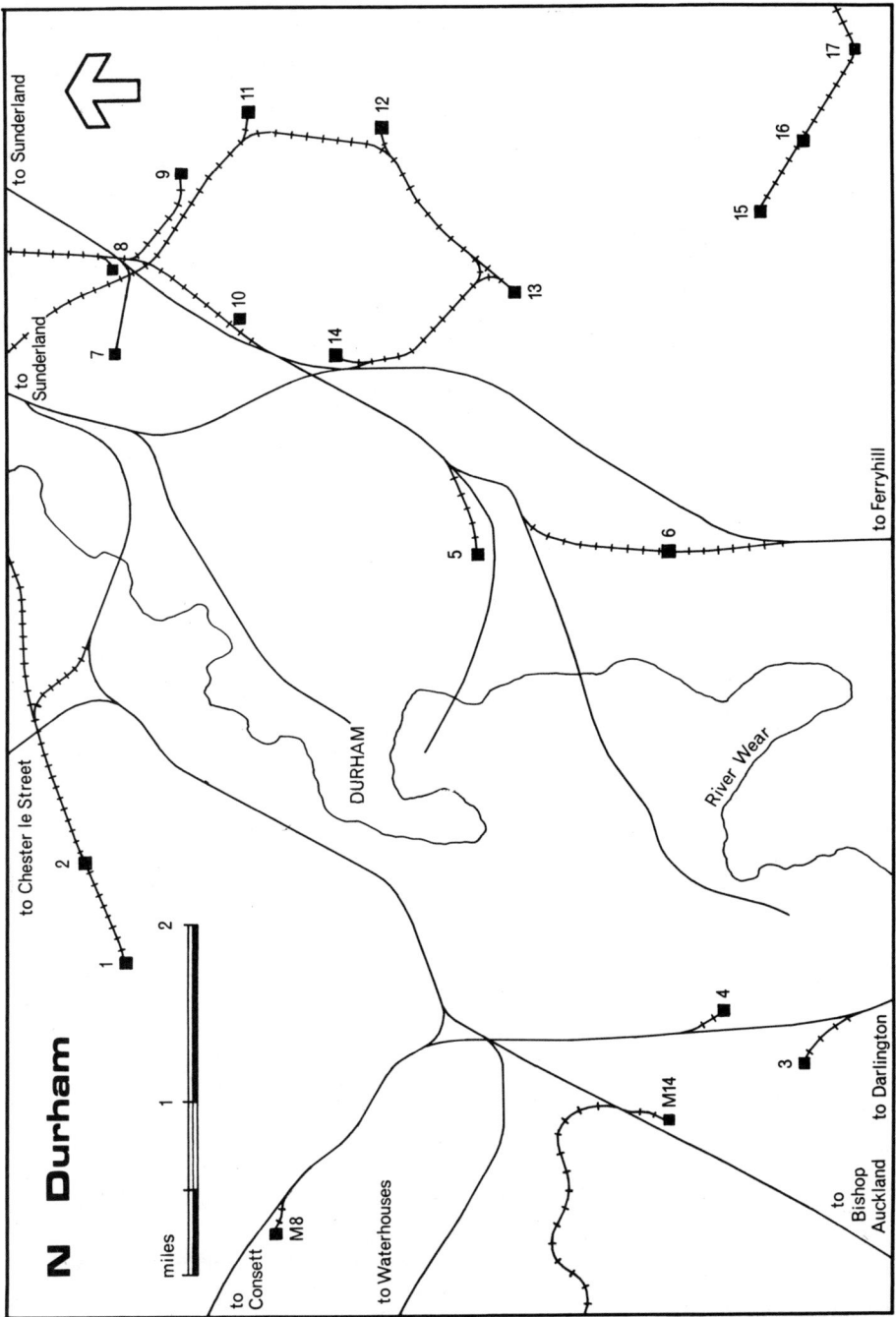

N Durham

to Sunderland

to Sunderland

to Sunderland

to Chester le Street

to Consett

to Waterhouses

to Bishop Auckland

to Darlington

to Ferryhill

DURHAM

River Wear

miles

M8

M14

1 2 3 4 5 6 7 8 9 10 11 12 13 14 15 16 17

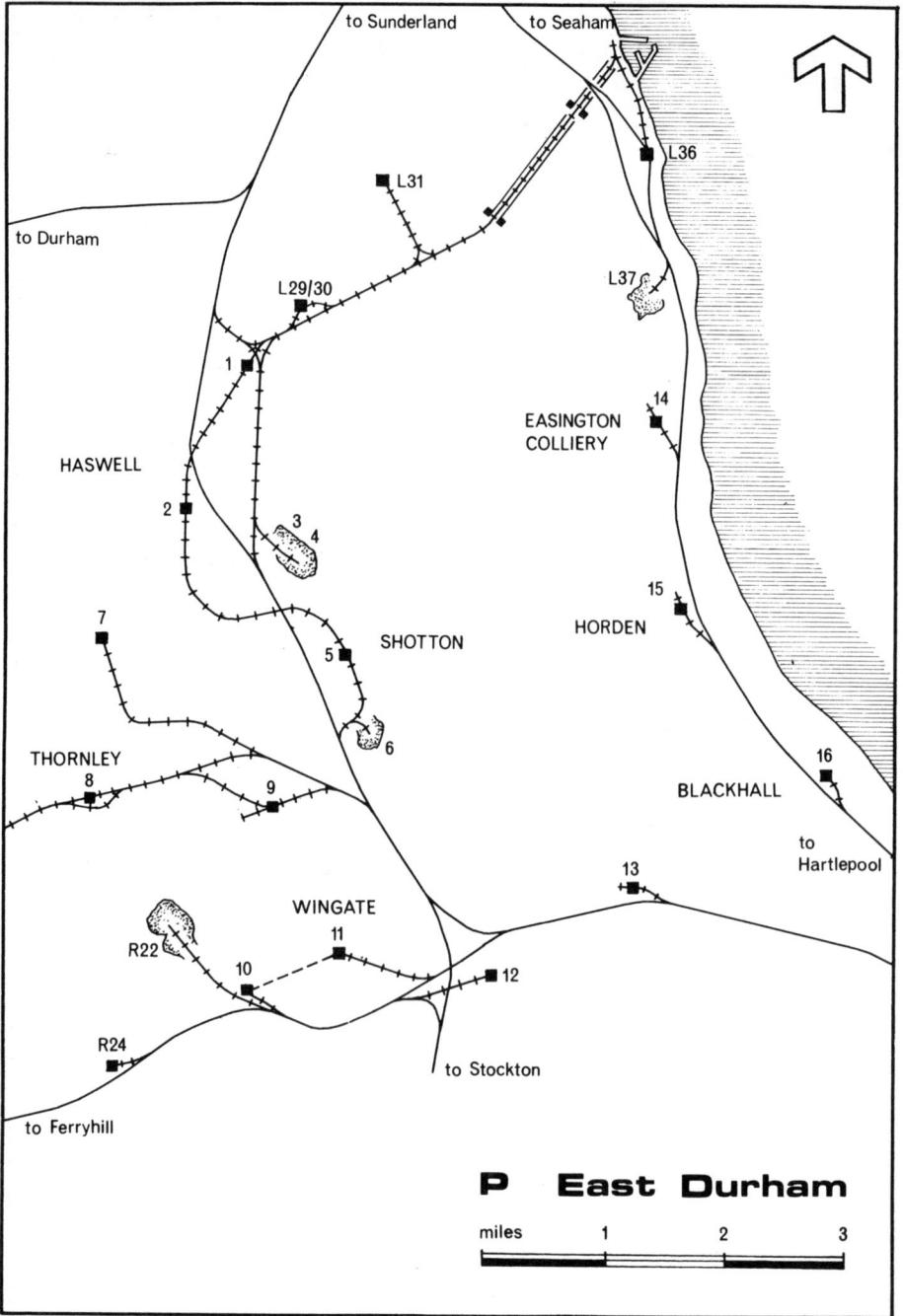

to Sunderland

to Seaham

L31

to Durham

L29/30

L36

L37

1

HASWELL

EASINGTON
COLLIERY

14

2

3 4

7

5

SHOTTON

HORDEN

15

6

THORNLEY

8   9

BLACKHALL

16

to Hartlepool

13

WINGATE

11

R22

10

12

to Stockton

R24

to Ferryhill

P East Durham

miles   1   2   3

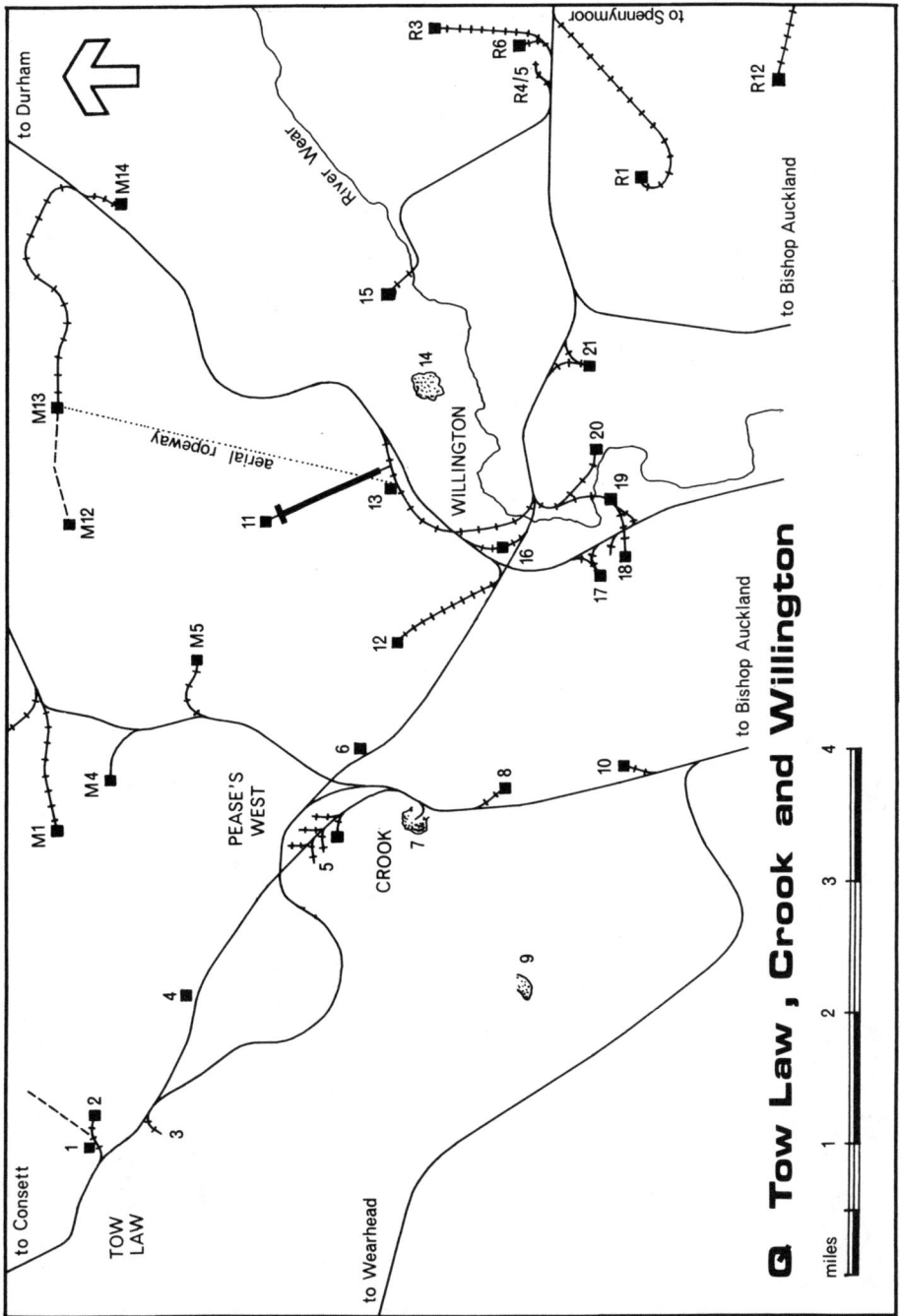

Q Tow Law, Crook and Willington

to Consett

to Durham

TOW LAW

River Wear

to Spennymoor

aerial ropeway

M13

M12

M14

M1

M4

M5

PEASE'S WEST

CROOK

WILLINGTON

to Wearhead

to Bishop Auckland

to Bishop Auckland

1
2
3
4
5
6
7
8
9
10
11
12
13
14
15
16
17
18
19
20
21

R1
R3
R6
R4/5
R12

miles

0 1 2 3 4

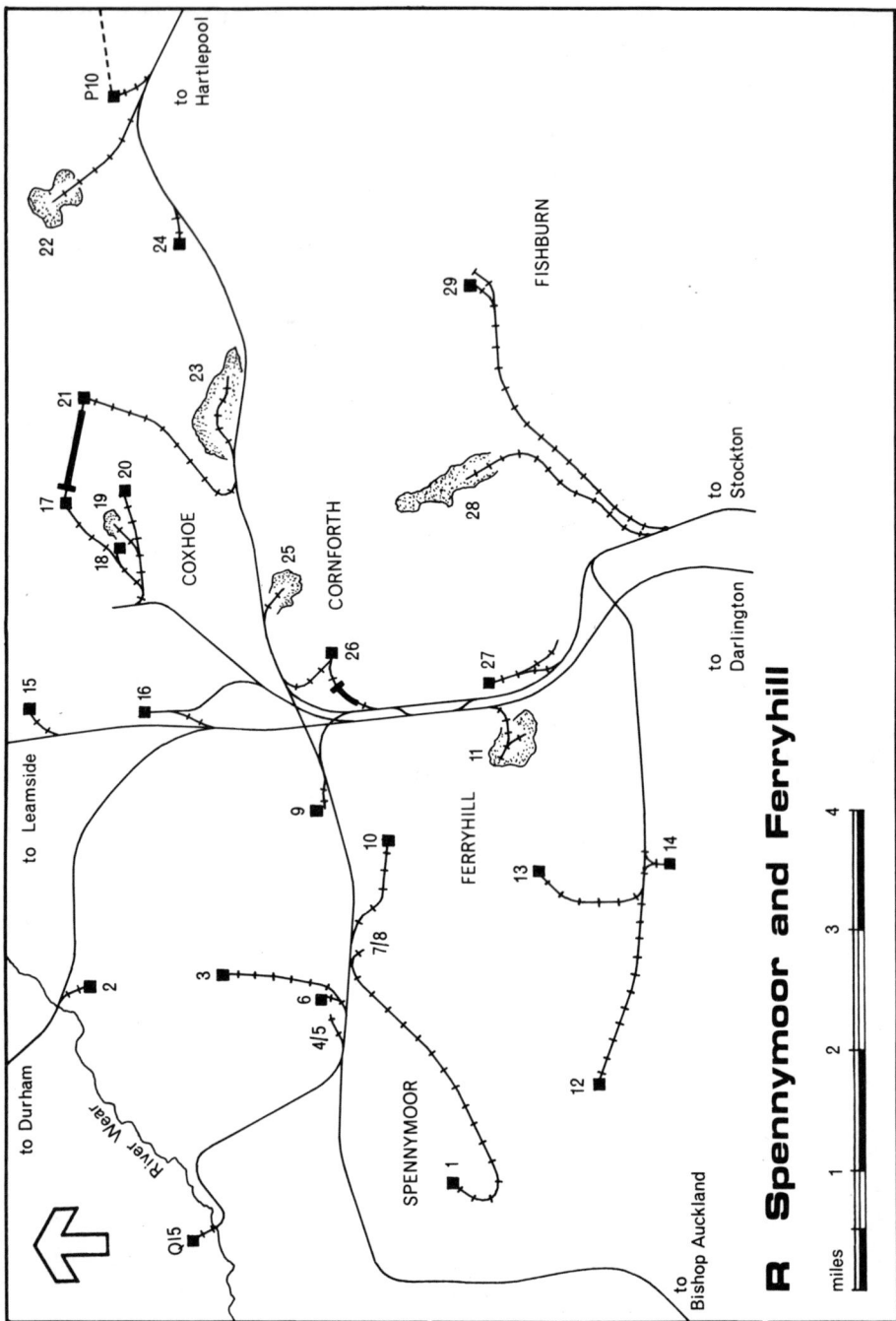

R Spennymoor and Ferryhill

to Durham

River Wear

to Leamside

to Hartlepool

22

24

P10

to Bishop Auckland

Q15

SPENNYMOOR

2

3

15

16

1

7/8

4/5

6

9

10

FERRYHILL

13

12

14

11

27

26

25

CORNFORTH

COXHOE

17

18

19

20

21

23

28

29

FISHBURN

to Stockton

to Darlington

miles

1   2   3   4

18

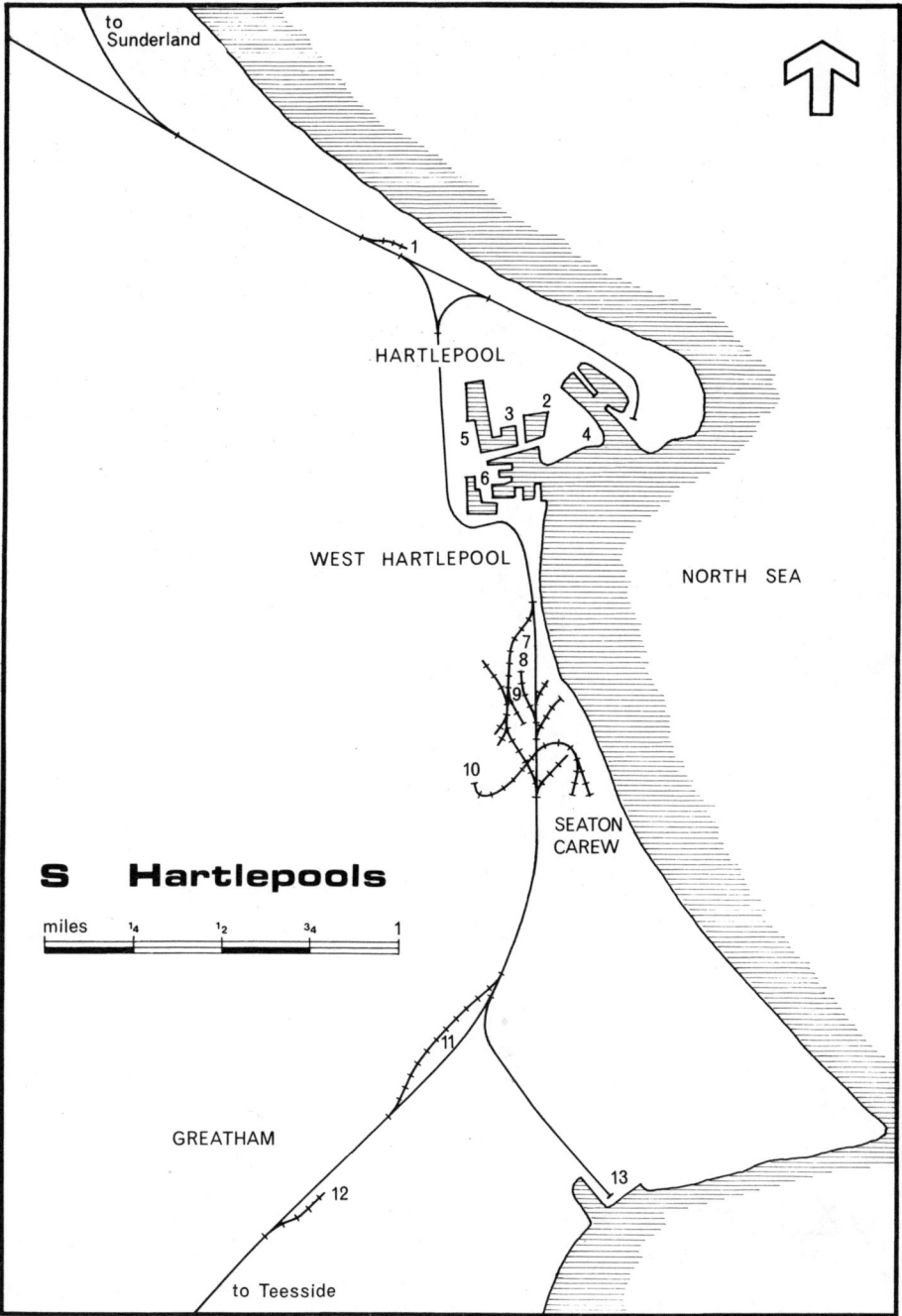

to
Sunderland

1

HARTLEPOOL

3 2
5 4
6

WEST HARTLEPOOL

NORTH SEA

7
8
9

10

SEATON
CAREW

S Hartlepools

miles ¼ ½ ¾ 1

11

GREATHAM

12

13

to Teesside

19

Bishop Auckland

to Spennymoor

25

23

24

22/28

21

to Durham

BISHOP
AUCKLAND

14

16

to Crook
Wearhead

18 19 20

15

WITTON
PARK

River Wear

13

WEST
AUCKLAND

12

10

Haggerleazes Branch

27

to
Darlington

SHILDON

9
11

COCKFIELD

1

7

26

COPLEY

2

BUTTERKNOWLE

6

8

3

5

4

WOODLAND

to Barnard Castle

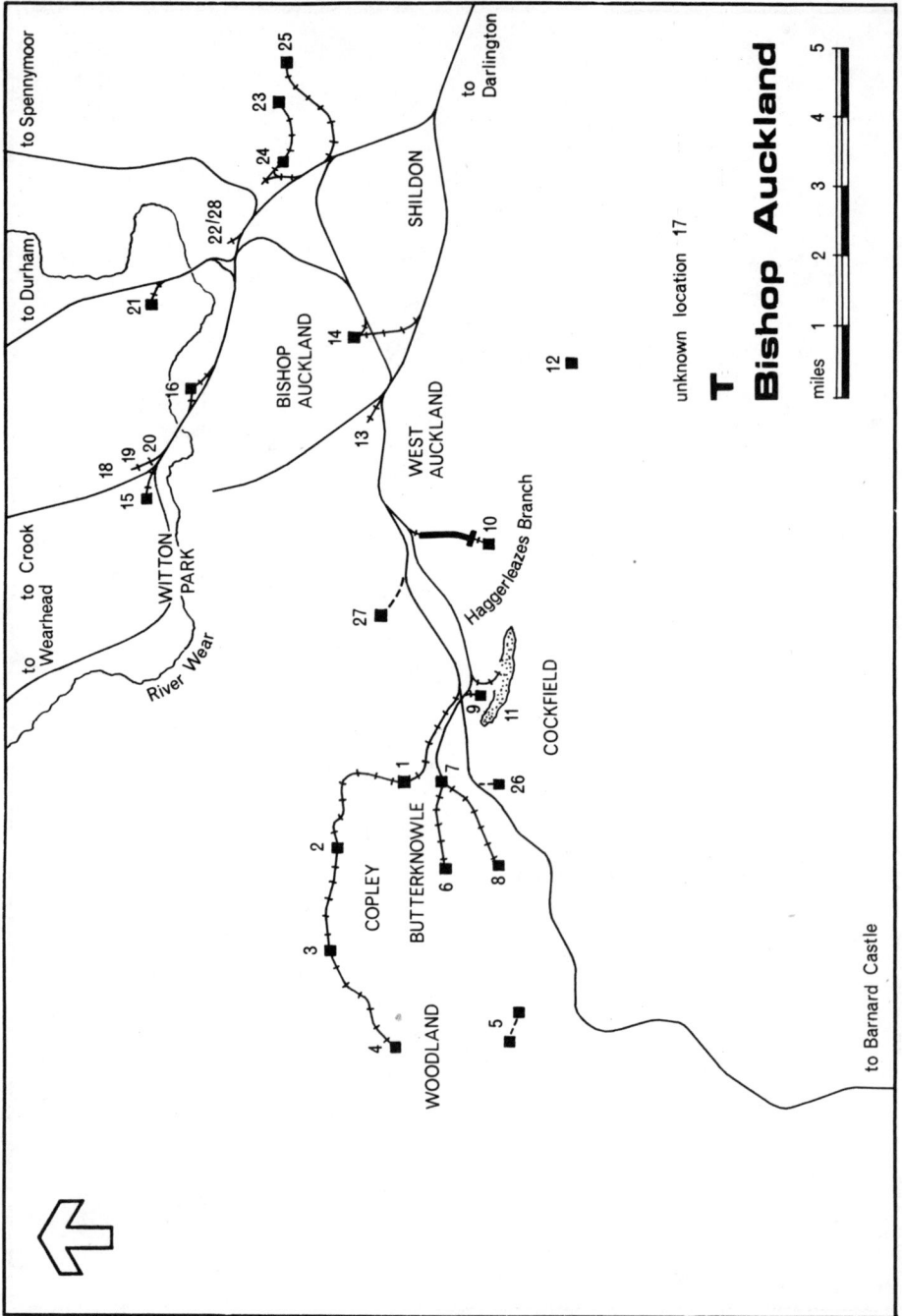

unknown location 17

T

miles 1 2 3 4 5

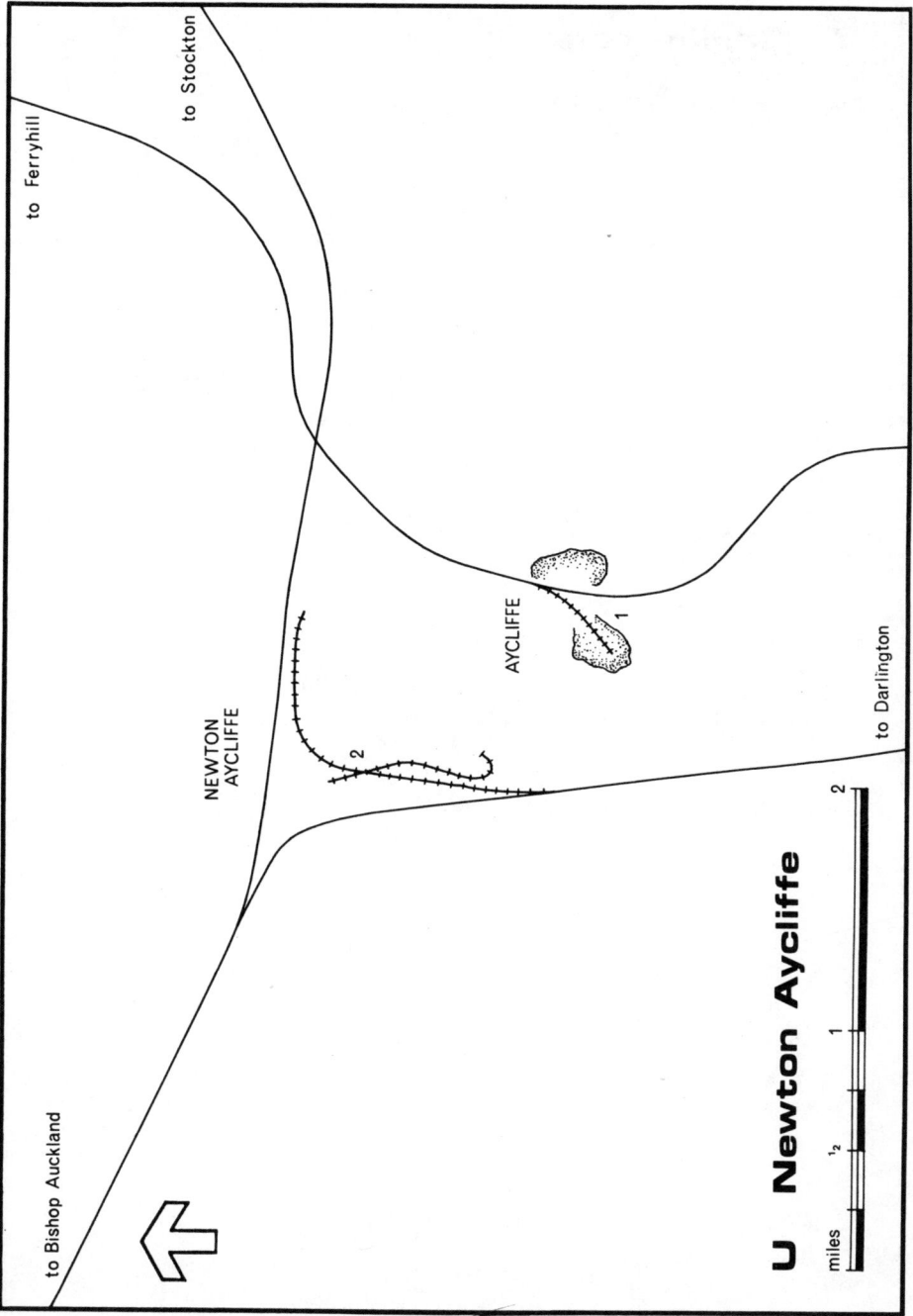

to Ferryhill

to Stockton

to Bishop Auckland

NEWTON
AYCLIFFE

AYCLIFFE

2

1

to Darlington

U Newton Aycliffe

miles

½   1   2

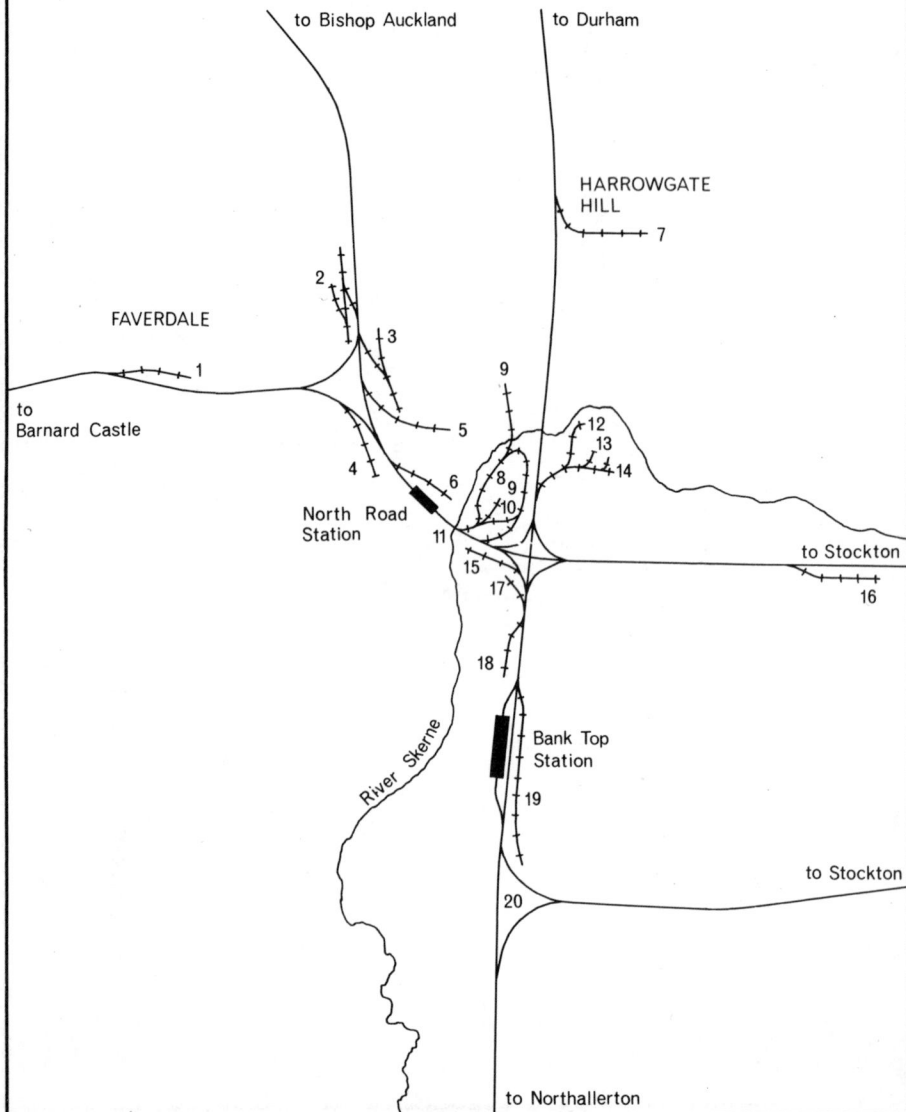

V Darlington

miles

to Bishop Auckland   to Durham

HARROWGATE HILL

7

FAVERDALE

2

3

1

to Barnard Castle

5

9

12
13
14

4

6

8 9

10

North Road Station

11

to Stockton

15

17

16

18

River Skerne

Bank Top Station

19

to Stockton

20

to Northallerton

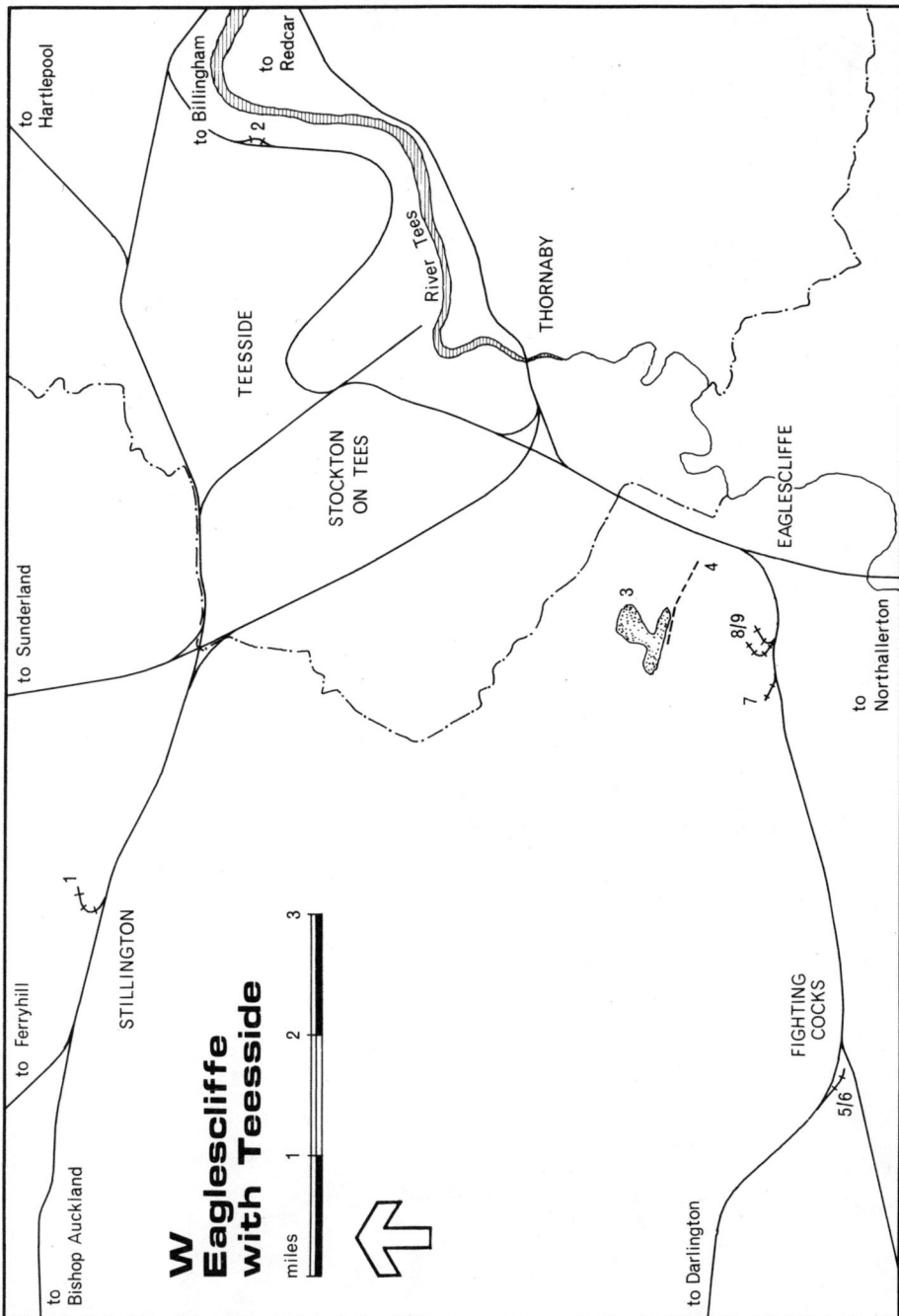

W
Eaglescliffe
with Teesside

miles 1   2   3

to Bishop Auckland
to Ferryhill
to Hartlepool
to Sunderland

STILLINGTON

to Billingham
to Redcar

TEESSIDE

River Tees

THORNABY

STOCKTON
ON TEES

EAGLESCLIFFE

to Northallerton

FIGHTING
COCKS

to Darlington

1
2
3
4
7
8/9
5/6

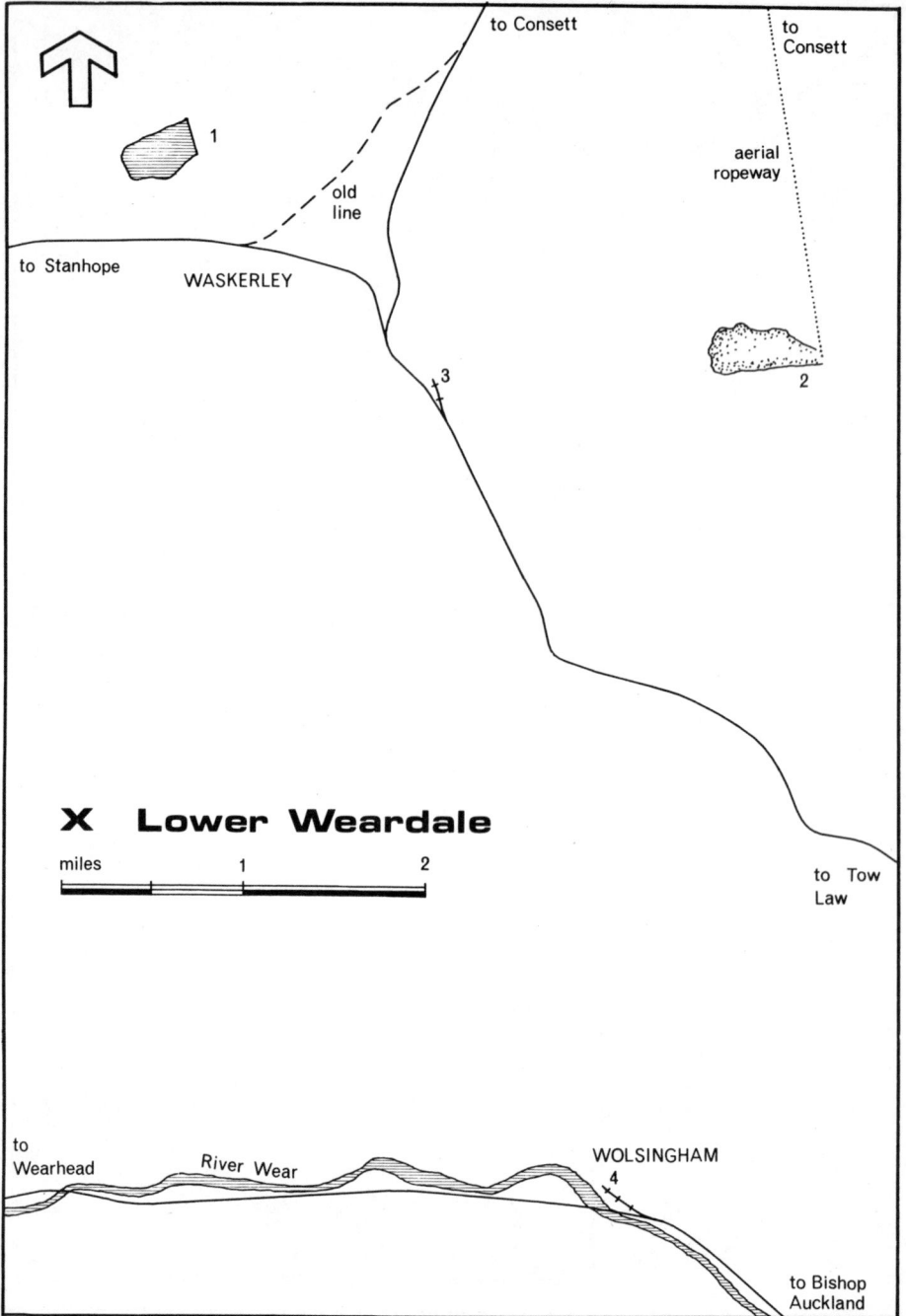

to Consett

to Consett

1

aerial
ropeway

old
line

to Stanhope

WASKERLEY

2

3

X Lower Weardale

miles   1   2

to Tow
Law

to Wearhead

River Wear

WOLSINGHAM

4

to Bishop
Auckland

24

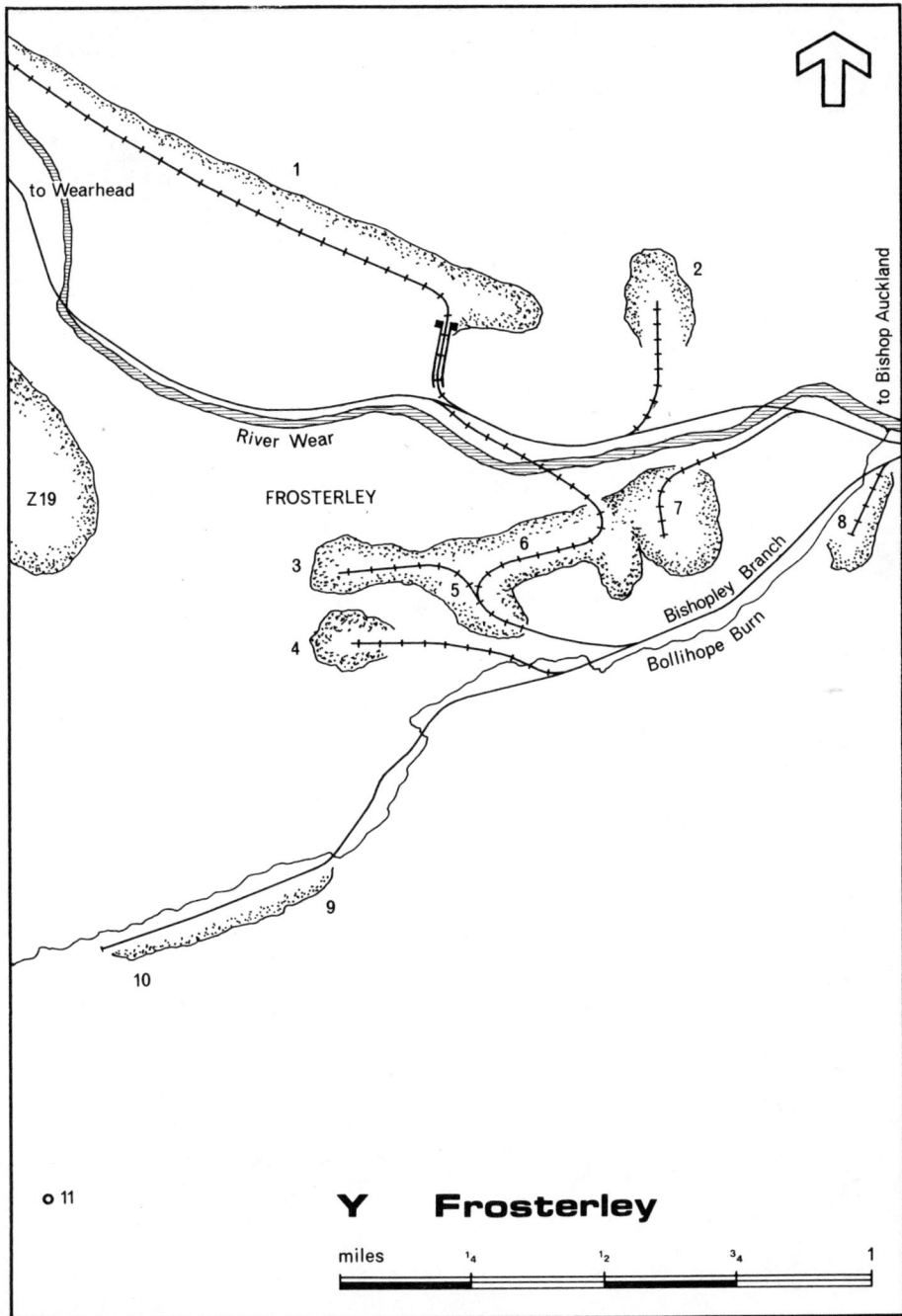

to Wearhead

1

2

River Wear

Z 19

FROSTERLEY

3

7

6

5

8

4

Bishopley Branch

Bollihope Burn

to Bishop Auckland

9

10

o 11

Y   Frosterley

miles $\frac{1}{4}$ $\frac{1}{2}$ $\frac{3}{4}$ 1

25

Upper Weardale

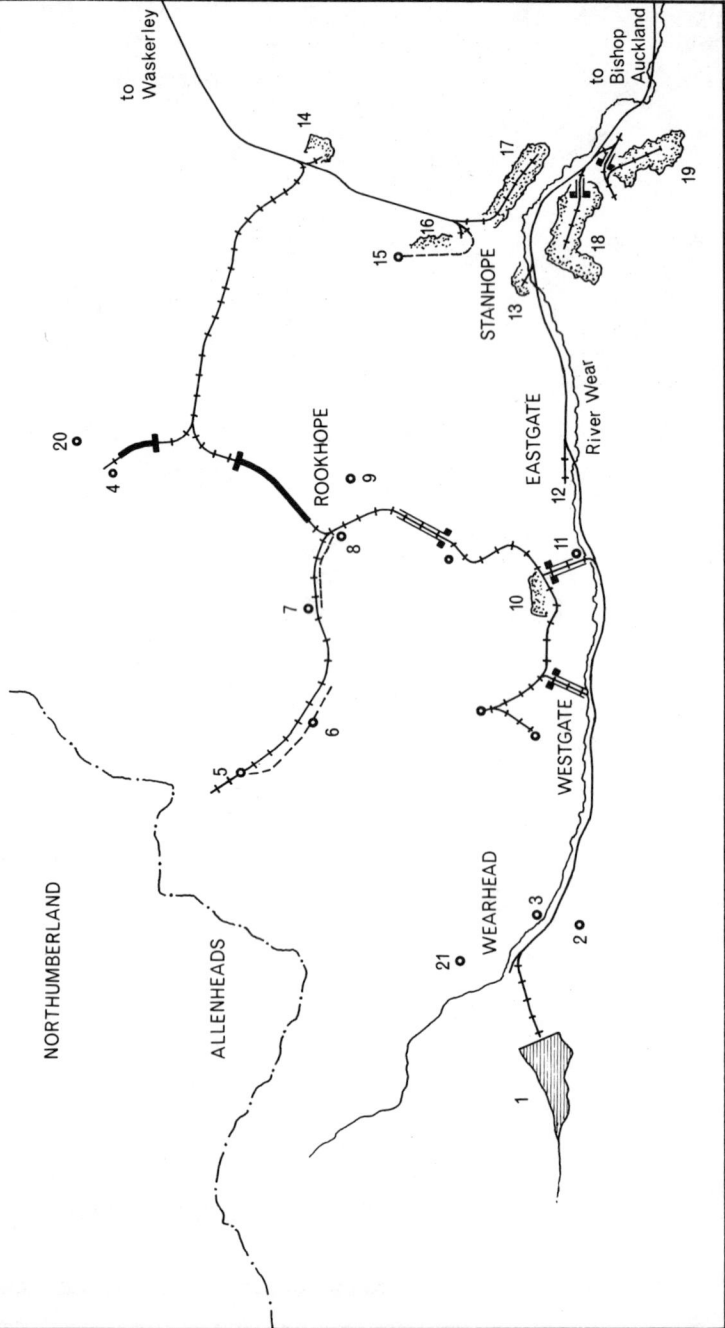

N

miles 1 2 3 4

NORTHUMBERLAND

ALLENHEADS

to Waskerley

14

16
15

17

STANHOPE

13

EASTGATE

River Wear

12

ROOKHOPE

20

4

9

8

7

11

10

5

6

WESTGATE

WEARHEAD

21

3

2

1

to Bishop
Auckland

18

19

SECTION 2

ALPHABETICAL LIST OF FIRMS

ABBEY WOOD COAL CO & FRANKLAND COAL CO (1934) LTD

L2 Both firms were owned by F.W.Blacklock, who purchased the Frankland Coal Co
(1934) Ltd in 1948. This firm owned Finchale Colliery (Map 85, NZ 293471),
a licensed mine near Finchale Abbey on R.Wear, though in fact the shaft
was used only for ventilation; the coal was drawn from a drift entrance
200 yards downstream from the Abbey, and the tubs were hauled up an incline
L1 to screens near the shaft. In 1952/3 Mr.Blacklock opened Abbey Wood Drift
(NZ 283466) under the title of Abbey Wood Coal Co, and linked it to
Finchale Colliery screens by a line 1¼ miles long. Tubs were hauled up an
incline 200 yards long, made by a wooden gantry on a gradient of 1 in 3,
and then taken to the screens by locomotive.
Both locomotives were constructed at Mr.Blacklock's scrap metal yard in
Gateshead. The second was unusual in that the engine drove a drum around
which a rope was wound once; as the drum revolved the loco pulled itself
and its load along. Both locomotives also worked underground as required.
The system had no main line rail connection, coal being taken by road to
a siding at Belmont on the BR Durham Gilesgate branch.
When coal working on the eastern side of the "take" ceased about 1953/4
the Frankland title was given up. Abbey Wood Drift was abandoned in
October 1955.

Gauge: 2' 0"

-		4wDMF	F.Blacklock c1952	(a)	(1)	
-		4wDMF	F.Blacklock c1953	(a)	(2)	

(a) constructed from various non-
locomotive parts

(1) loaned to Lanchester & Iveston
Coal Co Ltd for a fortnight
c/1954; believed stolen c/1956
(2) believed stolen c/1956

JOHN ABBOT & CO LTD, PARK IRON WORKS, GATESHEAD
(John Abbot & Co until 1864)

C4 Long-established firm (Map 78, NZ 256637), served by sidings N of NER
Gateshead-South Shields line, immediately W of Gateshead Station. The
works was probably shunted by horses before the arrival of first loco
below. The company absorbed its neighbours, Hawks, Crawshay & Co (q.v.),
about 1891, and went into voluntary liquidation in October 1909.

Gauge: 4' 8½"

-	0-4-0ST	OC	BH	13	1866	New	s/s
ADAMSON(?)	0-4-0ST	OC	AB	693	1891	New	(1)
HAWK	0-4-0ST	OC	BH	682	1882	(a)	(2)
ABBOT	0-4-0ST	OC	HL	2425	1899	New	(3)

Reputed to have built a loco for own use

(a) ex Hawks, Crawshay & Co,
Gateshead, c/1891

(1) if this loco was ADAMSON, it was
scr. on site by TWW c/1910
(2) to TWW, Charlton Works,
Sheffield, Yorks, W.R., c/1910
(3) to Skinningrove Iron Co Ltd,
Carlin How, Yorks, N.R. via TWW,
c/1910

<u>ANGLO-AUSTRAL MINES LTD</u>, COW GREEN MINES, near LANGDON BECK, TEESDALE

There were two mines here, a barytes mine (Map 84, NY 811305) and a lead
mine (NY 829313), which were connected by a line about 1¼ miles long. An
aerial ropeway then carried the ore from the eastern end of the line to a
point about ½m N of the Langdon Beck Hotel on the road between Alston and
Middleton-in-Teesdale. The barytes mine is said to have been worked by the
Hedworth Barium Co Ltd (q.v.) until about 1921, and then by the Consett
Iron Co Ltd for a short time, though this seems rather doubtful. No locomotives are thought to have been used here before the one given below.
The mines were abandoned in April 1954.

Gauge: 4' 8½"

		0-4-0ST	OC	KE		1923	(a)	s/s

(a) ex Gasswater Mine, Ayrshire,
    Scotland, c/1938

Gauge: Narrow

One or more battery locomotives were used underground from
October 1949, but details are lacking.

<u>ARMSTRONG-WHITWORTH ROLLS LTD</u> (subsidiary of Davy Ashmore Ltd from 10/1968)
(Armstrong Whitworth (Metal Industries) Ltd until 10/1968; Sir W.G.Arm-
strong Whitworth & Co (Ironfounders) Ltd until 15/6/1953; Sir W.G.Armstrong
Whitworth & Co (Engineers) Ltd until 10/4/1930; Sir W.G.Armstrong Whitworth
& Co Ltd until 1/1/1929; Sir W.G.Armstrong & Co Ltd until 1/1/1897)

<u>Close Works</u>, Gateshead. Map 78, NZ 258633

C6 Works served by sidings W of BR Gateshead-South Shields line, ½m E of
Gateshead Station. Shunting done by crane from September 1965.

Gauge: 4' 8½"

No.2	(form. 12)	0-4-0ST	OC	HL	2357	1896	(a)	Scr c/1955
	A.W.No.1	4wVBT	VCG	S	9558	1953	(b)	(1)
185	DAVID PAYNE	0-4-0DM		JF	4110006	1950	(c)	(2)

(a) ex Elswick Works, Newcastle-   (1) to Jarrow Works, 2/1965
    upon-Tyne   (2) to Jarrow Works, 9/1965
(b) New from S, via trials at
    Central Electricity Generating
    Board, Dunston G.S., 11/1953
(c) ex DL, Dock Street Foundry,
    Middlesbrough, Yorks, N.R.,
    5/1965

<u>Jarrow Works</u>, Jarrow. Map 78, NZ 321654
(Armstrong Whitworth (Metal Industries) Ltd until 10/1968; Jarrow Metal
Industries Ltd until 30/9/1960; subsidiary of Armstrong Whitworth (Metal
Industries) Ltd from 15/6/1953; previously subsidiary of Sir W.G.Armstrong
Whitworth & Co (Ironfounders) Ltd

E14 Works served by a branch (½m) from BR Gateshead-South Shields line at
      Jarrow Station. The main works was linked by a branch (1m) to another
E15 section of the works at NZ 323645, the line running alongside and then
      crossing the Bowes Railway (see John Bowes & Partners Ltd). A loco was
      occasionally borrowed from the adjacent works of Consett Iron Co Ltd (q.v.).
      Rail traffic ceased in 1969.
      In July 1970, the works, with the firm, was incorporated in the Davy Roll
      Co Ltd (q.v.).

Gauge: 4' 8½"

ELSIE	0-4-0ST	OC	HL	3895	1937	New	(1)
A.W.No.2 (form.No.1)	0-4-0ST	OC	RSH	7297	1945	New	(2)
A.W.No.1	4wVBT	VCG	S	9558	1953	(a)	(3)
185 DAVID PAYNE	0-4-0DM		JF	4110006	1950	(b)	(4)

(a) ex Close Works, Gateshead, 2/1965
(b) ex Close Works, Gateshead, 9/1965

(1) to Admiralty, Openshaw, Lancs, /1941
(2) scr 6/1965, but chassis rebuilt with diesel engine for furnace charging equipment
(3) boiler removed and frame converted to ladle carrier, /1967
(4) to Davy Roll Co Ltd, 7/1970

ASSOCIATED ELECTRICAL INDUSTRIES LTD, BIRTLEY
(W.T:Henley's Telegraph Works Co Ltd until 1/1/1960)

H30 Works (Map 78, NZ 272547) served by sidings E of BR Newcastle-Durham line, 1m S of former Birtley Station. Rail traffic ceased in 1970.

Gauge: 4' 8½"

-	4wDM		RH	265615	1948	New	Scr 6/1970

ASSOCIATED PORTLAND CEMENT MANUFACTURERS LTD, WEARDALE WORKS, near EASTGATE

Z12 Works(Map 84, NY 947385) opened in 1965, and served by sidings N of BR Wearhead Branch, ½m W of former Eastgate Station, but now at end of line. Works is alongside A 689 road from Eastgate to Westgate.

Gauge: 4' 8½"

-	4wDH		TH	148V	1965	(a)

(a) New, via International Engines Exhibition, Olympia, London, 4/1965

AYCLIFFE LIME & LIMESTONE CO LTD, AYCLIFFE
(latterly subsidiary of Gjers Mills & Co Ltd)

U1 Works and quarry (Map 85, NZ 283221) served by sidings W of BR Durham-Darlington line, immediately S of Aycliffe Station. Rail traffic was replaced by road transport in 1961, and the quarry has since closed.

Gauge: 4' 8½"

HAZELS	0-4-0WT	OC	CF	1189	1900	(a)		
			reb. Pilkington				Scr	/1951
-	4wT		Aycliffe			(b)	Scr	/1949
AYRESOME No.5	0-4-0ST	OC	MW	777	1881	(c)	Scr	/1956
AYRESOME No.12	0-4-0ST	OC	MW	1903	1916	(d)	Scr	4/1962

(a) ex Pilkington Bros Ltd, St. Helens, Lancs, via H.W. Johnson, Rainford, Lancs, dealer, /1923
(b) rebuilt from Foden lorry acquired from Davey Paxman & Co Ltd, Colchester, Essex, /1937
(c) ex Gjers Mills & Co Ltd, Middlesbrough, Yorks, N.R., 6/1950
(d) ex Gjers Mills & Co Ltd, Middlesbrough, Yorks, N.R., 3/1956

BATCHELOR, ROBINSON & CO LTD, HARTLEPOOL

S10 This metal processing works (Map 85, NZ 513309) is served by ½m branch W of
BR Hartlepool-Billingham line, 2¼m S of Hartlepool Station. A loco is only
used occasionally; most shunting is done by electric winches.

Gauge: 4' 8½"

No.2		0-4-0DM		JF	22488	1939	(a)	(1)
-		0-4-0DM		JF	4100012	1948	(b)	Scr 5/1973
-		0-4-0DM		DC	2652	1958	(c)	
-		0-4-0DM		DC	2655	1959	(d)	

(a) ex Nevill's Dock & Railway Co
    Ltd, Llanelli, Carms, 1964, loan
(b) ex Cerebos Foods Ltd, Greatham,
    8/1969
(c) ex Bristol Mechanised Coal Co
    Ltd, Filton, Gloucs, 11/1970
(d) ex Bristol Mechanised Coal Co
    Ltd, Filton, Gloucs, 3/1973

(1) ret. to Nevill's Dock & Railway
    Co Ltd, 4/1965

BEARPARK COAL & COKE CO LTD   (reg. 6/5/1872)

Bearpark Colliery, Bearpark. Map 85, NZ 243434

M8 This colliery opened in 1873, and was served by sidings W of LNER Consett-
Durham line, 1m N of Relly Mill Junction. The colliery locomotives also
shunted the adjacent coke ovens. The colliery was vested in NCB Northern
Division No.5 Area on 1st January 1947.

Gauge: 4' 8½"

	BRISTOL	0-6-0ST		FW			(a)	Scr
	WALKER	0-4-0ST	OC	FW		1861	(b)	Scr c/1915
	-	0-6-0ST	OC	FW	265	1875	New	Scr
(No.25)		0-6-0ST	OC	CF	1155	1898	New	(1)
	FLORENCE	0-6-0ST	OC	HC	880	1910	New	(1)
	NEWPORT	0-6-0ST	OC	FW			(c)	Scr
	"LITTLEBURN"	0-4-0ST	OC	KS	4143	1919	(d)	(1)
	MOSTYN	0-4-0ST	OC	LG≠		1906	(e)	(1)

≠ probably a rebuild of an older locomotive built by another firm

(a) the firm is known to have had an
    FW loco named BRISTOL, and an
    0-6-0ST with this name, believed
    to be FW 170, was dispatched
    from FW in 1/1873; these may be
    the same loco
(b) ex ?
(c) ex ? c/1914; could be FW 169
    /1872 offered for sale by Crown
    Coke Co Ltd, Consett, 1/1912
(d) ex Littleburn Colliery, c/1935
(e) ex East Hedley Hope Colliery for
    repairs, 4/1946

(1) to NCB No.5 Area, 1/1/1947

Bearpark Coke Ovens

These also began production in 1873. They consisted of rows, or "batteries"
of beehive ovens, along the top of which ran a tramway for the tubs used to
fill, or "charge", the ovens from above. In most places the tubs were
pushed by hand. These ovens closed in 1917, being replaced by new bye-
product ovens.

Gauge: 3' 0"

-	0-4-0TG	OC	JF	2820	1876	New	s/s
-	0-4-0TG	OC	JF	2821	1876	New	s/s
-	0-4-0TG	OC	JF	5006	1885	New⁄	s/s
-	0-4-0TG	OC	JF	5653	1888	New	s/s

⁄ confirmation that this loco was delivered here is lacking

East Hedley Hope Colliery, near Tow Law. Map 85, NZ 158404

M1 This colliery was originally opened in the 1870's and after various owners
and closures passed into the control of the Bearpark Coal & Coke Co Ltd in
June 1936. So far as is known there were no private locos at the colliery
before this date. It was served by a branch (1m) from the NER mineral line
linking the Deerness Valley and Stanley branches, and was vested in NCB
Northern Division No.5 Area on 1st January 1947.

Gauge: 4' 8½"

-		4wPM	Bearpark		(a)	Scr by /1946
-		4wPM	Bearpark		(a)	(1)
MOSTYN	0-4-0ST	OC	LG ⁄	1906	(b)	(2)

⁄ probably a rebuild of an older locomotive built by another firm

(a) rebuilt from road vehicles   (1) to NCB No.5 Area 1/1/1947
(b) ex Randolph Coal Co Ltd 4/1945   (2) to Bearpark Colliery for repairs
                                                  4/1946

Littleburn Colliery, Meadowfield. Map 85, NZ 255395

N4 This colliery was formerly owned by North Brancepeth Coal Co Ltd (q.v.);
it was taken over by Bearpark Coal & Coke Co Ltd and re-opened about
October 1931. It was closed in July 1935, but re-opened, without
locomotives, shortly before nationalisation, and vested in NCB Northern
Division No.5 Area on 1st January 1947. It was served by sidings E of
LNER line from Durham to Darlington, 2¼m S of Durham Station.

Gauge: 4' 8½"

"LITTLEBURN"	0-4-0ST	OC	KS	4143	1919	(a) (1)

(a) ex North Brancepeth Coal Co Ltd   (1) to Bearpark Colliery, c/1935
    c10/1931

BEDE METAL & CHEMICAL CO LTD, HEBBURN   (reg. 16/5/1872)

E8 Firm was a member of the industrial empire of Sir Charles Mark Palmer in
its early days. The works (Map 78, NZ 308654) was served by a branch (1m)
from BR Gateshead-South Shields line, ¼m E of Hebburn Station, which also
served the shipyards of R.& W.Hawthorn Leslie & Co Ltd and Palmers Hebburn.
The company went into liquidation in September 1957, and after demolition
in 1959 the site was used for an extension of Palmers Hebburn Yard, owned
by Vickers Armstrongs Ltd (q.v.).

Gauge: 4' 8½"

B M & C No.1	0-4-0ST	OC	BH	316	1874	New	
			reb. HL		1903		s/s
No.2	0-4-0ST	OC	HL	2152	1889	(a)	
			reb. HL		1914		Scr
BEDE No.3	0-4-0ST	OC	HL	3654	1927	New	s/s by /1956
No.4	0-4-0DM		HC	D607	1938	New	s/s by 1/1957

(a) ex John Bowes & Partners Ltd,
    Felling Colliery (c/1901?)

BIRTLEY BRICK CO LTD, UNION BRICKWORKS, BIRTLEY

H20 This company's brickworks (Map 78, NZ 266557 approx.) lay to the north of
Station Road in Birtley, and had no main line rail connection. In the late
1930's most of the clay quarries in the Birtley area operated internal
tramways, and although it is virtually certain that the loco below was
used here, confirmation is lacking. Loco haulage had been abandoned for
some time before the loco was sold.

Gauge: 2' 0"

83   LANCHESTER   0-4-0T   OC   AE   2071   1933   (a)   (1)

(a) ex Durham County Water Board,   (1) to R.R.Dunn, dealer, Bishop
    Burnhope Reservoir, /1937   Auckland, /1947; re-sold to
                                            Dinorwic Slate Quarries Co Ltd,
                                            Caerns, 7/49

BLAKE BOILER & ENGINEERING CO LTD, ALLIANCE WORKS, ALBERT HILL, DARLINGTON
(form. Darlington Wagon & Engineering Co Ltd, reg. 21/6/1884)

V14 Works (Map 85, NZ 299167) served by sidings E of LNER Durham-Darlington
line, 1m N of Darlington (Bank Top) Station. It lay immediately behind
(east of) the former Skerne Ironworks (q.v.), and had closed by 1939.

Gauge: 4' 8½"

    ALLIANCE   0-4-0ST   OC   (a)   s/s

    The firm may have had another loco before this one.

(a) origin unknown; said to have
    been rebuilt by HL

BLANCHLAND FLUOR MINES
(Blanchland Fluor Mines Ltd until 29/3/1970, when the firm became a
subsidiary of British Steel Corporation)

Z5 This firm owns Grove Rake Mine, near Rookhope (Map 84, NY 896442) and
Z4 Whiteheaps Mine, Ramshaw (Map 84, NY 948467). Grove Rake was formerly a
lead mine owned by Weardale Lead Co Ltd (q.v.), but it has latterly been
worked for fluorspar. In the 1950's it appears to have been owned by the
Grove Rake Mining Co Ltd as a subsidiary of Colville's Ltd, before
passing to the firm above. The mine, which consists of a main shaft and
a nearby drift, lies alongside a minor road from Allenheads to Rookhope,
about 3m from Rookhope, and there is no main line rail connection.
Whiteheaps Mine was originally an ironstone mine, but is also now worked
for fluorspar. Until about 1883 it was served by a branch (1½m) from the
Weatherhill & Rookhope section of the Weardale Iron Company's line (q.v.),
but since then it has had no rail connection.
Originally the underground system at Grove Rake was 1' 9" gauge. At
Whiteheaps it was 1' 7" at first, but was later altered to 2' 0".
However, about 1973 the gauge in both mines was altered to 1' 10". In
1974 the working locomotive allocation comprised three at Grove Rake shaft,
two at Grove Rake Drift and one at Whiteheaps, with quite frequent
transfers as required. For this reason the locomotive allocation is not
shown below.

Gauge: 1' 10" (underground)

-	0-4-0BE	WR				(a)
-	4wBE	WR	4812	1952		(b)
-	0-4-0BE	WR				(c)
-	0-4-0BE	WR	7291	1969	New	
-	0-4-0BE	WR	7481	1972	New	
-	0-4-0BE	WR	7549	1973	New	
-	0-4-0BE	WR		1974	New	

(a) ex Anglo-Austral Mines Ltd,
    Gasswater Mine, Ayrshire,
    Scotland; prev. 1' 7" gauge
(b) ex Force Crag Mines,Braithwaite,
    Cumberland, /1967
(c) ex Greenside Mining Co Ltd,
    Patterdale, Cumberland

BOLCKOW, VAUGHAN & CO LTD
(Bolckow, Vaughan & Co until 19/11/1864)

This vast industrial empire was founded in 1840 when Henry Bolckow (1806-1878) entered into partnership with John Vaughan (1799-1868) to build a small ironworks at Middlesbrough, which opened in May 1841. Their fortune was made ten years later when Vaughan discovered the Cleveland ironstone deposits. Their business fell into three sections - ironworks on Tees-side, collieries (usually in south-west Durham, and often with large numbers of coke ovens) and quarries in Weardale. Most survived to be absorbed into Dorman, Long & Co Ltd on 1st November 1929.

N.B. Not all the locomotive allocations shown below have been confirmed.

Auckland Park Colliery, near Bishop Auckland. Map 85, NZ 227285.

T24 Probably opened about 1870, and acquired by BV a few years later. It was situated on a short link from the branch ($\frac{1}{4}$m) to Black Boy Colliery (q.v.) from a junction 1m S of Bishop Auckland Station on LNER Bishop Auckland-Shildon line. The locos kept here also worked Black Boy Colliery until its closure. The colliery passed to Dorman, Long & Co Ltd on 1st November 1929.

Gauge: 4' 8½"

8		0-4-0ST	OC	BH	427	1877	New	s/s	
3		0-6-0ST	IC	MW	194	1866	(a)	Scr	/1927
101		0-6-0T	IC	HL	2429	1899	(b)	Scr	/1927
108	HECTOR	0-6-0ST	OC	HL	2613	1905	New	(1)	
113	PLUTO	0-6-0ST	OC	HL	2655	1906	New	(1)	
	HENRY CORT	0-4-0ST	OC	BH	607	1881	(b)	(1)	
	ACTIVE	0-4-0ST	OC	RS	3075	1901			
				reb. Ellis		1927	(c)	(1)	
	HARE	0-4-0ST	OC	GH		1908	(d)	(1)	

(a) ex Black Boy Colliery; probably   (1) to DL, 1/11/1929
    one or two other locos unknown
    also came from here
(b) ex Cleveland Works, Middles-
    brough, Yorks, N.R.
(c) ex Priestman Collieries Ltd,
    Blaydon Burn Colliery, via
    Ellis, Swalwell, /1927
(d) ex Newlandside Quarry by 7/1929

Collieries, ironworks and quarries of Bolckow Vaughan and Co Ltd

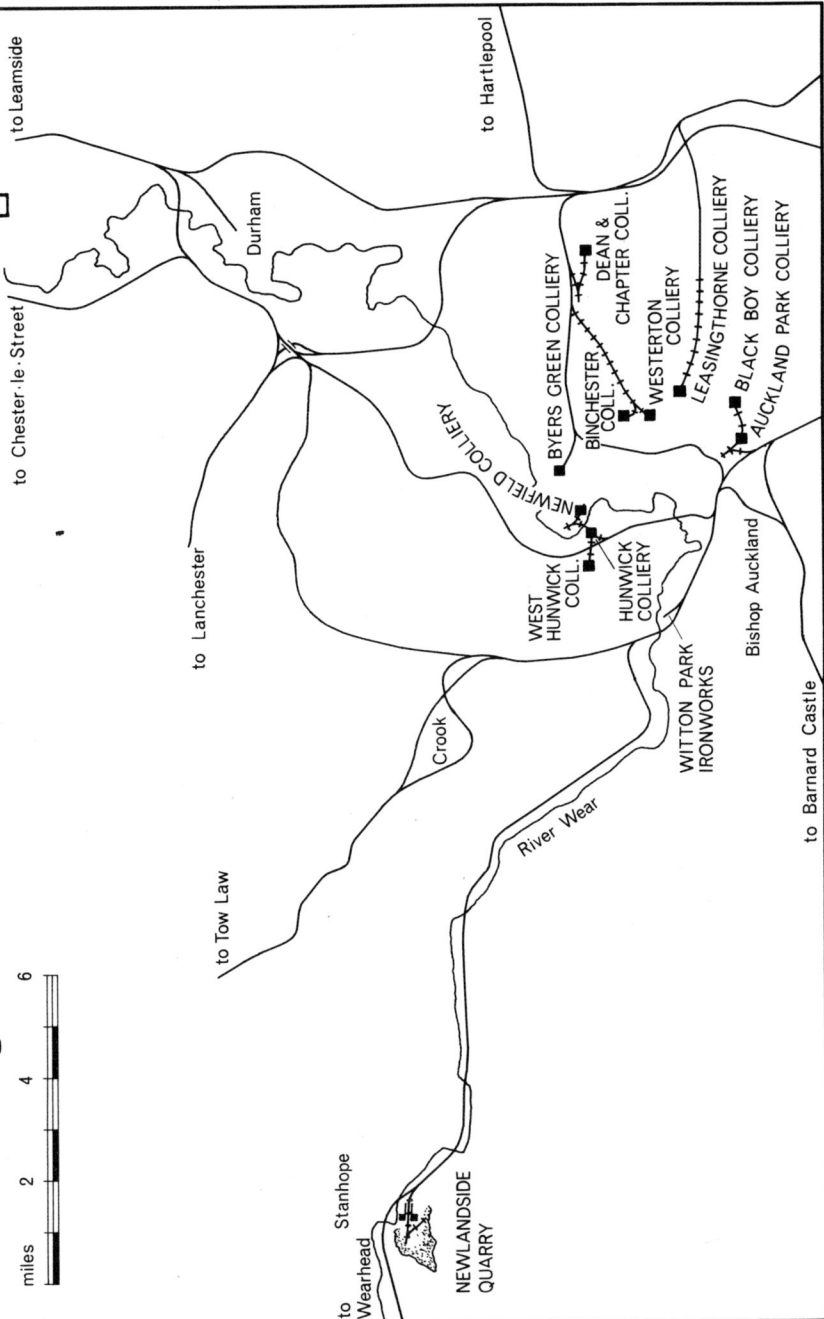

miles 2 4 6

to Leamside

to Hartlepool

to Chester·le·Street

Durham

to Lanchester

BYERS GREEN COLLIERY

DEAN & CHAPTER COLL.

BINCHESTER COLL.

WESTERTON COLLIERY

LEASINGTHORNE COLLIERY

BLACK BOY COLLIERY

AUCKLAND PARK COLLIERY

NEWFIELD COLLIERY

WEST HUNWICK COLL.

HUNWICK COLLIERY

Bishop Auckland

WITTON PARK IRONWORKS

to Barnard Castle

Crook

River Wear

to Tow Law

Stanhope

to Wearhead

NEWLANDSIDE QUARRY

35

Auckland Park Coke Ovens

These were adjacent to the colliery, and were of the beehive type, the
locos shunting the tubs along the top. Several BV collieries used coke
oven locomotives, but although they were all 0-4-0ST's of 3' 0" gauge,
most have not been positively identified - a number were also used at the
various Middlesbrough locations. The locos were BH 402/3 of 1876, 435/6
and 442 of 1877, 446/7 and 459 of 1878, 494/5 of 1879, 557/8 of 1880 and
595/6/7/8/9 and 601 of 1881. There were two working at Auckland Park by
January 1880, and they may have been here by November 1876. The ovens ceased
production in April 1909.

Gauge: 3' 0"

-		0-4-0ST	OC	BH		(a)	s/s
-		0-4-0ST	OC	BH		(a)	s/s

There may also have been transfers unknown.

(a) see list above

Binchester and Westerton Collieries, near Bishop Auckland.   Map 85,
NZ 237315.

R1   These two collieries were in fact the same site with regard to the surface,
but the shafts worked different seams underground, and they are always
listed separately. They were served by a branch (BV), 2¼m long, from
Binchester Junction on NER Ferryhill-Bishop Auckland line, 1m E of
Spennymoor Station. They were acquired from Nicholas Wood & Partners in
the 1860's. Binchester Colliery closed in January 1908, but Westerton
Colliery survived to be taken over by Dorman, Long & Co Ltd on 1st
November 1929, without locos.

Gauge: 4' 8½"

	ROCKET	0-6-0	OC	RS	15	1829	(a)	s/s
	TINY	0-4-0ST	OC	FJ	31	1864	(b)	(1)
7		0-6-0ST	OC	BH	391	1876	New	s/s
	COMET	0-4-0ST	OC	BH	544	1880	(c)	(1)

There were almost certainly other locos unknown.

(a) ex Stockton & Darlington   (1) to Newlandside Quarry by 5/1908
    Railway, No.7 ROCKET (may not
    have been owned by BV)
(b) ex Black Boy Colliery
(c) ex Cleveland Works, Middles-
    brough, Yorks, N.R. (?)

Binchester Coke Ovens

These lay adjacent to the colliery, and were operated in the same way as
Auckland Park. Locomotives were being used here by June 1878, and normally
there were two, though only one is recorded in January 1880. The ovens
ceased production in the quarter ending December 1908.

Gauge: 3' 0"

-		0-4-0ST	OC	BH	442	1877	New	s/s
-		0-4-0ST	OC	BH			(a)	s/s

There may also have been transfers unknown.

(a) see list under Auckland Park
Coke Ovens

Black Boy Colliery, Coundon Grange. Map 85, NZ 232284
(Black Boy Coal Co until 1871)

T23 This colliery was sunk in the late 1820's and was situated on a branch
(BV - 1m) from LNER Bishop Auckland-Shildon line, 1m S of Bishop Auckland
Station. The locos and responsibility for shunting the colliery were later
transferred to Auckland Park Colliery (q.v.), which was also served by the
same branch. Black Boy closed in December 1924.

Gauge: 4' 8½"

	-	0-4-0ST	OC	FJ	31	1864	New	(1)
No.3		0-6-0ST	IC	MW	194	1866	New	(2)

There were almost certainly other locos at the colliery,
but their identity is unknown.

(1) to Binchester Colliery
(2) to Auckland Park Colliery

Byers Green Colliery, Byers Green. Map 85, NZ 223335

Q21 This colliery was opened in January 1840, and was served by sidings S of
what was originally the West Durham Railway, ¼m E of Todhills Engine House.
After this line had been taken over by the NER, its rail access was altered
to a junction ½m W of Burnhouse Junction, which lay 2m W of Spennymoor
Station on the Ferryhill-Bishop Auckland line. The colliery closed in
April 1926.

A loco was recorded here in April 1871, but its identity is unknown.

Gauge: 4' 8½"

	-	0-4-0T	OC	FJ	47	1865	(a)	Scr by 1926
	CHEETHAM					1887?	(b)	(1)
110	HERCULES	0-6-0ST	OC	HL	2654	1906	(c)	(2)

(a) ex Robt. Sharpe & Sons, contrs,   (1) boiler exploded, 19/3/1901, but
    North Devon Rly contract, /1878   not seriously; s/s
(b) ex Cleveland Works, Middles-   (2) to Leasingthorne Colliery
    brough, Yorks, N.R., 9/1899
(c) ex Leasingthorne Colliery

Dean & Chapter Colliery, Ferryhill. Map 85, NZ 272331

R10 This colliery was opened in 1901, and was served by a branch (½m) from
NER Ferryhill-Bishop Auckland line, 1¼m E of Spennymoor Station. It passed
to Dorman, Long & Co Ltd on 1st November 1929.

Gauge: 4' 8½"

	HENRY CORT	0-4-0ST	OC	BH	607	1881	(a)	(1)
106	ERIMUS	0-6-0ST	OC	HL	2595	1904	(b)	(2)
116	GEORGE V	0-6-0ST	OC	HL	2833	1910	New	(2)
148	TAURUS	0-4-0ST	OC	HL	3384	1919	New	(2)
No.26	JOHN EVANS	0-6-0ST	IC	P	629	1896	(a)	(2)

(a) ex Cleveland Works, Middles-   (1) to Cleveland Works, Middles-
    brough, Yorks, N.R.   brough, Yorks, N.R.
(b) ex Cleveland Works ?   (2) to DL, 1/11/1929

37

<u>Leasingthorne Colliery</u>, near Coundon. Map 85, NZ 252304.

P12 Colliery acquired about 1873, and served by an extension (2m - BV) of NER
Chilton Branch. The colliery passed to Dorman, Long & Co Ltd on 1st
November 1929.

A loco was recorded here in November 1876, but its identity is unknown.

Gauge: 4' 8½"

	YORK	0-4-0ST	OC	BH	526	1880	New	s/s
14		0-6-0ST	IC	MW	1138	1889	New	Scr by 11/1929
102		0-4-0ST	OC	HL	2449	1900	New	(1)
107	ATLAS	0-6-0ST	OC	HL	2612	1905	New	(1)
110	HERCULES	0-6-0ST	OC	HL	2654	1906	New	(2)
120	LEEHOLME	0-4-0ST	OC	HL	2916	1912	New	(3)

(1) to DL, 1/11/1929
(2) to Byers Green Colliery, and ret;
    to DL, 1/11/1929
(3) sold for scrap, /1923

<u>Newfield Colliery</u>, Newfield. Map 85, NZ 205332.

Q20 This colliery was opened about 1840, and was originally served by a branch
(½m) from the West Durham Railway, ½m W of Todhills Engine House, but after
about 1891 by a branch from Hunwick Station on NER Durham-Bishop Auckland
Q19 line. Locos at the colliery also served <u>Hunwick Colliery</u> (NZ 210328), owned
by the Hunwick Coal Co until about 1876, and, via a ½m branch from Hunwick
Q18 Colliery, <u>West Hunwick Colliery</u> (NZ 195329), though this never seems to
have been owned by BV (see West Hunwick Refractories Ltd). Hunwick Colliery
was subsequently closed, but Newfield passed to Dorman, Long & Co Ltd on
1st November 1929.

A loco was recorded here in April 1871, and three in March
1890, but the only known information is that given below.

Gauge: 4' 8½"

	-	0-4-0T	OC	FJ	72	1867	(a)	(1)
	No.2	0-4-0ST	OC	BH			(b)	(2)
				reb. BV		1893		
	(No.1)	0-4-0ST	OC	P	916	1901	(c)	(2)

(a) New to Hunwick Coal Co; loco may   (1) to Hunwick Coal Co Ltd, West
    never have been owned by BV   Hunwick
(b) ex ?; may have been one of BH   (2) to DL, 1/11/1929
    427/8/9/431 (New to BV)
(c) ex Ramshaw Coal Co Ltd, Bishop
    Auckland, /1927

<u>Newfield Coke Ovens</u>

These were adjacent to the colliery, and were operated in the usual way.
A loco was being used here in November 1876. The ovens ceased production
in August 1913.

Gauge: 3' 0"

| | - | 0-4-0ST | OC | BH | | | (a) | s/s |
| No.1 | NEWFIELD | 0-4-0ST | OC | BH | 459 | 1878 | New? | s/s |

There may also have been transfers unknown.

(a) see list under Auckland Park
    Colliery

<u>Newlandside Quarry</u>, Stanhope. Map 84, NY 995383 (approx.)

Z18 This limestone quarry, opened in 1862 and taken over by BV about 1865,
became one of the largest in Weardale. It was served by a self-acting
incline, ¼m long, down to the NER Wearhead Branch, ¼m E of Stanhope
Station. It passed to Dorman, Long & Co Ltd on 1st November 1929.

There may well have been locos at the quarry before those given below.

Gauge: 4' 8½"

NEWLANDSIDE	0-4-0ST	OC	BH	365	1876	New	(1)
WITTON	0-4-0ST	OC	BH	367	1877	(a)	(2)
COMET	0-4-0ST	OC	BH	544	1880	(b)	s/s
TINY	0-4-0ST	OC	FJ	31	1864	(b)	s/s
HAVERTON	0-4-0ST	OC	AB	656	1890	(c)	(2)
HARE	0-4-0ST	OC	GH		1908	(d)	(3)

(a) ex Witton Park Ironworks (?)
(b) ex Binchester Colliery by 5/1908
(c) ex South Bank Works, Middles-
    brough, Yorks, N.R. by /1913
(d) ex Eston Mines, Yorks, N.R. by
    9/1914

(1) to unknown location; later at
    Parson Byers Quarry (see DL)
(2) to DL, 1/11/1929
(3) to Auckland Park Colliery by
    7/1929

<u>Witton Park Ironworks</u>, Witton Park. Map 85, NZ 174306.

T18 This works was opened in February 1846 and closed in 1882. It was served
by sidings ½m N of Etherley Station on NER Crook-Bishop Auckland line.
The site was taken over much later by Witton Park Slag Co Ltd (q.v.).

There may well have been locos at the works before those given below.

Gauge: 4' 8½"

VAUGHAN	0-4-0ST	OC	MW	416	1872	New	s/s
WITTON	0-4-0ST	OC	BH	367	1877	New	(1)
WEAR	0-4-0ST	OC	BH	368	1877	New	s/s
WHITWORTH	0-4-0ST	OC	BH	519	1879	New	s/s

(1) to Newlandside Quarry, Stanhope

JOHN BOWES & PARTNERS LTD
(John Bowes, Esq., & Partners until 21/7/1886; Marley Hill Coal Co until
11/1847)

This firm became one of the largest coal owners in North-East England,
with collieries in both Durham and Northumberland. The original partners
were John Bowes (1811-1885), William Hutt (1801-1882), Nicholas Wood
(1795-1865) and the Countess of Strathmore (1787-1860), who in the summer
of 1839 formed the Marley Hill Coal Company. Charles Mark Palmer
(1822-1907) became a full partner in 1846.

H10 Originally the partners owned only <u>Marley Hill Colliery</u>(Map 78, NZ 206575),
where a new sinking was opened in May 1840. In time nearly two dozen
collieries were to pass through their hands, but most of the important
ones in Co. Durham were eventually served by

<u>Bowes Railway</u> (Pontop & Jarrow Railway until 1932)
    This was basically put together in four sections. The first ran south-west
H6 from Marley Hill to <u>Burnopfield Colliery</u> (NZ 173562), which was acquired in
    November 1849, though the railway to it had been built in 1844-5. This line
H7 also served <u>Crookbank Colliery</u> (NZ 187571), acquired in December 1847, and
H11 <u>Andrews House Colliery</u> (NZ 205573). This colliery was acquired in the
    summer of 1852 and re-opened in December 1852, but was originally served by

sidings W of the NER Tanfield Branch; it was connected to the Partners'
line in 1854.

In February 1850, by an agreement back-dated to 1st January 1850, the
Partners took over the Springwell Railway and the collieries owned by Lord
Ravensworth & Partners (q.v.). This line had originally opened in January
H16 1826 to convey coal from Mount Moor Colliery (NZ 279577) and
F7   Springwell Colliery (NZ 285589) to
E13 Jarrow Staithes (NZ 318655). In May 1842 this line had been extended
H14 westwards to Kibblesworth Colliery (NZ 243562), owned by George Southern.

The Marley Hill line joined the (NER) Tanfield Branch at Bowes Bridge,
but with the acquisition of the Springwell line the Partners eventually
decided to link Marley Hill to Kibblesworth, so that all their coal could
be shipped at Jarrow. Kibblesworth Colliery was taken over in November 1851,
and the connecting link eventually opened in September 1854. At the same
H5   time the western end of the line was extended to a new colliery at Dipton
(NZ 158358), opened in April 1855. From Dipton to Jarrow was fifteen miles,
and the title "Pontop & Jarrow Railway" was given to it in November 1853.

In the winter of 1860 Crookbank Colliery was replaced by a new
H8   colliery at Byermoor (NZ 187573), while at the eastern end of the line the
D3   Partners acquired Wardley Colliery (NZ 306620) in April 1868, built a ½m
branch to it, and re-opened it in the summer of 1871. This colliery had
rather a short life, for in December 1911 coal winding ceased, and the
D4   colliery was replaced by Follonsby Colliery (NZ 313608), served by another
branch (¼m) and opened in June 1912. In July 1908 a new coking and bye-
products plant was opened at Marley Hill to replace the hundreds of beehive
H15 coke ovens at all the western collieries, and in 1914 Kibblesworth Grange
Drift (NZ 249564) was opened.

The economic depression between the wars resulted in the closure of
Andrews House Colliery in December 1920, to be followed by Springwell
(Vale Pit) (later name for Mount Moor Colliery) in May 1931, Springwell
Colliery itself in June 1932, Kibblesworth Grange Drift in December 1932
and Dipton Colliery in November 1940, the last causing the closure of the
railway between Dipton and Burnopfield. In the same year Follonsby Colliery
was sold to the Washington Coal Co Ltd, though it continued to be worked by
D5   Bowes Railway locomotives. On the credit side Monkton Coke Works (NZ
315626) was opened in April 1937 to replace the now obsolete plant at
H13 Marley Hill, and Blackburn Fell Drift (NZ 214573) followed in July 1937.

From Dipton to Birkheads Bank Top (NZ 222568), about 5¼ miles, locomotives were used, though until 1900 the ¼m section east of Burnopfield
Colliery was a rope-worked incline operated by a stationary engine. The
H12 loco shed was at Marley Hill. From Birkheads the wagons travelled over six
rope-worked inclines, the first and last being operated on the self-acting
principle and the other four by stationary engines. The Kibblesworth Engine
lowered the wagons down to the bottom of the Team Valley, whence the Black
Fell Engine hauled them up to Mount Moor. From here the Blackham's Hill
Engine hauled them up to its engine house before lowering them down to
Springwell Colliery, where the Railway's workshops were situated. After
descending the Springwell self-acting incline, the final four miles to
F2   Jarrow were worked by locomotives from a shed at Springwell Bank Foot.

A passenger service was operated from 1843 to 1872 between Springwell
Station, on a loop between the Railway and the (NER) line between Gateshead
and Sunderland, and Jarrow (Ellison Street). Also at Jarrow the Railway was
linked to the huge complex of Palmers Shipbuilding & Iron Co Ltd (q.v.),
served the paint works of Foster, Blackett & Wilson Ltd (q.v.) and had a
link with the NER line from Gateshead to South Shields at Pontop Junction,
½m W of Jarrow Station. In the west a link was put in to the Lintz Colliery
waggonway (see Lintz Coal Co) in 1867, but this was abandoned about 1870.

The Railway, together with the collieries at Burnopfield, Byermoor,
Marley Hill, Kibblesworth and Blackburn Fell Drift, and Monkton Coke Works,
passed to NCB Northern Division No.6 Area on 1st January 1947.

Ref: "The Bowes Railway" by C. E. Mountford, 1966.

PONTOP and JARROW (BOWES) RAILWAY and
Felling Colliery – John Bowes and Partners Ltd 1913

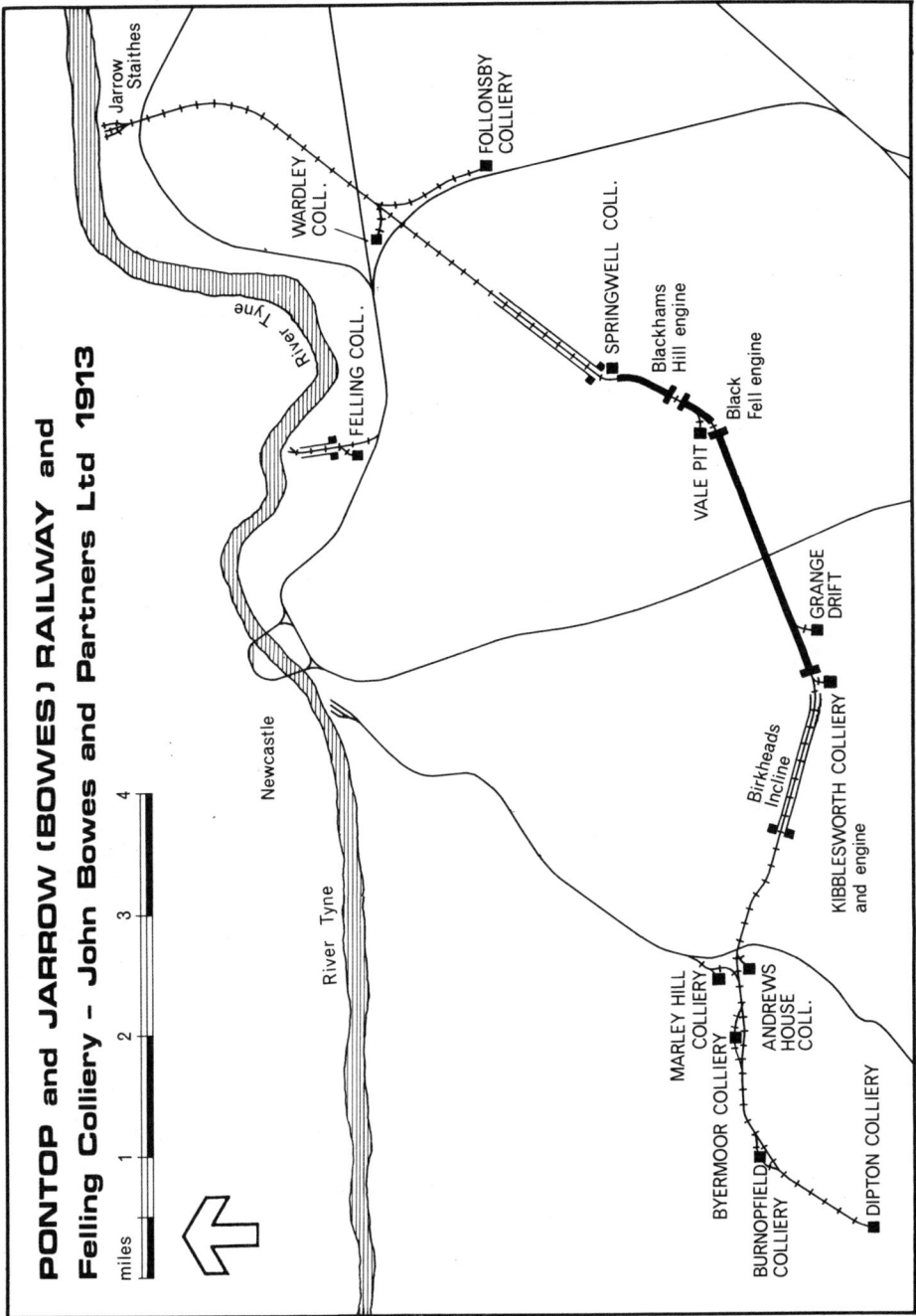

miles
0 1 2 3 4

River Tyne

Newcastle

Jarrow Staithes

FOLLONSBY COLLIERY

WARDLEY COLL.

SPRINGWELL COLL.

FELLING COLL.

River Tyne

Blackhams Hill engine

Black Fell engine

VALE PIT

GRANGE DRIFT

Birkheads Incline

KIBBLESWORTH COLLIERY and engine

MARLEY HILL COLLIERY

ANDREWS HOUSE COLL.

BYERMOOR COLLIERY

BURNOPFIELD COLLIERY

DIPTON COLLIERY

Not a great deal is known about the early locomotives, especially those at Marley Hill. A numbering scheme seems to have been introduced about 1860. The details given below for the first Nos. 3 to 8 must be regarded as largely conjectural, built up from the scraps of existing evidence. The loco sheds are coded as follows:

MH   Marley Hill
SBF   Springwell Bank Foot

Gauge: 4' 8½"

	BOWES	2-4-0?					(a)	MH s/s
	GIBSIDE	2-4-0	IC	RS			(a)	MH s/s
	STRATHMORE						(b)	SBF s/s
No.2		0-6-0	OC	RWH	476	1846	(c)	MH (1)

(a) the first loco to work at Marley Hill arrived in 6/1847; whether it was one of these locos is unknown
(b) ex Lord Ravensworth & Partners, 1/1/1850 ?
(c) ex NER, No.29, 11/1855

(1) to Northumberland & Durham Coal Co (subsidiary of John Bowes & Partners), Blackwall, London, by 1/1859

No.1	"BULL"	0-4-0	VC	RS	1	1826	(a)	SBF-MH (via RS reps) 1/1851 (1)
1		0-6-2ST	IC	BH	937	1888	New	SBF
				reb. HL		1901		Scr 9/1936
No.2		0-4-0	VC	RS	2	1826	(a)	SBF (2)
No.2	(later 2)	0-6-0	IC	RS	1516	1864	New	SBF
		reb. 0-6-0ST	IC	RS	2902	1898		Scr 3/1937
No.3	STREATLAM	0-4-0	OC	RS	795	1851	New	SBF (3)
No.3	(later 3)	0-6-2ST	IC	BH	938	1888	New	SBF-MH 11/34 -SBF 3/42 (4)
No.4	MARLEY HILL	0-4-0	OC	RS	816	1851	New	MH s/s c/1886
No.4	(later 4)	0-6-0ST	OC	BH	891	1887	New	MH-SBF 10/07 -MH 6/08 (5)
4		0-4-0ST	OC	KS	4030	1919	(b)	SBF (6)
No.5	DANIEL O'ROURKE	0-4-0ST	IC	Marley Hill		1854	New	MH Scr c/1885
No.5		0-6-0ST	OC	RWH	1986	1884	New✓	SBF-MH by /04 -SBF 1/32 Scr 9/1936
No.5		0-6-0T	IC	Ghd	7	1897	(c)	SBF Scr 10/1946
No.6		0-6-0	IC	RS	1074	1856	New	?-MH by 1885 s/s c/1890
No.6		0-4-0WT	OC	FJ	125	1874	(d)	MH (7)
No.6	(later 6)	0-6-0ST	OC	HL	2515	1901	New	MH-SBF 6/45
				reb. LG		1930		(4)
No.7							(e)	? s/s by 1874
No.7	(later 7)	0-6-0ST	IC	BH	304	1874	New	SBF-MH by /04 Scr /1933
7		0-4-0ST	OC	CF	1203	1901	(f)	SBF-MH 12/34 -SBF 5/38-MH 11/38-SBF 7/41 (8)
No.8							(e)	? s/s by 1882
No.8	(later 8)	0-6-0ST	IC	BH	692	1882	New	MH Scr c9/1934
No.8		0-6-0ST	IC	SS	4594	1900	(g)	SBF Scr 9/1946

No.9 (later 9)		0-6-0ST	IC	∅			(h)	MH-SBF ?/?
	reb.			RS	2821	1894		-MH 10/07-SBF
								6/08-MH 1/26
								-SBF 12/27-MH
								10/29-SBF 4/31
								Scr 2/1935
No.9		0-6-0PT	IC	SS	4051	1894		
	reb. Caerphilly							
						1930	(j)	SBF (9)
No.10 (HARTLEPOOL)		0-6-0	IC	TR	252	1854	New?	SBF (10)
	reb.	0-6-0ST	IC	BH		1877		
10		0-6-2ST	IC	BH	1071	1892	New	SBF Scr 10/
								1931
No.10		0-6-0PT	IC	NBL	16628	1905		
	reb.Sdn					1924	(k)	SBF (4)
No.11 (later 11)		0-6-0	IC	RS	1313	1860	New	SBF
	reb.	0-6-0ST	IC	RS		1875?		Scr /1915
11		0-6-0ST	OC	HL	3103	1915	New	MH-SBF 9/45
								(4)
No.12		0-6-0ST	IC	RS	1612	1864	New	SBF Scr /1885
12		0-6-0ST	OC	HL	2719	1907	New	MH (4)
No.13		0-6-0	IC	RS	1611	1864	New	SBF? Scr /1896
13		0-6-0ST	IC	HL	2545	1902	New	SBF-MH 7/31
								-SBF 11/37
								(4)
No.14		0-6-0ST	IC	RS	1800	1866	New	? (11)
14		0-6-2T	IC	CF	1158	1898	(m)	MH-SBF 3/14
								Scr 9/1923
14		0-6-0ST	IC	HL	3569	1923	New	SBF-MH 2/42
								(4)
15		0-6-0T	IC	HE	1506	1930	New	MH (4)
16		0-6-0ST	IC	VF	5288	1945	(n)	SBF (4)
17		0-6-0ST	IC	VF	5298	1945	(p)	MH (4)
39		0-6-0ST	IC	RWH	1422	1867	(q)	SBF (12)

✗ Delivered 3/1886.   ∅ Built by RS ?

(a) ex Lord Ravensworth & Partners, 1/1/1850
(b) ex Felling Colliery, 4/1926
(c) ex LNER, 1787, 8/1936
(d) ex Lord Dunsany & Partners, c/1890
(e) probably one of these was ex LNWR 54, 2-2-0 built Bury 1841, and delivered to Marley Hill 12/1855
(f) ex Felling Colliery, date unknown, but first recorded repair was 3/1932; ran as FELLING No.1 until 11/1934
(g) ex GWR, 713, 7/1936, via R.H. Longbotham & Co Ltd; arr. 8/1936
(h) ex ?, c/1860
(j) ex GWR, 717, 11/1934, via R.H. Longbotham & Co Ltd
(k) ex GWR, 725, 11/1934, via R.H. Longbotham & Co Ltd
(m) ex Harton Coal Co Ltd, South Shields, Marsden & Whitburn Colliery Railway, No.7, /1912, via Frazer
(n) ex WD, 75298, 4/1946; arr.5/1946
(p) ex WD, 75308, 4/1946; arr.5/1946

(1) converted to stationary boiler, and scr c/1887
(2) to Killingworth Colliery, Northumberland, /1863
(3) to Killingworth Colliery by /1880
(4) to NCB No.6 Area, 1/1/1947
(5) to Sir W.G.Armstrong Whitworth & Co Ltd(Lemington, Northumberland?) /1917
(6) ret. to Felling Colliery, 10/1927; to SBF, 12/1929; to MH (via WB reps), 9/1943; to NCB No.6 Area, 1/1/1947
(7) to Felling Colliery, c/1895
(8) loaned to Bedlington Coal Co Ltd, Northumberland, 11/1942; ret. to SBF,8/1944; scr 10/1946
(9) loaned to Harton Coal Co Ltd, Boldon Colliery, 2/1943; ret. to SBF, 8/1943; to MH, 10/1945; to NCB No. 6 Area, 1/1/1947
(10) to Killingworth Colliery by /1866; ret. to SBF, boiler exploded at Jarrow Staithes, 14/6/1882; to MH, c/1883; to Killingworth Colliery, c/1886
(11) to Carron Co, Falkirk, c/1880(?)

(q) hired from Lambton, Hetton   (12) ret. to Lambton, Hetton & Joicey
    Joicey Collieries Ltd, Lambton   Collieries Ltd, 3/1938
    Railway, 12/1937

<u>Felling Colliery</u>, Felling. Map 78, NZ 275624.
(Sir G.Elliot until 5/3/1883)

D1 This old colliery was the scene of a serious explosion in May 1812, in
which 91 people died, and which led directly to the invention of the
miners' safety lamp. It was served by sidings N. of the LNER Gateshead-
South Shields line, immediately W of Felling Station. The colliery also
had its own line to staithes on R.Tyne. It closed in April 1931.

Gauge: 4' 8½"

FELLING No.1	0-4-0ST	OC	BH	223	1871	New	s/s	
FELLING No.2	0-4-0ST	OC	BH	203	1871	New	(1)	
FELLING No.2	0-4-0ST	OC	HL	2152	1889	New	(2)	
BEACONSFIELD	0-4-0ST	OC	N			(a)	s/s	
ABBEY	0-4-0ST	OC	BH	317	1874	(b)	(3)	
FELLING No.2	0-4-0WT	OC	FJ	125	1874	(c)	Scr	/1917
FELLING No.1	0-4-0ST	OC	CF	1203	1901	New	(4)	
FELLING No.2	0-4-0ST	OC	KS	4030	1919	New	(5)	

(a) origin unknown   (1) to Marquis of Londonderry,
(b) hired from BH, /1892   Londonderry Railway, /1890
(c) ex Pontop & Jarrow Railway,   (2) to Bede Metal & Chemical Co Ltd,
    Marley Hill, c/1895   Hebburn (c/1901?)
                                     (3) ret. to BH
                                     (4) to Bowes Railway, Springwell
                                       Bank Foot, c3/1932
                                     (5) to Pontop & Jarrow Railway,
                                       Springwell Bank Foot, 4/1926;
                                       ret. 10/1927; to Springwell Bank
                                       Foot, 12/1929

<u>D. SEP. BOWRAN LTD</u>, SHIPCOTE WORKS, GATESHEAD

C17 A scrap-yard and works (Map 78, NZ 261629) on the site of the former BR
Park Lane Goods Depot, and served by sidings S of BR Gateshead-South
Shields line, ¼m E of Gateshead Station. The works did not have a loco
before the one below.

Gauge: 4' 8½"

-	0-4-0DM	RH	281270	1951	(a)	
No.5	0-6-0DM	HC	D835	1954	(b)	

(a) ex Hawthorn Leslie (Engineers)
    Ltd, St. Peter's Works,
    Newcastle, 4/1974
(b) ex CEGB, Stella South G.S., Blaydon

<u>BRITISH CHROME & CHEMICALS LTD</u>, EAGLESCLIFFE WORKS, URLAY NOOK
(subsidiary of Harrisons & Crosfield Ltd, who took over and set up a new
company using title of former owners (see below), 1/11/1973; Albright &
Wilson Ltd, Industrial Chemicals Division, until 1/11/1973; Albright &
Wilson Ltd, Associated Chemical Companies Division, until 6/1972; Assoc-
iated Chemical Companies (Fertilisers) Ltd until 1965; British Chrome &
Chemicals Ltd until 29/5/1958; Eaglescliffe Chemical Co Ltd until 1953;
Egglescliffe Chemical Co Ltd until 1938; orig. Egglescliffe Chemical Co)

W7 This works (Map 85, NZ 401147) was begun in 1833, shortly after the opening
of the Stockton & Darlington Railway, and is served by sidings N of the
present BR line, 1½m W of Eaglescliffe Junction. The works was shunted by
horses until the arrival of the first loco below.

Gauge: 4' 8½"

"COFFEE POT"	0-4-0VBT	IC				(a)	s/s after 1920
-	0-4-0ST	OC	HCR	139	1874	(b)	(1)
VICTORIA	0-4-0ST	OC	P	634	1897	(c)	Scr 3/1939
-	0-4-0ST	OC	AB	266	1884	(d)	(2)
-	0-4-0ST	OC	AB			(e)	s/s
PRINCESS ELIZABETH							
	0-4-0DM		JF	4200020	1947	New	(3)
PRINCESS MARGARET	4wDM		FH	3492	1951	New	
-	4wDM		FH	3808	1956	(f)	

(a) origin unknown
(b) ex Hogg & Henderson, dealers,
    Middlesbrough, Yorks, N.R.
(c) ex Linthorpe-Dinsdale Smelting
    Co Ltd, Middleton St. George
(d) ex Wake, Darlington, hire, /1917
(e) ex DL, Britannia Works, Middles-
    brough, Yorks, N.R., /1943
(f) ex Shawfield Works, Rutherglen,
    Glasgow, 10/1968

(1) to HC, /1914; re-sold to Hugh
    Symington & Co Ltd, Gretna
    contract, Cumberland, 5/1915
(2) ret. to Wake
(3) to Henderson Clark Ltd, Middles-
    brough, Yorks, N.R., for scrap,
    /1970

BRITISH CRANE & EXCAVATOR CORPORATION LTD, CROWN WORKS, PALLION, SUNDERLAND
(Steels Engineering Products Ltd until 28/3/1964 (both firms were
subsidiaries of Steel Group Ltd (Steel & Co Ltd until 1/10/1965))

K7 Works (Map 78, NZ 375580) was opened in late 1930's on the site of the
    former Egis Shipyard (see National Shipbuilders Securities Ltd). It was
    served by a branch (½m) from Pallion Station on BR Sunderland-Durham line,
    and was shunted by a loco from the adjacent shipyard of Short Bros Ltd
    (q.v.) until March 1956, when the work was taken over by a loco which the
    firm had built itself. Rail traffic ceased in 1967.

Gauge: 4' 8½"

-	4wDE	Coles	16640	1956	New	(1)

(1) to Crane Machinery Services Ltd,
    Feltham, Middlesex, 11/1967

BRITISH GAS CORPORATION, NORTHERN DIVISION
(Northern Gas Board until 1/1/1973)

Redheugh Works, Gateshead. Map 78, NZ 237625

C1 This works was closed at the time of the Corporation's creation, with the
    locomotive awaiting disposal.

Gauge: 4' 8½"

-	4wDM	RH	476140	1963	(a)	(1)

(a) ex Northern Gas Board, 1/1/1973

(1) to North of England Open-Air
    Museum, Marley Hill Loco Shed,
    for preservation, 3/1973

BRITISH RAILWAYS BOARD

Originally stockyards, depots, etc., were operated by locomotives in the capital stock list, but from about 1955 these duties were taken over by service locomotives belonging to the Chief Civil Engineer, though they too were included in capital stock. This continued until about the spring of 1969, when the duties were resumed by normal locomotives in capital stock.

Central Reclamation Depot and Croft Junction Storeyard, Darlington.

V20 The Reclamation depot, which was controlled by the Chief Civil Engineer, York, and the Croft Junction Storeyard, which came under the District Engineer, were situated together (Map 85, NZ 295130) about $\frac{1}{2}$m S of Darlington (Bank Top) Station on the BR Darlington-York line, in the triangle formed by the main line, the Stockton-Darlington line and the Geneva Loop. Both yards are now closed.

Gauge: 4' 8$\frac{1}{2}$"

87	4wDM	RH	463152	1961	New	(1)

(1) to Thornaby M.P.D. by 4/1969, and since scrapped

Etherley Tip, Witton Park. Map 85, NZ 174304.

T20 This tip for waste ballast is situated on BR Bishop Auckland-Wear Valley Branch, 2$\frac{1}{2}$m W of Bishop Auckland Station.

Gauge: 4' 8$\frac{1}{2}$"

56	4wDM	RH	338424	1955	(a)	(1)

(a) ex Chalk Lane Stockyard, Hull, Yorks, E.R.

(1) to Thornaby M.P.D. by 4/1969, and since scrapped

Permanent Way Stockyard, Low Fell, Gateshead. Map 78, NZ 248608.

C11 This stockyard lies W of BR Newcastle-Durham line, 2m S of Newcastle Central Station.

Gauge: 4' 8$\frac{1}{2}$"

83	4wDM	RH	432477	1959	New	(1)

(1) to Thornaby M.P.D. by 4/1969, and since scrapped

Rail Welding Depot, Dinsdale. Map 85, NZ 348138.

W6 This depot is served by sidings from Oak Tree Signal Box on BR Stockton-Darlington line, 3$\frac{1}{2}$m E of Darlington (Bank Top) Station.

Gauge: 4' 8$\frac{1}{2}$"

82	4wDM	RH	425485	1958	New	(1)

(1) to Thornaby M.P.D. by 4/1969, and since scrapped

BRITISH STEEL CORPORATION (Vesting day was 28/7/1967; but actual re-organisation did not occur until 1/7/1968, and a further re-organisation was carried out on 29/3/1970)

Blackdene Mine, Ireshopeburn, near Wearhead. Map 84, NY 868389.
(United Steel Companies Ltd, Ore Mining Branch, until 1/7/1968)

Z3 This is an old mine, worked by various companies for lead, and closed in the 1930's. It was re-opened to mine fluorspar in 1965, and was still being developed when nationalisation took place. The locomotives below work underground, but are usually brought to the surface at weekends. There is no main line rail connection.

Gauge: 2' 0" (underground)

	–	4wBE	GB	6017	1960	(a)	(1)
	–	0-4-0BE	WR	7056	1969	New	
	–	4wBE	GB	2996	1960	(b)	(1)
1	JOHN	4wBE	GB	6018	1960	(b)	(1)
	–	0-4-0BE	WR	7544	1972	New	
II		4wBE	CE	B0134A	1973	New	
I		4wBE	CE	B0134B	1973	New	

(a) ex Nettleton Top Mines, Lincs,   (1) to J.A.Lister & Sons Ltd,
    via Dragonby Shops, c6/1969;   Consett, for scrap, and removed
    prev. 2' 6" gauge   12/1974
(b) ex Nettleton Top Mines, Lincs.
    /1970; prev. 2' 6" gauge

Consett Works, Consett. General Steels Division.
(Northern Tubes Group until 29/3/1970; Consett Iron Co Ltd until 1/7/1968)

A large complex, covered by Map 84 NZ 0949/1049 and Map 78, NZ 0950/1050.
G13 The loco sheds are at Templetown NZ 109500.
    N.B. Other locomotives, not owned by the Corporation, were stored here
          between 1969 and 1973 awaiting restoration by their owners.

The Consett Works is also responsible for the locomotives at the Jarrow Works (see below), and so the following abbreviations have been used:

                    C   Consett Works
                    J   Jarrow Works

Gauge: 4' 8½"

B No.13	0-4-0ST	OC	HL	3953	1938	(a)	C	Scr 5/1971

(a) ex Consett Iron Co Ltd, 1/7/1968;
    stored.

1	0-6-0DM	HE	3504	1947	(a)	C	Scr 3/1970
2	0-6-0DM	HE	3580	1949	(a)	C	Scr 3/1970
3	0-4-0DM	HE	4010	1950	(a)	C	Scr 3/1970
4	0-4-0DM	HE	4011	1950	(a)	C	Scr 5/1970
5	0-6-0DE	WB/BT	3020	1951	(a)	C	Scr 5/1970
6	0-6-0DE	WB/BT	3021	1951	(a)	C	(2)
7	0-4-0DM	HE	4431	1953	(a)	C	(4)
8	0-4-0DM	HE	4432	1953	(a)	C	(4)
9	0-6-0DM	Consett		1956	(a)	C	Scr 2/1971
10	0-6-0DM	Consett		1958	(a)	C	
11	0-6-0DM	HE	4987	1956	(a)	C	Scr 2/1971
12	0-6-0DM	HE	4988	1957	(a)	C	Scr 2/1971
13	0-6-0DM	HE	4989	1957	(a)	C	Scr 2/1971
14	0-6-0DM	HE	5173	1957	(a)	C	
15	0-6-0DM	HE	5174	1957	(a)	C	Scr 11/1973
16	0-6-0DM	HE	5175	1957	(a)	C	Scr 2/1971

17		0-6-0DM	HE	5375	1958	(a) C	(3)	
18		0-6-0DM	HE	5376	1958	(a) C		
20		0-6-0DM	HE	5378	1958	(a) C-J 3/71		
21		0-6-0DM	HE	5379	1958	(a) C-J 12/69-C3/71		
22		0-6-0DM	HE	5380	1958	(a) C-J 8/75		
23		0-6-0DM	HE	5381	1958	(a) C		
24		0-4-0DM	HE	5384	1959	(a) C		
25		0-4-0DM	HE	5385	1959	(a) C-J 9/69-J 4/73		
28		0-6-0DH	HE	5392	1959	(a) C Scr 9/1970		
29		0-6-0DH	HE	5393	1959	(a) C	(5)	
30		0-6-0DH	HE	5394	1959	(a) C	(3)	
–		0-6-0DH	RR	10278	1968	(b) C	(1)	
17	(19 until 8/73)	0-6-0DM	HE	5377	1958	(c) C		
26		0-4-0DM	HE	5386	1959	(d) C-J 4/73		
31		0-6-0DH	RR	10285	1969	New C		
32		0-6-0DH	RR	10286	1969	New C		
33		0-6-0DH	RR	10287	1969	New C		
34		0-6-0DH	RR	10288	1969	New C		
35		4wDH	TH	221V	1970	New C		
36		4wDH	TH	222V	1970	New C		
37		4wDH	TH	223V	1970	New C		
38		4wDH	TH	224V	1970	New C		
39		0-6-0DH	RR	10289	1970	New C		
40		0-6-0DH	RR	10290	1970	New C		

≠ modified to work coke car at Fell Coke Works if required

(a) ex Consett Iron Co Ltd, 1/7/1968
(b) RR demonstration loco; ex Lindsay Oil Refinery Ltd, Immingham, Lincs, 2/1969
(c) ex Jarrow Works 10/1969
(d) ex Jarrow Works 12/1969

(1) to NCB Northumberland Area, Bates Colliery, Blyth, 4/1969; ret. to Consett, 6/1969; to British Steel Corporation, Ravenscraig Works, Motherwell, Lanarkshire, 7/1969
(2) to Trostre Works, Carmarthenshire, 8/1971
(3) to J.Lister & Sons Ltd, Consett, for scrap, 12/1972
(4) to J.Lister & Sons Ltd, Consett, for scrap, 8/1972; scr 6/1974
(5) sold for scrap, 11/1974

Gauge: 4' 8½"

E No. 1	2-4-0VBCr OC	BH	897	1887	(a) C		
E No. 6	0-4-0VBCr OC	BH	1049	1892	(a) C	Scr 2/1971	
E No. 9	2-4-0VBCr OC	RS	2854	1898	(a) C	(2)	
E No.10	0-4-0VBCr OC	CF	1206	1901	(a) C	(1)	

(a) ex Consett Iron Co Ltd, 1/7/1968

(1) to J.Lister & Sons Ltd, Consett, for scrap 9/1969
(2) dism; boiler fitted to E No.1, 1973

Fell Coke Ovens, Consett. NZ 0949 (locos used to haul coke cars)

Gauge: 4' 8½"

–	0-4-0WE	Goodman		1924	(a)
–	0-4-0WE	GB	2368	1952	(a)
		reb.Consett 1972			
–	4wWE	GB	420306	1972	New

(a) ex Consett Iron Co Ltd, 1/7/1968

<u>Darlington Forge Works</u>, Darlington. Map 85, NZ 295157.
(Darlington Forge Ltd (subsidiary of ESC) until 1/7/1968)

V9   This works, served by sidings N of BR Bishop Auckland-Darlington line,
     immediately N of Albert Hill Junction, was closed in February 1967, but
     survived to be included in the British Steel Corporation on 1st July 1968.
     The locomotives were occasionally used in salvage work before disposal.

Gauge: 4' 8½"

-	0-4-0ST	OC	RSH	7013	1940	(a)	Scr	/1970
No.46	0-4-0DM		HC	D1159	1961	(a)	(1)	
No.48	0-4-0DM		HC	D1161	1961	(a)	(1)	

(a) ex Darlington Forge Ltd,   (1) to Llanelly Steel Co Ltd,
    1/7/1968   Carmarthenshire, c6/1971, via
                                           Howard & Pepperell Ltd,
                                           Sheffield, Yorks, W.R.

<u>Hartlepool Works</u>, Hartlepool. General Steels Division.
(South Durham Steel & Iron Co Ltd until 29/3/1970; subsidiary of British
Steel & Tube Ltd from 22/6/1967, which was a subsidiary of British Steel
Corporation from 28/7/1967)

      This large complex (Map 85, NZ 5130/5131 and 5028/5029) is divided into
S9   two parts - the <u>North Works</u>, whose main entrance is at NZ 51**6318**, and the
S11 <u>South Works</u>, whose main entrance is at NZ 513291. The South Works loco
     shed (NZ 510288) provides locomotives for the whole complex, using both
     an internal link and running powers over the BR Cliff House Branch.
     Operations at the North Works have been reduced, and from 1971 only the
     coke ovens (in use) and the blast furnaces (not in use) have been retained.
     There are various access points from BR on the line between Hartlepool and
     Billingham.

     In 1973 it was proposed to re-number locomotives Nos. 2-11, 15, 16, 19 and
     450-454 to 960-977 in the same order, but only a few were actually carrying
     their new numbers when the scheme was abandoned, and the old numbers re-
     instated. Later in 1973 a new scheme was proposed, to add 900 to the same
     locomotives' existing numbers, but up to January 1974 no locomotive was
     carrying its new number.

Gauge: 4' 8½"

1	0-4-0DM	JF	4210146	1958	(a)	Scr 1/1973
2	0-6-0DH	JF	4240001	1959	(a)	
3	0-6-0DH	JF	4240002	1959	(a)	
4	0-6-0DH	JF	4240003	1959	(a)	
5	0-6-0DH	JF	4240004	1959	(a)	
6	0-6-0DH	JF	4240005	1960	(a)	
7	0-6-0DH	JF	4240006	1960	(a)	
8	0-6-0DH	JF	4240007	1960	(a)	
9	0-6-0DH	JF	4240008	1960	(a)	
10	0-6-0DH	JF	4240009	1960	(a)	
11	0-6-0DH	JF	4240011	1961	(a)	
15	0-4-0DH	JF	4220027	1964	(a)	
16	0-4-0DH	JF	4220028	1964	(a)	
19	0-4-0DM	JF	4210089	1953		
			reb. JF		1965	(a)	
20	0-4-0DM	JF	4210091	1954	(a)	Scr 1/1973
21	0-4-0DM	JF	4210094	1954		
			reb. JF		1966	(a)	(4)
22	0-4-0DM	JF	4210099	1955	(a)	Scr 1/1973
23	0-4-0DM	JF	4210102	1955	(a)	Scr 1/1973
24	0-4-0DM	JF	4210107	1955	(a)	Scr 7/1972
25	0-4-0DM	JF	4210110	1956	(a)	Scr 1/1973

27		0-4-0DM	JF	4210128	1957	(a)	Scr 7/1972
28		0-4-0DM	HC	D978	1957	(a)	
29		0-4-0DM	HC	D1052	1958	(a)	
No.30		0-4-0DM	HC	D1141	1959	(a)	
31		0-4-0DM	JF	4210148	1958	(a)	Scr 1/1973
33	BOYLE	0-4-0DE	RH	408309	1957	(a)	
34	(JAMES WATT)	0-4-0DE	RH	381757	1955	(a)	
32		0-4-0DM	HC	D1013	1957	(a)	Scr 9/1971
33		0-4-0DM	HC	D1081	1958	(a)	Scr 9/1971
36		0-4-0DM	HC	D1032	1958	(a)	Scr 7/1972
6	FARNDALE	0-6-0DE	YE	2719	1958	(b)	(1)
12	MARDALE	0-6-0DE	YE	2743	1959	(b)	(3)
11	LINGDALE	0-6-0DE	YE	2742	1959	(c)	(2)
1	ALLENDALE	0-6-0DE	YE	2629	1956	(d)	(3)
450		4wDH	TH	231V	1971	New	
451		4wDH	TH	232V	1971	New	
452		4wDH	TH	233V	1971	New	
453	(CHURCHILL)	4wDH	S	10025	1960	(e)	
454		4wDH	S	10018	1960	(f)	

(a) ex South Durham Steel & Iron Co Ltd, 29/3/1970
(b) on loan from ICI, Billingham Works, Teesside, to SDSI prior to 29/3/1970; on loan to BSC after that date
(c) ex ICI, Billingham Works, Teesside, 5/1970, loan
(d) ex ICI, Billingham Works, Teesside, 9/1970, loan
(e) ex Britannia Works, Middlesbrough, Teesside,10/1971
(f) ex Britannia Works, Middlesbrough, Teesside, 7/1972

(1) ret. to ICI, Billingham Works, Teesside, 5/1970
(2) ret. to ICI, Billingham Works, Teesside, 9/1970
(3) ret. to ICI, Billingham Works, Teesside, 4/1971
(4) to North Yorkshire Moors Railway, 5/1972

Gauge: 4' 8½"

-		4wWE	GB	1448	1936	(a)
-		0-4-0WE	GB	2937	1960	(b)
-		0-4-0WE	HL		1936	(c)

(a) ex South Durham Steel & Iron Co Ltd, 29/3/1970; at North Works
(b) ex South Durham Steel & Iron Co Ltd, 29/3/1970; at South Works
(c) ex Cleveland Coke Ovens, Middlesbrough, Teesside, 12/1971

Jarrow Works, Jarrow. General Steels Division.
(Northern Tubes Group until 29/3/1970; Consett Iron Co Ltd until 1/7/1968).

E17 This works (Map 78, NZ 324655) is served by ½m branch from BR Gateshead-South Shields line at Jarrow Station. Locomotives are the responsibility of Consett Works, and so the following abbreviations are used below:

C   Consett Works (q.v.)
J   Jarrow Works

Gauge: 4' 8½"

19		0-6-0DM	HE	5377	1958	(a) J-C 12/69
26		0-4-0DM	HE	5386	1959	(a) J-C 10/69-J 4/73
25		0-4-0DM	HE	5385	1959	(b) J-C 4/73
21		0-6-0DM	HE	5379	1958	(c) J-C 3/71
20		0-6-0DM	HE	5378	1958	(d) J
22		0-6-0DM	HE	5380	1958	(e)

(a) ex Consett Iron Co Ltd, 1/7/1968
(b) ex Consett Works, 9/1969
(c) ex Consett Works,12/1969
(d) ex Consett Works, 3/1971
(e) ex Consett Works, 8/1975

MARQUIS OF BUTE, GARESFIELD COLLIERY, HIGH SPEN

A3 This Colliery (Map 78, NZ 139598) was served by a private line, 5½m long,
to staithes on R. Tyne at Derwenthaugh. Part of the line was worked by
inclines, the remainder probably being worked by horses originally.
Whether the locos below worked at Garesfield Colliery or Derwenthaugh or
both is not definite. The colliery and its line were taken over by the
Consett Iron Co Ltd in 1891, and part of the route was later incorporated
in that company's Chopwell & Garesfield Railway (q.v.)

Gauge: 4' 8½"

GARESFIELD	0-4-0ST	OC	BH	854	1885	New	(1)
BURLEIGH	0-6-0ST	OC				(a)	(2)
BETTY	0-4-0ST					(b)	(1)

(a) ex ?, Leeds, Yorks, W.R., hire   (1) to Consett Iron Co Ltd /1891
(b) origin unknown   (2) ret. to hirer (by 3/1890?)

CARGO FLEET IRON CO LTD, WOODLAND COLLIERY, WOODLAND
(subsidiary of SDSI; Woodland Collieries Co Ltd (subsidiary of CFI) until
1914)

T4 This colliery (Map 84, NZ 066266) was situated at the end of a private
branch line, 4m long, which joined the NER Bishop Auckland-Barnard Castle
line 1½m NE of Cockfield Station. For the operation of this branch see
Woodland Collieries Co Ltd. The colliery closed in March 1921.

Gauge: 4' 8½"

-	0-6-0T	IC	Dar		1876	(a)	Scr c/1921
GEORGE	0-6-0ST	IC				(b)	s/s
No.1	0-4-0ST	OC	HL	2412	1899	(c)	(1)
-	0-4-0ST	OC	Joicey		1870	(d)	(2)

(a) ex Woodland Collieries Co Ltd,   (1) to Irchester Ironstone Co Ltd,
    /1914   Northants, c/1926
(b) ex ?, South Wales, c/1916   (2) to Cargo Fleet Works, Yorks,
(c) ex Weardale Steel, Coal & Coke   N.R., c/1923
    Co Ltd, Tudhoe, c/1918
(d) ex Cargo Fleet Works, Yorks,
    N.R., c/1920

CARLTON IRON CO LTD

This company operated on the southern edge of the Durham coalfield, and
was absorbed into Dorman, Long & Co Ltd on 2nd May 1923.

W1 Carlton Iron Works, Stillington. Map 85, NZ 373237.
(North of England Industrial Iron & Coal Co Ltd until 5/1877; owners until
4/1870 unknown)

This works probably opened in the late 1860's. It was served by sidings
N of NER Ferryhill-Stockton line, adjacent to Stillington Station.
It was taken over by Dorman, Long & Co Ltd on 2nd May 1923.

Gauge: 4' 8½"

3	COMTE DE PARIS	0-6-0ST	OC	BH	166	1870	New	Scr
6	LOTTIE	0-4-0ST	OC	HL	2110	1888	New	
				reb.		1906		(1)
5		0-4-0ST	OC	MW	60	1862	(a)	(2)
	CARLTON No.7	0-6-0ST	OC	HL	2607	1905	New	(3)
	CARLTON No.1	0-6-0ST	OC	HL	2732	1907	New	(3)
	CARLTON No.4	0-6-0ST	OC	VF	422	1858		
				reb.		1884		
				reb.		1903	(b)	(3)
	CARLTON No.2	0-6-0ST	OC	AB	1404	1915	New	(3)
6		0-6-0ST	OC				(c)	Scr

(a) ex Samuel Allsopp & Sons Ltd,
Burton-on-Trent, Staffs
(b) ex TWW, Sheffield, Yorks, W.R.,
c/1911; Rhymney Railway, O10,
until 5/1911
(c) origin unknown

(1) believed to have worked at Mainsforth Colliery at some period; to
DL, 2/5/1923
(2) believed to have worked at Mainsforth Colliery at some period; s/s
(3) to DL, 2/5/1923

<u>East Howle Colliery</u>, near Ferryhill. Map 85, NZ 291339.

R9 This colliery was opened in 1871, and was served by sidings N of NER
Ferryhill- Bishop Auckland line, ½m W of Coxhoe Junction. It was closed in
March 1905 after a fire, and replaced by Mainsforth Colliery (q.v.).

Two locos are recorded here in March 1890, but their identity
is unknown.

<u>Mainsforth Colliery</u>, Ferryhill Station. Map 85, NZ 307316.

R27 This colliery was begun in the 1870's, and coal was reached in June 1877,
but due to the depressed state of the industry the workings were then
closed down. Site work began again in 1900, and the colliery commenced
production in November 1905, to replace East Howle Colliery (q.v.). It was
served by ½m branch from NER Ferryhill-Stockton line, 1m S of Ferryhill
Station, and was taken over by Dorman, Long & Co Ltd on 2nd May 1923.

Which locos worked here is very uncertain, but it has been
suggested that the following did so at some period:

Gauge: 4' 8½"

5		0-4-0ST	OC	MW	60	1862	(a)	(1)
6	LOTTIE	0-4-0ST	OC	HL	2110	1888		
				reb.		1906	(a)	(1)

(a) ex Carlton Iron Works

(1) ret. to Carlton Iron Works (?)

<u>CASSOP COAL CO, NEW CASSOP</u>

N17 <u>Cassop Colliery</u> (Map 85, NZ 341382) was sunk by the Thornley Coal Co
(q.v.), probably in the 1840's, and was situated on a privately-owned
extension of what later became the NER Thornley Branch, about 1½m SW of
N15 Thornley Colliery. The branch ran on for another 1½m to <u>Cassop Moor</u>
N16 <u>Colliery</u> (NZ 320392), with <u>Cassop Vale Colliery</u> (NZ 334390) between the
two, though who owned these two is uncertain. The section between Cassop
Colliery and Thornley was worked by a stationary engine, but how the
remainder of the line was worked is not known. There was also a link from
R17 Cassop to <u>Crowtrees Colliery</u> (NZ 334379), worked by a stationary engine
near the latter colliery, to enable coal from the Coxhoe area to be shipped
at Hartlepool instead of Stockton. This link was opened in December 1839,
but it was later abandoned.

52

From 1850 onwards information about both the collieries and the method of
working the line becomes very confused. It would appear that both Cassop
Moor and Cassop Collieries were closed by the 1850's, and Cassop Vale
became Cassop Colliery (Vale Pit). By 1854 the owner was R.P.Philipson, a
Newcastle solicitor, who continued to work it until 1869. It does not
appear in N.E. Mining Institute records again until 1872, when the owners
are given as Robson & Co. This title appears for the next two years, but
1875 lists "The Owners of Cassop Colliery", and 1876-1877 give "George
Wythes". The title "Cassop Coal Co" only appears in the Manning Wardle
Order Book, and is not found in any North-East records.
It is also not known whether the stationary engine from the old Cassop
Colliery to Thornley was still in use in the 1870's. If it was,then
presumably the loco was used to bring wagons from the Vale Pit to the
incline.
The colliery closed in 1877, but even that does not end the confusion.
It has been suggested that the colliery was re-opened by the owners of
Whitwell Colliery, about ¼m to the north, and linked to the NER branch
there. The present authors can find no evidence of this at all, though
it may be possible that the owners of Whitwell Colliery leased the Cassop
Royalty and worked the coal through their own pit.

Gauge: 4' 8½"

	SWIFT	0-4-0		F&H			(a)	(1)
No.1	CASSOP	0-4-0ST	OC	MW	465	1873	New	(2)

(a) origin unknown   (1) offered for sale, 4/1868; s/s
                                      (2) to Clay Lane Iron Co Ltd, South
                                          Bank, Yorks, N.R.

CASTLE EDEN COAL CO LTD, CASTLE EDEN COLLIERY, near WELLFIELD
(reg. 6/10/1882)

P13 This colliery (Map 85, NZ 437381), on the south-eastern edge of the
    coalfield, was opened in 1840, and had various owners before coming to
    this company. It was served by sidings N of NER Hartlepool Branch,
    immediately W of Hesleden Station, and was worked by the NER until the
    arrival of the loco below. The colliery was flooded in November 1893 and
    closed in January 1894, the equipment being dismantled and auctioned in
    April 1894. It was later acquired by Horden Collieries Ltd (q.v.).

Gauge: 4' 8½"

-	0-4-0ST	OC	BH	613	1881	(a)	(1)

(a) ex West Hartlepool Steel & Iron   (1) to Hulam Coal Co Ltd, Hutton
    Co Ltd, West Hartlepool   Henry Colliery (c4/1894?)

CATERPILLAR TRACTOR CO LTD

Birtley Works, Birtley. Map 78, NZ 272552.
(The Birtley Co Ltd until 8/1956)

H31 This works was reconstructed from the premises of the former Birtley Iron
    Co Ltd (see Pelaw Main Collieries Ltd), and was originally served by a
    branch from the Pelaw Main Railway at "Birtley Tail", as well as by sidings
    E of LNER (BR) Newcastle-Durham line, ¼m S of the former Birtley Station.
    The works has been extensively re-developed by the present owners, and rail
    traffic ceased in July 1966.

Gauge: 4' 8½"

MC 156	0-4-0DM	JF	22900	1941	New	(1)

                                      (1) to S.Tynedale Rly. Preservation Socy,
                                          Slaggyford Stn,Cumberland, 8/1974

CENTRAL ELECTRICITY GENERATING BOARD
(Central Electricity Authority until 1/1/1958; British Electricity
Authority until 1/4/1955)

Darlington Generating Station. Map 85, NZ 294147.
(Darlington Corporation Electricity Dept. until 1/4/1948)

V18 This station was opened in December 1900, and was served by sidings W of
BR Durham-Darlington line, ½m N of Darlington (Bank Top) Station. Rail
traffic was replaced by road transport about 1964.

Gauge: 4' 8½"

JOHN HINKS	0-4-0ST	OC	RSH	7066	1942	New	s/s	c/1962
(No.11)	0-4-0ST	OC	HL	3641	1926	(a)	s/s	c/1968

(a) ex Carville G.S., Newcastle-
upon-Tyne, 9/1960

Sunderland Generating Station. Map 78, NZ 389574.
(Sunderland Corporation until 1/4/1948)

K18 Station served by sidings NE of NCB line from Deptford to Lambton Staithes,
about ¼m from BR junction. Rail traffic was replaced by road transport
about 1959.

Gauge: 4' 8½"

-	4wWE	BTH	1790	c1900	New	Scr	c/1953
-	4wWE	EE	1214	1942	New	Scr	/1963

Gauge: 2' 0"

-	4wPM (?)	FH			(a)	(1)
-	4wPM	L	20982	1943	New	s/s

(a) ex TWW, Sheffield, Yorks, W.R.,   (1) ret. to TWW, Sheffield, Yorks,
    hire, 8/1942; Buckton Quarry Co   W.R., by 3/1943
    Ltd, Stalybridge, Cheshire,
    until 12/1941

Shortly after the North-Eastern Electric Supply Co Ltd was formed in 1932,
it introduced a numbering scheme for its locomotives, based on their age,
at its North Tees, Dunston and Carville (Newcastle) Generating Stations.
This scheme was continued for some time after nationalisation, and was
extended to the new Stations, Stella South in Co. Durham and Stella North
and Blyth in Northumberland, though it never included the locomotives
already listed. What numbers, if any, the locomotives carried before the
introduction of the numbering scheme are not known.
In the list below North Tees Generating Station, although latterly in
Teesside, has been included for the sake of completeness. Gaps in the list
were allocated to locomotives at the Northumberland Generating Stations.

The following abbreviations are used:

D   Dunston Generating Station, Dunston. Map 78, NZ 238626.
        (North-Eastern Electric Supply Co Ltd until 1/4/1948;
        Newcastle-upon-Tyne Electric Supply Co Ltd until 30/9/1932)

B5   This Station was opened in July 1910, and is served by sidings
        from Dunston West Junction on BR Redheugh Branch.

NT   North Tees Generating Station, Haverton Hill. Map 85, NZ 478214.
        (North-Eastern Electric Supply Co Ltd until 1/4/1948;
        Cleveland & Durham Electric Power Ltd until 30/9/1932)

W2   This Station was opened in March 1921, and is served by sidings E of BR Haverton Hill-Stockton line, 1¼m S of Haverton Hill Station.

SS   <u>Stella South Generating Station</u>, near Blaydon. Map 78, NZ 174644.

Bl   This Station was opened in 1953, and is served by sidings N of BR Newcastle-Carlisle line, ½m E of Blaydon Station.

Gauge: 4' 8½"

No. 3		4wWE		DK		1908	New D		s/s c/1964
No. 4		4wWE		DK		1910	New D	(1)	
No. 5		4wBE		DK		1920	New NT-D		Scr /1953
No. 6		4wBE					New NT	(2)	
No. 7	(orig.No.1?)	4wBE					New NT		s/s
No. 8		0-4-0ST	OC	HL	3772	1930	New D		Scr 8/1968
No.10		0-4-0ST	OC	HL	3586	1924	New NT	(3)	
No.11		0-4-0ST	OC	HL	3641	1926	New D	(4)	
No.12		0-4-0ST	OC	HL	3651	1926	New NT-D c/62		
							-NT c6/63		Scr c/1968
No.13		0-4-0ST	OC	HL	3732	1928	(a) D	(5)	
No.14		0-4-0DE		AW	D21	1933	New D		
No.15		0-4-0ST	OC	RSH	7063	1942	New D	(6)	
69		0-6-0ST	IC	HC	1609	1934	(b) D	(7)	
No.16		0-4-0ST	OC	RSH	7359	1947	New NT	(8)	
No.17		0-4-0ST	OC	RSH	7679	1951	New D		Scr 8/1968
"No.18"		0-4-0ST	OC	HL	3090	1914	(c) SS	(9)	
19		0-6-0ST	IC	HC	1674	1937	(d) D	(10)	
No.20		0-4-0ST	OC	RSH	7743	1953	New SS		Scr 6/1971
-		4wVBT	VCG	S	9558	1953	(e) D	(11)	
21		0-4-0ST	OC	RSH	7796	1954	New SS	(12)	
No.22		0-4-0ST	OC	RSH	7744	1953	(f) SS	(13)	
No.25		4wVBT	VCG	S	9597	1955	(g) D	(14)	
No.26		0-4-0ST	OC	RSH	7798	1954	(h) NT		Scr 3/1970
No. 5		0-6-0DM		HC	D835	1954	(j) NT	(15)	
29		0-6-0DH		JF 4240013		1962	(k) SS		
2		4wDH		S	10003	1959			
				reb. TH		1969	(m) NT		
No.31		0-4-0DE		RH	412714	1957	(n) SS		
No.30		0-4-0DE		RH	412707	1957	(p) D		
55		0-4-0DE		RH	381751	1953	(q) D		
No. 1		0-6-0DH		JF 4240020		1964	(r) SS		

(a) ex Carville G.S., Newcastle, c/1936
(b) ex SRM, Dunston, /1947, hire
(c) ex G.E.Simm Ltd, dealer, 12/1952 prev. Royal Arsenal, Woolwich, London
(d) ex SRM, Dunston, No.82, 9/1950
(e) S demonstration loco, for trials, 9/1953
(f) ex Carville G.S., Newcastle, 3/1956
(g) ex Stella North G.S., Newburn, Northumberland
(h) ex Carville G.S., Newcastle, 9/1960
(j) ex Skelton Grange G.S., Yorks, N.R., 4/1967

(1) to Clayton & Davie, Dunston, for scrap, /1952
(2) scr and parts used to repair No.5
(3) to Skelton Grange G.S., Yorks, N.R., /1959
(4) to Carville G.S., Newcastle, c/1936
(5) to South Tynedale Railway Preservation Society, Slaggyford Station, near Alston, Northumberland, 12/1973
(6) to North Yorkshire Moors Railway Preservation Society Ltd, Goathland, Yorks, N.R., 6/1972
(7) ret. to SRM, Dunston, /1947
(8) to Mexborough G.S., Yorks, W.R., 9/1967

(k) ex Blyth G.S., Northumberland, 5/1968
(m) ex TH, 10/1969; prev. Bass, Mitchell & Butlers Ltd, Burton-on-Trent, Staffs
(n) ex Port of Tyne Authority, Albert Edward Dock, North Shields, Northumberland, 2/1970
(p) ex Port of Tyne Authority, Albert Edward Dock, North Shields, Northumberland,12/1971
(q) ex Port of Tyne Authority, Tyne Dock, 12/1971
(r) ex Drax G.S., near Selby, Yorks, W.R., 8/1972

(9) to Blyth G.S., Northumberland, 11/1955
(10) to Blyth G.S., Northumberland, 9/1952
(11) sold by S to Armstrong Whitworth (Metal Industries) Ltd, Close Works, Gateshead, 11/1953
(12) to North of England Open-Air Museum, Marley Hill Loco Shed, 5/1973 (property of Stephenson & Hawthorn Loco Trust)
(13) to Hams Hall G.S., Warwickshire, for repairs, c9/1959; ret. by 4/1960; to TWW, Sheffield, Yorks, W.R., 12/1968
(14) to Stella North G.S., Newburn, Northumberland
(15) to D.Sep.Bowran Ltd, Gateshead

CEREBOS FOODS LTD, GREATHAM, near HARTLEPOOL
(Cerebos Ltd until 1/1/1963)

S12 Works (Map 85, NZ 498267) served by sidings SE of BR Hartlepool-Billingham line, immediately S of Greatham Station. Rail traffic ceased in 1968.

Gauge: 4' 8½"

No.1	CEREBOS						(a)	s/s
	CEREBOS	0-4-0ST	OC	AB	773	1897	(b)	s/s
(No.1 MIDDLESBROUGH till 1920)								
8	CEREBOS	0-4-0ST	OC	AB	1768	1922	New	(1)
	-	4wPM		KC	1470	1926(?)	New	s/s
	CECIL	0-4-0ST	OC	RWH	1847	1881	(c)	s/s
	BESSIE	0-4-0ST	OC	HE	205	1878	(d)	(2)
	TEES-SIDE No.2	0-4-0ST	OC	MW	1327	1897	(e)	(3)
	CEREBOS	0-4-0DM		JF	4100012	1948	New	(4)

(a) ex ?, by /1910
(b) ex Sir W.G.Armstrong Whitworth & Co Ltd, Elswick Works, Newcastle, /1919
(c) ex Sir S.A.Sadler Ltd, Malton Colliery, via LG,c/1933
(d) ex Warner & Co Ltd, Cargo Fleet, Yorks, N.R., loan
(e) ex Tees Side Bridge & Engineering Works Ltd, Cargo Fleet, Yorks, N.R., 1/1947, loan

(1) to C.Herring & Son Ltd, Hartlepool,for scrap, 3/1968
(2) ret. to Warner & Co Ltd, Cargo Fleet, Yorks, N.R.
(3) ret. to Tees Side Bridge & Engineering Works Ltd, Cargo Fleet, Yorks, N.R., 5/1947
(4) to Batchelor, Robinson & Co Ltd, Hartlepool, 8/1969

CHARLAW & SACRISTON COLLIERIES CO LTD (reg. 12/8/1890)

This firm, an amalgamation of some smaller concerns, owned the

Sacriston Railway

H57 In its final form this ran from Witton Colliery (Map 85, NZ 233477) to Pelton Fell (Map 78, NZ 255519) on the LNER Pontop & Shields branch, a distance of 4¼ miles. ✗

✗ from 1831 to 1834 the line joined the Beamish Waggonway at Pelton Fell - see Lambton, Hetton & Joicey Collieries Ltd

56

H64   The first section of this, from Pelton Fell to <u>Waldridge Colliery</u> (NZ 250503) was opened in August 1831, probably using horses, though the last 300 yards up to Waldridge Colliery was almost certainly a self-acting incline originally. In August 1839 the line was extended from Bank Foot, Waldridge⧸ to <u>Charlaw Colliery</u> (subsequently re-named Witton Colliery),

H59 with <u>Sacriston Colliery</u> (NZ 237479) nearby. Most of this section was worked by the Sacriston Engine, which hauled wagons up from the north end of Sacriston Colliery yard up to the engine house before letting them down to Bank Foot, Waldridge. From the engine house short branches later ran to

H60 serve <u>West Edmonsley Colliery</u> (NZ 234492) and

H61 <u>Nettlesworth Colliery</u> (NZ 243492), and the engine also worked

H62 <u>Byron Colliery</u> (NZ 243498) on its northern side, though all three collieries seem to have been relatively short-lived.

    The replacement of horses by locomotives seems to have taken place much later than on other colliery railways. Locomotives were not used to shunt wagons at the western end of the line until after the formation of the firm above, while no locomotive is recorded at Bank Foot, Waldridge, until 1897. This section was operated for many years by the owners of Waldridge Colliery (latterly Priestman Collieries Ltd - q.v.), and not until 1924 did Charlaw & Sacriston Collieries take over the working, though a Priestman Collieries' loco continued to shunt Waldridge Colliery until its closure in April 1926.

H58   The Railway, together with Witton Colliery, <u>Shield Row Drift</u> (NZ 234475) and Sacriston Colliery, was vested in NCB Northern Division No.5 Area on 1st January 1947.

<u>Sacriston Colliery</u>

Gauge: 4' 8½"

	CHARLAW	0-4-0ST	OC	BH	1037	1891	New	(1)
	-	0-4-0ST	OC	MW	455	1874	(a)	(2)
1	SACRISTON	0-4-0ST	OC	CF	1210	1901	New	(3)
2	CHARLAW	0-4-0ST	OC	P	1180	1912	New	(3)

(a) ex P.H. & H.Hodgson, contrs,   (1) to W.Whitwell & Co Ltd,
    Workington, Cumberland   Thornaby, Yorks, N.R., /1912
                                       (2) to Raine & Co Ltd, Blaydon
                                       (3) to NCB No.5 Area, 1/1/1947

H63 <u>Bank Foot</u>, Waldridge (from 1924)

Gauge: 4' 8½"

	MARGARET	0-6-0ST	IC	AB	1005	1904	(a)
				reb.AB	8833	1924	(1)
	CECIL	0-6-0T	IC	HC	1524	1924	(a)	(1)

(a) ex Priestman Collieries Ltd,   (1) to NCB No.5 Area, 1/1/1947
    /1924

For locomotives at Waldridge Colliery see Priestman Collieries Ltd.

    ⧸ so termed to distinguish it from Waldridge Bank Foot
       on NER Pontop & Shields branch

<u>CHEMICAL & INSULATING CO LTD</u>, FAVERDALE, DARLINGTON (inc. in 1927)

V1 Works (Map 85, NZ 272165) opened in 1928, and originally served by sidings N of LNER/BR Darlington-Barnard Castle line, 1½m W of Darlington North Road Station, but latterly at the end of the line.

Gauge: 4' 8½"

-		4wWE	GEC	1928	New

A diesel locomotive was hired from BR Darlington for five days in October 1970

Gauge: 2' 0" (used internally in charging and discharging of indurating plant)

-	4wBE	GB	2848	1957	New

Gauge: 1' 8" (used in handling materials between sections of the processing plant)

-	4wPM			c1932	(a)	Scr c7/1967
-	4wPM			1935	(b)	Scr c7/1967
No.1	4wDM	RH	375360	1955	New	
(No.2)	4wDM	RH	402428	1956	New	
(No.3)	4wDM	RH	476124	1962	New	

(a) built by firm from Morris Cowley car
(b) built by firm from Morris Oxford car

CLARKE CHAPMAN-JOHN THOMPSON LTD, VICTORIA WORKS, GATESHEAD (Clarke, Chapman & Co Ltd until 27/7/1970; Clarke, Chapman & Co until 14/6/1893)

C9 Works (Map 78, NZ 263630) served by sidings N of BR Gateshead-South Shields line, 1m E of Gateshead Station. There was no rail traffic between 1969 and 1973.

Gauge: 4' 8½"

-	0-4-0CT	OC	HL	2249	1892	New	Scr 10/1955
(FOWNES)	0-4-0CT	OC	HL	2499	1901	(a)	Scr 5/1962
-	4wDM		RH	221642	1944	(b)	(1)
No.20	0-4-0DM		RH	327969	1954	(c)	

(a) ex Fownes Forge & Engineering Co Ltd, Tyne Dock
(b) ex Sevenoaks Brick Works Ltd, Kent, c/1953
(c) ex Port of Sunderland Authority, via Northern Supply Co, Sunderland, 6/1973

(1) to Leslie Sanderson Ltd, dealer, Birtley, 6/1969

CLEVELAND BRIDGE & ENGINEERING CO LTD, DARLINGTON (reg. 19/3/1877)

V19 Works (Map 85, NZ 295136) served by sidings immediately S of Bank Top Station, Darlington, on BR line from Darlington to York.

Gauge: 4' 8½"

ADAM	0-4-0ST	OC	P	1430	1916	(a)	
-	0-4-0ST	OC	Bwn	45285	1917	(b)	(1)
NAIROBI	0-6-0ST	OC	WB	2169	1922	(c)	(2)
-	4wDH		TH	111C	1961	(d)	

There may have been at least one other loco before those listed

(a) ex MOM, Chilwell, Notts, via TWW
(b) ex Willys-Overland-Crossley Ltd, Levenshulme, Lancs, via TWW, 1927
(c) ex Pauling, High Wycombe, Bucks, c/1939
(d) New to firm, but rebuild by TH of unidentified 0-4-0 steam loco

(1) to TWW, 1930; re-sold to Preston Corporation Gas Works, Lancs
(2) sold for scrap, c4/1961

CONSETT IRON CO LTD
(Derwent & Consett Iron Co Ltd until 4/4/1864; Derwent Iron Co until 20/7/1858)

The first blast furnace at Consett, originally known as Conside and consisting of only one farmhouse⁄, was built in 1840 to use local deposits of iron ore and coal, with limestone coming from Stanhope via the Stanhope & Tyne Railway. The Derwent Iron Company∅ expanded rapidly, but was brought down in the collapse of the Northumberland & Durham District Bank in 1857, and until its affairs were straightened out the concern was run jointly by the NER and the Stockton & Darlington Railway through a subsidiary company.

By 1860 there were eighteen blast furnaces, and eventually the company's furnaces, mills, collieries, coke ovens, bye-products plants, quarries and brickworks lay all around Consett, especially to the south and the east. Subsequently the company acquired collieries and quarries further away from the town, and brought its ore from Cleveland and abroad. In 1940 it also opened a works at Jarrow operated initially through a subsidiary company.

The collieries still working were vested in NCB Northern Division Nos. 5 and 6 Areas on 1st January 1947, and the company itself was merged into the British Steel Corporation on 1st July 1968.

The early development and working of the company's system around Consett is obscure. The same location may have been served by different lines at different times; lines were altered to make way for new development; in some cases the location is known but not its history, in others the reverse; while the nomenclature is frequently confusing. It would appear that the system was operated partly by locomotives and partly by stationary engines, and that some of the latter survived for many years, but again details are sketchy. The company also possessed extensive running powers over the NER, but again these fluctuated, and are not shown on the maps. By 1900 it would appear that all the company's works, etc., were operated by its own locomotives except Westwood Colliery (Map 78, NZ 113554), which was worked by the NER.

Besides small quarries and brickworks, the system around Consett, known latterly as 'Bank Top Home Railways' served the following locations:

G7 **Billingside Drift** (exact location doubtful). This may have been the site of workings known to have existed at NZ 124532, and served by a 2m line known originally as the Pont Burn Railway. This was worked at first by the Pont Engine at Leadgate near Bradley Iron Works, where the branch joined the NER, but later it was worked by locomotives. The drift was closed in January 1879.

G8 **Bradley Colliery** (NZ 124517). Also served by the Pont Burn line. Closure date not known, but probably before 1875.

G9 **Bradley Iron Works**, Leadgate. (NZ 121518), served by sidings N of NER Pontop & Shields branch, ½m W of Leadgate Station. Buildings latterly converted into workshops, and became NCB No.6 Area Central Workshops.

G11 **Brooms Drift** (NZ 138514 approx); lay about 1m N of Iveston village. The method of working is uncertain, but may have been via running powers over NER Pontop & Shields branch to a short branch about ½m E of Leadgate Station. The drift closed in 1883.

Consett Iron Works (including latterly the Fell and Templetown Coke Works – see below). A vast complex, mostly covered by NZ 0949/1049 and 0950/1050. There were a number of access points from the NER, the main one being at the Low Yard, about 1½m S of Blackhill Station.

G18 **Crookhall Colliery**, Consett. Originally NZ 127503, and served by a 1½m branch from the main complex, operated initially by the Crookhall Engine.

G15 On another link to this branch lay the **West Ellimore Pit** (NZ 120508).

⁄   The growing town was known as Berry Edge for a time.
∅   For the Derwent Iron Company's extensive railway activity see that
     entry.

CONSETT IRON CO. system up to c.1900

miles   ½   1   2

unknown location   G22
sites of other stationary
engines are uncertain

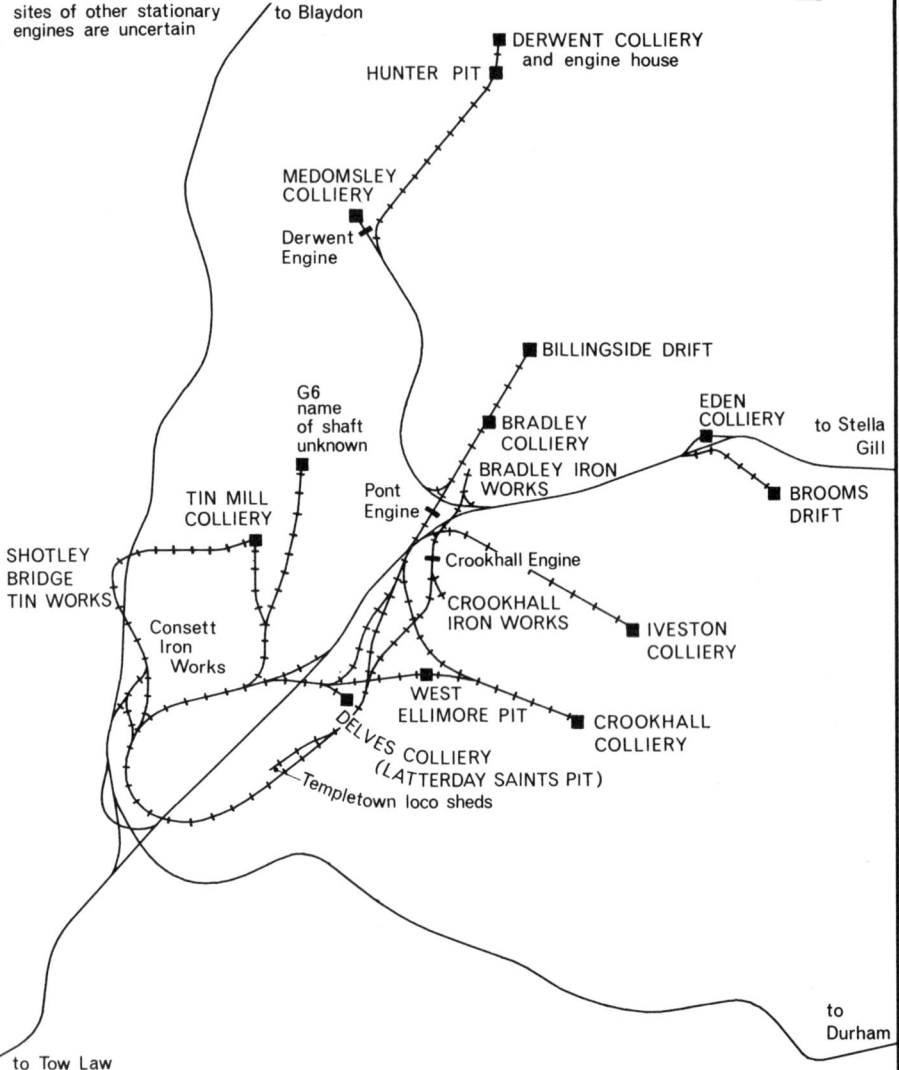

to Blaydon

DERWENT COLLIERY
and engine house

HUNTER PIT

MEDOMSLEY
COLLIERY

Derwent
Engine

BILLINGSIDE DRIFT

G6
name
of shaft
unknown

BRADLEY
COLLIERY

BRADLEY IRON
WORKS

EDEN
COLLIERY   to Stella
Gill

TIN MILL
COLLIERY

Pont
Engine

BROOMS
DRIFT

SHOTLEY
BRIDGE
TIN WORKS

Crookhall Engine

CROOKHALL
IRON WORKS

IVESTON
COLLIERY

Consett
Iron
Works

WEST
ELLIMORE PIT

CROOKHALL
COLLIERY

DELVES COLLIERY
(LATTERDAY SAINTS PIT)

Templetown loco sheds

to Tow Law

to
Durham

60

Later the title was given to other sinkings in the area, and latterly to
G14 the <u>Victory Pit</u> (NZ 113503). From here there ran a 2m narrow-gauge rope-
G20 worked line to <u>Woodside Winnings</u> (Map 85, NZ 138490) and <u>Humber Hill</u>
G21 <u>Drift</u> (NZ 140470). This unit was vested in NCB Northern Division No.6 Area
on 1st January 1947.
G16 <u>Crookhall Iron Works</u>, Consett, (NZ 118509). Opened in 1845, and served by
the main complex, with which it was eventually merged.
G14 <u>Delves Colliery</u>, Consett (NZ 113503). This colliery was sunk in 1847 , and
was served by a short branch from the main complex. From 1873 it was known
as the Latterday Saints Pit. It was closed in September 1913, but the site
was later re-opened as Crookhall Colliery (Victory Pit) - q.v.
G1 <u>Derwent Colliery</u>, Medomsley (NZ 123548), served by a 3m branch from the
NER Pontop & Shields branch at Leadgate. It was opened in 1856,
G2 and the title was latterly given to the <u>Hunter Pit</u>, to the south and sunk
in 1889. The first 1½ miles of the line were owned by the LNER until 1924,
when it was sold to the Company, who had always worked it. The last 1½
miles was originally an incline worked by the Derwent Engine at Medomsley
Colliery (q.v.). The colliery was vested in NCB Northern Division No.6
Area on 1st January 1947.
G10 <u>Eden Colliery</u>, Leadgate (NZ 134521). This was opened in 1850,
and was served by sidings N of NER Pontop & Shields branch, ½m E of
Leadgate Station, and reached via running powers over the NER. It was
vested in NCB Northern Division No.6 Area on 1st January 1947.
G19 <u>Iveston Colliery</u>, Iveston (NZ 133505). This colliery was won in June 1839
by Black, Reay & Co, and later taken over by the Company, who connected it
to the main complex by a branch 1½m long. It closed in January 1892.
G3 <u>Medomsley Colliery</u>, Medomsley, (NZ 115537), served by NER Medomsley Branch
(1½m), which was sold to the Company in 1924, and reached via running
powers from Consett. It was opened about 1841, and vested in NCB Northern
Division No.6 Area on 1st January 1947.
G5 <u>Tin Mill Colliery</u>, Blackhill, (NZ 104515). This was owned by the Shotley
Bridge Iron Co until 1866, and seems originally to have been called
Consett Colliery. It was linked to the main Consett system by a branch
(¼m), possibly worked by a stationary engine. Another branch (¼m) was
G6 later built to a quarry and a shaft as yet unidentified. In later years of
the nineteenth century the line to Consett was abandoned in favour of a
tramway direct to the "Tin Mill" (see below), but by the turn of the
century the old line had been re-instated, by which time the colliery was
also known as Mount Pleasant Colliery, Blackhill Colliery or Blackhill
Drift. It was closed in August 1910.

The company also worked:

G4 <u>Shotley Bridge Tin Works</u> (NZ 098515). This was owned by the Shotley Bridge
Iron Co (Shotley Bridge Tin Co and Richardson & Co are also found), and
was taken over by the Consett Iron Co Ltd in 1866. A branch ½m long
between the two works served the Tin Works. After the take-over this works
was reconstructed to manufacture iron plates and became an integral part
of the main complex, but the name "Tin Mill" remained in use for many
years.
H1 <u>South Medomsley Colliery</u>, near Dipton (NZ 144531). This was opened in 1861
as Pontop Hall Colliery by D. Baker & Co and served by an NER branch 1m
long from the Pontop & Shields branch, 1m E of Leadgate Station. The
Consett company worked the traffic on the branch from 1862 to 1884, when
the NER took over, the colliery owners (now The Owners of South Medomsley
Colliery) providing their own loco to shunt at the pit.

The details of locomotive operation in the early days are not clear.
Two returns of the Durham Coal Owners' Association, in April 1871 and
November 1876, list Billingside Drift, Eden, Iveston and Medomsley Collieries as having one locomotive each, but whether this was a permanent
allocation or whether a locomotive was supplied daily from Consett is not
known. A map of 1858 shows an "Engine Shed" at about the same place as the
G13 later large <u>Templetown Sheds</u> (NZ 109500), whence locomotives latterly

served the whole complex, and where complete overhauls, including new boilers and fireboxes, were done.

Ref : "Industrial Railway Record", Vol. 3, No.31.

The company also owned the

Chopwell & Garesfield Railway

In 1891 the company acquired from the Marquis of Bute (q.v.) Garesfield
A3 Colliery (NZ 139598) at High Spen, which was connected to staithes on R.
Tyne at Derwenthaugh by a line 5½m long, worked partly by inclines and
partly by locomotives. Between 1891 and 1897 this line was rebuilt, partly
A2 over a new route, and extended to a new colliery at Chopwell (NZ 115586),
a distance of about 2 miles. This line, now re-named the Chopwell & Garesfield Railway, and the last of the major colliery railways to be built,
was worked by locomotives from Chopwell to Thornley Bank Head, about 1½
miles E of Garesfield Colliery. Here a self-acting incline took the wagons
down to Winlaton Mill, where locomotives again took over. The loco sheds
were originally at Derwenthaugh and Garesfield, though later working on
the western section was transferred to a new shed at Chopwell, with only
one four-coupled saddletank being kept at Garesfield.
The line was opened in July 1899. This system was further extended by the

Whittonstall Railway

To develop their North-West Durham royalties still further, in 1907-1908
a narrow gauge line was built westwards from Chopwell to a new drift at
A1 Whittonstall in Northumberland (NZ 087572). This was about 2 miles long,
and worked originally by electric locomotives, the only example of narrow
gauge electric traction on the surface in Co. Durham. About 1930, however,
this was replaced by a main-and-tail rope haulage system, again a unique
example. A passenger service was also operated to carry men to and from
Whittonstall.

Ref : "Industrial Railway Record", Vol. 3, No.33.

The whole system passed to NCB Northern Division No.6 Area on 1st January
1947.

In the lists below the following abbreviations have been used:

Z17	AQ	Ashes Quarry, Stanhope (see below)
A2	Ch	Chopwell Colliery
G13	C	Consett Iron Works (Templetown Sheds)
B12	D	Derwenthaugh Loco Shed, Swalwell (also served Derwenthaugh Coke Works (NZ 193615) after 1929)
A3	G	Garesfield Colliery ⫻
E17	J	Jarrow Works (see below)
M7	LP	Langley Park Colliery (see below)

⫻ Short-term transfers between Derwenthaugh and Garesfield are not
recorded.

For ease of reference separate lists for Ashes Quarry, Jarrow and Langley
Park are included below, together with other locations which used locomotives.

N.B. In the lists below, where a Consett "rebuild" involved only an
identical new boiler, this is not shown.

Gauge: 4' 8½"

```
-              0-6-0   OC  TR    208  1852  New C  s/s
-              0-6-0   OC  TR    209  1852  New C  s/s
-              0-6-0   OC  TR    210  1852  New C  s/s
-              0-6-0?      TR    232  1853  New C  s/s
```

It is possible that one or more of these locomotives had inside cylinders.

```
-              0-4-0ST     Harris          New? C  s/s
-              2-4-0T  OC  RS   1085  1857  New C
          reb. 2-4-0      Con                      s/s
DERWENT        0-4-0ST OC  MW    112  1864  New C  (1)
BEN            0-4-0ST OC  FJ     87  1871  New C  s/s
```

> (1) apparently ret. to MW, who re-
> sold it to Pease, Hutchinson &
> Co, Darlington, c/1871

There were almost certainly other locomotives here in this early period, but no details survive, except that there may have been up to three Harris locos. Almost certainly at least three 0-4-0ST acquired before 1871 were included in B Nos. 4-9 below.

About 1872 the company decided to divide its locomotives into three classes. The 'A' class consisted of six-coupled engines, and was developed into a group of long-boilered pannier tanks. The 'B' class consisted of four-coupled saddletanks, later developed into three basic types - those with 12"x19" (later 13"x19") cylinders, those with 14"x22" cylinders and those with 16"x24" cylinders. The 'C' class was made up of four very small four-coupled saddletanks, and was eventually discontinued. Subsequently the company added the 'D' class, which was originally to contain crane tanks, but in which some four-wheeled cranes were later included, and the 'E' class, which consisted entirely of vertical-boilered cranes.

Gauge: 4' 8½"

```
A No.1    0-6-0ST IC  K    1843  1872  New C
                     reb. K        1886        Scr  9/1946
A No.1    0-6-0PT IC  RSH  7027  1941  New C  Scr c6/1960
A No.2    0-6-0ST IC  K    1844  1872  New C-G ?/?-C 7/20
                     reb. K        1888        -D 5/29-C 9/29
                     reb. HL
                          7008  1907        Scr   /1946
A No.2    0-6-0PT IC  RSH  7028  1941  New C-D 6/41-C
                                             12/46
                                             (1)
A No.3    0-6-0ST IC  K    1845  1872  New C
                     reb. BH       1889        Scr  4/1938
A No.3    0-6-0PT IC  HL   3951  1938  New C-D 12/46-C
                                             10/47
                                             Scr c6/1960
A No.4    0-6-0ST IC  K    1998  1874  New C-G 11/01-C /05
                     reb. HL       1892        -D 3/06-C 7/07
                                             Scr  5/1938
A No.4    0-6-0PT IC  HL   3952  1938  New C  (2)
A No.5    0-6-0PT IC  K    2509  1883  New C-D 12/22-C
                                             10/28-D 2/29-C
                                             5/35-D 6/36-C
                                             10/40-Ch 12/41
                                             (3)
A No.6    0-6-0PT IC  K    2510  1883  New C-D /19-C 10/23
                     reb. RS                   -D 1/24-Ch ?/?-
                          2915  1899        -C 9/29-Ch 2/30
                                             -C 11/34-Ch 1/35
```

							-C 11/40-D 1/41
							-C 4/42-D 3/44
							-C 7/46
							(3)
A No.7	0-6-0PT	IC	K	3905	1899	New	G-C ?/?-D 11/19
							-G ?/?-C 1/24
							-D 5/24-C 10/27
							-D 1/28-C 5/29
							-D 7/29-C 4/32
							-D 5/32-C 5/34
							(3)
A No.8	0-6-0PT	IC	K	3906	1899	New	G-C 11/99
							Scr 3/1950
A No.9 TAFF	0-6-0ST	IC	SS	2260	1872	(a)	C-G ?/?-C ?/?
		reb. AB					
				7952	1904		(4)
A No.9	0-6-0PT	IC	HL	3891	1936	New	C-D 7/46-Ch by
							12/46
							(3)
A No.10	0-6-0PT	IC	K	4051	1901	New	C-G 3/07-C 11/08
							-G 8/10-C 9/11
							-D 10/11-C 6/27
							-D 10/27-C 9/30
							-D 11/30-C 12/33
							-D 6/34-C 10/37
							-D 1/38-C 6/41
							-D 11/45-Ch ?/?
							-C 2/46-Ch 3/46
							-D 7/46
							(3)
A No.11	0-6-0PT	IC	HL	2641	1906	New	C-D 1/23-C 5/23
							-D 9/23-C 3/27
							-D 12/33-C 8/36
							-D 10/37-C 10/38
							-D 11/38-C 1/45
							-D 5/45
							(3)
A No.12	0-6-0PT	IC	HC	809	1907	New	D-C by 11/11
							-G 3/12-C 1/22
							-D 3/22-C 3/29
							-D 5/35-C 5/40
							-D 12/7/40
							-G 15/7/40
							-C 11/45
							Scr c6/1960
A No.13	0-6-0PT	IC	NLE	249	1908	New	G-C ?/?-D 4/14
							-C 6/14
							(3)
A No.14	0-6-0PT	IC	HL	3080	1914	New	C-D 9/30-C 12/30
							-D 3/31-C 5/32
							-D 10/38-C ?/?
							-D 1/45
							(3)
A No.15	0-6-0PT	IC	K	5179	1917	New C	(3)
A No.16	0-6-0PT	IC	HC	1448	1921	New C	(3)
A No.17	0-6-0PT	IC	HC	1449	1921	New	C-D 6/21-C 1/23
							-D 5/23-C 3/31
							-D 9/32-C 6/36
							-D 8/36-C 11/38
							-D 6/39-C 4/45
							-D 9/45-C 7/47
							Scr c6/1960
A No.18	0-6-0PT	IC	HL	3905	1937	New C	(3)
A No.19	0-6-0PT	IC	RSH	7029	1941	New C	(1)

(a) ex Brecon & Merthyr Railway,   (1) sold for scrap, 3/1962
    29, TAFF, via Bute Works   (2) converted to oil burning, /1951;
    Supply Co, 2/1899   removed, replaced and finally
                            removed, 4/1953; to NCB No.6
                            Area, Leadgate Shed, 11/1957
                  (3) to NCB No.6 Area, 1/1/1947
                  (4) sold for scrap, 10/1923

B No.1	0-4-0ST	OC	BH	289	1873	New C	(1)
B No.1	0-4-0ST	OC	HL	3390	1919	New C	Scr 7/1958
B No.2	0-4-0ST	OC	BH	326	1874	New C-AQ 2/15	
	reb. HL				1893	-C 4/1/28	
	reb. HL				1914	-D 20/1/28	
						-C 3/30-AQ 5/30	
						-C 5/50	
						Scr 7/1950	
B No.3	0-4-0ST	OC	BH	327	1874	New C	
	reb. BH				1889	(2)	
B No.3	0-4-0T	OC	HL	3495	1920	New C-AQ 1/21	
						-C 4/44	
						Scr /1952	
B No.4						(3)	
B No.4	0-4-0ST	OC	CF	1205	1901	New C-LP 12/05	
						-C 6/09	
						Scr 7/1950	
B No.5						(3)	
B No.5	0-4-0ST	OC	RS	2654	1888	New C	(4)
B No.5	0-4-0ST	OC	HL	3473	1920	New C	
	reb. Con				1952	Scr 5/1959	
B No.6						(3)	
B No.6	0-4-0ST	OC	HL	2235	1892	New C	(5)
B No.7						(3)	
B No.7	0-4-0ST	OC	RS	2655	1888	New C	(4)
B No.7	0-4-0ST	OC	HL	3474	1920	New C-J 2/44	
						-C 12/45	
						(6)	
B No.8						(3)	
B No.8						(7)	
B No.8	0-4-0ST	OC	BH	551	1880	New C	
B No.8	0-4-0ST	OC	HL	3475	1920	New C	Scr 4/1959
B No.9						(3)	
B No.9	0-4-0ST	OC	BH	552	1880	New C-AQ 10/17	
						-C 3/20-AQ 8/21	
						-C 3/33-AQ 3/44	
						-C 5/47	
						Scr 7/1950	
B No.10	0-4-0ST	OC	BH	328	1875	(a) C	
	reb.RS		2811		1893	(8)	
B No.10	0-4-0ST	OC	HL	3476	1920	New C-D 7/37-C 6/43	
						(9)	
B No.11	0-4-0ST	OC	BH	553	1880	New C	(1)
B No.11	0-4-0ST	OC	HL	3391	1919	New C	(6)
B No.12	0-4-0ST	OC	BH	698	1882	New C-AQ by /32	
						-C by 4/33	
						Scr 4/1936	
B No.12	0-4-0ST	OC	AB	2078	1939	New C	Scr 6/1958
B No.13	0-4-0ST	OC	HL	2176	1890	New C	(10)
B No.13	0-4-0ST	OC	HL	3953	1938	New C-J c/53-C 7/56	
						-J 5/57-C 3/67	
						(11)	
B No.14	0-4-0ST	OC	HL	2177	1890	New C	(12)
B No.14	0-4-0ST	OC	HL	3906	1937	New C	
	reb. Con				1951	(b)	(13)
B No.14	0-4-0F	OC	Con		1955	(c) C	Scr 3/1962
B No.15	0-4-0ST	OC	RS	2724	1890	New C	(14)
B No.15	0-4-0ST	OC	HL	3873	1936	New C	(15)

```
B No.16          0-4-0ST  OC  RS    2725  1890  New C-LP 12/20
                          reb. HL5809  1920      -C 6/40-LP 1/41
                                                   (16)
B No.17          0-4-0ST  OC  HL    2236  1892  New C   Scr /1928
B No.17          0-4-0ST  OC  HL    3753  1930  New C-D 9/31-C 5/39
                                                  -D 4/41-C 9/43
                                                   Scr 8/1958
B No.18          0-4-0ST  OC  BH     854  1885  (d) C-AQ ?/?
                                                  -C by 4/33
                                                   Scr /1942
B No.19          0-4-0ST  OC  BH    1113  1895  New Ch-C s/s c/1926
B No.19          0-4-0ST  OC  HL    3752  1930  New C   (6)
B No.20          0-4-0ST  OC  RS    2852  1897  New C   Scr /1929
B No.20          0-4-0ST  OC  HL    3745  1929  New C-D 5/39-C 8/39
                                                   (17)
B No.21          0-4-0ST  OC  HL    2377  1897  New Ch-C 6/12
                                                  -LP 12/28-C 1/29
                                                   (6)
B No.22          0-4-0ST  OC  CF    1163  1898  New C-LP by 5/37
                          reb.HL          1919     -C c/41
                                                   (6)
B No.23          0-4-0ST  OC  HL    2404  1899  New C   Scr 1/1921
B No.23          0-4-0ST  OC  HL    3744  1929  New C   (15)
B No.24          0-4-0ST  OC  AB     895  1901  New C-LP 12/37
                                                  -C 12/39
                                                   Scr 4/1959
B No.25          0-4-0ST  OC  HC     702  1904  New C-D 3/32-C ?/?
                                                  -LP 4/34-C 7/34
                                                  -D 9/34-C ?/?
                                                  -J 2/48-C 2/49
                                                   Scr 6/1950
B No.26          0-4-0ST  OC  HL    2639  1905  New C   (6)
B No.27          0-4-0ST  OC  HL    2640  1905  New C-LP 6/09
                                                  -C 12/20-D 10/29
                                                  -C 11/38
                                                   Scr 4/1959
B No.28          0-4-0ST  OC  HL    3003  1913  New C-LP 4/30-C 3/32
                                                   (18)
B No.29          0-4-0ST  OC  HL    3004  1913  New C-LP 10/33
                                                  -C 3/35-Ch 6/41
                                                  -C 8/43-J 11/53
                                                  -C by 4/55
                                                   Scr 6/1958
B No.30          0-4-0ST  OC  HL    3022  1913  New C-D 2/14-C 8/21
                                                  -D 12/35-C 4/40
                                                  -D 9/40-C ?/?
                                                  -J 12/45-C 4/48
                                                  -J 2/49
                                                   (19)
B No.31          0-4-0ST  OC  HL    3023  1913  New C-LP 9/25
                                                  -C 10/33-D 11/38
                                                  -J 7/43-C 3/45
                                                  -J  /53
                                                   (19)
B No.32          0-4-0ST  OC  HL    3251  1917  New C-G 3/30-C 9/41
                                                  -LP 3/42-C 9/43
                                                   Scr 6/1952
B No.33          0-4-0ST  OC  HL    3252  1917  New C-LP 10/36
                                                  -C 1/37-LP 1/40
                                                  -C c/41-J 6/42
                                                  -C 8/43
                                                   Scr 8/1955
B No.34          0-4-0ST  OC  HL    3253  1917  New C   Scr 6/1950
B No.35          0-4-0ST  OC  HL    3254  1917  New C-LP c/41
                                                   (16)
```

B No.36	0-4-0ST	OC	HL	3471	1921	New C-D 8/21-C 5/41 -D 4/42-C 12/46 Scr 8/1958
B No.37	0-4-0ST	OC	HL	3472	1921	New C-D 4/45-C 5/45 Scr 9/1959
B No.38	0-4-0ST	OC	HL	3496	1921	New C-D 11/21-C 3/27 -J 7/53 -C by 11/55 (20)
B No.39	0-4-0ST	OC	HL	3497	1921	New C (21)
B No.40	0-4-0ST	OC	RSH	7011	1940	New C Scr 7/1959
B No.41	0-4-0ST	OC	RSH	7016	1940	New C (15)
B No.42	0-4-0ST	OC	RSH	7022	1941	New C (22)
JARROW No.1	0-4-0ST	OC	AB	2091	1940	New C-J 3/41-C 2/44 -J 2/45-C /53 (23)
B 42	0-4-0ST	OC	Con		1954	(e) C-J 8/54 (24)

(a) built by BH with parts from old loco with boiler made at Consett in /1870
(b) reb. with frames, tanks and wheels from B No.42
(c) built from B No.14 (Con 1951) and wheels from E No.7
(d) ex Marquis of Bute, /1891
(e) built from parts of B No.14 (Con 1951) and JARROW No.1

(1) sold - for scrap? - 10/1919
(2) sold - for scrap? - /1919
(3) no records extant at Consett; probably one of early locos above
(4) to TWW, Tinsley Works, Sheffield, Yorks, W.R., 7/1920
(5) sold - for scrap? - /1926
(6) to NCB No.6 Area, 1/1/1947
(7) to Sir Hedworth Williamson's Limeworks Ltd, Fulwell, Sunderland, 10/1919
(8) sold - for scrap? - 3/1918
(9) to Seaham Harbour Dock Co Ltd, 3/1960
(10) to Steetley Lime and Basic Co Ltd, Coxhoe, 6/1923
(11) converted to oil-burning, 1954-1957; to British Steel Corporation, 1/7/1968
(12) to J. Tait & Partners, Middlesbrough, Yorks, N.R.; resold to Wingate Limestone Co Ltd, /1920
(13) scr /1954 and parts used to build B No.14 0-4-0F and B 42
(14) to Steetley Lime & Basic Co Ltd, Coxhoe, /1922
(15) to Seaham Harbour Dock Co Ltd, 2/1960; delivered 5/1960
(16) to NCB No.5 Area, 1/1/1947
(17) to Raine & Co Ltd, Blaydon, 8/1957
(18) to Darlington Rolling Mills Co Ltd, loan, 11/1944-12/1944; to NCB No.6 Area, 1/1/1947
(19) for subsequent history see Jarrow Works
(20) converted to oil burning, 4/1953; removed (at Jarrow), /1953; to Raine & Co Ltd, loan, /1958; to Seaham Harbour Dock Co Ltd, 2/1960; del. 5/1960
(21) scr at RSH c6/1952
(22) scr 5/1951 and parts used in rebuilding B No.14
(23) scr /1954 and parts used in building B 42

(24) built with oil-burning equipment; removed, /1956; for
subsequent history see Jarrow
Works

C No.1 (form. No.12)	0-4-0ST	OC	BH	191	1871	New C	(1)	
C No.2 (form. No.13)	0-4-0ST	OC	BH	192	1871	New C	(1)	
C No.3	0-4-0ST	OC	BH	247	1872	New C	(1)	
C No.4	0-4-0ST	OC	BH	248	1872	New C	(1)	

(1) all scr in early 1900's

D No.1	0-4-0CT	OC	D	1758	1883	New C	Scr	6/1927
D No.1	0-4-0CT	OC	AB	2111	1941	New C	Scr	7/1954
D No.2	0-4-0CT	OC	D	2063	1884	New C	Scr	6/1950
D No.3 "The Coffee Pot"	0-4-0VBCr	OC	BH	831	1885	New C	Scr	1/1940
D No.3	4wCr		Booth			(a) C	Scr	7/1950
D No.4	0-4-0CT	OC	D	2365	1888	New C	Scr	/1951
D No.5	0-4-0CT	OC	D	2366	1888	New C	Scr	/1927
D No.6	4wCr		TS	3469	1887	New C	(1)	
D No.6	4wCr		TS	13654	1941	New C	(2)	
D No.7	4wCr		TS		1891	New C	Scr by 1925	
D No.7	4wCr		TS	13653	1941	New C	(2)	
D No.8	4wCr		TS		1891	New C	Scr	3/1929
D No.8	4wCr		Priestman			(b) C	(3)	
D No.9	4wCr		TS	4731	1895	New C	Scr by 1925	
D No.9	4wCr		Priestman			(c) C	(4)	
D No.10	4wCr		TS	5784	1900	New C-D 3/00-C ?/? -D 9/21-C ?/? Scr 7/1950		
D No.11	4wCr		TS	5986	1901	New C	Scr	7/1950
D No.12	4wCr		TS	6199	1902	New C-J 5/46 (5)		
D No.13	4wCr		TS	8162	1913	New C	Scr	8/1953
D No.14	0-4-0CT	OC	NBL	21522	1917	New C	Scr 10/1952	
D No.15	4wCr		TS	9298	1919	New C	(6)	
D No.16	0-4-0CT	OC	AB	1665	1920	New C-J c7/52 (5)		
D 17	0-4-0CT	OC	AB	1715	1920	New C	Scr	2/1955
D No.18	4wCr		TS	9586	1920	New D-C 10/21 Scr 3/1955		
D No.19 KATIE	4wCr		TS	9634	1921	New C	Scr	6/1954
D 20	4wCr		Booth			(d) C	Scr	c/1962

(a) ex ?, 7/1940
(b) ex ?, 10/1940
(c) ex ?, 8/1940
(d) ex Head, Wrightson & Co Ltd, Stockton, 8/1957

(1) to ?, /1932
(2) to TWW, /1952
(3) to TWW, 5/1952
(4) to H.D.Ward Ltd, Wolsingham, for use as stationary boiler, 5/1952
(5) for subsequent history see Jarrow Works
(6) to TWW, 7/1952

E No.1	2-4-0VBCr	OC	BH	897	1887	New C	(1)	
E No.2	2-4-0VBCr	OC	BH	898	1887	New C	(2)	
E No.3	0-4-0VBCr	OC	BH	931	1888	New C	Scr	/1927
E No.4	0-4-0VBCr	OC	CoS	1749	1892	New C	Scr	3/1932
E No.5	0-4-0VBCr	OC	BH	1048	1892	New C	Scr	/1927
E No.6	0-4-0VBCr	OC	BH	1049	1892	New C	(1)	
E No.7	0-4-0VBCr	OC	BH	1051	1892	New C-D 9/28-C c2/29 (3)		

E No.8		0-4-0VBCr OC	RS	2853	1897	New C	Scr 7/1954
E No.9		2-4-0VBCr OC	RS	2854	1898	New C	(1)
E No.10		0-4-0VBCr OC	CF	1206	1901	New C	(1)
E No.11		0-4-0VBCr OC	CC	7519	1907	New C	Scr /1953
E No.12		0-4-0VBCr OC	CC	7520	1907	New C	Scr cl0/1962
E No.13 ROSIE		0-4-0VBCr OC	HL	2984	1913	New C-D 10/32
						(4)
E No.14		0-4-0VBCr OC	CoS	4101	1920	New C-D 6/28-C 1/33
						-D 6/33-C 10/33
						-D 6/34-C 8/34
						Scr c6/1961
E No.15		0-4-0VBCr OC	MF		1921	New C (5)
E No.16		0-4-0VBCr OC	MF		1921	New C Scr c/1962
E No.17		0-4-0VBCr OC	MF		1921	New C (6)

(1) to British Steel Corporation, 1/7/**1968**
(2) withdrawn 8/1955 and used for spares; finally scr by 2/1964
(3) scr /1954; wheels used in rebuilding B No.14
(4) to NCB No.6 Area, 1/1/1947
(5) to C.A.Parsons & Co Ltd, Newcastle, 8/1925
(6) dismantled and parts used to repair E No.16

1	0-6-0DM	HE	3504	1947	New C	(1)
2	0-6-0DM	HE	3580	1949	New C	(1)
3	0-4-0DM	HE	4010	1950	New C	(1)
4	0-4-0DM	HE	4011	1950	New C	(1)
5	0-6-0DE	WB/BT	3020	1951	New C	(1)
6	0-6-0DE	WB/BT	3021	1951	New C	(1)
7	0-4-0DM	HE	4431	1953	New C	(1)
8	0-4-0DM	HE	4432	1953	New C	(1)
9	0-6-0DM	Con		1956	New C	(1)
10	0-6-0DM	Con		1958	New C	(1)
11	0-6-0DM	HE	4987	1956	New C	(1)
12	0-6-0DM	HE	4988	1957	New C	(1)
13	0-6-0DM	HE	4989	1957	New C-J 1/67
					-C by 7/68
					(1)
14	0-6-0DM	HE	5173	1957	New C	(1)
15	0-6-0DM	HE	5174	1957	New C	(1)
16	0-6-0DM	HE	5175	1957	New C-J 9/61
					-C by 9/63
					(1)
17	0-6-0DM	HE	5375	1958	New C	(1)
18	0-6-0DM	HE	5376	1958	New C	(1)
19	0-6-0DM	HE	5377	1958	New C-J 4/68
					(2)
20	0-6-0DM	HE	5378	1958	New C	(1)
21	0-6-0DM	HE	5379	1958	New C-J 3/59-C 10/60
					-J 1/62-C 4/68
					(1)
22	0-6-0DM	HE	5380	1958	New C	(1)
23	0-6-0DM	HE	5381	1958	New C	(1)
24	0-4-0DM	HE	5384	1959	New C	(1)
25	0-4-0DM	HE	5385	1959	New C	(1)
26	0-4-0DM	HE	5386	1959	New C-J 3/64
					(2)
27	0-4-0DM	HE	5387	1959	New J-C 4/61-J 5/61
					(3)
28	0-6-0DH	HE	5392	1959	New C	(1)
29	0-6-0DH	HE	5393	1959	New C	(1)

	0-6-0DH	HE	5394	1959	New C (1)

(1) to British Steel Corporation, 1/7/1968
(2) for subsequent history see Jarrow Works
(3) to Raine & Co Ltd, Blaydon, loan, 1/1965; ret. to Consett, 2/1965; sold to Raine & Co Ltd, 2/1965

The company latterly operated three coke oven and bye-products plants, the Fell and the Templetown Works in the main complex at Consett, and the third at Langley Park Colliery. In 1929 a fourth plant was opened at Winlaton Mill. At least one coke oven loco, propelling the coke car between the ovens and the quenching tower, was used in this period, but at which works, and whether any more were used, is unknown. The Langley Park and Derwent-haugh Works passed to NCB Northern Division on 1st January 1947, and the Templetown Works closed in 1949.

Gauge: 4' 8½"

-	0-4-0WE	Goodman		1924	New? (1)
-	0-4-0WE	GB	2368	1952	New (1)

(1) to British Steel Corporation, 1/7/1968 (both at Fell Works)

Ashes Quarry, Stanhope. Map 84, NY 995397
(Ord & Maddison Ltd until 1900)

Z17 For many years the company did not own limestone quarries, as under an agreement dating back to the early years of the Derwent Iron Co the NER, as it became, agreed to supply limestone, and worked its own quarries in order to do so. This appears to have been abandoned about the turn of the century, when the company took over this quarry, which was probably begun in the 1870's. It lay to the north of Stanhope, and eventually expanded along the valley side towards Pease & Partners' Rogerley Quarry. It was served by sidings from the Crawleyside Incline of the NER Pontop & Shields branch, and was closed in 1949.
      It is not known whether locomotives were used during the ownership of Ord & Maddison Ltd, but this is probable. Under Consett ownership the first locomotive is not recorded here until 1915.

Gauge: 4' 8½"

B No.2	0-4-0ST	OC	BH	326	1874	(a) AQ-C 1/28 -D 20/1/28 -C 3/30-AQ 5/30 -C 5/50 (1)
B No.9	0-4-0ST	OC	BH	552	1880	(b) AQ-C 3/20 -AQ 8/21-C 3/33 -AQ 3/44-C 5/47 (1)
B No.3	0-4-0T	OC	HL	3495	1920	(c) AQ-C 4/44 (1)
B No.12	0-4-0ST	OC	BH	698	1882	(d) AQ-C by 4/33 (1)
B No.18	0-4-0ST	OC	BH	854	1885	(d) AQ-C by 4/33 (1)

There may have been other transfers unrecorded.

(a) ex Consett, 2/1915
(b) ex Consett, 10/1917
(c) ex Consett, 1/1921
(d) ex Consett, date unknown

(1) for subsequent history see main list

Butsfield Quarry, near Consett. Map 84, NZ 096445

X2 A large ganister quarry, 3¼m S of Consett. The quarry had no rail link, all the material being carried to Consett by aerial ropeway, but it operated an internal railway system until 1951. The quarry was not abandoned until some years afterwards.

Gauge: 3' 0"

CTS 1	0-4-0ST	OC	WB	2058	1917	(a)	Scr	/1951
-	0-4-0ST	OC	WB	2084	1919	(b)	Scr	10/1951
No.15	0-4-0ST	OC	HC	485	1897	(c)	Scr	/1951
FYLDE	0-4-0T	OC	P	1671	1924	(d)	Scr	/1951

(a) ex WD, Timber Supply Dept, by /1925
(b) ex DL, Burley Ironstone Quarries, Rutland, by /1929
(c) ex C.D.Phillips, Newport, Monmouthshire, /1935; form.GKN, Cyfarthfa Ironworks, Merthyr Tydfil, Glamorgan
(d) ex Davies, Middleton & Davis Ltd, Caerphilly, Glamorgan, c/1940

Chopwell Coke Ovens, Chopwell Colliery.

These were among the last beehive coke ovens to be built in Co. Durham. They were opened about 1897, and lay adjacent to the colliery. About 1901 they were modified to enable an electric locomotive to be used in shunting wagons carrying coal for charging the ovens, a line running along the top of each battery of ovens. They were also among the last beehive ovens to work, for they were not finally put out till about 1940.

Gauge: 4' 0"

-	4wWE	Coulson	c1901 New	(1)

(1) derelict from c/1940; to NCB No.6 Area, 1/1/1947

Derwenthaugh Loco Shed, Swalwell.

B12 Locomotives here are given, as far as they are known, in the main list, but the loco below was used here for some time as a stationary boiler.

Gauge: 4' 8½"

BETTY	0-4-0ST	OC		(a) s/s

(a) ex Marquis of Bute, /1891

Jarrow Works, Jarrow. Map 78, NZ 324655
(New Jarrow Steel Co Ltd until 6/1948, which was a subsidiary of Consett Iron Co Ltd from 1938 to 1948)

E17 This works was opened in 1940, and was served by a ½m branch from the BR Gateshead-South Shields line at Jarrow Station. It passed to the British Steel Corporation on 1st July 1968.

Gauge: 4' 8½"

JARROW No.1	0-4-0ST	OC	AB	2091	1941	(a) J-C 2/44 -J 2/45-C /53 (1)
B No.33	0-4-0ST	OC	HL	3252	1917	(b) J-C 8/43 (1)
B No.31	0-4-0ST	OC	HL	3023	1913	(c) J-C 3/45-J /53 Scr 3/1960
B No.7	0-4-0ST	OC	HL	3474	1920	(d) J-C 12/45 (1)
B No.30	0-4-0ST	OC	HL	3022	1913	(e) J-C 4/48 -J 2/49 Scr 6/1953
D No.12	4wCr		TS	6199	1902	(f) J Scr /1957
B No.25	0-4-0ST	OC	HC	702	1904	(g) J-C 2/49 (1)
D No.16	0-4-0CT	OC	AB	1665	1920	(h) J (2)
B No.38	0-4-0ST⚋	OC	HL	3496	1921	(j) J-C by 11/55 (1)
B No.29	0-4-0ST	OC	HL	3004	1913	(k) J-C by 4/55 (1)
B No.13	0-4-0ST	OC	HL	3953	1938	(m) J-C 7/56 -J 5/57 (3)
B 42	0-4-0ST⌀	OC	Con		1954	(n) J Scr 3/1960
21	0-6-0DM		HE	5379	1958	(p) J-C 10/60 -J 1/62-C 4/68 (1)
27	0-4-0DM		HE	5387	1959	New J-C 4/61 -J 5/61 (4)
16	0-6-0DM		HE	5175	1957	(q) J-C by 9/63 (1)
26	0-4-0DM		HE	5386	1959	(r) J (5)
13	0-6-0DM		HE	4989	1957	(s) J-C by 7/68 (1)
19	0-6-0DM		HE	5375	1958	(t) J (5)

⚋ oil-burning, 4/1953-c9/1953   ⌀ oil-burning, 1954-1956

(a) ex Consett, 3/1941
(b) ex Consett, 6/1942
(c) ex Derwenthaugh, 7/1943
(d) ex Consett, 2/1944
(e) ex Consett, 12/1945
(f) ex Consett, 5/1946
(g) ex Consett, 2/1948
(h) ex Consett, c7/1952
(j) ex Consett, 7/1953
(k) ex Consett, 11/1953
(m) ex Consett, c/1953
(n) ex Consett, 8/1954
(p) ex Consett, 3/1959
(q) ex Consett, 9/1961
(r) ex Consett, 3/1964
(s) ex Consett, 1/1967
(t) ex Consett, 4/1968

(1) for subsequent history see main list
(2) scr 1/1954, and boiler returned to Consett
(3) used as stationary boiler from /1961; to Consett, 3/1967
(4) loaned to Raine & Co Ltd, Blaydon, 1/1965; ret. to Consett, 2/1965; sold to Raine & Co Ltd, 2/1965
(5) to British Steel Corporation, 1/7/1968

M7 This colliery was opened in 1876, and was served by a branch, ½m long with
a reverse, from the NER Consett-Durham line (Lanchester Valley Branch), 4m
SE of Lanchester Station. The colliery lay north of the R. Browney, while
latterly the coking plant lay south of the river. Both passed to NCB
Northern Division No.5 Area on 1st January 1947.

Although at least one loco was almost certainly kept here from the opening
of the colliery, none is recorded before 1905.

Gauge: 4' 8½"

B No.5	0-4-0ST	OC	CF	1205	1901	(a) LP-C 6/09
						(1)
B No.27	0-4-0ST	OC	HL	2640	1905	(b) LP-C 12/20
						(1)
B No.16	0-4-0ST	OC	RS	2725	1890	(c) LP-C 6/40
			reb. HL			-LP 1/41
				5809	1920	(2)
B No.31	0-4-0ST	OC	HL	3023	1913	(d) LP-C 10/33
						(1)
B No.21	0-4-0ST	OC	HL	2377	1897	(e) LP-C 1/29
						(1)
B No.28	0-4-0ST	OC	HL	3003	1913	(f) LP-C 3/32
						(1)
B No.29	0-4-0ST	OC	HL	3004	1913	(g) LP-C 3/35
						(1)
B No.25	0-4-0ST	OC	HC	702	1904	(h) LP-C 7/34
						(1)
B No.33	0-4-0ST	OC	HL	3252	1917	(j) LP-C 1/37
						-LP 1/40-C c/41
						(1)
B No.22	0-4-0ST	OC	CF	1163	1898	(k) LP-C c/41
						(1)
B No.24	0-4-0ST	OC	AB	895	1901	(m) LP-C 12/39
						(1)
B No.35	0-4-0ST	OC	HL	3254	1917	(n) LP (2)
B No.32	0-4-0ST	OC	HL	3251	1917	(p) LP-C 9/43
						(1)

(a) ex Consett, 12/1905
(b) ex Consett, 6/1909
(c) ex Consett, 12/1920
(d) ex Consett, 9/1925
(e) ex Consett, 12/1928
(f) ex Consett, 4/1930
(g) ex Consett, 10/1933
(h) ex Consett, 4/1934
(j) ex Consett, 10/1936
(k) ex Consett, by 5/1937
(m) ex Consett, 12/1937
(n) ex Consett, c/1941
(p) ex Consett, 3/1942

(1) for subsequent history see main
    list
(2) to NCB No.5 Area, 1/1/1947

Whittonstall Railway

For the history and operation of this railway see the main notes. The
locomotives were kept at Chopwell No.3 Colliery, and were replaced by a
main-and-tail rope system about 1930.

Gauge: 2' 2"

-	0-4-4-0WE		Siemens		c1908	New	Scr c/1930
-	0-4-4-0WE		Siemens		c1908	New	Scr c/1930
WHITTONSTALL No.3	0-4-4-0WE		Hanomag	5968	1910	New	Scr c/1930

CONSETT WATER CO

X1 This company was formed in 1860, and constructed a number of reservoirs south-west of Consett. The biggest of these was the <u>Smiddy Shaw Reservoir</u> (Map 84, NZ 043463), and it is believed that the locomotive below worked there during its construction between 1870 and 1877, when it is said to have been linked to the NER Stanhope & Tyne branch near Waskerley.

Gauge: 4' 8½"

-		0-6-0	OC	Kitching	1840	(a)	(1)

(a) ex NER, c/1869; form. Stockton & Darlington Rly No.26, PILOT

(1) paraded at Stockton & Darlington Railway celebrations in 1875 as No.10 AUCKLAND; s/s

CORNFORTH LIMESTONE CO LTD, CORNFORTH LIMEWORKS & QUARRY, WEST CORNFORTH
(Member of Tarmac Group from 1/9/1973; previously subsidiary of F.W.Dobson & Co Ltd)

R25 Quarry (Map 85, NZ 317347) served by sidings S of BR mineral line from Garmondsway Quarry to Ferryhill, 2½m N of Ferryhill.

Gauge: 4' 8½"

-	4wPM	MR	2262	1923	(a)	
	reb. 4wDM			1934		(1)
-	4wDM	MR	5751	1937	New	(2)
-	4wDM	RH	236362	1946	New	(3)
R.F.SPALDING	4wDM	RH	262996	1949	New	
CORNFORTH	4wDM	RH	306087	1949	New	
(FRED DOBSON)	4wDM	RH	326071	1954	New(b)	

(a) ex MR, 9/1929
(b) to Hawthorn Limestone Co Ltd, Seaham, c/1965; ret. /1970

(1) to Dunlop Rim & Wheel Co Ltd, Coventry, Warwicks, via Bungey, /1949
(2) to Wagon Repairs Ltd, Gloucester
(3) to F.W.Dobson Ltd, Chilton Limeworks, by 9/1955

CROSSLEY SANITARY PIPES LTD, FIR TREE WORKS, near CROOK

Q9 Works (Map 85, NZ 134344) was built on the site of an old drift mine once owned by Bearpark Coal & Coke Co Ltd. It had no rail connection, the locos below being used only within the works. It was subsequently taken over by G.Strong, who replaced the system by cable haulage.

Gauge: 2' 0"

-	4wPM				(a)	Scr
-	4wDM	RH	247174	1947	New	Scr
-	4wDM	HE	3496	1947	(b)	(1)

(a) built with Morris engine, by firm
(b) ex NCB No.5 Area, Hole-in-the-Wall Colliery, Crook, by 4/1955, loan

(1) ret. to NCB No.5 Area, Hole-in-the-Wall Colliery, Crook

DEREK CROUCH (CONTRACTORS) LTD, NCBOE AUCKLAND PARK DISPOSAL POINT, BISHOP AUCKLAND

T24 This disposal point for opencast and other coal from south-west Durham was constructed on part of the Auckland Park Colliery site (Map 85, NZ 227285), and was served by a branch (½m) from BR Bishop Auckland-Darlington line, 1m S of Bishop Auckland Station. It was transferred to the firm above in March 1958, and was closed in September 1959.

For a full list of locomotives which have worked here see the list for NCB No.4 Area.

Gauge: 4' 8½"

No.1	"CLARENCE"	0-4-0ST	OC	BH	985	1890	(a)	Scr 2/1963
113	PLUTO	0-6-0ST	OC	HL	2655	1906	(b)	(1)
	DEREK CROUCH	0-6-0ST	IC	HE	3189	1944	(c)	(2)
	PATRIOT	0-6-0T	IC	BV		1920	(d)	Scr 3/1959

(a) ex NCB No.4 Area, 18/3/1958
(b) ex NCB No.4 Area, 18/3/1958, hire
(c) ex Coton Park Disposal Point, Derbyshire, 3/1958
(d) ex NCB No.4 Area, Mainsforth Colliery, loan, c11/1958

(1) ret. to NCB No.4 Area, Chilton Colliery, c5/1958
(2) to NCB No.5 Area, 11/1960; delivered to Brancepeth Colliery, 12/1960

CROWN COKE CO LTD, TEMPLETOWN, CONSETT   (reg. 9/1907)

G22 This firm owned a plant, the exact site of which is not known, which washed coke waste. It was linked to the railway system of the Consett Iron Co Ltd, from whom a loco was hired on occasions. It appears to have closed before the First World War.

Gauge: 4' 8½"

| - | | 0-6-0ST | OC | FW | 169 | 1872 | (a) | (1) |

(a) ex Sir B.Samuelson & Co Ltd, Newport Works, Middlesbrough, Yorks, N.R.

(1) advertised for sale, 1/1912; may be loco purchased by Bearpark Coal & Coke Co Ltd (q.v.) about /1915

DARLINGTON FORGE LTD
(subsidiary of English Steel Corporation from 1936; Darlington Forge Co Ltd (reg. c 1873) until 6/6/1919)

V9 The early history of this works (Map 85, NZ 295157) is confused with that of the South Durham Iron Co and the Darlington Steel & Iron Co Ltd (and its predecessors), both of whose works adjoined the Forge Works, and which were subsequently taken over after their owners had gone into liquidation. The Forge Works appears to have begun production in 1854, and was served by sidings N of NER Bishop Auckland-Darlington line immediately N of Albert Hill Junction. The works was closed in February 1967, but survived to be merged into the British Steel Corporation on 1st July 1968.

Gauge: 4' 8½"

-		0-6-0T	OC	BH			(a)	(1)
WOODBANK		0-4-0ST	OC	BH	387	1876	New	s/s
ADVANCE		0-6-0WT	OC				(b)	
	reb.	0-4-0ST	OC	BH				Scr c/1937
WOODBANK		0-4-0ST	OC	BH	1019	1891	New	Scr 3/1960
UNITY		0-4-0ST	OC	HL	2890	1911	New	Scr 2/1963
CONCORD		0-4-0ST	OC	HL	3300	1917	New	Scr 2/1960

(GEORGE VI)		0-4-0ST	OC	RSH	7013	1940	New	(2)
-		0-4-0ST	OC	HL	2839	1910	(c)	(3)
No.1		0-4-0ST	OC	HC	1199	1916	(d)	Scr c/1963
No.9		0-4-0ST	OC	HC	1688	1937	(e)	Scr 1/1960
No.46		0-4-0DM		HC	D1159	1959	New	(2)
No.48		0-4-0DM		HC	D1161	1959	New	(2)

(a) ex ?
(b) origin unknown
(c) ex TWW, Sheffield, Yorks, W.R., 9/1942, hire
(d) ex ESC, River Don Works, Sheffield, Yorks, W.R., 7/1954
(e) ex ESC, River Don Works, Sheffield, Yorks, W.R., 5/1956

(1) advertised for sale, 12/1878; s/s
(2) to British Steel Corporation, 1/7/1968
(3) to Tees Side Bridge & Engineering Co Ltd, Cargo Fleet, Yorks, N.R., 3/1944

DARLINGTON & SIMPSON ROLLING MILLS LTD, RISE CARR ROLLING MILLS, DARLINGTON

(Darlington Rolling Mills Co Ltd until 31/3/1945; this company was a subsidiary of Darlington & Simpson Rolling Mills Ltd from 7/6/1935; and a subsidiary of DL and BV from 1922; Sir Theodore Fry & Co Ltd until 1910; Fry, I'Anson & Co Ltd until 1906)

V2/3 The original works commenced production in 1868. Latterly the firm has had two works (Map 85, NZ 286164 and 284172), served by sidings from BR Bishop Auckland-Darlington line, ½m-1m N of Darlington (North Road) Station, with running powers between the two sections.

Gauge: 4' 8½"

✗		0-4-0ST		I'Anson			New	(1)
✗		0-4-0ST	OC	I'Anson		1875	New	(2)
-		0-4-0ST	OC	reb. HL	9242	1900	(a)	s/s
No.1		0-4-0ST	OC	HL	2039	1885	(b)	Scr
No.2		0-4-0ST	OC	reb. AB	9070		(a)	s/s
No.3		0-4-0ST	OC	reb. LG			(a)	s/s
	JUNO	0-4-0ST	OC	BH	606	1881	(c)	(3)
	WYLLIE	0-4-0ST	OC	BH	524	1880	(c)	(4)
	PRINCE	0-4-0ST	OC				(d)	s/s
No.1		0-4-0ST	OC	HL	3237	1917	(e)	(5)
No.2		0-4-0ST	OC	RSH	7073	1943	New	(6)
	B No.28	0-4-0ST	OC	HL	3003	1913	(f)	(7)
No.3		0-4-0ST	OC	RSH	7160	1945	New	(5)
No.4		0-4-0ST	OC	RSH	7660	1950	New	(8)
No.1		4wDH		TH	129V	1963	New	
No.2		4wDH		TH	131V	1963	(g)	

✗ one was named RISE CARR

(a) builders and origin unknown
(b) ex HL, Hebburn Shipyard, /1913
(c) ex BV, Cleveland Works, Middlesbrough, Yorks, N.R.
(d) ex BV, Cleveland Works, Middlesbrough, Yorks, N.R., in early 1920's (may be the LG hire loco named PRINCE)
(e) ex Palmers Shipbuilding & Iron Co Ltd, Jarrow, per TWW, after repair at HL, /1934
(f) ex Consett Iron Co Ltd, Consett, 11/1944, loan
(g) New ex TH, after demonstration at Firth Brown Ltd, Sheffield, Yorks, and East Midlands Gas Board, Car House Works, Rotherham, Yorks, 11/1963

(1) to R.W.Crosthwaite Ltd, Thornaby, Yorks, N.R.
(2) to Skerne Ironworks Co Ltd, Darlington
(3) to Gateshead County Borough, Saltmeadows Clearance Site, 1/1936
(4) ret. to BV, Cleveland Works, Middlesbrough, Yorks, N.R.
(5) to T.J.Thomson & Son Ltd, Stockton, for scrap, /1963
(6) to ? for scrap, /1963
(7) ret. to Consett Iron Co Ltd, 12/1944
(8) to W.Arnott Young & Co Ltd, Darlington, for scrap, 5/1965

DARLINGTON STEEL & IRON CO LTD, ALBERT HILL IRONWORKS, DARLINGTON
(Darlington Iron Co Ltd until 6/1882; William Barningham until c3/1873)

V8 The Albert Hill Works (Map 85, **NZ** 296158) began production in 1858-1859,
and was later joined by the Springfield Works on the opposite side of the
NER Durham-Darlington line, though whether this complex was served by
sidings from this line or from the Bishop Auckland-**D**arlington line is not
clear. The two works were connected by a rail link across the NER, over
which the company's locomotives ran. The firm produced only rails, and
went into liquidation in 1897. The Albert Hill site was later taken over
by Darlington Forge Co Ltd (q.v.) and the Springfield site by Robert
Stephenson & Co Ltd.

> **N.B.** How many locomotives the firm built for its own use is
> uncertain; other versions give a different number and
> different types.

Gauge: 4' 8½"

-	0-6-OT	OC	Wm.B		New	s/s
-	0-6-OT	OC	Wm.B		New	s/s
-	0-6-OT	OC	Wm.B		New	s/s
-	0-4-OST	OC	Wm.B	c1867	New	(1)
-	0-4-OST	OC	Wm.B	c1867	New	(1)

(1) to Sir B. Samuelson & Co Ltd,
    Slapewath Mines, Yorks, N.R. (?)

DAVY ROLL CO LTD, JARROW
(Armstrong-Whitworth Rolls Ltd until 7/1970 - q.v.)

E13 Works (Map 78, NZ 321654) served by sidings N of BR Gateshead-Tyne Dock
line, ½m W of Jarrow Station, but rail traffic had ceased in 1969.

Gauge: 4' 8½"

185	DAVID PAYNE	0-4-ODM	JF 4110006	1950	(a)	(1)

(a) ex Armstrong-Whitworth Rolls   (1) to Leslie Sanderson Ltd, dealer,
    Ltd, 7/1970   Birtley, 12/1970

DERWENT IRON CO

This company began operations at Consett (then called Conside) in 1840,
and expanded rapidly - so rapidly that within eighteen months of its
opening it had taken over part of a public railway, which it called the

Derwent Railway

The line concerned was the Stanhope & Tyne Railway, opened between Stanhope
and South Shields (32 miles) in September 1834. Despite the opening of
collieries along it, it was in continual financial difficulty because of
the high wayleave charges demanded for crossing land, as the line had been
built without an Act of Parliament. In **February** 1841 the company was
dissolved, and the railway divided into two sections. From the foot of the
Carr House East Incline near Conside to South Shields was taken over by a
new company, the Pontop & Shields Railway; the western end of the line
passed to the Derwent Iron Company, as it was so dependant upon the limestone quarried at Stanhope. This section was about 11 miles long, and
worked partly by horses and partly by inclines.
    To haul the wagons out of Weardale two tremendous inclines were
needed. The Crawleyside Incline had one section of 1 in 7¼, and the engine
could haul only two wagons at a time. Then the Weatherhill Engine brought
the wagons up to over 1400 feet, with an average gradient of 1 in 13. The
next section was relatively level, and was worked by horses as far as the
Parkhead Wheel, where a main-and-tail rope system brought the wagons to the

Meeting Slacks Engine. This engine also worked the incline on its eastern side, lowering the wagons down to the top of the Nanny Mayor's Incline, which was just over 1100 yards long and self-acting. For the next 1¼ miles the wagons were again hauled by horses, which were then taken round to the rear of the train to be put into 'dandy carts' so that the wagons could coast down to the edge of the Hownes Gill gorge. This was about 150 feet deep and 266 yards across, and worked by a very unusual method. In the bottom of the gorge was a stationary engine, which worked inclines on both sides down to it. The wagons were lowered down in cradles, one on each incline at a time, and turntables at the top and bottom enabled the wagons to be manoeuvred. This section rapidly became a bottleneck, as only about twelve wagons an hour could be dealt with. From the east side of the gorge the Carr House Engine hauled the wagons up the Carr House West Incline (1¼ miles) before lowering them ½ mile down the Carr House East Incline, the foot of which marked the end of the Derwent Iron Company's jurisdiction.

It seems, however, that the Iron Company had certain powers over the next 3¼ miles, as its successor, the Consett Iron Co Ltd, was to have in part later, for from the foot of the Carr House East Incline a branch ran northwards for 3 miles to serve Medomsley and Derwent Collieries, both owned by the Iron Company; and in December 1843 the Iron Company opened a line between the foot of the Annfield Plain East Incline (also known as the Loud Bank) on the Pontop & Shields to the Tanfield Branch of the Brandling Junction Railway at Tanfield Moor.

In 1844 the Iron Company received a report on the line from the Engineer to the Stockton & Darlington Railway, who saw the line as a means of extending their territory northwards. As a result of this report the working at Parkhead was altered, the horses being replaced by another main-and-tail rope system, this time worked from the Weatherhill Engine.

In the same year the Stockton & Darlington Railway agreed to extend their line from Bishop Auckland to Crook (operated through a subsidiary company, the Bishop Auckland & Weardale Railway). This extension was to join the Derwent Railway at the junction of the Meeting Slacks and Nanny Mayor's Inclines. Its construction was to be undertaken by another Stockton & Darlington Railway subsidiary, the Wear & Derwent Junction Railway, to whom the Iron Company was to sell its line, and this was completed in May 1845.

Nothing is known of whether the Iron Company used locomotives, either on the section between Nanny Mayor's Bank Foot and Hownes Gill, or to Medomsley Colliery and Annfield Plain West Bank Foot on the Pontop & Shields Railway.

Both sections of the former Stanhope & Tyne were later re-united under the North Eastern Railway.

In the middle 1850's the Iron Company was involved in a different scheme. To give a better outlet to Cumberland, the Company promoted the Stockton & Darlington & Newcastle & Carlisle Union Railway, which obtained its Act in July 1856. This was for a line 8 miles long to run between Cold Rowley, west of Hownes Gill on what was now the Stockton & Darlington Railway, and Stocksfield on the Newcastle & Carlisle Railway. About a mile had been built, when in November 1857 the Northumberland & Durham Bank failed, which precipitated the collapse of the Iron Company. The activities at Consett were rescued jointly by the North Eastern and Stockton & Darlington Railways, until in 1864 the Consett Iron Co Ltd (q.v.) was set up. The small section of line was subsequently incorporated into the iron works complex.

F.W.DOBSON & CO LTD, CHILTON, near FERRYHILL STATION
(Pease & Partners Ltd until c/1945 - q.v.)

R11 Quarry and limeworks (Map 85, NZ 302315) served by branch (½m) from BR Durham-Darlington line, ¼m S of Ferryhill Station. Operations were abandoned in December 1968.

Gauge: 4' 8½"

24		0-4-0ST	OC	HL	2453	1900	(a)	(1)
	F.W.DOBSON							
	(form. JAMES BLUMER)	4wDM		RH	236362	1946	(b)	Scr 11/1969

(a) ex PP, c/1945
(b) ex Cornforth Limestone Co Ltd,
    West Cornforth, by 9/1955

(1) to Hawthorn Limestone Co Ltd,
    Seaham Harbour, and ret; to
    T.J.Thomson & Son Ltd, Stockton,
    for scrap, 9/1955

DORMAN, LONG & CO LTD

Originally registered on 2nd November 1889, this firm greatly expanded its
activities with a number of amalgamations in 1923 and by absorbing Bolckow,
Vaughan & Co Ltd in 1929, when it became the largest industrial concern in
N.E. England. All the collieries except Newfield (see Dorman Long (Steel)
Ltd) passed to the NCB on 1st January 1947, and latterly Newfield Brick-
works was the only activity operated in Co. Durham.

> **N.B.** Information about the company's locomotive activity is
> very sketchy, and there were probably many more transfers,
> and even locomotives, than those shown below.

Auckland Park Colliery, near Bishop Auckland. Map 85, NZ 227285
(Bolckow, Vaughan & Co Ltd until 1/11/1929)

T24 This colliery was situated on a branch (¼m) from LNER Bishop Auckland-
Shildon line, 1m S of Bishop Auckland Station. The colliery ceased
production in 1943, but remained in use for pumping, and locomotives
continued to be sent to the workshops here for repairs. The colliery
passed to NCB Northern Division No.4 Area on 1st January 1947.

Gauge: 4' 8½"

	HENRY CORT	0-4-0ST	OC	BH	607	1881	(a)	(1)
	ACTIVE	0-4-0ST	OC	RS	3075	1901		
				reb.	Ellis	1927	(a)	(1)
108	HECTOR	0-6-0ST	OC	HL	2613	1905	(a)	(2)
113	PLUTO	0-6-0ST	OC	HL	2655	1906	(a)	(3)
	HARE	0-4-0ST	OC	GH		1908	(a)	(4)

(a) ex BV, 1/11/1929

(1) to NCB No.4 Area, 1/1/1947
(2) to Chilton Colliery, c/1934
(3) to Sherburn Hill Colliery
(4) to Newlandside Quarry by 8/1931

Bowburn Colliery, Bowburn. Map 85, NZ 304379
(Bell Bros Ltd until 2/5/1923)

R15 This colliery (not to be confused with an earlier Bowburn Colliery) was
opened in 1908, and lay E of LNER Leamside-Ferryhill line, 1½m N of
Tursdale Junction. For many years it was shunted by a steam crane, and no
locomotives are known prior to 1928. It was linked underground to Tursdale
Colliery (q.v.), with which it was merged after Tursdale ceased coal-
winding in June 1931, and it was vested in NCB Northern Division No.4 Area
on 1st January 1947.

Gauge: 4' 8½"

	HUGO	0-4-0ST	OC	MW	1517	1900	(a)	(1)
	COLONEL BELL	0-4-0ST	OC	MW	1697	1906	(b)	(2)
30		0-4-0ST	OC	P	669	1897	(c)	(3)
	MARY BELL	0-4-0ST	OC	MW	1422	1899	(d)	(4)
113	PLUTO	0-6-0ST	OC	HL	2655	1906	(e)	(5)
	CARLTON No.1	0-6-0ST	OC	HL	2732	1907	(f)	(5)

(a) ex Browney Colliery, /1928
(b) ex Tursdale Colliery by 8/1932
(c) ex Tursdale Colliery, /1933
(d) ex Tursdale Colliery by 5/1933
(e) ex Sherburn Hill Colliery
    4/1937
(f) ex Chilton Colliery, 5/1942

(1) to Parson Byers Quarry by 4/1929
(2) to Browney Colliery by 2/1936;
    ret. by 11/1936; to NCB No.4
    Area, 1/1/1947
(3) to Sherburn Hill Colliery
(4) to Mainsforth Colliery, /1933
(5) to NCB No.4 Area, 1/1/1947

Browney Colliery, near Meadowfield. Map 85, NZ 251389
(Bell Bros Ltd until 2/5/1923)

N3 This colliery was opened in 1879, and was served by sidings W of LNER
Durham-Darlington line, 1¼m S of Relly Mill Junction. It was closed in
July 1938 after partial flooding.

Gauge: 4' 8½"

ELSA	0-4-0ST	OC	MW	1328	1898	New	(1)	
SIR LOWTHIAN	0-4-0ST	OC	MW	1658	1905	New	Scr	/1938
-	0-4-0ST	OC	HG			(a)	Scr	
OLIVIA	0-4-0ST	OC	HL	3426	1919	(b)	(2)	
HUGO	0-4-0ST	OC	MW	1517	1900	(c)	(3)	
COLONEL BELL	0-4-0ST	OC	MW	1697	1906	(d)	(4)	

(a) ex Port Clarence Works, Port
    Clarence (now Teesside)
(b) ex Parson Byers Quarry, /1920
(c) ex Parson Byers Quarry in 1920's
(d) ex Bowburn Colliery by 2/1936

(1) to Parson Byers Quarry by 10/1918
(2) to Parson Byers Quarry by 9/1922
(3) to Bowburn Colliery, /1928
(4) ret. to Bowburn Colliery by
    11/1936

Carlton Iron Works, Stillington. Map 85, NZ 373237
(Carlton Iron Co Ltd until 2/5/1923)

W1 Works served by sidings N of LNER Ferryhill-Stockton line, adjacent to
Stillington Station. It closed about March 1930, and was dismantled during
the winter of 1930-1931. The last three locos worked slag. This site was
subsequently acquired by North Eastern Iron Refining Co Ltd (q.v.).

Gauge: 4' 8½"

	CARLTON No.1	0-6-0ST	OC	HL	2732	1907	(a)	(1)
	CARLTON No.2	0-6-0ST	OC	AB	1404	1915	(a)	(2)
	CARLTON No.4	0-6-0ST	OC	VF	422	1858		
				reb.		1884		
				reb.		1903	(a)	(3)
6	LOTTIE	0-4-0ST	OC	HL	2110	1888	(a)	Scr
	CARLTON No.7	0-6-0ST	OC	HL	2607	1905	(a)	(4)
	-	0-4-0ST	OC	HL	3169	1916	(b)	(5)
	-	0-4-0ST	OC	HC	324	1889		
				reb. Acklam	1926		(c)	(6)
	-	0-4-0ST	OC	CF	1199	1900	(d)	(7)

(a) ex Carlton Iron Co Ltd, 2/5/1923
(b) origin unknown
(c) ex Acklam Works, Middlesbrough,
    Yorks, N.R.; 9/1933
(d) ex Britannia Works, Middles-
    brough, Yorks, N.R.

(1) to Chilton Colliery, 8/1934
(2) to Cleveland Works, Middles-
    brough, Yorks, N.R.
(3) to Burley Ironstone Quarries,
    Rutland, c/1925
(4) to Chilton Colliery (c/1934?)
(5) to Acklam Works, Middlesbrough,
    Yorks, N.R.
(6) to Acklam Works, Middlesbrough,
    Yorks, N.R., 3/1934
(7) to Britannia Works, Middles-
    brough, Yorks, N.R., 1/1938

Collieries, ironworks and quarries of Dorman Long and Co Ltd

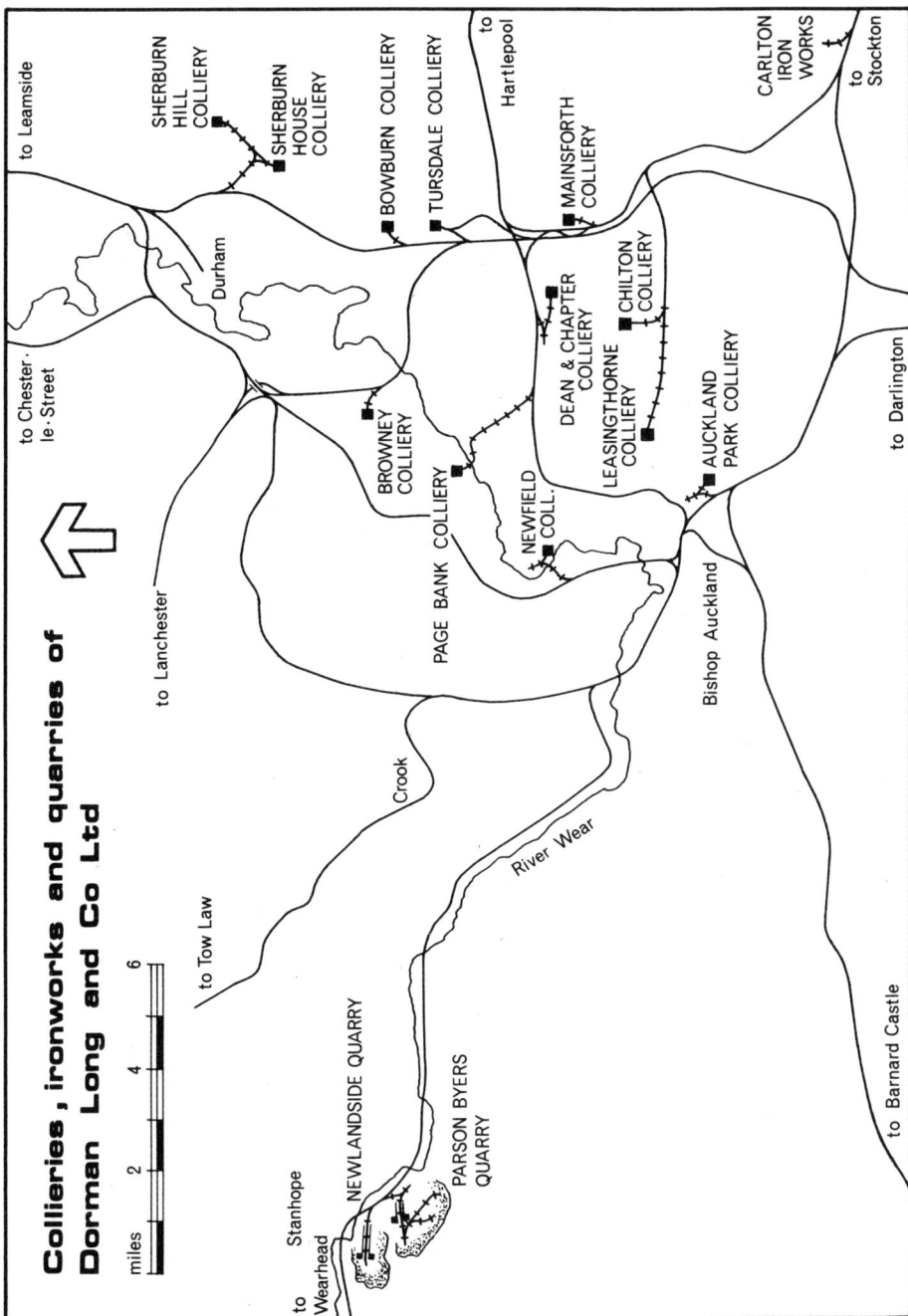

miles 2 4 6

to Leamside

to Chester-le-Street

SHERBURN HILL COLLIERY

SHERBURN HOUSE COLLIERY

BOWBURN COLLIERY

TURSDALE COLLIERY

to Hartlepool

MAINSFORTH COLLIERY

CARLTON IRON WORKS

to Stockton

Durham

DEAN & CHAPTER COLLIERY

CHILTON COLLIERY

BROWNEY COLLIERY

PAGE BANK COLLIERY

NEWFIELD COLL.

LEASINGTHORNE COLLIERY

AUCKLAND PARK COLLIERY

to Darlington

to Lanchester

Bishop Auckland

Crook

River Wear

to Tow Law

to Barnard Castle

to Stanhope Wearhead

NEWLANDSIDE QUARRY

PARSON BYERS QUARRY

81

Chilton Colliery, near Chilton Buildings. Map 85, NZ 278307

R13 Colliery formerly owned by Pease & Partners Ltd (q.v.), who had closed it
in 1930. It was re-opened by Dorman Long about July 1934. It was served by
a branch (¼m) from LNER Chilton branch, and passed to NCB Northern Division No.4 Area on 1st January 1947.

Gauge: 4' 8½"

120	CARLTON No.1	0-6-0ST	OC	HL	2732	1907	(a)	(1)
	CARLTON No.7	0-6-0ST	OC	HL	2607	1905	(b)	(2)
108	HECTOR	0-6-0ST	OC	HL	2613	1905	(c)	(3)
110	HERCULES	0-6-0ST	OC	HL	2654	1906	(d)	(4)
107	ATLAS	0-6-0ST	OC	HL	2612	1905	(e)	(5)

(a) ex Carlton Iron Works, 8/1934
(b) ex Carlton Iron Works, (c/1934?)
(c) ex Auckland Park Colliery, c/1934
(d) ex Leasingthorne Colliery by
    11/1937
(e) ex Leasingthorne Colliery by
    /1940

(1) to Bowburn Colliery, 5/1942
(2) to Sherburn Hill Colliery, /1940
(3) to Leasingthorne Colliery;
    ret. for reps, c6/1946;
    to NCB No.4 Area, 1/1/1947
(4) to Leasingthorne Colliery,
    (c6/1946?)
(5) to NCB No.4 Area, 1/1/1947

Dean & Chapter Colliery, Ferryhill. Map 85, NZ 272331
(Bolckow, Vaughan & Co Ltd until 1/11/1929)

R10 Colliery served by branch (½m) from LNER Ferryhill-Bishop Auckland line,
1¼m E of Spennymoor Station. It was vested in NCB Northern Division No.4
Area on 1st January 1947.

Gauge: 4' 8½"

No.26	(JOHN EVANS)	0-6-0ST	IC	P	629	1896	(a)	(1)
106	ERIMUS	0-6-0ST	OC	HL	2595	1904	(a)	(2)
116	GEORGE V	0-6-0ST	OC	HL	2833	1910	(a)	(2)
148	TAURUS	0-4-0ST	OC	HL	3384	1919	(a)	(3)
107	ATLAS	0-6-0ST	OC	HL	2612	1905	(b)	(4)
No.10		0-4-0ST	OC	BH	1095	1896	(c)	(5)
No.14		0-4-0ST	OC	HL	3248	1917	(d)	(6)
	CARLTON No.7	0-6-0ST	OC	HL	2607	1905	(e)	(2)
	ANGELA	0-4-0ST	OC	AE	1793	1918	(f)	(2)

(a) ex BV, 1/11/1929
(b) ex Leasingthorne Colliery,
    c/1930
(c) ex Vickers-Armstrongs Ltd,
    Elswick Works, Newcastle
(d) ex Port Clarence Works, Port
    Clarence, /1932 (now Teesside)
(e) ex Sherburn Hill Colliery,
    c/1943
(f) ex Burley Ironstone Quarries,
    Rutland, c/1946

(1) to Sherburn Hill Colliery
(2) to NCB No.4 Area, 1/1/1947
(3) to Mainsforth Colliery (after
    11/1941)
(4) to Leasingthorne Colliery, c/1931
(5) to Sherburn Hill Colliery, /1931
(6) to Warrenby Works, Redcar, Yorks,
    N.R.

Leasingthorne Colliery, near Coundon. Map 85, NZ 252304
(Bolckow, Vaughan & Co Ltd until 1/11/1929)

R12 Colliery served by 2m extension of LNER Chilton branch, and vested in NCB
Northern Division No.4 Area on 1st January 1947.

Gauge: 4' 8½"

102		0-4-0ST	OC	HL	2449	1900	(a)	Scr by 11/1937
107	ATLAS	0-6-0ST	OC	HL	2612	1905	(a)	(1)
110	HERCULES	0-6-0ST	OC	HL	2654	1906	(a)	(2)

108   HECTOR   0-6-0ST OC HL   2613 1905 (b) (3)

(a) ex BV, 1/11/1929
(b) ex Chilton Colliery

(1) to Dean & Chapter Colliery,
    c/1930; ret. c/1931; to Chilton
    Colliery by /1941
(2) to Chilton Colliery by 11/1937;
    ret. (c6/1946?); to NCB No.4
    Area, 1/1/1947
(3) to Chilton Colliery for reps,
    c6/1946

Mainsforth Colliery, Ferryhill Station. Map 85, NZ 307316
(Carlton Iron Co Ltd until 2/5/1923)

R27 Colliery served by branch (½m) from LNER Ferryhill-Stockton line, 1m S of
Ferryhill Station. Locos prior to Dorman Long ownership are not known. It
was vested in NCB Northern Division No.4 Area on 1st January 1947.

Gauge: 4' 8½"

No.	Name	Type		Builder	No.	Date		
No.1	"CLARENCE"	0-4-0ST	OC	BH	985	1890		
				reb.AB	2847	1904	(a)	(1)
104		0-6-0ST	IC	MW	1469	1900	(b)	Scr c/1943
	MARY BELL	0-4-0ST	OC	MW	1422	1899	(c)	(2)
	CHARLIE	0-4-0ST	OC	HC	1402	1922	(d)	(1)
148	TAURUS	0-4-0ST	OC	HL	3384	1919	(e)	(1)
30		0-4-0ST	OC	P	669	1897	(f)	(1)

(a) ex Port Clarence Works, Port
    Clarence (now in Teesside)
(b) ex Cleveland Works, Middles-
    brough, Yorks, N.R.
(c) ex Page Bank Colliery, /1931
(d) ex Tursdale Colliery, /1931
(e) ex Dean & Chapter Colliery,
    (after 11/1941)
(f) ex Sherburn Hill Colliery

(1) to NCB No.4 Area, 1/1/1947
(2) to Tursdale Colliery, /1931;
    ret. from Bowburn Colliery, /1933;
    to NCB No.4 Area, 1/1/1947

Newlandside Quarry, Stanhope. Map 84, NY 995383 (approx)
(Bolckow, Vaughan & Co Ltd until 1/11/1929)

Z18 This consisted of two huge limestone quarries on the south side of the
Wear Valley, served by a self-acting incline down to the LNER Wearhead
branch, ½m E of Stanhope Station. It was closed in May 1945, but has since
been re-opened by other owners, using road transport.

Gauge: 4' 8½"

No.	Name	Type		Builder	No.	Date		
	WITTON	0-4-0ST	OC	BH	367	1877	(a)	(1)
	HAVERTON	0-4-0ST	OC	AB	656	1890	(a)	(2)
	NEWPORT	0-4-0ST	OC	K			(b)	(3)
	HARE	0-4-0ST	OC	GH		1908	(c)	(4)
	HUGO	0-4-0ST	OC	MW	1517	1900	(d)	(5)
	ELSA	0-4-0ST	OC	MW	1328	1898		
				reb. R.Shaw		1925	(e)	(6)
	NEWLANDSIDE	0-4-0ST	OC	BH	365	1876		
				reb. Wake	2432		(e)	(7)
137	ARGYLE	0-4-0ST	OC	HL	3140	1915	(f)	(8)

(a) ex BV, 1/11/1929
(b) here, 11/1930; may be K 5115/
    1914 ex Newport Works, Middles-
    brough, Yorks, N.R.
(c) ex Auckland Park Colliery by
    8/1931

(1) to Parson Byers Quarry, c/1937
(2) to Parson Byers Quarry, c/1934;
    believed dism at Newlandside by
    10/1941; scr
(3) to Newport Works, Middlesbrough,
    Yorks, N.R.

(d) ex Parson Byers Quarry by
5/1932
(e) ex Parson Byers Quarry
(f) ex Cleveland Works, Middlesbrough, Yorks, N.R., /1935

(4) to Eston Mines, Yorks, N.R.;ret.
by 1941; to Parson Byers Quarry,
/1945
(5) to Cleveland Works, Middlesbrough, Yorks, N.R., and ret;
to Parson Byers Quarry, /1952
(6) to Cleveland Works, Middlesbrough, Yorks, N.R. in 1930's
and ret; to Parson Byers Quarry,
/1952
(7) to Cleveland Works, Middlesbrough,
Yorks, N.R., and ret; to Parson
Byers Quarry by 12/1939
(8) to Parson Byers Quarry, /1945

<u>Page Bank Colliery</u>, Page Bank. (sometimes called South Brancepeth Colliery)
Map 85, NZ 230359 (Bell Bros Ltd until 2/5/1923)

Q15 This colliery was opened about 1855, and was served by an NER branch 1½m
long from the Spennymoor-Bishop Auckland line, from a junction 1m W of
Spennymoor Station. From 1st January 1868 the branch was leased by Bell
Bros Ltd in order to run passenger trains to the colliery from Spennymoor,
though the NER provided the loco. In March 1890 the colliery is shown as
having two locomotives, and it would appear that by then the NER only ran
the train up to the bridge over the R.Wear, the colliery loco taking
charge for the remainder of the journey. The colliery closed in July 1931.
No details of locomotives before 1899 are known.

Gauge: 4' 8½"

MARY BELL	0-4-0ST	OC	MW	1422	1899	New	(1)
COLONEL BELL	0-4-0ST	OC	MW	1697	1906	New	(2)
HUGO	0-4-0ST	OC	MW	1517	1900	(a)	(3)

(a) ex Parson Byers Quarry by
10/1921

(1) to Mainsforth Colliery, /1931
(2) to Tursdale Colliery, 1/1927
(3) to Parson Byers Quarry by 2/1924

<u>Parson Byers Quarry</u>, near Stanhope. Map 84, NZ 000372 (approx)
(Bell Bros Ltd until 2/5/1923)

Z19 Another huge limestone quarry, begun in 1873, on the south side of the
Wear valley about half way between Stanhope and Frosterley. It was served
by a self-acting incline (¼m) down to the LNER Wearhead branch, 1m E of
Stanhope Station. It was closed in May 1958, but has since been re-opened
by other owners, using road transport.

Gauge: 4' 8½"

	-	0-4-0ST	OC	HH				(a)	Scr
	-	0-4-0ST	OC	HH				(a)	Scr
	HAWK	0-4-0ST	OC	H(L)		c1890		(a)	Scr c/1923
235	WASP	0-4-0ST	OC	MW	813	1881		(b)	Scr c/1943
No.2		0-4-0ST	OC	BH	992	1890		(c)	(1)
	HUGO	0-4-0ST	OC	MW	1517	1900		New	(2)
	PAULINE	0-4-0ST	OC	HL	2941	1912		New	s/s c/1953
	ELSA	0-4-0ST	OC	MW	1328	1898		(d)	
				reb.	R.Shaw	1925			(3)
	OLIVIA	0-4-0ST	OC	HL	3426	1919		New	(4)
	AILEEN	0-4-0ST	OC	HL	3572	1923		New	Scr /1959
	NEWLANDSIDE	0-4-0ST	OC	BH	365	1876		(e)	(5)
	HAVERTON	0-4-0ST	OC	AB	656	1890		(f)	(6)
	WITTON	0-4-0ST	OC	BH	367	1877		(g)	Scr
136	SALTBURN	0-4-0ST	OC	HL	3139	1919		(h)	Scr c9/1958
	HARE	0-4-0ST	OC	GH		1908		(j)	Scr c6/1958
137	ARGYLE	0-4-0ST	OC	HL	3140	1919		(j)	Scr c6/1958
No.22		0-4-0ST	OC	MW	756	1880		(k)	Scr 6/1958

(a) origin unknown
(b) ex Wake by 1/1928; orig. Lucas & Aird, contrs. used for removal of overburden
(c) ex ? (Bell Bros location unknown)
(d) ex Browney Colliery by 10/1918
(e) ex ? (DL location unknown)
(f) ex Newlandside Quarry, c/1934
(g) ex Newlandside Quarry, c/1937
(h) ex Cleveland Works, Middlesbrough, Yorks, N.R., /1941
(j) ex Newlandside Quarry /1945
(k) ex Warrenby Works, Redcar, Yorks, N.R., 12/1954

(1) converted to drive boring machine by 1919; apparatus later removed and sent to Tursdale Colliery c/1939
(2) to Page Bank Colliery by 10/1921; ret. by 2/1924; to Browney Colliery; ex Bowburn Colliery by 4/1929; to Newlandside Quarry by 5/1932; ex Newlandside Quarry, /1952; Scr 6/1958
(3) to Newlandside Quarry; ret. /1952; scr /1956
(4) to Browney Colliery, /1920; ret. by 9/1922; scr c9/1958
(5) to Newlandside Quarry by 12/1932; ret. by 12/1939; scr c6/1958
(6) believed dism at Newlandside Quarry by 10/1941 and scr there

Sherburn Hill Colliery, Sherburn Hill. Map 85, NZ 336427
(Sir B.Samuelson & Co Ltd until 2/5/1923; Lambton & Hetton Collieries Ltd until 1/1/1914; Lambton Collieries Ltd until 8/1911; Earl of Durham's Collieries Ltd until 26/6/1896; orig. Earl of Durham)

N12 This colliery was sunk in 1835, and was originally served by a long branch of the Earl of Durham's Railway, later the Lambton Railway, from Rainton. This was abandoned when the colliery changed hands in 1914, and all coal was dispatched via the colliery's other rail link, a 2m branch to LNER Leamside-Ferryhill line, joining immediately N of Sherburn Station. For the other collieries on this line, see Lambton, Hetton & Joicey Collieries Ltd. The loco shed was unusually sited underneath the screens. The colliery was vested in NCB Northern Division No.4 Area on 1st January 1947. The colliery was originally worked by locomotives of the Lambton·Railway, with a number being normally allocated to Sherburn Hill shed. In 1914 three passed to Sir B. Samuelson & Co Ltd and one was retained by the Railway.

Gauge: 4' 8½"

⚡		0-4-0ST	OC	HL	2530	1902	New	(1)
1		0-6-0ST	IC	H&C			(a)	
				reb.HL	9294	1914		(2)
2		0-6-0	IC	H&C	72	1866	(a)	
				reb. Ridley Shaw		1928		Scr c/1940
3		0-4-0ST	OC	H&C	79	1866	(a)	
				reb. Wake	1013	1914		Scr
4	VICTORIA	0-6-0ST	IC	HE	484	1889	(b)	s/s
64	"No.4"	0-6-0T	OC	HC	1335	1918	(c)	(2)
(153)	PATRIOT	0-6-0T	IC	BV		1920	(d)	(2)
No.26	JOHN EVANS	0-4-0ST	OC	P	629	1896	(e)	(2)
No.10		0-4-0ST	OC	BH	1095	1896	(f)	(2)
113	PLUTO	0-6-0ST	OC	HL	2655	1906	(g)	(3)
	CARLTON No.7	0-6-0ST	OC	HL	2607	1905	(h)	(4)
30		0-4-0ST	OC	P	669	1897	(j)	(5)

⚡ Lambton Railway 28

(a) ex Lambton & Hetton Collieries Ltd, 1/1/1914
(b) ex Hutchinson's Trustees, Widnes, Lancs, via Ralph Russell, /1916
(c) ex IWD Richborough, Kent
(d) ex Cleveland Works, Middlesbrough, Yorks, N.R.
(e) ex Dean & Chapter Colliery

(1) to Lambton & Hetton Collieries Ltd, 1/1/1914
(2) to NCB No.4 Area, 1/1/1947
(3) to Bowburn Colliery, 4/1937
(4) to Dean & Chapter Colliery
(5) to Mainsforth Colliery

(f) ex Dean & Chapter Colliery,
    /1931
(g) ex Auckland Park Colliery
(h) ex Chilton Colliery, /1940
(j) ex Bowburn Colliery

Tursdale Colliery, near Cornforth. Map 85, NZ 301360
(Bell Bros Ltd until 2/5/1923)

R16 This colliery was served by sidings E of LNER Leamside-Ferryhill line, 2½m
N of Ferryhill Station, and was acquired by Bell Bros Ltd in 1879. For
some time about the turn of the century it was also connected to the NER
Coxhoe Branch by a ½m NER link. Coal-winding ceased in June 1931, the
colliery being merged underground with Bowburn Colliery (q.v.), though the
shaft remained in use for pumping, and was vested in NCB Northern Division
No.4 Area on 1st January 1947

Gauge: 4' 8½"

	HUGH BELL	0-6-0ST	IC	HE			(a)	s/s
	COLONEL BELL	0-4-0ST	OC	MW	1697	1906	(b)	(1)
30		0-4-0ST	OC	P	669	1897	(c)	(2)
	CHARLIE	0-4-0ST	OC	HC	1402	1922	(d)	(3)
	MARY BELL	0-4-0ST	OC	MW	1422	1899	(e)	(4)
	-	0-4-0ST	OC	BH	992	1890	(f)	(5)

(a) ex ?, 3/1914   (1) to Bowburn Colliery by 8/1932
(b) ex Page Bank Colliery, 1/1927   (2) to Bowburn Colliery /1933
(c) ex Cleveland Works, Middles-   (3) to Mainsforth Colliery, /1931
    brough, Yorks, N.R.   (4) to Bowburn Colliery by 5/1933
(d) ex Frank Edmunds, /1930; form. (5) to NCB No.4 Area, 1/1/1947
    Birmingham Corporation Sewage
    Dept.
(e) ex Mainsforth Colliery, /1931
(f) ex Parson Byers Quarry, c/1939

DORMAN, LONG (STEEL) LTD
(Dorman, Long & Co Ltd until 2/10/1954)

Newfield Colliery & Brickworks, Newfield. Map 85, NZ 205332
(Bolckow, Vaughan & Co Ltd until 1/11/1929)

Q20 This works and drift were served by a branch (1m) from Hunwick Station on
BR Durham-Bishop Auckland line. The colliery became a licensed mine when
the coal industry was nationalised, and was abandoned in December 1959.
The brickworks, which manufactures firebricks, replaced its rail traffic
by road transport about 1962.

Gauge: 4' 8½"

No.2   0-4-0ST OC BH   ✦   1877
                           reb. BV   1893 (a) Scr   /1953
(No.1)   0-4-0ST OC P   916 1901 (a) Scr   c/1962
        BETTY   0-4-0ST OC AE 1769 1917 (b) Scr c11/1960
43   0-4-0ST OC DL   1949 (c) Scr   c/1962
                  ✦ probably one of BH 427/8/9/31

(a) ex BV, 1/11/1929
(b) ex WD, Tidworth, Hants, 3/1948
(c) ex Britannia Works, Middles-
    brough, Yorks, N.R., c11/1960

DOXFORD AND SUNDERLAND LTD
(Doxford and Sunderland Shipbuilding and Engineering Co Ltd until 23/3/1970;
William Doxford & Sons (Shipbuilders) Ltd until 1/4/1966; William Doxford
& Sons Ltd until 14/6/1961; William Doxford & Sons until 1/1/1891)

Pallion Yard, Sunderland. Map 78, NZ 377577 (approx)

K8 The early history of this yard is rather obscure. There were a number of
small shipbuilding yards in the Pallion area in the 1860's, and Doxford
appears to have begun his (or taken one over) in 1869, later taking over
neighbouring yards. The yard was served by sidings from BR Sunderland-
Durham line, E of Pallion Station, and rail traffic ceased in January 1971.
Only two locomotives are known before 1900; there may have been others.

Gauge: 4' 8½"

-		0-4-0ST	OC	BH	424	1878	New	(1)
GENERAL		0-4-0ST	OC	P	703	1899	New	Scr 5/1951
PALLION		0-4-0CT⟋	OC	HL	2517	1902	New	(2)
DEPTFORD		0-4-0T ⌀	OC	HL	2535	1902	New	Scr 4/1949
WEAR		0-4-0T ⌀	OC	HL	2551	1903	New	Scr 9/1952
HYLTON		0-4-0CT	OC	HL	2594	1905	New	Scr 9/1952
MILLFIELD		0-4-0CT	OC	HL	2632	1906	New	Scr 6/1938
GRINDON		0-4-0T ⌀	OC	AB	1305	1912	New	Scr 6/1969
BROWNIE		0-4-0CT	OC	HL	2550	1903	(a)	Scr 6/1969
ROKER		0-4-0CT	OC	RSH	7006	1940	New	(3)
HENDON		0-4-0CT	OC	RSH	7007	1940	New	(4)
SOUTHWICK		0-4-0CT	OC	RSH	7069	1942	New	(5)
MILLFIELD		0-4-0CT	OC	RSH	7070	1942	New	(6)
2		0-4-0ST	OC	HL	2989	1913	(b)	(7)
GENERAL		0-4-0ST	OC	P	2049	1944	(c)	(4)

⟋ crane removed for a time   ⌀ rebuilt from 0-4-0CT

(a) ex R.& W. Hawthorn Leslie
    (Shipbuilders) Ltd, Hebburn,
    /1940
(b) ex Wallsend & Hebburn Coal Co
    Ltd, Rising Sun Colliery, Walls-
    end, Northumberland, in period
    1939-1945, loan
(c) ex TWW, Grays, Middlesex,
    4/1951; prev. Morris Motors
    Ltd, Cowley, Oxfordshire

(1) to East & West Yorkshire Union
    Railway, 8, c/1903
(2) to D.W.Fickes, Dalescroft Rail-
    fans Club, Britannia Steelworks
    (BSC), Middlesbrough, Teesside,
    for restoration, 5/1971
(3) to D.W.Fickes, Dalescroft Rail-
    fans Club, Britannia Steelworks
    (BSC), Middlesbrough, Teesside,
    for restoration, 3/1971
(4) to Blaydon Metal Co Ltd, Blaydon,
    for scrap, 3/1971
(5) to Dinting Railway Centre Ltd,
    Dinting, Derbyshire, for
    restoration, 4/1971
(6) to A. Bloom, Bressingham Steam
    Museum, Bressingham, Norfolk,
    for restoration, 1/1971
(7) ret. to Wallsend & Hebburn Coal
    Co Ltd, Northumberland

DUNLOP, MEREDITH & CO LTD, CARR HOUSE IRONWORKS, STRANTON, WEST HARTLEPOOL
(Stranton Iron & Steel Works Ltd until 1/1874)

S7 Works (Map 85, NZ 515317?) served by sidings W of north end of NER Cliff
House Branch, and dismantled in 1887. The site is believed to have been
used later by Casebourne & Co Ltd, who did not employ locomotives.

Gauge: 4' 8½"

-	0-4-0ST	OC	BH	(a)	(1)
-	0-4-0ST	OC	BH	(a)	(1)

(a) origin unknown   (1) offered for sale, 5/1887; s/s

DUNSTON GARESFIELD COLLIERIES LTD, SWALWELL GARESFIELD COLLIERY, SWALWELL
(Company was Swalwell Garesfield Coal Co up to 1899; there were several
variations of title before the above was adopted in 1904)

B9 This was an old colliery (Map 78, NZ 205623) served by the NER Swalwell
Branch ($\frac{1}{2}$m) from Derwenthaugh on the NER Redheugh Branch. It was worked by
the NER until the arrival of the first loco below. The colliery closed in
August 1940. The site was later developed by NCBOE (q.v.).

Gauge: 4' 8$\frac{1}{2}$"

-	0-4-0ST	OC	BH	298	1875	(a)	(1)
PROSPECT	0-4-0ST	OC	HL	2479	1900	New	(2)

(a) ex NER, 996, via LG

(1) to LG; re-sold to Casebourne &
Co Ltd, Haverton Hill (now in
Teesside)
(2) to ICI Ltd, Dalbeattie, Kirk-
cudbrightshire, via Cohen, /1941

DURHAM & YORKSHIRE WHINSTONE CO LTD

Greenfoot Quarry, near Stanhope. Map 84, NY 983392
(orig. R. Summerson & Co Ltd - q.v.)

Z13 This quarry was apparently taken over from its previous owners in the late
1940's. It was served by sidings N of BR Wearhead Branch, 1$\frac{1}{4}$m W of Stanhope
Station, and was taken over by Tarmac Roadstone Ltd (q.v.) in October 1963.

Gauge: 2' 3$\frac{1}{2}$"

-	4wDM	RH	175420	1936	(a)	(1)

(a) ex R.Summerson & Co Ltd, c/1948   (1) to Tarmac Roadstone Ltd, 10/1963

Rogerley Quarry, Frosterley. Map 84, NZ 015377 (approx)
(PP until 1947)

Y1 This was a huge elongated quarry on the northern slopes of Weardale,
stretching from Frosterley almost all the way to Stanhope, a distance of
about 2m. When this firm took over, the rail link to Frosterley Station on
the BR Wearhead Branch was removed, but rail traffic continued within the
quarry between the face and a lorry loading platform. This working ceased
in 1954, and the system was dismantled in 1961. The quarry continues in
production, under different owners, using road transport.

Gauge: 4' 8$\frac{1}{2}$"

22	FROSTERLEY	0-4-0ST	OC	HL	2563	1903	(a)	s/s c1/1960

(a) ex PP, /1947

DURHAM COUNTY COUNCIL

The County County acquired a number of locomotives over the years,
principally for use on major roadworks for the movement of excavated
materials by means of skips, though the last two in the list were latterly
used in a slag works operated by the Council on the site of the works
formerly owned by the Linthorpe-Dinsdale Smelting Co Ltd (q.v.) at
Middleton St. George. When not in use the locomotives were kept at the
Council's Central Repair Depot, which was originally at Durham but was
later moved to Framwellgate Moor.

Gauge: 2' 0"

1		4wPM			1923	New	(1)
2		4wPM			1923	New	s/s
3		4wPM	KC	1652	1930	New	(2)
4		4wPM	KC	1655	1930	New	(2)
5		4wDM	RH	186322	1937	New	(3)
6		4wDM	RH	186342	1937	New	(4)

(1) to ?, /1948
(2) to Northumberland County Council,
      8/1950
(3) to A.M. Coke, Sleaford, Lincs, by
      1/1949; to Dinorwic Slate Quarr-
      ies Ltd, Caernarvonshire, via
      Bungey, 7/1950
(4) to Bungey, Hayes, Middlesex,
       /1950; re-sold to Dinorwic Slate
      Quarries Ltd, Caernarvonshire,
      8/1950

DURHAM COUNTY WATER BOARD

Burnhope Reservoir,   near Wearhead. Map 84, NY 845387 (approx)

Z1   This huge reservoir in Upper Weardale was begun in January 1931 and
completed in September 1937. During its construction it was served by a ½m
extension of the LNER Wearhead Branch, and an extensive 2' 0" gauge system
operated within the site.

Gauge: 4' 8½"

-		0-6-0ST	OC	AE	2000	1930	New	(1)
-		0-4-0ST	OC	AB	1988	1931	New	(2)

(1) to Newbiggin Colliery Co Ltd,
      Northumberland, c8/1934
(2) to Cambrian Wagon Works Ltd,
      Maindu Works, Cardiff, Glamorgan

Gauge: 2' 0"

1		4wPM		MR	5067	1930	New	(1)
2		4wPM		MR	5132	1930	New	(1)
3	"GREEN"	0-4-0WT	OC	AB	1855	1931	New	(2)
4	"RED"	0-4-0WT	OC	AB	1991	1931	New	(3)
5	"GREY"	0-4-0WT	OC	AB	1994	1931	New	(4)
6	"EDITH"	4wVBT	VCG	S	6902	1927	New	(5)
70		0-4-0WT	OC	AB	1995	1931	New	(6)
72	MIDGE	0-4-0ST	OC	KS	4290	1923	(a)	(7)
73	GNAT	0-4-0ST	OC	KS	4291	1923	(b)	(7)
74	BURNHOPE	0-4-2ST	OC	KS	1144	1911	(c)	(8)
75	WELLHOPE	0-4-2ST	OC	KS	1145	1912	(c)	(9)
76	IRESHOPE	0-4-2ST	OC	KS	1142	1911	(d)	(10)
77	KILLHOPE	0-4-2ST	OC	KS	1047	1908	(c)	(11)
78	HARTHOPE	0-4-2ST	OC	KS	1291	1915	(e)	(12)
79	"R.A.F."	0-4-0WT	OC	AB	1453	1918	(f)	(13)
80	WASP	0-4-0ST	OC	KS	4001	1918	(g)	(7)
81	DURHAM	0-4-0T	OC	AE	2066	1933	New	(3)
82	WEAR	0-4-0T	OC	AE	2067	1933	New	(3)
83	LANCHESTER	0-4-0T	OC	AE	2071	1933	New	(14)
84	AUCKLAND	0-4-0T	OC	AE	2072	1933	New	(15)
85	SUNDERLAND	0-4-0T	OC	AE	2073	1933	New	(2)
86	STANHOPE	0-4-2ST	OC	KS	2395	1917	(h)	(16)
87	"FOWLER"	0-6-0T	OC	JF	16991	1926	(j)	s/s

89

(a) ex Nelson Corporation, Upper Coldwell Reservoir, Lancs, 5/1932
(b) ex Nelson Corporation, Upper Coldwell Reservoir, Lancs, 7/1932
(c) ex Mowlem, Hants, /1932
(d) ex Pugsley, Bristol, 6/1932; form. Mowlem
(e) ex Royal Arsenal, Woolwich, London
(f) ex Admiralty, Air Service Construction Corps
(g) ex Air Ministry, Uxbridge, Middlesex
(h) ex Holloway Bros Ltd, contrs, Rosyth, Fife
(j) ex J.H.Dennis, Nocton Estates Light Railway, Lincs

(1) one of these went to Golightly, contr, Spennymoor; other s/s
(2) to Roads Reconstruction (1934) Ltd, Grovesend Quarry, Gloucs
(3) to Lord Penrhyn's Slate Quarries, Caernarvonshire, 10/1936
(4) to Lord Penrhyn's Slate Quarries, Caernarvonshire, 1/1938
(5) to Cliffe Hill Granite Co Ltd, Leics, /1935
(6) to Raisby Hill Limestone Co Ltd, Coxhoe
(7) to South Essex Waterworks Co Ltd, Essex, 1/1936
(8) to HE for scrap
(9) to HE, /1938; re-sold to an East African sugar factory per I.Gundle, 10/1940
(10) to Balfour, Beatty & Co Ltd, contrs, c4/1936
(11) to HE, /1938
(12) to HE, /1938; re-sold to East-woods Cement Ltd, Barrington, Cambs
(13) to Walton's Alston Limestone Co, Alston, Cumberland, /1938
(14) to Birtley Brick Co Ltd, Birtley, /1938
(15) to Roads Reconstruction (1934) Ltd, Vallis Vale Quarry, Somerset
(16) to Lord Penrhyn's Slate Quarries, Caernarvonshire, 12/1934

Location unknown

The locos below are listed as sold to the Board, but the Board now has no record of their location or work

Gauge: 2' 0"

–	4wDM	MR	7604	1939	New	(1)
–	4wDM	MR	7605	1939	New	(2)
–	4wDM	MR	7606	1939	New	(3)

(1) to Bungey, Hayes, Middlesex, /1950; re-sold to Norcon Ltd, Wimborne, Dorset
(2) to Bungey, Hayes, Middlesex, /1950
(3) to Bungey, Hayes, Middlesex, /1950; re-sold to NCB NE Division No.3 (Rotherham) Area, Denaby Main Colliery

DURHILLS LTD, COLLIER LAW QUARRY, near STANHOPE

Z14 A sand quarry (Map 84, NZ 004429), served originally by sidings from the LNER Pontop & Shields branch at Blanchland (Parkhead) Station, but from 1951 at the end of the line, 5m from Burnhill Junction, where there was a reverse for trains to and from the quarry. The locos below were used within the quarry, and were disused by 1954, the internal rail system having been dispensed with. The BR line was closed in April 1968, and the quarry is now worked by Thos. W. Ward Ltd under the title Dursand Quarry, using road transport.

Gauge: 2' 0"

-	4wDM	RH	166012	1932	(a)		Scr c/1955
-	4wDM	RH	177640	1936	(b)		Scr c/1955

(a) ex East Midland Gravel Co Ltd,
    Fengate Pits, Northants
(b) ex County Borough of Derby

EAGLESCLIFFE BRICKS LTD, EAGLESCLIFFE
(Cradock, Allison & Co Ltd until 1935)
COATHAM STOB ESTATES LTD, COATHAM STOB BRICKWORKS, near EAGLESCLIFFE
(both firms were subsidiaries of Crossley & Sons Ltd originally,
Crossley Building Products Ltd from c/1955)

W4 The Eaglescliffe Works (Map 85, NZ 419157) was begun just before the First
World War, and was served by sidings W of NER Stockton-Northallerton line,
¼m N of Eaglescliffe Station. This works was supplied by Witham Hall
Quarry, which lay immediately south of the works. At this time the firm's
trade was mainly in limestone, but about 1918 it opened a second quarry at
W3 Coatham Stob (NZ 411160), which was worked for the clay near the surface
and the whinstone about 180 feet down, and to which was laid a narrow
gauge line.
After Crossley & Sons Ltd took over they transferred the Coatham Stob
quarry to a new firm, Coatham Stob Estates Ltd, who in March 1938 opened a
modern brickworks on the quarry's northern side, though Eaglescliffe Bricks
Ltd continued to work the quarry as well for their own clay and whinstone,
and worked the traffic for both works. In late 1938, however, Coatham Stob
took over their own traffic, and subsequently helped to shunt Eaglescliffe's traffic also. At this period the Eaglescliffe line ran along the
southern side of the quarry, and loaded wagon bodies were lifted from the
quarry by various means and put on other frames to be taken down to Eaglescliffe. With the Witham Hall Quarry abandoned, the Coatham Stob Quarry was
extended westwards, and so the link between the two companies' systems was
removed, though Coatham Stob loaned Eaglescliffe a loco when necessary.

Whinstone working at the quarry ceased after the lower level was flooded,
Eaglescliffe's traffic then being mainly clay. The Coatham Stob system was
replaced by dumpers in 1962. Rail working to Eaglescliffe ceased in 1965,
and the brickworks there closed shortly afterwards, though its concrete
plant passed to Crossley Building Products Ltd. The Coatham Stob works
continues in production.

There are considerable difficulties concerning the locomotives used by the
two companies, the version the authors dislike least being given below.

Gauge: 2' 6"

ZURIEL	0-4-0T	OC	WB	1917	1910	(a)		Scr c/1946
MAGNET II	0-4-0ST	OC	WB	1877	1911	(b)		Scr c/1946
-	4wDM		HE	1929	1938	New		(1)
-	4wDM		RH	198245	1939	New		Scr c/1968
-	4wDM		RH			(c)		Scr /1969
-	4wDM		RH	242914	1946	New		Scr /1969
-	4wDM		HE	1929	1938	(d)		Scr c/1968

✗ owned by Eaglescliffe Bricks Ltd   ∅ owned by Coatham Stob Estates Ltd
N.B. Apart from locos that worked each other's traffic at Coatham Stob
Quarry, RH 242914/1946 was loaned to Eaglescliffe Bricks Ltd when
necessary.

HE 1929/1938 is believed never to have worked during its ownership
by Eaglescliffe Bricks Ltd

(a) ex Lunedale Whinstone Co,
    Middleton-in-Teesdale (c/1918?)
(b) ex F.B.Thompstone & Sons Ltd,
    Bosley, Cheshire, c/1925
(c) ex ?, /1942
(d) ex South Bank Brick Co Ltd,
    South Bank, Yorks, N.R., /1963 ∅

(1) to South Bank Brick Co Ltd,
    South Bank, Yorks, N.R., /1946 ∅

    ∅ this company was another subsidiary of Crossley & Sons Ltd

EASINGTON COAL CO LTD, EASINGTON COLLIERY, EASINGTON COLLIERY
(reg. 5/1/1899; latterly a subsidiary of Weardale Steel, Coal & Coke Co
Ltd)

P14 This colliery (Map 85, NZ 438442) was begun in 1901, but was not opened
until 1910 because of difficulties with the sinking. It was originally to
be linked to Seaham Harbour Docks by a branch of the Londonderry Railway
(see Marquis of Londonderry), but eventually it was served by sidings E of
LNER Seaham-West Hartlepool line, 4m S of Seaham Station. It was vested in
NCB Northern Division No. 3 Area on 1st January 1947.

Gauge: 4' 8½"

1		0-6-0ST	OC	AB	912	1901	New	(1)
-		0-4-0ST	OC	KS	4027	1919	(a)	(1)
-		0-6-0ST	OC	BH	704	1882	(b)	(1)
-		0-6-0ST	IC	VF	5305	1945	(c)	(1)

(a) ex Weardale Steel, Coal & Coke
    Co Ltd, Thornley Colliery, by
    5/1925
(b) ex Weardale Steel, Coal & Coke
    Co Ltd, Heights Quarry, /1943
(c) ex WD, 75315, 4/1946

(1) to NCB No.3 Area, 1/1/1947

EAST HETTON COLLIERIES LTD
(Walter Scott Ltd until 12/1935; East Hetton Coal Co Ltd until 19/5/1880)

East Hetton Colliery, near Kelloe. Map 85, NZ 346370

R21 Served by branch (2m) from LNER Wingate-Ferryhill line, 3½m N of Ferryhill
Station. Colliery may have been shunted for a time by the NER. It was
vested in NCB Northern Division No.4 Area on 1st January 1947.

Gauge: 4' 8½"

	-			TR	255	1855	New	s/s by 4/1871
	-			TR	256	1855	New	s/s by 4/1871
	EAST HETTON	0-4-0ST	OC	BH	267	1873	New	s/s
No.2		0-4-0ST	OC	BH	318	1874	New	s/s
	EAST HETTON	0-4-0ST	OC	HL	2279	1893	New	(1)
	WALTER SCOTT	0-6-0ST	IC	HL	2484	1900	New	(1)
	KELLOE	0-6-0ST	OC	P	525	1892	(a)	(2)
	KELLOE	0-4-0ST	OC	P	560	1893	(b)	(3)

(a) ex Crosby Mines, Lincs
(b) ex Trimdon Grange Colliery

(1) to NCB No.4 Area, 1/1/1947
(2) to Ridley Shaw, Middlesbrough,
    Yorks, N.R.
(3) to Trimdon Grange Colliery

<u>Trimdon Grange Colliery & Coking Plant</u>, Trimdon Grange. Map 85, NZ 366357
(orig. R.Forster)

R24 Sunk in 1845, this colliery was served by sidings N of LNER Wingate-
Ferryhill line, ¼m W of Trimdon Station. Around the turn of the century
the colliery was shunted by a loco summoned from East Hetton Colliery by
telephone, so that the colliery company presumably had running powers
between the two pits. There appear to have been frequent transfers later,
and the NER may also have shunted the colliery for a time. It was vested
in NCB Northern Division No.4 Area on 1st January 1947.

Gauge: 4' 8½"

-	0-6-0T	OC	AB	698	1891	New	s/s by 11/1896
KELLOE	0-4-0ST	OC	P	560	1893	(a)	(1)

(a) ex ICI, Winnington, Cheshire,   (1) to East Hetton Colliery, and ret;
    /1929   to NCB No.4 Area, 1/1/1947

<u>ELDON BRICKWORKS LTD</u>, ELDON, near BISHOP AUCKLAND

T25 This brickworks (Map 85, NZ 238280) was formerly attached to Eldon Colliery
(see Pease & Partners Ltd), which closed in July 1932. It was served by a
branch (1m) ½m N of Shildon Tunnel on LNER Bishop Auckland-Shildon line.
Rail traffic was later discontinued.

Gauge: 4' 8½"

-	4wDM	HE	1737	1935	New	(1)

(1) to North Eastern Trading Estates
    Ltd, Aycliffe Estate

<u>JAMES W. ELLIS ENGINEERING LTD</u>, HANNINGTON WORKS, SWALWELL
(Huwood-Ellis Ltd until 27/4/1970; James W. Ellis & Co Ltd until 8/3/1968;
subsidiary of Huwood Ltd from 1/1/1967; Hannington & Co Ltd until c/1903)

B7 This foundry and engineering works (Map 78, NZ 204627) was probably opened
just before the turn of the century, and was served by sidings S of NER
Redheugh Branch, 1½m E of Blaydon Station. The works was shunted by crane
in 1968 and 1969, and was closed in October 1971, having passed to Huwood
Ltd on 1st September 1971 (q.v.).

Gauge: 4' 8½"

REFORM	0-4-0ST	OC	AB	969	1903	New	(1)
-	0-6-0ST	IC	BH	716	1882		
			reb.		1906	(a)	(2)
-	0-4-0CT	OC	HL	2606	1905	(b)	Scr
-	0-4-0ST	OC	AE	1055	1874		
			reb.	Sdn	1892	(c)	(3)
PRESTON No.3	0-6-0ST	OC	HL	2737	1907	(d)	(4)
MARY ∅	0-4-0ST	OC	HL	3894	1936	New	Scr 11/1968
MARY	4wVBT	VCG	S	7852	1929	(e)	Scr /1962
-	4wDM		RH	305323	1951	(f)	(5)

   ∅ nameplates transferred to S 7852 from 1957 to 1962

(a) ex Harton Coal Co Ltd, /1910   (1) to APCM, Burham Works, Kent
(b) ex J.Spencer & Sons Ltd, Newburn (2) to Leversons Wallsend Collieries
    Steelworks, Northumberland,   Ltd, Usworth Colliery
    c/1923   (3) derelict by 6/1933; s/s
(c) ex Synthetic Ammonia & Nitrates   (4) to Horden Collieries Ltd, Horden
    Ltd, Billingham, c/1930?; see   Colliery, c/1939
    also Ministry of Munitions   (5) to Huwood Ltd, 1/9/1971
(d) ex U.A.Ritson & Sons Ltd,

Preston Colliery, North Shields,
Northumberland, by 6/1932
(e) ex BR, 68159, 3/1957
(f) ex South Western Gas Board,
Cheltenham Gas Works, Gloucs,
c8/1969

ENGLISH ELECTRIC CO LTD, STEPHENSON WORKS, DARLINGTON
(Robert Stephenson & Hawthorns Ltd until 1/1/1962 - q.v.)

V7 Works (Map 85, NZ 300166) served by sidings E of BR Durham-Darlington line,
1¼m N of Darlington (Bank Top) Station. It closed in March 1964. The
buildings have since been taken over by other firms, without rail traffic.

Gauge: 4' 8½"

D 0227"THE BLACK PIG"	0-6-0DH	VF	D227	1956				
		EE	2346	1956	(a)	Scr c/1965		

(a) ex Robert Stephenson & Hawthorns
Ltd, 1/1/1962

FENCE HOUSES BRICKWORKS LTD, LUMLEY QUARRY & BRICKWORKS, LUMLEY THICKS

L6 The rail system ran from the quarry (Map 78, NZ 307503) to a grinding
plant at the brickworks. Prior to the introduction of the loco below, the
tubs ran by gravity to the foot of an incline, whence they were hauled up
to the plant by a winch. In the latter part of 1955 loco working ceased
due to the uneven shape of the quarry floor through faulting, and extract-
ion from the quarry has since been handled by dumpers.

Gauge: 2' 0"

-	4wDM	RH	223716	1944	(a)	(1)

(a) ex Charles Wall Ltd, Globe   (1) to Thornton Engineering Co Ltd,
Works, Grays, Essex, via   Whitley Bay, Northumberland,
Grayston Plant & Engineering Co   c/1959
Ltd, c7/1953

FERENS & LOVE (1937) LTD
(Ferens & Love Ltd until 1937; orig. Ferens & Love)

Cornsay Colliery & Brickworks, Cornsay Colliery. Map 85, NZ 432170

M2 Colliery opened in 1868, and served by a branch (2¼m) from Flass Junction
on NER Waterhouses Branch. It became a licensed mine on 1st January 1947,
and was abandoned in September 1953, though the brickworks continued to
use rail transport until about 1962.

There was one loco here in April 1871 and November 1876, and two in March
1890, but their identity is unknown. One may be the first loco below.

Gauge: 4' 8½"

No.3	JOHN HARRIS (form. No.1)	0-4-0ST	OC	Harris?			(a)	s/s	
	CORNSAY	0-4-0ST	OC	HL	2478	1901	New	(1)	
No.2	JOHN OWEN	0-6-0ST	OC	FW	171	1872	(b)	Scr	/1952
1	KILMARNOCK	0-6-0ST	OC	AB	1497	1916	(c)	(2)	
	THORNCLIFFE	0-6-0ST	IC	MW	241	1867			
				reb.		1902			
				reb.		1932	(d)	Scr	/1952
	-	4wDM		FH	3374	1950	New	(3)	

(a) origin unknown   (1) to Hawthorn Limestone Co Ltd,
(b) ex Bute Works Supply Co. /1914;   Seaham Harbour

94

```
            until 8/1912 was GWR 1385        (2) to SDSI, Stockton Works,  /1943
    (c) ex MOM, Gretna, Cumberland            (3) to Smith, Patterson & Co Ltd,
    (d) ex Newton, Chambers & Co Ltd,             Blaydon, c/1962
        Yorks, W.R., 7/1946
```

Shincliffe Colliery, Shincliffe Colliery. Map 85, NZ 299399
(orig. Joseph Love & Partners; later Ferens & Love Ltd)

N6 This colliery was also opened in the 1860's, and was situated on a loop
between the NER Durham & Sunderland branch, ½m W of Sherburn House Station,
and Shincliffe Station on NER line from Leamside to Ferryhill. The colliery
is believed to have closed about 1877.

Gauge: 4' 8½"

JOHN BELL	0-6-0ST	IC	MW	148	1865	New	(1)
-	0-6-0ST	OC	BH	244	1873	New	(2)
SHINCLIFFE	0-4-0ST	✗					(3)

✗ The identity of this loco is disputed. The name may have been
carried by BH 244 at one time. It may possibly have been the
John Harris loco listed under Cornsay Colliery.

```
                        (1) sold c1914-1918; may have gone
                            to Cornsay Colliery
                        (2) apparently s/s by 11/1876
                        (3) to LG; became a hire loco named
                            PRINCE
```

FERGUSSON, WILD & CO LTD, STANHOPEBURN MINE, near STANHOPE

Z15 A mine with a long history of working for iron, lead and fluorspar, and
re-opened again for fluorspar in 1972. The locos below work and are charged
underground, but come to the surface at the Shield Hurst Level (Map 84, NY
987412). There is no main line rail connection. Mine taken over on 5th
April 1975 by Swiss Aluminium (U.K.) Ltd (q.v.).
Gauge: 1' 10"

-	0-4-0BE	WR			(a)	(1)
	0-4-0BE	WR	7644	1973	New	(1)

```
(a) ex Force Crag Mine Ltd,              (1) to Swiss Aluminium (U.K.) Ltd,
    Braithwaite, Cumberland,  /1973          4/1975
```

FLUORSPAR LTD, STANHOPEBURN MINE, near STANHOPE. Map 84, NY 987412
(subsidiary of Laporte Chemicals Ltd)

Z15 Originally an ironstone mine, and later worked by the Weardale Lead Co Ltd
(q.v.), it was acquired by the firm above in 1942 to work fluorspar. The
locos below worked underground, though their shed was on the surface, and
there was no main line rail connection. The mine closed in October 1964,
and the site was largely cleared in 1969-1970. (But see firm above)

Gauge: 1' 8"

-	4wBE	WR	3492	1946	(1)
-	4wBE				(2)
-	4wBE				(2)

```
                        (1) to Laporte Industries Ltd, Eyam,
                            Derbyshire,  /1966; reb. to 2' 0"
                            gauge and sent to Sallet Hole
                            Mine, Stoney Middleton, Derby-
                            shire
                        (2) to Laporte Industries Ltd, Eyam,
                            Derbyshire, and scrapped
```

<u>FORESTRY COMMISSION</u>, DINSDALE, DARLINGTON

Details unknown.

Gauge: 2' 0"

		4wPM	MR	9103	1942	New	s/s

<u>G. FOSTER</u>, RAMSHAW MINE, RAMSHAW

Z20 This little fluorspar mine (Map 84, NY 953474) operated both 1' 6" and
2' 0" gauge tub lines. The loco below was probably used to shunt tubs on
to a road transport hopper. The mine was closed about 1963, and the locomotive stored on the site. In 1973 working re-commenced (under different
owners?), using road transport.

Gauge: 2' 0"

		4wPM	MR	8614	1941	(a)

(a) ex Ewesley Quarry Co Ltd, Neth-
erwitton, Northumberland, c/1962

<u>FOSTER, BLACKETT & WILSON LTD</u>, TYNE LEAD WORKS, HEBBURN

E12 A long-established works (Map 78, NZ 317656) served by sidings from the
Pontop & Jarrow Railway of John Bowes & Partners Ltd (q.v.) W of the
staithes at Jarrow used between 1883 and 1936. Probably P&JR locos brought
the firm's traffic to and from the link with the NER at Pontop Junction,
Jarrow. The works continues in production, without rail traffic.

Gauge: 4' 8½"

	0-4-0ST	OC	P	1508	1918	New	(1)

(1) to Priestman's Whitehaven
Collieries Ltd, Whitehaven,
Cumberland, via Frazer, 4/1932

<u>FOWNES FORGE & ENGINEERING CO</u>, ST. BEDE'S WORKS, TYNE DOCK

E19 Works (Map 78, NZ 342650) served by branch (½m) N of NER Gateshead-South
Shields line, 1¼m W of Tyne Dock Station, and opened about August 1898.
It was closed some years later when the business was transferred to George
Fownes & Co of Cardiff.

Gauge: 4' 8½"

FOWNES	0-4-0CT	OC	HL	2499	1901	New	(1)

(1) to Clarke, Chapman & Co Ltd,
Gateshead

<u>FRAMWELLGATE COAL & COKE CO LTD</u>, FRAMWELLGATE COLLIERY, FRAMWELLGATE MOOR
(Framwellgate Coal & Coke Co until 13/1/1885)

This colliery consisted latterly of two pits, known as the High Pit or
N1/2 Cater House Pit (Map 85, NZ 261455) and the Low Pit (NZ 270445), about ½m
apart. The colliery was opened in 1842, and linked to the Londonderry
Railway by a branch from the Resolution Pit near Leamside (though part of
this line may have been owned by the Earl of Durham (q.v.). About 1859 it
was acquired by the Marquis of Londonderry, by which time it also had a
branch (3m) to Frankland Station on the NER line from Leamside Junction to
Newton Hall Junction. In 1878 it was purchased by Stevenson, Jacques & Co,
the owners of Acklam Iron Works, Middlesbrough, who apparently operated it
under the title of Framwellgate Coal Co. Whether the colliery company
remained a subsidiary of subsequent owners of the Acklam Works is unknown.

The company went into voluntary liquidation in July 1924.

For working in the days of the Londonderry Railway see the entry for the Marquis of Londonderry.

Gauge: 4' 8½"

-	0-4-0ST	OC	HCR	203	1878	New	s/s
CETEWAYO	0-4-0ST	OC	RWH	1789	1879	New	s/s
-	0-4-0ST					(a)	s/s c/1925

(a) origin unknown; may be one of
    the other locos listed

GATESHEAD COUNTY BOROUGH, SALTMEADOWS CLEARANCE SITE, GATESHEAD

C7 This was a large area (Map 78, NZ 2663) of derelict property which the Borough Council cleared for re-development, the job beginning in 1936 and being completed in the summer of 1937. To facilitate the removal of materials temporary sidings were laid from the LNER Gateshead-South Shields line.

Gauge: 4' 8½"

JUNO	0-4-0ST	OC	BH	606	1881	(a)	(1)
TOGO	0-4-0ST	OC	MW	1659	1905	(b)	s/s by 7/1937
54	0-6-0ST	IC	MW	1664	1905	(c)	(2)

(a) ex Darlington Rolling Mills Co   (1) to Short Bros Ltd, Sunderland,
    Ltd, via Rolling Stock Co Ltd,   9/1939
    1/1936   (2) to SLP, c12/1937
(b) ex Cochrane & Co Ltd, Middles-
    brough, Yorks, N.R., via
    Rolling Stock Co Ltd, 1/1936
(c) ex Sir W.G.Armstrong Whitworth
    & Co (Shipbuilders) Ltd,
    Walker-on-Tyne, Newcastle

WILLIAM GRAY & CO LTD
(William Gray & Co (1918) Ltd until 31/12/1922; William Gray & Co until 31/12/1918)

This shipbuilding firm went into voluntary liquidation in August 1962, and the plant was auctioned in May 1963.
The firm may well have had other locos besides those listed below.

Old Dockyard, West Hartlepool. Map 85, NZ 512332

S6 Served by sidings E of BR Seaham-West Hartlepool line, ½m N of West Hartlepool Station.

Gauge: 4' 8½"

WILLIAM GRAY No.2	0-4-0ST	OC	BH	908	1887	New	(1)
NUMBER ONE	0-4-0ST	OC	HL	3418	1919	New	(2)
-	0-4-0ST	OC	KS	3126	1918	(a)	(3)
-	4wDM		FH	3572	1952	(b)	(4)

(a) ex National Shipbuilding   (1) sold for scrap, c/1955
    Securities Ltd, Sunderland,   (2) to ?, c/1958
    3/1932   (3) to Central Marine Engineering
(b) ex Central Shipyard,. c/1958   Works
                                       (4) to J.B.White Ltd, scrap merch-
                                           ants, Thornaby, Yorks, N.R.,
                                           7/1963

Central Shipyard, Hartlepool. Map 85, NZ 515339 (approx)

S3 Opened in 1888, and served by sidings in the Hartlepool Docks complex.

Gauge: 4' 8½"

No.2	0-4-0ST	OC	MW	1020	1887	(a)	(1)
-	4wDM		FH	3572	1952	New	(2)
No.25	4wDM		RH	210479	1942	(b)	(3)

(a) ex Price & Wills, contrs,
    Tuxford, Notts
(b) ex Charles Young (Aldridge) Ltd,
    dealers, Aldridge, Staffs,
    c/1958; form. Air Ministry,
    Sealand, Flintshire

(1) to Michael Baum & Co Ltd,
    Middlesbrough, Yorks, N.R., for
    scrap, /1952
(2) to Old Dockyard, c/1958
(3) to TWW, Templeborough Works,
    Sheffield, Yorks, W.R., 5/1963;
    re-sold to South Western Gas
    Board, Bath Gas Works, Somerset,
    c2/1964

<u>Central Marine Engineering Works</u>, Hartlepool. Map 85, NZ 517340

S2 This was opened in 1884, and served by sidings in the Hartlepool Docks
    complex.

Gauge: 4' 8½"

SPEEDY	0-4-0CT	OC	HL	2334	1896	New	Scr		
-	0-4-0ST	OC	KS	3126	1918	(a)	Scr	/1963
WEST HARTLEPOOL No.2	0-4-0ST	OC	MW ✗						
			reb. Sir J.Jackson						
			Keyham		1903	(b)	(1)		

✗ plate read "Lennox, Lange & Co, 1882"

(a) ex Old Dockyard
(b) ex Admiralty, Devonport Yard,
    Devon, c/1935

(1) to Cox & Danks Ltd, contrs, /1948

<u>GREENSIDE SAND & GRAVEL CO LTD, FOLLY QUARRY, RYTON WOODSIDE</u>
(subsidiary of Sir Robert McAlpine & Sons Ltd)

A9 This quarry (Map 78, NZ 153625) operated an internal railway system, and
    may have had a standard gauge link to the Stella Coal Co Ltd's line to
    Greenside Colliery. The rail system was closed about 1958, and the quarry
    abandoned in July 1970.

Gauge: 2' 0"

-	4wDM		MR	8717	1941	(a)	(1)
-	4wDM		MR	8995	1946	(a)	(1)

(a) New to Sir Robert McAlpine &
    Sons Ltd, Hayes, Middlesex; to
    company above (on loan?) at
    unknown date

(1) locos used by RMA on contracts
    from /1958; stored at quarry
    from 5/1965; to Sir Robert
    McAlpine & Sons Ltd, Dunston,
    c6/1970, and scrapped at their
    Newcastle Workshops, 9/1970

<u>HAMSTERLEY COLLIERY LTD, HAMSTERLEY COLLIERY, near EBCHESTER</u>

G1 This colliery (Map 78, NZ 117565), opened about 1866, was really a drift.
    Tubs were hauled from the entrance to the screens via ¼m endless rope
    incline. The coal was then discharged into standard gauge wagons, via the
    screens, which lay alongside LNER Blackhill Branch, ½m E of High Westwood
    Station. The loco was used here, and kept in a shed ¼m W of the screens.
    The colliery was vested in NCB Northern Division No.6 Area on 1st January
    1947.

Gauge: 4' 8½"

BURNOPFIELD	0-4-0ST	OC	MW	1557	1902	New	Scr	/1933
HAMSTERLEY No.1	0-4-0ST	OC	HL	3467	1920	(a)	(1)	

(a) ex TWW, /1933; orig. Bombay   (1) to NCB No.6 Area, 1/1/1947
    Harbour Trust, India

S.HANRATTY, SCRAP IRON & STEEL MERCHANTS, WHESSOE ROAD, DARLINGTON

V6 This yard (Map 85, NZ 289158) is at the former North Road Station of BR
on the Bishop Auckland-Darlington line.

Gauge: 4' 8½"

-	0-4-0DM	HE	2839	1943	(a)

(a) ex Henry Williams Ltd,
    Darlington, c/1966

HARTLEY MAIN COLLIERIES LTD, PAGE BANK BRICKWORKS, PAGE BANK

Q14 This is believed to be the only example of a Northumberland colliery
company having operations in Co. Durham. Page Bank Brickworks lay adjacent
to Page Bank Colliery, which was closed by DL in July 1931 (q.v.). The
works (Map 85, NZ 228354) was taken over about 1933, but only operated for
2-3 years before being sold to the Page Bank Brick Co Ltd (q.v.).

Gauge: 2' 8½"

✗		4wPM	FH	1782	1931	(a)	(1)
✗		4wPM	FH	1892	1934	New	(1)
✗		4wPM	FH	1893	1934	New	
	reb.	4wDM					s/s

    ✗ numbered 17/18/19 in Hartley Main book list

(a) ex Cramlington Colliery, North-   (1) to Page Bank Brick Co Ltd,
    umberland; prev. 2' 4" gauge   c/1935

HARTON COAL CO LTD (Harton Coal Co formed in 1842; Harton Coal Co Ltd from
6/8/1885. Whitburn Coal Co formed in 1874; absorbed by Harton Coal Co Ltd
in 1891).

The history of this company's collieries and the railway system which
served them is exceptionally complicated. It is perhaps best taken in
chronological order, with the proviso that some of it is little more
than conjecture.

D11 Harton Colliery (Map 78, NZ 362642) was sunk in 1810, and it was probably
linked to the R.Tyne by a horse-worked waggonway. By 1844 it was owned by
the Harton Coal Co, who in that year opened what was known at first as
D9   Harton Colliery, but was later called St. Hilda's Colliery, in South
Shields (NZ 361667). At 1,260 feet this was then the deepest pit on the
Tyne, and it was linked to the river by a line about ¼m long, including a
short tunnel. It would seem that the old Harton Colliery was closed, at
least for a time, in the middle of the century. In 1869 the firm opened
D12 Boldon Colliery (NZ 347623), which was linked to the NER Pontop & Shields
branch near Brockley Whins. Almost certainly Boldon coal was shipped at the
St.Hilda Staithes, later known as Harton High Staithes (NZ 354662), as was
coal from Harton, and it seems that at this stage the NER worked the
traffic.

Meanwhile, away to the east, the Whitburn Coal Co had in May 1879 opened
D14 Whitburn Colliery (NZ 408637), and to serve this a line 3¼m long was built
from Whitburn Junction on the NER Pontop & Shields line. In March 1885
passenger services, on weekdays only, were begun, with stations at Westoe

99

Lane and Marsden, a beauty spot about ¼m N of the colliery. These had ceased by June 1887, but were re-commenced in March 1888 after Board of Trade approval. There were six trains daily (seven on Saturdays) and shortly afterwards a Sunday service was added. The 3rd class fares were 4d single and 6d return, and these remained the same until passenger services ceased in 1953 after nationalisation. This line was known as the Marsden Railway.

After the amalgamation in 1891 the new company acquired an old ballast railway which had formerly been used to carry ballast off-loaded from colliers to the Bents on the eastern side of the town. This ran past St. Hilda's Colliery, and seems to have been worked by a stationary engine. This was now linked up to the Marsden Railway east of Westoe Lane Station, giving Whitburn coal access to Harton High Staithes. Shortly after this the company built <u>Harton Low Staithes</u> about 300 yards further downstream, and linked them to the existing system by a steeply-graded line, including two tunnels, from St.Hilda's Colliery. This was followed by a new line, ¼m long, to Harton Colliery from a point near Whitburn Junction, and just north of this junction a large number of exchange sidings were built to cater for trains to and from Boldon, the Harton company now having acquired running powers over the NER. Running powers were also obtained over a section of the NER Pontop & Shields line between Dene Sidings and a junction E of St.Hilda's Colliery, to overcome congestion on the company's original line, which was only single track.

About 1908 the whole of the system in South Shields, including the NER Pontop line and the branch to Harton Colliery, was electrified on the overhead wire system. The electrification scheme was taken to a point 150 yards S of Mowbray Road Signal Box, though steam-hauled trains from Whitburn continued to work to Westoe Lane Station and to the Westoe exchange sidings, and trains from Boldon came into Dene Sidings.

D8 In 1913 the company opened <u>Westoe Colliery</u> (NZ 373668), about ½m E of St. Hilda's Colliery near Westoe Lane Station, but this was closed again shortly afterwards, and was not re-opened until 1947.

In the 1920's, because of a proposed new road between South Shields and Marsden, the Railway had to be moved 100 yards inland for a distance of ¼m at Marsden. This deviation, together with powers to work the line from Whitburn to Westoe Lane as a Light Railway, was granted by the Ministry of Transport in August 1926. This was opened about 1929, and the passenger service extended to a new station at Whitburn Colliery. The line was then controlled by three signal boxes, and the running time for the journey was 12 minutes. Just north of the colliery the line also served <u>Marsden Lime-</u>
D13 <u>stone Quarries</u> (NZ 405641), also owned by the company.

In August 1940 St. Hilda Colliery (as it was now known) closed, but the remaining collieries and railway system were vested in NCB Northern Division No.1 Area on 1st January 1947.

St. Hilda's Colliery

These locomotives are known to have worked here, but how it was worked before their arrival, and whether they survived until electrification, is not known.

Gauge: 4' 8½"

ST. HILDA No.2	0-4-0ST	OC	BH	515	1879	(a)	s/s
ST. HILDA No.1	0-4-0ST	OC	BH	516	1879	(a)	s/s

(a) ex Tyne Plate Glass Co, c/1891

South Shields, Marsden & Whitburn Colliery Railway (Marsden Railway until c1900-1906)

This title was given to the steam-worked section of the system between Whitburn Colliery and Westoe Lane Stations. The loco shed was at Whitburn.

Gauge: 4' 8½"

```
1                    0-6-0ST  IC  MW
                                  reb.
                                  Grange IW  1875? (a)  Scr  /1896
2                    0-6-0ST  OC  BH     504  1879  (b)  Scr  /1905
3                    0-6-0ST  IC  BH     716  1882
                                  reb.        1906  (b)  (1)
4                    0-6-0ST  IC  BH     826  1884  (b)
                                  reb.        1906
                                  reb.        1923       (2)
5                    0-6-0ST  IC  RS    2629  1887  New  Scr  /1922
5 (orig. 11)         0-6-0    IC  Ghd         1881  (c)  (2)
6                    0-4-0ST  OC  HE     286  1883  New  (3)
6                    0-6-0    IC  RS    2160  1874  (d)  Scr  /1912
6                    0-6-0    IC  RS    2056  1872
                                  reb. Ghd    1884  (e)  Scr 1/1930
6                    0-6-0    IC  Ghd         1882  (f)  (4)
6                    0-6-0    IC  RS    2587  1884  (g)  Scr  /1936
6                    0-6-0    IC  Ghd     23  1889
                                  reb.        1904  (h)  (2)
No.7                 0-6-2T   IC  CF    1158  1898  New  (5)
7                    0-6-0    IC  Ghd     38  1892
                                  reb.        1912  (j)  Scr  /1935
7                    0-6-0    IC  Ghd     43  1889
                                  reb.        1905  (k)  (6)
7                    0-6-0    IC  Dar    631  1898  (m)  Scr  /1946
8                    2-2-2WT  IC  SS    1501  1864  (n)  Scr  /1907
8                    0-6-0    IC  RS    1973  1870  (p)  Scr  /1929
8                    0-6-0    IC  Ghd      3  1889  (q)  (2)
9                    0-6-0    IC  Blyth & Tyne 1862 (r) Scr /1913
10                   0-6-0    IC  Blyth & Tyne 1862 (s) Scr /1914
10                   0-6-0    IC  RWH   1564  1873  (t)  Scr  /1931
11                   0-4-0ST  OC  MW                (u)  (7)
        LALEHAM      0-6-0ST  OC  AB    1639  1923  (v)  (2)
No.9                 0-6-0PT  IC  SS    4051  1894
                                  reb.
                                  Caerphilly  1930  (w)  (8)
```

(a) ex ?, to Whitburn Coal Co
(b) New to Whitburn Coal Co
(c) ex LNER, 396, /1925, via Frazer
(d) ex NER, 888, 12/1907
(e) ex NER, 786, 6/1912
(f) ex LNER, 1453, 2/1927
(g) ex LNER, 1486, 1/1930
(h) ex LNER, 1509, 8/1935
(j) ex LNER, 1616, 10/1929
(k) ex LNER, 776, 5/1935
(m) ex LNER, 1953, 5/1939
(n) ex Furness Rly, 22A, via Frazer,
    /1899
(p) ex NER, 718, 12/1907
(q) ex LNER, 869, 8/1931
(r) ex NER, 2255, 5/1900
(s) ex NER, 1712, 11/1900
(t) ex NER, 827, 9/1914
(u) ex ?, /1908
(v) ex Boldon Colliery

(1) to James W. Ellis & Co Ltd,
    Swalwell, /1910
(2) to NCB No.1 Area, 1/1/1947
(3) to Boldon Colliery by 10/1922
    (c/1907?)
(4) to Boldon Colliery, /1930
(5) to John Bowes & Partners Ltd,
    Pontop & Jarrow Railway, /1912,
    via Frazer
(6) to Boldon Colliery, c/1937
(7) fitted as armoured loco in 1914;
    Scr /1920
(8) ret. to Boldon Colliery, c7/1943

ex Boldon Colliery (on loan
     from John Bowes & Partners Ltd,
     Bowes Railway), c4/1943

Harton Railway

When the electrification referred to above was carried out, the company
built its own generating station to supply current at 540-575 volts, but
later a sub-station was built at Westoe Lane to draw on the local supply.
The majority of the electric locos were kept at a shed at Westoe (NZ
374667), but one or more were normally kept at Harton Colliery, and
usually one was kept at St. Hilda's Colliery (even after closure, when it
was left in the first tunnel if not required).

Gauge: 4' 8"

E	1		4wWE	Siemens		1907	New	(1)
E	2		4wWE	Siemens		1908	New	(1)
E	3		4w-4wWE	Siemens		1909	New⁄	(1)
E	4		4w-4wWE	Siemens		1909	New⁄	(1)
E	5		0-4-4-0WE	Siemens		1909	New⁄	(1)
E	6		0-4-4-0WE	Siemens		1910	New	(1)
E	7		4w-4wWE	KS	1202	1911	New	(1)
E	8		4w-4wWE	KS	1203	1911	New	(1)
E	9		4w-4wWE	AEG	1565	1913	New	(1)
E	10		4wWE	Siemens	862	1913	New	(1)

⁄ at Harton Colliery, 1/1/1947

(1) to NCB No.1 Area, 1/1/1947

Boldon Colliery, Boldon Colliery. (No loco allocations are known before
                                    1922)

Gauge: 4' 8½"

-			0-4-0ST	OC	HE	286	1883	(a)	s/s
1			0-6-0	IC	Ghd		1882	(b)	Scr c/1940
1			0-6-0T	IC	HC	332	1889	(c)	(1)
2			0-6-0	IC	Ghd	43	1889		
					reb.		1905	(d)	Scr /1939
3			0-4-0T	IC	Ghd	38	1888	(e)	(1)
4			0-6-0	IC	Ghd		1883	(f)	(1)
	LALEHAM		0-6-0ST	OC	AB	1639	1923	(g)	(2)
No.9			0-6-0PT	IC	SS	4051	1894		
					reb.				
					Caerphilly		1930	(h)	(3)

(a) ex SSMWCR, 6, by 10/1922   (1) to NCB No.1 Area, 1/1/1947
    (c/1907?)   (2) to SSMWCR
(b) ex SSMWCR, 6, /1930   (3) to SSMWCR, c4/1943; ret. c7/1943;
(c) ex GWR, 782, 11/1939   ret. to John Bowes & Partners
(d) ex SSMWCR, 7, c/1937   Ltd, 8/1943
(e) ex LNER, 24, via Frazer, 2/1931
(f) ex LNER, 1333, via Frazer, /1928;
    LNER until 8/1925
(g) ex Cohen /1929; prev. S.Pearson
    & Son Ltd, contrs
(h) ex John Bowes & Partners Ltd,
    Bowes Railway, 2/1943, loan

Marsden Limestone Quarries, Whitburn Colliery. Map 78, NZ 405641

D13 These were a group of quarries producing limestone dust for underground use
    at collieries and also limestone for general industrial use, and were cont-
    rolled by the manager of the nearby Whitburn Colliery. Standard gauge

wagons of the South Shields, Marsden & Whitburn Colliery Railway were
filled either from the kilns or the dust plant. The quarries passed to
NCB Northern Division No.1 Area on 1st January 1947.

Gauge: 2' 0"

-	4wDM	RH	187059	1937	(a)	(1)
-	4wDM	RH	189959	1938	(b)	(1)
-	4wDM	RH	189963	1939	(c)	(1)

(a) ex Thomas Mosdale & Son Ltd,   (1) to NCB No.1 Area, 1/1/1947
    Urmston, Lancs
(b) ex P.Caulfield & Co Ltd, Bonhill
(c) ex Charles Brand & Sons Ltd,
    Avonmouth contract, Somerset

HASWELL, SHOTTON & EASINGTON COAL & COKE CO LTD
(form. Haswell & Shotton Coal Co Ltd; orig. Haswell Coal Co)

This firm owned two collieries:

Haswell Colliery, Haswell. Map 85, NZ 375434

P2   This was a large colliery, opened in July 1835, and originally served by a
branch (1¼m) of the South Hetton Waggonway (q.v.). In September 1844 a
serious explosion occurred, in which 95 people were killed. Working to
South Hetton continued until at least 1859, but probably not long afterwards this was abandoned in favour of a new branch (½m) to what was to
become the NER Sunderland-Stockton line, ½m N of Haswell Station. In 1883
the NER took over the working of this branch, acquiring both the locomotives and the rolling stock, but it would seem that the company continued
to use its own locomotives for shunting at the colliery itself. It closed
in September 1896.

Shotton Colliery, Shotton. Map 85, NZ 398413

P5   This colliery, originally called Shotton Grange Colliery, was sunk in 1841,
and was at first served by a 2m extension of the South Hetton wagonway's
branch to Haswell, but this was later abandoned in favour of a ¾m branch
to the NER Sunderland-Stockton line, 1¼m N of Wellfield Junction. It is not
known whether the company used locomotives here, though it seems likely.
The colliery was closed in November 1877, but was re-opened in 1901 by
Horden Collieries Ltd (q.v.).

Gauge: 4' 8½"

HASWELL	0-6-0ST	IC	MW	242	1867	New	(1)
SHOTTON	0-6-0ST	IC	MW	479	1874	New	(2)
-	0-6-0ST	IC	MW	23	1861	(a)	s/s
-	0-4-0ST					(b)	(3)
-	0-4-0ST					(b)	(3)
-	0-4-0ST					(b)	(3)

(a) ex Backworth Collieries Ltd,   (1) to NER, 1883; became 1723, 1/1885
    Backworth, Northumberland   (2) to NER, 1883; became 1724, 1/1885
(b) origin unknown   (3) offered for sale, 8/1897; s/s

HAWKS, CRAWSHAY & CO, ENGINEERS, GATESHEAD

C5   A long-established firm (Map 78, NZ 258638), whose most famous work was
Robert Stephenson's High Level Bridge at Newcastle. The works was served
by sidings N of NER Gateshead-South Shields line, ¾m W of Gateshead East
Station. It was closed in September 1889 and the plant was acquired by their
near-neighbours, John Abbot & Co Ltd (q.v.).

    There may have been other locos besides the one listed.

Gauge: 4' 8½"

HAWK		0-4-0ST	OC	BH	682	1883	(a)	(1)

(a) New; believed to have been in   (1) to John Abbot & Co Ltd,
    part exchange for earlier (unid-   Gateshead, c8/1891
    entified) loco of same name

HAWTHORN AGGREGATES LTD, HAWTHORN QUARRY, near SEAHAM HARBOUR
(Hawthorn Limestone Co Ltd until c5/1970, which was latterly a subsidiary
of F.W.Dobson & Co Ltd until the same date)

L37 This limestone quarry (Map 85, NZ 437465) was opened in 1909, and served
by sidings W of BR line from Sunderland-Stockton, 2½m S of Seaham Station.
Rail traffic ceased in 1970.

Gauge: 4' 8½"

No.1		0-4-0ST	OC	BH	368	1877	(a)	
		reb.	LG					
		reb.	HL					Scr by 1947
No.2		0-4-0ST	OC	HL	2684	1907	(b)	
		reb. R.Shaw 1937						Scr by 1947
	CORNSAY	0-4-0ST	OC	HL	2478	1901	(c)	Scr by 1947
	-	0-6-0ST	IC	MW	1691	1907	(d)	(1)
	HAWTHORN	0-4-0ST	OC	RSH	7308	1946	New	(2)
24		0-4-0ST	OC	HL	2453	1900	(e)	(3)
	HAWTHORN No.5	4wDM		RH	326062	1952	New	Scr 3/1971
	FRED DOBSON	4wDM		RH	326071	1954	(f)	(4)

(a) ex BV, Cleveland Works,   (1) ret. to SLP
    Middlesbrough, Yorks, N.R.   (2) to Northern Gas Board, Thompson
(b) ex William Whitwell & Co Ltd,   Street Works, Stockton, via R.
    Thornaby, Yorks, N.R.   Shaw, c/1953
(c) ex Ferens & Love Ltd, Cornsay   (3) to F.W.Dobson & Co Ltd, Chilton
    Colliery   Limeworks, c/1955
(d) ex SLP, /1941, loan   (4) to Cornforth Limestone Co Ltd,
(e) ex F.W.Dobson & Co Ltd, Chilton   West Cornforth, c5/1970
    Limeworks, by 9/1950
(f) ex Cornforth Limestone Co Ltd,
    West Cornforth, c/1965

HAWTHORN LESLIE (SHIPBUILDERS) LTD, HEBBURN SHIPYARD, HEBBURN
(R.& W. Hawthorn,Leslie & Co Ltd until 1/7/1954; Andrew Leslie & Co until
4/3/1886)

E6 Yard served by branch (¼m) from BR Gateshead-South Shields line, ½m E of
Hebburn Station. The yard (Map 78, NZ 305652 (approx)) was among those absorbed into Swan Hunter & Tyne Shipbuilders Ltd (q.v.) on 1st January 1968.

Gauge: 4' 8½"

HEBBURN	0-4-0ST	OC	BH	202	1871	New	s/s	
HEBBURN	0-4-0ST	OC	BH	418	1877	New	s/s	
HEBBURN No.2	0-4-0ST	OC	BH	569	1880	New	s/s	
-	0-4-0ST	OC	HL	2039	1885	New	(1)	
SANDOW	0-4-0CT	OC	HL	2273	1893	New	Scr	1/1961
(BROWNIE)	0-4-0CT	OC	HL	2550	1903	New	(2)	
ATLAS	0-4-0ST	OC	HL	2917	1912	New	(3)	
AJAX	0-4-0ST	OC	HL	3319	1918	New	(4)	
HERCULES	0-4-0CT	OC	HL	2272	1893	(a)	Scr by 1939	
KELLY	0-4-0CT	OC	RSH	7126	1943	New	Scr	1/1961
-	0-4-0DM		RH	281270	1951	(b)	(5)	
TRIUMPH	0-4-0DM		RH	304472	1951	New	(6)	
APOLLO	0-4-0DM		RH	319288	1953	New	(6)	

104

(a) ex St. Peter's Shipyard, Walker-on-Tyne, Newcastle	(1) to Darlington & Simpson Rolling Mills Ltd, Darlington, /1913
(b) New for trials	(2) to William Doxford & Sons Ltd, Sunderland, /1940
	(3) to TWW, Templeborough Works, Sheffield, Yorks, W.R., 10/1951
	(4) to TWW, Templeborough Works, Sheffield, Yorks, W.R., 3/1953
	(5) to St. Peter's Works, Walker-on-Tyne, 2/1951
	(6) to Swan Hunter & Tyne Shipbuilders Ltd, 1/1/1968

W.HEDLEY

In the 1820's William Hedley (1779-1843), the famous enginewright from
Wylam in Northumberland, began to sink or acquire collieries in different
R17 parts of Durham. Among these were <u>Crowtrees Colliery</u>, Quarrington Hill
R20 (Map 85, NZ 334379), acquired in 1824, and <u>Coxhoe Colliery</u> (NZ 332363)
R18 and <u>West Hetton Colliery</u> (NZ 326368), near Quarrington Hill, in 1832.
Crowtrees and West Hetton Collieries were served by a branch of the
Clarence Railway from Coxhoe Station, while Coxhoe Colliery was served by
a second branch, and in 1835 Hedley obtained running powers over the
Clarence Railway in order to work his own trains to Stockton for shipment.
In December 1839, however, a short link, about ½m, worked by a stationary
engine, was opened between Crowtrees Colliery and Cassop Colliery on the
Cassop Moor waggonway (see Cassop Coal Co), which enabled Hedley's coal
to be shipped at Hartlepool.
The collieries subsequently fell into the hands of Ralph Ward Jackson
and the West Hartlepool Harbour and Railway Co (q.v.).
For other collieries owned by William Hedley see Holmside & South Moor
Collieries Ltd.

Gauge: 4' 8½"

TYNESIDE	✗	(a)	s/s
WYLAM	✗	(a)	s/s

   ✗ one is believed to have been built by RWH

(a) origin unknown

HEDWORTH BARIUM CO LTD,   JARROW

E18 Works (Map 78, NZ 341649) was served by ½m branch N of NER Gateshead-
South Shields line, 1½m W of Tyne Dock Station, and lay immediately W
of the works of Fownes Forge & Engineering Co (q.v.). It closed about
1922.

Gauge: 4' 8½"

-	0-4-0ST	OC	CF	1202	1901	New	(1)

(1) to Cleeve's Western Valleys Anthracite Collieries Ltd, Cwm Gorse Colliery, Glamorgan, c/1922

<u>HETTON COAL CO LTD</u> (Hetton Coal Co until 4/7/1884)

This company owned one of the most famous of the county's colliery railways:

Hetton Railway

L27 <u>Hetton Colliery</u> (Map 85, NZ 360469) was the first to be sunk through the magnesium limestone escarpment covering the eastern part of the coalfield, and the Railway was built to carry its coal to Sunderland, eight miles to the north-east. The company's managing partner was Nicholas Wood (1795-1865), and it was probably through him that George Stephenson was appointed Engineer in 1819. The line, which was the first in the world to be designed to use locomotives, was opened on 18th November 1822. The first 1½ miles from the colliery were worked by locomotives, and the next 1½ miles by two stationary engines. The first, at Copt Hill (originally known as the Byer Engine), hauled the wagons up to the engine house, where the ropes were changed for the engine to work them for a further ½m to an interchange point known as the "Flatt". From here they were hauled up to Warden Law (636 feet)(Map 78, NZ 368505). The wagons then descended four self-acting inclines to a marshalling yard at North Moor, Sunderland. The next two miles were originally worked by locomotives, but these were soon replaced by the Hunters Lane stationary engine at North Moor. The fifth incline mentioned in the account of the opening is believed to have been at the staithes (Map 78, NZ 390576).

In 1825 two branches were built, both worked by self-acting inclines. The
L26 first ran from Hetton Dene for ½m to <u>Eppleton Colliery</u> (NZ 364484), and the
L28 second ran from a point near Hetton Colliery for 1m S to <u>Elemore Colliery</u> (NZ 346356). It is possible about this time that loco working at the Hetton end of the line was replaced by horses for a time.

It would appear that the Hunters Lane Engine was replaced by locomotives in the 1890's. In 1895 locomotives took over on the Elemore branch, and in 1902 on the Eppleton branch.

The workshops for the Railway were at Hetton, not far from the loco shed. There was a link at Hetton with the NER Durham & Sunderland branch.

At the north end of Hetton Dene the line passed over the Londonderry Railway (Rainton & Seaham section), which, in addition to coal from Londonderry pits, also handled coal from the <u>North Hetton Coal Co Ltd</u>'s Hazard and Moorsley Collieries (q.v.) via a branch (1m) from Rainton Bridge. When this section of the Londonderry Railway closed in 1896 the North Hetton company took over the line between Rainton Bridge and Hetton and altered the north end to join the Hetton Railway.

In August 1911 the company amalgamated with Lambton Collieries Ltd. For details of the Railway's history thereafter see the entry for Lambton, Hetton & Joicey Collieries Ltd.

Gauge: 4' 8½"

-		0-4-0	VC	G.Stephenson	c1822	New	(1)
-		0-4-0	VC	G.Stephenson	c1822	New	(1)
-		0-4-0	VC	G.Stephenson	c1822	New	(1)
-		0-4-0	VC	G.Stephenson	c1822	New	(1)
-		0-4-0	VC	G.Stephenson	c1822	New	(1)

N.B. Three of these locomotives were named "Dart", "Tally-ho" and "Star".

                              (1) at least one, probably three,
                                  and possibly all five were
                                  numbered in the list below

Considerable uncertainty surrounds Nos 1, 3 and 4 in the list below.
In earlier sources 1 is given as 4, and said to be a 2-4-0 tender engine, rebuilt to 0-6-0ST at Hetton; the G.Stephenson loco is given as 3, though later photographs at Hetton show it with no number at all. 4 is given as 1. However, a photograph exists showing 1 (in 1911) as we have it below, and it is believed this loco is RS 1100.

						(a)	s/s
1	2-4-0T	OC	RS	1100	1857	New	(1)
2						(a)	s/s
2	0-6-0ST	IC	RWH	1969	1883	New	(1)
3	0-4-0	VC	G.Stephenson		c1822		
			reb.Hetton		1853		
			reb.Hetton		c1882		(2)
4	0-6-0	IC	RS	1649	1865	New	
reb.	0-6-0T	IC	Hetton				(1)
5	0-6-0	IC	RWH	1422	1867	New	
reb.	0-6-0ST	IC	Hetton				(1)
6	0-6-0ST	IC	RWH	1430	1868	New	(1)
7	0-6-0ST	IC	RS	1919	1869	New	(1)
8	0-6-0ST	IC	RWH	1478	1870	New	(1)
LYONS "Beetle No.1"	4wVB		Hetton		c1900	(b)⌿	(1)
EPPLETON "Beetle No.2"	4wVB		Hetton		c1900	(b)⌿	(1)

⌿ worked as colliery shunters

There may have been other locomotives unknown

(a) probably one of the G. Stephenson locomotives above
(b) assembled from various parts, not all locomotive in origin

(1) to Lambton & Hetton Collieries Ltd, 8/1911
(2) ceased to work about 1908-1911, and converted to stationary boiler to drive the saw-mill at Hetton Shops; to Lambton & Hetton Collieries Ltd, 8/1911

HOLMSIDE & SOUTH MOOR COLLIERIES LTD
(formed by amalgamation of T.Hedley & Bros Ltd and South Moor Colliery Co Ltd on 3/1/1925)

The collieries owned by both of the firms above had originally been owned by William Hedley (1779-1843) (see above). They form the only large group which was not a member of the Durham Coal Owners Association in the 19th century, and so much less is known about their early history.

Craghead Colliery, Craghead. Map 78, NZ 212506.
(T.Hedley & Bros Ltd until 3/1/1925; form T.Hedley & Bros; orig. W.Hedley)

H55 This colliery appears to have been sunk in the 1830's, and was linked to the Burnhope Waggonway (see Ritsons (Burnhope Collieries) Ltd), which ran from Burnhope Colliery to West Pelton, where it joined the Eden Incline of the NER Pontop & Shields Branch. Craghead Colliery lay 1¼m from the junction, and full wagons were taken to the top of the Craghead self-acting incline, whence they were lowered to the exchange sidings. Just north of
H56 the colliery a branch ran south-eastwards to Holmside Colliery (NZ 210498 approx), which was worked by locomotives from Craghead until its closure. Horses were used before the arrival of the (main) locos below. The colliery was vested in NCB Northern Division No.6 Area on 1st January 1947.

Gauge: 5' 0"

WYLAM DILLY	2-2-0⌿	VCG	Wm.Hedley	1813	(a)	(1)

⌿ all four wheels were driven

(a) ex Wylam Colliery, Wylam, Northumberland, c/1862; loco stored at Craghead, though occasionally steamed on a short section of track
(1) to Royal Scottish Museum, Edinburgh, for preservation, 10/1882

Gauge: 4' 8½"

HOLMSIDE	0-6-0ST					(a)	s/s
BURNHOPESIDE	0-6-0ST	OC	BH	888	1887	New	
			reb. HL		1931		(1)
CRAGHEAD	0-6-0ST	OC	BH	971	1890	New	
			reb. HL		1911		(2)
HOLMSIDE No.2	0-6-0ST	OC	CF	1204	1901	New	(2)
HOLMSIDE No.3							
(form. SOUTH MOOR No.3)	0-6-0ST	OC	HL	2956	1912	(b)	(1)

(a) origin unknown
(b) ex Morrison Busty Colliery

(1) to NCB No.6 Area, 1/1/1947
(2) to Morrison Busty Colliery by 8/1937

Morrison Busty Colliery, Annfield Plain. Map 78, NZ 176508
(South Moor Colliery Co Ltd until 3/1/1925; T.Hedley & Bros Ltd until 24/7/1889)

H35 This colliery was only one of a large number of pits collectively called South Moor Colliery. The Morrison Pit was served by a branch (1½m) from LNER Pontop & Shields Branch, 1½m E of Annfield Plain Station. The same
H37 branch also served the Charley Pit, about ½m NE. About ½m E of the
H40 junction of the branch above, sidings served the Louisa Pit (NZ 193527),
H39 from which a tramway ran southwards for about ½m to the Hedley Pit and the
H38 New South Moor Colliery (William Pit). The Morrison Pit itself was divided into two, the Busty Pit (above) and the North Pit, some 50 yards north, which was noteworthy as one of the only two places in the world where witherite (barium carbonate) existed in sufficiently large quantity to justify commercial exploitation; production continued into the 1940's. Besides the locos kept at the Morrison Pit, it would seem that a loco was also kept at the Louisa Pit. These two and the Hedley Pit, survived to be vested in NCB Northern Division No.6 Area on 1st January 1947.

Gauge: 4' 8½"

"CHUNKY"	0-4-0					(a)	s/s
SOUTH MOOR 2	0-6-0ST	OC	BH	1034	1891	New	
			reb.HL	3668	1904		(1)
SOUTH MOOR No.3	0-6-0ST	OC	HL	2956	1912	New	(2)
SOUTH MOOR No.4	0-6-0ST	OC	HL	3528	1922	New	(3)
CRAGHEAD	0-6-0ST	OC	BH	971	1890		
			reb.HL		1911	(b)	(3)
HOLMSIDE No.2	0-6-0ST	OC	CF	1204	1901	(b)	(3)
HOLMSIDE	0-6-0ST	OC	RSH	6943	1938	New	(3)

(a) origin unknown
(b) ex Craghead Colliery by 8/1937

(1) to Sir S.A.Sadler Ltd, Malton Colliery, after 1920
(2) to Craghead Colliery
(3) to NCB No.6 Area, 1/1/1947

Gauge: 3' 0" (may have worked on tramway between Louisa and Hedley Pits)

1							
	0-4-0ST	OC	BH	567	1880	(a)	s/s

(a) ex BH, reb. from 2' 0" gauge;
    prev. Birmingham Corporation Gas Dept.

HORDEN COLLIERIES LTD   (reg. 30/1/1900)

Created to exploit a royalty of 28 square miles, this was the last major new colliery company to be formed (except by amalgamation) in Co. Durham.

Locos were kept at:

Blackhall Colliery, Blackhall. Map 85, NZ 461396
P16 Opened in 1913, and served by sidings E of LNER Seaham-West Hartlepool
line, 1½m S of Horden Station. Vested in NCB Northern Division No.3 Area
on 1st January 1947

Horden Colliery and Coke Works, Horden. Map 85, NZ 442418
P15 Opened in 1902, and served by sidings W of LNER Seaham-West Hartlepool
line, ¼m N of Horden Station. Vested in NCB Northern Division No.3 Area
on 1st January 1947

Shotton Colliery and Coke Works, Shotton. Map 85, NZ 398413
P5 Formerly owned by Haswell, Shotton & Easington Coal & Coke Co Ltd (q.v.),
and closed in 1877. Re-opened by new owners in July 1901, and served by
branch (¼m) from LNER Sunderland-Stockton line, 1½m N of Wellfield Junction. The colliery was shunted by shire horses until after the First World
War. Vested in NCB Northern Division No.3 Area on 1st January 1947.

P13 The company also planned to re-open Castle Eden Colliery (see Castle Eden
Coal Co Ltd), but when the colliery was virtually ready to begin production
the "Depression" of the 1930's set in, and it remained only a pumping
station.

Gauge: 4' 8½"

No.1		0-6-0ST	OC	AB	1015	1904	New⧸ (1)
HORDEN		0-6-0ST	OC	P	1310	1914	New@ (1)
HORDEN No.2		0-6-0ST	OC	HL	3440	1920	Newø (1)
HORDEN No.3		0-6-0ST	OC	HL	3568	1923	Newø (1)
HORDEN No.4		0-6-0ST	OC	HL	2737	1907	(a)ø (1)
HORDEN No.5		0-6-0T	IC	RSH	7305	1946	Newø (1)

⧸   At Shotton Colliery,   1/1/1947
@   At Blackhall Colliery, 1/1/1947
ø   At Horden Colliery,   1/1/1947

(a) ex James W.Ellis & Co Ltd,   (1) to NCB No.3 Area, 1/1/1947
    Swalwell, c/1939

Gauge: 2' 8½" (Blackhall Colliery, underground)

-		0-4-0DM	HE	2980	1944	New	(1)

(1) to NCB No.3 Area, 1/1/1947

Gauge: 2' 8½" (Horden Colliery, underground)

-		0-4-0DM	HE	3330	1946	New	(1)

(1) to NCB No.3 Area, 1/1/1947

Shotton Brickworks, Shotton. Map 85, NZ 397404
P6 This was opened in 1904, and was served by a branch (¼m) from the colliery
line. By the mid-1920's a narrow gauge steam locomotive was being used to
pull full tubs of clay from the pit, which lay east of the works, up to the
kilns for processing, and this seems to have continued until just before
World War II. It is possible that there may have been more than one locomotive (not necessarily at the same time), but no details are known. The
works passed to NCB Northern Division No.3 Area on 1st January 1947.

HULAM COAL CO LTD, HUTTON HENRY COLLIERY, STATION TOWN
(form. Hutton Henry Coal Co Ltd)
P12 This colliery (Map 85, NZ 414367) was sunk in 1871 on the extreme south-
eastern edge of the coalfield, and was served by a branch (½m) from loop
between Wingate Junction and Wingate South Junction. The company went into
liquidation in 1897.

Gauge: 4' 8½"

-	0-4-0T	OC	HG	276	1871	(a)	(1)
-	0-4-0ST	OC	BH	613	1881	(b)	s/s

(a) ex Lloyd & Co, Middlesbrough,   (1) to LG, /1898
    Yorks, N.R.
(b) ex Castle Eden Coal Co Ltd,
    c4/1894

Gauge: 3' 0" (used on coke ovens?)

SHEILA	0-4-0ST	OC	BH	559	1880	(a)	s/s

(a) ex BV, (location unknown)

HUWOOD LTD, HANNINGTON WORKS, SWALWELL

B7 This works (Map 78, NZ 204627) was taken over from James W.Ellis Engineer-
    ing Ltd (q.v.), on 1st September 1971. It was closed in the following month
    for re-organisation, and rail traffic was not resumed when the works re-
    opened in 1972.

Gauge: 4' 8½"

-	4wDM	RH	305323	1951	(a)

(a) ex James W.Ellis Engineering
    Ltd, 1/9/1971

IMPERIAL CHEMICAL INDUSTRIES LTD, NOBEL DIVISION, HASWELL

P4 In 1923 ICI took over from Pease & Partners Ltd the Tuthill Limestone
    Quarry (q.v.), in which they built this works (Map 85, NZ 388426), a
    sabulite factory. It was served by a branch (½m) from the South Hetton
    Coal Co Ltd/NCB Pesspool Branch, which joined the LNER Sunderland-Stockton
    line 1m S of Haswell Station. The works closed about 1961.

Gauge: 4' 8½"

No.1		4wPM	Bg	3048	1942	New	
	reb. 0-4-0DM	Bg				(1)
(No.2)		4wPM	Bg	3051	1942	New	
	reb. 4wDM	Bg		1947		(1)

                              (1) to TWW, Haswell Station, for
                                  scrap, /1961

Gauge: 2' 0"

1	4wDM	RH	280865	1949	New	(1)
2	4wDM	RH	280866	1949	New	(1)

                              (1) to Shevington Works, near Wigan,
                                  Lancs, c/1962

IMPERIAL CHEMICAL INDUSTRIES (GENERAL CHEMICALS) LTD
(until 1931 entitled United Alkali Co Ltd, which was formed in 1890 by an
amalgamation of several firms, including Newcastle Chemical Works Co Ltd
and Charles Tennant & Partners Ltd)

Allhusen's Works, Gateshead. Map 78, NZ 2662/2663, 2762/2763.
(Newcastle Chemical Works Co Ltd until 1/11/1890; Charles Allhusen & Sons
until c6/1873)

C8 This large works, about ¼m long, was served by ½m branch from NER Gateshead
    -South Shields line, ½m E of Gateshead East Station. It was opened in 1834,
    and closed in 1937, the site being cleared by Gateshead Council (q.v.) and
    re-developed.

Gauge: 4' 8½"

	CHEMIST	0-4-0ST	OC	RS	2017	1873	New	s/s
2	CALCIUM	0-4-0ST	OC	RS	2124	1873	New	(1)
	✦	0-6-0ST	OC	RS	2381	1880	New	s/s
	✦	0-6-0ST	OC	RS	2554	1885	New	(2)
	CARBON	0-4-0ST	OC	RS	2637	1888	New	(3)
	SULPHUR	0-4-0ST	OC	RS	2668	1889	New	(3)
	SODIUM	0-4-0ST	OC	BH	935	1889	(a)	(4)
	JED	0-4-0ST	OC	P	1468	1917	New	(5)

✦ Some dispute exists concerning the names of these two locos.
RS 2381 is believed to have been originally ALFRED; it may later
have been SODIUM, and ended nameless. RS 2554 appears to have run
nameless for a time, and then became ALFRED, but by 1902 it was
SODIUM.

(a) ex South Stockton Iron Co Ltd,
    Yorks, N.R., by 3/1909

(1) to Billingham Division, Billingham
(2) to Billingham Division, Billingham
    /1927
(3) to Wallsend Works, Northumberland
(4) to the Owners of the Middles-
    brough Estate Ltd, Middlesbrough,
    Yorks, N.R.
(5) to Edward Collins Ltd, Kelvin-
    dale Paper Works, Glasgow

Tennant's Works, Hebburn. Map 78, NZ 301645
(Charles Tennant & Partners Ltd until 1/11/1890; Charles Tennant & Partners
until 1884(?)

E2 This works was served by sidings W of NER Gateshead-South Shields line, ¼m
W of Hebburn Station. It also had a self-acting incline to a wharf on R.
Tyne. The works closed in 1932, but the bauxite section, which lay on the
eastern side of the site, was taken over by International Aluminium Co Ltd
(q.v.).

Gauge: 4' 8½"

No.1	0-4-0ST	OC	BH	204	1871	New	s/s
No.2	0-4-0ST	OC	BH	305	1874	New	(1)
TENNANT'S No.3	0-4-0ST	OC	BH	881	1889	New	
			reb.	MW		1911		(1)
No.2	0-4-0ST	OC	P	452	1889	(a)	s/s

(a) ex Fleetwood Works, Lancs

(1) to International Aluminium Co
    Ltd, /1932

INKERMAN COLLIERY CO LTD, INKERMAN COLLIERY, TOW LAW

Q1 This was an old colliery (Map 84, NZ 114397), worked by the NER under
various owners, and latterly a licensed mine. It was served by sidings N of
BR line from Consett to Tow Law, 1m N of Tow Law Station. The loco below
was used to haul skips from opencast workings north of the colliery.

Gauge: 2' 0"

-	4wDM		RH	226268	1944	(a)	Scr c7/1967

(a) ex MOS, Ruddington Depot, Notts,
    c/1962

INTERNATIONAL ALUMINIUM CO LTD, TENNANT'S WORKS, HEBBURN

E3 The works (Map 78, NZ 306647) was taken over from ICI (General Chemicals)
Ltd in 1932. It was served by sidings N of LNER Gateshead-South Shields
line, ¼m W of Hebburn Station. It was closed in 1942 and dismantled in 1947.

Gauge: 4' 8½"

BAUXITE No.1	0-4-0ST	OC	BH	881	1889				
			reb.	MW		1911	(a)	Scr	/1947
BAUXITE No.2	0-4-0ST	OC	BH	305	1874	(a)	(1)		

(a) ex ICI (General Chemicals) Ltd, /1932

(1) to Cohen, /1947; presented to North Eastern Historical Engineering & Industrial Locomotive Society for preservation; presented to Science Museum, South Kensington, London, 10/1953

JOHNSONS (CHOPWELL) LTD, NCBOE DISPOSAL POINT, SWALWELL
(Mechanical Navvies Ltd until 29/7/1968; firm has operated the site for NCBOE from 1/2/1954)

B8 This disposal point for opencast coal from Co. Durham and southern Northumberland was opened in July 1945 and was constructed on the site of the former Swalwell Garesfield Colliery (see Dunston Garesfield Collieries Ltd), which was closed in 1940. The site (Map 78, NZ 205623) is served by the truncated remainder of the LNER Swalwell Branch from Derwenthaugh on BR Redheugh Branch.

For a complete list of locos before 1954 see NCBOE.

Gauge: 4' 8½"

-	0-6-0T	IC	RWH	1645	1875			
			reb.	York	1901	(a)	Scr	/1955
71495	0-6-0ST	IC	HC	1771	1944	(a)	(1)	
75167	0-6-0ST	IC	WB	2755	1944	(a)	Scr	10/1973
75169	0-6-0ST	IC	WB	2757	1944	(a)	(2)	
71511	0-6-0ST	IC	RSH	7165	1944	(b)	Scr	c8/1968
71515	0-6-0ST	IC	RSH	7169	1944	(c)	(3)	
12074	0-6-0DE		Derby		1950	(d)		
12088	0-6-0DE		Derby		1951	(e)		

(a) ex NCBOE, 1/2/1954
(b) ex Derek Crouch (Contractors) Ltd, Widdrington D.P., Chevington, Northumberland, 2/1962
(c) ex Richard Costain Ltd, Horton Grange D.P., Bebside, Northumberland, 9/1967
(d) ex BR, Crewe, Cheshire, 6/1972
(e) ex BR, Crewe, Cheshire, 7/1972

(1) to Richard Costain Ltd, Horton Grange D.P., Bebside, Northumberland, 3/1955
(2) to Sir James Miller & Partners Ltd, Widdrington South D.P., Chevington, Northumberland, c/1955
(3) to East Somerset Railway, Cranmore, Somerset, for preservation, 8/1973 (property of R.P. Weisham and N.J. Smith)

LAMBTON WAGGONWAY
This was owned by J.G. Lambton (1792-1840), later Earl of Durham (see below), and ran from Lambton Main Colliery and Lambton 'A' Pit near Fencehouses to Lambton Low Staith at Penshaw on R. Wear. Part of the waggonway was later incorporated into the Earl of Durham's Railway (q.v.).

Gauge: 4' 0"

-	4w + 4w	VC	✗	1814	New	(1)

✗ This was an articulated locomotive built by Phineas Crowther of the Ouseburn Foundry, Newcastle, to the design of William Chapman, of Murton House, Co. Durham. It was tried here on 24th December 1814, and pulled 18 loaded waggons weighing 54 tons up a gradient of 1 in 115 at 4 m.p.h.

(1) to Owners of Heaton Colliery, Newcastle-upon-Tyne, 7/1817

Private railways south of Sunderland in the 1860's

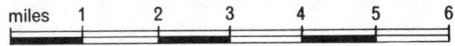

miles | 1 | 2 | 3 | 4 | 5 | 6

HETTON RAILWAY
LONDONDERRY RAILWAY
SOUTH HETTON RAILWAY
EARL OF DURHAM'S RAILWAY

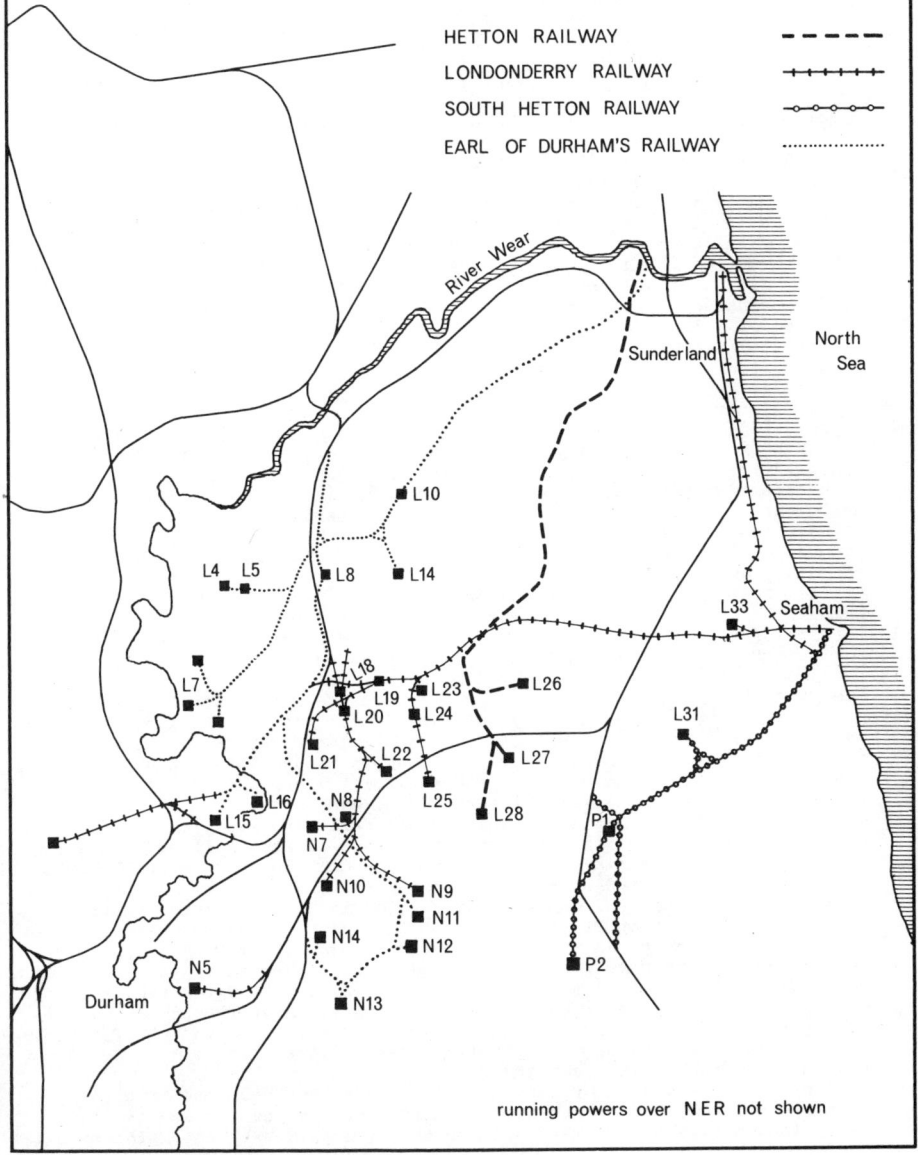

River Wear

Sunderland

North
Sea

L10

L4 L5   L8   L14

L33   Seaham

L7

L18
L19   L23   L26
L20   L24
L21   L22
L25   L27
L31
L28
L16   N8
L15   N7   P1

N10   N9
N11
N14   N12

N5   P2

Durham   N13

running powers over N E R not shown

LAMBTON, HETTON & JOICEY COLLIERIES LTD

This was the largest of the Co. Durham colliery companies, raising an average of four million tons per year from about 1910 onwards. The core of its activities was formed by the colliery interests of the Earls of Durham. In 1896 these were purchased by Sir J. Joicey, who formed Lambton Collieries Ltd on 26th June 1896. Under Lord Joicey, as he became, the firm in August 1911 absorbed the Hetton Coal Co Ltd and its subsidiary, the North Hetton Coal Co Ltd, to form Lambton & Hetton Collieries Ltd. On 26th November 1924 this firm finally amalgamated with James Joicey & Co Ltd to form Lambton, Hetton & Joicey Collieries Ltd.

The company owned several extensive railway systems, the largest being:

Lambton Railway (originally the Earl of Durham's Railway)

This can be traced back to three late eighteenth/early nineteenth century waggonways. The first was the Lambton waggonway (q.v.), which was joined by the Lumley waggonway at Burnmoor. The third was a waggonway from pits in the Newbottle area, which was opened by the Nesham family about 1815 (q.v.). This ran to the R. Wear at Sunderland, the most important colliery

L10 which it served being the Dorothea Pit (Map 78, NZ 334524) at Philadelphia. In 1819 J.G.Lambton (created Baron Durham in 1828 and Earl of Durham in 1833) purchased the Newbottle line, and joined the Lambton waggonway to it

L14 by means of a link between Burnmoor and Philadelphia. Houghton Colliery (NZ 338504) was sunk in 1821, and connected to the line by a branch (1m) from Philadelphia. At the same time workings were extended elsewhere,

L8 notably at Fencehouses, where the Lambton 'D' Pit (NZ 318507) was sunk in 1831.

N11 Also in 1831 sinkings were begun at Littletown Colliery (NZ 338436), and to serve this the waggonway was extended by about 5 miles from Rainton Meadows via a disused colliery known as the Resolution Pit. At the same time, presumably to cater for the increased traffic, considerable improvements were made to the older parts of the system. Part of the Nesham line between West Herrington and the Grindon Engine was replaced by a new line,

L7 and the Lumley waggonway, with its branch to Cocken Colliery (NZ 297474) and other small pits nearby, was also reconstructed, with stationary engines installed to replace horses.

Meanwhile there were further developments beyond Littletown. Sherburn Hill

N12 Colliery (NZ 336427) was sunk in 1835, to be followed not long after by

N13 Sherburn House Colliery (NZ 324417) and Sherburn Colliery (Lady Durham Pit)

N14 (NZ 315425), and these were served by a long branch from the Littletown

L15 line at Pittington. Then about 1840 a branch was built from the Resolution Pit to serve Frankland Colliery (NZ 296452), and about 1842 another branch was built from this line just south of the bridge over the R. Wear to

N2 serve Framwellgate Moor Colliery (NZ 270445), though this was not owned by the Earl. Later another short branch was built along the southern bank of

L16 the river to serve Brasside Colliery (NZ 305458).

This represented the maximum extent of the Earl's railway, and at this period most of the system was operated by rope-worked inclines. The section from Sherburn Colliery to Sherburn House Colliery was virtually level, and was probably worked by horses. From Sherburn House the waggons were drawn up to Sherburn Hill by a stationary engine there, whence there was an incline down to Low Pittington, the line being joined here at Bird-in-the-Bush Junction, by an incline from Littletown Colliery. From Low Pittington the waggons were hauled by an engine up to New Pittington, and this was followed by a self-acting incline (?) down to Pittington Village, both of these banks being very short. Near the tunnel under the Durham-Sunderland turnpike road the Belmont Engine worked the incline up from Pittington, and this was followed by a long self-acting incline (the Belmont Bank) down to Belmont Bottom, near the Resolution Pit.

From here to the bottom of the Junction Bank at Burnmoor the line was relatively level, and the horses here may have been superceded by the early locomotives below. The Junction Bank was worked by an engine situated

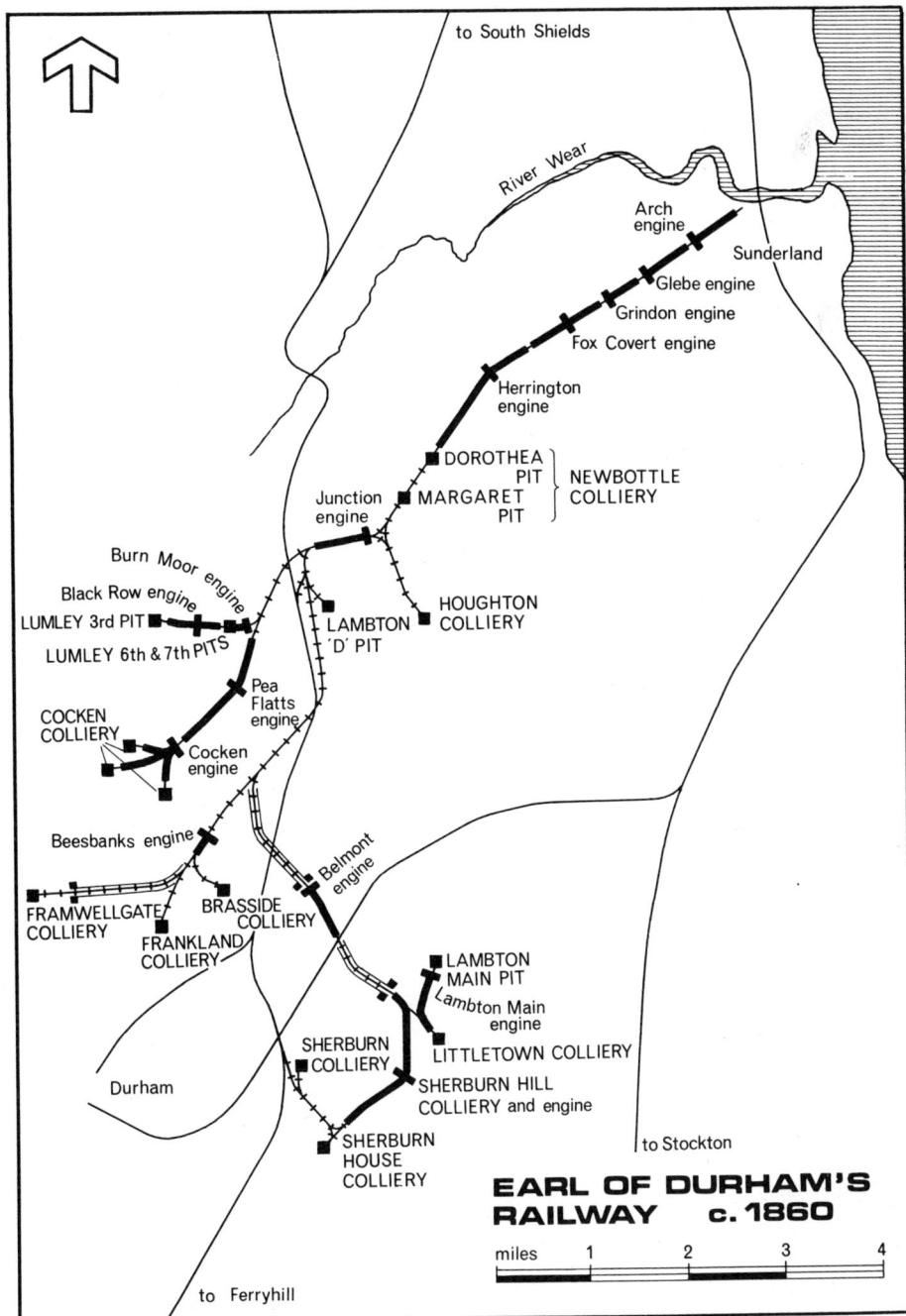

to South Shields

River Wear

Arch engine

Sunderland

Glebe engine

Grindon engine

Fox Covert engine

Herrington engine

DOROTHEA PIT

NEWBOTTLE COLLIERY

Junction engine

MARGARET PIT

Burn Moor engine

Black Row engine

LUMLEY 3rd PIT

HOUGHTON COLLIERY

LUMLEY 6th & 7th PITS

LAMBTON 'D' PIT

Pea Flatts engine

COCKEN COLLIERY

Cocken engine

Beesbanks engine

Belmont engine

FRAMWELLGATE COLLIERY

BRASSIDE COLLIERY

FRANKLAND COLLIERY

LAMBTON MAIN PIT

Lambton Main engine

SHERBURN COLLIERY

LITTLETOWN COLLIERY

Durham

SHERBURN HILL COLLIERY and engine

SHERBURN HOUSE COLLIERY

to Stockton

EARL OF DURHAM'S RAILWAY c. 1860

| miles | 1 | 2 | 3 | 4 |

to Ferryhill

115

near the Houghton Colliery branch junction.. The same engine may also
have worked traffic along this branch, but as the line was level it may
have been done by horses.

Beyond the Junction Engine the main line was level as far as Philadelphia,
from which the Herrington Engine hauled the waggons up the Herrington West
Bank and lowered them down the Herrington East Bank. From this point the
Fox Covert Engine took them to the summit of the line and lowered them
down to the Grindon Engine. There then followed three further inclines in
favour of the load, worked respectively by the Grindon Engine, the Glebe
Engine and the Arch Engine. At <u>Lambton Staithes</u> in Sunderland (Map 78, NZ
394574) there was another small engine which worked traffic to a landsale
yard.

K12

From Framwellgate Moor Colliery the first ½m may have been worked by
horses, and this was followed by a self-acting incline down to the R. Wear.
The branches to Frankland and Brasside Collieries were probably worked by
horses. From the east side of the river the waggons were drawn up a short,
steep incline by the Beesbanks Engine. From here to the Resolution Pit
junction may also have been worked by horses or the early locomotives.

The Lumley and Cocken branches were also worked by stationary engines. The
Black Row Engine, near Lumley Thicks, worked the line up from <u>Lumley Third
Pit</u> and dropped the waggons down to <u>Lumley Sixth</u> and <u>Seventh Pits</u>. From
here they were taken up to the junction with the main line by the Burnmoor
Engine. This section was virtually level, and may have been worked by main
-and-tail rope between the two engines. On the Cocken line the Cocken Engine drew waggons up from the various pits. The Pea Flatts Engine then
hauled them up the Pea Flatts Bank before dropping them down to the Sixth
and Seventh Pits. When the Great North of England Railway's line from
Rainton to Ferryhill was opened in 1844 a link was put in with the Earl's
railway at Sherburn Colliery. Similarly, a connection was put in to serve
Framwellgate Moor Colliery when the N.E.R. line from Leamside to Durham
was opened in 1857, though it seems that most of the traffic from here was
transferred on to the Londonderry Railway (Rainton & Seaham section) (q.v.)
via a long spur running east from a junction north of the Resolution Pit.
The system was operated as thus described until 1865, when the N.E.R.
opened a branch from their Durham-Sunderland line to Pallion. As a result
a tunnel was built to connect this with Lambton Staithes, and tender locomotives introduced to haul most of the Earl's traffic over the N.E.R. (via
running powers) from Penshaw to the Staithes and later to the new South
Dock. The old route over Grindon Hill seems to have been finally abandoned
about 1870. Loco working over the N.E.R. (with a reverse at both Penshaw

L3
L4/5

J1
J2

and Washington) to <u>Harraton Colliery</u> (NZ 291539) also seems to date from
this period, and <u>North Biddick Colliery</u> (NZ 307542) was similarly served
after it was acquired from Sir G. Elliott in 1894.

Following the introduction of locomotive working to Sunderland, the stationary engines were gradually replaced on the remaining sections of the
main line. Locomotives were kept at Sherburn Colliery by 1871, though re-
alignment and levelling of the line between Sherburn House and Pittington
was necessary before locos could work through from Sherburn to Belmont
Bank Head. The Belmont Bank remained a self-acting incline.

On the branches, Frankland Colliery seems to have closed by the 1860's,
together with the line to Framwellgate Moor Colliery, though this may have
lasted until about 1879. The lines to Brasside and Cocken closed with these
collieries in 1881, and with the closure of Lumley Second Pit in June 1877,

L4
J7

only <u>Lumley Sixth Pit</u> (NZ 309506) was now served by the branch (now loco-
worked) from Burnmoor. On the credit side, <u>New Herrington Colliery</u> (NZ
341533) was opened in 1874.

In August 1911 the <u>Hetton Railway</u> was taken over as a result of the amalgamation with the Hetton Coal Co Ltd. The staithes of the two companies
were adjacent, and were immediately linked by a tunnel. The two Railways
were also linked at their southern ends about 1917 by a long spur between
Rainton Meadows and Rainton Bridge on the line to North Hetton Colliery,
using part of the trackbed of the old Londonderry Railway (see Marquis of
Londonderry).

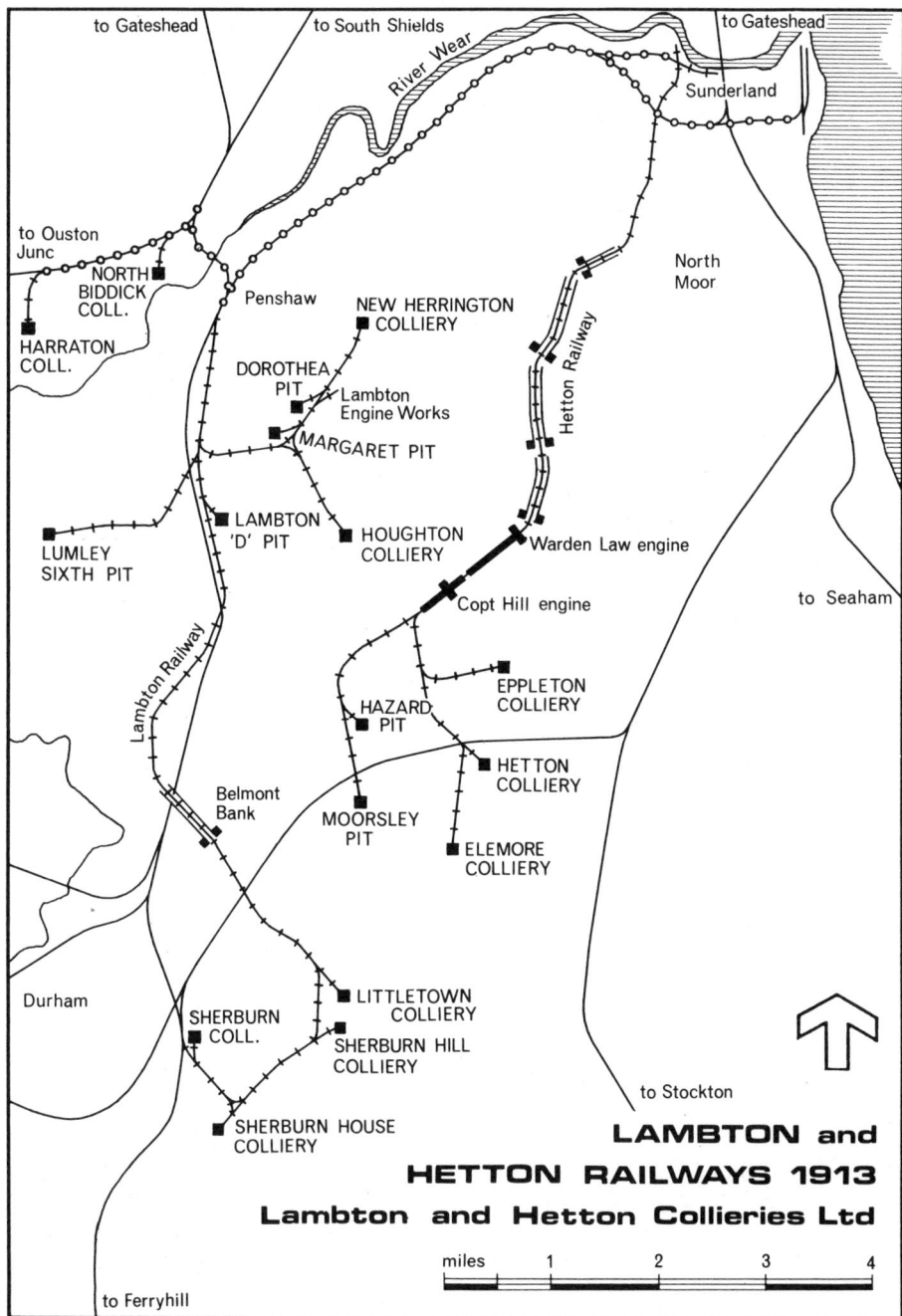

to Gateshead   to South Shields   to Gateshead

River Wear

Sunderland

to Ouston Junc

NORTH BIDDICK COLL.

HARRATON COLL.

Penshaw

North Moor

NEW HERRINGTON COLLIERY

DOROTHEA PIT

Lambton Engine Works

MARGARET PIT

Hetton Railway

LAMBTON 'D' PIT

HOUGHTON COLLIERY

Warden Law engine

LUMLEY SIXTH PIT

Copt Hill engine

to Seaham

Lambton Railway

HAZARD PIT

EPPLETON COLLIERY

Belmont Bank

HETTON COLLIERY

MOORSLEY PIT

ELEMORE COLLIERY

Durham

LITTLETOWN COLLIERY

SHERBURN COLL.

SHERBURN HILL COLLIERY

to Stockton

SHERBURN HOUSE COLLIERY

LAMBTON and HETTON RAILWAYS 1913

Lambton and Hetton Collieries Ltd

miles   1   2   3   4

to Ferryhill

Littletown Colliery closed in August 1913, and on 1st January 1914 the
Sherburn collieries were sold to Sir B. Samuelson & Co Ltd (see under DL).
As a result, the line from Rainton to Sherburn Hill was closed, though the
remaining section, from Sherburn Hill to Sherburn, was retained by the new
owners. Loco working to North Biddick Colliery ceased when the colliery
closed in June 1931, and the North Hetton branch was abandoned with the
closure of North Hetton Colliery in March 1935.

On 1st January 1947, when the remainder of the system and its collieries
were vested in NCB Northern Division No.2 Area, the line ran from Fence-
L9 houses, past Lambton Coke Works (NZ 318510) - opened in 1907, and Lambton
'D' Pit to Burnmoor Junction and Penshaw, with branches from Burnmoor to
Lumley Sixth Pit (1m); from Burnmoor to New Herrington Colliery, via
Dorothea Colliery (2m), and from Philadelphia to Houghton Colliery (1m).
The running powers over the LNER lines to Harraton Colliery and to Lambton
Staithes and South Dock in Sunderland from Penshaw were also vested in the
NCB.

L11 The main loco sheds were at Philadelphia (NZ 335524). Locos were also kept
at Sherburn Colliery, later replaced by a shed at Sherburn Hill Colliery,
to work the southern end of the system. A loco was kept at North Hetton
Colliery (Hazard Pit) until its closure, and one or two locos were also
kept at Harraton Colliery. After the amalgamation with the Hetton Railway
locos at the Staithes were kept on the Lambton side, and this shed also
supplied locos to work the Hetton Railway between the Staithes and the
North Moor Marshalling Yard, and also Silksworth Colliery (see below).
All repairs to Lambton Railway locos were carried out at the Lambton
L12 Engine Works (NZ 336525), which handled about twenty repairs a year, and
also took over all repairs to Hetton Railway locos from Hetton Shed after
the closure of Hetton Shops in the winter of 1934-1935.

Not a great deal is certain about the early locomotives, even to whether
some of those listed below were actually present. The Earl is said to have
had 18 locos in 1870, and the numbering scheme seems to date from shortly
afterwards, but nothing further can be stated with any confidence, except
that some of the locos un-numbered below must have been included. Several
of the early tender locos had a distinct affinity with RS design of the
period, but examination of the RS records has failed to produce any clue.

Gauge: 4' 8½"

PRINCE ALBERT	0-6-0		Hackworth		c1842	New	s/s
LAMBTON CASTLE						(a)	s/s
EARL GREY						(a)	s/s
ALBERT EDWARD	0-6-0		RWH	308	1839	(b)	s/s
-	0-6-0		reb.TR	213	1852	(c)	s/s
-	0-6-0		TR	236	1853	New	s/s
-	0-6-0		TR	251	1854	New	s/s
-	0-6-0ST	IC	H&C	21	1863	New	(1)
DURHAM	0-6-0ST	IC	MW	152	1865	New	s/s
-	0-6-0ST	IC	H&C	76	1866	New	(2)
-	0-6-0ST	IC	H&C	78	1866	New	s/s
-	0-6-0	IC				(d)	
reb.	0-6-0ST	IC	H&C	98	1870		s/s
-	0-6-0		Blair		c1865	(d)	s/s

(a) origin unknown
(b) ex Wingate Coal Co
(c) ex TR, /1852
(d) ex ?

(1) to HCR; rebuilt as HCR 170/1875,
    and re-sold to Commondale Brick
    & Tile Co, Yorks, N.R., 7/1875
(2) to HCR; rebuilt as HCR 171/1875,
    and re-sold to Stanton Iron Works
    Co Ltd, Teversal Colliery, Notts,
    11/1875

No.	Name	Type	Cyl	Builder	Works No.	Year	Status		
1		0-6-0	IC	H&C	71	1866	New ØØ	(1)	
2		0-6-0	IC	H&C	72	1866	New ØØ	(2)	
2		0-6-0ST	IC	RWH	1969	1883	(a)	Scr c/1939	
3		0-6-0	IC	BP	550	1865	New	(1)	
4		0-6-0	IC	RS ?					
		reb. BH			17	1866	New	(1)	
5		0-6-0	IC	H&C	30	1864	New ØØ	Scr c/1909	
5		0-6-2T	IC	RS	3377	1909	New	(1)	
6		0-6-0	IC	RS ⁄		1864	New	(1)	
7		0-6-0	IC	RS ⁄		1864	New	(1)	
8		0-6-0	IC	RS ⁄		1864	New	(1)	
9		0-6-0	IC	ED		1877	New	(1)	
10		0-6-0	IC	ED ?			New ?	Scr c/1909	
10		0-6-2T	IC	RS	3378	1909	New	(1)	
11		0-6-0	IC	ED ?			New ?	(3)	
11		0-4-0ST	OC	HC	1412	1920	New	(1)	
12		0-6-0	IC				New ?	Scr c/1912	
12		0-4-0ST	OC	HL	2789	1912	New	(1)	
13		0-4-0ST	OC	H&C	79	1866	New	(2)	
13		0-4-0ST	OC	HL	3055	1914	New ⁄⁄	(1)	
14		0-6-0ST	IC	H&C			(b)	(2)	
14		0-4-0ST	OC	HL	3056	1914	New	(1)	
15		0-4-0ST	OC	HCR	169	1875	New	(1)	
16		0-4-0ST	OC	H&C	96	1870	New	(1)	
17		0-4-0ST	OC	HCR	130	1873	New	(4)	
17		0-4-0ST	OC	MW	2023	1923	New %	(1)	
18		0-6-0ST	OC	BH	32	1867	New		
		reb. Dar				1918			
		reb.							
				HL	1491	1935		(1)	
19		0-4-0ST	OC	MW	344	1871	New	(1)	
20		0-6-0	IC	RS	2260	1876	New	(1)	
21		0-4-0ST	OC	RS	2308	1876	New	(1)	
22		0-4-0ST	OC	HC	230	1881	New	(1)	
23		0-4-0ST	OC	BH	688	1882	New %	(1)	
24		0-4-0ST	OC	BH	832	1885	New	(1)	
25		0-6-0	IC	ED		1890	New	(1)	
26		0-6-0	IC	ED		1894	New	(1)	
27		0-6-0ST	IC	RS	491	1846			
		reb.Ghd				1864			
		reb.Ghd				1873	(c)		
	reb.	0-6-0T	IC	reb.LEW		1904		(1)	
28		0-4-0ST	OC	HL	2530	1902	New	(1)	
29		0-6-2T	IC	K	4263	1904	New	(1)	
30		0-6-2T	IC	K	4532	1907	New	(1)	
31		0-6-2T	IC	K	4533	1907	New	(1)	
32		0-4-0ST	OC	HL	2826	1910	New ⁄⁄	(1)	
33		0-4-0ST	OC	HL	2827	1910	New	(1)	
34		0-4-0ST	OC	HL	2954	1912	New	(1)	
35		0-4-0ST	OC	HL	3024	1913	New %	(1)	
36	HAZARD	0-4-0ST	OC	P	615	1896	(d)	(1)	
37		0-6-0ST	IC	RWH	1430	1868	(e)	(5)	
38		0-6-0ST	IC	RWH	1478	1870	(f)	(6)	
39	(later No.39)	0-6-0ST	IC	RWH	1422	1867			
		reb.HL			2378		(g)	(7)	
40		0-6-0ST	IC	RS	1919	1869	(h)	(8)	
41		0-6-0T	OC	KS	3074	1917	(j)	(1)	
42		0-6-2T	IC	RS	3801	1920	New	(1)	
43		0-4-0ST	OC	GR	769	1920	New	(1)	
44		0-6-0ST	OC	MW	1934	1917	(k)	(1)	
45		0-6-0ST	IC	HL	2932	1912	(m)	(1)	
46		0-6-0T	IC	MW	1813	1913	(n)	(1)	
47		0-4-0ST	OC	HL	3543	1923	New	(1)	
48		0-4-0ST	OC	HL	3544	1923	New ⁄⁄	(1)	

49		0-4-OST	OC	MW	2035	1924	New %		(1)
50		0-4-OST	OC	MW	2036	1924	New %		(1)
51		4wBE		DK	9537	1918	(p)	Scr c/1937 ?	
52		0-6-2T	IC	NR	5408	1899	(q)		(1)
53		0-6-2T	IC	Cdf	302	1894	(r) %		(1)
54		0-6-2T	IC	Cdf	311	1897	(s)		(1)
55		0-6-2T	IC	K	3069	1887	(t) %		(1)
56		0-6-2T	IC	K	3580	1894	(u) %		(1)
57		0-6-2T	IC	HL	3834	1934	New		(1)
58		0-6-0ST	IC	VF	5299	1945	(v) ⌿⌿		(1)
59		0-6-0ST	IC	VF	5300	1945	(w)		(1)

∅∅ In its early years the firm of Hudswell & Clarke also gave works numbers to locomotive tenders. The tender of 1 was 73/1866, of 2 was 74/1866 and of 5 31/1864.

⌿ Attributed to Coulthard, but it seems likely that they were RS locos, Coulthard acting as agent.

⌿⌿ Hetton Loco Sheds, 1/1/1947   % Lambton Staithes, 1/1/1947
The majority of the remainder were at Philadelphia, but which locos were working at Harraton and Silksworth Collieries at Vesting Day is not known.

(a) ex Hetton Railway, 2
(b) presumably one of H&C 78 and 98 above
(c) built as 2-4-0 for Newcastle & Darlington Rly, No.22; NER 30 in 1854; reb. as 0-6-0 in 1864; reb. as 0-6-0ST in 1873; ex NER, 8/1898
(d) ex North Hetton Coal Co Ltd (see below); may have run as NORTH HETTON No.1 for a time; re-numbered in 1919
(e) ex Hetton Railway, 6; re-numbered in 1919
(f) ex Hetton Railway, 8; re-numbered in 1919
(g) ex Hetton Railway, 5; re-numbered in 1919
(h) ex Hetton Railway, 7; re-numbered in 1919
(j) ex ROD, 606, c/1920
(k) ex IWD, 23, Sandwich, Kent, c/1920
(m) ex Londonderry Collieries Ltd, Silksworth Colliery, c2/1920
(n) ex Lancaster's Steam Coal Collieries Ltd, Monmouthshire, GRIFFIN, 1/1923
(p) ex Philadelphia G.S. (see below), ELECTRIC No.1; re-numbered in 1925
(q) ex GWR, 426, per R.H.Longbotham & Co Ltd, 4/1929; orig. TVR, 85
(r) ex GWR, 448, per R.H.Longbotham & Co Ltd, 2/1930; orig. TVR, 26
(s) ex GWR, 475, per R.H.Longbotham & Co Ltd, 2/1930; orig. TVR, 64
(t) ex GWR, 159, per R.H.Longbotham & Co Ltd, 2/1931; orig. Cdf Rly, 28

(1) to NCB No.2 Area, 1/1/1947
(2) to Sir B. Samuelson & Co Ltd, 1/1/1914
(3) last recorded repair was 6/1914; s/s
(4) last recorded repair was 7/1921; s/s
(5) to Tanfield Lea Colliery
(6) to Tanfield Lea Colliery, 5/1938
(7) loaned to John Bowes & Partners Ltd, Bowes Railway, 12/1937; ret. 3/1938; loaned to WD, Central Ordnance Depot, Derby, 10/1940; overhauled at LMS Derby Works, 1941-1942; ret; to NCB No.2 Area, 1/1/1947
(8) to Handen Hold Colliery

(u) ex GWR, 156, per R.H.Longbotham
    & Co Ltd, 2/1931; orig. Cdf Rly,1
(v) ex WD, 75309, 4/1946
(w) ex WD, 75310, 4/1946

The Earl is known to have been using a number of compressed air locomotives underground by January 1878, but details are lacking.

Hetton Railway

For a description of this Railway see under Hetton Coal Co Ltd. After the formation of the new company in August 1911, a tunnel was built to link the two sets of staithes, and loco working on the Hetton side was supplied from Lambton Staithes shed. About 1917 the two railways were linked at their southern ends by a line from Nicholson's Pit on the Lambton Railway at Rainton Meadows to the Hazard Pit on the Hetton Railway's North Hetton branch. The new line utilised part of the trackbed of the former London-derry Railway (Rainton & Seaham section). The North Hetton line north of the Hazard Pit was later abandoned, and traffic - mostly small coal for Lambton Coke Works and rolling stock - was sent between the two lines via the LNER junctions at Hetton and North Hetton on the Sunderland-Durham Elvet line. Transfers of locos between Hetton and Philadelphia were quite frequent, and are not recorded. Hetton Workshops were closed in the winter of 1934-1935, all repairs then being done at Lambton Engine Works. The line, together with Elemore, Hetton and Eppleton Collieries, passed to NCB Northern Division No.2 Area on 1st January 1947.

Gauge: 4' 8½"

1		2-4-0T	OC	RS	1100	1857	(a)	s/s by 1919	
2		0-6-0ST	IC	RWH	1969	1883	(a)	(1)	
-		0-4-0	VC	G.Stephenson					
						c1822			
				reb.Hetton	1853				
				reb.Hetton	c1882		(b)	(2)	
4		0-6-0ST	IC	RS	1649	1865	(a)	(3)	
5		0-6-0ST	IC	RWH	1422	1867	(a)	(1)	
6		0-6-0ST	IC	RWH	1430	1868	(a)	(1)	
7		0-6-0ST	IC	RS	1919	1869	(a)	(1)	
8		0-6-0ST	IC	RWH	1478	1870	(a)	(1)	
	LYONS "Beetle No.1"	4wVB		Hetton		c1900	(a)	Scr c/1914	
	EPPLETON								
	"Beetle No.2"	4wVB		Hetton		c1900	(a)	Scr c/1914	

(a) ex Hetton Coal Co Ltd, 8/1911
(b) ex Hetton Coal Co Ltd, 8/1911;
    being used as stationary boiler
    in saw mill at Hetton Shops

(1) re-numbered in Lambton Railway
    list, /1919
(2) headed the Stockton & Darlington
    Railway centenary procession in
    steam, 9/1925; presented to York
    Railway Museum for preservation,
    7/1926
(3) last known repair was 6/1912; s/s

North Hetton Colliery, near Hetton

(North Hetton Coal Co Ltd until 8/1911; this company was originally a joint subsidiary of the Earl of Durham, the Marquis of Londonderry and the Hetton Coal Co.but became a subsidiary of the Hetton Coal Co alone about 1840)

L24 This colliery consisted of two pits - the Hazard Pit (Map 85, NZ 341478),
L25 sunk in 1818, and the Moorsley Pit (NZ 344466), sunk in 1826. A line 1½m long linked the two pits, and originally their coal was taken to staithes on R. Wear at North Biddick; but about 1833 this northern section was abandoned in favour of a link with the Londonderry Railway (Rainton & Seaham section) at Rainton Bridge, the line being operated by stationary engines at the two pits. Later a link was put in with the Durham & Sunder-

land Railway (later NER) at North Hetton. When the Londonderry Railway closed in 1896 it appears that the North Hetton company took over the section between Rainton Bridge and Hetton and altered the line to join the Hetton Railway (though this may have been done earlier). The stationary engines were replaced by locomotive working in 1902, the locomotive shed being at the Hazard Pit. For further development see the Hetton Railway above. The colliery closed in March 1935.

Gauge: 4' 8½"

HAZARD	0-4-0ST	OC	P	615	1896	(a)	(1)

(a) ex Vale of Neath Coal Co Ltd, Aberpergwm Colliery, Glamorgan, via Wake, /1902

(1) re-numbered in Lambton Railway list, /1919

Philadelphia Generating Station, Philadelphia. Map 78, NZ 334520.

L38 This station was built by the Company about 1918 to supply the Lambton Workshops and other colliery installations, and probably adjacent colliery houses. It later appears to have become part of the North-Eastern Electric Supply Co Ltd's system, though under what agreement is not known, and was subsequently closed.
The station initially had its own locomotive, but from about 1923 its repairs were included in colliery locomotive stock, into which it was eventually numbered in 1925. A small shed was provided for it in the main group of sheds.

Gauge: 4' 8½"

ELECTRIC No.1	4wBE	DK	9537	1918	New	(1)

(1) re-numbered into Lambton Railway list, /1925

Silksworth Colliery, Silksworth. Map 78, NZ 377541.

K15 This colliery was acquired from Londonderry Collieries Ltd in 1920, probably on 1st February. It was served by a branch (2¼m) from LNER Sunderland-Seaham line at Ryhope. The loco below was re-numbered into Lambton Railway stock, and transfers between Silksworth and Philadelphia arranged as required. The colliery was vested in NCB Northern Division No.2 Area on 1st January 1947.

Gauge: 4' 8½"

No.1 SILKSWORTH	0-6-0ST	IC	HL	2932	1912	(a)	(1)

(a) ex Londonderry Collieries Ltd, 1/2/1920 (?)

(1) re-numbered into Lambton Railway list, c2/1920

Beamish Railway
(James Joicey & Co Ltd until 26/11/1924; James Joicey & Co until 8/1/1886; orig. James Joicey)

The history of this line dates well back into the eighteenth century, when it ran from pits in the Beamish area to staithes on R. Wear at Fatfield. About 1853 it was taken over by Joicey, who had been rapidly expanding his colliery interests in West Durham. He linked it to the NER (Pontop & Shields branch) at Durham Turnpike (Ouston Junction), and abandoned the eastern section. About this time, but possibly in the 1830's, the line was reconstructed, and worked by a series of self-acting inclines and stationary engines, but very few details survive about them. The first locomotives arrived in 1872, but the total conversion to locomotive working does not seem to have been completed until some time afterwards.

H42 By 1913 the line ran from Beamish Mary Pit (Map 78, NZ 211536) and
H43 Beamish Air Pit (NZ 215534) to Beamish itself (1¼m). Here it was joined
H44 by branches from Beamish Second Pit (NZ 221537) and East Stanley Colliery
H45 (NZ 218539). From Beamish to Ouston Junction was 3½m. All locomotive
H46 repairs were done at Beamish Engine Works (NZ 222537), served by another
short branch at Beamish. The loco shed for the line was situated in the
Works compound. Beamish Mary and Beamish Second Pits survived to be vested
in NCB Northern Division No.5 Area on 1st January 1947.

Gauge: 4' 8½"

1	BEAMISH	0-6-0ST	IC	RS	2013	1872	New	Scr c/1939
2	STANLEY	0-6-0ST	IC	RS	2014	1872	New	(1)
3	TWIZELL	0-6-0T	IC	RS	2730	1891	New	(2)
4	LINHOPE	0-6-0T	IC	RS	2822	1895	New	(2)
No.5	MAJOR	0-6-0T	IC	K	4294	1905	New	
				reb. HL	2812	1931		(2)
	TANFIELD	0-4-0ST	OC	Joicey	377	1885	(a)	Scr c/1935

(a) ex Twizell Colliery   (1) to Handen Hold Colliery
                                           (2) to NCB No.5 Area, 1/1/1947

East Tanfield Colliery, near Tantobie. Map 78, NZ 194552.
(James Joicey & Co Ltd until 1917; James Joicey & Co until 8/1/1886;
orig. James Joicey)

H17 This colliery was sunk by Joicey in 1844, and was served by sidings W of
NER Tanfield Branch. It was sold to the East Tanfield Colliery Co Ltd in
1917 (see South Derwent Coal Co Ltd).

     There was a loco here by April 1871, but its identity is unknown.

Gauge: 4' 8½"

TANFIELD	0-4-0ST	OC	Joicey	377	1885	New	(1)
HARPERLEY	0-4-0ST	OC	Joicey	429	1894	New	Scr
SHIELD ROW	0-4-0ST	OC	HC		c1881		
			reb. LG		1914	(a)	(2)

(a) ex LG,   /1914   (1) to Twizell Colliery
                                           (2) to East Tanfield Colliery Co
                                               Ltd,   /1917

Handen Hold Colliery, West Pelton. Map 78, NZ 233526.
(James Joicey & Co Ltd until 26/11/1924; James Joicey & Co until 8/1/1886;
orig. James Joicey)

H49 This colliery was opened about 1858, and was served by sidings at the foot
of the Eden Incline on the NER Pontop & Shields branch. It was vested in
NCB Northern Division No.5 Area on 1st January 1947.

Gauge: 4' 8½"

	WHITEHALL	0-4-0ST	OC	AE	1387	1898	New/	Scr	/1939
	KYO	0-6-0ST	IC	RS	2993	1901	New	Scr	/1943
(2)	(STANLEY)	0-6-0ST	IC	RS	2014	1872	(a)	(1)	
38		0-6-0ST	IC	RWH	1478	1870	(b)	(2)	
40		0-6-0ST	IC	RS	1919	1869	(c)	(2)	

     / over the AE plate was fixed a second plate, reading Joicey 457/1898

(a) ex Beamish Railway   (1) derelict in retort house by
(b) ex Tanfield Lea Colliery   /1939; to NCB No.5 Area,
(c) ex Lambton Railway   1/1/1947
                                    (2) to NCB No.5 Area, 1/1/1947

South Tanfield Colliery, near Annfield Plain. Map 78, NZ 179521.
(James Joicey & Co Ltd at time of closure)

H36 This colliery was sunk in July 1837, and was served by sidings S of NER
Pontop & Shields branch 1½m E of Annfield Plain Station. It was closed in
November 1914.

There was a loco here by November 1896, but its identity is unknown.

Tanfield Lea Colliery, Tanfield Lea. Map 78, NZ 188544.
(James Joicey & Co Ltd until 26/11/1924; James Joicey & Co until 8/1/1886;
orig. James Joicey)

H18 This colliery was sunk in 1829, and acquired by Joicey in 1847. It was
latterly situated at the end of the NER Tanfield Branch, and appears to
have been worked by the NER until about 1900. It was vested in NCB
Northern Division No.6 Area on 1st January 1947.

Gauge: 4' 8½"

	LEIGH	0-4-0ST	OC	Joicey			(a)	s/s
	EDEN	0-4-0ST	OC	HL	2481	1900	New	(1)
38		0-6-0ST	IC	RWH	1478	1870	(b)	(2)
37		0-6-0ST	IC	RWH	1430	1868	(c)	(1)

(a) ex ?   (1) to NCB No.6 Area, 1/1/1947
(b) ex Lambton Railway, 5/1938   (2) to Handen Hold Colliery
(c) ex Lambton Railway

Twizell Colliery (later **Twizell Gate Colliery**), near West Pelton.
(James Joicey & Co Ltd until 26/11/1924; James Joicey & Co until 8/1/1886;
orig. James Joicey)

H47 This colliery (Map 78, NZ 223524) was opened by 1860, and was served by
sidings to the top of the Eden Incline on NER Pontop & Shields branch.
It was closed in July 1938. It may have had other locos, or have been
worked by NER.

Gauge: 4' 8½"

TANFIELD	0-4-0ST	OC	Joicey 377	1885	(a)	(1)

(a) ex East Tanfield Colliery   (1) to Beamish Railway

West Pelton Colliery (also known as **Alma Colliery**), Grange Villa.
(James Joicey & Co Ltd until 26/11/1924; James Joicey & Co until 8/1/1886;
orig. James Joicey)

H48 This colliery (Map 78, NZ 232515) was opened about 1858, and was connected
by a short branch to the NER Pontop & Shields branch at the foot of the
Eden Incline. It survived various closures to be vested in NCB Northern
Division No.5 Area on 1st January 1947. How it was worked latterly is not
certain.

Gauge: 4' 8½"

ALMA	0-4-0ST	OC	Joicey	(a)	Scr

(a) origin unknown

<u>LANCHESTER & IVESTON COAL CO LTD</u>, GREENWELL WOOD DRIFT, near LANCHESTER

H65 This drift (Map 85, NZ 168465) was a licensed mine, and had no main line
rail connection. The locos below were used both on the surface and
underground. The drift closed with the voluntary liquidation of the company in April 1966.

Gauge: 2' 0"

-	4wDMF		F. Blacklock				
					c1952	(a)	(1)
-	0-4-0DMF		HE	4991	1955	New	(2)
-	0-4-0DMF		HE	4979	1955	(b)	(2)

(a) ex Abbey Wood Coal Co, loan,   (1) ret. to Abbey Wood Coal Co
    c/1954   after a fortnight
(b) ex Weardale Lead Co Ltd,   (2) to Ayle Coal Co Ltd, Alston,
    Stotsfieldburn Mine, Rookhope,   Cumberland, 5/1966
    /1961

<u>LINTHORPE-DINSDALE SMELTING CO LTD</u>, MIDDLETON (or FIGHTING COCKS)
<u>IRONWORKS</u>, near MIDDLETON ST. GEORGE
(Dinsdale Smelting Co Ltd until 3/4/1903; Dinsdale Smelting Co until 1900;
form. James Tarbuck; see also below)

W5 This works (Map 85, NZ 348137) was opened in 1865 by the Middleton Iron
Co, and passed through various hands before being closed in 1882. Locos
may well have been used during this period, but no record survives. The
works was re-opened about 1892. It was served by sidings S of NER
Fighting Cocks Branch, ½m W of Oak Tree Junction.
The firm went into voluntary liquidation in August 1946, and the works
was sold in 1947. The slag heaps were later worked by Durham County
Council (q.v.), and the site used by British Railways (q.v.).

Gauge: 4' 8½"

VICTORIA	0-4-0ST	OC	P	634	1897	(a)	(1)
-	0-4-0ST	OC	MW	756	1880	(b)	(2)
DINSDALE No.1	0-4-0ST	OC	P	845	1900	New	(3)
DINSDALE No.2	0-4-0ST	OC	P	880	1901	New	(4)
DINSDALE No.3	0-4-0ST	OC	P	1058	1906	New	(3)
-	0-4-0VBT		Cochrane			(c)	(5)

  N.B. Works may also have had other locos on loan from Linthorpe
     Works, Middlesbrough, Yorks, N.R., from time to time.

(a) ex H.Lovatt Ltd, Hounslow,   (1) to Egglescliffe Chemical Co Ltd,
    Middlesex, contr   Urlay Nook
(b) ex E.Williams, Linthorpe   (2) to DL, Warrenby Works, Redcar,
    Ironworks, Middlesbrough,   Yorks, N.R., c/1946
    Yorks, N.R.   (3) to Gjers Mills & Co Ltd,
(c) ex Cochrane & Co Ltd, Middles-   Middlesbrough, Yorks, N.R.,
    brough, Yorks, N.R., c/1945   /1946
                                        (4) to DL, Lackenby Works, Middles-
                                            brough, Yorks, N.R. c/1946
                                        (5) sold for scrap, /1947; scr
                                            c/1950

LINTZ COLLIERY CO

Lintz Colliery (Anna Pit), near Burnopfield. Map 78, NZ 158561.

H3 This colliery was opened about 1855, and was served by a branch (1½m) from
the NER Tanfield Branch at White-le-Head, using a stationary engine to
haul wagons up from the colliery to the NER. In March 1867 the branch was
linked to the Pontop & Jarrow Railway (see John Bowes & Partners) at
Pickering Nook, where the Lintz line went under the P & JR, but the
traffic resumed its former route in 1870. The loco below would seem to
have been used only to shunt the colliery, which was closed in 1885.
It was however re-opened in 1889 by J. Shield (q.v.).

Gauge: 4' 8½"

-	0-4-0ST	OC	JF	2849	1876	New (1)

(1) offered for sale, 8/7/1887; s/s

West Lintz Drift, near Tantobie. Map 78, NZ 156548 (approx)

H4 Sometimes known as the Brass Thill Drift, this was opened in 1874, and
linked to the Anna Pit by a tramway 2m long. The drift would appear to
have been closed about 1878.

Ref: "Industrial Railway Record", No.15, p.95.

Gauge: 2' 0"

-	0-4-2ST	OC	BH	258	1874	New (1)

(1) offered for sale, 8/7/1887; s/s

LLOYDS (DARLINGTON) LTD, ALBERT HILL FOUNDRY, DARLINGTON

V11 This works (Map 85, NZ 295155) was taken over from Summerson's Foundries
Ltd (q.v.) about November 1967. Rail traffic had ceased some years before,
but the loco below was still on the premises.

Gauge: 4' 8½"

-	4wVBT	VCG	S	6076	1925	(a) Scr c2/1970

(a) ex Summerson's Foundries Ltd,
c11/1967

LONDON LEAD CO, CORNISH HUSH MINE, WHITFIELD BROW, near FROSTERLEY

Y11 This lead mine (Map 84, NZ 001335) was only one of quite a number of lead
mines in the Pennines worked by this company. Cornish Hush Mine is known to
have had a locomotive, and the loco below was delivered to the London Lead
Co, so it is thought they were one and the same. The mine lay about 1m SW
of the end of the NER Bishopley Branch, and it is possible that a later
road to the mine was constructed on the trackbed of a link to the NER. The
company surrendered its leases in 1883, though it is possible that the mine
continued working in a small way till about the turn of the century.
In 1970 it was re-opened to prospect for fluorspar (see Swiss Aluminium
Mining (U.K.) Ltd)

Gauge: 1' 10"

SAMSON	0-4-0WT	OCG	Lewin	1874	New s/s

MARQUIS OF LONDONDERRY

The 3rd Marquis of Londonderry (1788-1854), one of the most powerful and
autocratic coal owners of his time, gradually built up an extensive
railway system known as the

Londonderry Railway. This divided into two sections:

Rainton & Seaham section
The earliest collieries owned by the Londonderry family were in the
Rainton area, and coal from here was taken by short waggonways to the
R.Wear at Fatfield. In 1826 this system was extended to serve Londonderry
N9 Colliery (Map 85, NZ 334443) at Pittington, and sometimes known as
Pittington Colliery. This caused such an increase in traffic that the old
method of loading coal on to keels at Fatfield and subsequent transhipment
on to colliers at Sunderland was no longer adequate or economic. So the
Marquis decided to create a man-made port on the coast at Seaham, where
the foundation stone was laid on 27th November 1828. In conjunction with
this a new railway was built to connect with the old line at Rainton
Meadows. This line was worked entirely by ropes, and was opened on 25th
July 1831, most of the earlier line to Fatfield then being abandoned.

The southern extremity of the line was Londonderry Colliery, where,
certainly in later days the winding engine at the pit also worked the
first ½m of the Railway. Next came a steep, self-acting incline down to
Pittington village. Here a branch ½m long ran southwards to Broomside
N10 Colliery (NZ 317435), opened about 1835. The Flatts Engine, situated
near the junction of the branch, worked both the branch and also the next
section of the main line as far as Pittington Bank Foot, in both cases by
a form of main-and-tail haulage. At Pittington Bank Foot the line turned
under the Durham & Sunderland Railway (later NER), and ascended an incline
to Hindmarch's Engine, or Pittington Bank Engine, as it was known later.
N8 This engine also worked the Lady Seaham Pit (NZ 325453), near the foot of
the incline, and the main line northwards as far as the level crossing on
L22 Hetton Lane. Here a branch came up from the Alexandrina Pit (or Letch Pit)
(NZ 333464), sunk in 1824; this was worked by the Robney Engine, situated
near the junction with the main line. This engine may also have worked
the short section northwards to the Durham and Sunderland turnpike road,
where a long, self-acting incline known as Benridge Bank, took the line
down to Rainton Meadows. In 1838 the Durham & Sunderland Railway was
opened to this point, and gave access to shipping places at South Shields
via the Stanhope & Tyne Railway.
In the Rainton Meadows area several branches joined the line, notably from
L21 the Adventure Pit (NZ 315471), the
L19 Meadows Pit (NZ 324481), where there were large numbers of coke ovens, and
L20 Nicholson's Pit (NZ 327484). These three pits, with the Alexandrina Pit
above and the Plain Pit below, were collectively known as Rainton Colliery.
From the branch to Nicholson's Pit a long spur went off westwards to join
the Lambton Railway (q.v.) north of the Resolution Pit, and this was later
to become important. Not far from the junction of this branch at Rainton
L18 Meadows another branch ran northwards to serve in turn the Plain (or Plane)
L17 Pit (NZ 323487), Chilton Moor Workshops (NZ 323493) and Fencehouses Iron-
works (NZ 324498), though the last was not owned by the Marquis.
From Rainton Meadows the waggons were hauled eastwards to Rainton Bridge
by the Rainton Bridge Engine, which was situated at the junction with a
L23 branch running southwards to the Dunwell Pit (NZ 338485) and the North
Hetton Coal Company's Hazard and Moorsley Pits (see Lambton, Hetton &
Joicey Collieries Ltd). From Rainton Bridge the waggons were hauled up
first to the Rainton Engine, and then on to the Copt Hill Engine, passing
under the Hetton Railway (see Hetton Coal Co Ltd) in a short tunnel (the
two engine houses only a few yards apart).
From Copt Hill to Seaton Bank Top the line was fairly level, and so it was
worked by two main-and-tail sections (Warden Law Flat and the Long Run),

worked by the Warden Law Engine near Warden Law farm. At Seaton Bank Top
the line crossed the Durham & Sunderland Railway (later the NER), and for
a considerable time there was a connection between the two. The waggons
then descended the self-acting incline known as Seaton Bank, before being
hauled up the very short Londonderry Bank to the Sunderland and Stockton
turnpike road. The engine, situated near the level crossing, also worked
the Carr House Bank descending towards Seaham. In 1845 the Hetton and
North Hetton Coal Companies opened Seaton Colliery (NZ 409496) near the
top of this incline, and the working was altered so that the engine could
draw five waggons at a time into a siding, whence they could gravitate
L33 through the screens. In 1852 the Marquis opened Seaham Colliery, about
thirty yards to the east, but how this was worked is not clear; the
Londonderry family purchased the older pit in November 1864, and combined
the two into one unit. From the foot of the Carr House Incline another
self-acting incline, the Seaham or Polka Bank, took the waggons down to
Seaham Harbour and its docks.

Several extensions were made to this system, probably after the beginning
N2 of locomotive working. In 1859 Framwellgate Moor Colliery (NZ 207445)
was purchased, and reached from Rainton Bridge via the link with the
Lambton Railway, over which it would appear the Londonderry Railway had
running powers. About this time a Londonderry locomotive was working the
South Hetton Coal Company's Pesspool branch (q.v.) to Shotton Colliery,
though whether this was on hire or under a working agreement is not known.
Also about 1860 short branches were built from Seaham Harbour to Seaham
L39 Iron Works (NZ 433488), opened in 1859-1860, and the Seaham and London-
L40 derry Bottle Works (NZ 435487), which lay adjacent to each other. The NER
N7 too built branches to Belmont Colliery, which lay only yards from the
N5 Lady Seaham Pit, and to Old Durham Colliery (Lord Ernest Pit)(NZ 292415),
both from the Durham & Sunderland line, and it seems likely that the
Marquis had running powers to both, reaching the latter via a junction
with the NER on the Broomside Colliery branch.

It has been suggested that locomotive working on the more level parts of
the Rainton & Seaham section began as early as 1845, though evidence is
lacking. A locomotive was being used on the Framwellgate-Rainton section
(about 3½m) from 1859 onwards. At this time the Rainton area was still
being worked by stationary engines, but subsequently the Rainton Bridge
Engine was dispensed with, and by 1890 two locomotives were normally kept
at Rainton to serve the Alexandrina, Adventure and Meadows Pits. By this
time too the Warden Law Engine had been replaced by a loco shed at Warden
Law for the section between Copt Hill and Seaton Bank Top. By the early
1890's the 6th Marquis was facing serious financial problems, and further
economies were introduced. In the second half of 1892 the Londonderry
Engine was closed, and locomotive working introduced between Seaton Bank
Foot and Seaham Bank Head. About six months later the Rainton Incline was
abandoned, by extending the Copt Hill Incline half way down the Rainton
Bank, and introducing locomotive working over the remainder. Thus from
1893 only the Copt Hill, Seaton and Seaham Inclines were still in use.

Seaham & Sunderland section
Despite extensions to Seaham Harbour in 1838, shipping facilities became
inadequate for all the traffic coming down the line from Rainton, and also
from the South Hetton Waggonway (see South Hetton Coal Co) and its extension to Haswell and Shotton (see Haswell, Shotton & Easington Coal & Coke
Co Ltd). So a new line was put in hand to give access to the docks at
Sunderland. This line, six miles long, was opened on 3rd August 1854, and
passenger services were begun on 2nd July 1855. It began at Seaham Station
(NZ 424494) on a link between Seaham Bank and the Swine Lodge Incline on
the South Hetton line. It then ran north-westwards through Seaham Colliery
Station (NZ 421496), before turning north-eastwards to follow the coastline
to Ryhope, where there was another station, and then on to the docks at
Hendon. The passenger trains originally terminated at the Londonderry
Hendon Burn Station, but in October 1868 working was diverted into the NER

LONDONDERRY RAILWAY
Rainton & Seaham section c.1860

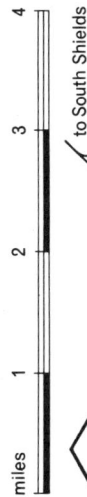

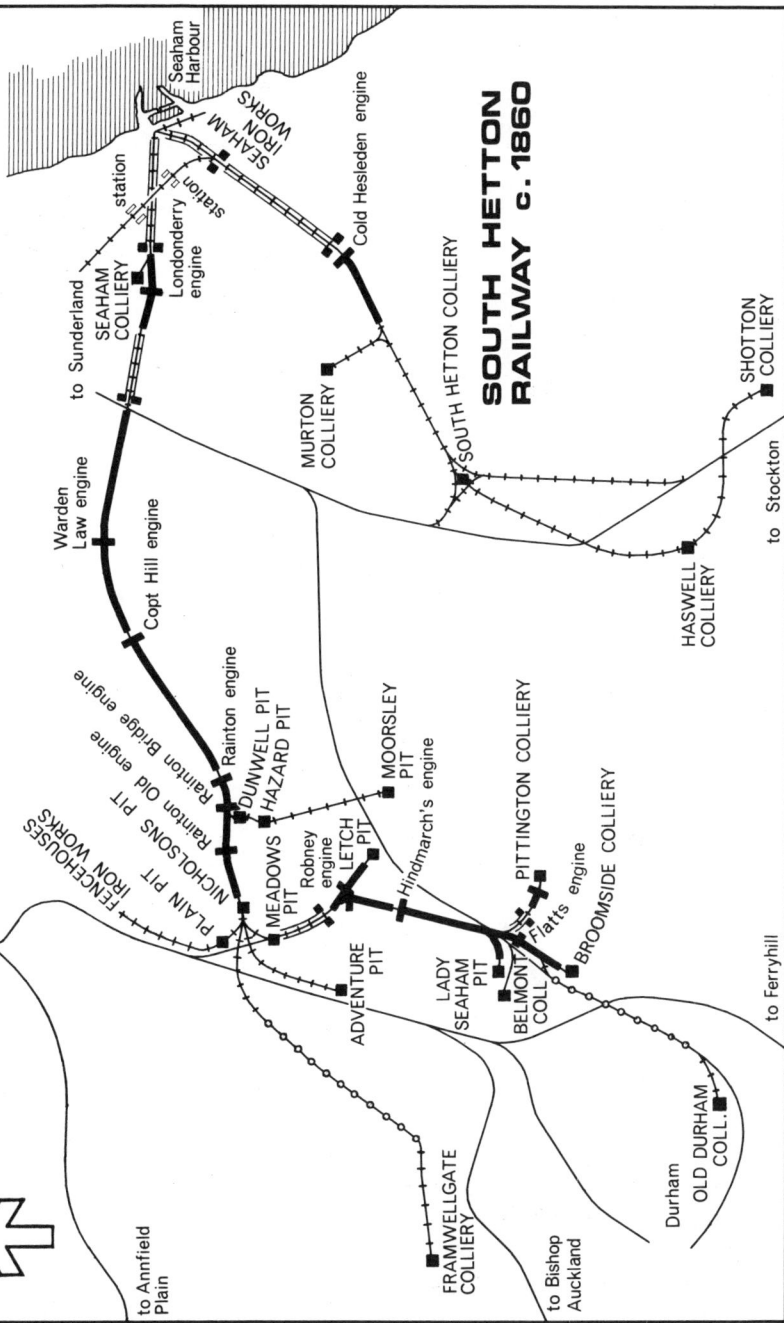

SOUTH HETTON
RAILWAY c.1860

Seaham Harbour
SEAHAM IRON WORKS
Cold Hesleden engine
Seaham station
Londonderry station
Londonderry engine
SEAHAM COLLIERY
to Sunderland
SOUTH HETTON COLLIERY
Warden Law engine
Copt Hill engine
MURTON COLLIERY
SHOTTON COLLIERY
to Stockton
HASWELL COLLIERY
Rainton engine
Rainton Bridge engine
Rainton Old engine
DUNWELL PIT
HAZARD PIT
MOORSLEY PIT
Hindmarch's engine
NICHOLSONS PIT
PLAIN PIT
FENCEHOUSES IRON WORKS
to South Shields
Robney engine
MEADOWS PIT
LETCH PIT
PITTINGTON COLLIERY
Flatts engine
BROOMSIDE COLLIERY
ADVENTURE PIT
LADY SEAHAM PIT
BELMONT COLL.
to Ferryhill
FRAMWELLGATE COLLIERY
to Anfield Plain
to Bishop Auckland
Durham
OLD DURHAM COLL.

miles
1 2 3 4

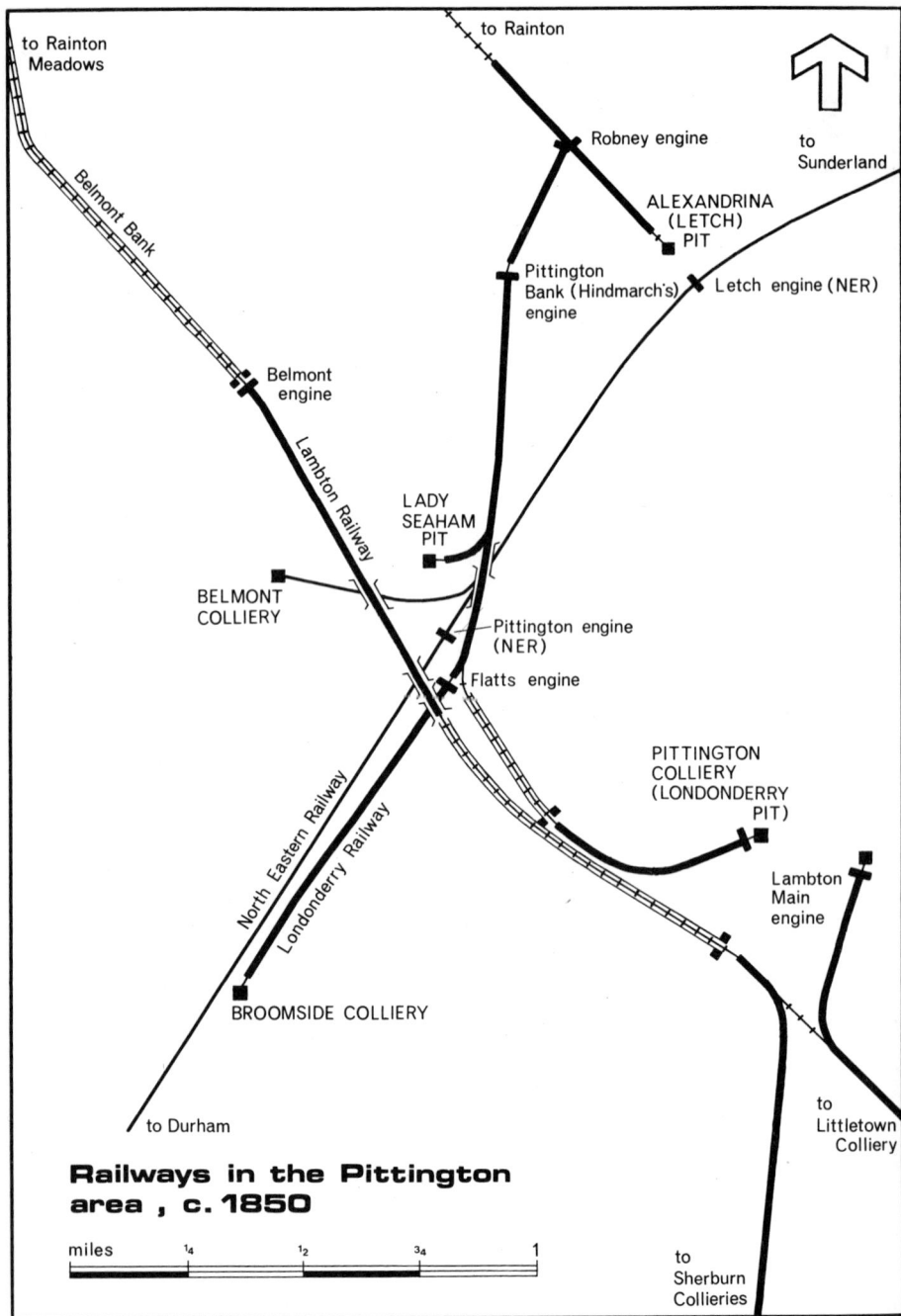

to Rainton Meadows

to Rainton

Belmont Bank

Robney engine

to Sunderland

ALEXANDRINA
(LETCH)
PIT

Pittington
Bank (Hindmarch's)
engine

Letch engine (NER)

Belmont
engine

Lambton Railway

LADY
SEAHAM
PIT

BELMONT
COLLIERY

Pittington engine
(NER)

Flatts engine

PITTINGTON
COLLIERY
(LONDONDERRY
PIT)

North Eastern Railway

Londonderry Railway

Lambton
Main
engine

BROOMSIDE COLLIERY

to Durham

to
Littletown
Colliery

**Railways in the Pittington
area , c. 1850**

miles   ¼   ½   ¾   1

to
Sherburn
Collieries

Hendon Station, and then in August 1879 into the Central Station in Sunderland. The Marquis had his own private station at Hallgarth (NZ 415504), ¼m N of Seaham Colliery Station. In 1859 a branch was opened from Ryhope to serve Ryhope Colliery (see Ryhope Coal Co Ltd), and this was extended in
K15 1871 to serve the Londonderry's new Silksworth Colliery,(NZ 377541).

In the early days the main workshops for the railway were at Chilton Moor (see above), but soon after the opening of the Sunderland line facilities began to be developed at Seaham, and in 1865-1866 quite extensive engineering and wagon shops were built adjacent to Seaham Station. The Chilton shops were closed in January 1866. For many years, however, the two sections were operated as almost seperate railways.

Old Durham Colliery closed in 1878, and in the same year Framwellgate Moor Colliery was sold to Framwellgate Coal Co (q.v.). In 1880 one of the most serious explosions in Co. Durham colliery history occurred at Seaham Colliery with 164 people killed. But it was not until the 1890's that the 6th Marquis began to encounter severe problems. Pittington Colliery, latterly owned by the North Hetton Coal Co Ltd, was closed in 1892, by which time most of the other collieries on the extremities of the system were closed. The Adventure Pit followed in March 1893, to be followed by the Alexandrina and Meadows Pits in November 1896. This meant the closure of the whole of the Rainton & Seaham section west of Seaham Colliery. The dismantling of the system was completed by the middle of December 1896, and the plant and five locomotives were to be offerred for sale from 9th-12th March 1897, though it would appear that only two locos were sold. The Adventure Pit was subsequently re-opened by the Rainton Colliery Co Ltd (q.v.) and survives to the present, while the other royalties were taken over by Lambton Collieries Ltd.

In January 1898 the Marquis decided to amalgamate the collieries, docks and railways into a limited company, but was subsequently compelled to treat the docks separately, as the extensions decided upon needed an Act of Parliament. This was obtained in July 1898, and in March 1899 the prospectus of the Seaham Harbour Dock Co Ltd (q.v.) was issued, the Marquis holding a controlling interest. Three locomotives were transferred to the new firm, but the date is uncertain. In May 1899 Londonderry Collieries Ltd was formed to take over Seaham and Silksworth Collieries and also a new sinking
L36 at Dawdon (NZ 436478), which was not destined to begin production until 1907. To serve this, and also another sinking at Easington four miles to the south, the Marquis, with the Seaham Harbour Dock Co Ltd and the Easington Coal Co Ltd, proposed to build a new branch. However, the NER, which had obtained running powers over the Sunderland section in 1894 (but apparently had never used them) was also planning to build a line from Seaham to Hartlepool, and the proposed Easington branch would appear to be designed to force the NER to purchase the Londonderry Railway. If so, it had the desired effect, for the NER rapidly came to terms, and under an Act of July 1900 amalgamation was sanctioned at a price of £400,000. The NER took possession of most of the system on 6th October 1900, and subsequently built its own branches to Seaham and Dawdon Collieries, though the private lines also continued in use. The engineering and wagon shops were not included in the sale, the former was closed in 1902 and a new loco shop for the Dock Company built in the Dock complex.

When the Duke of Wellington visited the Rainton area as a guest of the 3rd Marquis in 1827 he inspected a locomotive, but both its identity and ownership are disputed.

Ref: G. Hardy   "The Londonderry Railway". Goose, 1973.

Gauge: 4' 8½"

	FRANCIS ANNE	0-4-0	OC	RS	753	1849	(a)	s/s
1		0-6-0	IC	BH	34	1868	New	(1)
No.2	(CHEAPSIDE)	0-4-2	IC	Haigh		1841	(b)	
		reb. Seaham				1860		(2)
2		2-4-0T	IC	Seaham		1889	New	(1)
3		0-6-0	IC	TR	254	1855	New	
		reb. 0-6-0ST	IC	Seaham		1876		(3)
4		0-6-0	IC	RWH	479	1846	(c)	
		reb. 0-6-0ST	IC	Seaham		1885		(4)
No.5	SEFTON	0-4-2	OC	Tayleur	320?	1848	(d)	Scr /1858
5		0-6-0	IC	RWH			(e)	(5)
5		0-6-0	IC	Seaham		1885	New	(1)
6	CARADOC	0-6-0					(f)	(6)
6		0-4-0ST	OC	Harris		1868	New	
		reb. 0-6-0ST	IC	Seaham		1883		(4)
7		0-6-0	IC	RS	1073	1856	New	(7)
8		0-6-0	IC	RS	1075	1856	New	
		reb. 2-4-0T	IC	Seaham		1879		(1)
9		0-6-0	IC	RS	1096	1856	New	
		reb. 2-4-0T	IC	Seaham		1880		(1)
10		0-6-0	IC	RS	1217	1859	New	(1)
-		4-4-0	OC	RS	1206	1860	(g)	(8)
11		0-6-0	IC	RS	1326	1860	New	(1)
12		0-6-0	IC	RS	1327	1860	New	
		reb. 0-6-0ST	IC	Seaham		1877		(1)
-		0-6-0	OC	F&H			(h)	(9)
13		0-6-0	IC	RS	1416	1862	New	(1)
14		0-6-0	IC	RS	1417	1862	New	(1)
15		0-6-0	IC	Blair		1868	(j)	
		reb. Seaham				1887		(1)
16		0-4-0VBT	VC	HW	21	1870	New	(3)
17		0-4-0VBT	OC	HW	33	1873	New	
		reb. Seaham						(3)
18		0-4-0WT	OC	Lewin		c1875	New	(3)
19		0-4-0ST	OC	BH	203	1871	(k)	(10)
20		0-6-0	IC	Seaham		1892	New	(1)
21		0-4-4T	IC	Seaham		1895	New	(1)
-		0-4-4T	IC	Seaham			(m)	(11)

(a) ex Forster & Lawton, contrs for Sunderland section, c/1854
(b) ex L &YR, 139, 5/1854; orig. L &YR 35
(c) ex NBR, 32, /1855
(d) ex J.Blundell, dealer, 9/1855; orig. Lancashire, Crosby & Southport Rly, who sold loco in 1/1850
(e) origin unknown
(f) ex NER, c/1855; prev. York, Newcastle & Berwick Rly; possibly TR 182
(g) loco ordered for Turkey, but loaned by RS until delivery of RS 1326 and 1327
(h) ex ?, /1861
(j) origin doubtful; may be New
(k) ex John Bowes & Partners Ltd, Felling Colliery, /1890
(m) under construction when NER took over in 10/1900

(1) to NER, 6/10/1900
(2) s/s; some parts may have been used in new 2
(3) to Seaham Harbour Dock Co Ltd, /1899
(4) to ?; probably sold in 3/1897
(5) s/s; some parts may have been used in new 5
(6) to John Harris, Darlington, /1868, in part payment for new 6
(7) apparently being rebuilt as 0-6-0ST when NER took over in 10/1900; not included in sale, and apparently sold to Sir B.Samuelson & Co Ltd, Newport Works, Middlesbrough, Yorks, N.R.,c/1901
(8) ret. to RS
(9) scrapped, and parts used to drive the sawmill at Seaham by /1873
(10) to Rainton Colliery Co Ltd
(11) to Seaham Harbour Dock Co Ltd, /1901

LONDONDERRY COLLIERIES LTD

This was registered on 31st May 1899 to take over the collieries of the Marquis of Londonderry (q.v.). The railways to the collieries appear to have remained under the Londonderry Railway until the NER took over in October 1900, after which the NER worked Silksworth Colliery traffic, while the Seaham Harbour Dock Co Ltd handled traffic from Seaham Colliery. Gradually, however, the colliery firm purchased locomotives for shunting purposes.

Locomotives were kept at:

Dawdon Colliery, Dawdon. Map 85, NZ 436478.

L36 This colliery commenced sinking in 1899, and came into production in 1907. It was served by a short branch from Seaham Harbour (¼m), and also by a short loop from the NER Seaham-West Hartlepool line.

New Seaham (or Seaham) Colliery, Seaham Harbour. Map 85, NZ 413496.

L33 This was owned by the Marquis of Londonderry until 31st May 1899, and was linked to Seaham Harbour Docks by a self-acting incline (Seaham Bank - ¼m). It was also served by a NER branch (½m) from Seaham (formerly Seaham Colliery) Station, the two branches running alongside each other for most of their length.

Vane Tempest Colliery, near Seaham Harbour. Map 78, NZ 425503.

L32 This colliery was opened in 1928, and was served by a branch (½m) from LNER Sunderland-Seaham line, ½m N of Seaham Station.

All three collieries were vested in NCB Northern Division No.2 Area on 1st January 1947.

There were numerous transfers between these three collieries, which have not been recorded.

Gauge: 4' 8½"

SEAHAM	0-4-0ST	OC	HL	2701	1907	New	✗	(1)
DAWDON No.2	0-4-0ST	OC	HL	3492	1921	New	✗	(1)
LONDONDERRY	0-4-0ST	OC	AB	1724	1922	New	@	(1)
CASTLEREAGH	0-4-0ST	OC	AB	1885	1926	New	ø	(1)
VANE TEMPEST	0-6-0ST	OC	RS	4112	1935	New	ø	(1)
STEWART	0-4-0ST	OC	AB	2160	1943	New	@	(1)
WYNYARD	0-4-0ST	OC	AB	2165	1944	New	✗	(1)

✗ At Dawdon Colliery, 1/1/1947
@ At Seaham Colliery, 1/1/1947
ø At Vane Tempest Colliery, 1/1/1947

(1) to NCB No.2 Area, 1/1/1947

Seaham Wagon Works, Dawdon. Map 85, NZ 427491.

L35 Considerable doubt surrounds the background to these works. From 1866 the waggon shops for the Londonderry Railway lay adjacent to Seaham Station, and it is believed these continued in use until the Railway was taken over by the NER in 1900, after which they were closed. On the other hand, the oldest part of the Dawdon works' buildings were almost certainly built well back into the nineteenth century, and were designed for repairing "black waggons", which were used in the docks and on the Rainton & Seaham section of the Railway. Nor is the picture much clearer after 1900. The Dawdon works would appear to have been owned by Londonderry Collieries, but certainly many wagons from the Seaham Harbour Dock Co Ltd were also repaired here.

After the opening of the NER Seaham-West Hartlepool line in 1905, the works was served by sidings W of the line, ½m S of Seaham Station. It was shunted by horses until the arrival of the loco below, and was vested into NCB Northern Division No.2 Area on 1st January 1947.

Gauge: 4' 8½"

-	4wPM	MH	L116	1939	New	(1)

(1) to NCB No.2 Area, 1/1/1947

K15 Silksworth Colliery, Silksworth. Map 78, NZ 377541.

This colliery was owned by the Marquis of Londonderry until 31st May 1899, and was served by a branch of the Londonderry Railway 2¼m long from Ryhope, until that was taken over by the NER in October 1900. The loco below is believed to have worked only at the colliery, though running powers existed down to Ryhope. The colliery was sold to Lambton & Hetton Collieries Ltd in 1920, probably on 1st February.

Gauge: 4' 8½"

| No.1 | SILKSWORTH | 0-6-0ST | IC | HL | 2932 | 1912 | New | (1) |

(1) to Lambton & Hetton Collieries
Ltd, 1/2/1920 (?)

The firm also purchased the following underground locomotive for Vane Tempest Colliery :

Gauge: 2' 0"

| - | 4wBE | Atlas | 2456 | 1946 | New | (1) |

(1) to NCB No.2 Area, 1/1/1947

LOW BEECHBURN COAL CO LTD, LOW BEECHBURN COLLIERY, near CROOK (reg. 16/10/1889)

Q8 Some uncertainty exists regarding the location of this colliery. One version gives it as the later name of Thistleflat Colliery (Map 85, NZ 162347), which was served by sidings E of LNER Crook-Bishop Auckland line, ¼m S of Crook Station. Another version, however, gives the name to a shaft about a mile south on the same line, ¼m N of Beechburn Station. No other loco is known before the one below. The colliery was closed in January 1925, and sold to F.Hindley of Manchester in October 1930, but it was not re-opened, and was subsequently dismantled.

Gauge: 4' 8½"

| - | 0-4-0ST | OC | P | 644 | 1896 | (a) | s/s |

(a) ex Earl of Bradford's Collieries,
Great Lever, Lancs, via Cudworth
& Johnson, contrs, c/1923

MAWSON, CLARK & CO LTD, DUNSTON

B6 This works (Map 78, NZ 222628) manufactured grease and candles, and was served by sidings S of BR Redheugh Branch. It was shunted as required by a loco from Dunston G.S. from 1953 until its closure about 1955.

Gauge: 4' 8½"

| - | 0-4-0ST | OC | AB | 730 | 1893 | (a) | (1) |
| FRED | 0-6-0ST | OC | HE | 580 | 1893 | (b) | (2) |

(a) ex Hurst, Nelson & Co Ltd,
Motherwell, Lanarkshire
(b) ex A.J.Keeble (either from
Finedon, Northants, or Wissington, Norfolk) by 12/1916

(1) to TWW; re-sold to Gas, Light &
Coke Co Ltd, Beckton By-Products
Works, Essex, /1921
(2) sold for scrap, /1953

MID-DURHAM CARBONISATION CO LTD, STELLA GILL COKE WORKS, PELTON FELL
(Stella Gill Coke & Bye-Products Co Ltd until 3/10/1928)

H51 Coke works and bye-products plant (Map 78, NZ 260522) opened shortly after
the First World War, and served by sidings S of LNER Pontop & Shields
branch, ½m S of South Pelaw Junction. It was vested in NCB Nortnern
Division No.5 Area on 1st January 1947

It is believed that the company hired a loco from the Bank Foot, Waldridge,
loco shed of Charlaw & Sacriston Collieries Co Ltd (q.v.) when tne
Hawtnorn Leslie loco was out of commission and before the arrival of the
second loco.

Gauge: 4' 8½"

STELLA No.1	0-4-0ST	OC	HL	3504	1923	New	(1)
-	0-4-0ST	OC	P	1460	1916	(a)	(2)

(a) ex Washington Coal Co Ltd,   (1) to NCB No.5 Area, 1/1/1947
    Usworth Colliery   (2) ret. to Usworth Colliery

MINISTRY OF DEFENCE, ARMY DEPARTMENT
(form. War Department)

Royal Ordnance Factory, Birtley. Map 78, NZ 265564

H19 Formerly MOM and later a Royal Ordnance Factory (both q.v.). It is served
by sidings E of BR Newcastle-Durham line, ½m N of the former Birtley
Station.

Gauge: 4' 8½"

-		0-4-0DM	JF	22137	1937	(a)	(1)
-		0-4-0DM	AB	352	1941	(b)	(2)
853		0-4-0DM	JF	22976	1942	(c)	(3)
123	A7	0-4-0DM	DC/Bg	2157	1941	(d)	

(a) ex ROF   (1) to Bicester Workshops, Oxford-
(b) ex Puriton Ordnance Depot,   shire
    Somerset   (2) to North Eastern Iron Refining
(c) ex Bicester Workshops, Oxford-   Co Ltd, Stillington, 2/1962
    shire, c/1962   (3) to J.A.Lister & Sons Ltd,
(d) ex Bicester Workshops, Oxford-   Consett, for scrap, 12/1970
    shire, 12/1969

Burnhill Storage Depot, near Salter's Gate. Map 84, NZ 073433.
(form. Ministry of Public Building & Works; prev. Ministry of Works;
orig. MOS)

X3 Originally a war-time depot, and served by sidings E of LNER/BR line from
Consett to Tow Law, 1¼m S of Burnhill Junction, but latterly at the
northern end of the line. It was closed in March 1969.

Gauge: 2' 0"

-		4wDM	HE	2842	1942	New	(1)
-		4wDM	HE	2843	1942	New	s/s
-		4wDM	HE	2844	1942	New	(1)
(758079) ARMY No.20		4wDM	RH	211641	1942	(a)	(2)
(758115) ARMY No.23		4wDM	RH	226278	1944	(a)	(2)

(a) ex WD, East Riggs Depot,   (1) to WD, Bicester Workshops,
    Dumfriesshire, 2/1966   Oxfordshire, /1961
                                         (2) to East Riggs Depot, Dumfries-
                                             shire, /1970

MINISTRY OF DEFENCE, NAVY DEPARTMENT
(form. Admiralty)

Royal Navy Spare Parts Distribution Centre, Eaglescliffe. Map 85, NZ 410150

W9 Depot built on the site of works operated by Morris Motors Ltd for MOS during Second World War, and served by sidings N of BR Stockton-Darlington line, 1m W of Eaglescliffe Junction.

Gauge: 4' 8½"

	-	0-4-OST	OC	P	2048	1943	(a)	(1)
	-	4wDM		RH	224352	1945	(b)	(2)
No.1	YARD No.115	0-4-ODM		JF	22945	1941	(c)	(3)
No.2	YARD No.114	0-4-ODM		JF	22938	1941	(c)	(3)
YARD No.WD 6692/YARD No.736								
		0-4-ODM		RH	375717	1955	(d)	
EARL LEOFRIC OF MERCIA/		0-4-ODM		DC	2167	1942		
RISLEY YARD No.106 MED				VF	4859	1942	(e)	

(a) ex Morris Motors Ltd
(b) ex Rosyth Dockyard, Fifeshire, /1951
(c) ex Risley Depot, Lancs
(d) ex Ditton Priors Depot, Shropshire
(e) ex Risley Depot, Lancs, c/1970

(1) to Risley Depot, Lancs, c/1951
(2) to Rosyth Dockyard, Fifeshire
(3) to T.Ottewel & Co, Dewsbury, Yorkshire, W.R., for scrap c5/1967

MINISTRY OF MINES, COAL DISPOSAL POINT, SEATON CAREW

S13 A depot (Map 85, NZ 520270 approx) operated during the Second World War, and served by sidings at the end of the LNER Seaton Snook Branch.

Gauge: 4' 8½"

No.1	RISLEY	0-6-OST	IC	HC	1606	1929	(a)	(1)
200 (form. 108)	JEANETTE	0-6-OST	IC	HC	1699	1938	(a)	(1)
	NILE	0-6-OST	OC	AB	1770	1921	(b)	(2)

(a) ex SLP
(b) ex Pauling

(1) to SLP
(2) to Pauling by 1947

MINISTRY OF MUNITIONS (existed from 5/1915 to 3/1921)

National Projectile Factory, Birtley. Map 78, NZ 265564.

H19 This works was begun in August 1915 and commenced production in July 1916, being operated by the Belgian Government with Belgian workmen. Adjacent to it was a Cartridge Case Factory operated by Sir W.G.Armstrong, Whitworth & Co Ltd, who had constructed both factories for MOM. This large complex was served by sidings E of NER Newcastle-Durham line, ½m N of Birtley Station. After the War the complex became a Royal Ordnance Factory (q.v.).

Gauge: 4' 8½"

-	0-4-OST	OC	AE	1054	1874	(a)	s/s
-	0-4-OST	OC	AE	1055	1874		
	reb.	Sdn		1892	(b)	(1)	

(a) ex Powlesland & Mason, contrs, Swansea, Glamorgan, c/1915 orig. GWR 1331/2177
(b) ex Powlesland & Mason, contrs, Swansea, Glamorgan, c/1915 orig. GWR 1332/2178

(1) to ?, Billingham, by 1921

National Projectile Factory, Darlington.   Map 85, NZ 290160.
(National Shell Factory until 1/6/1918)

V5   This factory was built by Sir W.G.Armstrong, Whitworth & Co Ltd for MOM in
the summer of 1915 in part of the NER North Road Locomotive Works. It was
operated by the NER as sub-contractors to Armstrong Whitworth until 1st
July 1916 when it passed to the direct control of MOM, though still
managed by the NER. It was closed in 1919, the site being re-incorporated
into the main works.

Gauge: 4' 8½"

No.64		0-4-0ST	OC	AB	733	1893	(a)	(1)
	BEXHILL	0-6-0ST	IC	MW	1365	1898	(b)	(2)

(a) ex Hall, Richards & Co   (1) to Wake, /1919
(b) ex S.Pearson & Son Ltd, contrs   (2) to Wake, /1919; later to James
                                          Smith, Hamworthy, Dorset

MORRIS MOTORS LTD,   NUFFIELD WORKS,   EAGLESCLIFFE

W8   This was a metal produce recovery plant operated for the Air Ministry
during the Second World War. The factory (Map 85, NZ 410150) was served by
sidings N of LNER Stockton-Darlington line, 1m W of Eaglescliffe Junction.
It was closed after the War, and later taken over by the Admiralty (see
MODND).

Gauge: 4' 8½"

-	0-4-0ST	OC	P	2046	1943	New	(1)
-	0-4-0ST	OC	P	2047	1943	New	(2)
-	0-4-0ST	OC	P	2048	1944	New	(3)
-	0-4-0ST	OC	P	2049	1944	New	(2)
-	0-6-0T	OC	Davenport				
				2505	1943	(a)	(4)

(a) ex United States Army, WD 1940,   (1) to Cowley Works, Oxford
    6/1947   (2) to Cowley Works, Oxford, /1948
                                      (3) to Admiralty (with factory)
                                      (4) to Austin Motor Co Ltd, Birming-
                                          ham, per Abelson, 10/1949

NATIONAL COAL BOARD   -   see page 223

NATIONAL SHIPBUILDING SECURITIES LTD, EGIS SHIPYARD, PALLION, SUNDERLAND

K17 This yard (Map 78, NZ 373580) was opened in 1917 on the site of Thomas
Walter Oswald's Pallion yard (see also Doxford and Sunderland Ltd) under
the title of Egis Shipyard Ltd, the name being taken from the initial
letters of the four partners in the firm. It was taken over by William
Gray & Co (1918) Ltd on 1st January 1919, but later sold to the firm above.
It was closed from 1925 to 1927, and closed for good about 1932. The site
was later taken over by Steel & Co Ltd (see British Crane & Excavator
Corporation Ltd).

Gauge: 4' 8½"

-	0-4-0ST	OC	KS	3126	1918	New	(1)

                                 (1) to William Gray & Co Ltd,
                                     West Hartlepool, 3/1932

NESHAM FAMILY, NEWBOTTLE WAGGONWAY

This waggonway ran from collieries in the Newbottle area to the R.Wear at Sunderland. It was purchased in 1819 by J.G.Lambton, and later part was incorporated in the Earl of Durham's Railway (see Lambton, Hetton & Joicey Collieries Ltd).

Gauge: 4' 0" (?)

-	0-4-0	✗	1813	New s/s

✗ This loco was built by William Brunton at the Butterly Ironworks, Derbyshire. It had a single horizontal cylinder actuating a pair of legs (a "walking loco"). It was tested here on 31st July 1815, but the trial ended prematurely when the boiler exploded.

N.B. Most accounts wrongly refer to the trial as being on "The Earl of Durham's Railway".

NEW BRANCEPETH COLLIERY CO LTD, NEW BRANCEPETH COLLIERY & COKE WORKS, NEW BRANCEPETH

(orig. New Brancepeth Colliery Co; the firm was a subsidiary of Cochrane & Co Ltd until 12/1933, and thereafter a subsidiary of Weardale Steel, Coal & Coke Co Ltd)

M11 The colliery (Map 85, NZ, 222421) was opened in the 1850's, and was served by sidings S of NER Waterhouses Branch, ¼m W of Ushaw Moor Station. The colliery locos also shunted the coke works. It was vested in NCB Northern Division No.5 Area on 1st January 1947.

Gauge: 4' 8½"

	DESPATCH	0-4-0ST	OC	RWH	1019	1857	(a)	s/s
	COOMASSIE	0-4-0ST	OC	RWH	1635	1873	(a)	(1)
	-	0-4-0ST	OC	HL	2358	1896	(a)	(2)
	POWERFUL	0-6-0ST	OC	MW	1602	1903	(b)	(3)
	THE ALLY	0-6-0ST	OC	HL	3185	1916	(a)	(3)
4		0-6-0ST	OC	Joicey	210	1869		
				reb.Thornley	1924			
				reb.Thornley	1931		(c)	(3)
18		0-6-0ST	OC	RWH	1622	1874	(d)	(4)

(a) ex Cochrane & Co Ltd, Middles-brough, Yorks, N.R.
(b) ex Cochrane & Co Ltd, Middles-brough, Yorks, N.R., /1923
(c) ex Weardale Steel, Coal & Coke Co Ltd, Thornley Colliery
(d) ex Weardale Steel, Coal & Coke Co Ltd, Thornley Colliery, loan

(1) to Ammonia-Soda Co Ltd, Plumley Cheshire
(2) to Brunner, Mond & Co Ltd, Midd-lewich, Cheshire, per HL, 12/1916
(3) to NCB No.5 Area, 1/1/1947
(4) ret. to Weardale Steel, Coal & Coke Co Ltd, Thornley Colliery

New Brancepeth Coke Ovens

The colliery had quite a number of beehive coke ovens, and the locos below were introduced to shunt the tubs used to charge the ovens from the top. The beehives were replaced by new bye-product ovens and ceased production in October 1910, and the locos became redundant.

Gauge: 3' 0"

-	0-4-0TG	OC	JF	5661	1888	New	s/s
-	0-4-0TG	OC	JF	5883	1889	New	s/s

NEW BUTTERKNOWLE MARSFIELD COLLIERIES LTD
(New Butterknowle Colliery Co Ltd until 1910; prev. Butterknowle Colliery
Co Ltd (reg. 23/10/1885)

This company and its predecessors owned a number of small collieries on
the south-western corner of the coalfield:

Marsfield Colliery and Coke Ovens, Butterknowle. Map 84, NZ 105256.

T6 This colliery appears to have been opened in the latter half of the
nineteenth century. It was closed in 1910, together with its coke ovens.

New Butterknowle Colliery, Butterknowle. Map 84, NZ 111254.

T7 This colliery was open by 1870, and was closed about the First World War.

Quarry Drift, near Copley. Map 84, NZ 098246.

T8 This was a small drift, opened about 1900 and closed in 1910.

All three places were served by a system extending from the end of the NER
Haggerleazes Branch. New Butterknowle Colliery lay about 200 yards W of
the end of the NER line. The colliery line went on for about another 200
yards before dividing, one arm running SW for a mile to Quarry Drift
(possibly a rope-worked incline), and the other running NW for ½m to
Marsfield Colliery. The loco shed was at New Butterknowle Colliery.
The firm is also said to have owned Copley and Shotley Collieries, but the
location of these is uncertain. They do not appear to have been part of
the system above, and there is no record of whether they had their own
locomotives.

Gauge: 4' 8½"

COPLEY	0-4-0ST	OC				(a)	s/s
BUTTERKNOWLE	0-4-0ST	OC	HCR	107	1871	New	(1)
SHOTLEY	0-4-0ST	OC	BH	264	1873	New	s/s

(a) origin unknown   (1) offered for sale, 21/7/1910; s/s

Gauge: 3' 0" (line ran from Marsfield washery to the coke ovens)

FIREFLY	0-4-0T	OC	BH	252	1873	New	(1)

(1) to Lanark County Water Board,
Lanarkshire, /1910

NEWALLS INSULATION CO LTD
(Newall's Insulation & Chemical Co Ltd until 1/6/1971; Washington Chemical
Co Ltd until 1/10/1964; subsidiary of Turner & Newall Ltd from 12/2/1920)

Barnsdon Brickworks, Washington
This brickworks was part of the Washington complex (see below). The loco
below was usually used here, but was also found elsewhere on occasion.

Ref: "Industrial Railway Record", Vol.2, No.13

Gauge: 4' 8½"

No.2	0-4-0BE	HL	3584	1924ƒ	(a)	(1)

ƒ plate carried 1939

(a) ex RSH, Newcastle, 3/1939; built   (1) to J.Greenwood, Bishop Auckland,
for Wembley Exhibition, 1924   1/1966

Ford Quarry, South Hylton, Sunderland. Map 78, NZ 362572.

K2 A limestone quarry, served by sidings S of BR Sunderland-Durham line ½m NE
of South Hylton Station. The internal railway system was abandoned about
1965.

Gauge: 2' 0"

No.2		4wDM	HE	2982	1943	New	(1)
No.1		4wDM	HE	3098	1944	(a)	(1)

(a) ex MOS

(1) to R.Dunn, Bishop Auckland, 2/1967

Washington Works. Map 78, NZ 324557.

J6 A large industrial complex, served by sidings and branch (½m) just south of Washington Station on BR line from Pelaw to Penshaw. Rail traffic ceased in 1971.

Gauge: 4' 8½"

	–	0-4-0ST	OC	JF	1572	1872	New	s/s
	–	0-4-0ST	OC	FW	375	1878	New	s/s
	–	0-4-0ST	OC	HL	2247	1892	New	(1)
	SYLVIA	0-4-0ST	OC	HL	2645	1906	New	(2)
No.2		0-4-0ST	OC	HL	2780	1909	New	(3)
No.1	(form. No.3)	0-4-0ST	OC	HL	3349	1918	New	Scr 3/1967
No.2		0-4-0ST	OC	RSH	7068	1943	New	Scr 3/1967
No.3		0-4-0ST	OC	RSH	7117	1943	New	Scr 3/1967
	MURIEL	0-4-0DH		EE(V)	D1123	1966	New	(4)
	MARGARET	0-4-0DH		EE(V)	D1126	1966	New	(5)

(1) to PP, Bishop Middleham Quarry (c/1909?)
(2) to Trafford Park Works, Lancs, /1924
(3) to Trafford Park Works, Lancs, /1933
(4) to British Sugar Corporation, Wissington Works, Norfolk, 1/1970
(5) to Andrew Barclay, Sons & Co Ltd, Kilmarnock, Ayrshire, 4/1972

Gauge: 2' 0"

–		4wDM	MR	8747	1942	New	Scr c8/1967
–		4wDM	MR	40s273	1966	New	(1)

(1) to R.Dunn, Barnard Castle, 7/1972

NORTH BITCHBURN COAL CO LTD
(North Beechburn Coal Co Ltd until 14/2/1903; from about July 1927 the firm was a subsidiary of Pease & Partners Ltd, and went into voluntary liquidation on 15th July 1932, its holdings being divided among other Pease & Partners' subsidiaries)

Gordon House Colliery, Cockfield. Map 85, NZ 131249.

T9 This colliery was served by sidings S of NER Haggerleazes Branch, 2½m W of Spring Gardens Junction. It closed in August 1930, though it may have re-opened for a short time in 1932-1933.

Gauge: 4' 8½"

CARBON	0-4-0ST	OC	Grange Iron Wks	1866	(a)	(1)

May have had other locos unrecorded.

(a) ex ?

(1) to Randolph Colliery, /1931

<u>North Bitchburn Colliery & Brickworks</u>, near Howden-le-Wear
Map 85, NZ 166324.

Q10 Served by sidings E of NER Crook-Bishop Auckland line, ½m S of Beechburn
Station. The colliery and works were taken over by North Bitchburn
Fireclay Co Ltd (q.v.) on 5th May 1934.

Gauge: 4' 8½"

JESMOND	0-6-0T					(a)	(1)
CROSSFIELD	0-4-0T	OC	FJ	112	1873	(b)	(2)
—	0-4-0ST	OC	P	677	1897	(c)	(3)
HUSTLER	0-4-0ST	OC	P	1337	1913	New	(4)

(a) ex ?
(b) ex Carnforth Haematite Iron Co
    Ltd, Lancs, /1894
(c) ex North Lincs Iron Co Ltd,
    Scunthorpe, Lincs, /1911

(1) to North Bitchburn Fireclay Co
    Ltd, 5/5/1934
(2) to Rough Lea Colliery by /1926,
    and ret; to North Bitchburn
    Fireclay Co Ltd, 5/5/1934
(3) to Henry Stobart & Co Ltd,
    Thrislington Colliery, c/1932
(4) to Randolph Colliery, /1932

<u>Randolph Colliery</u>, Evenwood. Map 85, NZ 157249.
(orig. Pease & Partners Ltd)

T10 Served by a branch (1m) from NER Haggerleazes Branch, ¼m W of Spring
Gardens Junction. An incline worked by a stationary engine took wagons
down to the main line. The colliery passed to Randolph Coal Co Ltd in
January 1933.

Gauge: 4' 8½"

MOSTYN	0-4-0ST	OC	LG		1906	New⟋	(1)
CARBON	0-4-0ST	OC	Grange Iron Wks		1866	(a)	(1)
HUSTLER	0-4-0ST	OC	P	1337	1913	(b)	(1)

⟋ probably a rebuild by LG of an older loco
    built by another firm

There may have been other locos unrecorded.

(a) ex Gordon House Colliery, /1931 (1) to Randolph Coal Co Ltd, 1/1933
(b) ex North Bitchburn Colliery,
    /1932

<u>Rough Lea Colliery & Brickworks</u>, Hunwick. Map 85, NZ 194331.

Q17 This colliery was served by sidings W of NER Durham-Bishop Auckland line,
½m N of Hunwick Station. The colliery was closed in April 1926, but was
later re-opened by Henry Stobart & Co Ltd (q.v.).

It is uncertain which locos were here, but the colliery is believed to
have had the following:

Gauge: 4' 8½"

ARROW	0-4-0ST	OC	MW	498	1874	(a)	s/s after 2/1895
LILY	0-4-0ST	OC	MW	540	1875	(b)	(1)
ARROW	0-4-0ST	OC	BH	991	1890	(c)	s/s
THE COLONEL	0-4-0ST	OC	HG	251	1867	(d)	(2)
—	0-4-0T	OC	FJ	112	1873	(e)	(3)

(a) ex Casebourne & Co Ltd, Haverton Hill (now in Teesside)

(a) ex Casebourne & Co Ltd, Haverton
    Hill (now in Teesside)
(b) ex Rotherham, Masboro' & Holmes
    Coal Co, Yorks, W.R.
(c) ex North Eastern Steel Co Ltd,
    Middlesbrough, Yorks, N.R.
(d) ex Henry Stobart & Co Ltd,
    Newton Cap Colliery, /1924
(e) ex North Bitchburn Colliery by
    /1926

(1) to Wilson's Forge Ltd, Bishop
    Auckland, c/1930 (?)
(2) to Henry Stobart & Co Ltd,
    with colliery
(3) ret. to North Bitchburn Colliery

<u>Thrislington Colliery</u>, West Cornforth. Map 85, NZ 309338.
(Thrislington Coal Co Ltd until 1914; see also Rosedale & Ferryhill Iron
Co Ltd)

R26 This colliery had been opened in 1867, and was originally served by a
branch (½m) from Ferryhill Iron Works Junction on the NER Wingate-Ferryhill
line at West Cornforth Station. This link was subsequently abandoned in
favour of a new link to the NER Durham-Darlington line, ¼m N of Ferryhill
Station. This was an incline down to the main line worked by a stationary
engine. The colliery was taken over by Henry Stobart & Co Ltd in 1932.

Gauge: 4' 8½"

	ISABELLA	0-4-0ST	OC	BH	976	1889	New	s/s c/1930
	SIRDAR	0-4-0ST	OC	CF	1187	1899	New	s/s c/1930
9	-	0-4-0ST	OC	HL	2247	1892	(a)	(1)
8		0-4-0ST	OC	AB	1085	1907	(b)	(1)
		0-4-0ST	OC	HL	2798	1909	(c)	(1)

(a) ex PP, Bishop Middleham Quarry,
    in 1920's
(b) ex PP, Chilton Colliery, /1929
(c) ex PP, St Helen's Colliery,
    /1930

(1) to Henry Stobart & Co Ltd,
    15/7/1932

<u>NORTH BITCHBURN FIRECLAY CO LTD</u>

This company was formed on 5th May 1934 as a subsidiary of Pease & Partners
Ltd (q.v.) to take over the brickmaking activities of the group. It ceased
to be a PP subsidiary sometime after 1947, but in December 1962 it became
a subsidiary of Hepworth Iron Co Ltd, Sheffield, Yorks, W.R.

<u>Newton Cap Colliery & Brickworks</u>, near Bishop Auckland. Map 85, NZ 213308.
(Henry Stobart & Co Ltd until c4/1937)

T21 This colliery had been closed for some years before it was finally taken
over from Henry Stobart & Co Ltd (q.v.), and re-opened about April 1937.
It was served by a branch (¼m) from BR Durham-Bishop Auckland line, 1¼m N
of Bishop Auckland Station. The colliery became a licensed mine on 1st
January 1947, and was closed in 1967. The brickworks continues, without
rail transport.

Gauge: 4' 8½"

(COMET)	0-4-0ST	OC	MW	467	1873		
				reb. LG		(a)	Scr /1950
SAMSON	0-4-0DM		JF	4000013	1947	New	(1)
CONSTANTINE ⨯	0-4-0DM		JF	4110001	1949	New	(2)
BALLARAT ⨯	0-4-0DM		JF	4110002	1949	New	Scr /1964

⨯ it is possible that these names were reversed at some period

(a) ex Henry Stobart & Co Ltd,
    c4/1937

(1) to Rough Lea Colliery by 5/1951
(2) to North Bitchburn Colliery

North Bitchburn Colliery & Brickworks, near Howden-le-Wear. Map 85, NZ 166324.
(North Bitchburn Coal Co Ltd until 5/5/1934 - q.v.)

Q10 Served by sidings E of BR Crook-Bishop Auckland line, ½m S of Beechburn Station. The colliery became a licensed mine on 1st January 1947, and was closed in 1966. The brickworks continues, without rail transport.

Gauge: 4' 8½"

JESMOND	0-6-0T						(a)	(1)
-	0-4-0T	OC	FJ	112	1873		(a)	s/s c/1942
DAVID	0-4-0ST	OC	RSH	6940	1938		New	(1)
SAMSON	0-4-0DM		JF	4000013	1947		(b)	Scr /1968
CONSTANTINE	0-4-0DM		JF	4110001	1949		(c)	(2)

(a) ex North Bitchburn Coal Co Ltd, 5/5/1934
(b) ex Rough Lea Colliery
(c) ex Newton Cap Colliery

(1) to Rough Lea Colliery
(2) to John Brown (Land Boilers) Ltd, Dunbarton, c/1965

Rough Lea Colliery & Brickworks, Hunwick. Map 85, NZ 194331.
(Henry Stobart & Co Ltd until 5/5/1934 - q.v.)

Q17 Served by sidings W of BR Durham-Bishop Auckland line, ½m N of Hunwick Station. The colliery was subsequently closed, and the brickworks ceased to use rail transport about 1954.

Gauge: 4' 8½"

THE COLONEL	0-4-0ST	OC	HG	251	1867	(a)	s/s
GRETA	0-4-0ST	OC	HL	2139	1889	(b)	Scr c/1950
JESMOND	0-6-0T					(c)	Scr c/1940
DAVID	0-4-0ST	OC	RSH	6940	1938	(d)	(1)
SAMSON	0-4-0DM		JF	4000013	1947	(d)	(2)

(a) ex Henry Stobart & Co Ltd, 5/5/1934
(b) ex Cochrane & Co Ltd, Middlesbrough, Yorks, N.R., via Cohen, /1936
(c) ex North Bitchburn Colliery
(d) ex Newton Cap Colliery by 5/1951

(1) to NCB No.5 Area, Stella Gill Coke Ovens, 4/1954
(2) to North Bitchburn Colliery

NORTH BRANCEPETH COAL CO LTD, LITTLEBURN COLLIERY, MEADOWFIELD
(North Brancepeth Coal Co until 2/7/1890)

N4 This colliery (Map 85, NZ 255395) was opened in 1870, and was served by sidings W of NER Durham-Darlington line, 2¾m S of Durham Station. The colliery closed in August 1931, and the company went into liquidation, but about two months later working was re-commenced by Bearpark Coal & Coke Co Ltd (q.v.).

Gauge: 4' 8½"

-	0-6-0T	IC	JF	1541	1871	New	s/s ✦
-	0-4-0ST	OC	JF	2079	1874	New	s/s
WHITWELL	0-4-0ST	OC	BH	1096	1895	New	s/s
-	0-4-0ST	OC	KS	4143	1919	New	(1)

✦ A.R.Bennett's "Chronicles of Boulton's Siding" records that this loco was driving electric light plant at Brancepeth Colliery in 1924, but Brancepeth Colliery (owned by Strakers & Love - q.v.) would seem to be an error; probably the loco was still at Littleburn.

(1) to Bearpark Coal & Coke Co Ltd, c10/1931

NORTH EASTERN IRON REFINING CO LTD, STILLINGTON

W1 Works (Map 85, NZ 373237) was developed on the site of the former Carlton
Ironworks of Dorman, Long & Co Ltd (q.v.), and is served by sidings N of
BR Ferryhill-Stockton line, adjacent to the former Stillington Station.

Gauge: 4' 8½"

-	4wDM		RH	187071	1937	New	(1)
2	4wDM		RH	279593	1949	New	(1)
No.3	0-4-0DM		AB	352	1941	(a)	
-	4wDM		RH	312427	1951	(b)	

(a) ex WD, Birtley Ordnance Factory,
    2/1962
(b) ex Head, Wrightson & Co Ltd,
    Eaglescliffe (now in Teesside),
    9/1967

(1) to M.Henderson Clark Ltd,
    Thornaby, Yorks, N.R., 11/1968

NORTH EASTERN TRADING ESTATES LTD
Aycliffe Trading Estate, Aycliffe. Map 85, NZ 2723.

U2 This estate was developed on the site of ROF Aycliffe, and was served by
sidings from the BR Bishop Auckland-Darlington line at Heighington Station.
The shunting was contracted to BR from about 1963.

Gauge: 4' 8½"

ROF 9 No.7	0-4-0ST	OC	P	2016	1941	(a)	(1)
-	0-4-0ST	OC	P	2042	1943	(a)	(2)
-	4wDM		HE	1737	1935	(b)	(3)

(a) ex ROF Aycliffe
(b) ex Eldon Brickworks Ltd,
    Bishop Auckland

(1) to Team Valley Trading Estate,
    Gateshead, 8/1963
(2) to Team Valley Trading Estate,
    Gateshead, 8/1949
(3) to J.A.Lister & Sons Ltd,
    Consett, for scrap, c/1963

Team Valley Trading Estate, Gateshead. Map 78, NZ 2459 and 2460.

C12 This estate was opened in September 1937, and was served by sidings W of
BR Newcastle-Durham line, 3m S of Newcastle. The shunting was contracted
to BR in June 1966.

Gauge: 4' 8½"

No.1	0-6-0ST	OC	HL	3934	1937	New	Scr 11/1963
-	0-4-0ST	OC	P	2042	1943	(a)	Scr 1/1964
ROF 9 No.7	0-4-0ST	OC	P	2016	1941	(b)	(1)

(a) ex Aycliffe Trading Estate,
    8/1949
(b) ex Aycliffe Trading Estate,
    8/1963

(1) hired by NCB N&D No.5 Area to
    shunt Shop Pit section of Pelaw
    Main branch of Bowes Railway,
    8/1964-5/1966; Scr 6/1966

NORTHERN GAS BOARD (incorporated into British Gas Corporation 1/1/1973 - q.v.)

Darlington Gas Works, Darlington. Map 85, NZ 292154.
(Darlington Corporation until 1/5/1949)

V15 This works was served by sidings ½m S of North Road Station on BR Bishop
Auckland-Darlington line. Loco working ceased in 1965.

Gauge: 4' 8½"

```
TOM BARRON          0-4-0ST  OC  AB    1287  1914  New  Scr  /1951
-                   4wDM         RH  305320  1951  New  (1)
NORTHERN GAS BOARD
No.1                0-4-0ST  OC  P     2142  1953  (a)  (2)
```

(a) ex Thompson Street Gas Works,   (1) to Thompson Street Gas Works,
    Stockton, c9/1964   Stockton, /1964
                                     (2) to St.Anthony's Tar Works,
                                         Walker, Newcastle, /1965

Hendon Gas Works, Sunderland. Map 78, NZ 408555.

K13 Works served by sidings W of BR branch to Sunderland South Dock. It was
    closed in March 1969, and demolished by Golightly (Developments) Ltd in
    1970-1971.

Gauge: 4' 8½"

```
    A.M.No. 187     4wDM         RH  198325  1940  (a)  (1)
```

(a) ex Charles Jones (Aldridge) Ltd, (1) to Howden Gas Works, Willington
    Staffs, dealer, /1958; prev.   Quay, Northumberland, for reps,
    Air Ministry, Broadheath,   by 8/1959, and ret; to Golightly
    Cheshire   (Developments) Ltd, 12/1970; re-
                                          sold to Doxford and Sunderland
                                          Ltd, Wolsingham Works, 5/1972

Middleton Road Gas Works, West Hartlepool. Map 85, NZ 510334.
(Hartlepool Gas & Water Co Ltd until 1/5/1949)

S5 Works served by sidings E of BR Seaham-West Hartlepool line, ½m N of West
   Hartlepool Station. Rail traffic ceased about 1962.

Gauge: 4' 8½"

```
    HURWORTH        0-4-0ST  OC  BH     306  1873  New
                                 reb. Ridley          Scr  /1947
    -               4wDM         RH  235512  1945  New  (1)
```

                                     (1) to Thompson Street Gas Works,
                                         Stockton, /1962

Redheugh Gas Works, Gateshead. Map 78, NZ 237625.
(Newcastle-upon-Tyne & Gateshead Gas Co Ltd until 1/5/1949)

C1 Works opened in October 1876, and served by sidings S of BR Redheugh
   Branch. The coal carbonisation plant was closed in March 1967, but locomotive working was retained until 1972 to handle fuel oil and purification
   materials.

Gauge: 4' 8½"

```
    ALDERMAN HEDLEY   0-4-0ST  OC  BH    324  1874  New  s/s c/1900
    W.B.WILKINSON     0-4-0ST  OC  BH   1025  1891  New
                                     reb.HL      1902       (1)
    L.W.ADAMSON       0-4-0ST  OC  HL   2387  1897  New  Scr  /1938
    SIR W.H.
    STEPHENSON        0-4-0ST  OC  HL   2514  1901  New  (2)
    JAMES W.ELLIS     0-4-0ST  OC  HL   3573  1923  New  Scr  9/1963
    LT.COLONEL W.H.
    RITSON            0-4-0ST  OC  HL   3576  1923  (a)  (3)
    SIR CECIL A.
    COCHRANE          0-4-0ST  OC  RSH  7409  1948  New  (4)
    -                 0-4-0DM      RSH  7869  1956  (b)  (5)
    -                 0-4-0DM      RSH  7899  1958  New  (6)
    -                 4wDM         RH  476140  1963  New  (7)
```

```
        (a) ex Elswick Gas Works,          (1) to Elswick Gas Works, Newcastle,
            Newcastle, c/1947                   and ret; Scr 1/1952
        (b) ex RSH, hire, 8/1956           (2) to Elswick Gas Works, Newcastle,
                                               and ret; Scr 4/1957
                                           (3) to Elswick Gas Works, Newcastle,
                                               c/1948
                                           (4) to Hawthorn Locomotive Preservat-
                                               ion Group, NCB Backworth Sheds,
                                               Northumberland, for preservation,
                                               5/1971
                                           (5) ret to RSH,  /1958
                                           (6) to Elswick Gas Works, Newcastle,
                                               6/1964
                                           (7) to British Gas Corporation,
                                               1/1/1973
```

NORTHERN STONE FIRMS, SPRINGWELL QUARRIES, SPRINGWELL, near GATESHEAD

These workings for limestone date well back into the nineteenth century,
and were linked to the Blackham's Hill East Incline of the Pontop & Jarrow
Railway (see John Bowes & Partners Ltd) by a short branch near the bottom
F8 of the incline. The main quarry, (Map 78, NZ 284587) which lay to the south
of the P & JR, was latterly worked by a stationary engine, but in 1906 this
was replaced by a locomotive. This was found to be unsuitable, and horses
were substituted. The quarries continue to the present, without any rail
connection and under different ownership.

Gauge: 4' 8½"

```
No.9   DORIS          0-4-0ST  OC  MW   1150  1891  (a)  s/s c/1909
```

(a) ex Joseph Perrin & Co Ltd,
    Birkenhead, Cheshire, c10/1906

ORD & MADDISON LTD

Bishopley Quarries, near Frosterley

Y5 The main quarry in this group was <u>Bishopley Quarry</u> (Map 84, NZ 026363),
which was taken over from NER about 1875, and was served by sidings N of
NER Bishopley Branch, ½m from Bishopley Junction. East of it was <u>North
Y6 Bishopley Quarry</u>, (NZ 029365), also taken over about 1875, and which was
linked to its larger neighbour by a rope-worked incline operated by a
stationary engine. It was also linked from about 1875 to 1914 by a short
branch (½m) to Frosterley Station. About 1880 the firm began a new quarry
Y3 to the west of Bishopley Quarry. This was called <u>Brown's House</u> or <u>South
Bishopley Quarry</u>, and was served by an extension of the branch to Bishopley Quarry.
At least two or three locomotives are believed to have been used on this
system at any one time, but no details are known.
It is believed that all three quarries closed in March 1920. They were
taken over in the same year by Pease & Partners Ltd (q.v.).

<u>Lanehead Quarry</u>, Stanhope. Map 84, NY 990403.

Z16 This huge limestone quarry was acquired from the Wear Valley Railway in the
1850's. It was served by sidings W of the foot of the Crawleyside Incline
of the Wear Valley (later NER) Stanhope & Tyne Branch. The quarry was
exhausted about 1890, and the firm concentrated on Ashes Quarry, further to
the east. It is virtually certain that locomotives were used within the
quarry, but no details survive.

ORIGINAL HARTLEPOOL COLLIERIES CO LTD

The history of Thornley Colliery and the area around it is exceptionally complicated, and not fully known, the version below being that which the authors dislike least.

P8 Thornley Colliery (Map 85, NZ 365395) was opened in January 1835 by the Thornley Coal Co, and served by the Thornley branch of the Hartlepool Dock & Railway Co. A privately-owned extension of this line (2¼m) continued to collieries in the Cassop area (q.v.). About 1840 the
P7 Thornley Coal Co also opened Ludworth Colliery (NZ 363415), and linked it to the Thornley branch by a private line 1¼m long; how this line was worked is uncertain. By the late 1850's the two collieries, with Trimdon Colliery (NZ 378359)(also worked by what was now the NER), were owned by T.Wood, Burrell, Gurney & Co (who may still have been using the title Thornley Coal Co). In 1865 this firm disposed of Thornley and Ludworth Collieries, apparently to London Steam Collier & Coal Co Ltd (also recorded as London Steam Collieries Co), although these owners are not listed until 1866. About 1867 this firm began a new sinking at Wheatley
P9 Hill (NZ 385393), which was served by a 1m loop from the Thornley branch, and opened in 1869. By 1870 the three collieries had passed to Original Hartlepool Collieries Co Ltd.
In 1875 much of the surface of Thornley Colliery was destroyed in a fire, and the firm went bankrupt in 1877, all three collieries being offered for sale in May 1877. However, mining records continue to give the firm as the owners, so it was presumably they who (again) went bankrupt in April 1884. In 1885 the collieries were taken over by Weardale Iron & Coal Co Ltd (q.v.), but remained closed for some time: Thornley did not re-open until about May 1888.

Gauge: 4' 8½"

QUEEN	0-6-0ST	OC	BH	31	1867	New	(1)
PRINCESS	0-4-0ST	OC	MW	466	1873	New	(1)
ALBERT	0-4-0ST	OC	MW	492	1874	New	(1)

N.B. After the bankruptcy of 1884 the Thornley manager negotiated the sale of a loco to the NER, but the men tore up the track to prevent it leaving the colliery. As there is no trace of this in the NER records this arrangement was presumably rescinded.

(1) to Weardale Iron & Coal Co Ltd, /1885

THOMAS WALTER OSWALD, (also given as OSWALD & CO)

The history of this man is among the most involved in the county. In 1859 he took over Pallion High Yard in Sunderland from his father. In 1861 he went bankrupt, but he started again shortly afterwards. He also had a shipbuilding yard at North Dock, Sunderland, for a time. In 1870 he
K3 erected rolling mills at Castletown (NZ 366583), and also had a yard at South Dock. But in 1872 the mills were closed, and in 1875 he went bankrupt for a second time. He moved to Southampton, where he is believed to have failed yet again, after which he went to Milford Haven.
He is known to have owned at least three locomotives, which are listed in the "Engineer" of May 1877. This issue describes the sale of "Pallion Ironworks", but as Oswald is not known to have owned a works there, this is presumably an error for the Castletown works. Oswald's works were sold up in 1877, but the mills re-opened in 1881 under Wear Rolling Mills Co (q.v.). Later still the site became Hylton Colliery (see Wearmouth Coal Co Ltd). The Pallion shipyard was later merged into William Doxford & Sons (q.v.).

Gauge: 4' 8½"

WEAR	0-4-0ST	OC	HCR	101	1870	New	(1)
HYLTON	0-4-0ST	OC	BH	120	1871	New	(1)
PALLION	0-4-0ST	OC	BH	174	1871	New	(2)

(1) offered for sale, 5/1877; s/s
(2) offered for sale, 5/1877; to
C.D. Phillips, dealer, Newport,
Monmouthshire; to Griff Colliery
Co, Warwickshire, /1882

OWNERS OF PELTON COLLIERY LTD, PELTON COLLIERY, PELTON FELL
(Lord Dunsany & Partners until 6/1901; Owners of Pelton Colliery until
c/1881)

H52 This colliery (Map 78, NZ 255517) was served by sidings at the foot of the
Waldridge Incline on the NER Pontop & Shields branch. The colliery was
abandoned in April 1928, and the effects sold in October 1928, only to be
re-opened in 1929 by another firm, with the LNER working the traffic.

Gauge: 4' 8½"

No.1	0-4-0WT	OC	FJ	125	1874	New	(1)
PELTON	0-4-0ST	OC	HL	2073	1886	New	s/s

Two locomotives, details unknown, were offered for sale, 2/10/1928; s/s.

(1) to John Bowes & Partners Ltd,
Pontop & Jarrow Railway,
c/1890 (?)

OWNERS OF REDHEUGH COLLIERY, REDHEUGH COLLIERY, GATESHEAD

C3 This colliery was opened about 1872 (Map 78, NZ 244626), and was served
by sidings W of NER Newcastle-Durham line, ½m N of Bensham Station.
Normally the colliery was shunted by the NER, but the loco below is
believed to have worked here for a short time. The colliery was closed
in 1924.

Gauge: 4' 8½"

WYE	0-4-0ST	OC	MW	1037	1887	(a)	(1)

(a) ex C.Chambers, contr, c/1891,   (1) to Wallsend Slipway & Engineering
who had formerly used it on the   Co Ltd, Wallsend, Northumberland
Golden Valley Railway   (?), (c/1895?)

PAGE BANK BRICK CO LTD, PAGE BANK BRICKWORKS, PAGE BANK

Q14 This brickworks (Map 85, NZ 228354) was acquired from Hartley Main
Collieries Ltd (q.v.) about 1935. It had no main line rail connection,
and was closed in 1940 because of the wartime blackout restrictions.
The locos lay derelict for many years before being scrapped.

Gauge: 2' 8½"

-	4wPM		FH	1782	1931	(a)	Scr c/1963
-	4wPM		FH	1892	1934	(a)	Scr c/1963

(a) ex Hartley Main Collieries Ltd,
c/1935

PALMERS SHIPBUILDING & IRON CO LTD,   STEELWORKS & SHIPYARD,   JARROW
(Jarrow Iron Co until 21/7/1865)

E16 This shipyard (Map 78, NZ 318657 to 330657) ranks among the most famous in
the world. Begun by George and Charles Mark Palmer in 1852, it grew stead-
ily until it occupied ½m of river frontage and employed 7,000 men. It was
its boast that it took raw materials in and turned ships out without any-
thing leaving the site. It was served by sidings N of NER Gateshead-South
Shields line, ¼m W of Jarrow Station, and it also had a link to the Pontop
& Jarrow Railway of John Bowes & Partners Ltd. The firm fell victim to the
Depression, being taken over by National Shipbuilding Securities Ltd and
closed in June 1933.

Gauge: 4' 8½"

-		0-4-0ST	OC	HCR	32	1864	New	s/s
-		0-4-0T		RS	1619	1865	New	s/s
-		0-4-0T		RS	1801	1866	New	s/s
No. 5		0-4-0ST	OC	BH	62	1868	New	s/s
No. 6		0-4-0ST	OC	BH	128	1869	New	s/s
No. 7		0-4-0ST	OC	BH	216	1871	New	s/s
No. 8		0-4-0ST	OC	BH	176	1871	New	s/s
No. 9		0-4-0ST	OC	BH	315	1874	New	s/s
No.10		0-4-0ST	OC	BH	476	1879	New	s/s
	MIDGE	0-4-0ST	OC	BH	231	1872	(a)	s/s
	SLAVE	0-4-0CT/WT	OC	RWH	1877	1880	(b)	s/s
No. 4 (?)		0-4-0ST	OC	RWH	2026	1885	New	(1)
No.11 (?)		2-2-2CT	IC	HL	2113	1888	New	s/s
No.12		0-4-0ST	OC	HL	2135	1889	New	s/s
1		0-4-0ST	OC	HL	2169	1889	New	s/s
No.13		0-4-0ST	OC	HL	2666	1906	New	(2)
No.14		0-4-0ST	OC	HL	2667	1906	New	(2)
No.15		0-4-0ST	OC	P	1392	1915	New	(1)
No.16		0-4-0ST	OC	P	1413	1915	New	(1)
No.17		0-4-0ST	OC	HL	3237	1917	New	(3)
-		0-4-0ST	OC	KS	3097	1918	New	s/s after 12/1928
No.20		0-4-0ST	OC	KS	4029	1919	New	(1)
	HECTOR	0-4-0CT	OC	HL	2447	1900	(c)	s/s
	TEAM VALLEY	0-4-0ST	OC	HL	2489	1901	(a)	s/s
	FLOSSIE	0-4-0ST	OC	⚡			(d)	s/s

          ⚡ believed to have been either VF or WB

(a) ex T.D.Ridley, contr.   (1) to TWW, /1934
(b) ex W. Denny Bros, Dumbarton,   (2) to Palmers Hebburn Co Ltd, via
    /1885   TWW, /1934
(c) ex Hebburn Shipyard   (3) to Darlington Rolling Mills Co
(d) ex ?, contr.   Ltd, per TWW, after repair at
                                             HL, /1934

Gauge: 3' 0"

CHARGER	0-4-0ST	OC	WB	1381	1891	New	s/s

TWW used KING GEORGE 0-6-0ST IC HC 1040/1913 when dismantling the parts
of the site not taken over by other firms in 1937.

Hebburn Shipyard, Hebburn. Map 78, NZ 306653.
(Robert Stephenson & Co Ltd until 5/6/1912).

E7   This yard was served by a branch (¼m) from LNER Gateshead-South Shields
line, ½m E of Hebburn Station. It survived the collapse of 1933, to be
taken over by a new company, Palmers Hebburn Co Ltd (see Vickers Ltd) in
1934.

Gauge: 4' 8½"

COMET	0-4-0ST	OC	RS	2326	1888	New	s/s
EGBERT	0-4-0CT	OC	HL	2173	1890	New	(1)
HECTOR	0-4-0CT	OC	HL	2447	1900	New	(2)

Almost certainly there were other transfers between the Jarrow and Hebburn
yards after 1912, but details are unknown.

(1) to RS, Darlington
(2) to Jarrow Yard

PATONS & BALDWINS LTD, DARLINGTON

V16 Large woollen mill (Map 85, NZ 305153) on the north-east outskirts of
Darlington, and latterly at end of mineral line (1¼m) from BR Haughton
Lane Junction. Rail traffic ceased in 1973.

Gauge: 4' 8½"

PATONS	0-4-0F	OC	WB	2898	1948	New	
-	0-4-0D		RSH			(a)	(1)

(a) ex RSH, Darlington, hire, while   (1) ret. to RSH, Darlington, /1959
    WB at RSH for repairs, /1959

PEASE & PARTNERS LTD.
(formed on 19/8/1882 by an amalgamation of Joseph Pease & Partners, which
had previously operated the colliery interests of the Pease family, and
J.W.Pease & Co, whose main interests were in steel production)

The Pease family of Darlington built up one of the largest industrial
empires of the nineteenth century, with interests in collieries, coke
ovens, quarries, ironworks, brickworks, railways and other industrial
concerns in both Co. Durham and the North Riding of Yorkshire. Originally
these seem to have been run by different members of the family. Later
Pease & Partners became the centre of the empire, being responsible for
the collieries and quarries, while the other activities were controlled
by subsidiary companies, or by the personal holding of shares, e.g., in
North Eastern Railway. In the middle 1920's the empire fell on hard
times, and its activities were re-organised and shared among its subsidiaries. Today neither the firm or any of its empire remains.

The company is known to have carried out two separate numbering schemes
for its locomotives, the first about the turn of the century, and the
second about 1920. Complete details do not survive for either of these,
and very little is known about locomotive allocations, especially in
Weardale. There were undoubtably both more locomotives and more movements
than listed below, but the fragments here seem to be all that have been
recorded.

Q5 Bank Foot Coke Ovens, Crook. Map 85, NZ 158364.
Crook was the centre of the colliery empire. These ovens, which were
among the most famous and extensive in the country, were so called because
they were situated at the foot of the huge Sunniside Incline (eventually
NER) on the line from Tow Law to Crook. Locomotives from the shed here
also worked the adjacent Roddymoor Colliery (NZ 156365), sunk in 1844, and
latterly (probably) the "Pease's West Collieries" - West Emma (1846), West
Lucy (1849) and West Edward (1849), which seem later to have been absorbed
into the huge Roddymoor complex. The Ovens, together with Roddymoor
Colliery, were vested in NCB Northern Division No.5 Area on 1st January
1947.

Gauge: 4' 8½"

–		0-4-0ST	OC	JF	2078	1874	New	s/s
No.35		0-4-0T	OC	HL	2774	1909	New	Scr c/1920
14 (form. No.45)		0-4-0ST	OC	P	1467	1917	New	(1)
11 (form. No.32)		0-4-0T	OC	HL	2685	1906	(a)	(1)
13 (form. No.42)		0-4-0ST	OC	HL	2823	1910	(b)	(2)
No.10	CAROLINE	0-4-0ST	OC	BH	998	1891	(c)	Scr c/1939
12	PATRICIA	0-4-0ST	OC	HL	2993	1913	(d)	(1)

(a) ex Bowden Close Colliery
(b) ex Bowden Close Colliery
(c) ex Ushaw Moor Colliery
(d) ex Tees Ironworks, Cargo Fleet,
    Yorks, N.R.

(1) to NCB No.5 Area, 1/1/1947
(2) to Henry Stobart & Co Ltd,
    Thrislington Colliery, 9/1945

Gauge: 3' 0"

–	0-4-0BE	J.Booth		New	(1)

(1) to NCB No.5 Area, 1/1/1947

This loco was used to operate the coking car on the later ovens. It worked on a gantry, and when the ovens closed and the gantry was removed, the loco was marooned in its shed, and remained thus to be taken over by the NCB.

Gauge: 3' 0"

These locos worked on top of the ovens, but the first is believed to have worked on a different battery from the others. The latter were later replaced by conveyor belts.

–		0-4-0ST	OC	JF	5822	1888	New	s/s by 4/1901
15	(MIRIAM)	0-4-0ST	OC	⚹ reb. LG		c1900	(a)	(1)
–		0-4-0ST	OC	⚹ reb. LG		c1900	(a)	Scr /1935
–		0-4-0ST	OC	⚹ reb. LG		c1900	(a)	Scr
–		0-4-0ST	OC	⚹ reb. LG		c1900	(a)	Scr

  ⚹ These locos were MW 97/1863, 98/1863, 113/1864
    and BH 447/1878, acquired by LG from BV about 1900

(a) ex LG by 4/1901   (1) to NCB No.5 Area, 1/1/1947 (OOU)

Bishop Middleham Quarry, Bishop Middleham. Map 85, NZ 333320 (approx)

R28 A long, elongated limestone quarry, probably opened in the 1890's and closed in the 1930's, and served by a branch (1¼m) from LNER Ferryhill-Stockton line, just south of Chilton Branch Junction.

Gauge: 4' 8½"

No.6	0-4-0ST	OC	RS	2325	1894	New	(1)
No.16	0-4-0ST	OC	HL	2453	1900	New	(2)
20 (form. No.33)	0-4-0ST	OC	HL	2713	1907	New	(3)
9 (form. No.38)	0-4-0ST	OC	HL	2247	1892	(a)	(4)
10 (form. No.25)	0-4-0ST	OC	HL	2559	1903	(b)	(5)

(a) ex Washington Chemical Co Ltd,
    c/1909
(b) ex Bowden Close Colliery

(1) to Bowden Close Colliery
(2) to Chilton Limeworks
(3) to Henry Stobart & Co Ltd,
    Fishburn Colliery
(4) to North Bitchburn Coal Co Ltd,
    Thrislington Colliery, in 1920's
(5) to Henry Stobart & Co Ltd,

<u>Bowden Close Colliery</u>, Helmington Row. Map 85, NZ 184360

Q12 This colliery was sunk in 1845. It was served by a branch (¼m) from the West Durham Railway (later NER) at Sunny Brow, though from 1891 this branch was altered to join the NER line from Durham to Bishop Auckland, ¼m S of Willington Station. Probably at the same time the stationary engine which had hitherto worked the branch was replaced by locomotives. The colliery closed in June 1930.

Gauge: 4' 8½"

No.25		0-4-0ST	OC	HL	2559	1903	New	(1)
No.32		0-4-0T	OC	HL	2685	1906	New	(2)
No. 6		0-4-0ST	OC	RS	2325	1894	(a)	(3)
No.42		0-4-0ST	OC	HL	2823	1910	(b)	(4)
No.43		0-6-0T	OC	HL	3104	1915	New	(5)
26	HAREHOPE	0-4-0ST	OC	HL	2799	1909	(c)	(6)

(a) ex Bishop Middleham Quarry
(b) ex Thorne Colliery, Moorends, Yorks, W.R.
(c) ex Harehope Quarry, /1931

(1) to Bishop Middleham Quarry
(2) to Bank Foot Coke Ovens, Crook
(3) to Ushaw Moor Colliery
(4) to Bank Foot Coke Ovens, Crook
(5) to Henry Stobart & Co Ltd, Fishburn Colliery
(6) to Rogerley Quarry, Frosterley

<u>Broadwood Quarry</u>, Frosterley. Map 84, NZ 033366 (approx)

Y7 A large limestone quarry, served by a branch (¼m) 1m E of Frosterley Station on NER Wearhead Branch. The quarry closed about 1923, but was re-opened in 1926 by Witton Park Slag Co Ltd (q.v.)

Gauge: 4' 8½"

	EGYPT	0-6-0T	IC	JF	1539	1871	New	s/s

May have had other locomotives, unknown.

<u>Chilton Colliery</u>, Chilton Buildings. Map 85, NZ 278308

R13 This colliery was taken over in 1924 from the PP subsidiary company, Henry Stobart & Co Ltd (q.v.). It was served by a branch (1m) from NER Chilton Branch. It was closed in May 1930, but re-opened in July 1934 by Dorman, Long & Co Ltd (q.v.).

Gauge: 4' 8½"

WINDLESTONE	0-4-0ST	OC	AB	1085	1907	(a)	(1)
CHILTON No.3	0-6-0ST	IC	P	1219	1910	(a)	(2)

(a) ex Henry Stobart & Co Ltd, /1924

(1) to North Bitchburn Coal Co Ltd, Thrislington Colliery, /1929
(2) to Thorne Colliery, Moorends, Yorks, W.R.

<u>Chilton Limeworks & Quarry</u>, Chilton, near Ferryhill Station. Map 85, NZ 302315.

R11 This was quite a small limestone quarry on the site of Little Chilton Colliery (closed in 1865), served by a branch (½m) from LNER Durham-Darlington line, ¼m S of Ferryhill Station. It was sold to F.W.Dobson & Co Ltd (q.v.) about 1945.

Gauge: 4' 8½"

25	(form. No.22)	0-4-0ST	OC	HL	2456	1900	New	(1)	
17	GEORGE	0-4-0ST	OC	K	1705	1871			
				reb. J.Tait					
					90	1920	(a)	(2)	
24	(form. No.16)	0-4-0ST	OC	HL	2453	1900	(b)	(3)	

(a) ex Tees Ironworks, Cargo Fleet,
    Yorks, N.R.
(b) ex Bishop Middleham Quarry

(1) to Henry Stobart & Co Ltd,
    Fishburn Colliery
(2) to Tees Ironworks, Cargo Fleet,
    Yorks, N.R.
(3) to F.W.Dobson & Co Ltd, c/1945

Eldon Colliery, Shildon. Map 85, NZ 239280.
(South Durham Coal Co Ltd until 1903)

T25 This colliery appears to date from 1864 in its later form, and was served
by a branch (1m) ½m N of Shildon Tunnel on NER line from Bishop Auckland
to Shildon. The colliery was closed in July 1932, and dismantled in 1933-
1934 by TWW, who used 0-4-0ST OC AE 1631/1912 on the work. The adjacent
brickworks passed to Eldon Brickworks Ltd (q.v.).

Gauge: 4' 8½"

	ELDON	0-6-0ST	IC	MW	926	1884	New	s/s after 2/1916	
18	(form.No.3)	0-4-0ST	OC	HL	2185	1890	New	s/s	
	ELDON No.2	0-6-0ST	IC	MW	1566	1902	New	(1)	
	ELDON No.3	0-6-0ST	OC	P	1092	1906	New	(2)	
6	(form. No.34)	0-4-0ST	OC	AB	1085	1907	New	(3)	
	ELDON No.1	0-4-0ST	OC	Ridley	74	1920	New	(4)	
	RAKIE	0-4-0ST	OC	P	583	1894	(a)	(5)	

(a) ex Skinningrove Iron Co Ltd,
    Carlin How, Yorks, N.R., loan,
    /1924

(1) to Thorne Colliery, Moorends,
    Yorks, W.R., /1932
(2) to St. Helen's Colliery, c/1930
(3) to Henry Stobart & Co Ltd,
    Fishburn Colliery
(4) to TWW, /1932
(5) ret. to Skinningrove Iron Co Ltd,
    Carlin How, Yorks, N.R., /1925

Fineburn Quarry, near Frosterley. Map 84, NZ 010349 (approx)

Y9 This quarry was closed about 1896 by J.Walton & Co (q.v.) and re-opened by
PP in June 1910. It was situated at the end of the Bishopley Branch (see
below), about 3m from Bishopley Junction. When it was re-opened it is
believed to have had its own locomotive, but later it was worked by a loco
from the shed at Harehope Quarry (q.v.). It closed in 1925.

Frosterley Quarry, Frosterley. Map 84, NZ 032371.
(Rippon family until c/1875)

Y2 This quarry was begun in the late 1850's, and was served by a branch (½m)
N of NER Wearhead Branch, ½m E of Frosterley Station. The quarry was
closed in 1921. It is known to have had at least one locomotive at a time,
and the one below may have been one of them.

Gauge: 4' 8½"

No.26	FROSTERLEY	0-4-0ST	OC	HL	2563	1903	New	(1)	

(1) to Rogerley Quarry (c/1921 ?)

<u>Harehope Quarry</u>, near Frosterley. Map 84, NZ 038364.
(Harehope Gill Mining & Quarrying Co Ltd until 1915).

Y8 This quarry was begun in 1901, and was also worked for gannister until 1921. It was served by a branch (¼m) from the Bishopley Branch near Bishopley Junction. The quarry was closed in 1931. It is known to have had a number of locomotives, but the only one which seems certain is that given below.

Gauge: 4' 8½"

| 26(form.No.40) | HAREHOPE | 0-4-0ST | OC | HL | 2799 | 1909 | (a) | (1) |

(a) ex ?, c/1915 (?)   (1) to Bowden Close Colliery, /1931

Locomotives from Harehope Quarry also worked a number of other quarries served by the Bishopley Branch, viz:
Y5   <u>Bishopley Quarry</u> (NZ 026363)
Y3   <u>Brown's House or South Bishopley Quarry</u> (NZ 021360)
Y6   <u>North Bishopley Quarry</u> (NZ 029365)
Y9   <u>Fineburn Quarry</u> (NZ 010349) - see above
The first three were acquired from Ord & Maddison in 1920. Rail access was obtained by sidings into Bishopley Quarry, ½m from Bishopley Junction. South Bishopley was linked by an extension of this line, and North Bishopley by a rope-worked incline operated by a stationary engine. All four quarries ceased production in 1925, though North Bishopley (1938) and Harehope (1954) were later re-opened by other firms, without rail transport. All five quarries were served by the Bishopley Branch. This ran SW for 3m from Bishopley Junction, 1¼m E of Frosterley Station on LNER Wearhead Branch. Only the first 1¼m were owned by the LNER, the remainder always being privately owned, latterly by PP. In 1920 PP were granted full running powers over the whole of the branch, presumably so that locomotives from Harehope Quarry could also work traffic from the four quarries above.

<u>Lucy Pit</u>, Billy Row, near Crook.
This colliery was part of the "Pease's West Collieries" complex (see Bank Foot Coke Ovens, above), but the locomotives below are said to have worked here.

Gauge: 4' 8½"

| 1 | LOCOMOTION | 0-4-0 | VC | RS | 3 | 1825 | (a) | (1) |
| 25 | DERWENT | 0-6-0 | OC | Kitching | | 1845 | (b) | (2) |

(a) ex Stockton & Darlington Railway, /1850; used as a pumping engine
(b) ex NER, c/1869; orig. Stockton & Darlington Railway, 25

(1) ret. to Stockton & Darlington Railway, restored and placed on exhibition near North Road Station, Darlington, 6/1857; transferred to Bank Top Station, Darlington, /1890
(2) ret. to NER, 3/1898, and placed on Bank Top Station, Darlington, with LOCOMOTION above

<u>Rogerley Quarry</u>, Frosterley. Map 84, NZ 015377 (approx)
(Rippon family until c/1875)

Y1 A huge limestone quarry, eventually 2m long, on northern slopes of Weardale between Frosterley and Stanhope. It was originally linked to Frosterley Station by a self-acting incline, but at an unknown date this was altered to enable locomotives to be used. The scanty evidence suggests that there were two loco sheds, one in the quarry and the other at the bottom of the line near Frosterley Station. The quarry was sold to the Durham & Yorkshire Whinstone Co Ltd in 1947 (q.v.).

Gauge: 4' 8½"

21	MERRYBENT							
	(form. No.46)	0-4-0ST	OC	HL	3053	1914	(a)	(1)
22	FROSTERLEY							
	(form. No.26)	0-4-0ST	OC	HL	2563	1903	(b)	(2)
No.39		0-4-0ST	OC	HL	2798	1909	(c)	(3)
26	HAREHOPE	0-4-0ST	OC	HL	2799	1909	(d)	(1)

(a) ex Barton Limestone Co Ltd,   (1) to Tees Ironworks, Cargo Fleet,
    Yorks, N.R., c/1915   Yorks, N.R., /1947
(b) ex Frosterley Quarry (c/1921 ?)   (2) to Durham & Yorkshire Whinstone
(c) ex St. Helen's Colliery, /1926   Co Ltd, /1947
(d) ex Bowden Close Colliery,   (3) to St. Helen's Colliery, /1927
    c/1938

Gauge: 2' 6" (?)

-		0-4-0ST	OC					s/s

Nothing is known of this system, except that it was operating in 1903.

St. Helen's Colliery, St. Helen's Auckland. Map 85, NZ 196270.

T14 Sunk in 1831, this colliery was originally served by a branch (½m) from
the Stockton & Darlington Railway, but was latterly served by sidings N of
LNER line from Bishop Auckland to Barnard Castle, ½m E of St. Helen's
Auckland Station. The colliery closed in April 1926.

Gauge: 4' 8½"

No. 5	0-4-0ST	OC	BH	37	1867	New	s/s
8 (form. No.39)	0-4-0ST	OC	HL	2798	1909	(a)	(1)
30 (form. ELDON No.3)	0-4-0ST	OC	P	1092	1906	(b)	s/s

(a) ex Wooley Colliery by 1925   (1) to Rogerley Quarry, /1926; ret.
(b) ex Eldon Colliery, c/1930   1927; to North Bitchburn Coal
                                          Co Ltd, Thrislington Colliery,
                                          /1930

Stanley Colliery, near Waterhouses. Map 85, NZ 173397.

M4 This colliery was sunk in 1857 and served by sidings from NER Stanley
Branch, about 1½m S of Waterhouses Station. It is believed to have
usually been worked by the NER, but the loco below is shown as New to the
colliery, and although no locomotives were recorded in the 1870's, one is
again shown in March 1890. The colliery closed in November 1911.

Gauge: 4' 8½"

No. 8 STANLEY	0-4-0ST	OC	MW	144	1865	New	s/s (after 8/1903 ?)

Tuthill Quarry, near Haswell. Map 85, NZ 388426.
(Tuthill Limestone Co until 1899)

P3 This quarry was served by a branch (½m) from the South Hetton Coal Co
Ltd's Pesspool Branch, which joined the NER Sunderland-Stockton line
1m S of Haswell Station. The quarry closed after the First World War,
and the site was taken over by ICI in 1923 (q.v.).

Gauge: 4' 8½"

LADY CORNELIA	0-6-0ST	IC	MW	49	1862	(a)	s/s after 1895
-	0-4-0ST	OC	MW	498	1874	(b)	(1)
-	0-4-0ST	OC	RS	2875	1897	New	s/s
No.27	0-6-0ST	IC	P	1040	1905	New	(2)

(a) ex Brecon & Merthyr Railway,   (1) to Casebourne & Co Ltd, Haverton
    16, 2/1882   Hill (now Teesside)
(b) ex J.Whitham & Son, Leeds,   (2) to T.& R.W.Bower Ltd ⊀, Allerton
    Yorks, W.R.   Main Collieries, Yorks, W.R.

        ⊀ This firm was another PP subsidiary company

Ushaw Moor Colliery, Ushaw Moor. Map 85, NZ 220428.
(Henry Chaytor until 1893)

M10 This colliery was opened in 1866, and served by sidings N of LNER Waterhouses branch, 1m W of Ushaw Moor Station. It was vested in NCB Northern
Division No.5 Area on 1st January 1947.

Gauge: 4' 8½"

No.10 CAROLINE	0-4-0ST	OC	BH	998	1891	New	(1)
16 (form.No.6)	0-4-0ST	OC	RS	2325	1894	(a)	(2)
17 GEORGE	0-4-0ST	OC	K	1705	1871		
			reb.J.Tait	90	1920	(b)	(3)

(a) ex Bowden Close Colliery   (1) to Bank Foot Coke Ovens, Crook
(b) ex Tees Ironworks, Cargo Fleet, (2) to NCB No.5 Area, 1/1/1947
    Yorks, N.R., /1922   (3) to Tees Ironworks, Cargo Fleet,
                               Yorks, N.R.

Wooley Colliery, near Crook. Map 85, NZ 178385.

M5 This colliery was served by sidings on the NER Stanley Branch, about 2½m S
of Waterhouses Station. Its operation other than when the loco below was
present is uncertain. It closed in August 1931, but was re-opened before
nationalisation (without locomotives), and was vested into NCB Northern
Division No.5 Area on 1st January 1947.

Gauge: 4' 8½"

No.39	0-4-0ST	OC	HL	2798	1909	New	(1)

                    (1) to St. Helen's Colliery by 1925

Unknown location

Gauge: 4' 8½"

VICTORIA	0-4-0	IC	Bury		1838	(a)	s/s
No.24	0-4-0ST	OC	MW	573	1875		
			reb.LG		c1900	(b)	s/s
No.41	0-6-0ST	IC	HC	673	1906	(c)	s/s
7 CLEVELAND							
(form. No.44)	0-4-0ST	OC	MW	744	1880	(d)	s/s after 11/1929

(a) ex Manchester & Bolton Railway,
    120, 3/1854
(b) ex LG, c/1901; prev. NER 2054
(c) ex Whitaker Bros, contrs
(d) ex W. & I. Lant, contrs

PELAW MAIN COLLIERIES LTD
(Birtley Iron Co Ltd until 26/5/1926; orig Birtley Iron Co)
Birtley Iron Co was formed to operate the blast furnaces and iron works at
Birtley which commenced production in 1828; its collieries were run under
various titles - "Pelaw Main Collieries" till 1880; "Owners of Pelaw Main
Collieries" till 1900-1910; "Charles Perkins & Partners" and ending with
Pelaw Main Collieries. The furnaces were blown out in the early 1920's;
the iron works was re-organised under the title of The Birtley Co Ltd
about September 1930 (see Caterpillar Tractor Co Ltd) and the collieries
as above. The colliery firm passed into French control between the Wars.

N.B.   Besides their names, most of the firm's collieries were also
        allocated a letter at some period.

All of the company's collieries were served by

Pelaw Main Railway (first used in 1880's)
This railway has a long history, and its operation is perhaps the most
interesting in N.E.England. It begins with a new line opened on 17th May
1809 from Urpeth Colliery to staithes on R.Tyne at Bill Quay. The western
end of this line did not follow the route of the later line, but ran from
the colliery in a north-easterly direction up to a spot on Black Fell
marked on early O.S. maps as "Old Engine", which is believed to have been
the first stationary engine to have worked on a colliery waggonway. In
1814 this section was closed when the colliery passed to Benjamin Thompson,
who sank new collieries at Urpeth and Ouston, and built a new line to serve
them, joining the old line at Black Fell. He was a prominent advocate of
rope-worked inclines, and most of the system seems to have been worked in
this way.
By 1871 the focal point of the line was Birtley Iron Works, and the large
fan of sidings which lay on its north side, known for generations as
H28 "Birtley Tail". From here a long branch ran south-east to Ouston 'B' Coll-
H27 iery (Map 78,NZ 266545), Ouston 'A' Colliery (NZ 264535),
H26 Urpeth Busty Colliery (NZ 249536) and
H25 Urpeth 'C' Colliery (NZ 243545). From a junction north of Ouston 'A'
H53 Colliery another branch ran to South Pelaw Colliery (later known as 'E'
Pit)(NZ 264523), crossing the Beamish Railway on the level and with running
powers over a short section of the NER Pontop & Shields line to reach the
colliery. North-west from the "Tail" another branch ran to Bewicke Main
H23 Colliery (later known as the 'D' Pit) (NZ 254556), opened in May 1862.
The first stationary engine was situated at Urpeth Busty Colliery. Wagons
were hauled up from Urpeth 'C' Pit to the engine house, where the rope was
slipped from the front of the set by the first set rider. The set ran on
by momentum, and the same rope was then attached to the rear of the set for
it to be lowered down to Ouston 'A' Pit. From here a second stationary
engine lowered the wagons to the "Tail", though later this engine was
replaced by locomotive working. Whether the lines to Ouston 'B' Pit and
Bewicke Main were originally worked by ropes or horses is not known.
From "Birtley Tail" the wagons were hauled up the east side of the Team
Valley by two stationary engines. The first was situated near Birtley
Church, and worked the short section up to Birtley turnpike. From here to
the foot of the next incline the sets were worked by gravity and braked by
the set rider, and were then hauled up to Black Fell by a stationary engine
there, originally called the Black Fell Engine, but later known as the
Blackhouse Fell Engine, possibly to avoid confusion with the Black Fell
Engine on the nearby Pontop & Jarrow Railway. In 1904 the Birtley Church
Engine was dispensed with, and the whole line from the "Tail" to the
Blackhouse Fell Engine worked as one long bank.
Between the Blackhouse Fell Engine and the foot of the Eighton Banks West
Incline the line was flat, and originally worked by horses. But in 1821
Thompson converted it to rope haulage. Using the engines at Blackhouse
Fell and Eighton Banks to make a "reciprocating rope" system, he created
what was then the longest rope-worked incline in the country, nearly 1½
miles long, the difference in height between the engines being 178½ feet.
The Eighton Banks Engine worked a main-and-tail system on its east side as

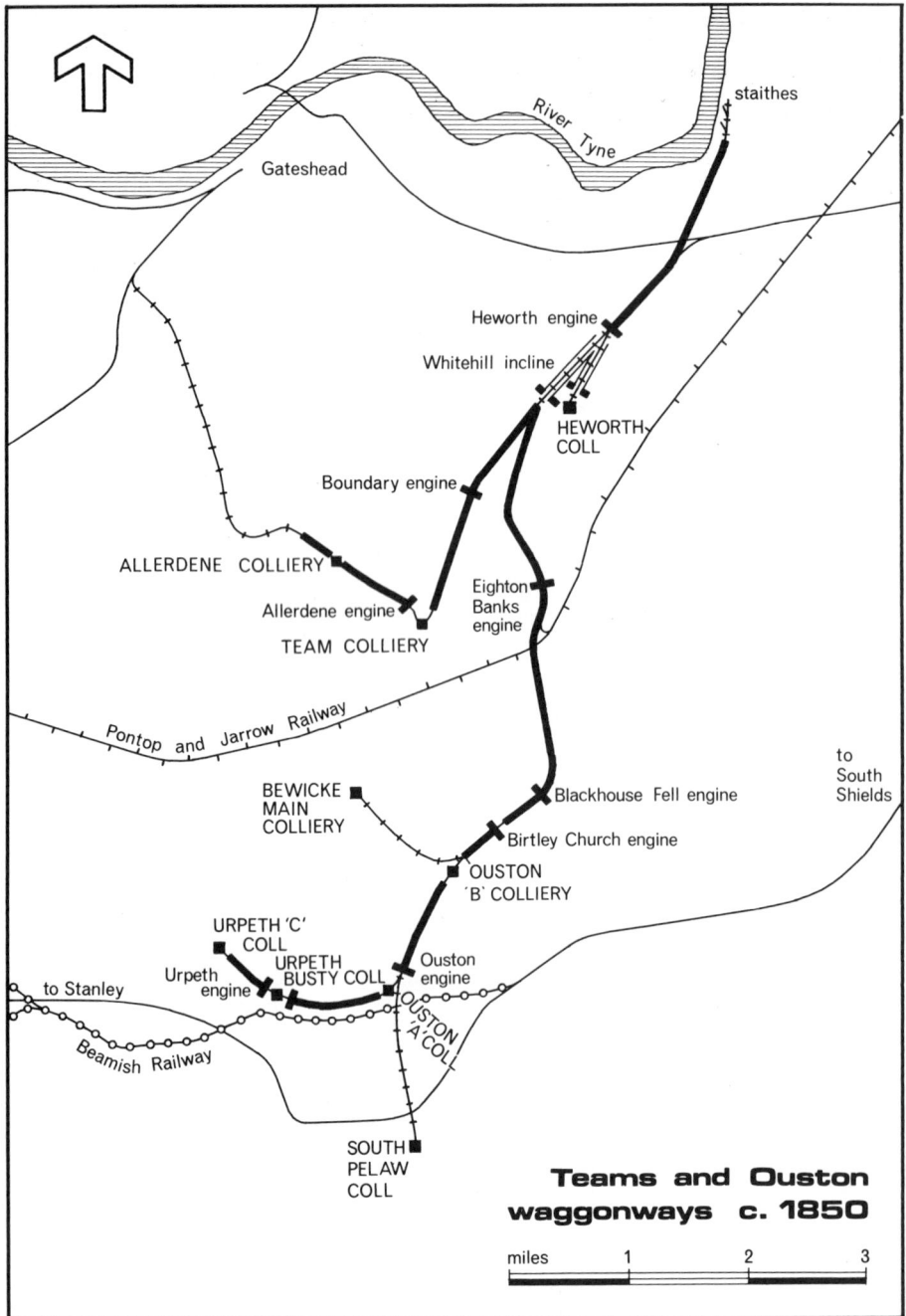

staithes

River Tyne

Gateshead

Heworth engine

Whitehill incline

HEWORTH COLL

Boundary engine

ALLERDENE COLLIERY

Eighton Banks engine

Allerdene engine

TEAM COLLIERY

Pontop and Jarrow Railway

to South Shields

BEWICKE MAIN COLLIERY

Blackhouse Fell engine

Birtley Church engine

OUSTON 'B' COLLIERY

URPETH 'C' COLL

URPETH BUSTY COLL

Urpeth engine

Ouston engine

to Stanley

OUSTON 'A' COLL

Beamish Railway

SOUTH PELAW COLL

Teams and Ouston waggonways c. 1850

miles   1   2   3

far as Whitehill Bank Top. Later both systems were replaced by locomotive working, and the Eighton Banks Engine was left to work only the steep ½m incline on its west side. The bank worked two sets at the same time, but its operation was curious in that at the top the kip was used for empties and there was only one road for fulls, so that as a full set on one side of the bank was followed by an empty set on the same side the ropes were crossed at the Bank Head on alternate sets. The locomotive working from Whitehill to the Bank Head was equally curious. The loco pulled the waggons to Eighton Banks, being attached to them by a chain about eight feet long. On approaching the Bank Head the chain was slipped, and the loco went ahead and into the loco shed siding while the wagons went past. When the end of the train had passed the points the loco came out to push the wagons up on to the kip.

From Whitehill a self-acting incline took the wagons down to the Heworth Engine, which in turn let sets of wagons down to Pelaw Main Staithes (NZ 300632). The working of this section was complicated by a link to Pelaw Station on the NER Gateshead-Tyne Dock line, and also by a junction F1 with a line to <u>Heworth Colliery</u> (NZ 284605) from the engine. Heworth Colliery was owned by a separate company, the Heworth Coal Co Ltd, whose staithes lay immediately downstream from the Pelaw Main Staithes. A self-acting incline brought the wagons down to the Heworth Engine, where a rope from the east drum was attached and the set then allowed to run forward for about 40 yards. The rope was then taken off, and twelve Pelaw Main wagons with a rope from the west drum run down to them for the journey to the staithes. Coming back the set was stopped in the same place, the Pelaw Main wagons hauled on to their kip, and then the Heworth rope attached for its set to be hauled into its kip. Heworth wagons to and from Pelaw Station were worked entirely by gravity. At both Pelaw Main and Heworth Staithes an incline worked by another stationary engine took the wagons down to the river, though the Heworth incline could only handle one wagon at a time, whereas the Pelaw Main incline could handle two. Pelaw Main horses and later locomotives shunted wagons at both staithes until about 1940, when the Heworth Staithes were burnt down and Heworth coal was shipped at the Pelaw Main Staithes.

At Whitehill this line was joined by another long line from collieries north of Birtley. These were originally owned by A.E.Burdon, but in 1882 they passed to the Birtley Iron Co, apparently as a result of a lost horse-racing wager.

This too was an old line, and originally its coal was shipped on to the Newcastle & Carlisle line at Dunston, but the link up to the Ouston waggonway at Whitehill also dates from an early period. At this time it served Teams (or Team) <u>Colliery</u>, which consisted of two pits about ½m apart - the
C15 <u>Shop Pit</u> (NZ 257586) near the bottom of the Team Valley, and the <u>Betty</u>
C16 <u>Pit</u> (NZ 265579), alongside the Great North Road. The line serving them ran up the valley to the Shop Pit Sidings at Lamesley, whence a stationary engine at the north end of the Betty Pit yard hauled the wagons up a single line incline to the Great North Road. This engine also worked the Shop Pit. Another engine hauled the wagons through to the south end of the Betty Pit yard, and also worked the Betty Pit, before being hauled up another single line incline by the Boundary Engine at Wrekenton. Later this engine, by then known as the Starrs Engine, took over the working of the Betty Pit,
C16 and also <u>Ravensworth Ann Colliery</u> on the same site after its opening in August 1930. In 1937 the line was rebuilt to pass under the Great North Road, which caused a complete reorganisation. A new engine house, known as King's Engine, was built for the Shop Pit Incline, while the old engine house was converted into a loco shed to house the locomotive to be used to shunt the colliery.

From the Starrs Engine the wagons were worked up to Whitehill by a main-and-tail system, but in 1909-1910 Gateshead Tramways extended their system out to Wrekenton, and to avoid problems where the ropes crossed the road a locomotive was introduced. The inclines on this section were unusual in that full wagons of coal, stones and materials commonly travelled in both directions, depending on their entry to the system and their destination. As might be expected, most of the early changes took place in the Birtley area. Ouston 'B' Colliery closed in 1875, and Urpeth Busty Colliery

Heworth staithes

Pelaw Main
staithes

Gateshead

Whitehill
incline

Heworth
engine

HEWORTH
COLL

Starrs
engine

RAVENSWORTH
SHOP PIT

Eighton
Banks
engine

Allerdene
engine

RAVENSWORTH
BETTY PIT

Pontop and Jarrow Railway

BEWICKE
MAIN COLL

Blackhouse
Fell engine

MILL DRIFT

RIDING DRIFT

BLACKHOUSE
'H' COLLIERY

OUSTON
'E' PIT

URPETH
'C' COLL

OUSTON
'B' COLL

OUSTON 'A' COLL

Urpeth
engine

Beamish Railway

OUSTON
WINNING

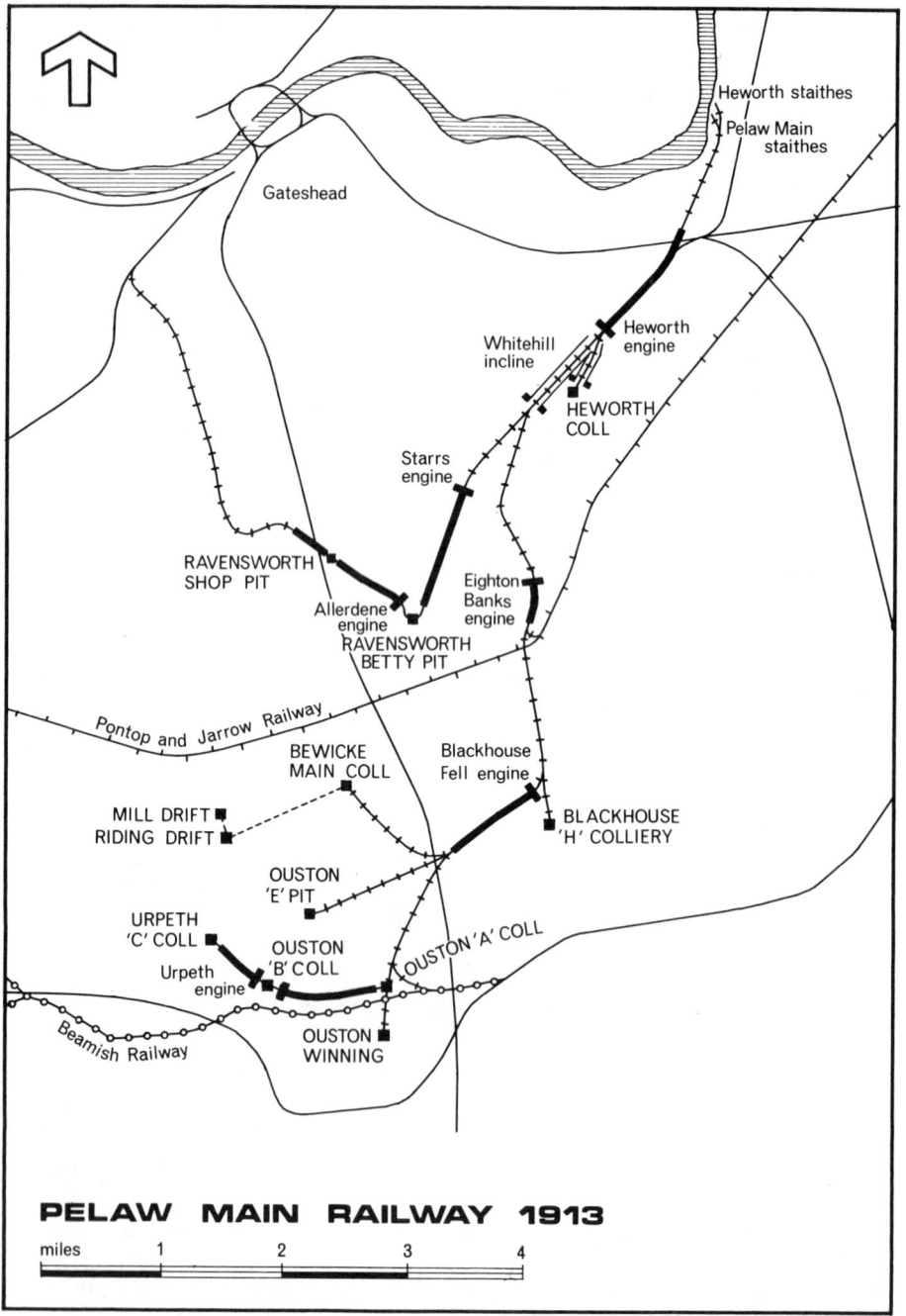

PELAW MAIN RAILWAY 1913

miles   1   2   3   4

eventually became Urpeth 'B' Colliery. South Pelaw Colliery closed about
1886 (re-opened in 1892 by South Pelaw Coal Co Ltd without locos), but was
H24 replaced in 1893 by Ouston 'E' Colliery (NZ 266548), served by another
branch westwards from the "Tail". Most of the South Pelaw line was
retained, however, for its southern end was modified to join the Beamish
Railway just west of the NER Durham Turnpike Junction. In 1901 the branch
to Ouston 'A' Colliery was extended beneath the Beamish Railway to Ouston
H29 Winning (NZ 264532), though this closed in 1915. In 1902 came an interest-
ing development when a narrow gauge line was built from Bewicke Main Coll-
H22 iery to Riding Drift (NZ 245553). This is believed to have been worked by
H21 a locomotive, and in 1907 a short branch was built from it to Mill Drift
(NZ 246555). This closed in April 1915, to be followed by the Riding Drift
in April 1926. Meanwhile Ouston 'A' Colliery closed in August 1924,
Urpeth 'B' about 1930 and Bewicke Main in January 1932.
On the east side of the valley a branch was built from the Blackhouse Fell
H32 Engine to Blackhouse 'H' Colliery (NZ 280556) (known locally as Wash Houses
Pit). This opened in 1913, but closed again in July 1914, and did not re-
open until 1920. It in turn was linked to a drift further down the hill-
side by a long curving 2' 0" gauge line about 1m long. This was worked by
a stationary engine at the Blackhouse screens, which hauled the tubs from
underground and up the hill on an endless rope. The system closed with
the abandonment of coal working in May 1932.
On the other side there was for many years a branch from Whitehill Junction
to White House Quarry, which lay immediately to the east. There is also a
strong tradition that in the 1890's another branch was laid west from
Whitehill to serve Sheriff Hill Colliery. This colliery, which was not
owned by the Birtley Iron Co, but by the Sheriff Hill Colliery Co Ltd (reg.
11/2/1890), consisted of three pits - the Fanny Pit (NZ 267603), the King
F5 Pit (NZ 273596) and Stormont Main Pit (NZ 276593). Of these, the last lay
almost alongside the Railway near the Springwell Road crossing, but does
not seem to have been linked to the Railway, and the branch above was
F3 probably built to the King Pit. It is further said to have been worked by
a stationary engine and been abandoned about 1895, though the King Pit at
least was working until the late 1920's.
Further down the line, Ravensworth Ann Colliery (see above) was opened in
C13 August 1930, to be followed in October 1936 by Ravensworth Park Drift
(NZ 242588) (sometimes known as Lady Park Drift), which was served by a
branch ½m long near the southern end of what was being developed as the
Team Valley Trading Estate. The line to Dunston was slightly re-aligned
when the Trading Estate was built, but Pelaw Main trains had priority over
C10 factory traffic. Meanwhile, further north, the Norwood Coking Plant
(NZ 238613) (see Priestman Collieries Ltd) had been opened in 1913 to
straddle the Dunston line, and sidings were laid into it to enable Pelaw
Main coal to be used.
A number of links with other lines have already been mentioned. The NER
Newcastle-Durham line subsequently passed over "Birtley Tail", and a link
was put in between the two lines. At the foot of the Eighton Banks Incline
the Pontop & Jarrow Railway of John Bowes & Partners Ltd (q.v.) passed
over the Pelaw Main line, and a link was put in to enable bricks from
Birtley to be sent on to the Pontop & Jarrow, though this was removed by
1923.
Apparently because of the company's French control, and the collapse of
France in 1940, Ouston 'E' Colliery closed in June 1940, to be followed
by Urpeth 'C' Colliery in October 1940, and no traffic passed over the
southern arm of the system until August 1946, when Ouston 'E' Colliery was
re-opened (Urpeth 'C' re-opened in 1947). The Railway and its collieries
passed to NCB Northern Division No.6 Area on 1st January 1947, though
Heworth Colliery passed to No.1 Area.

Locomotives first seem to have been used on the Ouston line in 1859, and
on the Team Colliery line in 1868, and were later introduced on all the
flatter sections of the system.

Locomotives were kept at:
    Birtley Iron Works   Pelaw Main Staithes ⨍
    Blackhouse Fell   Shop Pit sidings
    Eighton Banks (closed in 1940) Starrs
    Ouston 'E' Colliery (later)   Ravensworth Ann Colliery (after 1937)

⨍ only locos with cut-down mountings permitted.

The Workshops for the Railway were at Ouston 'E' Colliery.

Gauge: 4' 8½"

	PELAW	0-4-0WT	OC	H(L)	220	1859	New	s/s
	BEWICKE	0-6-0ST	OC	BH	52	1868	New	Scr 12/1929
	VICTORY	0-4-0ST	OC	John Harris	1863		(a)	Scr c/1900
	DERWENT	0-4-0ST	OC	John Harris	1865		(a)	Scr c/1900
	BYRON	0-4-0ST	OC	John Harris	1868		(a)	Scr c/1900
	BIRTLEY	2-4-0WT	OC	H(L)			(b)	
	reb.	0-6-0ST	OC	Birtley	c1871			Scr /1928
	PELAW	0-6-0T	OC	BH	60	1868	(c)	(1)
	OUSTON	0-6-0ST	OC	BH	602	1881	New	Scr 12/1929
	BURDON	0-6-0T	OC	BH	48	1868	(d)	Scr c/1920
	URPETH	0-4-0ST	OC	AB	3	1859	(e)	
				reb.AB	277	1884	(e)	(2)
	TYNE	0-4-0ST	OC	AB	786	1896	New	
				reb.AB		1940		(3)
	DERWENT	0-6-0ST	OC	AB	970	1903	New	
				reb.RSH		1945		(3)
	PELAW II	0-6-0ST	IC	Ghd		1874	(f)	Scr /1924
	ROSEBERY	0-6-0ST	IC	RS	2139	1873	(g)	Scr c/1930
	BALFOUR	0-6-0ST	IC	RS	2239	1875	(h)	Scr /1929
	GLADSTONE	0-6-0ST	IC	RS	2240	1875	(j)	Scr /1932
	SALISBURY	0-6-0ST	IC	RS	2244	1875	(k)	Scr /1925
6		4-4-0T	OC	BP	417	1864	(m)	(4)
	EAST CLIFF	0-6-0ST	IC	P	774	1899	(n)	Scr /1928
	OUSTON	0-6-0ST	IC	RWH	1657	1875	(p)	Scr /1928
	BYRON	0-6-0ST	IC	RWH	1662	1875	(q)	Scr /1928
	VICTORY	0-6-0ST	IC	RWH	1669	1875	(r)	Scr /1929
	LEAFIELD	0-6-0ST	IC	RWH	1666	1875	(s)	Scr c/1930
	MOSELEY	0-6-0ST	IC	Don	213	1876	(t)	Scr 8/1932
	CHARLES PERKINS	0-4-0T	OC	HL	2986	1913	New	(3)
24A		4-4-0T	OC	BP	770	1867		
		reb.				1880		
		reb.				1900	(u)	Scr /1932
26A		4-4-0T	OC	BP	772	1867		
		reb.				1901		
		reb.Neasden				1920	(v)	(3)
44A		4-4-0T	OC	BP	868	1869		
		reb.				1888		
		reb.				1902		
		reb.Neasden				1920	(w)	(3)
	BUSTY	0-4-0ST	OC	BH				
		reb.Ridley Shaw					(x)	Scr /1935
	CHARLES NELSON	0-4-0ST	OC	P	1748	1928	New	(3)
	HENRY C. EMBLETON	0-6-0T	OC	HL	3766	1930	New	(3)
	-	4wVBT	VCG	S	6936	1927⨍	New	Scr /1935
900		0-4-0T	IC	Ghd	35	1888	(y)	(3)
1308		0-4-0T	IC	Ghd	37	1891	(z)	(3)
1310		0-4-0T	IC	Ghd	38	1891	(aa)	(3)
	-	0-4-0ST	OC	RS	3057	1904	(bb)	(5)

⨍ Not delivered until 1930?

(a) ex contr. for NER Team Valley
    line, /1869
(b) ex CR, /1871
(c) ex I.C.Tone, contr., Sunderland,
    c/1873
(d) ex A.E.Burdon, /1882
(e) ex AB, /1884; prev. NBR, 241
(f) ex NER, 2289, via Frazer, 1/1904
(g) ex NER, 1670, /1905
(h) ex NER, 1673, /1905
(j) ex NER, 1674, /1905
(k) ex NER, 1676, /1905
(m) ex Metropolitan Rly, 6, via
    Frazer, /1906 ⚹
(n) ex S.Pearson & Son Ltd,
    Admiralty Harbour contract,
    Dover, Kent, 9/1908
(p) ex NER, 1350, via Frazer, 1/1910
(q) ex NER, 1355, via Frazer, 2/1910
(r) ex NER, 1362, 8/1910
(s) ex NER, 1359, 9/1910
(t) ex GNR, 606, via Wake, /1912
(u) ex Metropolitan Rly, 24A, via
    Frazer, /1922
(v) ex Metropolitan Rly, 26A, via
    Frazer, /1927
(w) ex Metropolitan Rly, 44A, via
    Frazer, /1927
(x) ex Ridley Shaw, Middlesbrough,
    Yorks, N.R., 4/1928
(y) ex LNER, 900, via Frazer, 5/1932
(z) ex LNER, 1308, via Frazer, /1932
(aa) ex LNER, 1310, via Frazer, /1932
(bb) ex U.A.Ritson & Sons Ltd, Burn-
    hope Colliery, loan, c/1930's

(1) to United National Collieries
    Ltd, Risca Colliery, Monmouth-
    shire, /1881
(2) to Steetley Lime & Basic Co Ltd,
    Coxhoe, c/1930
(3) to NCB No.6 Area, 1/1/1947
(4) to South Hetton Coal Co Ltd,
    c/1908 ⚹
(5) ret. to U.A.Ritson & Sons Ltd,
    Burnhope Colliery

⚹ confirmation that this loco worked on the Pelaw Main system
  is lacking

Gauge: Narrow

    A narrow gauge locomotive was used on the line from Bewicke 'D' Pit
    to the Riding Drift about 1902, but no other details are known.

PELTON BRICK CO LTD, PELTON FELL

H50 Quarry and brickworks (Map 78, NZ 254517) opened in 1940, and served by
an internal rail system, which was replaced by dumpers about 1967.

Gauge: 2' 0"

| - | | 4wDM | RH | 213836 | 1942 | (a) | (1) |
| - | | 4wDM | RH | 375696 | 1954 | New | (2) |

(a) ex RH; prev. MOS

(1) to R.P.Morris, Longfield, Kent,
    9/1968; doubtful whether actually
    transferred; s/s
(2) to M.E.Engineering Ltd,
    Cricklewood, Middlesex, /1968

PICKFORD, HOLLAND & CO LTD, ECLIPSE SILICA BRICKWORKS, CROOK

Q7 Works (Map 85, NZ 159351) served by sidings W of BR Crook-Bishop Auckland line, ¼m S of Crook Station. Rail traffic ceased in 1965.

Gauge: 4' 8½"

-		0-4-0ST	OC	BH			(a)	s/s
-		4wPM		FH	1829	1933	New	(1)
-		4wDM		RH	207102	1941	New	(2)
-		4wDM		RH	443644	1961	New	(3)

(a) origin unknown

(1) to Dunlop Rubber Co Ltd, Glasgow
(2) to RH for overhaul, 6/1961; to Blaenavon Works, Monmouthshire, 9/1961
(3) to TWW, Templeborough Works, Sheffield, Yorks, W.R., 7/1965; re-sold to C.F.Booth Ltd, Rotherham, Yorks, W.R., c/1966

PORT OF SUNDERLAND AUTHORITY, SOUTH DOCK, SUNDERLAND
(River Wear Commissioners until 1/10/1972)

K10 The River Wear Commissioners were created in 1859. In 1972 their operations were taken over by Sunderland Corporation under the title above. The loco shed (Map 78, NZ 409573) is situated in the docks complex.

Gauge: 4' 8½"

1		0-6-0ST	IC	MW	17	1860	New	Scr	c/1900
No.1		0-4-0ST	OC	HL	2589	1904	(a)		
				reb.	HL	1933		(1)	
	R.W.C. No.2	0-6-0ST	IC	MW	57	1862	New	(2)	
3		0-4-0ST	OC	HE	14	1866	New	Scr	
	R.W.C. No.4	0-4-0ST	OC	AB	52	1866	New	Scr	c/1930
5		0-4-0ST	OC	BH	173	1871	New	Scr	/1930
No.6		0-6-0ST	OC	FW	140	1872	New	(2)	
	R.W.C. No.7	0-6-0ST	OC	HC	266	1883	New		
				reb.		1908		Scr	c/1930
No.9	GNAT	0-4-0ST	OC	RWH	2029	1885	New		
				reb.		1936		Scr	9/1960
No.10		0-4-0ST	OC	HC	221	1881	(b)		
				reb.		1908			
				reb.		1937		(3)	
No.12		0-4-0ST	OC	AB	805	1897	New		
				reb.		1910			
				reb.		1937		Scr	/1956
No.13		0-4-0ST	OC	AB	1127	1907	New		
				reb.		1930		(4)	
No.14		0-6-0T	OC	HC	1039	1913	New		
				reb.		1938		(4)	
No.15		0-4-0ST	OC	P	1761	1929	New	(4)	
No.16		0-4-0ST	OC	P	1589	1928	(c)	(5)	
No.17		0-6-0T	OC	AB	2029	1937	New	(6)	
No.18		0-4-0DM		RH	243081	1948	New	(7)	
No.19		0-4-0DM		RH	304471	1951	New	(8)	
No.20		0-4-0DM		RH	327969	1954	New	(9)	
No.21		0-4-0DE		RH	395294	1956	New		
No.22		0-4-0DE		RH	416210	1957	New		

(a) ex Lever Bros (Port Sunlight) Ltd, Port Sunlight, Cheshire
(b) ex Wear Rolling Mills Co Ltd, Sunderland

(1) to TWW, for scrap, /1953
(2) for sale, 7/1904; scr c/1910
(3) to Thomas Young & Sons (Ship-breakers) Ltd, Sunderland, for scrap, 9/1956; scr 5/1957

(c) ex ICI Ltd, Billingham Works,
/1932

(4) to Thomas Young & Sons (Ship-
breakers) Ltd, Sunderland, for
scrap, 10/1959
(5) to TWW, /1953
(6) to TWW, Templeborough Works,
Sheffield, Yorks, W.R., 6/1950;
re-sold to NCB N.E. Div. No.1
Area, Maltby Main Colliery,
Maltby, Yorks, W.R., 7/1952
(7) to NCB Coal Products Division,
Northern Region, Monkton Coking
Plant, 12/1970
(8) to Scottish Pulp & Paper Mills
Ltd, Fort William, Inverness-
shire, Scotland, 1/1970, per R.R.
Britton Ltd, Cranrose, Dorset
(9) to Clarke - Chapman - John
Thompson Ltd, Gateshead, via
Northern Supply Co, Sunderland,
6/1973

Gauge: 1' 8" (locos used on repairs to breakwaters)

8	(form. MIDGET)	0-4-0ST	OC	DK	262	1883	New	Scr c/1930
11	(form. WASP)	0-4-0ST	OC	DK	266	1891	New	Scr c/1930

PORT OF TYNE AUTHORITY
(Tyne Improvement Commission until 1/8/1968)

The Commission was originally created in 1850, and operated docks on both
sides of the river. It is also known to have used locomotives on river
bank works. The main office is at Bewick Street, Newcastle.

South Pier Works, South Shields. Map 78, NZ 373677.

D6 This works has no main line rail connection.

Gauge: 4' 8½"

GERALDINE	0-4-0ST	OC	BH	369	1876	New	Scr	/1934
GROYNE								
(form. No.1 ETHEL)	0-4-0ST	OC	BH	288	1873	(a)	(1)	
6 (46) PEREYRA	0-4-0ST	OC	MW	1042	1888			
	reb.	TJR		1914	(b)	Scr 6/1949		
7 (47) BELLE VUE	0-4-0ST	OC	P	1099	1907			
	reb.	Adams		1937	(c)	Scr c/1949		
48	4wDM		RH	294263	1950	(d)		

(a) ex Albert Edward Dock, North
Shields, Northumberland
(b) ex TJR by 8/1928
(c) ex Adams, Newport, Monmouthshire, /1937; prev. New
Westbury Iron Co Ltd, Wilts
(d) ex Tyne Dock, /1950

(1) to North Pier Works, Tynemouth,
Northumberland

Tyne Dock, Tyne Dock. Map 78, NZ 3465/3565.
(operated by LNER until 1/5/1937)

D10 A vast docks complex, originally opened in March 1859, with various
access points from BR.
There may have been other locomotive loans from Albert Edward Dock,
North Shields, Northumberland, besides those listed below, both before
and after 1938. Rail traffic ceased in 1973.

Gauge: 4' 8½"

11		0-6-0ST	OC	RS	3072	1901	(a)	(1)
21	(1 until 1949)	0-6-0ST	OC	P	1952	1938	New	(2)
22	(2 until 1949)	0-6-0ST	OC	P	1953	1938	New	(3)
23	(3 until 1949)	0-6-0ST	OC	P	1954	1938	New	(3)
24	(4 until 1949)	0-6-0ST	OC	P	1955	1938	New	(4)
25	(5 until 1949)	0-6-0ST	OC	AE	1618	1912	(b)	(5)
26	(6 until 1949)	0-6-0ST	OC	P	1616	1923	(b)	(6)
7		0-6-0ST	OC	BH	666	1882	(b)	(7)
27	(7 until 1949)	0-6-0ST	OC	RSH	7212	1945	New	(3)
28	(8 until 1949)							
	(5 until 1945)	0-6-0ST	OC	BH	645	1881	(b)	s/s c/1950
29	(9 until 1949)	0-6-0ST	OC	BH	373	1875	(b)	Scr 10/1950
No.1		0-6-0ST	OC	RSH	7138	1944	(c)	(8)
-		4wDM		RH	294263	1950	New	(9)
50		0-6-0DM		AB	380	1950	New	(10)
51		0-6-0DM		AB	381	1951	New	(11)
52		0-6-0DM		AB	382	1951	New	(12)
53		0-4-0DE		RH	323600	1953	New	(13)
54		0-4-0DE		RH	349087	1954	New	(14)
55		0-4-0DE		RH	381751	1955	New	(15)
56		0-4-0DE		RH	381752	1955	New	(16)
57		0-4-0DE		RH	381753	1955	New	(17)
58		0-4-0DE		RH	381755	1955	New	

(a) ex Albert Edward Dock, North
Shields, Northumberland, loan,
/1938
(b) ex Albert Edward Dock, North
Shields, Northumberland, /1940
(c) ex Albert Edward Dock, North
Shields, Northumberland, /1949

(1) ret. to Albert Edward Dock, North
Shields, Northumberland, c/1938
(2) to Albert Edward Dock, by 7/1954;
ret. by 4/1955; to Albert Edward
Dock, /1955
(3) to Albert Edward Dock, /1955
(4) to Albert Edward Dock by 7/1954
(5) to Albert Edward Dock, c/1951
(6) to Albert Edward Dock, 7/1954
(7) to Albert Edward Dock, /1945
(8) to Albert Edward Dock by 7/1952
(9) to South Pier Works, South
Shields, /1950
(10) to TWW, Templeborough Works,
Sheffield, Yorks, W.R., 5/1963
(11) to Albert Edward Dock, 10/1955;
ret; to TWW, Templeborough Works,
Sheffield, Yorks, W.R., 5/1963
(12) to Leslie Sanderson Ltd, dealer,
Birtley, /1963
(13) to Albert Edward Dock; ret.1/1959;
to Albert Edward Dock; ret.1/1960;
to Albert Edward Dock; ret. /1962;
to TWW, Templeborough Works,
Sheffield, Yorks, W.R., 10/1968
(14) to Albert Edward Dock; ret;
cannibalised as source of spares
for other locomotives
(15) to Central Electricity Generating
Board, Dunston G.S., 12/1971
(16) to TWW, Templeborough Works,
Sheffield, Yorks, W.R., 10/1968
(17) to TWW, Templeborough Works,
Sheffield, Yorks, W.R., 2/1970;
re-sold to Albright & Wilson Ltd,
Portishead, Somerset, 6/1971

<u>PRIESTMAN COLLIERIES LTD</u>

The foundation of this company is a little obscure, but it would appear that on 1st January 1899 the owners of Blaydon Burn, Lilley, Victoria Garesfield and Waldridge Collieries (who had been collaborating together for some time, but whose titles at the time are uncertain - see below) amalgamated to form <u>The Owners of the Priestman Collieries</u>. The limited company with the shorter title was registered on 14th December 1903 upon the absorption of Axwell Park Colliery, previously owned by Hannington & Co Ltd.

<u>Axwell Park Colliery</u>, Swalwell. Map 78, NZ 202618.
(Hannington & Co Ltd until 14/12/1903)

B10 This colliery, also known as Axwell Garesfield, or simply Axwell Colliery, is believed to have been sunk in 1856, and appears to have been shunted for many years by horses. It was served by sidings alongside LNER Blackhill Branch, ¼m S of Swalwell Station. It was vested in NCB Northern Division No.6 Area on 1st January 1947.

Gauge: 4' 8½"

AXWELL	0-4-0ST	OC	HL	2330	1896	New	(1)

(1) to NCB No.6 Area, 1/1/1947

<u>Axwell Park Coke Ovens</u>.

These were adjacent to the colliery, and the loco below worked the coke car. They ceased production in April 1930.

Gauge: 4' 8½"

-	0-4-0WE		New?	Scr

<u>Blaydon Burn Colliery</u>, Blaydon Burn. Map 78, NZ 166624.
(Joseph Cowan & Co until 1/1/1899)

A10 This colliery consisted of two pits, the Bessie and the Mary, and was opened in the 1850's. Shortly afterwards an extensive brickworks was also developed. The complex was served by a branch 1¼m long from NER Newcastle -Carlisle line, ¼m W of Blaydon Station. Not long after the turn of the century the <u>Ottovale Coke Ovens</u> (bye-product) were built nearby, and they and the colliery were vested into NCB Northern Division No.6 Area on 1st January 1947.

No locomotives are known before 1896.

Gauge: 4' 8½"

BLAYDON BURN No.1	0-4-0ST	OC	RS	2840	1896	New	Scr	/1926
ENTERPRISE	0-4-0ST	OC	CF	1190	1900	New	Scr	/1935
VENTURE	0-4-0ST	OC	CF	1198	1901	New	Scr	/1929
ACTIVE	0-4-0ST	OC	RS	3075	1901	New	(1)	
INDUSTRY	0-4-0ST	OC	HC	749	1906	New	(2)	
ENERGY	0-4-0ST	OC	HC	764	1906	New		
			reb.HL					
				8860	1934		(2)	
BETTY	0-4-0ST	OC	RS	3376	1909	New	(2)	
GEORGE	0-4-0ST	OC	HC	1190	1916	(a)	(3)	
NELL	0-4-0ST	OC	HC	1191	1916	New	(4)	
GERALD	0-4-0ST	OC	HL	2426	1899	(b)	(2)	
CLAUDE	0-4-0ST	OC	HL	2349	1896	(b)	(5)	
BLAYDON BURN No.2	0-4-0ST	OC	HC	1514	1923	New	(2)	

(a) believed ordered by Priestman
Collieries Ltd, but delivered
to Sir W.G.Armstrong Whitworth
& Co Ltd, Lemington, Newcastle-
upon-Tyne, by MOM
(b) ex Blaydon Main Colliery

(1) to BV, Auckland Park Colliery,
via James W. Ellis & Co Ltd,
Swalwell, /1927
(2) to NCB No. 6 Area, 1/1/1947
(3) ex Sir W.G.Armstrong Whitworth &
Co Ltd, Lemington, Newcastle-
upon-Tyne; to Ashington Coal Co
Ltd, Northumberland, /1916; ret.
to Blaydon Burn Colliery, /1918;
to Brims & Co Ltd, contrs, Newcastle, and ret; to Ashington
Coal Co Ltd, loan, /1925; ret.
/1926; to NCB No.6 Area,1/1/1947
(4) to Norwood Coke Ovens, c/1930
(5) to Waldridge Colliery, /1916;
ret. /1917; to Waldridge Colliery and ret; to NCB No.6 Area,
1/1/1947

<u>Blaydon Main Colliery</u>, Blaydon. Map 78, NZ 188632.
(Stella Coal Co Ltd until 1908 - q.v.)

B3 This colliery was served by a branch (½m) from NER Blackhill Branch, ½m W
of Blaydon Station. It was closed in March 1921.

Gauge: 4' 8½"

CLAUDE	0-4-0ST	OC	HL	2349	1896	(a)	(1)
GERALD	0-4-0ST	OC	HL	2426	1899	(a)	(1)

(a) ex Stella Coal Co Ltd, /1908   (1) to Blaydon Burn Colliery

<u>Lilley Drift and Brickworks</u>, Rowlands Gill. Map 78, NZ 168591.
(Joseph Cowan & Co until 1/1/1899)

A12 This small unit appears to have been started in the 1870's, and was served
by sidings W of NER Blackhill Branch, ½m N of Rowlands Gill Station. For
some time after 1896 it was connected to Blaydon Burn Colliery by an aerial
ropeway. It was vested in NCB Northern Division No.6 Area on 1st January 1947.

Gauge: 4' 8½"

INDUSTRY	0-4-0ST	OC				(a)	s/s c/1905
ASHINGTON	0-4-0ST	OC	B	303	1883		
			reb.RS	2987	1900	(b)	(1)

(a) origin unknown   (1) to NCB No.6 Area, 1/1/1947
(b) ex Ashington Coal Co Ltd, North-
umberland, via RS, /1900 (?)

<u>Norwood Coke Ovens</u>, Gateshead. Map 78, NZ 238613.
(Teams By-Product & Coke Co Ltd until 1930)

C10 This large complex was begun in 1912, and linked at its northern end to the
NER Tanfield Branch immediately N of Ellison Road crossing. The southern
end was served by a link to the Pelaw Main Railway's line to Dunston (see
Pelaw Main Collieries Ltd). Its owners went into voluntary liquidation in
May 1930, and the works were taken over by Priestman Collieries Ltd shortly
afterwards. It was vested in NCB Northern Division on 1st January 1947, and
its locomotives included in the No.6 Area list.

Gauge: 4' 8½"

TEAMBY							
(form. ASHBOURNE)	0-6-0ST	IC	HC	439	1896	(a)	s/s
ERNEST BURY	0-6-0ST	OC	HL	3282	1917	New	(1)
NELL	0-4-0ST	OC	HC	1191	1916	(b)	(1)

```
            VENTURE          0-4-0ST   OC  HL   2837  1910  (c)  (1)
            HASWELL          0-6-0T    IC  HC   1251  1917  (d)  (1)
```

(a) ex Naylor Bros, contrs, Harrow,   (1) to NCB No.6 Area, 1/1/1947
    Middlesex, /1913
(b) ex Blaydon Burn Colliery, c/1930
(c) ex HL, /1931; prev. Marston,
    Thompson & Evershed Ltd, Burton-
    on-Trent, Staffs
(d) ex Victoria Garesfield Colliery

Victoria Garesfield Colliery, Rowlands Gill. Map 78, NZ 145580.
(Owners of Victoria Garesfield Colliery until 1/1/1899; Priestman & Peile
until c1/1897; prev. Victoria Garesfield Colliery Co; orig. Thomas Ramsey)

A11 This colliery was sunk about 1860, and was served by a branch (1½m) from
NER Blackhill Branch, immediately W of Rowlands Gill Station. West of the
colliery were the Whinfield Ovens, the last 193 working beehive ovens in
the country. They and the colliery were vested in NCB Northern Division
No.6 Area on 1st January 1947.

Gauge: 4' 8½"

```
            VICTORIA No.1    0-4-0T    OC  MW                 (a)  s/s
            VICTORIA No.2    0-6-0ST   IC  FJ    167  1879  New   Scr
            VICTORIA No.3    0-6-0ST   IC  RS   2620  1887  New   s/s
            VICTORIA No.4    0-6-0ST   IC  RS   2847  1896  New
                                          reb.      1904         (1)
            VICTORIA No.5    0-6-0ST   IC  RS   2879  1900  New
                                          reb.HL 4861 1925        (2)
            HASWELL          0-6-0T    IC  HC   1251  1917  New   (3)
```

(a) origin unknown   (1) to Ashington Coal Co Ltd, North-
                                          umberland, and ret; to NCB No.6
                                          Area, 1/1/1947
                                      (2) to NCB No.6 Area, 1/1/1947
                                      (3) to Norwood Coke Ovens

Waldridge Colliery, Waldridge. Map 78, NZ 250501.
(Waldridge Coal Co Ltd until 1/1/1899; The Owners of Waldridge Collieries
until c/1895; the Owners of Victoria Garesfield Colliery until c/1893;
form. Thiedmann & Wallis)

H64 This colliery was linked by a short branch to the Sacriston Railway (see
Charlaw & Sacriston Collieries Co Ltd) at Bank Foot, Waldridge, the section
from here to Pelton Fell being owned and operated by Priestman Collieries
Ltd and their predecessors. This section was opened in August 1831, but no
locomotives are recorded before 1897. There were two loco sheds, one at the
colliery itself and one at Bank Foot, Waldridge, at the junction of the
branch and the main line. In 1924 control was handed over to Charlaw &
Sacriston Collieries Co Ltd, but Priestman Collieries Ltd continued to
work the colliery until its closure in April 1926.

Gauge: 4' 8½"

```
            WALDRIDGE    ⟋    0-4-0ST   OC  BH    546  1881  New  (1)
            CECIL        ⟋⟋   0-6-0ST   IC  AB    803  1897  New  s/s by  1924
            WALDRIDGE No.2 ⟋  0-4-0ST   OC  HC    674  1903  New
                                            reb.HL 4161 1925       (2)
            MARGARET     ⟋⟋   0-6-0ST   IC  AB   1005  1904  New  (3)
            CLAUDE       ⟋    0-4-0ST   OC  HL   2349  1896  (a)  (4)
            FAITH        ⟋    0-4-0ST   OC  HC   1201  1916  New  Scr c/1926
            CECIL        ⟋⟋   0-6-0T    IC  HC   1524  1924  New  (3)
```

            ⟋   shedded at the colliery
            ⟋⟋ shedded at Bank Foot, Waldridge

(a) ex Blaydon Burn Colliery, /1916; (1) to HC, /1903, in part exchange
    ret. /1917; ex Blaydon Burn   for new loco
    Colliery   (2) to Watergate Colliery, /1926
                                       (3) to Charlaw & Sacriston Collieries
                                           Co Ltd, /1924
                                       (4) to Blaydon Burn Colliery

Watergate Colliery, near Sunniside. Map 78, NZ 222599.

A15 This colliery was opened in 1926, and was served by sidings E of LNER
    Tanfield Branch, 2¼m from Dunston. It was vested in NCB Northern
    Division No.6 Area on 1st January 1947.

Gauge: 4' 8½"

	WALDRIDGE No.2	0-4-0ST	OC	HC	674	1903		
				reb.HL	4161	1925	(a)	(1)

(a) ex Waldridge Colliery, /1926   (1) to NCB No.6 Area, 1/1/1947

RAINE & CO LTD
(B.W. & G.Raine until 8/10/1891)

Delta Iron & Steel Works, Swalwell. Map 78, NZ 208633.

B4 This long-established works is served by sidings W of BR mineral line from
    Blaydon to Gateshead (the Redheugh Branch) 1½m E of Blaydon Station.

Gauge: 4' 8½"

	NORTH STAR	0-4-0ST	IC	JF			(a)	s/s
	-	0-4-0ST	OC	MW	455	1874	(b)	s/s
	-	0-4-0ST	OC	BH	852	1885	(c)	s/s
	BEATTY	0-6-0ST	IC	MW	1669	1905	(d)	(1)
	DELTA 1924	0-4-0ST	OC	AE	1932	1924	New	Scr 10/1957
No.2		0-4-0ST	OC	WB	2664	1942	(e)	Scr c/1959
	B No.20	0-4-0ST	OC	HL	3745	1929	(f)	s/s c/1965
No.7		0-4-0ST	OC	AB	1337	1913	(g)	(2)
13		0-4-0ST	OC	AB	2118	1941	(h)	s/s c/1965
	-	0-6-0DM		HC	D624	1942	(j)	(3)
	-	0-4-0DM		HE	5387	1959	(k)	(3)
	-	0-4-0DM		AB	384	1951	(m)	(3)
41		0-4-0ST	OC	RSH	7674	1951	(n)	(4)
1	(form.21)	0-4-0DE		BP	7946	1961		
				BT	339	1961	(p)	
2	(form.22)	0-4-0DE		BP	7947	1961		
				BT	340	1961	(p)	(5)
	SIR WILLIAM	0-4-0DE		BP	7873	1962		
				BT	443	1962	(p)	

(a) origin unknown
(b) ex Charlaw & Sacriston Collier-
    ies Co Ltd
(c) ex J.Spencer & Sons Ltd,
    Newburn, Newcastle-upon-Tyne
(d) ex Bradford Corporation, Water-
    works Dept., Nidd Valley Light
    Railway
(e) ex C.A.Parsons & Co Ltd,
    Newcastle, per A.W.Wanless & Co,
    Newcastle, 9/1953
(f) ex Consett Iron Co Ltd, Consett,
    8/1957
(g) ex Millom Hematite Ore & Iron Co
    Ltd, Millom, Cumberland, 6/1959

(1) withdrawn /1957 and used as a
    stationary boiler; scr /1959
(2) to Clayton & Davie, Dunston,
    for scrap, 5/1962
(3) to T.J.Thomson & Son Ltd,
    Teesside, for scrap, 4/1971
(4) ret. to NCB Northumberland Area,
    Burradon Colliery, 8/1969
(5) dismantled and used for spares
    from 1973

(h) ex G.Stephenson (Builders & Con-
    tractors) Ltd, Bishop Auckland,
    c3/1962; prev. ROF Linwood,
    Renfrewshire, Scotland
(j) ex TWW, Templeborough Works,
    Sheffield, Yorks, W.R., c5/1964;
    prev. Shell-Mex & B.P.Ltd, Hull
(k) ex Consett Iron Co Ltd, loan,
    1/1965; ret. 2/1965; purchased,
    2/1965
(m) ex Leslie Sanderson Ltd, Birtley,
    c/1968; prev. Lever Bros Ltd,
    Port Sunlight, Cheshire
(n) ex NCB Northumberland Area,
    Rising Sun Colliery, Wallsend,
    4/1969, loan
(p) ex Parkgate Iron & Steel Co Ltd,
    Sheffield, Yorks, W.R., 9/1970

Winlaton Mill Works, Winlaton Mill. Map 78, NZ 186604.

A13 This works was served by sidings from the Chopwell & Garesfield Railway of
the Consett Iron Co Ltd (q.v.). It was closed about 1918. The site is
now the workshops of NCB Clockburn Drift (q.v.).

Gauge: 4' 8½"

-	0-4-0VB		(a)	Scr c/1900
-	0-4-0ST		(b)	s/s
-	0-4-0ST		(c)	s/s

(a) origin unknown
(b) ex ?
(c) ex ?

RAINTON COLLIERY CO LTD, ADVENTURE COLLIERY, WEST RAINTON

L21 This colliery (Map 85, NZ 315471) was formerly owned by the Marquis of
Londonderry (q.v.) and served by the Londonderry Railway (Rainton & Seaham
Section). It was re-opened by its new owners about the turn of the century,
and served by sidings E of NER Sunderland-Durham line, ½m N of Leamside
Station. It was worked by the NER from 1903, and was vested in NCB Northern
Division No.2 Area on 1st January 1947.

Gauge: 4' 8½"

-	0-4-0ST	OC	(a)	(1)

(a) ex Marquis of Londonderry,   (1) to Seaham Harbour Dock Co Ltd,
    Londonderry Railway, c/1898;   /1903
    probably BH 203/1871

RAISBY QUARRIES LTD, GARMONDSWAY QUARRY, near COXHOE
(Raisby Hill Limestone Co Ltd until 1947; prev. Raisby Basic Co Ltd;
Raisby Basic Co until 30/9/1882)

R23 This huge limestone quarry and works (Map 85, NZ 353345) was originally
served by sidings N of NER Wingate-Ferryhill line, but has latterly been
at the end of the line, 4m N of Ferryhill Station.

Gauge: 4' 8½"

BESSIE	0-4-0ST	OC	HE	240	1880	(a)	s/s by 6/1928
-	0-4-0ST	OC	AB	1289	1912	New	(1)
10(orig. No.1 VICTORY)	0-4-0ST	OC	P	1544	1919	New	(2)
11(orig. No.2;later No.1)	0-4-0ST	OC	P	1637	1923	New	Scr c/1965

No.3		0-4-0ST	OC	P	1648	1923	New	Scr	/1969
	MOS No.2L	0-4-0ST	OC	AB	2119	1941	(b)	Scr	c6/1970
	–	4wDH	S		10031	1960	(c)	(3)	
	–	4wDH	S		10077	1961	New		

(a) ex South Stockton Iron Co,
    Yorks, N.R., by 7/1897
(b) ex G.Stephenson (Builders & Con-
    tractors) Ltd, Bishop Auckland,
    by 4/1959; prev. ROF Linwood,
    Renfrewshire, Scotland
(c) S demonstration loco; ex ICI
    Ltd, Billingham, c9/1960

(1) to Wilsons & Clyde Coal Co Ltd,
    Glencraig Colliery, Fifeshire,
    Scotland, /1936
(2) parts used to repair No.3, /1960;
    remainder scrapped between 1960
    and 1964
(3) sold by S to Dorman Long (Steel)
    Ltd, Middlesbrough, Yorks, N.R.,
    and delivered 4/1961

Gauge: 2' 0" (used within quarry for a time)

70		0-4-0WT	OC	AB	1995	1931	(a)	(1)
6		4wPM	MR		4045	1926	(b)	s/s
	–	4wPM	MR				(c)	s/s

(a) ex Durham County Water Board
(b) ex Francois Cementation Co Ltd,
    Kendal, Westmorland, /1940
(c) origin unknown

(1) to Dinorwic Slate Quarries Co
    Ltd, Caernarvonshire, /1948

RAMSHAW COAL CO LTD

Very little is known about this firm, or which collieries it owned. In 1937
it is listed as owning Ramshaw No.1 and Ramshaw No.2 Collieries (both later
nationalised - see NCB) and a small mine at West Auckland, but there is no
record of loco working at any of these. It is believed that the loco below
T27 worked at screens (Map 85, NZ 151262) situated alongside the LNER Bishop
Auckland-Barnard Castle line, ¼m E of Evenwood Station. These screens were
fed by a narrow gauge line (rope-worked ?) which drew coal from two drifts
known as Carterthorne Colliery.

Gauge: 4' 8½"

1	0-4-0ST	OC	P	916	1901	(a)	(1)

(a) ex ?   (1) to BV, Newfield Colliery, /1927

RANDOLPH COAL CO LTD, RANDOLPH COLLIERY & COKE WORKS, EVENWOOD
(subsidiary of PP; North Bitchburn Coal Co Ltd until 1/1933)

T10 Colliery (Map 85, NZ 157249) served by branch (1m) from LNER Haggerleazes
Branch, ¼m W of Spring Gardens Junction. An incline (1260 yds) worked by a
stationary engine took wagons down to the LNER. The unit was vested in NCB
Northern Division No.4 Area on 1st January 1947.

Gauge: 4' 8½"

CARBON	0-4-0ST	OC	Grange Iron Wks				
					1866	(a)	s/s
MOSTYN	0-4-0ST	OC	LG	⌀	1906	(a)	(1)
HUSTLER	0-4-0ST	OC	P	1337	1913	(a)	(2)
RANDOLPH	0-4-0ST	OC	RSH	7043	1942	New	(2)
WINSTON	0-4-0ST	OC	RSH	7159	1945	New	(2)

⌀ probably a rebuild by LG of an older locomotive built by another firm

(a) ex North Bitchburn Coal Co Ltd,
    1/1933

(1) to Bearpark Coal & Coke Co Ltd,
    East Hedley Hope Colliery,
    4/1945
(2) to NCB No.4 Area, 1/1/1947

<u>RANDOLPH COKE & CHEMICAL CO LTD</u>, RANDOLPH COKE WORKS, EVENWOOD
(company formed in 1957 as a subsidiary of North Eastern Tar Distillers
(Sadlers) Ltd to take over Randolph Coke Works from NCB Durham No.4 Area
in May 1957.

T10 Coke works (Map 85, NZ 157249) served by a branch (1m) from BR Haggerleazes
Branch, ¼m W of Spring Gardens Junction. An incline (1260 yds) worked by a
stationary engine took wagons down to BR. The works closed in September
1968, but was re-opened in the following month as a subsidiary of Millom
Hematite Ore & Iron Co Ltd, Cumberland, without rail transport.

Gauge: 4' 8½"

RANDOLPH	0-4-0ST	OC	RSH	7043	1942	(a)	(1)
(WINSTON)	0-4-0ST	OC	RSH	7159	1945	(a)	(1)

(a) ex NCB No.4 Area, 20/5/1957   (1) to C. Herring & Son Ltd,
                                            Hartlepool, for scrap, 3/1969;
                                            not removed until autumn 1969

<u>RANSOME HOFFMANN POLLARD LTD</u>, ANNFIELD PLAIN
(Ransome & Marles Bearing Co Ltd until 1/1/1970)

H34 Works (Map 78, NZ 160508) opened in 1951 and served by sidings S of BR
mineral line from Annfield Plain to Consett (Pontop & Shields branch),
1m W of former Annfield Plain Station.

Gauge: 4' 8½"

-	4wDM	RH	305302	1951	New	(1)
-	4wDM	RH	275881	1949	(a)	

(a) ex Newark Works, Notts, 3/1971   (1) to Newark Works, Notts, 3/1971

<u>LORD RAVENSWORTH & PARTNERS</u>

This partnership, known locally as "The Grand Allies", was at the
beginning of the nineteenth century the most powerful in the country.
F7 In February 1824 it opened a new colliery at <u>Springwell</u>, near Gateshead,
and to convey coal from this colliery (Map 78, NZ 285589) and <u>Mount Moor</u>
H16 <u>Colliery</u> (NZ 279577), about ¼m to the west, to the R. Tyne at Jarrow,
they commissioned their former enginewright, George Stephenson, to build
a new line, which was opened in January 1826. Coal from Mount Moor was
hauled up a short incline to a stationary engine at Blackham's Hill, whence
it was let down to Springwell. Then came a self-acting incline down to the
Leam Lane, whence locomotives took over for the run to Jarrow (4m). In
1840 Mount Moor Colliery was closed, but in June 1842 the line was extended
H14 westwards to <u>Kibblesworth Colliery</u> (NZ 243562), owned by George Southern,
by means of two more inclines, both worked by stationary engines. In
February 1850 Springwell and Mount Moor Collieries were taken over by
John Bowes, Esq., & Partners (q.v.), the agreement being backdated to 1st
January 1850. Kibblesworth Colliery followed in November 1851, and all
subsequently became part of the Pontop & Jarrow Railway. A passenger
service had also been operated over part of the line from 1843.
The loco shed was at Springwell Bank Foot.

Ref: "The Bowes Railway" by C.E.Mountford, 1966.

Gauge: 4' 8½"

No.1		0-4-0	VC	RS	1	1826	New	(1)
No.2		0-4-0	VC	RS	2	1826	New	(1)
	STRATHMORE						(a)	(1)

(a) origin unknown; believed to have (1) to John Bowes, Esq., & Partners,
    been here   1/1/1850

REDHEUGH IRON & STEEL CO (1936) LTD, TEAMS, GATESHEAD

C2 Works (Map 78, NZ 235623) served by sidings N of LNER Tanfield Branch,
about ¼m S of junction with Redheugh Branch. So far as is known the works
has never had any standard gauge locomotives; the one below is believed to
have been used for transferring ladles of molten metal between different
parts of the works.

Gauge: 2' 6"

-		4wPM	FH	2064	1937	New	s/s

G.RENNOLDSON, SOUTH SHIELDS

D16 The location of this engineering works is uncertain.

Gauge: 4' 8½" (?)

-				(a)	(1)

(a) believed to have been made at   (1) exploded, 20/11/1837
    the works in 1837

A.REYROLLE & CO LTD, HEBBURN

E4 Works consists of two units, the Hebburn Works (Map 78, NZ 304644), lying
W of BR line from Gateshead to South Shields, ½m W of Hebburn Station, and
E5 the New Town Works (NZ 308647), immediately E of the line at Hebburn
Station. One locomotive was used at each works, and also for shunting
between the two works using running powers over BR. Rail traffic ceased
in 1970.

Gauge: 4' 8½"

1		4wBE	EE	512	1920	New	Scr 1/1971
2		0-4-0DM	AW	D22	1933	New	(1)

(1) to W.F. & J.R.Shepherd Ltd, Byker,
    Newcastle-upon-Tyne, 12/1970

THOMAS RICHARDSON & SONS LTD, HARTLEPOOL IRON WORKS, HARTLEPOOL
(Thomas Richardson & Sons until 1894)

S4 Works (Map 85, NZ 521336) served by sidings in Hartlepool Docks complex.
In the 1850's the firm built a number of locomotives, but most of its work
was concerned with marine engines. The works was acquired on 29th October
1900 by Richardsons, Westgarth & Co Ltd (q.v.).

> The firm is believed to have had one or more locos built by
> John Harris of Darlington before those listed below, and may
> well have had other locos afterwards.

Gauge: 4' 8½"

No.2		0-4-0ST	OC	HE	30	1869	New	(1)
No.3		0-4-0ST	OC	HE	60	1871	New	(2)
No.4		0-4-0ST	OC	HE	78	1872	New	(3)
No.5		0-4-0ST	OC	HE	80	1873	New	(4)

(1) to Hull Dock Co, Hull, Yorks,
    E.R., via HE, 12/1873
(2) to Hutchinson's Trustees, Widnes,
    Lancs, by 10/1897
(3) to Terry, Greaves & Co, Old
    Roundwood Colliery, Wakefield,
    Yorks, W.R., by 1/1876
(4) to Tees Conservancy Commissioners,
    Middlesbrough, Yorks, N.R., by 10/1875

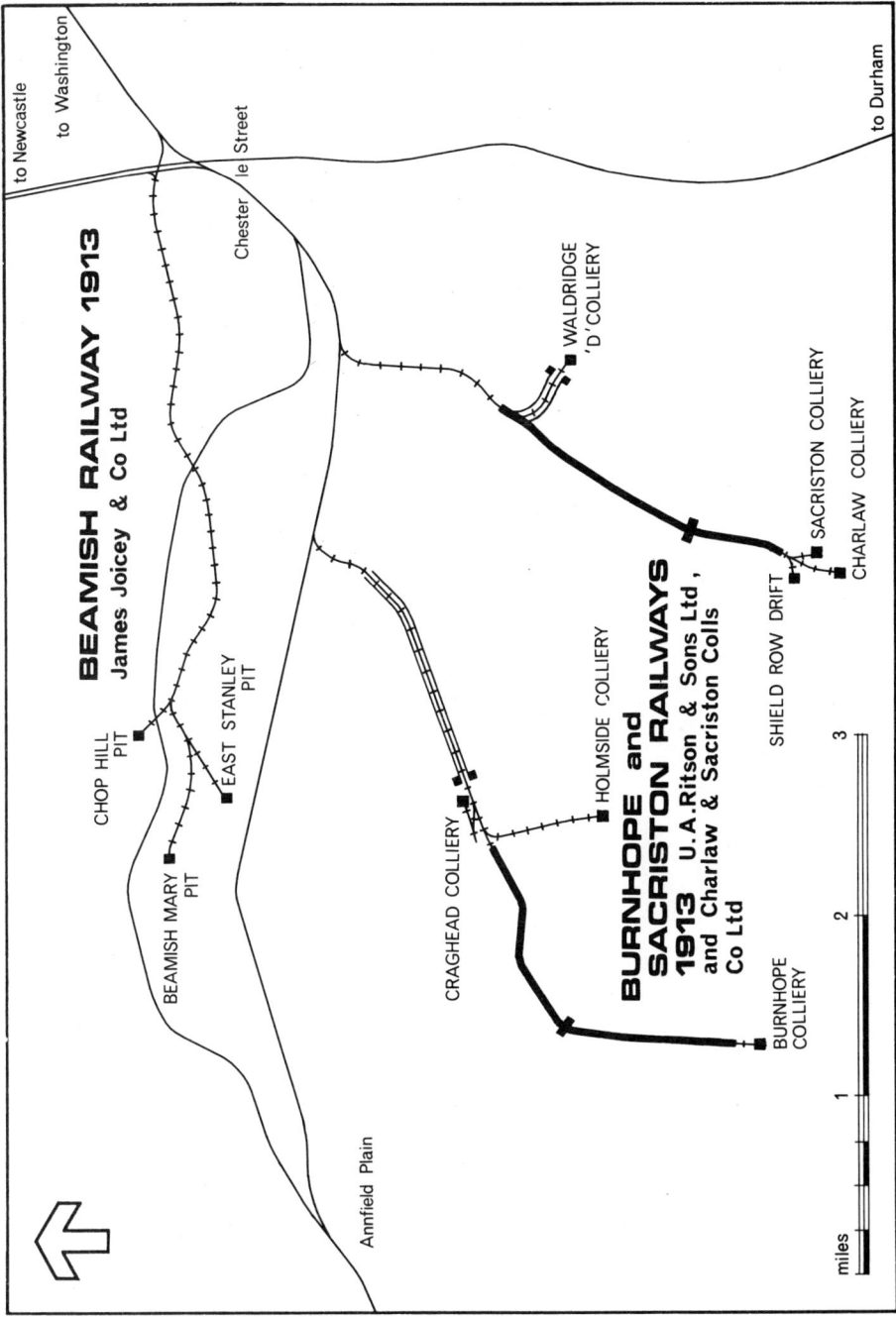

BEAMISH RAILWAY 1913
James Joicey & Co Ltd

BURNHOPE and
SACRISTON RAILWAYS
1913 U.A.Ritson & Sons Ltd,
and Charlaw & Sacriston Colls
Co Ltd

to Newcastle
to Washington
Chester le Street
to Durham

WALDRIDGE
'D' COLLIERY

SACRISTON COLLIERY

CHARLAW COLLIERY

SHIELD ROW DRIFT

HOLMSIDE COLLIERY

CHOP HILL
PIT

EAST STANLEY
PIT

BEAMISH MARY
PIT

CRAGHEAD COLLIERY

BURNHOPE
COLLIERY

Annfield Plain

miles

1   2   3

175

RICHARDSONS WESTGARTH (HARTLEPOOL) LTD, HARTLEPOOL ENGINE WORKS, HARTLEPOOL
(Richardsons, Westgarth & Co Ltd until 3/1938; subsidiary of Richardsons
Westgarth Group)

S4 Works (Map 85, NZ 521336) formerly owned by Thomas Richardson & Sons Ltd
(q.v.) in Hartlepool Docks complex. The sidings from the south were removed
about 1958, and rail traffic from the north via the No.1 Swing Bridge was
discontinued about 1962, all traffic then being taken by road.

Gauge: 4' 8½"

	-	0-4-0T	HH				(a)	(1)	
	FOREST	0-4-0T					(b)	(2)	
	-	0-4-0ST	OC	AB ∕		1883	(c)	Scr c/1922
533		0-4-0ST	OC	AB	823	1898	(d)	(3)	
	-	0-4-0ST	OC	P	1510	1919	New	Scr	/1962
	WEAVER	0-4-0ST	OC	MW	1072	1888	(e)	(4)	

∕ carried Lennox Lange plate

(a) ex ?   (1) for sale, 7/1903; s/s by /1909
(b) ex ?, hire (?)   (2) to ?, ex hire (?)
(c) ex contr., Hartlepool, (Torbuck?)   (3) to Ashmore, Benson, Pease & Co
(d) ex R.Hickman, Middlesbrough,   Ltd, Stockton, c/1922
    Yorks, N.R.   (4) ret. to T.J.Thomson & Son Ltd,
(e) ex T.J.Thomson & Son Ltd,   Stockton, ex hire
    Stockton, hire, /1947

RITSONS (BURNHOPE COLLIERIES) LTD, BURNHOPE COLLIERY, BURNHOPE

H54 This colliery (Map 85, NZ 191482) was sunk in 1845, and was linked by the
Burnhope Waggonway to the Stanhope & Tyne Railway (later NER) at West Pelt-
on. Wagons from the colliery were hauled by a stationary engine up to the
top of the moor to the north of the colliery, and then let down to Craghead
Colliery, whence the traffic was worked by Holmside & South Moor Collieries
Ltd (q.v.) and their predecessors. When a locomotive was first used at
Burnhope for shunting is not known. The colliery was taken over in 1939 by
Bearpark Coal & Coke Co Ltd, and shunting at the colliery was resumed by
the stationary engine. The colliery, by then also drawing on a number of
nearby drifts, was vested in NCB Northern Division No.6 Area on 1st January
1947.

Gauge: 4' 8½"

	-	0-4-0ST	OC				(a)	(1)
	BURNHOPE	0-4-0ST	OC	RS	3057	1904	New	(2)

(a) origin unknown   (1) to RS, /1904, in part exchange
                                         for new loco
                                     (2) loaned to Pelaw Main Collieries
                                         Ltd, and ret; to SDSI, West
                                         Hartlepool, /1939

ROBINSON & HANNON LTD, TYNEDALE WORKS, BLAYDON

B2 This works (Map 78, NZ 190637) was part of the site formerly owned by Smith,
Patterson & Co Ltd (q.v.), and was served by sidings N of BR Newcastle-
Carlisle line, ½m E of Blaydon Station. Rail traffic ceased in 1966.

Gauge: 4' 8½"

	-	4wDM	FH	3374	1950	(a)	(1)

(a) ex Smith, Patterson & Co Ltd,   (1) hired to Cox & Danks Ltd for dis-
    1/1/1965   mantling BR Blackhill Branch, and
                                         ret. 7/1965; to T.Turnbull Ltd,

JOHN ROGERSON & CO LTD, WOLSINGHAM STEELWORKS, WOLSINGHAM
(John Rogerson & Co until 1887)

X4 This works (Map 84, NZ 082372) was begun in 1864 by C.Attwood, and was
taken over by John Rogerson & Co in 1885. It was served by sidings N of NER
Wearhead Branch, ½m E of Wolsingham Station. John Rogerson & Co Ltd sold
out in 1930. For later history see Wolsingham Steel Co Ltd. A loco shed to
house "three small locomotives" was being built here in March 1893, but
their identity is unknown. In later years shunting was done by steam crane.

Gauge: 4' 8½"

No.1			P			(a)	s/s
No.2		0-4-0ST	OC	P	1460	1916	New (1)

(a) origin unknown

(1) to Leversons Wallsend Collieries
Ltd, Usworth Colliery, via C.W.
Dorking & Co Ltd

ROLLING STOCK & ENGINEERING CO LTD, NESTFIELD WORKS, ALBERT HILL,DARLINGTON
(form. Rolling Stock Co Ltd; orig. Darlington Rolling Stock Co Ltd)

V12 Works (Map 85, NZ 298159) served by sidings E of BR Durham-Darlington line
1¼m N of Darlington (Bank Top) Station. Rail traffic ceased in 1968.

Gauge: 4' 8½"

NESTFIELD	0-4-0ST	OC				(a)	
			reb.HL	9492	1908		s/s c/1931
No.4	0-4-0ST	OC	HL	2533	1902	(b)	Scr /1952
-	4wDM		RH	305303	1951	New	(1)

(a) origin unknown
(b) ex Samuel Tyzack & Co Ltd,
    Sunderland, 4/1937

(1) to Llanelli Steel Co Ltd, Llan-
    elli, Carmarthenshire, 6/1968

ROSEDALE & FERRYHILL IRON CO LTD (reg. 6/1864)

Ferryhill Iron Works (Map 85, NZ 304335) was opened in 1859 by James Morrison; in fact the works was not at Ferryhill, but West Cornforth. In 1867
R26 the firm opened Thrislington Colliery, a few yards to the north, by which
time it also owned ironstone mines in North Yorkshire. The ironworks was
served by an NER branch (1¼m) from Ferryhill Station on the Durham-Darlington line, while the colliery was served by a private branch (½m) from
Ferryhill Iron Works Junction on the NER Wingate-Ferryhill line at West
Cornforth Station. The two locations were linked, and it is assumed that
the locomotives below were used indiscriminately. The firm failed in January 1879. The ironworks were eventually purchased by John Rogerson & Co,
and were dismantled in 1882, apparently without being re-started. The
colliery passed to the Thrislington Coal Co Ltd, (q.v.), using different
rail access.

Gauge: 4' 8½"

-	0-4-0ST	OC	MW	199	1866	(a)	(1)
FERRYHILL	0-4-0ST	OC	BH	22	1867	New	s/s
JAMES MORRISON	0-4-0ST	OC	BH	95	1869	New	s/s
EDDIE (form.							
THRISLINGTON)	0-4-0ST	OC	BH	354	1875	New	s/s

(a) ex W.Ritson, contr,NER Allendale
    Branch, Northumberland, /1867

(1) to BV, Cleveland Works, Middles-
    brough, Yorks, N.R.

Two "7 in.tank locomotives", almost certainly from Ferryhill Ironworks,
were offered for sale in the "Colliery Guardian" of 6th June 1873. Their

identity and fate is unknown.

ROYAL ORDNANCE FACTORIES

<u>Aycliffe Factory</u>, Aycliffe.   Map 85, NZ 2723.
U2 Factory opened in 1941, and served by sidings from LNER Bishop Auckland-Darlington line, at Heighington Station. The premises were later acquired by North Eastern Trading Estates Ltd, (q.v.).

Gauge: 4' 8½"

ROF 9 No.1	0-4-0DM		JF	22934	1941	New	(1)
ROF 9 No.2	0-4-0DM		JF	22943	1941	New	(2)
ROF 9 No.3	0-4-0ST	OC	HC	1722	1941	New	(3)
ROF 9 No.4	0-4-0DM		JF	22948	1941	New	(4)
ROF 9 No.5	0-4-0ST	OC	RSH	7046	1941	New	(5)
ROF 9 No.6	0-4-0DM		JF			(a)	s/s
ROF 9 No.7	0-4-0ST	OC	P	2016	1941	New	(6)
ROF 9 No.8	0-4-0ST	OC	P	2042	1943	New	(6)

(a) origin doubtful

(1) to SR, 400S, /1946
(2) to Vickers-Armstrongs Ltd, Squires Gate, Lancs, 2/1946
(3) to Pilkington Bros Ltd, St.Helens, Lancs, 3/1946
(4) to R.S.Hayes Ltd, Bridgend, Glamorgan
(5) to Pilkington Bros Ltd, St.Helens, Lancs, 6/1946
(6) to North Eastern Trading Estates Ltd, Aycliffe

<u>Birtley Factory</u>, Birtley. Map 78, NZ 265564.
H19 Formerly owned by MOM, and latterly by MOD, Army Dept (both q.v.). Served by sidings E of LNER Newcastle-Durham line, ½m N of Birtley Station.

Gauge: 4' 8½"

-	0-4-0DM		JF	22137	1937	New	(1)

(1) to MOD, Army Dept

<u>Spennymoor Factory</u>, Spennymoor. Map 85, NZ 267337 (approx)
R7 Opened about 1938, and closed about 1946. Served by sidings from LNER Spennymoor-Ferryhill line, 1m E of Spennymoor Station. Site later developed as a Trading Estate.

Gauge: 4' 8½"

-	0-4-0ST	OC	HC	1507	1923	(a)	(1)

(a) ex Shaw's Glazed Brick Co Ltd, Darwen, Lancs, via TWW, 2/1938

(1) to MOS, Kings Newton Depot, Derbyshire

<u>RYHOPE COAL CO LTD</u>, RYHOPE COLLIERY, RYHOPE
(form. Ryhope Coal Co)

K16 Colliery (Map 78, NZ 399575) was opened in 1859, and was served by a branch (¾m) of the Londonderry Railway (NER from October 1900) from Ryhope Station. The colliery was vested in NCB Northern Division No.1 Area on 1st January 1947.

Gauge: 4' 8½"

No.2	0-6-0ST	IC	MW	274	1870	New	s/s after 2/1889

-	0-6-0ST	IC	BH	716	1883		
			reb.		1906	(a)	s/s
-	0-4-0ST	OC	AB	1082	1907	New	(1)
1	0-6-0ST	OC	P	1403	1916	New	(2)
2	0-6-0ST	OC	P	1455	1918	New	(2)
No.3	0-6-0T	IC	Dar	480	1892	(b)	(2)

(a) ex Leversons Wallsend Collieries Ltd, Usworth Colliery

(b) ex LNER, 1144, 6/1938

(1) to Wake, Darlington, c/1916; re-sold to Workington Iron & Steel Co Ltd, Cumberland, /1916

(2) to NCB No.1 Area, 1/1/1947

SIR S.A.SADLER LTD

Hamsteels Colliery, near Quebec. Map 85, NZ 184432.
(Joseph Johnson (Durham) Ltd until 1/4/1923; Sir S.A.Sadler Ltd until 1917; form. Hamsteels Colliery Co; orig. Owners of Hamsteels Colliery)

M9 Colliery was opened in 1867, and was served by sidings N of 1¼m private branch which served Cornsay Colliery (see Ferens & Love (1937) Ltd) from Flass Junction on NER Waterhouses Branch. The colliery closed in July 1924, but was re-opened in May 1932, with an aerial ropeway to Malton Colliery. It was vested in NCB Northern Division No.5 Area on 1st January 1947.

Gauge: 4' 8½"

HAMSTEELS	0-6-0ST	IC	MW	480	1874	New	s/s after 10/1910
WHITWORTH (HAMSTEELS by 8/1922)	0-6-0ST	IC	MW	569	1875	New	
			reb. MW		1922		(1)

(1) to Malton Colliery, c/1924

Gauge: 2' 10" (used on coke ovens)

HAMSTEELS No.3	0-4-0ST	OC	BH	439	1877	New	s/s
-	0-4-0ST	OC	BH	856	1885	(a)	s/s

(a) ex Bowling Iron Co Ltd, Bradford, Yorks, W.R., by 4/1901

Malton Colliery & Coke Works, near Lanchester. Map 85, NZ 180461.
(form. Love & Son)

M6 Colliery was opened in 1870, and consisted of a number of scattered drifts. Coal came to sidings S of LNER Lanchester-Durham line, 1m SE of Lanchester Station. It was vested in NCB Northern Division No.5 Area on 1st January 1947.

Gauge: 4' 8½"

BOBS	0-6-0ST	OC	HCR	176	1876	(a)	
			reb. Worth & Mackenzie, Stockton			Scr	/1914
BASIL ✗ (form. WILBERFORCE)	0-4-0ST	OC	I'Anson		1875	(b)	(1)
CECIL	0-4-0ST	OC	RWH	1847	1881	(c)	(2)
BASIL ✗	0-6-0ST	OC	BH	1034	1891		
			reb. HL	3668	1904	(d)	(3)
HAMSTEELS	0-6-0ST	IC	MW	569	1875		
			reb. MW		1922	(e)	(3)
SILKSTONE	0-6-0ST	IC	MW	341	1871		
			reb.		1903		
			reb.		1925		
			reb.		1935	(f)	(3)

✗ This was a painted name, which was first carried by the I'Anson loco, and was then transferred to BH 1034

(a)	ex Cliffe Coal & Fireclay Co Ltd, Wakefield, Yorks, W.R., c/1887	(1) to South Medomsley Colliery Co Ltd, via R.Shaw, c/1945
(b)	ex Skerne Ironworks Co Ltd, Darlington	(2) to Cerebos Ltd, Greatham, via LG, c/1933
(c)	ex Sir B.Samuelson & Co Ltd, Newport Works, Middlesbrough, Yorks, N.R., c/1916	(3) to NCB No.5 Area, 1/1/1947
(d)	ex South Moor Colliery Co Ltd, c/1923	
(e)	ex Hamsteels Colliery, c/1924	
(f)	ex Newton, Chambers & Co Ltd, Sheffield, Yorks, W.R., 6/1946	

SEAHAM HARBOUR DOCK CO LTD

This company was formed in 1899 during the re-organisation of the industrial interests of the 6th Marquis of Londonderry (q.v.).

L34 Initially it took over Seaham Harbour Docks, probably with the three dock locomotives owned by the Londonderry Railway. In October 1900 the Railway was absorbed by the NER, but the branches to Seaham Colliery ($\frac{1}{2}$m) and the sinking at Dawdon ($\frac{1}{4}$m) were excluded, and it would seem that these were then worked by the Dock Co, though eventually locomotives were introduced by Londonderry Collieries Ltd (q.v.) for shunting at the collieries them-selves. Besides this traffic, the Docks were also served by the railway from South Hetton and Murton Collieries (see South Hetton Coal Co Ltd). All these lines to the Docks passed to the NCB in 1947.
The loco shed is at Map 85, NZ 431494.

Gauge: 4' 8$\frac{1}{2}$"

16		0-4-0VBT	VC	HW	21	1870	(a)	(1)
17		0-4-0VBT	OC	HW	33	1873		
				reb.Seaham			(a)	(2)
18		0-4-0WT	OC	Lewin	c1875		(a)	
	reb.	0-4-0T	OC	Seaham				
	reb.	0-4-0ST	OC	Seaham		1927		(7)
3		0-6-0	IC	TR	254	1855		
	reb.	0-6-0ST	IC	Seaham		1876	(b)	Scr
1	SEATON	0-6-0T	IC	Seaham		1902	(c)	Scr 5/1962
19		0-4-0ST	OC	BH	203	1871	(d)	Scr c3/1939
	REX	0-4-0ST	OC	MW	838	1885	(e)	Scr /1939
	DICK	0-4-0ST	OC	HE	628	1895	(e)	Scr 12/1963
	SEAHAM	0-6-0ST	OC	P	1052	1905	New	Scr /1961
	SILKSWORTH	0-6-0ST	OC	P	1083	1906	New	Scr 7/1963
	MILO	0-6-0ST	IC	RS	2241	1875	(f)	Scr 7/1963
	AJAX	0-6-0	IC	Blyth & Tyne	1867		(g)	Scr /1926
	MARS	0-6-0ST	IC	RS	2238	1875	(h)	Scr 7/1963
	CLIO	0-6-0	IC	Ghd		1875	(j)	Scr /1955
	JUNO	0-6-0ST	OC	HL	3527	1922	New	Scr 1/1967
	NEPTUNE	0-6-0ST	OC	HL	3898	1936	New	Scr 1/1967
	SENTINEL	4wVBT	VCG	S	9575	1954	(k)	Scr 6/1965
	TEMPEST	4wVBT	VCG	S	9618	1956	New	(3)
	–	4wVBT	VCG	S	9619	1957	New	(4)
	–	0-6-0DE		YE	2668	1956	(m)	(5)
18		0-6-0ST	OC	BH	32	1867		
				reb.HL	1491	1935	(n)	Scr 12/1963
44		0-6-0T	OC	MW	1934	1917		
				reb.LEW		1951	(n)	Scr 7/1963
	B No.10	0-4-0ST	OC	HL	3476	1920	(p)	Scr 12/1966
	B No.15	0-4-0ST	OC	HL	3873	1936	(q)	Scr 12/1963
	B No.23	0-4-0ST	OC	HL	3744	1929	(q)	Scr c6/1967
	B No.38	0-4-0ST	OC	HL	3496	1921	(q)	Scr c6/1967

	B No.41	0-4-0ST	OC	RSH	7016	1940	(q)	Scr	2/1967
	-	4wDH		TH	104C	1960	(r)	Scr	1/1975
No.1		0-4-0ST	OC	HL	3354	1918	(s)	Scr	2/1964
	S D S & I Co No.3	0-4-0ST	OC	HL	3355	1918	(s)	Scr	c6/1967
10		0-4-0ST	OC	HL	3352	1918	(t)	Scr	3/1967
52		0-4-0ST	OC	RSH	7340	1946	(t)	Scr	11/1966
173		0-4-0ST	OC	HL	3919	1937	(t)	Scr	9/1967
183		0-4-0ST	OC	RSH	7347	1947	(t)	(6)	
24		0-4-0ST	OC	RSH	7342	1947	(u)	Scr	12/1966
25		0-4-0ST	OC	RSH	7345	1947	(u)	Scr	11/1966
54		0-4-0ST	OC	RSH	7346	1947	(u)	Scr	12/1966
177		0-4-0ST⁄	OC	RSH	7036	1940	(u)	Scr	c6/1967
D1		0-6-0DH		EE(V)	D1191	1967	New		
D2		0-6-0DH		EE(V)	D1192	1967	New		
D3		0-6-0DH		EE(V)	D1193	1967	New		
D4		0-6-0DH		EE(V)	D1194	1967	New		
D5		0-6-0DH		EE(V)	D1195	1967	New		

⁄ converted to oil firing by 7/1965

(a) ex Marquis of Londonderry,
Londonderry Railway, /1899
(b) ex Marquis of Londonderry,
Londonderry Railway, /1899;
ownership doubtful; believed to
have been used in sinking of
Dawdon Colliery
(c) under construction as 0-4-4T at
Seaham Engine Works when Londonderry Railway taken over by NER
in 10/1900; completed as shown
(d) ex Rainton Colliery Co Ltd,
/1903
(e) ex S.Pearson & Son Ltd, contrs
for Seaham South Dock, /1905
(f) ex NER, 1662, 7/1907
(g) ex NER, 1927, 9/1907
(h) ex NER, 1661, 12/1908
(j) ex NER, 125, 12/1911
(k) S demonstration loco; ex S,
9/1956; purchased, 11/1956
(m) YE demonstration loco; ex NCB
Northern (Northumberland &
Cumberland) No.3 Area, Ashington
Colliery, 9/5/1958
(n) ex NCB No.2 Area, 2/1960
(p) ex Consett Iron Co Ltd, 3/1960
(q) ex Consett Iron Co Ltd, 2/1960;
delivered 5/1960
(r) reb. of TEMPEST, ex TH, via DL,
Lackenby Works, Middlesbrough,
Yorks, N.R., trials, 10/1960
(s) ex SDSI, West Hartlepool,
11/1961
(t) ex DL, Acklam Works, Middlesbrough, Yorks, N.R., 6/1963
(u) ex DL, Britannia Works,
Middlesbrough, Yorks, N.R.,
11/1963

(1) to HW for preservation, 6/1959
(2) to HW for preservation, 6/1962
(3) to TH for conversion to DH, /1959
(4) ret. to S by 2/1958
(5) to Appleby-Frodingham Steel Co
Ltd, Lincs, 15/5/1958, ex trial
(6) to W.F.Smith Ltd, Seaham Harbour,
for scrap, c12/1967
(7) to North of England Open-Air
Museum, Beamish, for preservation,
1/1975

<u>SEATON CAREW IRON CO LTD</u>,   SEATON CAREW IRONWORKS,   WEST HARTLEPOOL
(reg. 25/4/1882)

S8   This company was formed to take over the blast furnaces formerly owned by
the West Hartlepool Iron Co, which had failed in 1875 (see entry for South
Durham Steel & Iron Co Ltd).   The works (Map 85, NZ 518309 (approx)) was
served by sidings from NER West Hartlepool-Billingham line, 1¼m S of West
Hartlepool Station.   The works passed into the control of the East Coast
Steel Corporation in 1919, and was subsequently taken over by the adjacent
South Durham Steel & Iron Co Ltd, though this may have occurred earlier
than the usually quoted date of 1928.

Gauge: 4' 8½"

GLADYS	0-4-0ST	OC	AB			(a)	(1)
DAISY	0-4-0ST	OC	P	467	1888	New	(1)
WALTER MORRISON	0-4-0ST	OC	P	657	1897	New	(1)
FRANCIS	0-4-0ST	OC	HL	2378	1898	New	(1)
AILEEN	0-4-0ST	OC	HL	2445	1899	New	(1)
MAJOR	0-4-0ST	OC	AB	1363	1914	New	(1)
COLONEL	0-4-0ST	OC	AB	1501	1917	New	(1)
1918	0-4-0ST	OC	AB	1609	1918	New	(1)

(a) origin unknown; may have been   (1) to SDSI, (1928?)
    AB 299/1888, known to have been
    delivered to West Hartlepool

<u>SHELL-MEX & B.P. LTD</u>,   JARROW

E20 A large oil depot (Map 78, NZ 338655) served by a branch (¼m) from BR
Gateshead- South Shields line, ¼m E of Jarrow Station.   Shunting has been
done by BR from 1964.

Gauge: 4' 8½"

No.16 (THE ERNEST BRIERLEY) 0-4-0DM	DC	2164	1941	(a)	(1)

(a) ex Trafford Park Works,   (1) to Salt End Works, Hull, Yorks,
    Manchester, /1950   E.R., via Bg for repairs, 1/1965

<u>J. SHIELD</u>,   ANNA PIT,   near BURNOPFIELD

H3   This colliery (Map 78, NZ 158561) was formerly Lintz Colliery, closed by
the Lintz Coal Co (q.v.) about 1885.   In 1889 it was re-opened by Mr.Shield,
who used horses to shunt the colliery and built a self-acting incline down
to the South Garesfield Colliery sidings N of Lintz Green Station on the
NER Blackhill Branch.   The colliery was taken over by the South Garesfield
Colliery Co Ltd (q.v.) about 1895.

Gauge: 4' 8½"

LINTZ No.1	0-4-0ST	OC	West Hartlepool	(a)	(1)

(a) ex NER, 1778, 7/1893   (1) to South Garesfield Colliery Co
                                               Ltd, c/1895

SHORT BROS LTD, PALLION, SUNDERLAND

K6 Shipbuilding yard (Map 78, NZ 375580) served by a branch (½m) from Pallion
Station on BR Sunderland-Durham line. The company's locos also shunted
the adjacent works of Steels Engineering Products Ltd (q.v.) until 1956.
The firm went into voluntary liquidation in April 1964.

Gauge: 4' 8½"

-	0-4-0ST	OC	Butterley			(a)	(1)
-	0-4-0ST	OC	P	971	1903	New	(2)
-	0-4-0ST	OC	HL	2496	1901	(b)	(3)
-	0-4-0ST	OC	BH	606	1881	(c)	s/s
BASIL	0-4-0ST	OC	I'Anson		1875	(d)	s/s
YARD No.249	4wVBT	VCG	S	9563	1954	New	s/s c/1964

(a) ex Butterley Co Ltd, Derbyshire
(b) ex Ewesley Quarry Co Ltd,
     Northumberland
(c) ex Gateshead County Borough,
     9/1939
(d) ex South Medomsley Colliery Co
     Ltd, c/1945

(1) to Sadler & Co Ltd, Middles-
     brough, Yorks, N.R.
(2) to J.C.Wight Ltd, Pallion,
     Sunderland, for scrap, /1954
(3) to Sir Hedworth Williamson's
     Limeworks Ltd, Fulwell,
     Sunderland, /1940

SHOTTON BRICK CO LTD, SHOTTON BRICKWORKS, SHOTTON COLLIERY
(subsidiary of John W. Pearson & Co Ltd, Middlesbrough, Yorks, N.R.)

P6 This brickworks and its quarry (Map 85, NZ 397404) were taken over from
NCB Durham No.3 Area about 1953, and closed about 1959. It was served
by the NCB branch to Shotton Colliery, which joined the BR Sunderland-
Stockton line, 1¼m N of Wellfield Junction.

Gauge: 2' 6"

-	4wDM	HE	4400	1954	New	s/s
-	4wDM	HE	5282	1957	New	s/s

SKERNE IRONWORKS CO LTD, SKERNE IRONWORKS, ALBERT HILL, DARLINGTON
(Pease, Hutchinson & Co until 1872)

V13 This works (Map 85, NZ 298159) was opened in 1864, and was served by
sidings E of NER Durham-Darlington line, 1¼m N of Darlington (Bank Top)
Station. Its later history is a little uncertain. It appears to have
closed in 1889, and in May 1889 the auction of works equipment included
two locomotives, which may have been the two below. It would seem,
however, that the works was later re-opened by Wake & Carr (q.v.).

Gauge: 4' 8½"

-	0-4-0ST	OC	MW	112	1864	(a)	s/s
-	0-4-0ST	OC	I'Anson		1875	(b)	(1)

(a) ex MW, c/1871; prev. Consett
     Iron Co Ltd
(b) ex Fry, I'Anson & Co Ltd,
     Darlington

(1) to Sir S.A.Sadler Ltd, Malton
     Colliery

SLATER & CO (LIMESTONE) LTD, MARSDEN QUARRIES, near WHITBURN

D13 This group of five limestone quarries, not all of them in production, was purchased from NCB N&D No.1 Area in September 1965, and all rail transport was immediately replaced by road haulage.

Gauge: 2' 0"

-	4wDM	RH	177535	1936	(a)	(1)
-	4wDM	RH	187059	1937	(a)	(1)
-	4wDM	RH	189959	1938	(a)	(2)
-	4wDM	RH	189963	1939	(a)	(3)
-	4wDM	RH	287662	1950	(a)	(1)

(a) ex NCB No.1 Area, 9/1965

(1) sold for scrap, c/1967
(2) parts sent to Newlandside Quarry (owned by firm); remainder sold for scrap
(3) to North of England Open Air Museum, Brancepeth Store, c/1967

HOWARD SMITH (HENDON) LTD, HENDON PAPER MILLS, GRANGETOWN, SUNDERLAND
(Hendon Paper Works Co Ltd until 1/1/1963)

K14 Works (Map 78, NZ 410550) was served by sidings W of BR mineral line from Grangetown to South Dock, Sunderland. Rail traffic ceased in 1965.

Gauge: 4' 8½"

-	0-4-0ST	OC	AB	1256	1912	New	Scr
HENDON	4wVBT	VCG	S	7062	1927	New	s/s c/1958
HENDON	4wDM		FH	3865	1958	New	(1)

(1) to NCB Yorkshire No.7 Area, Old Roundwood Colliery, via FH, c10/1965

SMITH, PATTERSON & CO LTD, PIONEER FOUNDRY, BLAYDON

B2 Works (Map 78, NZ 190637) served by sidings N of BR Newcastle-Carlisle line, ½m E of Blaydon Station. The firm went into voluntary liquidation in September 1964, and part of the works was later purchased by Robinson & Hannon Ltd (q.v.).

Gauge: 4' 8½"

BUTTERFLY	0-4-0ST	OC	MW	942	1885	(a)	s/s after 11/1896
PIONEER	0-4-0ST	OC	HE	18	1867		
			reb. HC		1906	(b)	(1)
JUBILEE	0-4-0ST	OC	HL	3577	1923	New	Scr /1964
TEES-SIDE No.2	0-4-0ST	OC	MW	1327	1897		
			reb.Galloways	1922			
			reb.Teesside	1936		(c)	(2)
-	4wDM		FH	3374	1950	(d)	(3)

(a) ex C.Braddock, Golborne, Lancs
(b) ex Walter Scott & Co, contrs
(c) ex Tees Side Bridge & Engineering Works Ltd, Cargo Fleet, Yorks, N.R., /1947, loan
(d) ex Ferens & Love (1937) Ltd, Cornsay Brickworks, c/1962

(1) to Edward Lloyd Ltd, Sitting-bourne, Kent, /1942
(2) ret. to Tees Side Bridge & Engineering Works Ltd, Cargo Fleet, Yorks, N.R., /1947
(3) to Robinson & Hannon Ltd, 1/1/1965

SOUTH DERWENT COAL CO LTD

East Tanfield Colliery, near Tantobie. Map 78, NZ 194552.
(East Tanfield Colliery Co Ltd until 1930; James Joicey & Co Ltd until
1917 - q.v.)

H17 Colliery served by sidings E of LNER Tanfield Branch, and vested in NCB
Northern Division No.6 Area on 1st January 1947.

Gauge: 4' 8½"

STANLEY No.2	0-4-0ST	OC	HC		c1881			
			reb.	LG		1914	(a)	(1)
STANLEY No.1	0-4-0ST	OC	AB	1659	1920	New	(1)	
-	0-4-0ST	OC	AB	973	1903	(b)	(2)	

(a) ex James Joicey & Co Ltd, /1917 (1) to NCB No.6 Area, 1/1/1947
(b) ex West Stanley Colliery   (2) to Burdale Quarries Ltd, Yorks,
                                          N.R., via Wilson, North Grimston,
                                          c/1924

West Stanley Colliery, Stanley. Map 78, NZ 193526.
(F.H.Burns until 1909; Burns & Clark until 1891)

H41 This colliery, sunk in 1832, was served by sidings S of LNER Pontop &
Shields branch, 2½m E of Annfield Plain Station. On 16th February 1909
it was the scene of the worst disaster in Durham mining history when an
explosion killed 168 men and boys. The colliery closed in March 1936.

Gauge: 4' 8½"

-	0-4-0ST	OC	MW	14	1860	New	s/s
BENTON	0-4-0ST	OC	HCR	103	1871	New	(1)
BENTON	0-4-0ST	OC	BH	1032	1891	New	(2)
ROTHERSYKE	0-4-0T	OC	FJ	187	1882	(a)	(3)
BENTON	0-4-0ST	OC	AB	973	1903	New	(4)
-	0-4-0ST	OC	CF	1193	1900	(b)	(5)

(a) ex Cleator & Workington Junction (1) to BH, /1891, in part exchange
    Railway, No.1   for new loco
(b) ex South Garesfield Colliery Co   (2) to Sir W.G.Armstrong Whitworth &
    Ltd, c/1929   Co Ltd, Puzzulio Shipyard, Italy
                                        (3) to C.D.Phillips, dealer, Newport,
                                        Monmouthshire, c/1899
                                        (4) to East Tanfield Colliery
                                        (5) to Cowpen Coal Co Ltd, North-
                                        umberland, /1937

SOUTH DURHAM IRON CO, ALBERT HILL, DARLINGTON

V10 This works (Map 85, NZ 295157 (approx)) was begun in 1855, and was closed
in 1883. Three years later it was taken over by the adjacent Darlington
Forge Co Ltd (q.v.), and merged into that firm's premises. It was served
by sidings from Albert Hill Junction, E of North Road Station on NER
Bishop Auckland-Darlington line.

Gauge: 4' 8½"

HARRY TURNER	0-4-0ST	OC	MW	447	1873	New	(1)

Believed to have had at least two other locomotives, named
BLACK DWARF and BLACK PRINCE.

                                      (1) to Bowesfield Iron Co Ltd,
                                            Stockton

SOUTH DURHAM STEEL & IRON CO LTD

(subsidiary of British Steel & Tube Ltd from 22/6/1967, which was a subsidiary of the British Steel Corporation between 1/7/1968 and 29/3/1970, when the Corporation was re-organised (q.v.).

This very large company was begun in December 1898 by W.C.Gray, a prominent West Hartlepool shipbuilder, with the amalgamation of West Hartlepool Steel & Iron Co Ltd, Stockton Malleable Iron Co Ltd and Moor Steel & Iron Co Ltd, also of Stockton. In 1900 control passed to Sir Christopher Furness, who was building a sizeable industrial empire. The details are not fully clear, but they would appear to be as follows: In September 1899 Furness re-organised the Weardale Steel, Coal & Coke Co Ltd (q.v.), which in 1901 took over the Cargo Fleet Iron Co Ltd of Middlesbrough, but which was transferred to SDSI about 1904; thereafter the Weardale company, which had now lost all its steel-making interests, became a subsidiary of either SDSI or Cargo Fleet Iron Co Ltd, though which is not clear.

At the end of the First World War SDSI was a leading member of the East Coast Steel Corporation, which took over Cochrane & Co Ltd, of Ormesby, Yorks, N.R., in 1918 and Seaton Carew Iron Co Ltd (q.v.) in 1919. Cochrane's became a subsidiary of SDSI about 1923, but the Seaton Carew company was fully absorbed, allegedly in 1928. From this period both Cochrane's and the Weardale company acquired subsidiary colliery companies, including the Easington Coal Co Ltd (q.v.) and the New Brancepeth Colliery Co Ltd (q.v.), both of which used locos, and the Trimdon Coal Co Ltd and the Wingate Coal Co Ltd, both without locos. It would also seem that the South Hetton Coal Co Ltd (q.v.) became a member of the group, apparently as a direct subsidiary of SDSI. As with other steel companies, the colliery interests were nationalised on 1st January 1947.

After overtures over a number of years, a scheme of amalgamation with Dorman, Long & Co Ltd and Stewarts & Lloyds Ltd was implemented on 22nd June 1967, under which Dorman Long & Co Ltd became British Steel & Tube Ltd and took over the other two as subsidiary companies. This company, together with SDSI, was taken over by British Steel Corporation on 23rd July 1967 (Vesting Day as 1st July 1968), but SDSI retained its identity until the Corporation's re-organisation of 29th March 1970.

West Hartlepool Works, later the **North Works**, Hartlepool.
Map 85, NZ 518309 (approx).
(West Hartlepool Steel & Iron Co Ltd until 29/12/1898)

S9   This works was begun about 1864 by Pile, Spence & Co, a shipbuilding and steamship company in West Hartlepool. This firm failed in 1866, and in July 1868 the works passed to Thomas Richardson & Sons, who also owned the Hartlepool Iron Works (q.v.). They in turn sold it in June 1874 to West Hartlepool Iron Co Ltd, but this firm failed too in 1875, and the works remained closed until offered for sale in March 1880. The rolling mills at the works were taken over by West Hartlepool Steel & Iron Co Ltd, while another new company, the Seaton Carew Iron Co Ltd (q.v.), formed in 1882, took over the blast furnaces. When the two works were re-united in the 1920's (see above), the Seaton Carew works blast furnaces were put out, and iron continued to be brought to West Hartlepool from the Cargo Fleet works in Middlesbrough until 1937-1938, when the whole West Hartlepool works was modernised and equipped with its own coke ovens and blast furnaces.

After the opening of the South Works in 1960 all locomotives were eventually transferred there, and the few remaining steam locomotives lay around in various parts of the works until scrapped.

Very little is known about the locomotives believed to have been owned by the West Hartlepool Steel & Iron Co Ltd, but about ten locos may have been taken over in 1898, most of which apparently survived only a few years.

Gauge: 4' 8½"

WEST HARTLEPOOL No.1

	WEST HARTLEPOOL No.1								
		0-4-0ST	OC	BH	613	1881	New	(1)	
No.1							(a)	s/s	
No.1		0-4-0ST	OC	HL	2412	1899	New	(2)	
No.1		0-4-0ST	OC	HL	3354	1918	New	(3)	
No.2							(a)	s/s	
No.2	NESSIE	0-4-0ST	OC	HE	177	1877	(b)	Scr	c/1924
No.3		0-4-0ST	OC	HL	2134	1889	New	Scr	c/1918
	S D S & I Co No.3	0-4-0ST	OC	HL	3355	1918	New	(3)	
No.4							(a)	s/s	
No.4		0-4-0ST	OC	HE	608	1895	(b)	Scr	/1958
No.5		0-4-0ST	OC	Grange Iron Wks		1873	New?	Scr	c/1918
No.5		0-4-0ST	OC	KS	3095	1918	New	Scr	/1969
No.6							(a)	s/s	
No.6		0-4-0ST	OC	HE	951	1907	New	Scr	c/1956
No.7							(a)	s/s	
No.7		0-4-0ST	OC	HE	1086	1911	(n)	Scr	c/1958
No.8							(a)	s/s	
No.8		0-4-0ST	OC	HE	1108	1912	New	Scr	c/1956
No.9							(a)	s/s	
No.9		0-4-0ST	OC	HE	413	1887	(b)	s/s after 1917	
No.9		0-4-0ST	OC	HE	894	1905	(c)	Scr	
No.9		0-4-0ST	OC	RS	3057	1904	(d)	Scr	c/1956
No.10							(a)	s/s by /1917	
No.10		0-4-0ST	OC	HE	1405	1920	New	Scr	c/1960
No.11							(a)	s/s by /1917	
No.11	STANGHOW	0-4-0CT	OC	HL	2516	1902	(e)		
	reb.	0-4-0T	OC	SDSI		1941		Scr	c/1953
No.12		0-4-0ST	OC	MW	1967	1918	New	Scr	/1969
	GLADYS	0-4-0ST	OC	AB			(f)	(4)	
	DAISY	0-4-0ST	OC	P	467	1888	(f)	Scr	c/1936
	WALTER MORRISON	0-4-0ST	OC	P	657	1897	(f)	Scr	c/1936
	FRANCIS	0-4-0ST	OC	HL	2378	1898	(f)	(5)	
	AILEEN	0-4-0ST	OC	HL	2445	1899	(f)	Scr after 1945	
	MAJOR	0-4-0ST	OC	AB	1363	1914	(f)	(6)	
	COLONEL	0-4-0ST	OC	AB	1501	1917	(f)	(7)	
1918		0-4-0ST	OC	AB	1609	1918	(f)	(8)	
No.13		0-4-0ST	OC	HL	3935	1937	New	Scr	/1953
No.14		0-4-0ST	OC	AB	2105	1940	New	Scr	c6/1960
No.15		0-4-0ST	OC	RSH	7045	1942	New	(9)	
-		0-4-0DM		HE	2652	1942	New	(10)	
No.16		0-4-0ST	OC	HE	1087	1911	(g)	Scr	c/1956
No.17		0-4-0ST	OC	AE	1801	1918	(h)	Scr	c/1956
No.18		0-4-0DM		JF	4210086	1953	New	(11)	
No.19		0-4-0DM		JF	4210089	1953	New	(10)	
No.20		0-4-0DM		JF	4210091	1954	New	(10)	
No.21		0-4-0DM		JF	4210094	1954	New	(10)	
No.22		0-4-0DM		JF	4210099	1955	New	(10)	
No.23		0-4-0DM		JF	4210102	1955	New	(10)	
No.24		0-4-0DM		JF	4210107	1955	New	(10)	
No.25		0-4-0DM		JF	4210110	1956	New	(10)	
No.26		0-4-0DM		JF	4160009	1953	(j)	(12)	
No.27		0-4-0DM		JF	4210128	1957	New	(10)	
No.28		0-4-0DM		HC	D978	1957	New	(10)	
No. 1		0-4-0DM		JF	4210146	1958	(k)	(13)	
No.29		0-4-0DM		HC	D1052	1958	New	(10)	
No.30		0-4-0DM		HC	D1141	1959	New	(10)	
31		0-4-0DM		JF	4210148	1958	(m)	(10)	
32		0-4-0DM		JF	4210147	1958	(m)	(11)	

(a) ex West Hartlepool Steel & Iron
    Co Ltd, 29/12/1898 (conjectural)
(b) ex Moor Works, Stockton,(c/1907?)
(c) ex Malleable Works, Stockton,
    /1936
(d) ex Ritsons (Burnhope Collieries)
    Ltd, /1939
(e) ex Cochrane & Co Ltd, Middles-
    brough, Yorks, N.R.
(f) ex Seaton Carew Iron Co Ltd,
    /1928
(g) ex Malleable Works, Stockton,
    /1949
(h) ex T.J.Thomson & Son Ltd,
    Stockton, /1949; prev. Furness
    Shipbuilding Co Ltd, Haverton
    Hill (now in Teesside)
(j) ex Malleable Works, Stockton,
    /1957
(k) ex South Works by 8/1958
(m) ex South Works by 1/1960
(n) ex Malleable Works, Stockton
    by 7/1912

(1) to Castle Eden Coal Co Ltd
(2) to Weardale Steel, Coal & Coke
    Co Ltd, Tudhoe, /1917
(3) to Seaham Harbour Dock Co Ltd,
    11/1961
(4) to Wake, Darlington, /1935
(5) boiler fitted to AILEEN c/1940;
    remainder scrapped
(6) to Irchester Ironstone Co Ltd,
    Northants, 11/1957
(7) to Cargo Fleet Works, Yorks,
    N.R., 11/1957
(8) to Irchester Ironstone Co Ltd,
    Northants, 2/1959
(9) to Cargo Fleet Works, Yorks,
    N.R. 6/1957
(10) to South Works Loco Shed, c/1963
(11) to Cargo Fleet Works, Yorks,
    N.R., 12/1962
(12) to Malleable Works, Stockton,
    1/1962
(13) ret. to South Works, 9/1958;
    to North Works by 12/1958;
    ret. to South Works, 3/1959;
    to North Works, c3/1962;
    ret. to South Works, c9/1962

North Works Coke Ovens (used for working coke car)

Gauge: 4' 8½"

-	4wWE	GB	1448	1936	New	(1)

(1) to British Steel Corporation,
    29/3/1970

North Works Cogging Shop (used for working furnace ladles)

Gauge: 2' 6"

-	4wDM	HE	3308	1946	New	s/s c/1954
-	4wRE	SDSI			New	s/s

South Works, West Hartlepool (Greatham). Map 85, NZ 5028 and 5029.

S11 This huge new works was built on the site of the former West Hartlepool
Airport, and was opened in August 1960. It is connected by an internal rail
system to the North Works, about 1¼miles to the north, and also has links
with the BR Hartlepool-Billingham line. The South Works Loco Shed (NZ
510288) took over all locomotive working about 1963. The works passed under
the direct control of the British Steel Corporation on 29th March 1970.

Gauge: 4' 8½"

1	(form. No.1)	0-4-0DM	JF	4210146	1958	New	(1)
No.2		0-4-0DM	JF	4210147	1958	New	(2)
No.3		0-4-0DM	JF	4210148	1958	New	(2)
2	(form. No.2)	0-6-0DH	JF	4240001	1959	New	(3)
3	(form. No.3)	0-6-0DH	JF	4240002	1959	New	(3)
4	(form. No.4)	0-6-0DH	JF	4240003	1959	New	(3)
5	(form. No.5)	0-6-0DH	JF	4240004	1959	New	(3)
6	(form. No.6)	0-6-0DH	JF	4240005	1960	New	(3)
7	(form. No.7)	0-6-0DH	JF	4240006	1960	New	(3)
8	(form. No.8)	0-6-0DH	JF	4240007	1960	New	(3)
9	(form. No.9)	0-6-0DH	JF	4240008	1960	New	(3)
10	(form. No.10)	0-6-0DH	JF	4240009	1960	New	(3)

11	(form. No.11)	0-6-0DH	JF	4240011	1961	New	(3)
-		0-4-0DM	HE	2652	1942	(a)	(4)
19	(form. No.19)	0-4-0DM	JF	4210089	1953	(a)	
			reb. JF		1965		(3)
20	(form. No.20)	0-4-0DM	JF	4210091	1954	(a)	(3)
21	(form. No.21)	0-4-0DM	JF	4210094	1954	(a)	
			reb. JF		1966		(3)
22	(form. No.22)	0-4-0DM	JF	4210099	1955	(a)	(3)
23	(form. No.23)	0-4-0DM	JF	4210102	1955	(a)	(3)
24	(form. No.24)	0-4-0DM	JF	4210107	1955	(a)	(3)
25	(form. No.25)	0-4-0DM	JF	4210110	1955	(a)	(3)
27	(form. No.27)	0-4-0DM	JF	4210128	1957	(a)	(3)
28	(form. No.28)	0-4-0DM	HC	D978	1957	(a)	(3)
29	(form. No.29)	0-4-0DM	HC	D1052	1958	(a)	(3)
No.30		0-4-0DM	HC	D1141	1959	(a)	(3)
31		0-4-0DM	JF	4210148	1958	(a)	(3)
15		0-4-0DH	JF	4220027	1964	New	(3)
16		0-4-0DH	JF	4220028	1964	New	(3)
33	BOYLE	0-4-0DE	RH	408309	1957	(b)	(3)
34	JAMES WATT	0-4-0DE	RH	381757	1955	(b)	(3)
12	MARDALE	0-6-0DE	YE	2743	1959	(c)	(3)
32		0-4-0DM	HC	D1013	1957	(d)	(3)
33		0-4-0DM	HC	D1081	1958	(d)	(3)
36		0-4-0DM	HC	D1032	1958	(d)	(3)
6	FARNDALE	0-6-0DE	YE	2719	1958	(e)	(3)

(a) ex North Works, c/1963
(b) ex ICI, Burn Naze Works, Lancs, 3/1965
(c) ex ICI, Billingham Works, Teesside, 1/1970, loan
(d) ex Cargo Fleet Works, Yorks, N.R., 2/1970, for scrap
(e) ex ICI, Billingham Works, Teesside, 3/1970, loan

(1) to North Works by 8/1958; ret. to South Works, 9/1958; to North Works by 12/1958; ret. to South Works, 3/1959; to North Works, c3/1962; ret. to South Works, c9/1962; to British Steel Corporation, 29/3/1970
(2) to North Works by 1/1960
(3) to British Steel Corporation, 29/3/1970
(4) to Bell & Sons (Doncaster) Ltd, Port Clarence, Teesside, 3/1968

South Works Coke Ovens (used for working coke car)

Gauge: 4' 8½"

-		0-4-0WE	GB	2937	1960	New	(1)

(1) to British Steel Corporation, 29/3/1970

SOUTH GARESFIELD COLLIERY CO LTD

H2 This firm began operations in August 1887 at South Garesfield Colliery (Map 78, NZ 157572), which was worked by the NER from sidings N of Lintz Green Station on NER Blackhill Branch. About 1895 the company took over
H3 the Anna or Lintz Pit (NZ 158561) from J. Shield (q.v.), which was connected to the South Garesfield sidings by a self-acting incline. About
H4 1900 the company expanded further by opening the Esther Pit (NZ 156548) (almost certainly the former West Lintz Drift of the Lintz Coal Co - q.v.) and laid a line 2m long to it. The loco was kept at the Lintz Pit to work to the Esther Pit and to shunt wagons up to the bank head. The two pits closed in March 1929, but South Garesfield Colliery was vested in NCB Northern Division No.6 Area on 1st January 1947.

Gauge: 4' 8½"

LINTZ No.1	0-4-0ST	OC	West Hartlepool	(a)	(1)
LINTZ No.2	0-4-0ST	OC	CF	1193 1900	New	(2)

(a) ex J.Shield, Anna Pit, c/1895

(1) to CF for repairs, /1899, but
found impractical; pieces
returned to construct underground
haulage engine, c/1900
(2) to South Derwent Coal Co Ltd,
West Stanley Colliery, c/1929

SOUTH HETTON COAL CO LTD
(latterly a subsidiary of SDSI; South Hetton Coal Co until 18/7/1874)

The opening of Seaham Harbour by the Marquis of Londonderry (q.v.) in 1831
encouraged the development of the coalfield south-west of the new town,
P1 and on 5th August 1833 South Hetton Colliery (Map 85, NZ 383453) was
opened, together with a railway 4m long to Seaham Docks. This line was
P2 extended for a further 1¼ miles to Haswell Colliery (NZ 375434) when it
opened on 2nd July 1835, the Haswell Coal Co being a partnership of some of
the same men who owned South Hetton Colliery. In 1841 the railway was
P5 extended for a further two miles to Shotton Colliery (NZ 398413), also
owned by the Haswell Coal Co, while to the east of South Hetton Murton
L31 Colliery (NZ 399473) was opened in April 1843 after five years' work and
an outlay of a quarter of a million pounds (mainly because of difficulties
with quicksand), and linked to the line by a branch (¼m). Meanwhile the
system had been linked in November 1835 by a branch (1½m) known as the
Pespool Branch to what was later the NER Sunderland-Stockton line, ½m S of
Haswell Station, and later another link was added, also from South Hetton
Colliery, to join the same NER line ¼m S of South Hetton Station.
How the line was worked in its early days is uncertain. The first loco-
motives below are thought to have worked between Shotton, Haswell and
South Hetton, to a point about ¼m east of the last-named colliery. From
here a steeply-graded section known as the Long Run took the waggons down
to the triangular junction with the Murton branch, and this is believed to
have been a self-acting incline. From here the waggons ascended Hesleden
Bank and then descended Stony Cut Bank and Swine Lodge Bank to reach
Seaham Docks. At Hesleden Bank Head stood the Cold Hesleden Engine, but it
is uncertain whether it worked the banks on both sides or whether the
Stony Cut Bank was self-acting.
To make matters even more confused, it is known that a locomotive from the
Londonderry Railway (see Marquis of Londonderry) was working the Pespool
Branch in 1859, but under what arrangement and for how long is unknown.

In the late 1880's it would seem that the company was trying to abandon its
inclines, for it was trying to get the NER to make a branch to Murton
Colliery and Lord Londonderry to build a new line from Hesleden Bank Head
down to Seaham Docks. Both ideas proved abortive, and it would seem that
it was shortly after this that locomotive working was extended right
through to Hesleden, with the Cold Hesleden Engine being abandoned and the
Stony Cut Bank, now definitely self-acting, re-named Hesleden Bank. By
this time, too, the section between Shotton and South Hetton had been
closed, possibly as early as the 1860's, and so the railway was now in the
form in which it was to remain until nationalisation.
All locomotives were kept at South Hetton Colliery, where all repairs were
also done. In later years it was an industrial archaeologist's paradise,
for the firm was still using the original buildings and much old machinery,
while "black waggons", the later version of the old chaldrons, were in
regular use and no locomotive had been built later than 1886.
On 1st January 1947 both South Hetton and Murton Collieries were incorporated into NCB Northern Division No.2 Area.

SOUTH HETTON
RAILWAY 1913
(South Hetton Coal
Co Ltd)

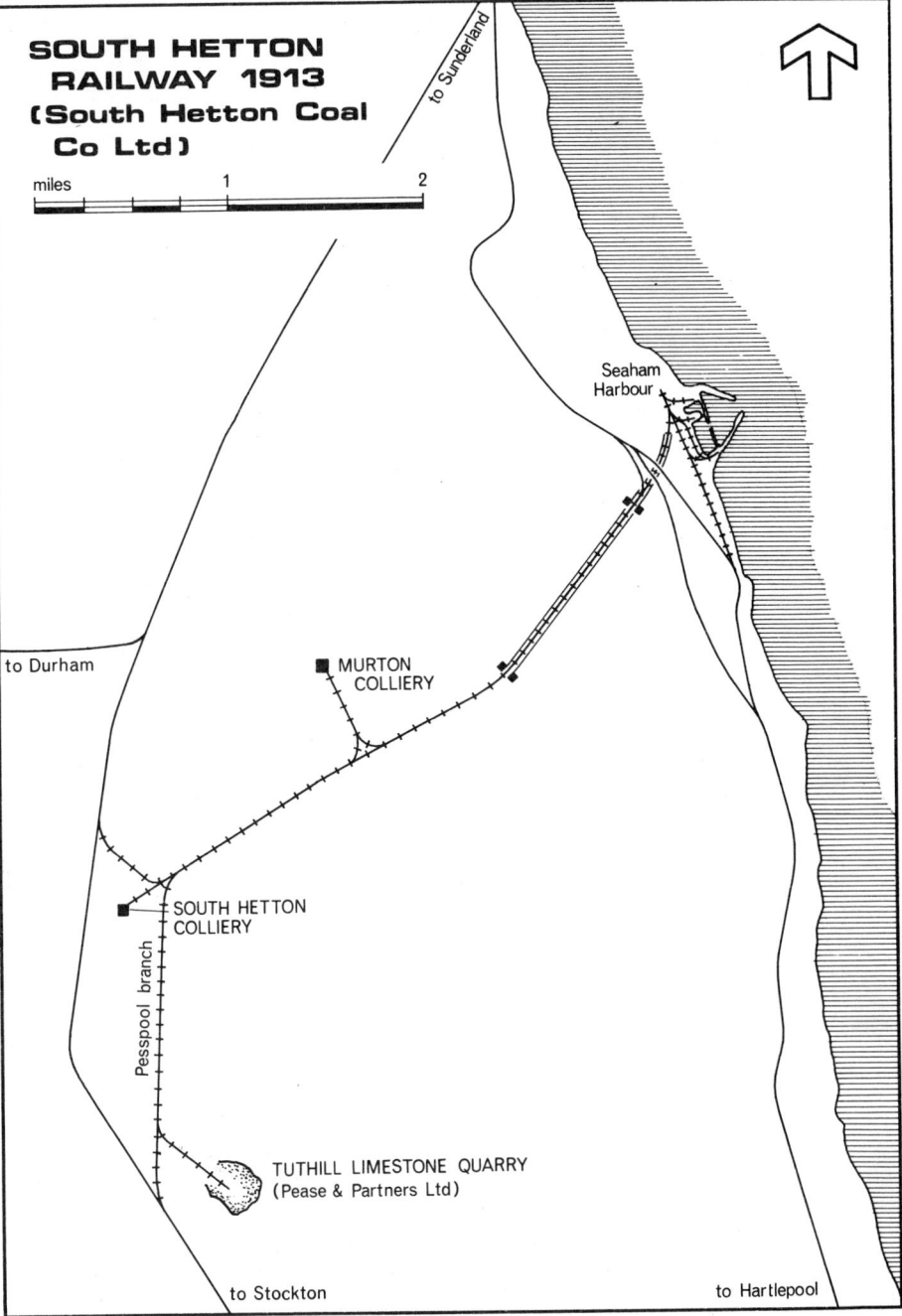

to Sunderland

miles
1
2

Seaham
Harbour

to Durham

■ MURTON
   COLLIERY

■ SOUTH HETTON
   COLLIERY

Pesspool branch

TUTHILL LIMESTONE QUARRY
(Pease & Partners Ltd)

to Stockton

to Hartlepool

191

Gauge: 4' 8½"

No.	Name	Type	Cyl	Builder	No.	Date	Note	Disposal	
	BRADYLL	0-6-0	OC	Hackworth	≠		New	(1)	
	KELLOR	0-6-0	OC	Hackworth	≠		New	Scr	
	PRINCE ALBERT	0-6-0	OC	Hackworth	≠		New	Scr	
	WELLINGTON	0-6-0	OC	Hackworth	≠		New	Scr	
	DILIGENCE	0-4-0	VC	RS	6	1829			
	reb.	0-6-0	OC	Hackworth		1834	(a)	s/s	
No.1		0-6-0	IC	TR	265	1854		New	s/s
No.2 (?)		0-6-0	IC	RS	1913	1869		New	s/s
1		0-6-0ST	OC	BH	355	1875		New	(2)
2	HAVERHILL	0-6-0T	OC	SS	2358	1873	(b)	(2)	
3		0-4-2ST	IC	BP	190	1860	(c)	Scr	/1902
No.3	GLAMORGAN	0-6-0T	IC	HE	396	1886			
				reb.Baker		1907	(d)	(2)	
No.4		0-6-0ST	IC	MW	697	1878		New	
				reb.S.Hetton		1913		(2)	
No.5		0-6-0ST	IC	MW	758	1881		New	
				reb.S.Hetton		1910		(2)	
-		4-4-0T	OC	BP	425	1864	(e)	(3)	
6		4-4-0T	OC	BP	417	1864	(f)		
	reb.	0-6-0T	OC	South Hetton		1909		(2)	
No.7		0-6-0ST	IC	Joicey	305	1883		New	
				reb.		1906			
				reb.Coulson		1935		(2)	
8		0-6-0T	IC	RS	625	1848			
				reb.		1866	(g)		
				reb.S.Hetton		1923		(2)	
9	SIR GEORGE	0-6-0ST	IC	RS	624	1848			
				reb.		1865	(h)	(2)	
10	WHITFIELD	0-6-0ST	IC	SS	1011	1857			
				reb.EV		1904	(j)	(2)	
11		0-6-0ST	IC	VF	5308	1945	(k)	(2)	
12		0-6-0ST	IC	VF	5309	1945	(m)	(2)	

≠ building dates are disputed

(a) ex Stockton & Darlington Railway, No.4, DILIGENCE, 2/1841
(b) ex Colne Valley & Halstead Rly, /1889; prev. Cornwall Minerals Rly
(c) ex Colne Valley & Halstead Rly, No.2, /1894; prev. North London Railway
(d) ex P.Baker & Co Ltd, dealer, Cardiff, Glamorgan, c/1907; prev. T.A.Walker, contr.
(e) ex Metropolitan Rly, 14, /1905
(f) ex Birtley Iron Co Ltd by 1908 (?); prev. Metropolitan Railway, 6
(g) ex Alexandra (Newport & South Wales) Docks & Rly, No.2, /1898; prev. LNWR
(h) ex Alexandra (Newport & South Wales) Docks & Rly, No.1, /1898; prev. LNWR
(j) ex Ebbw Vale Steel & Iron Co Ltd, Ebbw Vale, Glamorgan, /1907
(k) ex WD, 75318, 4/1946
(m) ex WD, 75319, 4/1946

(1) wdn /1875; used for many years as a snow plough; to NCB No.2 Area, 1/1/1947
(2) to NCB No.2 Area, 1/1/1947
(3) believed that parts used in re-building of 6, with remainder scr, c/1909

SOUTH MEDOMSLEY COLLIERY CO LTD,   SOUTH MEDOMSLEY COLLIERY, near DIPTON
(The Owners of South Medomsley Colliery Ltd (reg.17/2/1898) until 1/5/1931)

H1 This colliery was opened in 1861, when it was known as Pontop Hall Colliery
and owned by D.Baker & Co. It was linked by an NER branch (1m) to NER
Pontop & Shields Branch, 1m E of Leadgate Station, but from 1862 it was
worked by the Derwent & Consett Iron Co (later the Consett Iron Co Ltd -
q.v.). In 1864 the Ann Pit was sunk at Pontop Hall, and this later became
known as South Medomsley Colliery. The Consett Iron Co Ltd continued to
work the traffic until 1884, when the NER took over the branch working and
the colliery company acquired a loco for shunting at the pit. The colliery
was vested in NCB Northern Division No.6 Area on 1st January 1947.

Gauge: 4' 8½"

SOUTH MEDOMSLEY	0-4-0ST	OC	B	315	1884	New	(1)
-	0-4-0ST	OC	AB	1811	1923	New	(2)
BESSIE	0-4-0ST	OC	HE	205	1878	(a)	(3)
BASIL	0-4-0ST	OC	I'Anson		1875	(b)	(4)

(a) ex Warner & Co Ltd, Cargo Fleet,   (1) to North Eastern Steel Co Ltd,
    Yorks, N.R., loan, /1944   Acklam, Yorks, N.R., c/1930
(b) ex R.Shaw, Middlesbrough, Yorks,   (2) to NCB No.6 Area, 1/1/1947
    N.R., c/1945; prev.Sir S.A.Sadler   (3) ret. to Warner & Co Ltd, Cargo
    & Co Ltd, Malton Colliery   Fleet, Yorks, N.R., /1944
                                        (4) to Short Bros Ltd, Sunderland,
                                            c/1945

SPENCER & CO

Bishopley Crag Quarry, near Frosterley. Map 84, NZ 021360.

Y4 This quarry was begun about 1871, and acquired by this firm about the
middle 1870's. It was served by a branch N of NER Bishopley Branch at White
Kirkley. The quarry was exhausted by about 1902, and the firm opened

Bollihope Quarry, near Frosterley. Map 84, NZ 010350 (approx)

Y10 This quarry was begun about 1902, but had a life of only a few years.

It is known that the firm used locomotives at both of these quarries, and
also had running powers over part of the NER Bishopley Branch, but no
details of them survive.

STEETLEY DOLOMITE (QUARRIES) LTD, COXHOE
(subsidiary of Steetley Co Ltd from 3/1951; Steetley Co Ltd until 3/1951;
Steetley Lime & Basic Co Ltd until 22/3/1944)

R19 Works and huge limestone quarry (Map 85, NZ 328366 (approx)), served by
branch (½m) from BR Coxhoe Branch. The works closed in March 1967, after
which BR took over the shunting of quarry traffic.

Gauge: 4' 8½"

-		0-4-0ST	OC	AB	233	1881	(a)	Scr
No.15		0-4-0ST	OC	AB	688	1891	(b)	
				reb.AB		1946		(1)
COXHOE No.1		0-4-0ST	OC	BH	1038	1893		
				reb.CF		1901	(c)	
				reb.YE		1925		
				reb.YE		1933		(2)
B No.15		0-4-0ST	OC	RS	2724	1890	(d)	s/s by 1951
B No.13		0-4-0ST	OC	HL	2176	1890	(e)	(1)
SENTINEL 1		4wVBT	VCG	S	7669	1928	New	s/s c/1949
KITCHENER		0-4-0ST	OC	AB	3	1859		
				reb.AB 277		1884	(f)	Scr
COXHOE No.2		0-4-0ST	OC	RSH	6939	1938	New	(3)
COXHOE No.3		0-4-0ST	OC	RSH	6963	1939	New	(3)

(No.4)		0-4-0ST	OC	HC	1734	1942	New	(4)	
-		0-4-0ST	OC	P	2032	1942	(g)	(4)	
		0-4-0ST	OC	HC	1733	1943	(h)	(5)	
COXHOE No.4		0-4-0ST	OC	HC	1735	1942	(j)	Scr c2/1967	
COXHOE No.1		0-4-0ST	OC	RSH	7819	1954	New	Scr 5/1967	
-		0-4-0DE		YE	2779	1960	New	(6)	

(a) ex Lonsdale Hematite Iron Co
   Ltd, Whitehaven, Cumberland
(b) ex Armstrong, Whitworth & Co
   Ltd, Newcastle-upon-Tyne
(c) ex Clifton & Kersley Coal Co
   Ltd, Lancs, via CF, /1901
(d) ex Consett Iron Co Ltd, /1922
(e) ex Consett Iron Co Ltd, 6/1923
(f) ex Pelaw Main Collieries Ltd,
   c/1930
(g) ex Ocean Salts Ltd, Harrington,
   Cumberland, /1945 ∅
(h) ex Ocean Salts Ltd, Harrington,
   Cumberland, /1948 ∅
(j) ex British Periclase Co Ltd,
   West Hartlepool, /1954 ∅

(1) to TWW, Haswell, for scrap,
   12/1959
(2) to Steetley Works, Notts, /1917;
   ret. by 1938; to William Cory &
   Son Ltd, Purfleet, Essex, /1947
(3) to TWW, Haswell, for scrap,
   5/1960
(4) to Birmingham Corporation Gas
   Dept., Swan Village Gas Works,
   1/1947
(5) to Magnesium Electron Ltd,
   Hapton, Norfolk, 4/1955
(6) to Steetley Ground Limestone Co
   Ltd, Rainbow Bridge Quarry,
   Conisborough, Yorks, W.R.,
   11/1967 ∅

∅ these companies were all subsidiaries of Steetley Co Ltd

Gauge: 4' 8½"

The loco below, called a "tram" by the men, had a skip at each end which was filled with limestone and coke and lifted up to a set of kilns. A winch was previously used. The kilns were demolished in 1962.

-	0-2-4DM					(a)	s/s c/1967

(a) origin unknown - may have been
   built at Coxhoe; had engine
   HE 84868/1959

Gauge: 3' 5½"

This loco hauled large hopper wagons under kilns to collect the dolomite remaining after the limestone had been burned. The loco had three booms to three overhead wires.

-	4wWE	GB	2319	1950	New	s/s c/1967

Gauge: 2' 0"

This system was used to haul loaded tubs of coke and stone to another set of kilns, where the tubs were emptied into skips for lifting up to the top of the kilns.

-	4wBE	GB	2130	1948	New	s/s c/1967
-	4wBE	WR	5115	1953	New	s/s c/1967
-	4wBE	WR	5316	1955	New	s/s c/1967

Gauge: 2' 0"

These locos are believed to have worked within the quarry for a time.

-	4wDM				(a)	Scr
-	4wDM	RH	211683	1941	(b)	Scr

(a) origin unknown
(b) ex Rainbow Bridge Quarry,
   Conisborough, Yorks, W.R.

STEETLEY (MFG) LTD, PALLISER WORKS, HARTLEPOOL
(Steetley Magnesite Co Ltd until 29/12/1969; British Periclase Co Ltd
until 27/10/1952 (formed 3/8/1937) - all three companies were/are
subsidiaries of Steetley Co Ltd)

S1 Works (Map 85, NZ 507352) was begun in 1937 to produce magnesia from sea-
water. It is served by sidings E of BR Seaham-Hartlepool line at Cemetary
North Junction.

Gauge: 4' 8½"

MARS	0-4-0T	OC	AE	1701	1915	(a)	s/s
P.W. 1	0-4-0ST	OC	HC	1735	1942	New	(1)
-	0-4-0DM		RH	327966	1954	New	
-	0-4-0DM		HC	D1346	1965	(b)	
03 154	0-6-0DM		Sdn		1960	(c)	(2)

May also have had 0-4-0ST OC HC 1734/1942 from Steetley Lime & Basic Co
Ltd, Coxhoe, sometime between 1943 and 1945.

(a) ex Sharp, Jones & Co Ltd, Brank-   (1) to Steetley Dolomite (Quarries)
    some, Dorset, per MOS, /1942   Ltd, Coxhoe, /1954
(b) ex Scottish Gas Board, Provan   (2) ret. to BR, 3/1974
    Works, Lanarkshire, 7/1971
(c) ex BR, Thornaby, Teesside, hire,
    2/1974

STELLA COAL CO LTD
(form. Stella Coal Co)

The history of this company stretched back into the eighteenth century.
A number of its collieries were latterly served by their own railway
system, viz:

A5 Addison Colliery, Ryton. Map 78, NZ 168643. Sunk before 1870.
A6 Emma Colliery, Ryton (also known as Towneley Colliery). Map 78, NZ 144639.
    Sunk before 1870.
A8 Greenside Colliery, Greenside. Map 78, NZ 139619. Opened about August 1907.
A7 Stargate Colliery, near Ryton. Map 78, NZ 161634. Sunk in 1872.

The central point of the system was Stargate Colliery. From here ran
branches to Emma Colliery (1¼m), worked by stationary engine (latterly
hauling two wagons at a time), and to Greenside Colliery (2¼m), normally
worked by a locomotive kept there. From Stargate a self-acting incline took
the wagons down to sidings E of Addison Colliery, which lay alongside LNER
Newcastle-Carlisle line, 1¼m W of Blaydon Station. Both Stargate and
Addison Collieries had locomotives for shunting, and the workshops were
also at Addison Colliery.

Locomotives were also kept at:

Blaydon Main Colliery, Blaydon. Map 78, NZ 188632.
B3 This colliery was sunk before 1870, and was owned for some time by G.H.
Ramsey. It was served by a branch (½m) from NER Blackhill Branch, ½m W of
Blaydon Station. The colliery was sold in 1908 to Priestman Collieries Ltd
(q.v.).

Clara Vale Colliery, Clara Vale. Map 78, NZ 132651.
A4 This colliery was opened in July 1893, and served by sidings N of LNER
Newcastle-Carlisle line, 1m E of Wylam Station.

All collieries except Blaydon Main passed to NCB Northern Division No.6
Area on 1st January 1947.

Locomotives were frequently transferred between different collieries, and
so only the allocation at Vesting Day is shown.

Lines and collieries of Stella Coal Ltd 1913

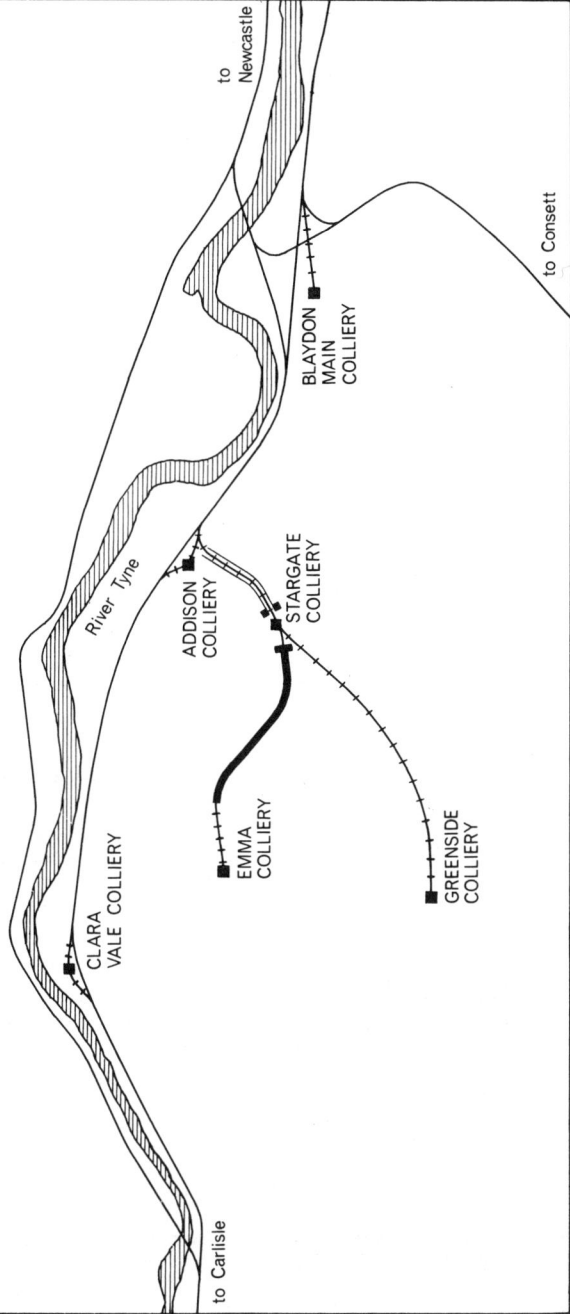

miles

1   2

to Newcastle

to Consett

BLAYDON
MAIN
COLLIERY

River Tyne

ADDISON
COLLIERY

STARGATE
COLLIERY

EMMA
COLLIERY

GREENSIDE
COLLIERY

CLARA
VALE COLLIERY

to Carlisle

Gauge: 4' 8½"

STELLA	0-4-0ST	OC	AB	70	1868	New		(1)
TOWNELEY	0-4-0ST	OC	RWH	1726	1875	New	s/s	
HEDGEFIELD	0-4-0ST	OC	RWH	1817	1880	New	s/s	
TOWNELEY	0-4-0ST	OC	HL	2199	1891	New	s/s	
MARLEY	0-4-0ST	OC				(a)	Scr	
CLARA	0-4-0ST	OC	HL	2281	1895	New ∅		(2)
CLAUDE	0-4-0ST	OC	HL	2349	1896	New		(3)
GERALD	0-4-0ST	OC	HL	2426	1899	New		(3)
STELLA	0-4-0ST	OC	HL	2583	1904	New		
			reb.HL		1931		≠	(4)
JOAN	0-4-0ST	OC	HL	2617	1905	New @		(2)
MURIEL	0-4-0ST	OC	HL	2694	1907	New @		(2)
ADDISON	0-4-0ST	OC	HL	2702	1907	New	Scr	
EMMA	0-4-0ST	OC	HL	2740	1908	New ≠		(2)
VICTORY	0-4-0ST	OC	HL	3438	1920	New ≠≠		(2)

∅ At Clara Vale Colliery, 1/1/1947
≠ At Addison Colliery,   1/1/1947
@ At Stargate Colliery,   1/1/1947
≠≠ At Greenside Colliery, 1/1/1947

(a) ex "a local colliery"

(1) to ?, Scotland
(2) to NCB No.6 Area, 1/1/1947
(3) to Priestman Collieries Ltd with
    Blaydon Main Colliery, /1908
(4) loaned to ICI Ltd, Billingham,
    1928-1931; to NCB No.6 Area,
    1/1/1947

ROBERT STEPHENSON & HAWTHORNS LTD, HARROWGATE HILL, DARLINGTON
(subsidiary of VF from 1944; Robert Stephenson & Co Ltd until 6/1937;
Robert Stephenson & Co (1914) Ltd until 5/1919; Robert Stephenson & Co Ltd
until 13/3/1914)

V7 Works (Map 85, NZ 300166) opened in 1901, and served by sidings E of BR
Durham-Darlington line, 1¾m N of Darlington (Bank Top) Station. The works
passed to the control of English Electric Co Ltd (q.v.) on 1st January 1962.

Gauge: 4' 8½"

	PHOENIX	0-4-0ST	OC	RS		c1905	(a)	Scr	c/1938
(614)	EGBERT	0-4-0CT	OC	HL	2173	1890	(b)		
				reb.RS		1918		Scr	11/1952
(615)	WINSTON CHURCHILL	0-6-0ST	IC	MW	2025	1923	(c)	(1)	
No.755		0-4-0ST	OC	RSH	7675	1951	(d)	(2)	
	-	0-4-0DM		RSH	7869	1956	(e)	(3)	
D 0227	"THE BLACK PIG"	0-6-0DH		VF	D227	1956			
				EE	2346	1956	(f)	(4)	

(a) constructed from loco ex Burn-
    hope Colliery and a Joicey loco
    built in 1880
(b) ex Hebburn Works
(c) ex Cadbury Bros Ltd, Blackpole
    Works, Worcestershire
(d) ex Forth Banks Works, Newcastle,
    /1951 (painted at Darlington)
(e) ex Northern Gas Board, Redheugh
    Works, Gateshead, /1958
(f) ex BR after trials, c/1960

(1) to Guy Pitt & Co Ltd, Dudley,
    Worcs, 5/1946
(2) to NCB East Midlands Division
    No.3 Area, 6/1961
(3) to Northern Gas Board, Carlisle
    Works, Cumberland, /1960 (fitted
    with new plates dated 1960)
(4) to English Electric Co Ltd,
    1/1/1962

HENRY STOBART & CO LTD
(Henry Stobart & Co until 24/11/1893; subsidiary of PP by 3/1920)

Chilton Colliery, Chilton Buildings. Map 85, NZ 278308.
(South Durham Coal Co Ltd until 1903; South Durham Coal Co until 1888; orig. Chilton Coal Co)

R13 This colliery was opened in 1872, and was served by a 1m branch from NER
Chilton Branch. The locos below may also have worked at Windlestone Coll-
R14 iery (NZ 284296), which was owned by Pease & Partners Ltd, and was served
by sidings S of NER Chilton Branch about ½m E of junction of line to
Chilton Colliery. Windlestone Colliery was closed in October 1924, and
Chilton Colliery was taken over by Pease & Partners in the same year.

Gauge: 4' 8½"

CHILTON	0-6-0ST	IC	MW	324	1871	(a)	s/s
-	0-6-0ST	IC	MW	693	1878	(b)	(1)
CHILTON No.1	0-6-0ST	OC	AB	961	1902	New	(2)
CHILTON No.2	0-6-0ST	OC	AB	1097	1907	New	(2)
CHILTON No.3	0-6-0ST	IC	P	1219	1910	New	(3)
WINDLESTONE	0-4-0ST	OC	AB	1085	1907	(c)	(3)

(a) ex Eckersley & Bayliss, contrs   (1) to South Leicestershire Colliery
(b) ex Logan & Hemingway, contrs   Co Ltd
(c) ex Fishburn Colliery   (2) to Fishburn Colliery
                           (3) to Pease & Partners Ltd, /1924

Etherley Colliery, Witton Park.

T15 This colliery consisted of three pits, viz. Jane Pit (Map 85, NZ 171304),
served by sidings W of NER Bishop Auckland-Crook line, ¼m N of Etherley
T16 Station; George Pit (NZ 185301), served by sidings N of Bishop Auckland-
T17 Crook line, ¼m E of Etherley Station, and the John Pit, whose location is
uncertain. Originally the John Pit was worked by a stationary engine, but
a locomotive is recorded here in November 1876, with two more serving the
Jane and George Pits. The John and Jane Pits appear to have closed before
1900, but the George Pit, latterly known as Old Etherley Colliery (Bush
Pit), closed in 1917.

It is assumed that more locomotives worked here than those below.

Gauge: 4' 8½"

RESOLUTE	0-4-0ST	OC	K	1508	1868	(a)	(1)
ETHERLEY	0-4-0ST	OC	HCR	129	1873	New	s/s
NILE	0-4-0ST		K	?		(a)	(2)

(a) origin unknown   (1) to Fishburn Colliery, c/1912
                           (2) to Fishburn Colliery (?)

Fishburn Colliery & Coke Works, Fishburn. Map 85, NZ 361318.

R29 This colliery, opened in 1914, was the last to be sunk in this south-
eastern part of the coalfield. It, and a coking plant opened later, was
served by a branch (2½m) from LNER Ferryhill-Stockton line, ¼m N of
Sedgefield Station. It was vested in NCB Northern Division No.4 Area on
1st January 1947.

Gauge: 4' 8½"

	RESOLUTE	0-4-0ST	OC	K	1508	1868	(a)	Scr	/1915
	NILE	0-4-0ST		K	?		(b)	s/s	
1	(FISHBURN)	0-6-0ST	IC	P	1423	1916	New		
				reb.TIW May 1936				(1)	
	-	0-4-0ST	OC	Bwn			(c)	(2)	
	-	0-4-0ST	OC	Bwn			(d)	s/s	
	-	0-4-0ST	OC	T.D.Ridley			(e)	(3)	

```
6                       0-4-0ST  OC  AB  1085  1907  (f)  (4)
       -                0-6-0ST  OC  AB   961  1902  (g)  s/s
       -                0-6-0ST  OC  AB  1097  1907  (h)  s/s
3    (TORONTO)          0-4-0ST  OC  P   1194  1912  (j)
                        reb.TIW June 1938              (1)
4                       0-6-0T   OC  HL  3104  1915  (k)
                        reb.TIW Dec  1936              (1)
20                      0-4-0ST  OC  HL  2713  1907  (m)
                        reb. F'burn
                                 Apr  1945            (1)
25                      0-4-0ST  OC  HL  2456  1900  (n)  (1)
```

(a) ex Etherley Colliery, c/1912   (1) to NCB No.4 Area, 1/1/1947
(b) ex Etherley Colliery   (2) to ?,Sunderland
(c) ex Wake, /1917; prev. ROD   (3) to ?, Bishop Auckland
(d) origin unknown; believed to   (4) to Chilton Colliery
    have been here
(e) ex T.D.Ridley, hire
(f) ex PP, Eldon Colliery
(g) ex Chilton Colliery
(h) ex Chilton Colliery
(j) ex Newton Cap Colliery
(k) ex PP, Bowden Close Colliery
(m) ex PP, Bishop Middleham Quarry
(n) ex PP, Chilton Limeworks

Newton Cap Colliery, near Bishop Auckland. Map 85, NZ 213308.

T21 Served by branch (¼m) from LNER Durham-Bishop Auckland line, 1¼m N of
    Bishop Auckland Station. It was closed about 1934, and taken over by North
    Bitchburn Fireclay Co Ltd about April 1937.

    There may well have been other locomotives besides those listed below.

    Gauge: 4' 8½"

```
        THE COLONEL     0-4-0ST  OC  HG   251  1867  New  (1)
        (COMET)         0-4-0ST  OC  MW   467  1873  (a)  (2)
        TORONTO         0-4-0ST  OC  P   1194  1912  New  (3)
```

(a) ex LG; NER 2252 until 5/1902   (1) to North Bitchburn Coal Co Ltd,
                                          Rough Lea Colliery, /1924
                                      (2) to North Bitchburn Fireclay Co
                                          Ltd, c4/1937
                                      (3) to Fishburn Colliery

Rough Lea Colliery, Hunwick. Map 85, NZ 194331.
(North Bitchburn Coal Co Ltd originally - q.v.).

Q17 This colliery was served by sidings W of LNER Durham-Bishop Auckland line,
    ½m N of Hunwick Station. It had been closed by North Bitchburn Coal Co Ltd
    in April 1926, and it was taken over by North Bitchburn Fireclay Co Ltd on
    5th May 1934. Which locomotives were present during the short period of
    Stobart ownership is uncertain, but that below is believed to have been one.

    Gauge: 4' 8½"

```
        THE COLONEL     0-4-0ST  OC  HG   251  1867  (a)  (1)
```

(a) ex North Bitchburn Coal Co Ltd   (1) to North Bitchburn Fireclay Co
                                          Ltd, 5/5/1934

Thrislington Colliery, West Cornforth. Map 85, NZ 309338.
(North Bitchburn Coal Co Ltd until 15/7/1932 - q.v.)

R26 This colliery was connected to the LNER Durham-Darlington line, ½m N of
    Ferryhill Station, by an incline worked by a stationary engine at the coll-

iery. It was vested in NCB Northern Division No.4 Area on 1st January 1947.

Gauge: 4' 8½"

9		0-4-0ST	OC	HL	2247	1892	(a)	
		reb.TIW June 1935						(1)
6		0-4-0ST	OC	AB	1085	1907		
		reb.TIW Jan 1938					(a)	(2)
8		0-4-0ST	OC	HL	2798	1909		
		reb.TIW Sept 1935					(a)	(2)
7		0-4-0ST	OC	P	677	1897		
		reb.TIW Apr 1935					(b)	(2)
10		0-4-0ST	OC	HL	2559	1903	(c)	(3)
13		0-4-0ST	OC	HL	2823	1910	(d)	(2)

(a) ex North Bitchburn Coal Co Ltd,
    15/7/1932
(b) ex North Bitchburn Coal Co Ltd,
    North Bitchburn Colliery, /1932
(c) ex PP, Bishop Middleham Quarry,
    /1938
(d) ex PP, Bank Foot Coke Ovens,
    Crook, 9/1945

(1) to PP, Tees Ironworks, Cargo
    Fleet, Yorks, N.R., 12/1946
(2) to NCB No.4 Area, 1/1/1947
(3) to PP, Thorne Colliery, Moorends,
    Yorks, W.R., /1941

<u>STRAKERS & LOVE LTD</u>   (Strakers & Love until 13/5/1925)

<u>Brancepeth Colliery</u>, Willington. Map 85, NZ 205357.

Q13 Opened in April 1842, and originally connected by a branch (1¼m, including
a self-acting incline) to the West Durham Railway at Todhills Bank Foot;
but after the opening in 1857 of the NER Durham-Bishop Auckland line the
colliery was linked to this, as its sidings lay N of the line, ½m N of
Willington Station. About 1940 the colliery was linked to Brandon Pit House
Colliery (q.v.) by an aerial ropeway. It passed to NCB Northern Division
No.5 Area on 1st January 1947.
All repairs to the company's locomotives were done at Brancepeth Shops.

Gauge: 4' 8½"

No.1	BRANCEPETH	0-6-0ST	IC	MW	104	1864	New	(1)	
	BRANDON	0-6-0ST	IC	MW	200	1867	New		
		reb.				1881			
		reb.				1895			
		reb.				1909			
		reb.				1925			(2)
	OAKENSHAW	0-4-0ST	OC	HCR	124	1871	(a)	(3)	
	TIGER	0-4-0ST	OC	MW	320	1870	(b)		
		reb.				1881			(4)
	BRANCEPETH	0-6-0ST	IC	MW	775	1882	New		
		reb.				1897			
		reb.				1911			
		reb.				1927		Scr	/1937
	HELMINGTON	0-6-0ST	OC	RWH	1882	1882	New		
	reb.	0-4-0ST	OC	Brancepeth		1897			
		reb.				1905			
		reb.				1923			(2)
	HOWDEN DENE No.1	0-6-0T	OC	HL	2880	1911	New	(5)	
	JUPITER	0-4-0ST	OC	MW	1880	1915	(c)	(6)	
	WILLINGTON	0-4-0ST	OC	AE	1509	1907			
		reb.TJR				1920		(d)	(7)
	STAGSHAW	0-6-0ST	OC	HL	3513	1927	New	(2)	
	MEADOWFIELD	0-6-0ST	OC	FW	289	1876			
		reb.RWH				1881			
		reb.				1893			
		reb.				1907		(e)	Scr 3/1934
	HOWDEN DENE No.2	0-6-0ST	OC	RS	4113	1937	New	(2)	

∅ HOWDEN DENE until 1937

(a) ex Brandon Colliery, /1880
(b) ex Brandon Colliery, /1881
(c) ex Vickers Ltd, Barrow-in-
    Furness, Lancs, 6/1920
(d) ex TJR, Crymlyn Burrows Depot,
    Swansea, Glamorgan, 12/1920
(e) ex Brandon Colliery, c/1933

✗ TEST until 1921

(1) to Brandon Colliery, /1880
(2) to NCB No.5 Area, 1/1/1947
(3) to Oakenshaw Colliery by 3/1890;
    ret. (from Willington Colliery)
    /1932; Scr c/1933
(4) to Willington Colliery by 3/1890
(5) to Brandon Colliery, 3/1925; ret.
    /1946; to NCB No.5 Area,1/1/1947
(6) to Brandon Colliery, 4/1923
(7) to Brandon Colliery, 10/1921

Brancepeth Coke Ovens & Bye-Product Plant.

The colliery was one of the most famous in Durham for its coke. This plant
was opened in 1937, and lay to the north of the colliery. Ordinary traffic
was handled by the colliery locos, but the loco below was used to haul a
coking car along the discharge side of the ovens to the quenching tower.

Gauge: 4' 8½"

| | 0-4-OWE | HL | 3859 | 1937 | New | (1) |

(1) to NCB No.5 Area, 1/1/1947

The locos below were used during the construction of the above plant in
1935-1937. Whether they were owned by Strakers & Love Ltd or by a
contractor is uncertain.

Gauge: 2' 0"

| | 4wDM | RH | 175121 | 1935 | New | (1) |
| | 4wDM | RH | 175399 | 1935 | New | (2) |

(1) to Geo. Porter,Bellshill, 8/1936;
    later to Guanogen Ltd, Castle
    Bromwich, Warwickshire, via
    Cohen, Kingsbury
(2) ret. to RH, 10/1936; re-sold to
    Rowhedge Sand & Ballast Co Ltd,
    Brook Pits, Essex, 11/1936

Brandon Colliery, Brandon. Map 85, NZ 245400.

M14 Opened in 1844, and latterly served by sidings S of LNER Durham-Bishop
Auckland line, 1m S of Relly Mill Junction.
    In 1923 a heavily-graded branch (2m) was built from the colliery to Brandon
M13 Pit House Colliery (NZ 215404), then being sunk. When this colliery was
opened in April 1926 severe restrictions were placed on locomotive working.
Both collieries passed to NCB Northern Division No.5 Area on 1st January 1947.

Gauge: 4' 8½"

	TIGER	0-4-0ST	OC	MW	320	1870	New		(1)
	OAKENSHAW	0-4-0ST	OC	HCR	124	1871	New		(2)
No.1	BRANCEPETH	0-6-0ST	IC	MW	104	1864	(a)	(3)	
	STAGSHAW	0-4-0ST	OC	RWH	1821	1880	New		
				reb.		1891			
				reb.		1906		Scr 4/1927	
	MEADOWFIELD	0-6-0ST	OC	FW	289	1876			
				reb.RWH		1881	(b)		
				reb.		1893			
				reb.		1907		(4)	
	WILLINGTON	0-4-0ST	OC	AE	1509	1907			
				reb.TJR		1920	(c)	(5)	
	JUPITER	0-4-0ST	OC	MW	1880	1915	(d)	(6)	

```
            HOWDEN DENE No.1 ⊀ 0-6-0T    OC   HL    2880  1911  (e)  (7)
            LEAZES               0-6-0ST   OC   HL    3830  1934  New  (5)
    75256                        0-6-0ST   IC   WB    2779  1945  (f)  (5)

            ⊀ HOWDEN DENE until 1937
```

(a) ex Brancepeth Colliery, /1880	(1) to Brancepeth Colliery, /1881
(b) ex RWH, /1881	(2) to Brancepeth Colliery, /1880;
(c) ex Brancepeth Colliery, 10/1921	ret. (from Oakenshaw Colliery),
(d) ex Brancepeth Colliery, 4/1923	/1893; to Willington Colliery,
(e) ex Brancepeth Colliery, 3/1925	c/1914
(f) ex WD, 75256, 4/1946	(3) withdrawn /1882; re-sold to MW
	c/1886
	(4) to Brancepeth Colliery, c/1933
	(5) to NCB No.5 Area, 1/1/1947
	(6) loaned to Witton Park Slag Co
	Ltd, Etherley, /1931, and ret;
	to NCB No.5 Area, 1/1/1947
	(7) loaned to ICI, Billingham, /1928;
	ret. by 2/1929; to Brancepeth
	Colliery, /1946

<u>Oakenshaw Colliery</u>, Oakenshaw. Map 85, NZ 200376.

Q11 This colliery, opened in 1855, was also known as Brancepeth 'B' Pit. It was
linked to Brancepeth Colliery sidings by an incline, 1¼m long, worked by a
stationary engine at the colliery, although the full waggons were travell-
ing downhill. Production ceased in March 1940, although the colliery continued as a pumping station. The greater part of the incline is now a road.
Locomotives do not appear to have been used here normally, but the
following is recorded.

Gauge: 4' 8½"

```
    OAKENSHAW        0-4-0ST   OC   HCR    124  1873  (a)  (1)
```

(a) ex Brancepeth Colliery by 3/1890   (1) to Brandon Colliery, /1893

<u>Willington (or Sunnybrow) Colliery</u>, Sunnybrow. Map 85, NZ 194343.

Q16 This colliery also appears to have opened in the 1840's. Later it was
sometimes known as 'Z' Pit. Originally it was served by sidings N of the
West Durham Railway near Todhills Bank Foot, but later its sidings were
linked to the NER Durham-Bishop Auckland line, ½m S of Willington Station.
It was closed in 1932, being connected underground to Brancepeth.
Undoubtedly more locomotives worked here than those listed below;
HELMINGTON is said to have been working here in 1905.

Gauge: 4' 8½"

```
    -                0-6-0ST   IC   HCR    45   1865  New  s/s by 3/1890
    TIGER            0-4-0ST   OC   MW     320  1870
                               reb.            1881  (a)
                               reb.            1891
                               reb.            1901       s/s after
                                                          11/1926
    OAKENSHAW        0-4-0ST   OC   HCR    124  1871  (b)  (1)
```

(a) ex Brancepeth Colliery by 3/1890   (1) to Brancepeth Colliery, /1932
(b) ex Brandon Colliery, c/1914

<u>R.SUMMERSON & CO LTD</u>

<u>Cockfield Quarry</u>, Cockfield. Map 84, NZ 113251 to Map 85, NZ 143244.

T11 A long, elongated quarry about 1¼m long, served by a branch (½m) S of LNER
Haggerleazes Branch, 2m W of Spring Gardens Junction. It appears to have
closed shortly after the Second World War.

Gauge: 2' 3½"

W.SUMMERSON	0-4-0ST	OC	HE	567	1892	New	s/s	
ROSEBERRY	0-4-0ST	OC	BH	1065	1892	(a)	(1)	

(a) ex Gribdale Mining Co Ltd, Great   (1) to Greenfoot Quarry, and ret;
    Ayton, Yorks, N.R., /1926   Scr c12/1950

Greenfoot Quarry, near Stanhope. Map 84, NY 983392.

Z13 Another large limestone quarry, originally owned by Ord & Maddison Ltd, and
served by sidings N of LNER Wearhead Branch, 1¼m W of Stanhope Station.
About 1948 it was taken over by Durham & Yorkshire Whinstone Co Ltd (q.v.).

Gauge: 2' 3½"

ROSEBERRY	0-4-0ST	OC	BH	1065	1892	(a)	(1)
-	4wDM		RH	175420	1936	(b)	(2)

(a) ex Cockfield Quarry   (1) to Cockfield Quarry
(b) ex West Hunwick Silica &   (2) to Durham & Yorkshire Whinstone
    Firebrick Co Ltd   Co Ltd, c/1948

SUMMERSON'S FOUNDRIES LTD
(Thomas Summerson & Sons Ltd until 9/1947)

V11 Albert Hill Foundry, Darlington. Map 85, NZ 295155.

Works served by sidings from Albert Hill Junction on LNER Bishop Auckland-
Darlington line, ½m E of Darlington (North Road) Station. In 1960 shunting
was taken over by a crane, and about November 1967 the works passed to
Lloyd's (Darlington) Ltd (q.v.).

Gauge: 4' 8½"

HERALD							
(form. HASKIN)	0-4-0CT	OC	HL	2468	1900	New	Scr
-	0-6-0ST	IC	MW	1513	1901	(a)	(1)
JEANIE	0-6-0T	IC	HC	694	1904	(b)	(2)
-	4wVBT	VCG	S	6076	1925	(c)	(3)

(a) ex John Scott, contr.   (1) to Vivian & Sons Ltd, Landore,
(b) ex T.Wrigley, Prestwich, Lancs,   Glamorgan, via G.Trollope & Sons
    hire, 2/1922   (2) ret. to T.Wrigley, 4/1922
(c) ex Derwent Valley Light Railway,   (3) to Lloyd's (Darlington) Ltd,
    Yorks, E.R., /1926   c11/1967

Trading Estate Works, Spennymoor. Map 85, NZ 267337 approx.

R8 This works opened in 1950, and was served by sidings within the Spennymoor
Trading Estate complex, which was served by sidings S of BR Spennymoor-
Ferryhill line, 1m E of Spennymoor Station. Rail traffic ceased about
1965, and the works also subsequently passed to Lloyd's (Darlington) Ltd.

Gauge: 4' 8½"

-	0-4-0DM		JF	4110008	1950	New	(1)

(1) to Leslie Sanderson Ltd, dealer,
    Birtley, c/1966; re-sold to APCM,
    Penarth Works, Glamorgan, c/1967

SWAN HUNTER SHIPBUILDERS LTD
(Swan Hunter & Tyne Shipbuilders Ltd until 28/1/1969)

Hebburn Yard, Hebburn. Map 78, NZ 305652 (approx)
(R. & W. Hawthorn Leslie (Shipbuilders) Ltd until 1/1/1968)

E6 This yard is served by a branch (¼m) N of BR Gateshead-South Shields
    line, ½m E of Hebburn Station. Immediately east of this yard is the
E7 Palmers Hebburn ship-repairing yard, which was taken over by Swan Hunter
    Shiprepairers Ltd on 19th August 1972, but the locomotives below work
    solely in the Hebburn Yard.

Gauge: 4' 8½"

        TRIUMPH   0-4-0DM   RH 304472 1951 (a)
        APOLLO   0-4-0DM   RH 319288 1953 (a)

(a) ex R. & W. Hawthorn Leslie
    (Shipbuilders) Ltd, 1/1/1968

SWISS ALUMINIUM MINING (U.K.) LTD
(Star Aluminium Co Ltd until 7/1971; Anglo-Swiss Alumimium Co Ltd until
c5/1971)

Cambo Keels Mine, near Eastgate. Map 84, NY 935383.
(Operated for Maddison & Brown from 1971; orig. Maddison & Brown)

Z11 This mine is situated below the A689 road between Eastgate and Westgate.
    It appears to have been driven in 1847 as a drainage drift to the Slitt
    mines (see entry for Weardale Iron Co Ltd), probably by the Beaumont
    family, who controlled much of the Upper Weardale mining industry in the
    19th century. It seems later to have been worked for lead, and abandoned
    in 1938. It was worked between 1948 and 1961 by Anglo-Austral Mines Ltd,
    and re-opened by Messrs. Maddison and Brown, two local men, to prospect
    for fluorspar in February 1969. None of the earlier owners are believed
    to have used locomotives. The locomotives below normally work underground,
    though the 1' 8" gauge loco shed is on the surface. There is no main line
    rail connection.

Gauge: 2' 0"

              -                4wBE   GB 420288 1971 (a)

(a) ex Cornish Hush Mine, /1975;
    loco stored

Gauge: 1' 8"

              -                0-4-0BE   WR 7377 1970 New
              -                4wBE ⤳   WR 2489 1943 (a)

              ⤳ formerly 0-4-0BE

(a) ex Force Crag Mines Ltd, Braith-
    waite, Cumberland, hire, 3/1973;
    purchased, 6/1973; prev. 1' 10"
    gauge

Gauge: 60cm

-	4wBE	WR	7624	1975	New

Cornish Hush Mine, Whitfield Brow, near Frosterley. Map 84, NZ 001335.

Y11 This was an old lead mine, formerly owned by the London Lead Co Ltd (q.v.),
and closed between 1880 and 1900. It was re-opened in August 1970 to
prospect for fluorspar, but operations here were suspended in 1975. The
only access to it is by a long private road.

Gauge: 2' 0"

-	4wBE	GB	420288	1971	New	(1)

(1) to Cambo Keels Mine to be stored,
/1975

Stanhopeburn Mine, Stanhope. Map 84, NY 987412.
(Fergusson, Wild & Co Ltd until 5/4/1975)

Z15 This old mine, worked by a variety of previous owners for ironstone, lead
and fluorspar, passed to these owners in April 1975. The locomotives
below work underground, though their shed is on the surface. There is no
main line rail connection.

Gauge: 2' 0"

-	4wBE	WR			(a)
-	4wBE	WR	7644	1973	(a)

(a) ex Fergusson, Wild & Co Ltd,
3/1975

TARMAC ROADSTONE LTD, GREENFOOT QUARRY, near STANHOPE

Z13 This quarry (Map 84, NY 983392) was taken over from Durham & Yorkshire
Whinstone Co Ltd in October 1963, and was served by sidings N of BR
Wearhead Branch, 1¼m W of Stanhope Station. Internal rail traffic was
replaced by road transport shortly after the take-over, and the quarry
ceased production about 1965.

Gauge: 2' 3½"

-	4wDM	RH	175420	1936	(a)	s/s c/1969

(a) ex Durham & Yorkshire Whinstone
Co Ltd, 10/1963

THARSIS SULPHUR & COPPER CO LTD, TYNE WORKS, HEBBURN

E1 Works (Map 78, NZ 302642) served by sidings W of LNER Gateshead-South Shields line, ½m W of Hebburn Station. It closed about 1939.

Gauge: 4' 8½"

COLIN McANDREW	0-4-0ST	OC	AB	1223	1911	(a)	(1)

(a) ex Colin McAndrew Ltd, Edinburgh,   (1) to N. Greening & Sons Ltd,
    Scotland   Warrington, Lancs, c/1939

TYNE PLATE GLASS CO, SOUTH SHIELDS

D16 Works (Map 78, NZ 359668?) was served by sidings adjacent to NER South Shields Low Station. It passed into the hands of Charles Mark Palmer in 1860, but continually lost money, and was closed in 1891.

Gauge: 4' 8½"

A.M.P.	0-4-0ST	OC	BH	515	1879	New	(1)
C.M.P.	0-4-0ST	OC	BH	516	1879	New	(1)

(1) to Harton Coal Co Ltd, St.Hilda
Colliery, South Shields,
c/1891 (?)

SAMUEL TYZACK & CO LTD, MONKWEARMOUTH IRONWORKS, SUNDERLAND
(Samuel Tyzack & Co until 5/12/1889)

K9 Works (Map 78, NZ 398585) served by sidings E of LNER Gateshead-Sunderland line, ½m N of Monkwearmouth Station. It closed in 1937.

Gauge: 4' 8½"

No.1	0-4-0ST	IC	JF	1568	1871	New	s/s
No.2	0-4-0ST	OC	BH	529	1880	New	s/s
No.3	0-4-0ST	OC	BH	1098	1896	New	(1)
No.4	0-4-0ST	OC	HL	2533	1902	New	(2)

(1) to TWW, 9/1937
(2) to Rolling Stock Co Ltd,
Darlington, 4/1937

J. VAUGHAN, AUCKLAND IRONWORKS, BISHOP AUCKLAND

Not a great deal is certain about either the works or its owners. The
T28 former (Map 85, NZ 211294?) appears to have been opened in the late 1860's and was served by sidings N of NER Bishop Auckland-Darlington line, immediately E of Bishop Auckland Station. The works is later recorded as owned by Thomas Vaughan, though this family does not appear to have had any connection with the Vaughans of Bolckow & Vaughan. The works is believed to

have closed in May 1877, and it is possible that parts of the site were
later taken over by Robert Wilson & Sons (q.v.) and Lingford, Gardiner &
Co Ltd.

Gauge: 4' 8½"

AUCKLAND	0-4-0ST	OC	MW	270	1869	New	(1)	
AUCKLAND	0-4-0ST	OC	MW	87	1864	(a)	s/s	

(a) ex Smith, Knight & Co, contrs,   (1) ret. to MW, and re-sold to Henry
    Wakefield, Yorks, W.R. ?   Lee & Son, contrs, Beverwijk,
                                      Holland, 9/1870

VICKERS LTD, PALMERS HEBBURN YARD, HEBBURN
(Vickers-Armstrongs (Shipbuilders) Ltd until 1/4/1965; Vickers-Armstrongs
Ltd until 1/7/1955; Palmers Hebburn Co Ltd until 1/1/1947)

E7 This yard (Map 78, NZ 306653) was taken over by Palmers Hebburn Co Ltd
after the collapse of Palmers Shipbuilding & Iron Co Ltd (q.v.). It was
served by a branch (½m) N of BR Gateshead-South Shields line, ½m E of
Hebburn Station. The ship-repairing facilities were discontinued in
September 1970, and were purchased by Swan Hunter Shiprepairers Ltd in
August 1972. The marine works continues to be operated by Vickers Ltd,
but road transport took over from rail about 1972.

Gauge: 4' 8½"

PALMERS No.1	0-4-0ST	OC	HL	2666	1906	(a)	Scr c12/1959
PALMERS No.2	0-4-0ST	OC	HL	2667	1907	(a)	Scr c12/1959
PALMERS No.1	4wDM		FH	3890	1958	New	(1)
PALMERS No.2	4wDM		FH	3891	1958	New	

(a) ex Palmers Shipbuilding & Iron   (1) to TH, Kilnhurst, Yorks, W.R.,
    Co Ltd, via TWW, /1934   6/1968; re-sold to South Wales
                            Warehouses Ltd, Penarth, Glamor-
                            gan, 10/1968

WAKE & CARR, SKERNE IRONWORKS, ALBERT HILL, DARLINGTON

V13 This works (Map 85, NZ 298159) was formerly owned by Skerne Ironworks Co
Ltd (q.v.), and was served by sidings E of NER Durham-Darlington line, 1¼m
N of Darlington (Bank Top) Station. After the closure of the works by its
previous owners in 1889 its equipment was auctioned; but it would seem that
it was subsequently re-opened, probably by the above partnership, though
this is not fully clear. The works was finally closed in 1899, and its
effects auctioned in November 1899.

Gauge: 4' 8½"

       The sale details of November 1899 include a "six-coupled locomotive,
       two four-wheeled locomotives and a four-wheeled vertical boilered
       locomotive", but no identification has yet proved possible.

WALLSEND & HEBBURN COAL CO LTD, HEBBURN COLLIERY, HEBBURN
(reg. 15/2/1892)

This colliery was owned by a number of previous firms, the last being the
Tyne Coal Co Ltd, who worked it between 1867 and 1892. The earliest pit
was sunk in 1792, and later the colliery consisted of three pits - the
E10 'A' Pit (Map 78, NZ 315653),
E11 'B' Pit (NZ 318650) and
E9 'C' Pit (NZ 308650), the last two being linked to the 'A' Pit by waggonways
which then ran on to staithes on the R.Tyne. The 'B' Pit was closed in the
nineteenth century, and after the opening of the NER Gateshead-South
Shields line in 1872 the colliery was linked to it by a branch ½m E of
Hebburn Station. It was closed in March 1931.

An unusual feature of its locomotive stock was the battery locomotives used after 1921.

Gauge: 4' 8½"

No.1		0-6-0T	IC	JF	1542	1871	New	s/s
No.2		0-4-0ST	OC	BH	237	1873	New	s/s
No.2		0-4-0ST	OC	BH	762	1883	New	s/s
No.3		0-4-0ST	OC	BH	763	1883	New	s/s
No.4		0-4-0WT	OC	EB	30	1891	(a)	s/s
No.1		4wBE		EE	518	1921	New	s/s
No.2		4wBE		EE	519	1921	New	s/s
No.3		4wBE		EE	570	1923	New	s/s

(a) ex "a glass works"
    (in South Shields?)

J.WALTON & CO, FINEBURN QUARRY, near FROSTERLEY

Y9 This quarry (Map 84, NZ 010349 approx) was opened about 1871, and lay at the end of the NER Bishopley Branch, about 3m from Bishopley Junction. It was closed about 1896, but later re-opened by Pease & Partners Ltd (q.v.).

It is believed that the firm used locomotives within the quarry, but no details survive.

WASHINGTON COAL CO LTD   (reg. 10/2/1895)
(subsidiary of Denaby & Cadeby Main Collieries Ltd, Yorkshire)

Usworth Colliery, Usworth. Map 78, NZ 315584.
(Leversons Wallsend Collieries Ltd until 1940; Jonassohn, Gordon & Co Ltd until c/1920; John Bowes & Partners Ltd until 1897; Elliot & Jonassohn until 20/3/1882; orig. G.Elliot)

J5 This colliery was opened in 1845, and was latterly served by sidings E of LNER line from Pelaw to Washington, ½m N of Usworth Station. After disposing of its locomotives the colliery was shunted by the LNER, and passed to NCB Northern Division No.1 Area on 1st January 1947.

Gauge: 4' 8½"

USWORTH		0-4-0ST	OC	BH	38	1867	New	s/s
-		0-6-0ST	IC	BH	716	1883		
				reb.		1906	(a)	(1)
-		0-4-0ST	OC	P	1460	1916	(b)	(2)

(a) ex James W.Ellis & Co Ltd,
    Swalwell
(b) ex John Rogerson & Co Ltd, Wol-
    singham, via C.W.Dorking & Co Ltd

(1) to Ryhope Coal Co Ltd
(2) to Mid-Durham Carbonisation Co
    Ltd, and ret; to NCB No.1 Area,
    1/1/1947

WEAR STEEL CO LTD, CASTLETOWN IRONWORKS, SUNDERLAND
(Wear Rolling Mill Co Ltd until 1888; orig. Wear Rolling Mills Co Ltd)

K3 This works (Map 78, NZ 366583) had been closed in 1875 following the bankruptcy of Thomas Walter Oswald (q.v.), and was re-opened by its new owners in 1881. It was served by sidings S of NER Hylton, Southwick & Monkwearmouth Branch, 1½m W of Monkwearmouth. It closed in September 1894. The site and certain buildings were subsequently used in the sinking of Hylton Colliery, which was begun by Wearmouth Coal Co Ltd (q.v.) in April 1897.

Gauge: 4' 8½"

-		0-4-0ST	OC	HC	221	1881	New	(1)
-		0-4-0ST	OC	AB	641	1889	New	s/s

(1) to River Wear Commissioners,
    Sunderland

<u>WEARDALE LEAD CO LTD</u>   (reg. 21/6/1883)
(subsidiary of ICI Ltd from 1962)

This company,formed in June 1883 and reconstituted in 1900, entered the
lead industry when it was already in decline, but managed to maintain a
successful, if precarious existance for many years, until the great
expansion in fluorspar mining changed its fortunes.

None of the company's mines have had main line rail connections.

<u>Barbury Mine</u>, Ireshopeburn. Map 84, NY 865385.

Z2 This was a relatively short-lived mine. The date when locomotive haulage
was first used underground is uncertain. The mine was abandoned in April
1959.

Gauge: 2' 0" (underground)

| | - | 0-4-0BE | WR | 5601 | (a) | (1) |

May have had other locomotives unknown.

(a) origin unknown   (1) to Redburn Mine

<u>Bolts Burn Mine</u>, Rookhope. Map 84, NY 937425.

Z8 This was an old, rich lead mine in the centre of Rookhope, taken over by
the company in 1884. The ore from here was taken about ½m up Rookhope Burn
to the Lintzgarth Smelter (NY 926428). This was originally done by horses
operating a 2' 6" gauge line; but about 1913 this was re-laid as a 1' 10"
gauge locomotive-worked line. The loco shed at Rookhope was built alongside
the standard gauge shed of the Weardale Iron Company, and the Lead Company's
traffic was carried over the Iron Company's line to the junction with the
NER Stanhope & Tyne Branch at Parkhead until the former closed about 1923.
The smelter closed in September 1919, and the mine followed in 1932.

Gauge: 1' 10"

No.2   0-4-0ST OC HL   3029 1913 New s/s

<u>Burtree Mine</u>, Cowshill. Map 84, NY 859412.

Z21 This again would appear to be an old lead mine re-opened to prospect for
fluorspar, probably in 1970.

Gauge: 2' 0" (underground)

	-	4wBE	CE	5889	1971	New		
	-	4wBE				(a)	Scr	/1973
		4wBE	WR	7789	1975	New		

(a) ex Redburn Mine, c/1972

<u>Grove Rake Mine</u>, near Rookhope. Map 84, NY 895441.

Z5 This mine lay further up Rookhope Burn, about 3m from Rookhope. It had
originally been worked for ironstone by Weardale Iron Co, and was served by
their branch from Rookhope to Frazer's Hush.Ironstone working ceased in
1875, and the railway lifted. It was re-opened for lead in the 1880's, and
a narrow gauge line built on the opposite side of the burn to carry ore
from the mine down to cleaning plants at Rispey, about 1¼m away. Later this
line also served Wolf's Cleugh Mine (q.v.). From Rispey the ore was carried
by horse and cart down to the Lintzgarth Smelter. The mine was abandoned in
1903, but was re-opened much later for fluorspar (see Blanchland Fluor
Mines).

Gauge: 2' 6"

No.1   0-4-0ST OC BH   981 1889 New (1)

(1) to Stanhopeburn Mine, /1909

Redburn Mine, Rookhope.   Map 84, NY 927431.

Z7 This was originally a lead mine, situated close to the Lintzgarth Smelter,
and abandoned in 1935. It was re-opened to mine fluorspar in 1962. A small
narrow-gauge surface system was operated from about 1965 to 1971,
sometimes using one of the underground battery locomotives in addition to
those listed below.

Gauge: 2' 0"

No.1	(RS 71)	4wDM	MR	7808	1937	(a)	Scr 5/1973
	RS 83	4wDM	MR	7815	1941	(b)	(1)
	RS 82	4wDM	MR	7814	1940	(c)	Scr 5/1973

(a) ex ICI Ltd, Tunstead Limeworks,   (1) used for spares, and remainder
    Derbyshire, 6/1965   Scr c/1967
(b) ex ICI Ltd, Tunstead Limeworks,
    Derbyshire, c/1965, for spares
(c) ex ICI Ltd, Tunstead Limeworks,
    Derbyshire, c/1969

Gauge: 2' 0"   (underground)

-	4wBE	WR	5299	1955	New	
-	4wBE	WR	5601		(a)	
-	4wBE	WR	6805	1964	New	
-	4wBE	WR	4184	1947	(b)	
-	4wBE	WR			(b)	(2)
-	4wBE	GB	420167	1969	New	(1)
-	4wBE	GB	420253	1970	New	
-	4wBE	GB		1973	New	

(a) ex Barbury Mine   (1) ret. to GB, 2/1969
(b) ex Stotsfieldburn Mine, c/1969   (2) to Burtree Mine, c/1972

Stanhopeburn Mine, Stanhope. Map 84, NY 987412.

Z15 This was another old mine, which had been served by a standard gauge branch
(1½m) from the foot of the NER Stanhope & Tyne Branch at Crawleyside. It
was worked by horses, and probably owned by the Weardale Iron Co, who had
ironstone mines lower down the burn. It was re-opened by the Lead Company
in 1906, and a narrow gauge line built on the standard gauge track bed.
Locomotive haulage was replaced by horses about 1930, and about 1937 the
mine was sold to a local man, J.G.Beaston. In 1942 it passed to Fluorspar
Ltd (q.v.), by which time a road had been built on the railway trackbed.

Gauge: 2' 6"

| No.1 | "LITTLE SALLY" | 0-4-0ST | OC | BH | 981 | 1889 | (a) | Scr /1937 |

(a) ex Grove Rake Mine, /1909

Stotsfieldburn Mine, Rookhope. Map 84, NY 943423.

Z9 This mine, lying to the south of Rookhope, was opened in 1914. It was
using battery locomotives underground by 1948, and in later years it also
had a locomotive on the surface. It was abandoned in November 1966, and
the site was cleared and levelled in 1969.

Gauge: 2' 0" (may have been 1' 10")

| - | | 0-4-0DM | HE | 4979 | 1955 | (a) | (1) |
| RS 52 | | 4wDM | MR | 5683 | 1935 | (b) | Scr c/1969 |

(a) ex Coldbury Lead Co Ltd,　　　　(1) to Lanchester & Iveston Coal Co
　　Northumberland　　　　　　　　　　Ltd, /1961
(b) ex ICI Ltd, Hindlow Limeworks,
　　Derbyshire, c/1960

Gauge: 2' 0" (underground)

-	4wBE	WR			(a)	(1)
-	4wBE	WR			(a)	(1)
-	4wBE	WR			(a)	(1)
-	4wBE	WR	4184	1947	(b)	(2)

(a) origin unknown　　　　　　　　　(1) cannibalised to make one good
(b) ex Greenside Mining Co Ltd,　　　　loco, which was sent to Redburn
　　Patterdale, Westmorland　　　　　　Mine c/1969; other remains scrapped
　　　　　　　　　　　　　　　　　　(2) to Redburn Mine, c/1969

Wolf's Cleugh Mine, near Rookhope. Map 84, NY 902432.

Z6　This mine lay in Rookhope Burn, about 1½m NW of the village. It was worked
by the company from 1901 to 1912, utilising the line from Grove Rake to
Rispey. It was re-opened in 1946, and locomotive haulage underground was
introduced in March 1954. The mine was abandoned in December 1955.

Gauge: 2' 0" (?) (underground)

　　　　Details of battery loco(s) unknown.

WEARDALE STEEL, COAL & COKE CO LTD
(Weardale Iron & Coal Co Ltd until 28/9/1899; Weardale Iron Co until
23/7/1863; see also below)

This company was formed in 1846, and built ironworks on the western edge of
the Durham coalfield to use local coal and iron ore from Weardale. By the
turn of the century these were exhausted, and in 1899 the firm was reconstituted by Sir Christopher Furness, the shipbuilding and steamship magnate.
In 1901 the firm took over the Cargo Fleet Iron Co Ltd of Middlesbrough,
and ceased its own steel making activities, but in 1904, with the new Cargo
Fleet Works under construction, that company was sold to the South Durham
Steel & Iron Co Ltd, of which Furness was also chairman. Thereafter the
company became a member of the South Durham group of companies, but whether
of South Durham direct or of the Cargo Fleet company is uncertain. Latterly
it supplied the coal and limestone needs of the group, either directly or
through subsidiary companies.

The firm owned two major iron works, viz:

Tow Law Iron Works, Tow Law. Map 84, NZ 117387.

Q3　This was opened in 1846, and was situated S of NER Consett-Bishop Auckland
line at Tow Law Station. It closed about 1887.

Tudhoe Iron Works, Spennymoor. Map 85, NZ 260338.

R4　This was opened in 1853, and was served by sidings N of NER Ferryhill-
Bishop Auckland line E of Spennymoor Station. It closed in 1875, but was
rebuilt and re-opened in 1879. Steel production ceased abruptly in November
1901, though it seems that the works was not completely closed for some
years afterwards. It was eventually dismantled by T.W.Ward Ltd between 1912
and 1914, though its coke ovens continued in production (see below).

To bring iron ore and limestone to these works the company built an
extensive railway system in Weardale. The first section was

Weatherhill & Rookhope Railway

This was built during 1846, and ran from a junction with the Wear & Derwent
Junction Railway's Stanhope & Tyne section (later NER) at Parkhead (later
Blanchland) (Map 84, NZ 003431). This section, 5¼m long, rose to 1670 feet,

and was worked by a locomotive kept about 4½ miles from Parkhead, at Bolts
Law (NY 949442), whence an incline, 2000 yards long and worked by a
stationary engine, took the line down to Rookhope.
Rookhope remained the terminus for some years, and not until the middle
1850's does the line seem to have been extended to the ironstone mines in
Upper Weardale north of Westgate. This section was called

Middlehope & Rookhope Railway

Very little is known about its early operation. It is possible that all
but the far western section was worked by ropes. There is known to have
been an engine house at Bishops Seat, and this may have operated some form
of main-and-tail system, with a self-acting incline from Smailes Burn down
into Rookhope. In later years the flatter sections were worked by locomotives from sheds at Rookhope (NY 937427) and Heights Quarry (NY 925388),
leaving only the Smailes Burn Incline. Its operation was curious, for
since loaded wagons travelled in both directions, the counterbalance was
provided by old locomotive tenders filled with water, the amount of water
depending on the load and the direction of travel. From Rookhope the line
Z8 served <u>Bolts Burn</u> lead mine (NY 937425, not owned by the company), <u>Smailes</u>
Z10 <u>Burn Mine</u> (NY 941415), <u>Heights Quarry</u>,
<u>Slitt Pasture Mine</u> (NY 915390) and <u>West Slitt Mine</u> (NY 903593, a lead mine
also not owned by the firm), which was the end of the line, 11½m from
Parkhead. Below the line in Middlehope were more lead mines, which are
believed to have had their own internal narrow-gauge system worked by
horses, with a lift to raise their ore up to the Iron Company's line.
To cater for iron ore from the company's other mines further up Weardale,
a depot was opened at Scutterhill, above Westgate (NY 915388).

Probably about 1865 two long branches were built. The first ran
from a point between Parkhead and Bolts Law north-westwards to ironstone
Z4 mines at <u>Sike Head</u> (NY 950464) and <u>Ramshaw</u> (NY 948467). Between these two
mines was an incline worked by a stationary engine at the former, but the
remainder was locomotive-worked. The second ran from Rookhope to ironstone
mines at Frazers Hush at the head of Rookhope Burn. This was 4½m long, and
entirely loco-worked. En route it served <u>Lintzgarth Smelt Mill</u> (NY 927428,
Z7 not owned by the company), <u>Rispey Mine</u> (NY 912427) and <u>Grove Rake Mine</u>
Z5 (NY 895441), before ending at <u>Frazers Hush</u> (NY 8844).

With no "main line" railway in Upper Weardale for most of the
century the Iron Company's line carried a considerable amount of ordinary
commercial traffic to and from places such as Wearhead, Westgate and
Rookhope, and to facilitate this the firm built an incline, worked by a
stationary engine, from their Scutterhill Depot down into the village of
Westgate. This was about ¼m long, and probably opened in the late 1860's.
The firm also ran a passenger service between Parkhead and Bolts Law
(possibly including the Ramshaw branch) for many years.

In the slump of the mid 1870's the Slitt Mines ceased production,
and the section beyond Scutterhill was closed, as were the branches to
Frazers Hush and Ramshaw. With the opening of the NER line to Wearhead in
1895 the section west of Heights Quarry, with the incline to Westgate, was
also closed.

In 1915, to handle increased production from Heights Quarry, the
company built a self-acting incline about ¼m long from the quarry down to
the NER line in the valley below. This was known as the Cambo Keels
Incline, and was built by German prisoners of war.

The whole of what was left of the system was officially closed in
March 1923, though the line was left intact, and horses continued to pull
supplies from Parkhead to Bolts Law, while for many years this section was
also used by gentlemen for grouse shooting from a battery-driven open truck.
The track was eventually lifted about 1940-1942.

The company also used locomotives at the following locations, though
whether this was throughout the life of the location is not known:

Black Prince Colliery, Tow Law. Map 84, NZ 117397.

Q2 Probably opened in the 1850's, and served by a branch (½m) from NER
Consett-Bishop Auckland line, ½m W of Tow Law Station. It was closed
between 1914 and 1923, and finally shut down in June 1929.

Croxdale Colliery, Croxdale. Map 85, NZ 266371.

R2 This colliery should not be confused with an earlier Croxdale Colliery
(NZ 267393) with a different rail link and not owned by this company. This
later colliery, about 1½m S of the earlier one, was opened about 1875, and
served by a branch (¼m) from NER Durham-Darlington line at Croxdale
Station. It was closed in March 1915.

M3 **Hedley Hill Colliery**, near Waterhouses. Map 85, NZ 165412.

This colliery was probably opened in the 1870's, and was served by a
branch (½m) from Ivesley Station on the NER line between Waterhouses and
Crook. It was closed in 1908-1912, 1914-1915, 1921-1923, and finally shut
down in November 1929.

P8 **Thornley Colliery**, Thornley. Map 85, NZ 365395.
    Acquired from Original Hartlepool Collieries Co Ltd (q.v.) in 1885,
P7 together with **Ludworth Colliery** (NZ 363415) and **Wheatley Hill Colliery**
P9 (NZ 385393). All three collieries were closed at the time of acquisition.

Thornley Colliery, re-opened in May 1888, was served by a branch (2m - NER)
from NER Sunderland-Stockton line, 1m N of Wellfield Junction. Wheatley
Hill was served by a 1m loop from this branch, and Ludworth by a branch
(1¼m - NER/private) from a point 1m W of Thornley. Normally all locos
were kept at Thornley, but in March 1890 one is recorded at both of the
other collieries. Ludworth suffered closure between 1902 and 1908, and
was finally closed in March 1921. The other two collieries survived to be
vested in NCB Northern Division No.3 Area on 1st January 1947.

Tudhoe Colliery, Tudhoe. Map 85, NZ 257356.

R3 This colliery dates from 1864-1865, and was served by a branch (1m) from
NER Ferryhill-Bishop Auckland line, ½m E of Spennymoor Station. Near the
R6 southern end of this branch was **Tudhoe Grange Colliery** (NZ 265338), but
this was closed in March 1885. Tudhoe Colliery was closed in September 1935.

Tudhoe Coke Ovens, Spennymoor. Map 85, NZ 261338.

R5 These survived the closure of Tudhoe Ironworks to be vested in NCB Northern
Division on 1st January 1947, the locomotives being administered by No.4 Area.

So far as is known, no locomotives worked at the company's other locations,
though "coke oven apparatus engines", which may be locomotives, are
recorded in March 1890 at Black Prince Colliery (1), Tudhoe Colliery (1)
Q4 and West Thornley Colliery (NZ 133386) (1).

Ref: T.E.Rounthwaite. "Railways in Weardale". R.C.T.S., 1965.

The very small amount of information known about the location of these
locomotives is given. It is assumed that the majority of the remainder
worked mainly at Tow Law or Tudhoe. The main workshops were at Tudhoe
until that works closed, when they were transferred to Thornley Colliery.

BL	Bolts Law	R	Rookhope
BP	Black Prince Colliery	T	Thornley Colliery
HQ	Heights Quarry	TC	Tudhoe Coke Ovens

Gauge: 4' 8½"

No.	Name	Type	Cyl	Builder	Works No	Date	Orig	Disposal
	-	0-4-2		Fairbairn		1842	(a)	s/s
	BELLOROPHON	0-6-0		Hackworth?			(b)	BL Scr c/1900
	JENNY LIND	0-6-0		Hackworth?			(b)	BL Scr c/1900
No. 1	JOHN RENNIE	0-4-0ST	OC	GW		1861	(b)	Scr
No. 1		0-4-0ST	OC	N	2280	1878	(c)	(1)
No. 1		0-4-0ST	OC	CF	1196	1900	New	Scr
2		0-6-0ST		reb.Thornley		1920	(b)	Scr
3	CRAWLEYSIDE	0-4-0T	OC	GW		1864	New?	s/s
4	(WEARDALE)	0-4-0ST	OC	Joicey	210⊘	1869	New	
	reb.	0-6-0ST	OC					BL
				reb.Thornley		1924		
				reb.Thornley		1931	T	(2)
5	CHARLES ATTWOOD	0-4-0T	OC	GW	172	1863	New?	s/s
5		0-6-0ST	OC	BH (?)			(b)	
				reb.Thornley		1925	TC	(3)
6	TOW LAW	0-6-0	IC	J.Bond,Tow Law	⊘		New	
	reb.	0-6-0ST	IC					BP-T c/1914
								Scr c/1915
6		0-4-0ST	OC	KS	4027	1919	New	T	(4)
7	SPAWOOD	0-4-0ST	OC	Joicey		1872	New	
				reb.Tudhoe		1903		(1)
8	MIDDRIDGE	0-4-0ST	OC	Joicey		1870	New	(1)
9	SEDGEFIELD	0-4-0ST	OC	Joicey		1874	New	R Scr /1924
10		0-4-0VB	G	HW			(b)	s/s
10	MICKLETON	0-4-0ST	OC	AB	305	1888	(d)	
	(later BELMONT)							(1)
11	ZEPHYR	0-4-0ST		J.Bond,Tow Law			New	s/s
12	(STAR)	0-4-0ST	OC	Tow Law			New	
				reb.Tudhoe		1909		s/s
13	CROXDALE	0-4-0ST	OC	Joicey	c1875		New	
	reb.	0-6-0ST	OC					s/s
14	(BLACK PRINCE)	0-4-0ST	OC	Joicey			New?	
	reb.	0-6-0ST	OC	Tudhoe		1899		
				reb.Thornley		1928	T	(5)
15	(WOLSINGHAM)	0-6-0ST	OC	Tow Law		1873	New	
				reb.Tudhoe		1895		
				reb.Tudhoe Coll.		1905		Scr
16	TUDHOE	0-6-0T	OC	BH	57	1868	New	Scr
16		0-4-0ST	OC	AB	1066	1906	New	Scr
17	BISHOP MIDDLEHAM	0-6-0ST	OC	RWH	1554	1872	New	(6)
17		0-6-0T	OC	KS	3098	1918	(e)	T
				reb.Thornley		1938		(5)
18	(SUNDERLAND BRIDGE)	0-6-0ST	OC	RWH	1622	1874	New	T	(7)
No.19		0-6-0ST	OC	BH	704	1882	New	
				reb.Tudhoe		1909		HQ (8)
20		0-6-0ST	OC	Tow Law			New	
				reb.Tudhoe		1908		R Scr c/1939
21	QUEEN	0-6-0ST		BH	31	1867	(f)	T
				reb.Tudhoe		1896		(9)
No.21		0-4-0ST	OC	KS	4028	1919	New	TC (3)
No.22	PRINCESS	0-4-0ST	OC	MW	466	1873	(f)	T	(10)
23	ALBERT	0-4-0ST	OC	MW	492	1874	(f)	T Scr after 10/1906
24		0-6-0ST	OC	AB	1321	1913	New	
				reb.Thornley		1921		
				reb.Thornley		1929	T	(5)
25		0-4-0ST	OC	P	521	1891	(g)	R s/s c/1928
26		0-4-0ST	OC	D	2051	1884	New	(1)
27		0-6-0T	OC	KS	3100	1918	(e)	
				reb.Thornley		1942	T	(5)
No. 1		0-4-0ST	OC	HL	2412	1899	(h)	(11)
	-	0-6-0ST	IC	VF	5307	1945	(j)	T	(5)

┌ may be 240   ∅ built 1870-1874

(a) ex L&YR, 141, ELBE, 1/1855
(b) origin unknown
(c) ex Yorkshire & Derbyshire Iron
    Co
(d) ex J.Torbuck, dealer, Middles-
    brough, Yorks, N.R.
(e) ex Furness Shipbuilding Co Ltd,
    Haverton Hill in 1920's
(f) ex Original Hartlepool Collier-
    ies Co Ltd, /1885
(g) ex Broomhill Collieries Ltd,
    Northumberland
(h) ex South Durham Steel & Iron Co
    Ltd, West Hartlepool, /1917
(j) ex WD, 75317, /1946

(1) to Cargo Fleet Iron Co Ltd,
    Yorks, N.R.
(2) to New Brancepeth Colliery Co Ltd
(3) to NCB No.4 Area, 1/1/1947
(4) to Easington Coal Co Ltd by
    5/1925
(5) to NCB No.3 Area, 1/1/1947
(6) to Broomhill Collieries Ltd,
    Northumberland
(7) loaned to New Brancepeth Colliery
    Co Ltd, and ret; to NCB No.3
    Area, 1/1/1947
(8) to Easington Coal Co Ltd, /1943
(9) to ?, Liverpool area, /1921
(10) to Wake & Hollis Ltd, contrs
(11) to Cargo Fleet Iron Co Ltd,
    Woodland Colliery, c/1918

Gauge: 3' 0" (worked at Tudhoe Ironworks Rolling Mill)

-		0-4-0ST	OC	JF	c1893	(a)	(1)
-		0-4-0ST	OC	JF		(a)	(1)
-		0-4-0ST	OC	Miller,Coatbridge	(a)	(1)

(a) origin unknown   (1) to TWW, /1912

Gauge: 2' 8" (worked at Tow Law Ironworks)

| LITTLE GRIMSBY | 0-4-0ST | OCG | I.W.Boulton | 1860 | (a) | Scr |

(a) ex I.W.Boulton, Ashton-under-
    Lyne, Lancs, /1865 (reb. from
    2' 0" gauge, /1864)

WEARMOUTH COAL CO LTD
(Bell, Stobart & Co until 1/1/1878; W.Bell & Partners until c/1870

K11 For many years this firm owned only Monkwearmouth (later Wearmouth)
     Colliery in Sunderland (Map 78, NZ 394578). Opened in June 1835 after nine
     years' work, it was for many years the deepest mine in the world. Its coal
     was originally all shipped on to R.Wear, but later it was served by sidings
     S of NER Hylton, Southwick & Monkwearmouth Branch, ½m W of Monkwearmouth
     Junction.
K4   In 1900 the firm opened Hylton Colliery (NZ 366583) on the site of the
     former Castletown Ironworks (see Wear Steel Co Ltd). This lay 1¼m further
     west along the same NER branch, and running powers between the two collier-
     ies were acquired. One four-coupled loco was normally kept at Hylton, being
     changed as required. Both collieries were vested in NCB Northern Division
     No.1 Area on 1st January 1947.

Gauge: 4' 8½"

-		0-4-0ST	OC	JF	2834	1876	New	s/s
No.2		0-4-0ST	OC	BH	395	1878	New	Scr c/1922
PHYLLIS		0-6-0ST	IC	AB	833	1898	New	
		reb.HL			7866	1915		(1)
GEORGE		0-6-0ST	IC	AB	909	1901	New	(2)
BUNNY		0-6-0T	IC	AB	911	1901	New	
(form. ALEXANDRA)		reb.HL			6429	1913		(1)
WILL		0-6-0T	IC	AB	999	1904	New	(1)
JEAN		0-6-0T	IC	HL	2769	1909	New	(1)
No.3		0-4-0ST	OC	HL	2784	1909	New	(3)

No.5		0-4-OST	OC	HL	2824	1910	New	(1)
No.1		0-4-OST	OC	HL	3494	1922	New	(1)
No.2		0-4-OST	OC	HL	3493	1922	New	(1)
No.4		0-4-OST	OC	RSH	6945	1938	New	(1)
No.3		0-4-OST	OC	RSH	7307	1946	New	(1)
	DIANA	0-6-OT	IC	RSH	7304	1946	New	(1)

(1) to NCB No.1 Area, 1/1/1947
(2) to WD, Longmoor, Hants; believed
    sunk in the Channel during World
    War I
(3) to RSH, Newcastle, for repairs,
    /1945, but found impractical
    and scrapped 4/1946

WEST HARTLEPOOL HARBOUR & RAILWAY CO

As this was a public railway this company is strictly outside the scope of
this book, but as its involvement in colliery history is so complicated, a
brief note was thought to be worthwhile.

This company, an amalgamation of smaller concerns, received its Act in May
1853. Fearing competition for the West Hartlepool coal traffic from other
neighbouring railways, it began both to acquire collieries on its system
and to build up a system of steamships. As it was exceeding its parliament-
ary powers in doing so, the collieries were actually owned by its chairman,
Ralph Ward Jackson (regarded as the founder of the town of West Hartlepool).
By 1860 he owned eleven collieries, viz.

R1 Binchester Colliery, near Bishop Auckland. Map 85, NZ 237315.

R18 Bowburn Colliery, near Quarrington Hill. Map 85, NZ 326368.
    (N.B. This was formerly known as West Hetton Colliery (see W.Hedley);
    it was not the Bowburn Colliery later owned by Bell Bros Ltd).

Q21 Byers Green Colliery, Byers Green. Map 85, NZ 223335.

    Little Chilton Colliery, Ferryhill Station. Map 85, NZ 302315.
    (N.B. This was the site of the later Chilton Quarry (see Pease & Partners
    Ltd); it was not the Chilton Colliery of later years)

R20 Coxhoe Colliery, Coxhoe. Map 85, NZ 332363.
    (Also known as West Hetton Colliery (Coxhoe Pit). See W.Hedley.

R17 Crowtrees Colliery, Quarrington Hill. Map 85, NZ 334379.
    (Also known as West Hetton Colliery (Crowtrees Pit). See W.Hedley.

    Heugh Hall Colliery, Quarrington Hill. Map 85, NZ 324379.

    South Kelloe Colliery, Quarrington Hill. Map 85, NZ 338367.

    Merrington Colliery, Spennymoor. Map 85, NZ 252338.
    N.B. This colliery was contiguous with Whitworth Colliery (not owned by
    Jackson)

Q20 Newfield Colliery, Newfield. Map 85, NZ 205332.

Q15 Page Bank Colliery, Page Bank. Map 85, NZ 230359.

An investigation into the affairs of the company resulted in Jackson transferring all the collieries to the Railway on 23rd February 1860, and his
eventual resignation from the Board in April 1862, though he was exonerated.
The Board was instructed to dispose of the collieries, but through the
depressed state of the coal trade was unable to do so for some time. Little
Chilton was closed in 1865, but five were sold in that year - Binchester
and Newfield to Hunwick & Newfield Coal Co (later to BV), Byers Green to
Bolckow, Vaughan & Co Ltd (q.v.), Merrington to R.S.Johnson & Co, and Page
Bank to Bell Bros Ltd (see DL).
On 1st July 1865 the Railway was absorbed by the North Eastern Railway,
together with the five remaining collieries. These were offered for sale on
27th March 1866, and all were purchased by J.Morrison & Co. They, and Merrington, continued to be worked by the NER; the others all subsequently used

their own locomotives.
A number of WHHR locomotives were also not taken over by the NER, some of
them considerably newer than those which did change hands. The fate of
these is at present unknown.

WEST HUNWICK REFRACTORIES LTD, HUNWICK
(West Hunwick Silica & Firebrick Co Ltd until 6/1963; Hunwick Coal Co until
4/1922; prev. West Witton Ganister and Firebrick Co Ltd)

Q18 Works and associated mine and quarry (Map 85, NZ 194331) served by sidings
W of BR Durham-Bishop Auckland line, ½m N of Hunwick Station. Rail traffic
ceased in 1968.

Gauge: 4' 8½"

-		0-4-0T	OC	FJ	72	1867	(a)	s/s
WEST HUNWICK No.2	0-4-0ST	OC	CF	1183	1899	(b)	
				reb. R.Shaw	1949			Scr c/1958
WEST HUNWICK No.3	4wDM		RH	421417	1958	New	(1)	

(a) ex Hunwick Coal Co, Hunwick   (1) to Rugby Portland Cement Co Ltd,
    Colliery   Strood, Kent, 5/1969
(b) ex PP, Tees Bridge Ironworks,
    Stockton

Gauge: 2' 4"

-	4wDM	RH	175420	1936	New	(1)

                  (1) to R.Summerson & Co Ltd,
                      Greenfoot Quarry, Stanhope

WHESSOE LTD, WHESSOE FOUNDRY, HOPETOWN, DARLINGTON
(Whessoe Foundry & Engineering Co Ltd until 8/11/1945; Whessoe Foundry Co
Ltd until 9/4/1920; Charles I'Anson & Co until 30/4/1891; see also below)

V4 Works (Map 85, NZ 285160 approx) was begun by William Lister, and passed
into the control of the Kitching brothers in the 1850's. In 1860 the
Kitchings sold their nearby railway works to the Stockton & Darlington
Railway, and handed over control of the former Lister works to a cousin,
Charles I'Anson.
The works are served by sidings S of a loop between Stooperdale Junction
and Hopetown Junction, Darlington.

There were very probably more locos than those listed below, but details
are lacking.

Gauge: 4' 8½"

	INFLEXIBLE	0-4-0ST	OC	MW	575	1875			
				reb.MW		1901	(a)	(1)	
(314)	MONARCH	0-4-0ST	OC	P	1210	1910	(b)	(2)	
	ACKLINGTON	0-6-0ST	OC	reb.Ridley		1903	(c)	s/s	
	HEMINGWAYS	0-4-0ST	OC	TW			(d)	s/s	
	EAST LAYTON	0-4-0ST	OC	HL	2871	1911	(e)	(3)	
982		0-4-0T	IC	Dar		1923	(f)	(4)	
(316)	DERWENT II	0-4-0DE		RH	312988	1952	New		

(a) ex Wake, Darlington; form.   (1) sold for scrap, /1927
    Talk O' Th' Hills Collieries   (2) to Ashmore, Benson, Pease & Co
    Ltd, Staffs   Ltd, Stockton, per Cox & Danks,
(b) ex Penderyn Limestone Quarries   c/1953
    (Hirwaun) Ltd, /1927   (3) ret. to Fawcett Limestone Co Ltd,
(c) origin unknown   Yorks, N.R.
(d) ex WD, Purfleet, Essex   (4) ret. to LNER, /1937
(e) ex Fawcett Limestone Co Ltd,
    Yorks, N.R., loan

(f) ex LNER, 982, /1937, loan

WIGGINS TEAPE LTD, HYLTON MILL, SOUTH HYLTON, SUNDERLAND
(Ford Paper Mills Ltd until 1/3/1968; Ford Paper Works Ltd until c/1932;
subsidiary of Alex. Pirie & Sons Ltd from c/1932; all these firms were
subsidiaries of Wiggins Teape Ltd)

K1 Works (Map 78, NZ 361574) was opened in 1838, and was subsequently served
by a connection N of the LNER/BR Sunderland-Durham line, ½m N of Hylton
Station, though latterly at the end of the line. An incline worked by a
stationary engine took the wagons down into the works. It was closed in
July 1971.

Gauge: 4' 8½"

FORD		0-4-0ST	OC	BH	188	1872	(a)	s/s
FORD		0-4-0ST	OC	MW	1323	1896	(b)	Scr c/1930
-		0-4-0ST	OC	HC	535	1900	(c)	s/s
-		0-4-0ST	OC	HC	1207	1916		
				reb.		1926	(d)	Scr /1962
-		4wVBT	VCG	S	6310CH	1926	(e)	(1)
-		4wPM		H	965	1930	New	(2)
HYLTON		4wDH		FH	3967	1961	New	(3)

(a) ex I.C.Tone, contr, Alexandra
Bridge, Sunderland, c/1903
(b) ex T.Mitchell, contr, Woodhouse
Hill, Yorks, W.R.
(c) ex TWW, Charlton Works, Sheffield, Yorks, W.R., 1/1920;
prev. James Pain
(d) ex Cohen, c/1926; prev.Greenwood
& Batley Ltd, Leeds, Yorks, W.R.
(e) ex S, /1929, for trials

(1) to Clay Cross Co Ltd, Grin
Quarry, Derbyshire, c/1929, via S
(2) to Lytham Motive Power Museum,
Lytham, Lancs, /1972
(3) to Ely Works, Cardiff, Glamorgan,
c7/1971

WIGGLESWORTH COLLIERY CO LTD, HOLLY MOOR COLLIERY, COCKFIELD

T26 This very small colliery (Map 84, NZ 115246), which is also recorded as
Holy Moor and Hollymoor, probably dates from the turn of the century.
From the shaft (drift?) a narrow gauge tramway ran down to screens along-
side the LNER line from Bishop Auckland to Barnard Castle, ½m NE of
Cockfield Station. Loco working had been abandoned by 1929, though the
colliery continued for a few more years under different owners.

Gauge: 2' 0"

-		4wVBT	VCG	S	6770CH≠	1926	(a) (1)

≠ A 2' 0" gauge locomotive at the Cliffe Hill Granite Co Ltd in
Leicestershire (officially S 6751CH) incorrectly carried Sentinel
plates 6770CH. It is not known whether the reverse is true.

(a) New; said to have replaced an
earlier conventional locomotive
(1) to Northumberland Whinstone Co
Ltd, Northumberland, by 6/1929

HENRY WILLIAMS LTD, RAILWAY APPLIANCE WORKS, ALBERT HILL, DARLINGTON

V17 This works (Map 85, NZ 296152) was begun in 1883, and was served by sidings
SW of Albert Hill Junction on BR Bishop Auckland-Darlington line, ½m E of
Darlington (North Road) Station. It is not known whether there were any
locomotives before 1927. Rail traffic ceased about 1965.

Gauge: 4' 8½"

-	0-4-0PM	HR	908	1927	New	(1)
	0-4-0DM	HE	2839	1943	New	(2)

                                          (1) to Rolling Stock Co Ltd, Eryholme
                                              Junction, Yorks, N.R. c/1943
                                          (2) to Hanratty Bros Ltd, Darlington,
                                              c/1966

SIR HEDWORTH WILLIAMSON'S LIMEWORKS LTD, FULWELL, SUNDERLAND

K5 The early history of this huge complex is obscure. By the 1850's there were
seven limestone quarries in the Southwick and Fulwell areas of Sunderland,
though some were not being worked. At this time two separate railway
systems were operated. The first ran from Thistley Hall Quarry (Map 78,
NZ 379598) to the Wear Lime Works on the bank of the R.Wear (NZ 390583) a
distance of about 1¼ miles, and included an engine house and a "windlass".
The second ran from Carley Hill Quarry (immediately NE of Thistley Hall
Quarry), down to Carley Limeworks, which lay immediately to the east of the
other works, and this line too had an engine house known as the Carley Hill
Engine. Whether the lines were under the same ownership is not known, as is
whether or not locomotives were used. Later both lines were abandoned in
favour of a link to the NER Gateshead-Sunderland line, ½m N of Fulwell
Station, and a limeworks was built near the quarries, which had expanded
and become known as Southwick and Fulwell Quarries. The complex was closed
in February 1957, and much of the site has been cleared and levelled.

Gauge: 4' 8½"

TEDDY (form.FRITZ)	0-4-0ST	OC	BH	1026	1891	New	Scr	
TEDDY	0-4-0ST	OC	BH	1114	1895	New	s/s	
DOROTHY	0-4-0ST	OC	BH	1121	1895	New	s/s	
RACEY	0-4-0ST	OC	BH	1122	1895	New	s/s	
PHYLLIS	0-4-0ST	OC	LE	230	1897	New	(1)	
SYLVIA	0-4-0ST	OC	LE	238	1899	New	Scr	/1927
CHARLES HEDWORTH	0-4-0ST	OC	HC	683	1903	New	(2)	
JOE	0-4-0ST	OC	HL	2431	1899	(a)	(3)	
BILLY	0-4-0ST	OC	BH	551	1880	(b)	s/s	
ELIZABETH	0-4-0ST	OC	HC	1484	1922	New	(4)	
FRITZ	0-4-0ST	OC	HC	1493	1923	New	(4)	
PHYLLIS	4wVBT	VCG	S	5988CH	1925	(c)	(5)	
CHARLES HEDWORTH	4wVBT	VCG	S	6218CH	1926	(d)	(6)	
SYLVIA	0-4-0ST	OC	HC	1599	1927	New	(4)	
BILLY	0-4-0ST	OC	HL	3806	1934	New	(5)	
TEDDY	0-4-0ST	OC	HL	3887	1936	New	(5)	
NICHOLAS	0-4-0ST	OC	HL	2496	1901	(e)	(4)	

(a) ex John Hill & Co, Middlesbrough, (1) reb. at Fulwell to S 5988, /1925
    Yorks, N.R., 12/1914   (2) reb. to S 6218, /1926
(b) ex Consett Iron Co Ltd, 10/1919   (3) to Kirkby Stephen Works, West-
(c) reb. from LE 230   morland, c/1951
(d) reb. from HC 683   (4) scr on site by TWW, /1957
(e) ex Short Bros Ltd, Pallion,   (5) to Kirkby Stephen Works, West-
    Sunderland, /1940   morland
                                       (6) to Kirkby Stephen Works, West-
                                           morland, and ret; scr by 1949

WILSONS FORGE LTD, BISHOP AUCKLAND
(form. Wilsons Forge (1929) Ltd; orig. Robert Wilson & Sons Ltd)

T22 Works (Map 85, NZ 213293) served by sidings N of BR Bishop Auckland-Shildon
line, ½m E of Bishop Auckland Station. Rail traffic ceased about 1958.

Gauge: 4' 8½"

-	0-4-0ST	OC	MW	540	1875	(a)	s/s c/1946
-	0-4-0ST	OC	AE	1613	1911	(b)	(1)

(a) ex North Bitchburn Coal Co Ltd,   (1) sold for scrap, 4/1959
    c/1930 (?)

219

(b) ex Cohen, Wood Lane, London,
    c/1946; prev. Cordes (Dos Works)
    Ltd, Newport, Monmouthshire

WINGATE COAL CO, WINGATE GRANGE COLLIERY, WINGATE

P11 This colliery (Map 85, NZ 398373) was opened in 1839, and was served by a
     branch (½m) of the Great North of England, Clarence & Hartlepool Junction
     Railway, which after various amalgamations eventually became part of the
     NER. It would appear that at first, as on the Clarence Railway, the coal
     owners ran their own trains to Hartlepool Docks; later the railway took
     over control of the traffic. The colliery survived to be vested in NCB
     Northern Division No.3 Area on 1st January 1947.

Gauge: 4' 8½"

-	0-6-0		RWH	297	1839	New	s/s
-	0-6-0		RWH	308	1839	New	(1)
ROYAL GEORGE	0-6-0	VC	Hackworth		1828	(a)	s/s
VICTORY	0-6-0	VC	Hackworth		1829	(b)	s/s

(a) ex Stockton & Darlington Rly,   (1) to Earl of Durham
    No.5, ROYAL GEORGE, 12/1840
(b) ex Stockton & Darlington Rly,
    No.8, VICTORY, 2/1841

WINGATE LIMESTONE CO LTD, WINGATE QUARRY, near TRIMDON COLLIERY

R22 Quarry (Map 85, NZ 373377) was served by a branch (1m) N of LNER Wingate-
     Ferryhill line, ¼m E of Trimdon Station. Its locomotives were maintained
     by South Hetton Coal Co Ltd. It closed in May 1930.

Gauge: 4' 8½"

WINGATE	0-4-0ST		AB			(a)	(1)
BIRKBECK	0-4-0ST					(b)	(1)
GREENSIDE	0-4-0ST					(b)	(1)
HOLMLEA	0-4-0ST	OC	MW	1887	1915	New	(2)
CARMEL	0-4-0ST	OC	MW	1911	1917	New	(3)
-	0-4-0ST	OC	HL	2177	1890		
			reb. J.Tait				
				100	1920	(c)	(4)

(a) origin doubtful; may be   (1) one four-coupled saddletank with
    AB 662/1890   outside cylinders was offered for
(b) origin unknown   sale 5/1915; may have been one of
(c) ex J.Tait, Middlesbrough, Yorks,   these; otherwise s/s
    N.R., /1920; prev. Consett Iron   (2) to RS, /1933, via W.Blenkinsop,
    Co Ltd   Middlesbrough; re-sold to G. & T.
                                          Earle Ltd, Hessle, Yorks, E.R.,
                                          3/1934
                                      (3) to RS, /1933, via W.Blenkinsop,
                                          Middlesbrough; re-sold to
                                          S.Taylor, Frith & Co Ltd, Dove
                                          Holes, Derbyshire, per J.C.Oliver
                                          Ltd, c/1935
                                      (4) to W.Blenkinsop, Middlesbrough,
                                          /1933

WITTON PARK SLAG CO LTD

Broadwood Quarry, near Frosterley. Map 84, NZ 033366 (approx)

Y7 This quarry had been closed by Pease & Partners Ltd in 1923, and was re-
    opened by these owners in 1926. It was served by a branch (½m) 1m E of
    Frosterley Station on LNER Wearhead Branch. The rail traffic was later
    taken over by the LNER.

Gauge: 4' 8½"

-	4wPM	MR			(a)	s/s
-	4wPM	MR	1951	1920	(b)	s/s

(a) origin unknown
(b) ex ?, /1930

Gauge: 2' 0" (used within quarry)

-	0-4-0ST	OC	KS			(a)	s/s by 1939
JIMMY	0-4-0ST	OC	KS	4246	1922	(b)	Scr by 1939
-	4wPM	MR		4577	1930	New	s/s

(a) origin unknown
(b) ex R.H.Neal,contr

Etherley Works, Witton Park. Map 85, NZ 174306 (approx)

T19 This works processed slag from the former Witton Park Ironworks of Bolckow, Vaughan & Co Ltd (q.v.). It was served by sidings ½m N of Etherley Station on LNER Crook-Bishop Auckland line. Work appears to have ended about 1931.

Gauge: 4' 8½"

AUBREY LAWRENCE	0-4-0ST	OC	KS	2399	1917	(a)	s/s c/1932
JUPITER	0-4-0ST	OC	MW	1880	1915	(b)	(1)

Two standard gauge locomotives were offered for sale in April 1927.

(a) ex MOM, Sutton Oak, Lancs
(b) ex Strakers & Love Ltd, Brandon
    Colliery, loan, /1931

(1) ret. to Strakers & Love Ltd,
    /1931

Gauge: 2' 0"

-	4wPM	MR	3833	1926	New	s/s

WOLSINGHAM STEEL CO LTD, WOLSINGHAM
(Doxford and Sunderland Ltd until 1/11/1972; Doxford and Sunderland Shipbuilding and Engineering Co Ltd until 23/3/1970; see also below)

X4 Works (Map 84, NZ 082372) is served by sidings N of BR Wearhead Branch, ½m E of Wolsingham Station (closed). Locomotives were used here when it was owned by John Rogerson & Co Ltd (q.v.), but under later ownership and the majority of Doxfords' ownership shunting was done by steam cranes.

Gauge: 4' 8½"

(No.1)	4wDM	RH	432480	1959	(a)	
(No.2)	4wDM	RH	198325	1940	(b)	(1)

(a) ex Golightly (Developments) Ltd,
    Ferryhill, 11/1970; prev.
    Northern Gas Board, Commercial
    Street Gas Works, Middlesbrough,
    Teesside
(b) ex Golightly (Developments) Ltd,
    Ferryhill, 5/1972; prev.
    Northern Gas Board, Hendon Gas
    Works, Sunderland

(1) used as source of spares for
    RH 432480

NICHOLAS WOOD & PARTNERS

Nicholas Wood (1795-1865), sometime Viewer of Killingworth Colliery in Northumberland and associate of George Stephenson, subsequently became both a noted mining engineer and colliery owner, with interests in John Bowes, Esq., & Partners, the Hetton Coal Co, the Harton Coal Co, and this firm above, which appears to date from the 1850's.
The collieries below used locomotives under subsequent owners, and it is possible that they may have done under Wood's ownership, though nothing has yet come to light.

Black Boy Colliery, Coundon Grange. Map 85, NZ 232284.

T24 This colliery, sunk in the late 1820's, was served by a branch (1m) from NER Bishop Auckland-Shildon line, 1m S of Bishop Auckland Station. It was later owned by the Black Boy Coal Co (an alternative name for Nicholas Wood & Partners?) and then by Bolckow, Vaughan & Co Ltd (q.v.).

Leasingthorne Colliery, near Coundon. Map 85, NZ 252304.

R12 This colliery was served by an extension of NER Chilton Branch. It was later owned by Bolckow, Vaughan & Co Ltd (q.v.).

Westerton Colliery, near Bishop Auckland. Map 85, NZ 237315.

R1 This colliery was served by a branch (2¼m) from Binchester Junction on NER Ferryhill-Bishop Auckland line. It too later came under the control of Bolckow, Vaughan & Co Ltd (q.v.).

WOODLAND COLLIERIES CO LTD
(Woodland Collieries Co until 11/1880; latterly subsidiary of Cargo Fleet Iron Co Ltd)

Not a great deal is known about either this company or the collieries which it owned. It would appear that the firm owned the four collieries served by the Woodland Branch, which joined the NER Bishop Auckland-Barnard Castle line 1¼m NE of Cockfield Station. These collieries were **Morley Colliery** (Map 84, NZ 105266?), **Crane Row Colliery** (NZ 093276), **Crako Scar Colliery** (NZ 082276) and **Woodland Colliery** (NZ 066266). The branch, about 4½ miles long, was opened about 1863, and worked by the NER until 1885, when the colliery owners took over. It would appear that at least at one time the usual method of working the branch was to assemble sets of 50-60 wagons at Woodland, and then let the wagons coast down to the NER with men sitting on the brake handles, and the loco following behind to haul back the empties.
Morley and Crane Row Collieries had closed by 1913, and shortly afterwards Crake Scar followed. Woodland Colliery was taken over in 1914 by Cargo Fleet Iron Co Ltd (q.v.), who continued working the branch until the final closure in March 1921.

Gauge: 4' 8½"

T1
T2
T3
T4

NELSON	0-6-0ST	OC	K	1786	1871	(a)	s/s
-	0-4-0ST	OC	B	208	1873	(b)	(1)
ELEANOR	0-6-0ST	OC	AB	694	1891	New	s/s
-	0-6-0T	IC	Dar		1876	(c)	(2)

(a) ex Charles Nelson, contr.,
    Middlesbrough, Yorks, N.R.,
    /1885
(b) ex J.Torbuck, Middlesbrough,
    Yorks, N.R., hire, /1886
(c) ex NER, 1293, 4/1911

(1) boiler exploded, 11/1886
(2) to Cargo Fleet Iron Co Ltd,
    /1914

SECTION 3

NATIONAL COAL BOARD

NATIONAL COAL BOARD

On 1st January 1947 collieries in Durham, Northumberland and Cumberland were vested into the Northern Division (ND) of the NCB, which was sub-divided as follows:

No. 1 Area	North-East Durham	(N1/D1)
No. 2 Area	Mid-East Durham	(N2/D2)
No. 3 Area	South-East Durham	(N3/D3)
No. 4 Area	South-West Durham	(N4/D4)
No. 5 Area	Mid-West Durham	(N5/D5)
No. 6 Area	North-West Durham	(N6/D6)
No. 7 Area	Southern Northumberland	(N7)
No. 8 Area	Central Northumberland	(N8)
No. 9 Area	Northern Northumberland	(N9)
No.10 Area	Cumberland	

Coking plants were controlled directly by the Division, but their locomotives were the responsibility of the Area in which the plant was situated. Mines producing less than 150 tons per week remained privately-owned, but became "licensed mines".

On 1st January 1950 the Northern Division was divided into the Durham Division (DD) (Nos. 1 to 6 Areas as before) and the Northern (Northumberland & Cumberland) Division (N(N&C) (Nos. 7 to 10 Areas being re-numbered Nos. 1 to 4).

In April 1959 Sherburn Hill Colliery was transferred from No.4 Area to No.3 Area.

On 1st January 1963 the former No.5 Area was divided between Nos.4 and 6 Areas, the latter then becoming No.5 Area.

In addition, coking plants were transferred to the new Coal Products Division (Northern Region) (CPD), which also took over coke car locomotives and shunting locomotives at Norwood Coking Plant, though locomotives used for shunting at the other plants remained under the control of the Areas, as before.

On 1st January 1964 the Areas in Northumberland, by now reduced to two, were combined with the five in Durham to form the Northumberland & Durham Division (N&D), the Durham Areas retaining their former numbers.

On 28th June 1965 the former No.2 Area was divided between Nos.1 and 3 Areas, and in addition Ryhope Colliery was transferred from No.1 to No.3 Area.

On 26th March 1967 the Northumberland & Durham Division was abolished. Nos.1 and 5 Areas combined to form the North Durham Area (NDM) and Nos.3 and 4 Areas combined to form the South Durham Area (SDM). In Northumberland the two Areas combined to form the Northumberland Area. In addition, the Area Workshops were transferred to the new Workshops Division.

On 1st April 1973 the Coal Products Division, which had previously been re-organised in January 1970 and January 1973, was converted into a new fully-controlled subsidiary, National Smokeless Fuels Ltd (NSF).

On 1st April 1974 the Northumberland, North Durham and South Durham Areas were combined to form the North-East Area (NE), with headquarters at Coal House, Team Valley, Gateshead.

Note: From the early years of nationalisation each Area was divided into "Groups", lettered from 'A' upwards. In Durham these sometimes affected locomotive numbering, as the Group Engineer was directly responsible for locomotives within his Group. They were abolished on 26th March 1967.

1. ALPHABETICAL LIST OF LOCATIONS IN CO. DURHAM

(a) where locomotives have been used or stored
(✓ indicates locomotives used underground)

ADDISON COLLIERY, Ryton. Map 78, NZ 168643.
(Stella Coal Co Ltd; N6 from 1/1/1947; D6 from 1/1/1950; D5 from 1/1/1963)
  A5   Colliery sidings lay S of BR Newcastle-Carlisle line, 1¼m W of Blaydon
       Station. Closed 22nd February 1963.

ALLERDENE SHOP PIT LOCO SHED (Pelaw Main Railway) - see SHOP PIT

AREA APPRENTICE TRAINING CENTRE, Tursdale. Map 85, NZ 303359.
(Opened D4; N&D4 from 1/1/1964; SDM from 26/3/1967)
  R16   Narrow gauge diesel locomotive allocated for training purposes from
       January 1967. Under re-organisation of training this section was
       closed in 1968.

AREA APPRENTICE TRAINING CENTRE, Usworth. Map 78, NZ 315584.
(Opened D1; N&D1 from 1/1/1964; NDM from 26/3/1967)
  J5   Narrow gauge diesel locomotive allocated for training purposes from
       January 1961, latterly as a static exhibit. This type of training was
       transferred with the locomotive to North Durham Engineering Centre in
       September 1970, and the Usworth Centre was closed on 6th January 1973.

AREA ENGINEERING CENTRE, Annfield Plain. Map 78, NZ 176508.
(officially known as NORTH DURHAM ENGINEERING CENTRE, and formerly as
MORRISON APPRENTICE TRAINING CENTRE)
(Opened D6; D5 from 1/1/1963; N&D5 from 1/1/1964; NDM from 26/3/1967)
  H66   Narrow gauge locomotives allocated for training purposes (surface
       railway system) from October 1965, which became the centre's only
       activity from 3rd April 1973 until its final closure in December 1973.

AREA MACHINERY STORES, Blackhall. Map 85, NZ 461397.
(formerly AREA CENTRAL STORES)
(Opened by D3; N&D3 from 1/1/1964; SDM from 26/3/1967)
  P16   Spare underground locomotives kept here. Closed in 1968, and converted
       into colliery fitting shops.

AREA MACHINERY STORES, Stella Gill, Pelton Fell. Map 78, NZ 262522.
(known as STELLA GILL STORES)
(Opened by D5; N&D5 from 1/1/1964; NDM from 26/3/1967; NE from 1/4/1974)
  H51   Building part of former Stella Gill Coking Plant (demolished).
       Spare narrow gauge surface and underground locomotives stored here up
       to 9/1972. **Closed on**

AREA MACHINERY STORES, Tursdale. Map 85, NZ 303360.
(NE from 1/4/1974).
  R16   Buildings in Central Workshops, Tursdale, used to store spare
       underground locomotives from 1/1975.

AREA MACHINERY STORES, Whitburn. Map 78, NZ 411634.
(Opened by D1; N&D1 from 1/1/1964; NDM from 26/3/1967; NE from 1/4/1974)
  D15   Buildings in Central Workshops, Whitburn, used to store spare
       underground locomotives.

AREA TRAINING CENTRE, Seaham. Map 85, NZ 412498.
(Opened by D2; N&D2 from 1/1/1964; N&D3 from 28/6/1965; SDM from 26/3/1967;
NE from 1/4/1974)
  L33   Narrow gauge diesel locomotives were first allocated for training
       purposes in July 1965, but under re-organisation of training this

section was discontinued in 1966. It was re-opened in the autumn of 1973, with enlarged facilities, including a skid track.

ARNGHYLL COLLIERY, near Copley.   Colliery comprised two drifts - Cowley Drift, Map 84, NZ 067245, and Busty Drift, NZ 072243. (Opened by N4 in 1947; D4 from 1/1/1950)
  T5   Cowley Drift lay alongside the unfenced road which joined the B6282 road from Woodland to Eggleston. It seems probable that the two drifts were connected by a narrow gauge line, on which diesel locomotives were used. At least one of the locomotives was not flameproofed, which suggests that they did not work underground from the surface. The colliery had no main line rail connection, and was closed on 5th May 1951.

AUCKLAND PARK DISPOSAL POINT,   near Bishop Auckland. Map 85, NZ 227285. (Opened by Ministry of Fuel & Power, and operated by DL (?) from c/1945, and N4 from 1/1/1947; N4 became D4 on 1/1/1950, and overall control passed to NCBOE on 1/4/1952; operated by Derek Crouch (Contractors) Ltd from 18/3/1958)
  T24 Auckland Park Colliery was closed in 1943, but towards the end of the Second World War, probably in 1945, the old colliery screens and weighbridge were re-opened to handle local opencast coal. They were served by a private branch (½m) from a junction 1m S of Bishop Auckland Station on BR Bishop Auckland-Shildon line. After nationalisation of the coal industry the Point became a Deep Mines Establishment operated by No.4 Area, and its locos were included in No.4 Area stock. New screens were built for NCBOE adjacent to the colliery in the mid-1950's, and in March 1958 No.4 Area gave up its operation to private contractors, the colliery site then being partially cleared. The Disposal Point was closed on 11th September 1959, and the site cleared in 1963.

AXWELL PARK COLLIERY, Swalwell. Map 78, NZ 202618. (Priestman Collieries Ltd; N6 from 1/1/1947; D6 from 1/1/1950).
  B10 Colliery sidings lay E of BR line from Blaydon to Blackhill, ¼m S of Swalwell Station. It was closed on 7th August 1954.

BANK FOOT COKE OVENS, Crook. Map 85, NZ 158364. (Pease & Partners Ltd; ND from 1/1/1947; DD from 1/1/1950).
  Q5   The plant consisted of ovens, refinery and tar distillation unit, and was part of the extensive Roddymoor complex at Pease's West. It was served by a branch (½m) from a junction immediately N of Crook Station on BR line from Crook to Tow Law. It was closed in October 1960.

BANK FOOT, WALDRIDGE, LOCO SHED (Sacriston Railway). Map 78, NZ 247502. (Charlaw & Sacriston Collieries Co Ltd; N5 from 1/1/1947; D5 from 1/1/1950).
  H63 Loco shed was situated near junction of main line and former branch to Waldridge Colliery (closed). Locomotives worked trains through to Pelton Fell exchange sidings on BR mineral line from Pelton Fell to Annfield Plain (Pontop & Shields branch). The shed closed with the Railway in February 1955.

BEAMISH ENGINE WORKS, Beamish (Beamish Railway). Map 78, NZ 222537. (Lambton, Hetton & Joicey Collieries Ltd; N5 from 1/1/1947; D5 from 1/1/1950; D5 (new) from 1/1/1963).
  H46 The loco shed for the Railway was situated inside the works compound. Locomotives worked trains from Beamish Mary Colliery (1¼m W of shed) and Beamish Second Colliery (adjacent to Engine Works) through to Ouston Junction (BR), 3½m E of shed. In 1955 traffic was diverted at West Pelton via a newly-constructed link to Handen Hold Colliery, which took over the one remaining Beamish Engine Works duty as from 7th August 1963.

BEAMISH MARY COLLIERY, near Stanley. Map 78, NZ 211536. (Lambton, Hetton & Joicey Collieries Ltd; N5 from 1/1/1947; D5 from 1/1/1950; D5 (new) from 1/1/1963; N&D5 from 1/1/1964).

H42   Served by Beamish Railway (q.v.). Colliery was closed on 26th March 1966.

BEAMISH RAILWAY
(Lambton, Hetton & Joicey Collieries Ltd; N5 from 1/1/1947; D5 from 1/1/1950; D5 (new) from 1/1/1963; N&D5 from 1/1/1964).

Railway ran from Beamish Mary Colliery to Ouston Junction (BR - Map 78, NZ 273536), a distance of 4¼ miles. Short branches served Beamish Second Colliery and Beamish Engine Works, where the one loco shed was situated.

In 1955 a ½m link was built between the Railway at West Pelton and Handen Hold Colliery on the BR mineral line from Pelton Fell to Annfield Plain (Pontop & Shields branch), in order that the section of Railway between West Pelton and Ouston Junction might be closed. In August 1963 Beamish Engine Works Loco Shed was closed, and all working transferred to Handen Hold Colliery shed.

The remainder of the Railway was closed with Beamish Mary Colliery on 26th March 1966.

BEAMISH SECOND COLLIERY, Beamish. Map 78, NZ 221537.
(Lambton, Hetton & Joicey Collieries Ltd; N5 from 1/1/1947; D5 from 1/1/1950).

H44   Served by a short branch of the Beamish Railway at Beamish. The colliery was closed on 9th November 1962.

BEARPARK COLLIERY & COKE OVENS, Bearpark. Map 85, NZ 243434.
(Bearpark Coal & Coke Co Ltd)

COLLIERY   :- N5 from 1/1/1947; D5 from 1/1/1950; D4 from 1/1/1963; N&D4 from 1/1/1964; SDM from 26/3/1967; NE from 1/4/1974).

COKE OVENS :- ND from 1/1/1947; DD from 1/1/1950.

M8   The colliery was served by sidings W of BR Consett-Durham line, 1m N of Relly Mill Junction. The colliery locos shunted the coke ovens until their closure in April 1960. Rail traffic was replaced by road haulage in September 1962.

BILDERSHAW COLLIERY, near West Auckland. Map 85, NZ 195244.
(Opened by D4)

T12   This drift mine had no connection to a main line railway. It lay near to the A68 road, SE of West Auckland. Narrow gauge diesels were used from 1952, but how is uncertain. It closed on 16th October 1956.

BLACKBURN FELL DRIFT, near Sunniside. Map 78, NZ 214573.
(John Bowes & Partners Ltd; N6 from 1/1/1947; D6 from 1/1/1950; D5 from 1/1/1963; N&D5 from 1/1/1964; NDM from 26/3/1967; NE from 1/4/1974)

H13   Served by Bowes Railway until 30th March 1970, when rail traffic was replaced by road transport.

BLACK FELL LOCO SHED, Eighton Banks, near Gateshead. Map 78, NZ 281577.
(NE Area)

H69   On the closure of the Bowes Railway in 1974 the Black Fell Incline was converted into a 1¼m 3' 0" gauge test track for underground locomotives, with a loco shed made from part of the kip at the bank head. The line was brought into operation in January 1975.

BLACKHALL COLLIERY, Blackhall. Map 85, NZ 461396.
(Horden Collieries Ltd; N3 from 1/1/1947; D3 from 1/1/1950; N&D3 from 1/1/1964; SDM from 26/3/1967; NE from 1/4/1974).

P16   The colliery is served by sidings E of BR Seaham-Hartlepool line, 1¼m S of former Horden Station. A narrow gauge diesel loco is used in the colliery stockyard.

⨍   The 2' 8½" system underground, used only for man-riding, was replaced by the 2' 0" system used in the rest of the colliery in 1962.

BLACKHOUSE FELL LOCO SHED, near Birtley (Pelaw Main Railway). Map 78,NZ 282562
(Pelaw Main Collieries Ltd; N6 from 1/1/1947; D6 from 1/1/1950)
   H33   This loco shed housed one loco, which took trains from the top of the
        Blackhouse Fell Incline (NZ 280560) to the foot of the Eighton Banks
        Incline (NZ 277576), a straight run of about one mile. The shed closed
        with the remainder of this section of the Railway in January 1959.

BLAYDON BURN COLLIERY, Blaydon. Map 78, NZ 166624.
(Priestman Collieries Ltd; N6 from 1/1/1947; D6 from 1/1/1950)
   A10   The colliery was served by an NCB branch (1¼m) from junction 1¼m W of
        Blaydon Station on BR Newcastle-Carlisle line. The colliery consisted
        of two pits - the Mary Pit, closed on 28th March 1953, and the Bessie
        Pit, closed on 3rd November 1956.

BOLDON COLLIERY, Boldon Colliery. Map 78, NZ 347623.
(Harton Coal Co Ltd; N1 from 1/1/1947; D1 from 1/1/1950; N&D1 from 1/1/1964;
NDM from 26/3/1967; NE from 1/4/1974)
   D12   Colliery is served by sidings W of BR Harton-Washington mineral line,
   ⊀   1½m S of Harton Junction, and latterly at end of line. NCB locos have
        running powers over BR from the colliery to Whitburn Junction, on a
        spur immediately N of Tyne Dock Station on BR Gateshead-South Shields
        line, in order to gain access to Dene Sidings on the Harton Railway
        and allow Boldon coal to be shipped at Harton Low Staithes. They also
        have running powers through Tyne Dock Station to interchange sidings
        ¼m N, giving access to Harton High Staith. Latterly loco repairs have
        been done at Westoe Lane Loco Sheds (q.v.); these short-term transfers
        are not recorded.
        A narrow gauge battery loco is used in the colliery stockyard, etc.

BOWBURN COLLIERY, Bowburn. Map 85, NZ 304379.
(Dorman, Long & Co Ltd; N4 from 1/1/1947; D4 from 1/1/1950; N&D4 from 1/1/1964;
SDM from 26/3/1967)
   R15   Colliery sidings lay E of Leamside-Ferryhill line (BR), 1½m N of
   ⊀   Tursdale Junction. The colliery was linked underground to the former
        Tursdale Colliery (q.v.). It was closed on 22nd July 1967.

BOWES RAILWAY
(John Bowes & Partners Ltd; N6 from 1/1/1947; D6 from 1/1/1950; D5 from
1/1/1963; N&D5 from 1/1/1964; NDM from 26/3/1967; NE from 1/4/1974)
        This Railway ran from Burnopfield Colliery to Jarrow Staithes, a
        distance of 13m. Besides Burnopfield Colliery, the Railway since 1947
        has served Byermoor Colliery, High Marley Hill Drift, Marley Hill
        Colliery, Blackburn Fell Drift, Kibblesworth Colliery, Springwell
        Workshops, Wardley No.1 Colliery (latterly called Usworth Colliery)
        via ¼m branch, Monkton Coal Preparation Plant and Monkton Coking Plant.
        Jarrow Staithes are operated by the Port of Tyne Authority (Tyne
        Improvement Commission until 1/8/1968).
   H12   Locomotives from Marley Hill Loco Shed handled traffic between
        Burnopfield Colliery, etc, to Birkheads Bank Top (NZ 222568), a
        distance of 2¼m. The next six miles were worked by six inclines,
        operated variously by gravity or stationary engines, taking the wagons
   F2   to Springwell Bank Foot (NZ 296605), whence locomotives from the shed
        there took trains to Wardley, Monkton and Jarrow.
        The section between Burnopfield and the marshalling yard west of
        Marley Hill Colliery was closed in August 1968, to be followed by the
        section between Blackburn Fell Drift and Kibblesworth in March 1969.
        The now isolated section around Marley Hill continued operating until
        30th July 1970. In 1971 the loco shed was taken over by the North of
        England Open-Air Museum.
        With the closure of Kibblesworth Colliery in October 1974 the remaining
        five inclines were closed, except that the former Springwell Incline
        was kept open until November 1974 for wagon repairs at Springwell
        Workshops. Usworth Colliery closed in August 1974, but its branch
        remains open to handle waste from Monkton Coal Preparation Plant.

In 1955 a short loop was built between Blackham's Hill (NZ 283583) on
the Bowes Railway to Eighton Banks (NZ 281583) on the Pelaw Main
Railway. In January 1959 the remaining section of the latter became a
branch of the Bowes Railway 6¼m long. This served Ravensworth Park
Drift, Ravensworth Shop Colliery and Ravensworth Ann Colliery, with
C14/16   loco sheds at Shop Pit, Ravensworth Ann Colliery and Starrs
F4   (Wrekenton), and two more inclines, both worked by stationary engines;
for full details see PELAW MAIN RAILWAY.
In May 1963 the working at the western end of this branch was re-
organised; the section from the southern end of the Team Valley
Trading Estate to Dunston (BR) was closed, and traffic between
Ravensworth Park Drift and the foot of the Allerdene Incline was taken
over by a loco hired from the Team Valley Trading Estate, the Shop Pit
loco shed being used only for repairs until August 1964, when it was
closed. It was re-opened temporarily between 6th and 21st September
1965, and in May 1966 it was restored to full working when the NCB
again took over full control of the traffic.
In March 1968 coal-winding at the Ravensworth Ann Colliery shaft
ceased, its coal being drawn instead via Ravensworth Park Drift
(renamed Ravensworth Ann Colliery). As a result the Ravensworth Ann
loco shed was closed, wagons from the Starrs Incline being allowed to
run right through the former colliery yard. In April 1973 Ravensworth
Ann Colliery was merged with Kibblesworth Colliery, and so this last
remaining section of the Pelaw Main Railway closed on 18th April 1973.
The Bowes Railway originally had two links with BR, one at Bowes
Bridge, Marley Hill, with the Tanfield Branch (closed in August 1962)
and the other at Pontop Junction, Jarrow, ½m W of Jarrow Station on
the BR Gateshead-South Shields line, which remains in full use.
H14   A locomotive was used temporarily at Kibblesworth Colliery in 1964,
while from 1964 locomotives were sometimes brought in for repairs or
F6   scrap to Springwell Workshops, which closed in March 1975.

BRADLEY DRIFT, Leadgate. Map 78, NZ 118528.
(Opened D6; D5 from 1/1/1963; N&D5 from 1/1/1964)
G23   This drift was served by locos from Leadgate Loco Shed (q.v.).
It was closed on 25th September 1966.

BRANCEPETH COLLIERY & COKING PLANT, Willington. Map 85, NZ 205357.
(Strakers & Love Ltd)
         COLLIERY   :- N5 from 1/1/1947; D5 from 1/1/1950; D4 from 1/1/1963;
                         N&D4 from 1/1/1964; SDM from 26/3/1967.
         COKING PLANT :- ND from 1/1/1947; DD from 1/1/1950; CPD from 1/1/1963.
Q13   The colliery sidings lay N of BR Durham-Bishop Auckland line, ½m N of
Willington Station. The coking plant lay at the E end of the complex.
In March 1967 the ovens and the C.A.L. plant were closed, and on 1st
April 1967 shunting at the plant was taken over by CPD, who hired one
of the colliery locos to do so. The colliery closed on 22nd July 1967,
to be followed by the coking plant's benzole refinery and boiler plant
in December 1967.
The colliery was connected to Brandon Pit House Colliery by an aerial
ropeway, though latterly this was disused.

BRANDON 'C' COLLIERY, Brandon, near Durham. Map 85, NZ 245400.
(Strakers & Love Ltd; N5 from 1/1/1947; D5 from 1/1/1950)
M14   The colliery sidings lay S of BR Durham-Bishop Auckland line, 1m S of
Relly Mill Junction, and at the northern end of the NCB branch to
Brandon Pit House Colliery, with which it was merged from 20th August
1960.

BRANDON PIT HOUSE COLLIERY, near Meadowfield. Map 85, NZ 215404.
(Strakers & Love Ltd; N5 from 1/1/1947; D5 from 1/1/1950; D4 from 1/1/1963;
N&D4 from 1/1/1964; SDM from 26/3/1967)
M13   The colliery was served by a steeply-graded branch (NCB - 2m) from a
junction with the BR Durham-Bishop Auckland line, 1m S of Relly Mill

Junction. It was also connected to Brancepeth Colliery by an aerial
ropeway, though latterly this was disused. From 1950 to 1958 coal was
brought to Brandon Pit House from West Brandon Drift by a narrow gauge
line 1m long. A narrow gauge loco was also used in the colliery stockyard.
On 20th August 1960 the colliery was merged with Brandon 'C' Colliery,
and it was closed on 15th March 1968.

BURNHOPE COLLIERY, Burnhope. Map 85, NZ 191482.
(Bearpark Coal & Coke Co Ltd; N6 from 1/1/1947)
  H54   This colliery did not use a locomotive, but is included here for the
       sake of completeness. It was situated at the end of the Burnhope
       Railway, an extension of the NCB line from Craghead Colliery. Wagons
       from the colliery were hauled by the Bank Top stationary engine up to
       Burnhope Moor and then let down to Craghead, whence they were worked
       by Craghead locos. An aerial ropeway 4½m long also took coal to
       Langley Park Colliery. The colliery was closed on 22nd July 1949.

BURNOPFIELD COLLIERY, Burnopfield. Map 78, NZ 173562.
(John Bowes & Partners Ltd; N6 from 1/1/1947; D6 from 1/1/1950; D5 from
1/1/1963; N&D5 from 1/1/1964; NDM from 26/3/1967)
  H6   Colliery situated at the western end of the Bowes Railway and worked
      by locos from Marley Hill Shed. It was closed on 9th August 1968.

BYERMOOR COLLIERY, Byermoor. Map 78, NZ 187573.
(John Bowes & Partners Ltd; N6 from 1/1/1947; D6 from 1/1/1950; D5 from
1/1/1963; N&D5 from 1/1/1964; NDM from 26/3/1967)
  H8   Colliery served by the Bowes Railway, and worked by locos from Marley
      Hill Shed. It was closed on 2nd February 1968.

CENTRAL WORKSHOPS, BRADLEY, Leadgate. Map 78, NZ 118517.
(Consett Iron Co Ltd; N6 from 1/1/1947; D6 from 1/1/1950; D5 from 1/1/1963;
N&D5 from 1/1/1964; Workshops Div. from 26/3/1967)
  G9   Served by sidings N of line from Ouston Junction to Consett (BR) at
      Leadgate, but worked by locos from Leadgate Loco Shed until June 1965,
      when the rail connection was removed. Major loco repairs ceased in
      February 1963, but minor repairs to locos from Leadgate continued
      until June 1965. The workshops were closed on 7th March 1969.

CENTRAL WORKSHOPS, PHILADELPHIA, commonly known as LAMBTON ENGINE WORKS.
Map 78, NZ 336525.
(Lambton, Hetton & Joicey Collieries Ltd; N2 from 1/1/1947; D2 from 1/1/1950;
N&D2 from 1/1/1964; N&D3 from 28/6/1965; Workshops Div. from 26/3/1967;
NE from 1/4/1974. N.B. Between 28/6/1965 and 26/3/1967 the Wagon Shop was
administered by N&D1)
  L12   The main locomotive repair works in Co. Durham, both for surface and
      underground locomotives, for all Durham Areas.
      Surface locos: repaired in the loco erecting shop. Transfers to the
      Works up to April 1974 only shown in loco lists if they involved a
      change of Area.
      Underground locomotives: usually repaired in the fitting shop.
      Transfers shown in loco lists if the loco was returned to a different
      colliery from which it had been sent.
      The Works is served by sidings E of the Lambton Railway at Philadelphia.

CENTRAL WORKSHOPS, TURSDALE, near Cornforth. Map 85, NZ 303360.
(Opened by D4 in 1952; N&D4 from 1/1/1964; Workshops Div. from 26/3/1967;
NE from 1/4/1974)
  R16   Works served by sidings E of BR Leamside-Ferryhill line, immediately N
      of Tursdale Junction. This works also carried out repairs to narrow
      gauge surface and underground locomotives for No.3 Area. Major standard
      gauge loco repairs ceased in January 1961.

CENTRAL WORKSHOPS, WHITBURN. Map 78, NZ 411634.
(Opened by D1; N&D1 from 1/1/1964; Workshops Div. from 26/3/1967; NE from
1/4/1974)
    D15   Works served by a link from South Shields, Marsden & Whitburn Colliery
           Railway at Whitburn Colliery. Major locomotive repairs ceased in May
           1965, and rail traffic ceased in June 1968.

    N.B. All Central Workshops were known as Area Central Workshops until
         26/3/1967.

CHILTON COLLIERY, Chilton Buildings. Map 85, NZ 278308.
(Dorman, Long & Co Ltd; N4 from 1/1/1947; D4 from 1/1/1950; N&D4 from 1/1/1964)
    R13   Colliery connected by a 1m branch to NCB line from junction with BR
     ⚒   Ferryhill-Stockton line, 2¼m S of Ferryhill Station, to Leasingthorne
           Colliery (formerly LNER Chilton Branch). The colliery was merged with
           Dean & Chapter Colliery on 28th May 1960, but maintained a separate
           allocation for underground locomotives until the closure of the complex
           on 15th January 1966.

CHOPWELL COLLIERY, Chopwell. Map 78, NZ 114586.
(Consett Iron Co Ltd; N6 from 1/1/1947; D6 from 1/1/1950; D5 from 1/1/1963;
N&D5 from 1/1/1964)
    A2   This colliery consisted of three separate pits (Nos. 1, 2 and 3), and
           with Whittonstall Drift, was part of the Chopwell Unit. It was served
           by the Chopwell & Garesfield Railway (later Derwenthaugh Railway)
           until February 1961, when road transport took over. The Unit closed on
           25th November 1966, though the three Chopwell shafts had ceased to
           raise coal before this.

CHOPWELL & GARESFIELD RAILWAY   (later DERWENTHAUGH RAILWAY)
(Consett Iron Co Ltd; N6 from 1/1/1947; D6 from 1/1/1950; D5 from 1/1/1963;
N&D5 from 1/1/1964; NDM from 26/3/1967)
           This Railway ran from Chopwell Colliery to Derwenthaugh Staithes at
           Swalwell (Map 78, NZ 204634), a distance of about 7½m. Besides
           Chopwell Colliery, the Railway has served since 1947 Garesfield Coll-
           iery, Clockburn Drift and Derwenthaugh Coking Plant. In addition, the
           Railway was linked to Whittonstall Drift by a narrow gauge line.
    A2   Locomotives from a shed at Chopwell worked trains through to Thornley
           Bank Head (NZ 165604), where a self-acting incline took the wagons
           down to Winlaton Mill. The remaining section was worked by locomotives
    B12   from Derwenthaugh Shed.
    A3   There was also a small loco shed at Garesfield Colliery, where one
           loco was kept for shunting.
           Derwenthaugh Staithes closed in 1960, and the section between Chopwell
           and Winlaton Mill followed in February 1961, since when Clockburn
           Drift has been the westernmost extremity of the line. The wagon shops
           are at Derwenthaugh.
           The Railway is linked to BR by a junction on the BR Redheugh Branch,
           1¼m E of Blaydon Station.

CLARA VALE COLLIERY, Clara Vale. Map 78, NZ 132651.
(Stella Coal Co Ltd; N6 from 1/1/1947; D6 from 1/1/1950; D5 from 1/1/1963;
N&D5 from 1/1/1964)
    A4   Colliery served by sidings N of BR Newcastle-Carlisle line, 1m E of
           Wylam Station. It was closed on 5th February 1966.

CLOCKBURN DRIFT, Winlaton Mill. Map 78, NZ 186604.
(Opened by D6 in 1952; D5 from 1/1/1963; N&D5 from 1/1/1964; NDM from 26/3/1967;
NE from 1/4/1974)
    A14   This is not a drift in the usual sense, but a large horizontal boring
     ⚒   driven from Winlaton Mill to Marley Hill Colliery, a distance of just
           over two miles. It was opened in 1952 to enable coal from Marley Hill
           Colliery to be used at Derwenthaugh Coking Plant. The original intent-
           ion was to continue westwards to Byermoor and possibly Burnopfield
           Colliery, but this was never done. Coal working was also done from the

tunnel, notably in the Three Quarter Drift, about ¼m from the entrance. The tunnel is laid with two 3' 6" gauge tracks, and locomotives bring trains of tubs out to a tippler plant for transfer into standard gauge wagons on the Chopwell & Garesfield (Derwenthaugh) Railway.

CONSETT IRON WORKS LOCO SHEDS, Templetown, Consett. Map 78, NZ 109500.
(Owned by Consett Iron Co Ltd)
G13   Locos from here continued to work collieries etc., handed over to the NCB at Vesting Day until January 1949, when the new NCB Loco Shed at Leadgate was opened.

CRAGHEAD COLLIERY, Craghead. Map 78, NZ 212506.
(Holmside & South Moor Collieries Ltd; N6 from 1/1/1947; D6 from 1/1/1950; D5 from 1/1/1963; N&D5 from 1/1/1964; NDM from 26/3/1967)
H55   Colliery served by NCB branch (1¼m) from BR Pontop & Shields line
╱   between Stanley and Pelton Fell (latterly Grange Villa to Pelton Fell). Locos took full wagons to Craghead Bank Top, ½m from the colliery, where a self-acting incline took them down to the BR exchange sidings, where until 1965 another loco worked. The system was replaced by road haulage from 1st July 1966, and the colliery was closed on 11th April 1969.

CROOKHALL COLLIERY, Consett.
(Consett Iron Co Ltd; N6 from 1/1/1947; D6 from 1/1/1950; D5 from 1/1/1963; N&D5 from 1/1/1964)
G13   This colliery consisted latterly of three units – Victory Pit
G20   (Map 78, NZ 113503), and Woodside Winnings (Map 85, NZ 138490) and
G21   Humber Hill Drift (NZ 140470), which were linked to the Victory Pit by a narrow gauge rope-worked line 2m long. The Victory Pit was part of the Consett Iron Works complex, and was shunted by locos from Templetown until January 1949, when the working was transferred to the new Leadgate shed. The colliery closed on 9th November 1963, but its coal preparation plant remained open (with rail traffic) until 21st December 1965.

DAWDON COLLIERY, Seaham. Map 85, NZ 436478.
(Londonderry Collieries Ltd; N2 from 1/1/1947; D2 from 1/1/1950; N&D2 from 1/1/1964; N&D3 from 28/6/1965; SDM from 26/3/1967; NE from 1/4/1974)
L36   The colliery is served by sidings W of a short loop from BR Seaham-
╱   Hartlepool line. It is also linked by a branch (¼m) to Seaham Harbour Docks. A narrow gauge surface system was opened in 1973. The colliery also uses various transport systems underground.

DEAF HILL COLLIERY, Deaf Hill. Map 85, NZ 372368.
(Trimdon Coal Co Ltd; N3 from 1/1/1947; D3 from 1/1/1950; N&D3 from 1/1/1964)
P10   This colliery was served by sidings N of BR Wingate-Ferryhill line, 1m W of Wingate Junction, and was worked by BR until 1955. In that year it was reconstructed, and a 2' 0" gauge line, worked by locomotives, was built to take Deaf Hill coal to Wingate Grange Colliery Washery, 1¼m away, though some coal continued to be dispatched via BR. The narrow gauge line was closed in October 1962, except for the system immediately around the colliery. In March 1964 a standard gauge NCB loco was allocated to the colliery to carry out early morning shunting. The colliery was closed on 25th February 1967.

DEAN & CHAPTER COLLIERY, Ferryhill. Map 85, NZ 272331.
(Dorman, Long & Co Ltd; N4 from 1/1/1947; D4 from 1/1/1950; N&D4 from 1/1/1964)
R10   This colliery lay alongside the old A1 road at Ferryhill, and was
╱   served by a ½m branch from BR Spennymoor-Ferryhill line, 1¼m E of Spennymoor Station. It was amalgamated with Leasingthorne Colliery (q.v.) on 1st January 1950, and also Chilton Colliery on 28th May 1960, though the latter retained its separate locomotive allocation. The whole complex was closed on 15th January 1966.
A narrow gauge loco was latterly used in the colliery yard.

DERWENT COLLIERY, Medomsley. Map 78, NZ 123548.
(Consett Iron Co Ltd; N6 from 1/1/1947; D6 from 1/1/1950; D5 from 1/1/1963;
N&D5 from 1/1/1964)
G2   Colliery was served by a branch (3m) from a junction at Leadgate, 1m N
      of Consett Station, on BR Pontop & Shields branch. It was worked via
      running powers over BR by NCB locos, first from Consett Iron Works,
      but from January 1949 by locos from the new Leadgate Shed. Loco
      working was replaced by road transport during the winter of 1960-1961,
      and the colliery closed on 21st November 1964.

DERWENTHAUGH COKING PLANT, Winlaton Mill. Map 78, NZ 193615.
(Consett Iron Co Ltd; ND from 1/1/1947; DD from 1/1/1950; CPD from 1/1/1963;
National Smokeless Fuels Ltd from 1/4/1973)
B11   Served by locos from Derwenthaugh Loco Shed on Chopwell & Garesfield
      Railway. An electric loco is used to haul the coke car. When this is
      under repair a loco is normally hired from North -East Area (latterly).
      In 1971 the ovens were rebuilt, and a diesel loco was purchased to
      haul the car, but in the event was not used.

DERWENTHAUGH LOCO SHED, Swalwell. (Chopwell & Garesfield Railway)
Map 78, NZ 204631.
(Consett Iron Co Ltd; N6 from 1/1/1947; D6 from 1/1/1950; D5 from 1/1/1963;
N&D5 from 1/1/1964; NDM from 26/3/1967; NE from 1/4/1974)
B12   Since 1947 locos from this shed have worked Derwenthaugh Staithes
      (closed 1960), Derwenthaugh Coking Plant and Clockburn Drift.
      Originally locos took trains from the foot of Thornley Incline at
      Winlaton Mill (NZ 186607) to the coking plant or the staithes, but in
      1961 the section of railway west of Winlaton Mill was closed, making
      Clockburn Drift the end of the line. The wagon shops are a few yards
      SE of the loco shed.
      BR locos work on to the system via a junction with the Redheugh
      Branch, 1½m E of Blaydon Station.

DERWENTHAUGH RAILWAY - see CHOPWELL & GARESFIELD RAILWAY

DOROTHEA COLLIERY, Philadelphia. Map 78, NZ 334524.
(Lambton, Hetton & Joicey Collieries Ltd; N2 from 1/1/1947; D2 from 1/1/1950)
L10   The colliery was served by the Lambton Railway as part of the
      Philadelphia complex. It was merged with Herrington Colliery on 29th
      December 1956.

EASINGTON COLLIERY, Easington Colliery. Map 85, NZ 438442.
(Easington Coal Co Ltd; N3 from 1/1/1947; D3 from 1/1/1950; N&D3 from 1/1/1964;
SDM from 26/3/1967; NE from 1/4/1974)
P14   Colliery served by sidings W of BR Seaham-Hartlepool line, 4m S of
 ⁄   Seaham Station.
      A 2' 0" gauge system was at one time used underground for development
      purposes, but the whole colliery was subsequently converted to 3' 0"
      gauge.

EAST HEDLEY HOPE COLLIERY, near Tow Law. Map 85, NZ 158404.
(Bearpark Coal & Coke Co Ltd; N5 from 1/1/1947; D5 from 1/1/1950)
M1   The colliery was served by a BR branch (2¼m) from Waterhouses Station
      on BR Waterhouses Branch. It was closed on 31st January 1959.

EAST HETTON COLLIERY, near Kelloe. Map 85, NZ 346370.
(East Hetton Collieries Ltd; N4 from 1/1/1947; D4 from 1/1/1950; N&D4 from
1/1/1964; SDM from 26/3/1967; NE from 1/4/1974)
R21   Colliery served by NCB branch (2m) from BR Wingate-Ferryhill line,
      3½m N of Ferryhill Station.
      A narrow gauge loco is used in the colliery stockyard.

EAST TANFIELD COLLIERY, near Tantobie. Map 78, NZ 194552.
(South Derwent Coal Co Ltd; N6 from 1/1/1947; D6 from 1/1/1950; D5 from
1/1/1963; N&D5 from 1/1/1964)
  H17 Colliery served by sidings W of BR Tanfield Branch. Its rail traffic
       was replaced by road transport in April 1958, and the colliery was
       closed on 9th January 1965.

EDEN COLLIERY, Leadgate. Map 78, NZ 134521.
(Consett Iron Co Ltd; N6 from 1/1/1947; D6 from 1/1/1950; D5 from 1/1/1963;
N&D5 from 1/1/1964; NDM from 26/3/1967; NE from 1/4/1974)
  G10 Colliery served by sidings N of BR Pontop & Shields branch, 1½m N of
       Consett Station, but worked by NCB locos, first from Consett Iron
       Works and later from Leadgate Shed, exercising running powers over BR.
       This working was replaced by road transport in July 1965. It was
       merged with South Medomsley Colliery on 30th December 1961. The main
       shaft and its buildings were closed on 23rd October 1967, since when
       its coal has been drawn from the Main Coal Drift (NZ 142517).

EIGHTON BANKS LOCO SHED (Pelaw Main Railway), Galloping Green.
Map 78, NZ 281582.
(Pelaw Main Collieries Ltd; N6 from 1/1/1947; D6 from 1/1/1950)
  F9 Locos from here handled trains between the top of the Eighton Banks
      Incline to the top of the Whitehill Incline at Heworth (NZ 279603),
      a distance of 1¼m. The shed is said to have been closed in December
      1948, but locos continued here until about 1954. Latterly traffic was
      handled by locos from the Starrs Loco Shed at Wrekenton (q.v.).

ELEMORE COLLIERY, Easington Lane. Map 85, NZ 356456.
(Lambton, Hetton & Joicey Collieries Ltd; N2 from 1/1/1947; D2 from 1/1/1950;
N&D2 from 1/1/1964; N&D3 from 28/6/1965; SDM from 26/3/1967)
  L28 Colliery was served by the Hetton Railway until 9th September 1959.
   /   Thereafter it was linked to the Top Level of the Hawthorn Combined
      Mine, which was officially opened on 2nd January 1960. The inclusion
      of Elemore in this scheme, which was not intended originally, necess-
      itated the conversion of the 2' 3½" gauge system to 2' 0", a job not
      finally completed till 1961. The Elemore section was also the only
      part of the Hawthorn system to use diesel, rather than battery,
      locomotives. The colliery closed on 2nd January 1974.

EMMA COLLIERY, Ryton. Map 78, NZ 144639.
(Stella Coal Co Ltd; N6 from 1/1/1947; D6 from 1/1/1950; D5 from 1/1/1963;
N&D5 from 1/1/1964; NDM from 26/3/1967)
  A6 The colliery was served by a branch (1¼m) of the Stella Unit Railway
      from Stargate Colliery. Originally this branch was worked by a stat-
      ionary engine hauling two wagons at a time, but in 1948 this was re-
      placed by loco working from Stargate, subject to certain restrictions.
      Rail traffic was replaced by road transport in August 1961, and the
      colliery closed on 19th April 1968.

EPPLETON COLLIERY, near Hetton-le-Hole. Map 85, NZ 364484.
(Lambton, Hetton & Joicey Collieries Ltd; N2 from 1/1/1947; D2 from 1/1/1950;
N&D2 from 1/1/1964; N&D3 from 28/6/1965; SDM from 26/3/1967; NE from 1/4/1974)
  L26 Colliery was served by the Hetton Railway until 9th September 1959.
   /   Thereafter it was linked to the Bottom Level of the Hawthorn
      Combined Mine, which was officially opened on 2nd January 1960,
      but retaining its separate identity.
      A narrow gauge locomotive is used in the colliery stockyard.

FISHBURN COLLIERY & COKING PLANT, Fishburn. Map 85, NZ 361318.
(Henry Stobart & Co Ltd)
  COLLIERY   : - N4 from 1/1/1947; D4 from 1/1/1950; N&D4 from 1/1/1964;
                    SDM from 26/3/1967.
  COKING PLANT : - ND from 1/1/1947; DD from 1/1/1950; CPD from 1/1/1963;
                    National Smokeless Fuels Ltd from 1/4/1973.
  R29   Unit served by a NCB branch (3½m) from BR Ferryhill-Stockton line,
  ⚲   ½m N of former Sedgefield Station. In May 1954 a new coking plant was
           opened. The colliery locos also shunted the coking plant, which uses
           an electric loco to shunt the coke car. The colliery was closed on
           30th November 1973, but rail traffic continued to the coal preparation
           plant (closed October 1974) and the coking plant. On 17th February
           1975 the coking plant took over responsibility for the locomotives.

GARESFIELD COLLIERY, High Spen. Map 78, NZ 139598.
(Consett Iron Co Ltd; N6 from 1/1/1947; D6 from 1/1/1950)
  A3   This colliery was served by the Chopwell & Garesfield Railway (q.v.).
           A small loco was kept here for shunting the colliery, but loco
           transfers between here and Derwenthaugh were so frequent as to be
           impossible to record. The colliery was closed on 29th January 1960.

GREENSIDE COLLIERY, Greenside. Map 78, NZ 139620.
(Consett Iron Co Ltd; N6 from 1/1/1947; D6 from 1/1/1950; D5 from 1/1/1963;
N&D5 from 1/1/1964)
  A8   Colliery served by Stella Unit Railway via branch (2¼m) from Stargate
           Colliery. In August 1961 rail haulage was replaced by road transport.
           The colliery was closed on 23rd July 1966.

HAMSTERLEY COLLIERY, Hamsterley. Map 78, NZ 117565.
(Hamsterley Colliery Ltd; N6 from 1/1/1947; D6 from 1/1/1950; D5 from 1/1/1963;
N&D5 from 1/1/1964; NDM from 26/3/1967)
  G1   The colliery screens lay ½m E of High Westwood Station on BR Blackhill
           Branch. Tubs from the colliery (which was really a drift) were hauled
           up to the screens via ¼m endless rope incline, and the coal was dis-
           charged into standard gauge wagons. The loco was used here, and kept
           in a shed ¼m W of the screens. The system was replaced by road trans-
           port in June 1953, and the colliery closed on 2nd February 1968.

HANDEN HOLD COLLIERY, West Pelton. Map 78, NZ 233526.
(Lambton, Hetton & Joicey Collieries Ltd; N5 from 1/1/1947; D5 from 1/1/1950;
new D5 from 1/1/1963; N&D5 from 1/1/1964; NDM from 26/3/1967)
  H49   The colliery was served by sidings N of BR Pontop & Shields line. It
           was connected to the Beamish Railway by a ½m branch in 1954-1955, and
           took over all loco working on that Railway in August 1963. The shunting
           was taken over by BR from 24th December 1966, and the colliery closed
           on 1st March 1968.

HARRATON COLLIERY, near Chester-le-Street. Map 78, NZ 291539.
(Lambton, Hetton & Joicey Collieries Ltd; N2 from 1/1/1947; D2 from 1/1/1950;
N&D2 from 1/1/1964)
  J1   This colliery was served by sidings S of BR mineral line from Wash-
           ington to Ouston Junction, but was worked by Lambton Railway locomo-
           tives exercising running powers over BR from Penshaw North Junction
           (immediately N of Penshaw Station on Durham-Sunderland line), with a
           reverse at Washington. A loco was also kept at the colliery for shunt-
           ing, but the early transfers are not fully known. It closed on 29th
           May 1965.

HARTON COLLIERY, South Shields. Map 78, NZ 362642.
(Harton Coal Co Ltd; N1 from 1/1/1947; D1 from 1/1/1950; N&D1 from 1/1/1964;
NDM from 26/3/1967)
  D11   Colliery served by a branch (¼m) of Harton Railway from Dean Sidings

Harton Railway 1967

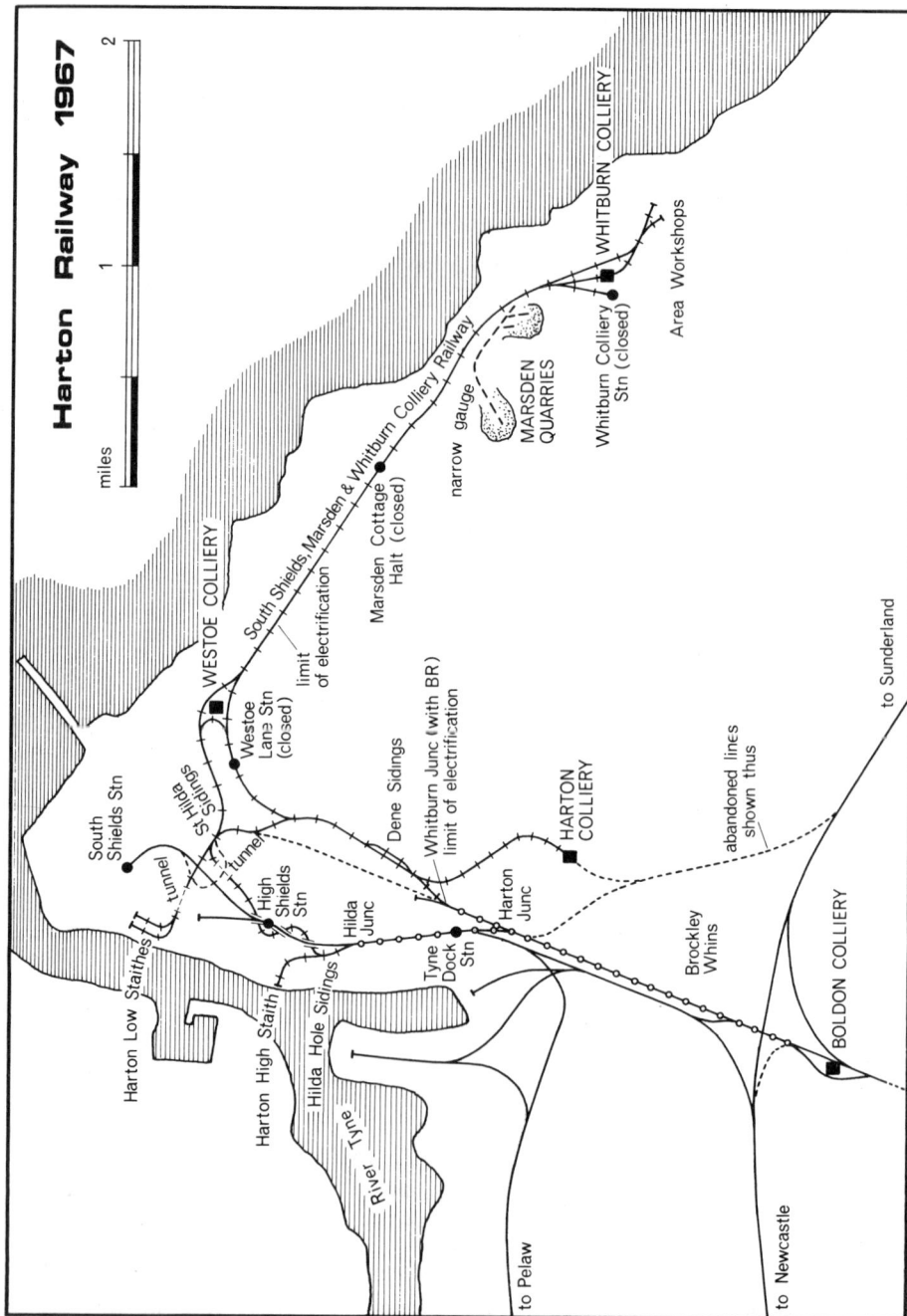

miles

WHITBURN COLLIERY

Area Workshops

Whitburn Colliery
Stn (closed)

MARSDEN
QUARRIES

narrow gauge

Marsden Cottage
Halt (closed)

South Shields, Marsden & Whitburn Colliery Railway

limit
of electrification

WESTOE COLLIERY

Westoe
Lane Stn
(closed)

Dene Sidings

Whitburn Junc (with BR)
limit of electrification

HARTON
COLLIERY

South
Shields Stn

St Sidings

High
Shields Stn

Hilda
Junc

Harton
Junc

tunnel

tunnel

Brockley
Whins

abandoned lines
shown thus

BOLDON COLLIERY

Harton Low Staithes

Tyne
Dock Stn

Harton High Staith

Hilda Hole Sidings

River Tyne

to Pelaw

to Newcastle

to Sunderland

236

(Whitburn Junction), but was allocated one loco for shunting.
A narrow gauge loco was used on an extensive surface system.
The colliery closed on 25th July 1969.

HARTON RAILWAY
(Harton Coal Co Ltd; N1 from 1/1/1947; D1 from 1/1/1950; N&D1 from 1/1/1964;
NDM from 26/3/1967; NE from 1/4/1974)
This railway absorbed the South Shields, Marsden & Whitburn Colliery
Railway (q.v.) in November 1953.
The original Harton system is electrified (overhead wire), and worked
by locomotives from Westoe Lane Loco Shed (Map 78, NZ 374667). If one
takes Westoe Colliery as the centre, three lines radiated outwards.
The one running due west runs to Harton Low Staithes (NZ 359660). This
line is about 1¼m long, and includes one (originally two) tunnel. From
it a branch (¼m) runs to Harton High Staithes, about 300 yards up-
stream from the Low Staithes, and now only used for the shipment of
stone. The second line runs south-westwards, originally to Harton
Colliery, but now only as far as Dean Sidings (2¼m), from which a
short link runs to Whitburn Junction and thence to Harton Junction on
BR Gateshead-South Shields line, W of Tyne Dock Station. Dene Sidings
act as the interchange point not only for traffic from BR, but also
for trains from Boldon Colliery, using running powers over BR. The
lines to the Staithes and to Dean Sidings are linked by the "Pontop"
line, originally a disused BR line, but rebuilt by the NCB for electric
locos in 1965.
The third line was the SSMWCR, which ran south-east from Westoe to
Whitburn Colliery, following the A183 road from South Shields to
Sunderland for most of its three miles. This was worked by locomotives
from a shed at Whitburn, and was never electrified. Until September
1965 this line also served Marsden Quarries, and there was a link to
the Central Workshops, Whitburn, ¼m S of the colliery. This line
closed with Whitburn Colliery in June 1968.

HAWTHORN COMBINED MINE & COKING PLANT, near Murton.
COMBINED MINE : - Map 85, NZ 390458. Opened by D2; N&D2 from 1/1/1964;
                  N&D3 from 28/6/1965; SDM from 26/3/1967; NE from 1/4/1974.
COKING PLANT : - Map 85, NZ 390460. Opened by DD; CPD from 1/1/1963;
                  National Smokeless Fuels Ltd from 1/4/1973.
L29   The combined mine was officially opened on 2nd January 1960 to wind
       all coal formerly raised at Elemore, Eppleton and Murton Collieries,
       though these collieries retain their separate identities and under-
       ground responsibilities up to 200 yards from the Hawthorn shaft.
L30   The coking plant was commissioned in November 1958, and uses an
       electric loco to haul the coking car.
       Both locations are served by locos from South Hetton Shed, which is
       controlled by Hawthorn. Colour light signals are used in the vicinity
       of the complex. Most coal and coke is dispatched via the links with BR
       at South Hetton, while the stone and washery waste is sent to Seaham
       Harbour for disposal at sea (see South Hetton Colliery entry).

HERRINGTON COLLIERY, New Herrington. Map 78, NZ 341533.
(Lambton, Hetton & Joicey Collieries Ltd; N2 from 1/1/1947; D2 from 1/1/1950;
N&D2 from 1/1/1964; N&D1 from 28/6/1965; NDM from 26/3/1967; NE from 1/4/1974)
J7   This colliery is served by the Lambton Railway. It was merged with
⌐   Dorothea Colliery on 29th December 1956.
       Narrow gauge locos are used in the colliery stockyard,etc.

HETTON COLLIERY, Hetton-le-Hole. Map 85, NZ 360469.
(Lambton, Hetton & Joicey Collieries Ltd; N2 from 1/1/1947; D2 from 1/1/1950)
L27   This colliery was served by the Hetton Railway, and was closed on
       22nd July 1950.

HETTON RAILWAY
(Lambton, Hetton & Joicey Collieries Ltd; N2 from 1/1/1947; D2 from 1/1/1950)
This Railway ran from Elemore Colliery at Easington Lane to Hetton
Staithes on the R. Wear at Sunderland, a distance of 9m. At Hetton-le-
Hole there were branches to Hetton Colliery ($\frac{1}{2}$m) and Eppleton Colliery
($\frac{3}{4}$m). Locomotives from Hetton Loco Shed (Map 85, NZ 358472) collected
wagons from these three collieries and took them to the bottom of the
Copt Hill Incline at Hetton Dene (NZ 351491), 2$\frac{1}{4}$m from Elemore. They
were then hauled by a stationary engine up to Copt Hill, where the
ropes were changed to allow the engine to haul the wagons northwards
to an interchange point known as "The Flatts". From here they were
hauled up to the 600ft summit at Warden Law (Map 78, NZ 368505). The
wagons then descended four self-acting inclines to a marshalling yard
at North Moor, Sunderland. Just north of this a link between the
Railway and Silksworth Colliery was built not long after nationalisation; this was $\frac{3}{4}$m long, and steeply graded. The main line continued
to Hetton Staithes (NZ 390576) via a narrow tunnel, which necessitated
cut-down cab mountings. Hetton Staithes were connected to Lambton
Staithes to the east by a short tunnel, and latterly all coal was
shipped here. The loco shed was also at Lambton Staithes, and locos
from here also worked Silksworth Colliery, though the colliery had one
loco for shunting, and was also served by a BR mineral branch (2$\frac{1}{4}$m)
from Ryhope.
With the imminent opening of Hawthorn Combined Mine, the Railway
between Elemore and North Moor was closed on 9th September 1959.
The George Stephenson stationary engine at Warden Law was dismantled
for preservation in the North of England Open-Air Museum. For the
subsequent history of the remaining section between Silksworth and
Lambton Staithes see the entries for these locations.
All major locomotive repairs were carried out at Lambton Engine Works.

HEWORTH COLLIERY, Gateshead. Map 78, NZ 284605.
(Heworth Coal Co Ltd; N1 from 1/1/1947; D1 from 1/1/1950)
F1   The colliery lay east of the Whitehill Incline of the Pelaw Main
⨯   Railway, to which it was linked at the bottom by a self-acting incline
$\frac{1}{2}$m long. It closed on 29th June 1963.

HIGH MARLEY HILL DRIFT, Byermoor. Map 78, NZ 191572.
(Opened by D6; D5 from 1/1/1963)
H9   This lay $\frac{1}{2}$m E of Byermoor Colliery on the Bowes Railway, and was worked
by locos from Marley Hill Shed. It was closed on 29th June 1963.

HOLE-IN-THE-WALL COLLIERY, Crook. Map 85, NZ 168362.
(W. Craggs & Sons Ltd; N5 from 1/1/1947; D5 from 1/1/1950; D4 from 1/1/1963;
N&D4 from 1/1/1964)
Q6   This colliery, begun in 1935, consisted of three drift mines - Hole-in-
the-Wall, Stonechester and Dowfold Drifts, all of which were worked by
narrow gauge surface locomotives. No locomotives were used before
Vesting Day, and there was no main line rail connection.
It was closed on 21st November 1964, though certain areas of working
had ceased previously.

HORDEN COLLIERY & COKING PLANT, Horden. Map 85, NZ 442418.
(Horden Collieries Ltd)
  COLLIERY   : - N3 from 1/1/1947; D3 from 1/1/1950; N&D3 from 1/1/1964;
                 SDM from 26/3/1967; NE from 1/4/1974.
  COKING PLANT : - ND from 1/1/1947; DD from 1/1/1950.
P15   This unit was served by sidings W of Seaham-Hartlepool line (BR), $\frac{1}{4}$m N
⨯   of the former Horden Station. The colliery locos shunted the coking
plant until its closure in January 1959.
Narrow gauge locomotives are used in an extensive surface system.
Underground there were originally two systems, but the 2' 8$\frac{1}{2}$" system
was converted to the 2' 0" system operating in the remainder of the
colliery about 1959.

HOUGHTON COLLIERY, Houghton-le-Spring. Map 78, NZ 338504.
(Lambton, Hetton & Joicey Collieries Ltd; N2 from 1/1/1947; D2 from 1/1/1950;
N&D2 from 1/1/1964; N&D1 from 28/6/1965; NDM from 26/3/1967; NE from 1/4/1974)
L14   This colliery was served by a branch (1m) from Houghton Junction on the
Lambton Railway. Rail traffic ceased in February 1975.

HYLTON COLLIERY, Castletown, near Sunderland. Map 78, NZ 366583.
(Wearmouth Coal Co Ltd; N1 from 1/1/1947; D1 from 1/1/1950; N&D1 from 1/1/1964;
NDM from 26/3/1967; NE from 1/4/1974)
K4   The colliery is situated at the end of the BR Hylton Branch (1½m) from
Monkwearmouth; but it was also formerly worked by NCB locos from
Wearmouth Colliery, using running powers. The BR locos used the south-
ern track and the NCB locos the northern track, crossing BR at both
Wearmouth and Hylton. This working ceased in August 1971.
One loco was used for shunting here, but transfers are only listed from
January 1958. Rail traffic ceased in February 1975.

KIBBLESWORTH COLLIERY, Kibblesworth. Map 78, NZ 243562.
(John Bowes & Partners Ltd; N6 from 1/1/1947; D6 from 1/1/1950; D5 from
1/1/1963; N&D5 from 1/1/1964; NDM from 26/3/1967; NE from 1/4/1974)
H14   Colliery lay at the top of Kibblesworth Incline on the Bowes Railway.
The screens lay about ¼m down the incline on its south side, and wagons
were worked into the sidings by the Kibblesworth Stationary Engine,
though shunting of wagons within the sidings was carried out by another
hauler. During a breakdown of this hauler in 1964 the sidings were
shunted by a locomotive. From 24th April 1973 all former Ravensworth
Ann Colliery coal was also drawn at Kibblesworth Colliery, which closed
on 4th October 1974.

LAMBTON COKING PLANT, Fencehouses. Map 78, NZ 318510.
(Lambton, Hetton & Joicey Collieries Ltd; ND from 1/1/1947; DD from 1/1/1950;
CPD from 1/1/1963; National Smokeless Fuels Ltd from 1/4/1973)
L9   Served by a branch (½m) from Burnmoor Junction on the Lambton Railway,
and worked by Lambton Railway locomotives.
An electric loco is used for hauling the coking car.

LAMBTON 'D' COLLIERY, Fencehouses. Map 78, NZ 318507.
(Lambton, Hetton & Joicey Collieries Ltd; N2 from 1/1/1947; D2 from 1/1/1950;
N&D2 from 1/1/1964)
L8   This colliery was served by an extension of the Lambton Railway branch
to Lambton Coking Plant. It was closed on 27th February 1965, but the
coal preparation plant remains open.

LAMBTON ENGINE WORKS, Philadelphia - see CENTRAL WORKSHOPS, PHILADELPHIA

LAMBTON RAILWAY
(Lambton, Hetton & Joicey Collieries Ltd; N2 from 1/1/1947; D2 from 1/1/1950;
N&D2 from 1/1/1964; N&D1 from 28/6/1965; NDM from 26/3/1967; NE from 1/4/1974)
The main NCB section of this famous railway runs from Herrington
Colliery to Penshaw Sidings, E of BR Sunderland-Durham line alongside
Penshaw Station. Since 1947 this has served, besides Herrington Coll-
iery, Lambton Engine Works, Dorothea Colliery, Houghton Colliery (via
a 1m branch from Houghton Junction, Map 78, NZ 332518), Lambton 'D'
Colliery, Lambton 'D' Coal Preparation Plant and Lambton Coking Plant
(all via ½m branch from Burnmoor Junction (NZ 317517) and Lumley Sixth
Colliery (via another branch (1m) from Burnmoor Junction, and since
closed). From Penshaw, Lambton Railway locomotives had running powers
over BR to reach Harraton Colliery via Penshaw North Junction and a
reverse at Washington, a distance of 3m; these powers were given up
with the closure of the colliery in 1965. From Penshaw NCB locos also
had running powers over the BR Sunderland-Durham line for 4½m to
Lambton Staithes, Sunderland, which were reached by a branch (1m) from

a junction ¼m E of Pallion Station. Running powers were also exercised on to South Dock. The former were given up with the closure of Lambton Staithes on 6th January 1967, and the latter followed on 18th January 1967.

At Lambton Staithes there was a tunnel to the adjoining Hetton Staithes of the Hetton Railway, and coal from Elemore, Eppleton and Silksworth Collieries was also shipped at Lambton Staithes latterly. From Herrington Colliery to the Staithes was approximately 9¼m.

The main loco sheds are at Philadelphia (see below), but locos were also kept at Harraton Colliery and Lambton Staithes, as well as Silksworth Colliery and Hetton on the Hetton Railway. The Railway's steam locomotives were replaced by diesels on 16th February 1969. The sections of the Railway controlled by the NCB are fully equipped with signal boxes and either semaphore or colour light signals.

LAMBTON RAILWAY LOCO SHEDS, Philadelphia. Map 78, NZ 335524.
L11 These lie just to the north of the Philadelphia level crossing on the A182 road from Washington to Houghton-le-Spring. In the days of the steam locos four sheds were in use. Two were long, narrow sheds on either side of the main line, but the eastern one was bricked up for a time, apart from a small annexe on the eastern side. A third, 4-road shed, was situated near this one, and was also used for storing locos; this was demolished in 1972. About 100 yards north, adjacent to Lambton Engine Works, was a fourth shed, where washing out and minor repairs were done.
With the reduction of duties due to colliery closures, and the arrival of diesels, all this accommodation was not needed, and so the southern end of the western narrow shed was bricked up and the shed itself divided into a repair shop and a running shed (2-road).

LAMBTON STAITHES, Sunderland. Map 78, NZ 394574.
(Lambton, Hetton & Joicey Collieries Ltd; N2 from 1/1/1947; D2 from 1/1/1950; N&D2 from 1/1/1964; N&D1 from 28/6/1965)
K12 These were the older type of staith with spouts. They were served by a branch (1m - NCB) from BR Sunderland- Durham line (Deptford branch), but worked by Lambton Railway locomotives from Philadelphia. The loco shed at the Staithes supplied Hetton Staithes also (via a short tunnel), and worked the Hetton Railway from North Moor Yard to the staithes, as well as Silksworth Colliery, though one loco was kept at the latter for local shunting. When the Staithes closed on 6th January 1967 Silksworth Colliery took over responsibility for its own locomotives.

LANGLEY PARK COLLIERY & COKING PLANT, Langley Park. Map 85, NZ 211457.
(Consett Iron Co Ltd)
COLLIERY : - N5 from 1/1/1947, D5 from 1/1/1950; D4 from 1/1/1963; N&D4 from 1/1/1964; SDM from 26/3/1967; NE from 1/4/1974.
COKING PLANT : - ND from 1/1/1947; DD from 1/1/1950.
M7 Served by sidings N of Lanchester-Durham line (BR), 3¼m SE of Lanchester Station. The colliery locos also shunted the coking plant until its closure on 25th March 1961. Rail transport was replaced by road haulage in April 1965, and the colliery closed on 31st October, 1975.

LEADGATE LOCO SHED, Leadgate. Map 78, NZ 119515.
(Opened by N6; D6 from 1/1/1950; D5 from 1/1/1963; N&D5 from 1/1/1964)
G17 This shed was opened in January 1949 to house the locos previously kept at Consett Iron Works. Locos from here worked Crookhall, Derwent, Medomsley and Eden Collieries (the latter via running powers over BR), and the Area Central Workshops, Bradley. The working to Derwent and Medomsley was relinquished to road transport during the winter of 1960-1961, and the working to Eden followed in July 1965. The shed finally closed on 21st December 1965 with the closure of Crookhall Washery.

<u>LEASINGTHORNE COLLIERY</u>, near Coundon. Map 85, NZ 252304.
(Dorman, Long & Co Ltd; N4 from 1/1/1947; D4 from 1/1/1950)
  R12   This colliery was served by an extension (NCB - 2m) of the BR Chilton
       Branch. As from 1st January 1950 it was merged with Dean & Chapter
       Colliery, but locos were occasionally sent to the workshops here for
       repairs until about 1954.

<u>LILLEY DRIFT</u>, Rowlands Gill. Map 78, NZ 168591.
(Priestman Collieries Ltd; N6 from 1/1/1947; D6 from 1/1/1950)
  A12   A small drift mine, supplying a brickworks, and served by sidings W of
       BR Blackhill Branch, ½m N of Rowlands Gill Station. The drift was
       closed on 5th January 1957, but the brickworks continues, without rail
       transport.

<u>LOUISA COLLIERY</u>, Stanley. Map 78, NZ 193527.
(Holmside & South Moor Collieries Ltd; N6 from 1/1/1947; D6 from 1/1/1950)
  H40   This colliery was served by sidings N of BR Pontop & Shields branch at
   ⨍   Stanley, but worked by locos from Morrison Busty Colliery exercising
       running powers over BR from Annfield Plain. In the years immediately
       after Vesting Day a loco is sometimes shown as allocated here (for
       local shunting). The colliery was merged with Morrison Busty Colliery
       on 31st December 1965, but a separate allocation for underground locos
       was maintained until loco haulage in this area of the colliery ceased
       in 1967.

<u>LUMLEY SIXTH COLLIERY</u>, Lumley. Map 78, NZ 309506.
(Lambton, Hetton & Joicey Collieries Ltd; N2 from 1/1/1947; D2 from 1/1/1950;
N&D2 from 1/1/1964; N&D1 from 28/6/1965)
  L5   Served by the Lambton Railway via a 1m branch from Burnmoor Junction.
       The colliery was closed on 22nd January 1966.

<u>MAINSFORTH COLLIERY</u>, Ferryhill Station. Map 85, NZ 307316.
(Dorman, Long & Co Ltd; N4 from 1/1/1947; D4 from 1/1/1950; N&D4 from 1/1/1964;
SDM from 26/3/1967)
  R27   The colliery was served by a branch (NCB - ¼m) from BR Ferryhill-
   ⨍   Stockton line, from a junction ¼m S of Ferryhill Station.
       A narrow gauge loco was used in the colliery stockyard.
       The colliery was closed after serious flooding on 6th December 1968.

<u>MALTON COLLIERY & COKING PLANT</u>, near Lanchester. Map 85, NZ 180461.
(Sir S.A.Sadler Ltd)
  <u>COLLIERY</u>   : - N5 from 1/1/1947; D5 from 1/1/1950.
  <u>COKING PLANT</u> : - ND from 1/1/1947.
  M6   Served by sidings S of BR Lanchester-Durham line, 1m SE of Lanchester
       Station. The colliery was a group of small drifts. The colliery locos
       shunted the coking plant until its closure in July 1949, and their
       remaining work was taken over by BR about 1956. The colliery closed on
       22nd July 1961.

<u>MARLEY HILL COLLIERY</u>, near Sunniside. Map 78, NZ 206575.
(John Bowes & Partners Ltd; N6 from 1/1/1947; D6 from 1/1/1950; D5 from
1/1/1963; N&D5 from 1/1/1964; NDM from 26/3/1967; NE from 1/4/1974)
  H10   Served by sidings from the Bowes Railway. In 1952 the colliery was
   ⨍   linked to Clockburn Drift (q.v.), from which time most of the coll-
       iery's output was dispatched this way, but a small amount was still
       sent up the shafts to be handled by the Bowes Railway until July 1971.

<u>MARLEY HILL LOCO SHED</u> (Bowes Railway). Map 78, NZ 207573.
(John Bowes & Partners Ltd; N6 from 1/1/1947; D6 from 1/1/1950; D5 from
1/1/1963; N&D5 from 1/1/1964; NDM from 26/3/1967)
  H12   This loco shed served the western end of the Bowes Railway, working
       Burnopfield, Byermoor and Marley Hill Collieries, and High Marley Hill
       and Blackburn Fell Drifts. Wagons from these places were latterly
       assembled in the Marley Hill marshalling yard and then taken to

Birkheads Bank Top (NZ 222568). Working west of the yard ceased in
August 1968, to be followed by working east of the shed in March 1970.
The handling of Marley Hill Colliery coal for transfer to road trans-
port continued until 30th July 1970, when the shed finally closed.
The building was taken over by the North of England Open-Air Museum
in 1971.
The shed also handled repairs to locomotives at East Tanfield and
Tanfield Lea Collieries, and also occasionally for other collieries.

MARSDEN QUARRIES, near Whitburn Colliery. Map 78, NZ 405641.
(Harton Coal Co Ltd; N1 from 1/1/1947; D1 from 1/1/1950; N&D1 from 1/1/1964)
   D13   These were a group of five quarries producing limestone dust for
         underground use at collieries, and also limestone for general
         industrial use. They were controlled by the manager of the nearby
         Whitburn Colliery. A 2' 0" gauge system was operated in the quarries,
         with a loco shed and workshops. Standard gauge wagons of the South
         Shields, Marsden & Whitburn Colliery Railway (later Harton Railway)
         were filled either from the kilns (put out about 1954) or from the
         dust plant. The quarries were sold to Slater & Co (Limestone) Ltd in
         September 1965.

MEDOMSLEY COLLIERY, Medomsley. Map 78, NZ 115536.
(Consett Iron Co Ltd; N6 from 1/1/1947; D6 from 1/1/1950; D5 from 1/1/1963;
N&D5 from 1/1/1964; NDM from 26/3/1967)
   G3   The main colliery, known as the Hunter Pit, was served by a branch
         (NCB - 1½m) from a junction at Leadgate, 1m N of Consett Station,
         on BR Pontop & Shields branch, but it was worked by NCB locos, first
         from Consett Iron Works, and from January 1949 from the new shed at
         Leadgate, using running powers across BR. Loco working was replaced
         by road haulage during the winter of 1960-1961. The shaft was closed
         on 2nd August 1963, but coal continued to be drawn via Elm Park Drift
         (NZ 106530) until its closure on 6th October 1972.

MONKTON COAL PREPARATION PLANT, Wardley. Map 78, NZ 314627.
(Opened by D6 in 1956; D5 from 1/1/1963; N&D5 from 1/1/1964; NDM from
26/3/1967; NE from 1/4/1974)
   D5   Worked by locos from the Springwell Bank Foot shed of the Bowes
         Railway, but operated internally by gravity.

MONKTON COKING PLANT, Wardley. Map 78, NZ 315626.
(John Bowes & Partners Ltd; ND from 1/1/1947; DD from 1/1/1950; CPD from
1/1/1963; National Smokeless Fuels Ltd from 1/4/1973)
   D5   This plant is situated on the opposite side of the Bowes Railway
         to the Coal Preparation Plant, to which it is linked by conveyor belt.
         It is shunted by locos from the Railway's Springwell Bank Foot Loco
         Shed, but has used both electric and diesel locos to haul the coke car.

MORRISON BUSTY COLLIERY, Annfield Plain. Map 78, NZ 176508.
(Holmside & South Moor Collieries Ltd; N6 from 1/1/1947; D6 from 1/1/1950;
D5 from 1/1/1963; N&D5 from 1/1/1964; NDM from 26/3/1967)
   H35   This colliery was originally served by a branch (1¼m) from BR Pontop
    ⁄   & Shields branch at Annfield Plain. After the section of this between
         Grange Villa and Stanley was closed, trains were re-routed to come
         up to South Moor and then reverse back to junction on BR line from
         Beamish to Annfield Plain at Oxhill, ¼m N of the former Annfield
         Plain Station. The colliery locos also worked Louisa Colliery, Stanley,
         by exercising running powers over BR until 31st December 1955, when
         the two collieries were merged, though their underground locomotive
         allocations were kept separate until the working in the Louisa area
         ceased in 1967. The colliery closed on 5th October 1973.

MURTON COLLIERY, Murton. Map 85, NZ 399473.
(South Hetton Coal Co Ltd; N2 from 1/1/1947; D2 from 1/1/1950; N&D2 from
1/1/1964; N&D3 from 28/6/1965; SDM from 26/3/1967; NE from 1/4/1974)
    L31   This colliery was originally served by a branch (¼m) from the NCB line
    ✗   from South Hetton to Seaham Harbour, and was worked by locos from
          South Hetton Loco Sheds. As from 2nd January 1960 this colliery,
          together with Eppleton & Elemore Collieries, was linked underground
          to the new Hawthorn Combined Mine, though retaining its separate
          identity and underground loco allocation. The branch to the Seaham
          Harbour line was then lifted.
          A narrow gauge loco is used on an extensive surface system.

NEW BRANCEPETH COLLIERY & COKING PLANT, New Brancepeth. Map 85, NZ 222421.
(New Brancepeth Colliery Co Ltd)
    COLLIERY   : - N5 from 1/1/1947; D5 from 1/1/1950.
    COKING PLANT : - ND from 1/1/1947; DD from 1/1/1950.
    M11   Served by sidings S of BR Waterhouses branch ¼m S of Ushaw Moor
          Station. The colliery locos shunted the coking plant until the closure
          of the colliery on 17th July 1953, after which they became the respon-
          sibility of the coking plant. When this too was closed, in July 1957,
          the site was cleared to become a coal stocking site.

NEW BRANCEPETH COAL STOCKING SITE, New Brancepeth. Map 85, NZ 222421.
(Opened by D5 about 1958; D4 from 1/1/1963; N&D4 from 1/1/1964)
    M11   This was opened about 1958 on the site of the former New Brancepeth
          Colliery and Coking Plant. It was served by sidings S of BR Water-
          houses branch, ¼m S of Ushaw Moor Station. When stocks had been built
          up one loco was stored in the loco shed and all sidings and rail
          access removed. In October 1963 the site was re-opened and the sidings
          re-laid, locos being used until the exhaustion of stocks in March 1964.

NORTH DURHAM ENGINEERING CENTRE, Annfield Plain. - see AREA ENGINEERING CENTRE,
Annfield Plain.

NORWOOD COKING PLANT, Gateshead. Map 78, NZ 238613.
(Priestman Collieries Ltd; ND from 1/1/1947; DD from 1/1/1950; CPD from
1/1/1963). Locos administered by N6 from 1/1/1947; D6 from 1/1/1950;
CPD from 1/1/1963; National Smokeless Fuels Ltd from 1/4/1973.
    C10   At its southern end the plant was linked to the Pelaw Main Railway's
          line to Dunston. This was closed in May 1963.
          At its northern end there was a link to the BR Tanfield Branch
          immediately N of Ellison Road crossing. This link was abandoned in
          1962 in favour of a new rail connection with the BR mineral line from
          Blaydon to Low Fell, immediately to the north of the plant.

OUSTON 'E' COLLIERY, Ouston. Map 78, NZ 266548.
(Pelaw Main Collieries Ltd; N6 from 1/1/1947; D6 from 1/1/1950)
    H24   Served by the Pelaw Main Railway. The colliery was merged with Urpeth
          'C' Colliery on 30th March 1957, and was closed on 31st January 1959.
          N.B. Some transfers shown to this location were probably transfers to
               the Loco Repair Shops of the Pelaw Main Railway, which were part
              of the colliery complex.

PEASE'S WEST GARAGE, Crook. Map 85, NZ 158366 (approx)
(Opened by D5 in 1959; D4 from 1/1/1963; N&D4 from 1/1/1964)
    Q5   This was a building in the Roddymoor complex used for storing narrow
          gauge diesel locomotives (surface) which were surplus to requirements.
          It was opened in December 1959 and closed in September 1964.

PELAW MAIN RAILWAY
(Pelaw Main Collieries Ltd; N6 from 1/1/1947; D6 from 1/1/1950)
    This Railway consisted basically of two arms, which joined at White-
hill, near Gateshead (Map 78, NZ 279602), and then ran to the Pelaw
Main Staithes (NZ 300632) on the R.Tyne.

    Southern arm : wagons from Ouston 'E' and Urpeth 'C' Collieries were

H24   brought by the locos from the shed at Ouston 'E' Colliery to the fan
of sidings known as "Birtley Tail" (NZ 272554) at the foot of the
Blackhouse Fell Incline. The stationary engine at the top of this
incline hauled the wagons up to the engine house, opposite to which

H33   was the Blackhouse Fell Loco Shed (NZ 280560). The loco kept here
handled traffic over the next mile to the foot of the Eighton Banks
Incline, whence the wagons were hauled up to the Eighton Banks Engine
House (NZ 280583). Traffic between here and Whitehill Washery and Yard

F9   was handled either by a loco from the Eighton Banks Loco Shed or from
F4   the Starrs Loco Shed at Wrekenton. This arm was approximately 4¼ miles.

    Northern arm : On the western end of this full wagons originally

C14   travelled in both directions. From the Shop Pit sidings (NZ 253587) a
loco from the shed would take trains to Allerdene Sidings, Dunston,
which were exchange sidings with BR. This line, 2m long, had a short
branch to Ravensworth Park Drift about ½m N of the loco shed, and
passed through the Team Valley Trading Estate. Latterly very little
coal was sent this way, though there was a considerable traffic in
timber from BR.

    Traffic going in the direction of Whitehill was pushed up to the top
of the Shop Pit sidings to be taken up the Allerdene Incline to
Ravensworth Ann Colliery. The Kings Engine House, situated at the north
end of the colliery yard, also shunted Ravensworth Shop Colliery, about
two-thirds the way down the Incline, and the Ravensworth Ann stone heap.

C16   A loco was kept here to shunt the colliery yard, and also to push
wagons to the foot of the Starrs Incline, whence they were hauled up

F4   to Wrekenton (NZ 273594). A loco from the Starrs Loco Shed then took
trains to Whitehill. From the Shop Pit sidings to Whitehill was
approximately 4 miles.

    At Whitehill there was a washery, and wagons were then shunted to the
top of the Whitehill self-acting Incline. At the foot of this the
Railway was joined by another incline, from Heworth Colliery. At Whitehill Bank Foot was the Heworth Engine, and to handle the wagons from
two destinations a curious method of working was adopted. Wagons from
Heworth were attached to a rope from the east drum, and the set then
allowed to run forward about 40 yards. The rope was then taken off, and
twelve Pelaw Main wagons with a rope from the west drum run down to
them for the journey to the staithes. Coming back the set was stopped
in the same place, the Pelaw Main wagons hauled on to their kip, and
then the Heworth rope attached for its wagons to be hauled on to their

D2   kip. A loco from the shed at the staithes shunted wagons in the sidings
there (a loco with cut-down mountings was necessary because of a
narrow bridge), but another incline worked by a stationary engine
lowered wagons down to the river. From Whitehill to the staithes was
approximately 2½ miles.

    On 31st January 1959 the sections between Ouston 'E' Colliery and the
Eighton Banks Engine House, and Whitehill to the A185 road (NZ 297624),
about ¼m S of the staithes, were closed. Traffic from the northern
arm was then brought up to Whitehill, where the washery and sidings
were subsequently removed, and then pushed down the remaining part of
the southern arm to Eighton Banks. Here a short link, about 200
yards long, had been built in 1955 to connect with the Blackham's
Hill East Incline of the Bowes Railway, and the wagons were taken via
this to Springwell. From then onwards the working and locomotive
repairs were an integral part of the Bowes Railway (q.v. for subsequent
history). This final section closed on 18th April 1973.

PELAW MAIN STAITHES LOCO SHED, Bill Quay. Map 78, NZ 300632.
(Pelaw Main Collieries Ltd; N6 from 1/1/1947; D6 from 1/1/1950; D5 from
1/1/1963; N&D5 from 1/1/1964)
   D2   A small shed for locos shunting wagons in the sidings, etc., above
        Pelaw Main Staithes (see Pelaw Main Railway). After the closures of
        January 1959 this section was left isolated, and coal was brought by
        road to be transferred into railway wagons prior to shipment. The
        shed was closed in May 1964.

PHILADELPHIA LOCO SHEDS, Lambton Railway - see LAMBTON RAILWAY LOCO SHEDS,
Philadelphia.

RANDOLPH COLLIERY & COKING PLANT, Evenwood. Map 85, NZ 157249.
(Randolph Coal Co Ltd)
   COLLIERY   : - N4 from 1/1/1947; D4 from 1/1/1950.
   COKING PLANT : - ND from 1/1/1947; DD from 1/1/1950.
   T10   Served by a branch (1m) from BR Haggerleazes Branch, ½m W of Spring
        Gardens Junction. An incline (1260 yds) worked by a stationary engine
        took wagons down to BR. Originally the colliery locos also shunted the
        coking plant, but on 20th May 1957 they and the coking plant were sold
        to Randolph Coke & Chemical Co Ltd, after which they were hired to
        shunt the colliery. This closed on 17th February 1962.

RAVENSWORTH ANN COLLIERY, near Birtley. Map 78, NZ 265579.
(Pelaw Main Collieries Ltd; N6 from 1/1/1947; D6 from 1/1/1950; D5 from
1/1/1963; N&D5 from 1/1/1964; NDM from 26/3/1967)
   N.B.   This colliery was combined with Ravensworth Betty Colliery, and
        sometimes known under that title; also known locally as Team or
        Teams Colliery.
   C16   This colliery was situated originally alongside the A1 road, ½m N of
        the Birtley boundary. It lay between the Allerdene and Starrs Inclines
        of the Pelaw Main Railway, but used its own loco to shunt wagons
        between the two, and also in its colliery yard. The loco shed was the
        former engine house for the Allerdene Incline.
        On 8th March 1968 the Ann Pit shaft ceased to be a coal-drawing shaft,
        and from 11th March 1968 Ann Pit coal was drawn via the former Ravens-
   C13   worth Park Drift, which then became known as Ravensworth Ann Colliery.
        Loco working also ceased, all the work being done by rope. In April
        1973 the colliery was merged with Kibblesworth Colliery (q.v.), and
        from 24th April 1973 all coal was drawn at Kibblesworth.

RAVENSWORTH PARK DRIFT, near Lamesley. Map 78, NZ 242588.
(Pelaw Main Collieries Ltd; N6 from 1/1/1947; D6 from 1/1/1950; D5 from
1/1/1963; N&D5 from 1/1/1964; NDM from 26/3/1967)
   N.B.   Sometimes known as Lady Park Drift.
   C13   This drift was originally served by a short branch (½m) from the Pelaw
        Main Railway's line to Dunston, but from May 1963 it was at the end of
        the line. The drift itself was closed on 9th March 1968, but was re-
        opened two days later as part of Ravensworth Ann Colliery, whose title
        it then took.

RAVENSWORTH SHOP COLLIERY, near Lamesley. Map 78, NZ 257586.
(Pelaw Main Collieries Ltd; N6 from 1/1/1947; D6 from 1/1/1950)
   N.B.   Sometimes known as Allerdene Shop Pit, or much more commonly, simply
        as "the Shop Pit".
   C15   Worked by the Kings Engine on the Pelaw Main Railway. It was closed on
        23rd February 1962.

RODDYMOOR COLLIERY, Crook. Map 85, NZ 158366.
(Pease & Partners Ltd; N5 from 1/1/1947; D5 from 1/1/1950; D4 from 1/1/1963)
   Q5   The colliery was part of the extensive complex which included the Bank
        Foot Coke Ovens, and was served by the same branch (½m) from a junction
        immediately N of Crook Station on BR line from Crook to Tow Law. It was

merged with Wooley Colliery (see ⊁ b) on 1st April 1951. It was shunted
by locos from the Bank Foot Coke Ovens until September 1960, when it
received its own allocation. Rail traffic was replaced by road haulage
in March 1962, and the colliery was closed on 10th August 1963.

RYHOPE COLLIERY, Ryhope. Map 78, NZ 399535.
(Ryhope Coal Co Ltd; N1 from 1/1/1947; D1 from 1/1/1950; N&D1 from 1/1/1964;
N&D3 from 28/6/1965)
K16   The colliery was served by a BR branch (⅞m) from BR Sunderland-Seaham
⊁   line. Loco haulage underground was replaced by tractors and conveyors
       in 1964-1965. The colliery was closed on 25th November 1966.

SACRISTON COLLIERY, Sacriston. Map 85, NZ 234478.
(Charlaw & Sacriston Collieries Co Ltd; N5 from 1/1/1947; D5 from 1/1/1950;
new D5 from 1/1/1963; N&D5 from 1/1/1964; NDM from 26/3/1967; NE from 1/4/1974)
H59   The colliery was served by the Sacriston Railway until February 1955,
⊁   when the railway was replaced by road haulage.
       Locomotive haulage underground was dispensed with in 1962.

SACRISTON RAILWAY
(Charlaw & Sacriston Collieries Co Ltd; N5 from 1/1/1947; D5 from 1/1/1950)
       This Railway ran from Witton Colliery to Pelton Fell, a distance of
H59   approximately 4¼ miles. Locomotives from a shed at Sacriston Colliery
       served Witton Colliery and Shield Row Drift, and assembled wagons at
       the foot of an incline at the north end of Sacriston Colliery yard.
       A stationary engine at Edmonsley next hauled them up to the engine
H63   house and let them down to the Bank Foot, Waldridge. Locos from a shed
       here then handled traffic to exchange sidings with the BR Pontop &
       Shields line at Pelton Fell. The Railway ran adjacent to Nettlesworth
       Drift and Pelton Colliery (see ⊁ b), but there was no rail connection.
       The Railway was closed in February 1955, coal traffic being taken over
       by road transport.

SEAHAM COLLIERY, Seaham. Map 85, NZ 413496.
(Londonderry Collieries Ltd; N2 from 1/1/1947; D2 from 1/1/1950; N&D2 from
1/1/1964; N&D3 from 28/6/1965; SDM from 26/3/1967; NE from 1/4/1974)
N.B.   Formerly known as New Seaham Colliery.
L33   The colliery is served by a BR branch (½m) from BR Seaham-Hartlepool
       line, just S of Seaham Station, and is also connected to Seaham
       Harbour Docks, the two lines running alongside each other for most of
       their length. Originally the NCB line was a self-acting incline, but in
       1965 locomotives were allowed to work over it, though it continued to
       work wagons of stone by the rope for some months afterwards. It was
       converted to a single line track, and the rope removed in the early
       months of 1968.

SEAHAM WAGON WORKS, Dawdon. Map 85, NZ 427491.
(Londonderry Collieries Ltd; N2 from 1/1/1947; D2 from 1/1/1950; N&D2 from
1/1/1964; N&D3 from 28/6/1965; SDM from 26/3/1967; NE from 1/4/1974)
N.B.   After the NCB re-organisation of 1967 this works was not taken over
       by the Workshops Division, but remained under South Durham Area,
       except that it was controlled by the Engineering Department rather
       than the Production Dept.
L35   This works is served by sidings W of BR Seaham-Hartlepool line, ½m S
       of Seaham Station, and is reached via running powers over BR from
       Seaham Docks.

SHERBURN HILL COLLIERY, Sherburn Hill. Map 85, NZ 336427.
(Dorman, Long & Co Ltd; N4 from 1/1/1947; D4 from 1/1/1950; D3 from 4/1959;
N&D3 from 1/1/1964)
N12   This colliery was connected by a branch (NCB - 2m) to BR line from
⊁   Leamside to Ferryhill, immediately N of Sherburn Station. The loco shed
       was unusual in being sited underneath the colliery screens. It was
       closed on 7th August 1965.

SHIELD ROW DRIFT, Sacriston. Map 85,NZ 234475.
(Charlaw & Sacriston Collieries Co Ltd; N5 from 1/1/1947)
   H58   Served by sidings from the Sacriston Railway, and closed in April 1948.

SHOP PIT, near Lamesley - see RAVENSWORTH SHOP PIT

SHOP PIT LOCO SHED, near Lamesley (Pelaw Main Railway). Map 78, NZ 253587.
(Pelaw Main Collieries Ltd; N6 from 1/1/1947; D6 from 1/1/1950; D5 from
1/1/1963; N&D5 from 1/1/1964; NDM from 26/3/1967)
   C14   The loco kept here originally handled traffic between the Shop Pit
         sidings at the foot of the Allerdene Incline and Allerdene Sidings,
         Dunston (NZ 235617), which were exchange sidings with BR. This line,
         about 2m long, had a short branch to Ravensworth Park Drift about ½m
         N of the loco shed, and passed through the Team Valley Trading Estate,
         near the north end of which was a link to Norwood Coking Plant. In May
         1963 the Dunston traffic ceased, leaving the loco to work wagons
         between Ravensworth Park Drift and the foot of the incline. To do this
         a loco was hired from the Trading Estate via another link 200 yards
         north of the shed. The shed itself was used only for repairs until
         August 1964, when it was closed. It was re-opened temporarily from 6th
         to 21st September 1965 following an embankment slip which prevented
         access to the Estate loco, and in May 1966 it was restored to full
         working when the NCB resumed control of the traffic. The shed was
         finally closed on 18th April 1973 following the merger of Ravensworth
         Ann and Kibblesworth Collieries (q.v.).

SHOTTON COLLIERY & COKING PLANT, Shotton Colliery. Map 85,NZ 398413.
(Horden Collieries Ltd)
   COLLIERY   : - N3 from 1/1/1947; D3 from 1/1/1950; N&D3 from 1/1/1964;
                     SDM from 26/3/1967.
   COKING PLANT : - ND from 1/1/1947; DD from 1/1/1950.
   P5   Served by NCB branch (¼m) to BR Sunderland-Stockton line, 1¼m N of
   ∕   Wellfield Junction. The colliery locos also shunted Shotton Brickworks
         until it was sold to Shotton Bricks Ltd (q.v.) about 1953, and the
         coking plant until its closure in May 1958. The colliery was closed on
         1st September 1972.

SILKSWORTH COLLIERY, Silksworth, near Sunderland. Map 78,NZ 377541.
(Lambton, Hetton & Joicey Collieries Ltd; N2 from 1/1/1947; D2 from 1/1/1950;
N&D2 from 1/1/1964; N&D1 from 28/6/1965; SDM from 26/3/1967)
   K15   On Vesting Day this colliery was served by a BR branch (2¼m) to the
   ∕   Sunderland-Seaham line at Ryhope, with NCB running powers to Ryhope.
         Shortly after nationalisation a short link (½m) was built from the
         colliery to the Hetton Railway, just south of the North Moor Yard.
         After the closure of Lambton Staithes on 6th January 1967 all traffic
         was dispatched via the BR line, with the exception of wagons to a
         landsale depot in Sunderland via the Hetton line. The colliery closed
         on 5th November 1971.

SOUTH HETTON COLLIERY, South Hetton. Map 85, NZ 383453.
(South Hetton Coal Co Ltd; N2 from 1/1/1947; D2 from 1/1/1950; N&D2 from
1/1/1964; N&D3 from 28/6/1965; SDM from 26/3/1967; NE from 1/4/1974)
   P1   Served by NCB line (4m) to Seaham Harbour Docks, of which the last 1¼m
   ∕   consists of two self-acting inclines - Hesledon No.1 (Stony Cut) and
         No.2 (Swine Lodge). There are two links with BR at South Hetton - one,
         via the Pesspool Branch to the Sunderland-Stockton line ½m S of the
         former Haswell Station, and the other by a short link to the same line
         ½m N of the former South Hetton Station; latterly the BR track between
         these two junctions has been removed. At Swine Lodge Bank Head, at the
         Dawdon end of the line, there was a second kip, operated by BR, from
         which a short incline (350 yds) provided a link to the BR Seaham-
         Hartlepool line, ½m S of Seaham Station; this working was discontinued
         about 1964. Latterly all coal has been dispatched via BR at South
         Hetton, and all stone via the NCB line to Seaham.

The NCB line also served Murton Colliery via a ¼m branch until 1960, when that colliery's coal, together with Eppleton and Elemore Collieries, was drawn at the new Hawthorn Combined Mine. This, with its associated coking plant, was constructed about ½m E of South Hetton Colliery, and on its opening took over responsibility for railway operation and repairs. Colour light signals were erected in the area around Hawthorn, and the locomotives fitted with radio-telephone, though this was later abandoned. This shed was the last to operate regular steam working in Co. Durham.

The loco haulage underground at South Hetton Colliery was only used temporarily during development work. A narrow gauge loco was used in the colliery stockyard until 1971, when a dumper took over.

SOUTH MEDOMSLEY COLLIERY, near Dipton. Map 78, NZ 144531.
(South Medomsley Colliery Co Ltd; N6 from 1/1/1947; D6 from 1/1/1950)
  H1   This colliery was served by a branch (NCB - 1m) from the BR Annfield Plain-Consett line, 1m N of Leadgate Station. It was merged with Eden Colliery on 30th December 1961 and the site cleared.

SOUTH PELAW COLLIERY, near Chester-le-Street. Map 78, NZ 264523.
(South Pelaw Coal Co Ltd; N5 from 1/1/1947; D5 from 1/1/1950; new D5 from 1/1/1963; N&D5 from 1/1/1964)
  H53 This colliery was served by sidings S of BR Ouston Junction-Annfield Plain line, ½m S of Ouston Junction. It had not previously used its own locomotive, but did so between 1948 and 1954; otherwise it was shunted by BR. It was closed on 3rd January 1964.

SOUTH SHIELDS, MARSDEN & WHITBURN COLLIERY RAILWAY
(Harton Coal Co Ltd; Nl from 1/1/1947; Dl from 1/1/1950)
       This Railway ran from Whitburn Colliery to South Shields, a distance of 3 miles, much of it alongside the A183 road from South Shields to Sunderland. It served Whitburn Colliery and Marsden Quarries. It was the only NCB Railway in Co.Durham to operate public passenger services, and stations were provided at Whitburn Colliery, Marsden and Westoe Lane in South Shields. The passenger service was withdrawn on 22nd November 1953, from which date the line was merged into the Harton Railway. The station at Whitburn survived until the clearance of the Whitburn Colliery site in 1968; that at Westoe Lane may still be seen.
  D14 The loco shed was at Whitburn Colliery.

SPRINGWELL BANK FOOT LOCO SHED, Bowes Railway. Map 78, NZ 296605.
(John Bowes & Partners Ltd; N6 from 1/1/1947; D6 from 1/1/1950; D5 from 1/1/1963; N&D5 from 1/1/1964; NDM from 26/3/1967; NE from 1/4/1974)
  F2   This shed is situated 100 yards north of the foot of the Springwell Incline, and handles traffic between Springwell Bank Foot and Jarrow, a distance of 3½ miles. It also serves Monkton Coal Preparation Plant, Monkton Coking Plant and Usworth Colliery (formerly Wardley No.1 or Follonsby Colliery), the latter via a ½m branch. In 1959 it took over responsibility for all repairs to locomotives on the remainder of the Pelaw Main Railway, and latterly locomotives from other collieries have also been sent here for repairs.

SPRINGWELL WORKSHOPS, Springwell. Map 78, NZ 285588.
(John Bowes & Partners Ltd; N6 from 1/1/1947; D6 from 1/1/1950; D5 from 1/1/1963; N&D5 from 1/1/1964; Workshops Division from 26/3/1967; NE from 1/4/1974)
  F6   General Workshops for the Bowes Railway and its wagons, though equipment for local collieries was also repaired, and from 1966 wagons from other locations were also occasionally sent here for repair. In August 1964 a small locomotive repair bay was opened here, and from September 1965 locomotives awaiting disposal were also brought here. The buildings lay on both sides of the Railway at the interchange point between the Blackham's Hill East and Springwell Inclines, and wagon movements were performed by a number of small winches. The Wagon shops closed in November 1974, though the Engineering Shops continued in operation until March 1975.

STARGATE COLLIERY, Stargate, near Ryton. Map 78, NZ 161634.
(Stella Coal Co Ltd; N6 from 1/1/1947; D6 from 1/1/1950; D5 from 1/1/1963)
  A7   This colliery was served by the Stella Unit Railway, with its own loco
        shed, until August 1961, when the railway was replaced by road haulage.
        It was closed on 29th June 1963.

STARRS LOCO SHED, Wrekenton. (Pelaw Main Railway). Map 78, NZ 273594.
(Pelaw Main Collieries Ltd; N6 from 1/1/1947; D6 from 1/1/1950; D5 from
1/1/1963; N&D5 from 1/1/1964; NDM from 26/3/1967)
  F4   Locos from this shed handled traffic between the top of the Starrs
        Incline and Whitehill Yard. Between 1948 and 1954 they also took over
        the working between Eighton Banks and Whitehill. In January 1959 this
        was re-organised, and the Starrs loco then took all Pelaw Main traffic
        up to Whitehill, pushed it round to Eighton Banks, over the link to
        the Bowes Railway and into Springwell Colliery, though in periods of
        heavy traffic two locomotives were used, the working being divided at
        Whitehill. In 1971 the reverse at Whitehill was replaced by a curve,
        so that the loco headed the train for the whole journey. On 18th April
        1973 this section of the railway was finally closed, though the shed
        remained open for salvage work for about a week afterwards.

STELLA GILL COKING PLANT, Pelton Fell. Map 78, NZ 260522.
(Mid-Durham Carbonisation Co Ltd; ND from 1/1/1947; DD from 1/1/1950)
Locos administered by N5 from 1/1/1947; D5 from 1/1/1950; new D5 from 1/1/1963.
  H51   Served by sidings S of BR Pontop & Shields line, ½m S of South Pelaw
        Junction. The plant was closed in April 1962, but the loco continued
        to be used on salvage work and the clearance of coke stocks until
        November 1963.

STELLA GILL WITHDRAWN MACHINERY STORES, Pelton Fell. Map 78, NZ 262522.
(Opened by N&D5; NDM from 26/3/1967; NE from 1/4/1974)
  H51   When the Stella Gill coking plant site was cleared, one building and a
        small compound were retained as a withdrawn machinery stores. From
        February 1970 spare narrow gauge surface and underground locomotives
        have occasionally been kept here. It was closed on

STELLA UNIT RAILWAY
(Stella Coal Co Ltd; N6 from 1/1/1947; D6 from 1/1/1950)
  A7   The central point of this system was Stargate Colliery. To Stargate
        ran a branch from Emma Colliery (1¼m). At Vesting Day this line was
        worked by a stationary engine, but in 1948 this was abandoned in
        favour of loco working by locos from Stargate shed. Also to Stargate
  A8   ran a branch (2¼m) from Greenside Colliery. At first this was worked
        by a loco kept at Greenside, but about January 1960 this job was also
        taken over by Stargate shed. From Stargate a self-acting incline took
        the wagons down to sidings S of BR Newcastle-Carlisle line, 1m W of
        Blaydon Station. The system was closed in August 1961 in favour of
        road transport.

SWALWELL DISPOSAL POINT, Swalwell. Map 78, NZ 205623.
(Opened by Ministry of Fuel & Power 7/1945; NCBOE from 1/4/1952; operated for
NCBOE by Mechanical Navvies Ltd from 1/2/1954, and Johnsons (Chopwell) Ltd
from 29/7/1968)
  B8   This disposal point for opencast coal from Co. Durham and southern
        Northumberland was constructed on the site of the former Swalwell
        Garesfield Colliery, and is served by sidings S of BR Redheugh Branch.

TANFIELD LEA COLLIERY, Tanfield Lea. Map 78, NZ 188544.
(Lambton, Hetton & Joicey Collieries Ltd; N6 from 1/1/1947; D6 from 1/1/1950)
  H18   Situated at the end of the BR Tanfield Branch, 7m from Redheugh.
        The colliery was closed on 25th August 1962.

THORNLEY COLLIERY, Thornley. Map 85, NZ 365395.
(Weardale Steel, Coal & Coke Co Ltd; N3 from 1/1/1947; D3 from 1/1/1950;
N&D3 from 1/1/1964; SDM from 26/3/1967)
P8   This colliery was served by a BR branch (2m) from the Sunderland-
      Stockton line, 1m N of Wellfield Junction. Until 1959 Thornley locos
      also worked Wheatley Hill Colliery. The colliery closed on 9th January
      1970, but its coal preparation plant continued in operation (q.v.).

THORNLEY COAL PREPARATION PLANT, Thornley. Map 85, NZ 365395.
(Opened by D3; N&D3 from 1/1/1964; SDM from 26/3/1967; NE from 1/4/1974)
P8   Served by a BR branch (2m) from Sunderland-Stockton line, 1m N of
      Wellfield Junction, this survived the closure of the colliery until
      31st January 1976, though rail traffic ceased on 10th January.

THRISLINGTON COLLIERY & COKING PLANT, West Cornforth. Map 85, NZ 309338.
(Henry Stobart & Co Ltd)
   COLLIERY   : - N4 from 1/1/1947; D4 from 1/1/1950; N&D4 from 1/1/1964.
   COKING PLANT : - ND from 1/1/1947; DD from 1/1/1950.
R26   This was connected to the BR Durham-Darlington line, ¼m N of Ferryhill
 ⚡   Station, by an incline (½m) worked by a stationary engine. The
      colliery locos shunted the coking plant until its closure in April
      1954. The colliery was closed on 4th March 1967, but its coal
      preparation plant continued in operation (q.v.).

THRISLINGTON COAL PREPARATION PLANT, West Cornforth. Map 85, NZ 309338.
(Opened by D4; N&D4 from 1/1/1964; SDM from 26/3/1967)
R26   This continued in operation after the closure of Thrislington
      Colliery, and for a time continued to be linked to the BR Durham-
      Darlington line, ¼m N of Ferryhill Station, by an incline (½m)
      worked by a stationary engine; but latterly all coal was brought to
      and from the plant by road. It closed on 26th March 1970.

TRIMDON GRANGE COLLIERY & COKING PLANT, Trimdon Grange. Map 85, NZ 366356.
(East Hetton Collieries Ltd)
   COLLIERY   : - N4 from 1/1/1947; D4 from 1/1/1950; N&D4 from 1/1/1964;
                     SDM from 26/3/1967.
   COKING PLANT : - ND from 1/1/1947; DD from 1/1/1950.
R24   Served by sidings N of BR line from Wingate Junction to Ferryhill,
      ¼m W of Trimdon Station; but after the closure of this line between
      Trimdon Grange and Garmondsway Quarry the colliery stood at the end
      of the line, 2½m from Wingate Junction. The colliery locos shunted
      the coking plant until its closure in April 1962. The colliery was
      closed on 16th February 1968, though after clearance the area was
      used as a coal stocking site for a time. The whole site has now
      been cleared.

TUDHOE COKING PLANT, Spennymoor. Map 85, NZ 261338.
(Weardale Steel, Coal & Coke Co Ltd; ND from 1/1/1947; DD from 1/1/1950)
Locos administered by N5 from 1/1/1947; D5 from 1/1/1950; D4 from c/1950.
   R5   This plant was served by sidings N of BR line from Ferryhill to
        Bishop Auckland, ½m E of Spennymoor Station. It was closed in
        August 1955.

TURSDALE COLLIERY, near Cornforth. Map 85, NZ 292360.
(Dorman, Long & Co Ltd; N4 from 1/1/1947)
   R16 This colliery was closed at Vesting Day, though its shaft was part of
        the workings of Bowburn Colliery. The site was subsequently cleared
        for the new Area Central Workshops of No.4 Area (opened in 1952),
        though the shaft remained open for a training face underground. It
        was served by sidings E of BR Leamside-Ferryhill line, immediately N
        of Tursdale Junction.

TWIZELL BURN DRIFT, Grange Villa. Map 78, NZ 232515.
(Lambton, Hetton & Joicey Collieries Ltd; N5 from 1/1/1947)
  H67   Served by the Beamish Railway. This drift worked the Five Quarter
         seam, and was closed on 1st July 1948.

TWIZELL BURN/ALMA DRIFT, Grange Villa. Map 78, NZ 233516 (approx)
(Opened by N5; D5 from 1/1/1950)
  H68   This drift was also served by the Beamish Railway. It worked the
         Main Coal seam, and was closed on 2nd March 1955.

URPETH 'C' COLLIERY, Urpeth. Map 78, NZ 243546.
(Pelaw Main Collieries Ltd; N6 from 1/1/1947; D6 from 1/1/1950)
  H25   This colliery, served by the Pelaw Main Railway, was closed at Vesting
         Day. It was re-opened in 1947, and merged with Ouston 'E' Colliery on
         30th March 1957.

USHAW MOOR COLLIERY, Ushaw Moor. Map 85, NZ 220428.
(Pease & Partners Ltd; N5 from 1/1/1947; D5 from 1/1/1950)
  M10   This colliery was served by sidings N of BR Waterhouses Branch, 1m W
         of Ushaw Moor Station. The shunting was taken over by BR in 1948.
         It closed on 5th August 1960.

USWORTH COLLIERY, Usworth. Map 78, NZ 315584.
(Washington Coal Co Ltd; N1 from 1/1/1947; D1 from 1/1/1950)
  J5   This colliery was served by sidings W of BR line from Pelaw to
         Washington, ½m N of Usworth Signal Box. On 2nd January 1959 it was
         combined with Wardley No.1 and Wardley No.2 Collieries, the Usworth
         shaft then being used for man-riding only. See also next entry.

USWORTH COLLIERY, White Mare Pool. Map 78, NZ 313608.
(NDM from 26/3/1967; NE from 1/4/1974)
  D4   This colliery was originally Wardley No.1 Colliery (q.v.), and was
   ⧸   also known locally as Follonsby Colliery. In 1959 it became the coal-
         drawing shaft for the unit formed by it, Wardley No.2 and Usworth
         shafts. On 2nd January 1969 its name was changed to Wardley/Usworth
         Colliery, and on 20th January 1969 to Usworth Colliery. Thus latterly
         Usworth Colliery consisted of two shafts about a mile apart, this one
         for coal-winding, and the other (see above) for man-riding. This shaft
         was served by a branch (½m) of the Bowes Railway from Wardley Yard,
         and also by sidings E of BR line from Pelaw to Washington, 1¼m S of
         Pelaw Station. The colliery closed on 8th August 1974.
         A narrow gauge locomotive was used in the colliery stockyard
         intermittently from 1959 to 1969.

VANE TEMPEST COLLIERY, Seaham. Map 78, NZ 425503.
(Londonderry Collieries Ltd; N2 from 1/1/1947; D2 from 1/1/1950; N&D2 from
1/1/1964; N&D3 from 28/6/1965; SDM from 26/3/1967; NE from 1/4/1974)
  L32   Colliery served by ½m branch from BR Sunderland-Hartlepool line,
   ⧸   ½m N of Seaham Station.

VICTORIA GARESFIELD COLLIERY, Rowlands Gill. Map 78, NZ 145580.
(Priestman Collieries Ltd; N6 from 1/1/1947; D6 from 1/1/1950)
  A11   This was served by an NCB branch (1½m) from immediately N of Rowlands
         Gill Station on BR Blackhill branch. Nearby were the Whinfield
         Beehive Coke Ovens, the last working beehive ovens (193) in Co. Durham.
         They ceased production in May 1958, and a small number are preserved
         on site. The colliery locos shunted the ovens until closure. The
         colliery closed on 13th July 1962.

WARDLEY COLLIERY, White Mare Pool. Map 78, NZ 313608.
(Washington Coal Co Ltd; Nl from 1/1/1947; Dl from 1/1/1950; N&Dl from
1/1/1964; NDM from 26/3/1967)
> N.B. Properly known as Wardley No.1 Colliery, and locally known as
>   Follonsby Colliery. See also below.
> D4   Served by a branch (¼m) of the Bowes Railway from Wardley Yard, and
> ✗   also by sidings E of BR line from Pelaw to Washington, 1¼m S of Pelaw
>   Station.
>   On 2nd January 1959 it was combined with Usworth Colliery, which, with
>   Wardley No.2 Colliery (NZ 306620), re-opened at the same time, became
>   man-riding shafts only, all coal being wound at the Wardley No.1 shaft.
>   On 2nd January 1969 this shaft was re-named Wardley/Usworth, and on
>   20th January 1969 it became Usworth Colliery (q.v.). Wardley No.2
>   Colliery shaft was closed on 29th April 1971. The colliery closed on
>   8th August 1974.
>   A narrow gauge battery loco was used in the colliery stockyard.

WASHINGTON 'F' COLLIERY, Washington. Map 78, NZ 303574.
(Washington Coal Co Ltd; Nl from 1/1/1947; Dl from 1/1/1950; N&Dl from
1/1/1964; NDM from 26/3/1967)
> J3   This colliery was situated at the end of a BR branch (1¼m) from the
> ✗   Pelaw-Washington line, from a junction immediately S of Washington
>   Station. Shunting was done by BR, but from February 1963 a loco was
>   allocated to bring coal from Washington Glebe Colliery, ½m down the
>   branch, to a landsale depot at the 'F' Pit. The colliery closed on
>   21st June 1968, but the landsale depot continued until April 1969.

WASHINGTON GLEBE COLLIERY, Washington. Map 78, NZ 308563.
(Washington Coal Co Ltd; Nl from 1/1/1947; Dl from 1/1/1950; N&Dl from
1/1/1964; NDM from 26/3/1967)
> J4   Served by the same BR branch as to Washington 'F' Colliery, and also
>   shunted by BR, but after the closure of the Washington 'F' landsale
>   depot in April 1969 its loco was stored here until cut up in August
>   1970. The colliery closed on 4th August 1972.

WATERGATE COLLIERY, near Sunniside. Map 78, NZ 222599.
(Priestman Collieries Ltd; N6 from 1/1/1947; D6 from 1/1/1950; D5 from
1/1/1963; N&D5 from 1/1/1964)
> A15   This colliery was served by sidings E of BR Tanfield Branch, 2¼m from
> ✗   Dunston. It was closed on 20th August 1964.

WEARMOUTH COLLIERY, Sunderland. Map 78, NZ 394578.
(Wearmouth Coal Co Ltd; Nl from 1/1/1947; Dl from 1/1/1950; N&Dl from 1/1/1964;
NDM from 26/3/1967; NE from 1/4/1974)
> K11   Served by sidings S of BR Hylton branch, ½m W of Monkwearmouth Junc-
> ✗   tion. NCB locos also worked traffic between Wearmouth and Hylton
>   Colliery, using running powers over BR; this duty ceased in August 1971.
>   Coal shipments from Wearmouth Staithes ceased in 1969, and subsequently
>   much of the colliery surface layout was re-designed, only one loco
>   being retained for shunting wagons less than 21 tons.
>   A narrow gauge loco is used on an extensive surface system.

WEST AUCKLAND COAL PREPARATION PLANT, West Auckland. Map 85, NZ 183267.
(Opened by D4; N&D4 from 1/1/1964; SDM from 26/3/1967)
> T13   This was a new washery opened in 1956 to deal with coal from various
>   sources in S.W.Durham. It was served by sidings immediately W of West
>   Auckland Station on BR Bishop Auckland-Barnard Castle line, and was
>   closed on 18th August 1967.

WEST BRANDON DRIFT, near Waterhouses. Map 85, NZ 198402.
(Opened by D5)
> M12   This drift was opened in 1950, and connected to Brandon Pit House
>   Colliery by a narrow gauge line 1m long. It was closed on 22nd August
>   1958.

WEST THORNLEY COLLIERY, near Tow Law. Map 85, NZ 133386.
(Weardale Steel, Coal & Coke Co Ltd; N5 from 1/1/1947; D5 from 1/1/1950;
D4 from 1/1/1963; N&D4 from 1/1/1964)
   Q4   A narrow gauge loco was used on the surface here between April 1956
        and October 1957. The colliery closed on 6th November 1965.

WESTOE COLLIERY, South Shields. Map 78, NZ 373368.
(Harton Coal Co Ltd; N1 from 1/1/1947; D1 from 1/1/1950; N&D1 from 1/1/1964;
NDM from 26/3/1967; NE from 1/4/1974)
   D8   This colliery, re-opened in 1947, is served by the Harton Railway, and
   ⚹   is one of the largest in N.E.England. Narrow gauge locomotives were
        used in mine car sidings from May 1974.

WESTOE LOCO SHED, South Shields. (Harton Railway). Map 78, NZ 374667.
(Harton Coal Co Ltd; N1 from 1/1/1947; D1 from 1/1/1950; N&D1 from 1/1/1964;
NDM from 26/3/1967; NE from 1/4/1974)
   D7   This is the loco shed for the Harton Railway electric locos (except
        for the one formerly kept at Harton Colliery). A repair bay is
        incorporated in the shed buildings.

WHEATLEY HILL COLLIERY, Wheatley Hill. Map 85, NZ 385393.
(Weardale Steel, Coal & Coke Co Ltd; N3 from 1/1/1947; D3 from 1/1/1950;
N&D3 from 1/1/1964; SDM from 26/3/1967)
   P9   This colliery was served by a loop line from the BR Thornley branch.
        It was originally worked by locos from Thornley Colliery, but in 1959
        it was allocated its own loco, with a new loco shed. The colliery was
        closed on 3rd May 1968.

WHITBURN COLLIERY, Whitburn Colliery. Map 78, NZ 408637.
(Harton Coal Co Ltd; N1 from 1/1/1947; D1 from 1/1/1950; N&D1 from 1/1/1964;
NDM from 26/3/1967)
  D14   This colliery lay at the southern end of the South Shields, Marsden &
   ⚹   Whitburn Colliery Railway, later the Harton Railway. The loco shed for
        the railway was at the southern end of the colliery. It was closed on
        7th June 1968.

WHITTONSTALL DRIFT, near Whittonstall, Northumberland. Map 78, NZ 087573.
(Consett Iron Co Ltd; N6 from 1/1/1947; D6 from 1/1/1950; D5 from 1/1/1963;
N&D5 from 1/1/1964)
   A1   There were two drifts here, the second, opened in 1960, being about ¼m
        E of the first. They were connected to Chopwell Colliery by the Whitt-
        onstall Railway, a narrow gauge line 2m long, worked by a main-and-tail
        rope system, unique on the surface in Co.Durham. The main engine house
        was at Chopwell, with another engine at Whittonstall to shunt the
        drifts themselves. Originally a passenger service for the miners was
        provided between Chopwell & Whittonstall, but this was subsequently
        discontinued. The drifts closed on 25th November 1966.
 N.B. Whittonstall was included with Chopwell Colliery for official purposes.

WINGATE GRANGE COLLIERY, Wingate. Map 85, NZ 398373.
(Wingate Coal Co Ltd; N3 from 1/1/1947; D3 from 1/1/1950)
  P11   This colliery was served by a BR branch (½m) from Wingate-Ferryhill
        line, immediately E of Wingate Station, and was originally shunted by
        BR. In 1955 it was linked by a narrow gauge line to Deaf Hill Colliery,
        and to handle the increased output a standard gauge loco was allocated
        to Wingate Grange in December 1955. The colliery was closed on 26th
        October 1962.

WITTON COLLIERY, Sacriston. Map 85, NZ 238461.
(Charlaw & Sacriston Collieries Co Ltd; N5 from 1/1/1947; D5 from 1/1/1950;
new D5 from 1/1/1963; N&D5 from 1/1/1964)
  H57   Situated at the southern end of the Sacriston Railway. After the clos-
        ure of the Railway in February 1955 it was served by road transport.
        It was closed on 8th January 1966.

ADVENTURE COLLIERY, West Rainton.	Map 85, NZ 315471	
BARCUS CLOSE COLLIERY, near Burnopfield.	Map 78, NZ 173578	Closed
BARLOW TOWNELEY DRIFT, Barlow.	Map 78, NZ 150607	Closed
BRUSSLETON COLLIERY, near West Auckland.	Map 85, NZ 207249	Closed
CAUSEY MILL DRIFT, near Stanley.	Map 78, NZ 223533	Closed
CHESTER SOUTH MOOR COLLIERY, Chester Moor.	Map 85, NZ 268494	Closed
COCKEN DRIFT, Cocken.	Map 85, NZ 283472	Closed
DUNSTON (also known as DUNSTON & ELSWICK) COLLIERY	Map 78, NZ 228625	Closed
ELDON DRIFT, Eldon, near Shildon.	Map 85, NZ 250278	Closed
ESH COLLIERY, Esh Winning.	Map 85, NZ 195423	Closed
ESPERLEY LANE DRIFT, Evenwood.	Map 85, NZ 140238	Closed
FENHALL DRIFT, near Lanchester.	Map 85, NZ 167484	Closed
GRANGE COLLIERY, Belmont.	Map 85, NZ 302447	Closed
GREENCROFT TOWER COLLIERY, Annfield Plain.	Map 78, NZ 167502	Closed
HAGGS LANE DRIFT, near Shildon.	Map 85, NZ 206256	Closed
HAMSTEELS COLLIERY, near Esh Winning.	Map 85, NZ 182431	Closed
HARBOUR HOUSE DRIFT, near Leamside.	Map 85, NZ 288471	Closed
HEDLEY COLLIERY, South Moor.	Map 78, NZ 193524	Closed
KIMBLESWORTH COLLIERY, Kimblesworth.	Map 85, NZ 261469	Closed
LANCHESTER TOWNELEY DRIFT, near Lanchester.	Map 85, NZ 180461	Closed
LITTLEBURN COLLIERY, Meadowfield, near Durham.	Map 85, NZ 255395	Closed
MARSHALL GREEN COLLIERY, Witton-le-Wear.	Map 85, NZ 156317	Sold
METAL BRIDGE DRIFT, near Ferryhill.	Map 85, NZ 290350	
MIDDRIDGE DRIFT, near Shildon.	Map 85, NZ 245268	Closed
NETTLESWORTH DRIFT, near Waldridge (includes	Map 85, NZ 254493	Closed
DENE DRIFT at Waldridge)	Map 78, NZ 247502	Closed
NEW SHILDON COLLIERY, Shildon.	Map 85, NZ 220256	Closed
NORTH TEES COLLIERY, near Winston.	Map 84, NZ 123164	Closed
PELTON COLLIERY, Pelton.	Map 78, NZ 255517	Closed
PHOENIX DRIFT, near Greenside.	Map 78, NZ 137628	Closed
PRINCES STREET DRIFT, near Shildon.	Map 85, NZ 201263	Closed
QUARRY DRIFT (originally known as ETHERLEY DENE		
DRIFT), near Bishop Auckland.	Map 85, NZ 205292	Closed
RAMSHAW No.1 COLLIERY, near West Auckland.	Map 85, NZ 165273	Closed
RAMSHAW No.2 COLLIERY, near West Auckland.	Map 85, NZ 170267	Closed
ROSE COTTAGE DRIFT, near Annfield Plain.	Map 85, NZ 175497	Closed
SOUTH GARESFIELD COLLIERY, near Burnopfield.	Map 78, NZ 157572	Closed
SOUTH SHILDON COLLIERY, Shildon.	Map 85, NZ 233253	Closed
STAINDROP FIELD HOUSE COLLIERY, near Evenwood Gate.	Map 85, NZ 175249	Closed
STANLEY BURN DRIFT, Prudhoe.	Map 85, NZ 115626	Closed
STANLEY COTTAGE DRIFT, near Billy Row.	Map 85, NZ 171391	Closed
TANFIELD MOOR COLLIERY, Tantobie.	Map 78, NZ 169545	Closed
TUDHOE MILL DRIFT, Tudhoe.	Map 85, NZ 252355	Closed
TUDHOE PARK COLLIERY, Tudhoe.	Map 85, NZ 268357	Closed
WATERHOUSES COLLIERY, Waterhouses.	Map 85, NZ 185411	Closed
WESTERTON COLLIERY, Westerton.	Map 85, NZ 237318	Closed
WHITWORTH PARK COLLIERY, Spennymoor.	Map 85, NZ 250340	Closed
WOOLEY COLLIERY, near Crook.	Map 85, NZ 178385	⨍

⨍ merged with Roddymoor Colliery (see a)

2. <u>ALPHABETICAL LIST OF LOCATIONS IN NORTHUMBERLAND</u>
(using locomotives on the formation of
North-East Area on 1st April 1974)

(∤ indicates locomotives used underground)

<u>AREA MACHINERY STORES</u>, Seaton Delaval. Map 78, NZ 301762.
(known as SEATON DELAVAL YARD)

> Buildings part of former Seaton Delaval Colliery, and used to store
> spare underground locomotives. Closed on 27th March 1975.

<u>AREA TRAINING CENTRE</u>, Ashington. Map 78, NZ 264879.

> Narrow gauge locomotive used for training purposes.

<u>ASHINGTON LOCO SHED</u>, Ashington. Map 78, NZ 263881.

> Works Ashington Colliery (NZ 265882), and controls locomotives at
> Lynemouth Colliery (q.v.). Also handles materials traffic for
> Woodhorn Colliery (NZ 289884) and Ellington Colliery (q.v.).

<u>BACKWORTH COLLIERY</u>, Backworth. Map 78, NZ 304719.
(normally known as ECCLES COLLIERY)

> Locos work the colliery, and also traffic between Backworth and
> Weetslade Coal Preparation Plant (q.v.). Last steam-worked shed in
> Northumberland; replaced by diesels in January 1976.

<u>BATES COLLIERY</u>, Blyth. Map 78, NZ 304823.

> Colliery has a second loco shed at NZ 309823. Locos also work between
> colliery and former Isabella Pit sidings (1¼m S) and shunt the staithes.

<u>BRENKLEY COLLIERY</u>, Seaton Burn. Map 78, NZ 223743.

> A drift mine, from which mine cars are worked by a 2' 6" gauge main-
> and-tail rope system to screens at Seaton Burn Yard (NZ 239728). Here
> the coal is transferred into standard gauge wagons, worked originally
> by locomotives from Burradon, but latterly from Weetslade.

<u>BURRADON LOCO SHED</u>, Burradon. Map 78, NZ 276722.

> There was also a second loco shed at NZ 274725, latterly disused.
> Locos worked traffic at Burradon Colliery (NZ 274726), closed on
> 21st November 1975, Havannah and Brenkley Collieries, Weetslade Coal
> Preparation Plant and Coal Depot, and the stone disposal point at
> NZ 283736. The shed was closed on 3rd Jan 1976 and its locos transferred
> to a new shed at Weetslade.

<u>CENTRAL WORKSHOPS</u>, Ashington. Map 78, NZ 260881.

> From March 1967 a number of underground locomotives from Durham have
> been repaired here. Repairs to surface locomotives ceased in March 1975.

<u>DUDLEY COLLIERY</u>, Dudley. Map 78, NZ 259738.

<u>ELLINGTON COLLIERY</u>, Ellington. Map 78, NZ 283917.

∤   All coal from this colliery is drawn at Lynemouth Colliery, but the
> colliery retains its separate identity for materials and man-riding.
> Narrow gauge locomotives are used in the colliery stockyard.
> Although the colliery also retains a separate underground locomotive
> allocation, in practice the underground complex with Lynemouth is
> treated as one unit.

HAVANNAH COLLIERY, Hazlerigg. Map 78, NZ 217718.

    A drift mine, worked by locomotives originally from Burradon, but latterly from Weetslade.

LYNEMOUTH COLLIERY, Lynemouth. Map 78, NZ 298905.

    Locomotives are permanently kept here, but switched by Ashington Loco Shed if necessary.
A narrow gauge locomotive is used at the entrance of Bewick Drift (NZ 303906), ½m from main shafts.

NETHERTON COLLIERY, Bedlington. Map 78, NZ 240826.

    This colliery was closed at the date of re-organisation, and its locomotives were awaiting disposal.

SHILBOTTLE COLLIERY, Shilbottle. Map 71, NU 215080.

    N.B. This colliery and Whittle Colliery (q.v.) are situated on an isolated part of the coalfield in North Northumberland.

WEETSLADE COAL PREPARATION PLANT, near Burradon. Map 78, NZ 256724.

    Originally worked by locomotives from Burradon Loco Shed, but took over the locomotives and duties of Burradon upon its closure on 3rd Jan 1976.

WHITTLE COLLIERY, Newton-on-the-Moor. Map 71, NU 176064.

    Locomotives work traffic between the drift entrance and the screens at the main colliery site (NU 174067) and down to BR via a 5m branch. Narrow gauge locomotives are used in the colliery stockyard and also to transport men and materials to the drift entrance, the line running alongside the standard gauge line.

GENERAL NOTES

    The list of NCB locomotives which follows has been divided up into six main sections, viz:

1. Surface locomotives, Areas 1-6, 1947-1967
2. Surface locomotives, North and South Durham Areas, 1967-1974
3. Surface locomotives for the North-East Area (including locomotives previously in the Northumberland Area), 1974 onwards
4. Locomotives owned by National Smokeless Fuels Ltd (Coal Products Division from 1963-1973)
5. Underground locomotives, 1947-1974 (see also note at beginning of this section)
6. Underground locomotives for the North-East Area (including locomotives previously in the Northumberland Area), 1974 onwards

    Each NCB location at which locomotives have been either used or stored has been given an abbreviation, and a list of these appears at the beginning of the entry for each Area.
    Any location which was closed during its operation by an Area is shown thus.
    The locomotives acquired from constituent companies in 1947 are shown in the alphabetical order of those companies, and are listed in order of age. Locomotives purchased by the NCB are then added in chronological order of acquisition. In subsequent re-organisations constituent Areas have been similarly treated, the locomotives grouped under each colliery.

On 28th June 1965 this Area was enlarged by the addition of the northern half of the former No.2 Area.

On 26th March 1967 this Area was combined with the former No.5 Area to form the new North Durham Area (q.v.).

This Area took over 21 steam locomotives, 10 electric locomotives and 3 narrow gauge diesel locomotives. No numbering scheme was introduced, either for them or new locomotives, though the latter were sometimes included in a former colliery numbering scheme, as at Wearmouth Colliery. In 1963 'B' Group locomotives were numbered from 1 in a scheme based on order of acquisition, but the number 8 was omitted when the locomotives were painted, the last two becoming 9 and 10.

New diesel locomotives acquired in 1965-1966 were numbered in a Divisional series beginning at No. 500, but the number 508 was also omitted.

The Area operated two railways:

Harton Railway, incorporating South Shields, Marsden & Whitburn Colliery Railway, with loco sheds at:

Ha	Harton Colliery, near South Shields
We	Westoe Colliery, South Shields
Wh	Whitburn Colliery

Lambton Railway (from June 1965), with loco sheds at:

LS	Lambton Staithes, Sunderland (closed 6/1/1967)
P	Lambton Railway Loco Sheds, Philadelphia
Sk	Silksworth Colliery, Sunderland

Other locations

UTC	Area Apprentice Training Centre, Usworth
B	Boldon Colliery
Hn	Herrington Colliery, New Herrington
Hy	Hylton Colliery, Castletown
LEW	Lambton Engine Works, Philadelphia
MQ	Marsden Quarries, near Whitburn (sold 9/1965)
R	Ryhope Colliery (to No.3 Area, 6/1965)
U	Usworth Colliery (combined with Wardley Colliery, 1/1959)
Wa	Wardley Colliery, White Mare Pool
WF	Washington 'F' Colliery
Wm	Wearmouth Colliery, Sunderland

Gauge: 4' 8½"

4		0-6-0	IC	Ghd		1883	(a)	B-Wh c/50	Scr 6/1952
3		0-4-0T	IC	Ghd	38	1888	(a)	B-U /48	Scr /1952
	BOLDON No.1 (orig. No.1)	0-6-0T	IC	HC	332	1889	(a)	B	Scr 3/1958
5		0-6-0	IC	Ghd		1881	(a)	Wh	Scr 2/1953
4		0-6-0ST	IC	BH	826	1884	(a)	Wh	Scr /1948
8		0-6-0	IC	Ghd	3	1889	(a)	Wh	Scr 8/1954
6		0-6-0	IC	Ghd	23	1889	(a)	Wh	Scr 6/1951

```
(1)       LALEHAM              0-6-0ST  OC  AB    1639  1923  (a)  Wh-B 2/60
                                                                      Scr  6/1964
3         (orig. No.3)         0-6-0T   IC  Dar    480  1892  (b)  R       Scr  1/1960
1                              0-6-0ST  OC  P     1403  1916  (b)  R       (1)
(2)                            0-6-0ST  OC  P     1455  1918  (b)  R       (1)
          -                    0-4-0ST  OC  P     1460  1918  (c)  U       Scr   /1948
          PHYLLIS              0-6-0ST  IC  AB     833  1898  (d)  Wm      Scr 11/1953
          BUNNY                0-6-0T   IC  AB     911  1901  (d)  Wm      Scr  6/1963
          WILL                 0-6-0T   IC  AB     999  1904  (d)  Wm-Hy 12/66
                                                                      (2)
          JEAN                 0-6-0T   IC  HL    2769  1909  (d)  Wm      (2)
          DIANA                0-6-0T   IC  RSH   7304  1946  (d)  Wm      (2)
No.1                           0-4-0ST  OC  HL    3494  1922  (d)  Wm      Scr  6/1959
No.2                           0-4-0ST  OC  HL    3493  1922  (d)  Wm      (2)
No.3                           0-4-0ST  OC  RSH   7307  1946  (d)  Wm      Scr  9/1966
No.4                           0-4-0ST  OC  RSH   6945  1938  (d)  Wm      Scr  9/1966
No.5                           0-4-0ST  OC  HL    2824  1910  (d)  Wm      Scr  6/1959
(71485); later (7294);         0-6-0ST  IC  RSH   7294  1945  (e)  B-Wh 2/59-B 4/62
4 from 1963; "10" from                                                -Wh 26/5/62
3/1966                                                                -B 30/5/62-Wh 11/62
                                                                      -WF 2/63-Wm 3/66
                                                                      (2)
(7132); 5 from 1963            0-6-0ST✓ IC  RSH   7132  1944  (f)  B-Wh 9/48-B 5/54
                                                                      -Wh 6/64-B 12/65
                                                                      -Wm 6/66
                                                                      (2)
(No.9); 2 from 1963            0-6-0STø IC  HE    3191  1944  (g)  Wh-LEW /51-Wh 4/52
"2B" from 12/65                                                       -LEW 5/52-Wh 6/52
                                                                      -B c/56-Wh 2/61
                                                                      -P 12/65-Wm 6/66
                                                                      (2)
(10)      (3) from 1963        0-6-0ST  OC  RSH   7339  1947  New  Wh-WF 3/66
                                                                      (2)
          BOLDON No.1513       0-6-0ST  IC  HC    1513  1924
                                        reb HC          1947  (h)  Wh-B by 9/48
                                                                      -Wh 1/50-B 2/50
                                                                      Scr 12/1959
          (USWORTH No.1)       0-4-0ST  OC  RSH   7414  1948  New  U-Hy 1/58-Wm 12/63
7 from c/1959                                                         -Hy 9/64-Wm 6/65
                                                                      -Hy c10/65
                                                                      Scr 11/1966
"4"                            0-6-0    IC  Ghd     28  1897  (j)  B-Wh 3/56
                                                                      Scr  7/1956
No.6                           0-4-0ST  OC  RSH   7535  1949  New  Wm-Hy 6/65
                                                                      Scr  9/1966
(7603); 6 from 1963            0-6-0ST  OC  RSH   7603  1949  New  Wh-B 9/61-Wh 11/62
                                                                      -B 7/64
                                                                      (2)
No.2                           0-6-0ST  OC  RSH   7599  1949  (k)  Wm      (3)
(7695); 7 from 1963            0-6-0ST  OC  RSH   7695  1951  New  Wh-B 2/58-Wh 7/59
                                                                      -B 4/65(2)
(7749); 9 from 1963            0-6-0ST  OC  RSH   7749  1952  New  Wh-B 7/58-Wh 2/59
                                                                      -B 2/61-Wh 5/62
                                                                      -B 11/62-Wh 12/62
                                                                      -B 5/63-Wh 4/65
                                                                      (2)
          (USWORTH No.2)       0-4-0ST  OC  RSH   7807  1954  New  U-Wm 1/58-Hy 9/64
8 from c/1959                                                         -Wm 10/65-Hy 12/66
                                                                      (2)
(7811);10 from 1963            0-6-0ST  OC  RSH   7811  1954  New  Wh-B 7/59-LEW 2/60
                                                                      -B 5/60-Wh 2/61
                                                                      -B 8/62-Wh 9/62
                                                                      -B 12/62-Wh 6/65
                                                                      (2)
```

3		0-6-0ST	OC	RSH	7689	1951	(m)	Wm	(2)
4		0-6-0ST	OC	RSH	7690	1951	(m)	Wm-Hy 12/66	(2)
-		0-4-0DH		AB	478	1963	New	Hy-Wm 10/64	(2)
No.501		0-6-0DH		HE	6612	1965	New	Wm	(2)
1		0-6-0DH		NBL	27410	1955	(n)	LS-P 12/66	(2)
2	(No.2 until 7/65)	0-6-0ST	OC	RSH	7599	1949	(n)	P	(2)
3		0-6-0ST	OC	RSH	7687	1951	(n)	P	(2)
4		0-6-0ST	OC	RSH	7688	1951	(n)	P	(2)
5		0-6-2T	IC	RS	3377	1909	(n)	P	(2)
7		0-6-0ST	IC	HE	3820	1954	(n)	P	(2)
8		0-6-0ST	OC	RSH	7691	1952	(n)	P	(2)
10		0-6-2T	IC	RS	3378	1909	(n)	P	(2)
11		0-4-0ST	OC	HC	1412	1920			
		reb		HC		1948	(n)	P	(4)
27		0-6-0T	IC	RS	491	1846			
		reb		Ghd		1864			
		reb		Ghd		1873			
		reb		LEW		1904	(n)	P	(2)
28		0-4-0ST	OC	HL	2530	1902	(n)	P	(2)
29		0-6-2T	IC	K	4263	1904	(n)	P	(2)
30		0-6-2T	IC	K	4532	1907	(n)	P	(2)
31		0-6-2T	IC	K	4533	1907	(n)	P	(2)
32		0-4-0ST	OC	HL	2826	1910	(n)	LS	(2)
33		0-4-0ST	OC	HL	2827	1910	(n)	P-Wm 12/66	(2)
34		0-4-0ST	OC	HL	2954	1912	(n)	LS-Sk 12/66	(2)
35		0-4-0ST	OC	HL	3024	1913	(n)	P-LS 6/65-Sk 12/66	(2)
37		0-4-0ST	OC	RSH	7755	1953	(n)	LS-P 1/67	(5)
38		0-4-0ST	OC	RSH	7756	1953	(n)	P	(6)
No.39		0-4-0ST	OC	RSH	7757	1953	(n)	LS-P 3/66-Wm 3/67	(2)
42		0-6-2T	IC	RS	3801	1920	(n)	P	(2)
45		0-6-0ST	IC	HL	2932	1912	(n)	P	(2)
47		0-4-0ST	OC	HL	3543	1923	(n)	P-LS 2/66-P 1/67	(2)
51		0-6-0ST	IC	RSH	7101	1943	(n)	LS-P 2/66	(2)
52		0-6-2T	IC	NR	5408	1899	(n)	P	(2)
53		0-6-2T	IC	Cdf	302	1894	(n)	P	Scr 10/1966
58		0-6-0ST	IC	VF	5299	1945	(n)	LS-Wm 9/66-P 3/67	(2)
59		0-6-0ST	IC	VF	5300	1945	(n)	P	(2)
60		0-6-0ST	IC	HE	3686	1948	(n)	P	(7)
63		0-6-0ST	OC	RSH	7600	1949	(n)	P	(2)
2505/78		4wDM		FH	3852	1957			
		reb		NCB		1958	(n)	P-Hy 9/65	(2)
No.505		0-6-0DH		HE	6616	1965	New	Wh	(2)
No.506		0-6-0DH		HE	6617	1965	New	Wh	(2)
No.507		0-6-0DH		HE	6618	1965	New	Wh-B 19/5/66 -Wm 30/5/66-B 6/66	(2)
No.509		0-6-0DH		AB	514	1966	New	Wh	(2)
1	(form. E1)	4wWE		Siemens		1907	(a)	We	(2)
2	(form. E2)	4wWE		Siemens		1908	(a)	We	(2)
E3		4w-4wWE		Siemens		1909	(a)	Ha	(2)
4	(form. E4)	4w-4wWE		Siemens		1909	(a)	Ha-We c/51	(2)

E5		0-4-4-0WE	Siemens		1909	(a)	Ha-We	c/51
								Scr 10/1965
E6		0-4-4-0WE	Siemens		1910	(a)	We	(8)
7	(form. E7)	4w-4wWE	KS	1202	1911	(a)	We	
			reb NCB		1953			(2)
8	(form. E8)	4w-4wWE	KS	1203	1911	(a)	We	(2)
9	(form. E9)	4w-4wWE	AEG	1565	1913	(a)	We	(2)
E10		4wWE	Siemens	862	1913	(a)	We	(2)
No.11		4w-4wWE	EE	1795	1951			
			Bg	3351	1951	New	We	(2)
No.12		4w-4wWE	EE	1794	1951			
			Bg	3350	1951	New	We	(2)
No.13		4w-4wWE	EE	2308	1957			
			Bg	3469	1957	New	We	(2)
No.14		4w-4wWE	EE	2599	1959			
			Bg	3519	1959	New	We	(2)
No.15		4w-4wWE	EE	2600	1959			
			Bg	3520	1959	New	We	(2)
-		4wDMTW	Bg	3585	1962	New	We	(2)

ø Fitted with Giesl ejector,
   2/1961

≠ Fitted with HE mechanical stoker,
   6/1964, but subsequently removed

(a) ex Harton Coal Co Ltd, 1/1/1947
(b) ex Ryhope Coal Co Ltd, 1/1/1947
(c) ex Washington Coal Co Ltd, 1/1/1947
(d) ex Wearmouth Coal Co Ltd, 1/1/1947
(e) ex WD, 71485, 4/1947
(f) ex WD, 75182, /1947
(g) ex WD, 75140, 6/1947
(h) ex WD, 70069, via HC, 12/1947;
    delivered 1/1/1948
(j) ex BR, NE Region, 5626, 4/1948
(k) ex No.2 Area, Philadelphia, loan,
    /1951
(m) ox DL, Lackenby Works, Middles-
    brough, Yorks, N.R., 12/1962
(n) ex No.2 Area, 28/6/1965

(1) to No.3 Area, 28/6/1965
(2) to North Durham Area, 26/3/1967
(3) ret. to No.2 Area, Philadelphia,
    c7/1951
(4) to No.3 Area, Dawdon Colliery,
    loan, 2/1966; ret. 7/1966; to North
    Durham Area, 26/3/1967
(5) to No.3 Area, Dawdon Colliery,
    loan, 1/1967; to South Durham Area,
    loan, 26/3/1967
(6) to No.3 Area, Seaham Colliery,
    7/1965
(7) to No.3 Area, Dawdon Colliery,
    7/1965
(8) to Area Central Workshops, Whitburn,
    for conversion to diesel railcar,
    10/1962; plan abandoned, and remains
    of loco scrapped 1/1966

Gauge: 2' 8½"

-		0-4-0DMF	HE	2980	1944	(a)	UTC	(1)

(a) ex No.3 Area, Blackhall Colliery,
    underground, 1/1961, for training
    instruction (static exhibit)

(1) to North Durham Area, 26/3/1967

Gauge: 2' 6"

-		4wBE	GB	2573	1955			
			reb NCB		1958	(a)	B	(1)

(a) ex Westoe Colliery, underground,
    5/1960

(1) to North Durham Area, 26/3/1967

Gauge: 2' 0"

-		4wDM	RH	187059	1937	(a)	MQ	(1)
-		4wDM	RH	189959	1938	(a)	MQ	(1)
-		4wDM	RH	199963	1939	(a)	MQ	(1)
-		4wDM	RH	287662	1950	New	MQ	(1)
-		4wDM	RH	177535	1936	(b)	MQ	(1)

No.1		4wDM	RH	371541	1954	(c)	Hn-LEW	/65
								(2)
No.2		4wDM	RH	371551	1954	(c)	Hn	(2)

(a) ex Harton Coal Co Ltd, 1/1/1947
(b) ex F.H.Lloyd & Co Ltd, Wednesbury,
    Staffs (?),c/1952
(c) ex No.2 Area, 28/6/1965

(1) to Slater & Co (Limestone) Ltd,
    9/1965
(2) to North Durham Area, 26/3/1967

| - | | 4wBE | GB | 2378 | 1953 | (a) | Wa | (1) |
| - | | 4wBE | GB | 2572 | 1955 | (b) | Ha | (2) |

(a) ex Wardley Colliery, underground,
    3/1959
(b) ex Area Central Workshops,
    Whitburn, 6/1964; prev. Heworth
    Colliery, underground

(1) returned underground by 11/1961;
    returned to surface by 11/1964;
    to North Durham Area, 26/3/1967
(2) to North Durham Area, 26/3/1967

No.2 (Mid-East Durham) Area

On 28th June 1965 this Area was divided between No.1 and No.3 Areas.

This Area received 75 locomotives. One of these was what was left of an old Hackworth engine, which was subsequently preserved at Lambton Engine Works, and another was a loco at Seaham Wagon Works which never appeared in official loco lists.

For the remainder a numbering scheme was introduced in 1948. The 54 locomotives working on the Lambton Railway kept their original numbers; locomotives at South Hetton were allocated Nos. 61 to 72, and those at the Seaham Collieries Nos. 81 to 87, the last on an age basis. New locomotives were allocated blank numbers in the list according to the location to which they were sent.

The Area operated two railways:

Hetton Railway, with loco sheds at:

| He | Hetton-le-Hole (closed 9/1959) |
| Sk | Silksworth Colliery, Sunderland |

Lambton Railway, with loco sheds at:

Hr	Harraton Colliery, near Chester-le-Street (closed 29/5/1965)
LS	Lambton Staithes, Sunderland
P	Lambton Railway Loco Sheds, Philadelphia

Other locations

Da	Dawdon Colliery
Ep	Eppleton Colliery, near Hetton-le-Hole
Hn	Herrington Colliery, New Herrington
LEW	Lambton Engine Works, Philadelphia
Mu	Murton Colliery
Se	Seaham Colliery
SWW	Seaham Wagon Works, Dawdon
SoH	South Hetton Colliery
VT	Vane Tempest Colliery, Seaham

Gauge: 4' 8½"

–	0-6-0	OC	Hackworth	✗	(c)	SoH-LEW c/48 (preserved) (1)
1	0-6-0	IC	H&C	71	1866	(a)	P Scr 8/1954
1	0-6-0DH		NBL	27410	1955	New	P-He 9/56-LS 12/56 (1)
No.2	0-6-0ST	OC	RSH	7599	1949	New	P (2)
3	0-6-0	IC	BP	550	1865	(a)	P Scr 10/1954
3	0-6-0ST	OC	RSH	7687	1951	(m)	P (1)
4	0-6-0	IC	RS ?				
	reb		BH	17	1866	(a)	P Scr 10/1954
4	0-6-0ST	OC	RSH	7688	1951	(m)	P (1)
5	0-6-2T	IC	RS	3377	1909	(a)	P (1)
6	0-6-0	IC	RS ?		1864	(a)	P (3)
6	0-6-0PT	IC	LEW		1958	(j)	P Scr 10/1964
7	0-6-0	IC	RS ?		1864	(a)	P Scr c3/1952
7	0-6-0ST	IC	HE	3820	1954	New	P (1)
8	0-6-0	IC	RS ?		1864	(a)	P (3)
8	0-6-0ST	OC	RSH	7691	1952	(m)	P (1)
9	0-6-0	IC	ED		1877	(a)	P (4)
10	0-6-2T	IC	RS	3378	1909	(a)	P (1)
11	0-4-0ST	OC	HC	1412	1920	(a)	P-He by 5/51-P /55
	reb		HC		1948		-He /57-P /59 (1)
12	0-4-0ST	OC	HL	2789	1912	(a)	P-He c8/50-P /59 -Da /60 (5)
13	0-4-0ST	OC	HL	3055	1914	(a)	He-VT /60-P 2/61 -VT 8/61 (5)
14	0-4-0ST	OC	HL	3056	1914	(a)	P-He /52-VT /60 -P 24/1/61 -Se 27/1/61 -P 5/61-Da 10/62 (5)
15	0-4-0ST	OC	HCR	169	1875	(a)	P (6)
16	0-4-0ST	OC	HCR	96	1870	(a)	P Scr 2/1952
17	0-4-0ST	OC	MW	2023	1923	(a)	LS-He /52-LS c/53 -P /58 Scr 8/1960
18	0-6-0ST	OC	BH	32	1867		
	reb		HL	1491	1935	(a)	P-VT c4/58-P /59 (7)
19	0-4-0ST	OC	MW	344	1871	(a)	P-SoH 11/47 Scr 8/1954
20	0-6-0	IC	RS	2260	1876	(a)	P Scr c8/1960
21	0-4-0ST	OC	RS	2308	1876	(a)	P Scr /1954
22	0-4-0ST	OC	HC	230	1881	(a)	P Scr c6/1958
23	0-4-0ST	OC	BH	688	1882	(a)	LS-P c/51 Scr 1/1963
24	0-4-0ST	OC	BH	832	1885	(a)	P (8)
25	0-6-0	IC	ED		1890	(a)	P Scr 5/1960
26	0-6-0	IC	ED		1894	(a)	P Scr 12/1962
27	0-6-0T	IC	RS	491	1846		
	reb		Ghd		1864		
	reb		Ghd		1873		
	reb		LEW		1904	(a)	P-SoH 3/52-P 9/53 (9)
28	0-4-0ST	OC	HL	2530	1902	(a)	P (1)
29	0-6-2T	IC	K	4263	1904	(a)	P (1)
30	0-6-2T	IC	K	4532	1907	(a)	P (1)
31	0-6-2T	IC	K	4533	1907	(a)	P (1)
32	0-4-0ST	OC	HL	2826	1910	(a)	He-P 1/47-He /51 -VT c/54-Hr /55

No.	Name	Type		Maker	Works	Year		Notes
								-P /56-LS 8/62 (1)
33		0-4-0ST	OC	HL	2827	1910	(a)	P-He c3/54-LS /60 -P /61 (1)
34		0-4-0ST	OC	HL	2954	1912	(a)	P-LS /50-P /53 -LS /60-P 12/62 -LS 6/64 (1)
35		0-4-0ST	OC	HL	3024	1913	(a)	LS-P 3/60-LS 5/61 (1)
36	(HAZARD)	0-4-0ST	OC	P	615	1896	(a)	P-SoH 3/48-P /51 -VT c/57-Se c4/58 -P /60-VT 5/61 -P 4/62-Se 5/62 -P 6/62 Scr 1/1963
37		0-6-0ST	IC	RWH	1430	1868	(g)	P Scr /1951
37		0-4-0ST	OC	RSH	7755	1953	New	LS-P /57-LS 12/60 (1)
38		0-4-0ST	OC	RSH	7756	1953	New	LS-VT 2/61-P 5/61 -Hr 10/64-P 6/65 (1)
39		0-6-0ST	IC	RWH	1422	1867	(a)	P (3)
39	(later No.39)	0-4-0ST	OC	RSH	7757	1953	New	P-LS /59-Sk 9/63 -LS by 6/64 (1)
41		0-6-0T	OC	KS	3074	1917	(a)	P-He /51 (10)
42		0-6-2T	IC	RS	3801	1920	(a)	P (1)
43		0-4-0ST	OC	GR	769	1920	(a)	P-Sk /52-P /54 -Sk /56-P c/57 -LS /58-Sk /59 -LS /60-Sk /61 -Se 5/61 (5)
44	"THE CAMEL"	0-6-0ST	OC	MW	1934	1917	(a)	
	reb	0-6-0T	OC	LEW		1951		P-LS /52-P /55 (7)
45		0-6-0ST	IC	HL	2932	1912	(a)	P-SoH 11/49-P /52 -He /56-P 2/58 (1)
46		0-6-0T	IC	MW	1813	1913	(a)	P-He /51-LS /55 -He /57-P /58 Scr 4/1960
47		0-4-0ST	OC	HL	3543	1923	(a)	P-He /50-P /52 -LS /54-P 2/59 -LS 10/60 (1)
48		0-4-0ST	OC	HL	3544	1923	(a)	He-SoH 8/4/57 -He 11/4/57-LS /60 -P c6/60-Hr 3/62 -P 10/64-Se 4/65 (5)
49		0-4-0ST	OC	MW	2035	1924	(a)	LS-He by 4/52 -P c/57-Hr 5/61 -P 3/62-Da 5/64 (5)
50		0-4-0ST	OC	MW	2036	1924	(a)	LS-P /54 (11)
50		0-4-0ST	OC	LEW		1957	(h)	P-LS 4/57-VT 11/58 (5)
51		0-6-0ST	IC	RSH	7101	1943	(e)	P (12)
52		0-6-2T	IC	NR	5408	1899	(a)	P-SoH 11/50-P 1/51 -LS /54-P /56

No.	Name	Type	Cyl	Bldr	Works No	Date	Orig	Disposal
								-LS /59-P /60 (1)
53		0-6-2T	IC	Cdf	302	1894	(a)	LS-P /52-LS /55 -P /58 (1)
54		0-6-2T	IC	Cdf	311	1897	(a)	P-LS /51-P 4/55 Scr 9/1958
55		0-6-2T	IC	K	3069	1887	(a)	LS-P /51-LS /56 -P /59 Scr c8/1961
56		0-6-2T	IC	K	3580	1894	(a)	LS-P /51 Scr 1/1964
57		0-6-2T	IC	HL	3834	1934	(a)	P Scr 5/1964
58		0-6-0ST	IC	VF	5299	1945	(a)	He-P /51-LS /59 (1)
59		0-6-0ST	IC	VF	5300	1945	(a)	P-LS 3/52-He /54 -P /57-SoH 1/59 -LS 4/62-P 1/64 (1)
60		0-6-0STø	IC	HE	3686	1948	New	P-He /57-P /60 (13)
(61)	1	0-6-0ST	OC	BH	355	1875	(b)	SoH Scr 3/1950
61		0-6-0ST	IC	HE	3821	1954	New	SoH (5)
(62)	2 HAVERHILL	0-6-0T	OC	SS	2358	1873	(b)	SoH (14)
62		0-6-0ST	IC	HE	3687	1949	New	SoH (5)
(63)	3 GLAMORGAN	0-6-0T	IC	HE	396	1886	(b)	SoH (14)
63		0-6-0ST	OC	RSH	7600	1949	New	SoH-P 11/58 (1)
64	(4 until 1948)	0-6-0ST	IC	MW	697	1878	(b)	SoH Scr 9/1954
64		0-6-0DH		NBL	27763	1959	New	SoH (5)
(65)	5	0-6-0ST	IC	MW	758	1881	(b)	SoH (14)
65		0-6-0DH		NBL	27764	1959	New	SoH (5)
(66)	6	0-6-0T	OC	BP	425	1864		
		reb SoH				1910	(b)	SoH (14)
66		0-6-0DH		NBL	27765	1959	New	SoH (5)
(67)	7	0-6-0ST	IC	Joicey	305	1883	(b)	SoH (14)
67	GORDON	0-6-2T	IC	Cdf	306	1897	(f)	SoH (15)
68	(8 until 1948)	0-6-0T	IC	RS	625	1848		
		reb				1866		
		reb				1923	(b)	SoH Scr 11/1953
68		0-6-0ST	IC	HE	3784	1953	New	SoH (5)
(69)	9 SIR GEORGE	0-6-0ST	IC	RS	624	1848		
		reb				1905		
		reb				1911	(b)	SoH Scr 11/1953
69		0-6-0STø	IC	HE	3785	1953	New	SoH (5)
(70)	10 WHITFIELD	0-6-0ST	IC	SS	1011	1857	(b)	SoH (14)
71	(11 until c/1950)	0-6-0ST	IC	VF	5308	1945	(b)	SoH (5)
72	(12 until c/1950)	0-6-0ST	IC	VF	5309	1945	(b)	SoH (5)
81	SEAHAM	0-4-0ST	OC	HL	2701	1907	(d)	Da-P 7/62 Scr 5/1964
82	DAWDON No.2	0-4-0ST	OC	HL	3492	1921	(d)	Da-P 2/62 Scr 1/1964
83	(LONDONDERRY)	0-4-0ST	OC	AB	1724	1922	(d)	Se-He /56-Se c4/56 (5)
84	CASTLEREAGH	0-4-0ST	OC	AB	1885	1924	(d)	VT-Se /55-VT /56 (5)
85	VANE TEMPEST	0-6-0ST	OC	RS	4112	1935	(d)	VT-P 8/60 Scr 1/1964
86	STEWART	0-4-0ST	OC	AB	2160	1943	(d)	Se (5)
87	WYNYARD	0-4-0ST	OC	AB	2165	1944	(d)	Da-VT /50-Da /52 (5)
-		4wPM		MH	L116	1939	(d)	SWW (5)
-		4wDM		LEW		c1955	(n)	SWW (5)
2505/78		4wDM		FH	3852	1957		
		reb NCB				1958	(k)	P (1)
-		4wDH		TH	105V	1962	(p)	P-Se-P (16)

264

⚡ date of building doubtful
∅ fitted with mechanical stoker, HE 3686 in 3/1962 and HE 3785 in 5/1964

(a) ex Lambton, Hetton & Joicey
Collieries Ltd, 1/1/1947
(b) ex South Hetton Coal Co Ltd,
1/1/1947
(c) ex South Hetton Coal Co Ltd,
1/1/1947; loco derelict and parts
missing
(d) ex Londonderry Collieries Ltd,
1/1/1947
(e) ex WD, Antwerp, Belgium, 75065,
6/1947
(f) ex WD, Longmoor, Hants, 70205, 1/1948
(g) ex No.6 Area, Morrison Busty Colliery, 10/1949
(h) rebuild of 50 MW 2036/1924 with
boiler from 24 BH 832/1885, 4/1957
(j) built from parts of 6 RS?, 8 RS? and
39 RWH 1422/1867, 7/1958; other
parts of these locos scrapped /1951
(k) ex No.5 Area, Brandon Pit House
Colliery, 2/1962
(m) ex DL, Acklam Works, Middlesbrough,
Yorks, N.R., 12/1962; delivered
1/1963
(n) built from Aveling Baring dumper
(p) ex Tees Side Bridge & Engineering Co
Ltd, 10/9/1962 for trials

(1) to No.1 Area, 28/6/1965
(2) to No.1 Area, Wearmouth Colliery,
and ret by 7/1951; to Dawdon Colliery, 1/1961; to Philadelphia,
c4/1961; to No.1 Area, 28/6/1965
(3) parts used to build 6 0-6-OPT;
remains of 6 Scr /1951; of 8 Scr
/1952 and of 39 Scr /1951
(4) to No.5 Area, Brandon Colliery,
8/1961, as stationary boiler for
heating colliery baths (loan);
ret. 6/1962; loaned to No.5 Area,
Brancepeth Colliery, for same
purpose, 9/1962; to No.4 Area,
1/1/1963; and purchased 10/1963
(5) to No.3 Area, 28/6/1965
(6) to No.8 (Central Northumberland)
Area, Horton Grange Colliery,
c/1948; loan; ret. c/1950. Scr
2/1962
(7) to Seaham Harbour Dock Co Ltd,
2/1960
(8) withdrawn /1956, and boiler used
to rebuild 50 MW 2036/1924;
remains Scr 5/1959
(9) withdrawn /1963: awaiting decision
on future; to No.1 Area, 28/6/1965
(10) to No.5 Area, Brandon Colliery,
loan, 11/1959; ret. 15/2/1961; to
No.3 Area, Horden Colliery,
21/2/1961, loan; ret. 7/1961; to
No.3 Area, Blackhall Colliery,
loan, 4/1962; ret. 7/1962; to No.5
Area, Brandon Pit House Colliery,
loan, 11/1962; to No.4 Area,
1/1/1963; ret. 12/1963; Scr 10/1964
(11) withdrawn 1/2/1956; rebuilt with
boiler from 24 BH 832/1885 - see (h)
(12) to No.7 (South Northumberland)
Area, Rising Sun Colliery, loan,
by 3/1949; to No.8 (Central Northumberland) Area, Seaton Delaval
Colliery, c6/1949; to No.4 Area,
Chilton Colliery, 11/1949; to No.5
Area, Brandon Colliery, 1/1950; to
No.4 Area, Chilton Colliery,
23/6/1950; to No.4 Area, Dean &
Chapter Colliery, 26/6/1950;
finally ret. to Philadelphia,
4/1952; to South Hetton Colliery,
7/1952; ret. to Philadelphia,
12/1955; to No.1 Area, 28/6/1965
(13) to No.6 Area, Springwell Bank Foot,
loan, 9/1962; to No.3 Area, Sherburn Hill Colliery, 10/1962; to
No.3 Area, Blackhall Colliery,
3/1963; ret. to Philadelphia,
4/1965; to No.1 Area, 28/6/1965
(14) Scr between 18/5/1948 and 20/7/1948
(15) to British Railways (WR), Caerphilly Works, for preservation,
1/1962

Gauge: 2' 0"

No.1		4wDM	RH	371541	1954	New	Hn	(1)	
No.2		4wDM	RH	371551	1954	New	Hn	(1)	
-		4wDM	RH	223747	1944	(a)	SoH	(2)	

(a) ex East Midlands Division, Lea   (1) to No.1 Area, 28/6/1965
    Hall Colliery, Staffs, 5/1956   (2) to No.3 Area, 28/6/1965

-		4wBE	Atlas	2458	1946	(a)	Ep-Se 9/63		
							Scr	/1964	
-		4wBE	WN	BS1312/1	1955	(b)	Mu	(1)	
-		4wBE	WN	BS199/2	1954	(c)	Ep	(1)	
-		4wBE	WN	TJ189/3	1952	(d)	Mu	(1)	

(a) ex Eppleton Colliery, underground, (1) to No.3 Area, 28/6/1965
    8/1959
(b) ex Murton Colliery, underground,
    12/1959
(c) ex Eppleton Colliery, underground,
    via LEW (reps), 3/1963
(d) ex Murton Colliery, underground,
    3/1964

No.3 (South-East Durham) Area

On 28th June 1965 this Area was enlarged by the addition of the southern
half of the former No.2 Area, together with Ryhope Colliery from No.1 Area.

On 26th March 1967 this Area was combined with the former No.4 Area to
form the new South Durham Area (q.v.)

No numbering scheme was introduced by this Area for the 16 locomotives
acquired from its constituent owners, and locomotives taken over from other
Areas continued to carry their former names or numbers. Seven locomotives were
acquired by the Area on its own account; one was numbered, two were named and
the remainder carried neither number nor name.

Locations

STC   Area Training Centre, Seaham (no locos from 10/1966)
Bl   Blackhall Colliery
Da   Dawdon Colliery
DH   Deaf Hill Colliery (closed 25/2/1967)
E   Easington Colliery
Ep   Eppleton Colliery, Hetton-le-Hole
H   Horden Colliery
LEW   Lambton Engine Works, Philadelphia
Mu   Murton Colliery
R   Ryhope Colliery (closed 25/11/1966)
Se   Seaham Colliery
SWW   Seaham Wagon Works, Dawdon
SH   Sherburn Hill Colliery (closed 7/8/1965)
Sh   Shotton Colliery
SoH   South Hetton Colliery
T   Thornley Colliery
VT   Vane Tempest Colliery, Seaham
WH   Wheatley Hill Colliery
WG   Wingate Grange Colliery (closed 26/10/1962)

Gauge: 4' 8½"

No.	Name	Type	Cyl	Builder	Works No	Year	Note	History
19		0-6-0ST	OC	BH	704	1882	(a)	E-Bl by 4/50-E c/51 Scr /1958
1		0-6-0ST	OC	AB	912	1901	(a)	E Scr c/1957
6		0-4-0ST	OC	KS	4027	1919	(a)	E Scr 8/1964
-		0-6-0ST	IC	VF	5305	1945	(a)	
				reb WB	7613	1959		E (1)
	(HORDEN)	0-6-0ST	OC	P	1310	1914	(b)	Bl-Sh c/52-Bl 11/56 -H c6/58-Sh 1/60 -E 9/60-Sh 11/60 -T c4/61-Sh c7/61 (1)
	HORDEN (No.4)	0-6-0ST	OC	HL	2737	1907	(b)	H-Bl 12/54-H 7/55 -Bl 6/57-H 7/61 Scr 6/1966
	HORDEN No.2	0-6-0ST	OC	HL	3440	1920	(b)	
				reb WB	6292	1962		H (1)
	HORDEN No.3	0-6-0ST	OC	HL	3568	1923	(b)	H-Bl c/54-Sh /56 -H c/57-Bl 3/59 Scr 4/1964
	HORDEN (No.5)	0-6-0T	IC	RSH	7305	1946	(b)	H-Bl 1/63 (1)
(No.1)		0-6-0ST	OC	AB	1015	1904	(b)	Sh-H /55-Sh c/57 (1)
14		0-6-0ST	OC	Joicey				
				reb Tudhoe		1899		
				reb Thornley		1928	(c)	T Scr c10/1949
18		0-6-0ST	OC	RWH	1622	1874	(c)	T Scr 8/1956
No.24		0-6-0ST	OC	AB	1321	1913		
				reb Thornley		1929	(c)	T-E /58-Se 5/66 (1)
No.17		0-6-0T	OC	KS	3098	1917		
				reb Thornley		1938	(c)	T (1)
No.27		0-6-0T	OC	KS	3100	1917		
				reb Thornley		1942	(c)	T-WH 7/65-T c9/65 (1)
-		0-6-0ST	IC	VF	5307	1945	(c)	
				reb HE	58936	1959		T-Bl /47 -LEW (reps) 10/63 -Bl 5/64 (1)
-		6wDM		KS	4421	1929	(d)	WG-DH 3/64 (1)
No.2		0-6-0DM		AB	423	1958	New	T-WH /59 (1)
	ACTIVE	0-4-0ST	OC	RS	3075	1901		
				reb R.Shaw		1931		
				reb NCB		1954	(e)	SH-T 7/60 Scr 5/1963
148	TAURUS	0-4-0ST	OC	HL	3384	1919	(e)	SH-H (via HE reps) 7/61-T c3/63 (1)
	MONTY	0-6-0ST	IC	RSH	7146	1944	(e)	SH-Bl 9/59-SH 1/60 -H 11/60-SH 3/64 -H 8/65 (1)
6D		0-6-0DM		HE	5342	1958	(e)	SH-LEW c2/62 -SH 5/62-E 11/65 (1)
10D		0-6-0DM		HE	5304	1959	(f)	SH-R (via AB reps) 11/65-Se 11/66 (1)
41		0-6-0T	OC	KS	3074	1917	(g)	H (2)

No.	Name	Type		Builder	Works No.	Date		Disposal		
60		0-6-0ST⚡	IC	HE	3686	1948	(h)	SH-Bl	3/63	(3)
	HORDEN No.1	0-6-0DH		AB	488	1964	New	H	(1)	
	EASINGTON No.1	0-6-0DH		AB	491	1964	New	E	(1)	
-		0-6-0DH		AB	498	1965	New	Bl	(1)	
1		0-6-0ST	OC	P	1403	1916	(j)	R	(4)	
(2)		0-6-0ST	OC	P	1455	1918	(j)	R	(4)	
12		0-4-0ST	OC	HL	2789	1912	(k)	Da	(1)	
14		0-4-0ST	OC	HL	3056	1914	(k)	Da-VT (via LEW reps) 10/65	(1)	
49		0-4-0ST	OC	MW	2035	1924	(k)	Da	(1)	
87	WYNYARD	0-4-0ST	OC	AB	2165	1944	(k)	Da	Scr	11/1966
43		0-4-0ST	OC	GR	769	1920	(k)	Se	Scr	2/1967
83	(LONDONDERRY)	0-4-0ST	OC	AB	1724	1922	(k)	Se	(1)	
48		0-4-0ST	OC	HL	3544	1923	(k)	Se	(1)	
86	STEWART	0-4-0ST	OC	AB	2160	1943	(k)	Se	Scr	2/1967
-		4wPM		MH	L116	1939	(k)	SWW	(5)	
-		4wDM		LEW		c1955	(k)	SWW	(1)	
71		0-6-0ST	IC	VF	5308	1945	(k)	SoH	(1)	
72		0-6-0ST	IC	VF	5309	1945	(k)	SoH	(1)	
62		0-6-0ST	IC	HE	3687	1949	(k)	SoH	(1)	
68		0-6-0ST	IC	HE	3784	1953	(k)	SoH	(1)	
69		0-6-0ST∅	IC	HE	3785	1953	(k)	SoH	(1)	
61		0-6-0ST	IC	HE	3821	1954	(k)	SoH	(1)	
64		0-6-0DH		NBL	27763	1959	(k)	SoH	(1)	
65		0-6-0DH		NBL	27764	1959	(k)	SoH	(1)	
66		0-6-0DH		NBL	27765	1959	(k)	SoH	(1)	
13		0-4-0ST	OC	HL	3055	1914	(k)	VT	(6)	
50		0-4-0ST	OC	MW	2036	1924				
		reb LEW				1957	(k)	VT	(1)	
84	CASTLEREAGH	0-4-0ST	OC	AB	1885	1926	(k)	VT	(1)	
38		0-4-0ST	OC	RSH	7756	1953	(m)	Se	(1)	
11		0-4-0ST	OC	HC	1412	1920				
		reb HC				1948	(n)	Da	(7)	
37		0-4-0ST	OC	RSH	7755	1953	(p)	Da	(1)	
-		0-4-0DH		AB	523	1967	New	Se	(1)	
-		0-4-0DH		AB	524	1967	New	Se	(1)	
-		0-4-0DH		AB	547	1967	-	(8)		
-		0-4-0DH		AB	548	1967	-	(8)		
-		0-6-0	OC	Hackworth	⚡⚡		(k)	LEW preserved	(9)	

⚡ fitted with Hill-Bigwood mechanical stoker, subsequently removed
∅ fitted with HE mechanical stoker, 4/1964
⚡⚡ date of building doubtful

(a) ex Easington Coal Co Ltd, 1/1/1947
(b) ex Horden Collieries Ltd, 1/1/1947
(c) ex Weardale Steel, Coal & Coke Co Ltd, 1/1/1947
(d) ex Ravenglass & Eskdale Railway, via R.R.Dunn (dealer), Bishop Auckland, 12/1955
(e) ex No.4 Area (with colliery), 4/1959
(f) ordered by No.4 Area, but delivered new to No.3 Area
(g) ex No.2 Area, Philadelphia, loan, 2/1961
(h) No.2 Area loco; ex No.6 Area, Springwell Bank Foot, 10/1962
(j) ex No.1 Area, 28/6/1965
(k) ex No.2 Area, 28/6/1965
(m) ex No.1 Area, Philadelphia, 7/1965
(n) ex No.1 Area, Philadelphia, loan, 2/1966
(p) ex No.1 Area, Philadelphia, loan, 1/1967

(1) to South Durham Area, 26/3/1967
(2) to No.2 Area, Philadelphia, 5/1961; loaned from there to Blackhall Colliery, 4/1962; ret. 7/1962
(3) to No.2 Area, Philadelphia, 4/1965; purchased from No.1 Area, 7/1965; and del. to Dawdon Colliery; to South Durham Area, 26/3/1967
(4) sold for scrap, 1/1967
(5) loco out of use; to South Durham Area, 26/3/1967
(6) sold for scrap, 8/1966
(7) to No.1 Area, Philadelphia, 7/1966
(8) ordered by No.3 Area, but not delivered before reorganisation
(9) to Workshops Division, 26/3/1967

Gauge: 2' 3½"

-	0-4-0DMF	HE	3524	1947	(a)	STC	Scr 10/1966
-	0-4-0DMF	HE	4631	1953	(a)	STC	Scr 10/1966
-	0-4-0DMF	HE	4632	1953	(a)	STC	Scr 10/1966

(a) ex Elemore Colliery, underground,
    7/1965

Gauge: 2' 0"

-	4wDM	RH	217986	1942	(a)	H	(1)
-	4wDM	RH	211614	1941	(b)	H	(1)
-	0-4-0DM	RH	338425	1955	New	DH-H 1/66 (1)
-	0-4-0DM	RH	338426	1955	New	DH-B1 3/67 (1)
-	0-4-0DM	HE	4502	1954	(c)	DH	(2)
-	0-4-0DM	RH	393979	1956	New	DH	(1)
-	0-4-0DM	RH	392157	1956	(d)	B1-LEW 10/66 (1)
-	4wDM	RH	223747	1944	(e)	SoH	Scr 9/1966
-	4wDM	RH	223690	1944	(f)	SoH	(1)

(a) ex ?, 9/1948
(b) ex Bungey, c/1951
(c) ex Horden Colliery, underground,
    9/1955
(d) ex No.4 Area, Fishburn Colliery,
    underground, 10/1962
(e) ex No.2 Area, 28/6/1965
(f) ex ?, Newcastle-upon-Tyne, dealer,
    3/1966; prev. R.W.Bell & Co Ltd,
    contrs, Newcastle-upon-Tyne

(1) to South Durham Area, 26/3/1967
(2) to Shotton Colliery for reps,
    5/1959, prior to being sent
    underground (q.v.)

-	4wBE	WN	BS199/2	1954	(a)	Ep	(1)
-	4wBE	WN	TJ189/3	1952	(a)	Mu	(1)
-	4wBE	WN	BS1310/2	1955	(a)	Mu	Scr 12/1966

(a) ex No.2 Area, 28/6/1965

(1) to South Durham Area, 26/3/1967

No.4 (South-West Durham) Area

On 1st January 1963 this Area was enlarged by the addition of the
greater part of the former No.5 Area.

On 26th March 1967 this Area was combined with the former No.3 Area
to form the new South Durham Area (q.v.).

This Area did not introduce any numbering scheme for the 40 locomotives
acquired from its constituent companies. Steam locomotives purchased new from
1949 onwards were numbered in a series from No.50 upwards, while new diesel
locomotives purchased between 1956 and 1959 were numbered from 1 upwards,
suffixed by 'D', though this was not fully maintained. Second-hand locomotives,
and those acquired from the old No.5 Area continued to carry their former names
or numbers.

Locations

TTC	Area Apprentice Training Centre, Tursdale
TCW	Area Central Workshops, Tursdale
A	Arnghyll Colliery, near Copley (closed 5/5/1951)
AuP	Auckland Park Disposal Point (operated for (latterly) NCBOE - to Derek Crouch (Contractors) Ltd, 3/1958)
Bs	Bildershaw Colliery, near West Auckland (closed 16/10/1956)
Bo	Bowburn Colliery
Bp	Brancepeth Colliery, Willington
BPH	Brandon Pit House Colliery, near Meadowfield
C	Chilton Colliery (merged with Dean & Chapter Colliery, 28/5/1960)
D&C	Dean & Chapter Colliery, Ferryhill (closed 15/1/1966)
EH	East Hetton Colliery, near Kelloe
F	Fishburn Colliery
HW	Hole-in-the-Wall Colliery, Crook (closed 21/11/1964)
LP	Langley Park Colliery
Le	Leasingthorne Colliery, near Coundon (merged with Dean & Chapter Colliery, 1/1/1950)
M	Mainsforth Colliery, Ferryhill Station
NB	New Brancepeth Coal Stocking Site (closed 3/1964)
PWG	Pease's West Garage, Crook (closed 9/1964)
Ra	Randolph Colliery, Evenwood (locos sold, 5/1957)
SH	Sherburn Hill Colliery (to No.3 Area, 4/1959)
Th	Thrislington Colliery, West Cornforth (closed 4/3/1967) Thrislington Coal Preparation Plant, West Cornforth
TG	Trimdon Grange Colliery
TC	Tudhoe Coking Plant (locos administered by this Area; to No.5 Area, c/1950)
Tu	Tursdale Colliery, Cornforth (loco stored)
WA	West Auckland Coal Preparation Plant

Gauge: 4' 8½"

	HENRY CORT	0-4-0ST	OC	BH	607	1881	(a)	AuP	Scr	1/1949	
	ACTIVE	0-4-0ST	OC	RS	3075	1901					
				reb R.Shaw		1931					
				reb NCB		1954	(a)	AuP-M 2/50-Le c/53 -M c/53-SH 7/58			
								(1)			
113	COLONEL BELL	0-4-0ST	OC	MW	1697	1906	(a)	Bo	Scr	c11/1949	
	PLUTO	0-6-0ST	OC	HL	2655	1906	(a)	Bo-C 6/47 -AuP 11/49-C 2/51 -AuP 3/58			
								(2)			
107	CARLTON No.1	0-6-0ST	OC	HL	2732	1907	(a)	Bo	(3)		
	ATLAS	0-6-0ST	OC	HL	2612	1905	(a)	C-AuP 12/51 -D&C c1/55-F 6/57 -M 7/58-TCW 6/64		Scr	10/1964
108	HECTOR	0-6-0ST	OC	HL	2613	1905	(a)	C-AuP 6/48 -D&C 9/48		Scr	6/1960
106	ERIMUS	0-6-0ST	OC	HL	2595	1904	(a)	D&C-M c/55 -D&C by 7/55		Scr	4/1963
116	CARLTON No.7	0-6-0ST	OC	HL	2607	1905	(a)	D&C	Scr	8/1959	
	GEORGE V	0-6-0ST	OC	HL	2833	1910	(a)	D&C	Scr	12/1962	
	ANGELA	0-4-0ST	OC	AE	1793	1918	(a)	D&C-C 1/51 -AuP 2/51-M 12/51 -TCW 12/61		Scr	5/1963
110	HERCULES	0-6-0ST	OC	HL	2654	1906	(a)	Le-C by 10/48 -TCW 12/60-WA 1/62			

```
                                                      -Bp (reps) 5/65
                                                      -WA 8/65
                                                         (4)
No.1  "CLARENCE"    0-4-0ST  OC  BH      985   1889
                                reb AB  2847   1904  (a)  M-AuP 6/47-M c8/48
                                                         -AuP 4/49-Ra 6/49
                                                         -M c/55-Ra c/56
                                                         -AuP c/56
                                                            (5)
30                 0-4-0ST  OC  P       669   1897
                                reb R.Shaw     1930  (a)  M-Bo c8/47
                                                         -M c10/47-TG 12/49
                                                          Scr    /1952
      MARY BELL    0-4-0ST  OC  MW     1422   1899  (a)  M-TG c8/47
                                                          Scr   8/1951
148   TAURUS       0-4-0ST  OC  HL     3384   1919  (a)  M-SH 11/57
                                                            (1)
      CHARLIE      0-4-0ST  OC  HC     1402   1922  (a)  M      Scr   9/1959
No.10              0-4-0ST  OC  BH     1095   1896  (a)  SH     Scr   4/1959
No.26 (JOHN EVANS) 0-4-0ST  OC  P       629   1896  (a)  SH     Scr   6/1954
No. 1              0-6-0ST  IC  H&C
                                reb HL 9294   1914  (a)  SH-AuP c7/48
                                                          Scr   1/1949
No. 4              0-6-0T   OC  HC     1335   1918  (a)  SH     Scr   4/1959
      PATRIOT      0-6-0T   IC  BV            1920  (a)  SH-Bo c7/47
                                                         -AuP 1/54-M c/57
                                                            (6)
"No.2"             0-4-0ST  OC  BH      992   1890  (a)  Tu     Scr    /1952
      KELLOE       0-4-0ST  OC  P       560   1893
                                reb R.Shaw     1930  (b)  EH     Scr   4/1949
      EAST HETTON  0-4-0ST  OC  HL     2279   1893  (b)  EH     Scr   9/1951
49    (WALTER SCOTT) 0-6-0ST IC HL     2484   1900  (b)  EH-D&C c/52
                                                          Scr    /1956
      HUSTLER      0-4-0ST  OC  P      1337   1913  (c)  Ra     Scr  12/1948
      RANDOLPH     0-4-0ST  OC  RSH    7043   1942  (c)  Ra     (7)
      WINSTON      0-4-0ST  OC  RSH    7159   1945  (c)  Ra     (7)
20                 0-4-0ST  OC  HL     2713   1907  (d)  F      Scr   7/1966
3                  0-4-0ST  OC  P      1194   1912  (d)  F      Scr   c/1957
No.4               0-6-0T   OC  HL     3104   1915  (d)  F      Scr   9/1958
1                  0-6-0ST  IC  P      1423   1916  (d)  F      Scr   c/1957
7                  0-4-0ST  OC  P       677   1897  (d)  Th     Scr   c/1950
25                 0-4-0ST  OC  HL     2456   1900  (d)  Th-F/54 Scr  6/1958
6                  0-4-0ST  OC  AB     1085   1907  (d)  Th     Scr  c1/1952
8                  0-4-0ST  OC  HL     2798   1909  (d)  Th     Scr   7/1963
13                 0-4-0ST  OC  HL     2823   1910  (d)  Th-EH 3/47
                                                         -Bo c12/48-EH 1/59
                                                          Scr   6/1963
5                  0-6-0ST  OC  BH(?)
                                reb HL        1910
                                reb Thornley  1925  (e)  TC     (8)
21                 0-4-0ST  OC  KS     4028   1919  (e)  TC     (8)
      MONTY (75196 0-6-0ST  IC  RSH    7146   1944  (f)  D&C-C 3/48-SH 1/49
        until 4/1948)                                       (1)
No.140             0-6-0T   OC  HC     1821   1948  New  C-M 12/60
                                                            (4)
51                 0-6-0ST  IC  RSH    7101   1943  (g)  C      (9)
No.50              0-4-0ST  OC  AB     2277   1950  New  Th     (4)
No.51              0-4-0ST  OC  AB     2276   1949  New  M-EH 3/62-D&C 11/65
                                                           (10)
No.52              0-4-0ST  OC  AB     2275   1949  New  Bo     (4)
21 (No.53 until 1953) 0-4-0ST OC RSH   7539   1949  New  EH     Scr  c8/1966
22 (No.54 until 1953) 0-4-0ST OC AB    2320   1952  New  EH-TG 5/64-EH 8/64
                                                           (4)
No.55              0-4-0ST  OC  AB     2321   1952  New  TG     (4)
No.56.             0-4-0ST  OC  AB     2322   1952  New  Bo-EH 5/64
                                                           (11)
```

271

No.	Name	Type		Builder	Works No.	Year		Disposal
No.57		0-4-0ST	OC	AB	2341	1953	New	Th (4)
1D		0-6-0DM		HE	4986	1956	New	D&C-EH (via HE reps) 10/66 (4)
D2		0-6-0DM		RH	395303	1956	New	WA-F 3/10/57 -WA 8/10/57 -Bp (reps) 9/63 -WA 11/63 (4)
58		0-4-0ST	OC	HL	2639	1905	(h)	WA-TCW 11/61 Scr 6/1963
AMW & B No.129		0-6-0T	OC	HC	1541	1924	(j)	F Scr 7/1966
3D		0-6-0DM		HE	5302	1958	(k)	M (4)
-		0-6-0DM		RH	408296	1957	New	F (4)
5D		0-6-0DM		HE	5341	1958	New	F (4)
6D		0-6-0DM		HE	5342	1958	New	SH (1)
7D		0-6-0DM		HE	5177	1958	New	D&C-EH 12/65 (4)
8D		0-6-0DM		HE	5303	1958	New	Bo (4)
9D		0-6-0DM		HE	5382	1958	New	D&C-F 1/66 (4)
10D		0-6-0DM		HE	5304	1959	-	(12)
11D		0-6-0DM		HE	5305	1959	New	M (4)
501		0-4-0ST	OC	AB	2281	1950	(m)	Be-LP 1/63-EH 4/65 -D&C 11/65 (10)
9		0-6-0	IC	ED		1877	(n)	Bp Scr 8/1965
11		0-4-0T	OC	HL	2685	1906		
				reb RSH/NCB		1958	(m)	Bp-EH 5/63-TG 6/64 -EH 12/64 Scr 3/1966
	HOWDEN DENE No.1	0-6-0T	OC	HL	2880	1911	(m)	Bp (4)
	CECIL	0-6-0T	IC	HC	1524	1924	(m)	Bp Scr 11/1964
	STAGSHAW	0-6-0ST	OC	HL	3513	1927		
				rob HE/NCB		1961	(m)	Bp (4)
	HOWDEN DENE No.2	0-6-0ST	OC	RS	4113	1937	(m)	Bp (4)
505		0-6-0ST	IC	HE	3819	1954	(m)	Bp (4)
	THE ALLY	0-6-0ST	OC	HL	3185	1916	(m)	BPH Scr 11/1965
41		0-6-0T	OC	KS	3074	1917	(p)	BPH (13)
14		0-4-0ST	OC	P	1467	1917	(m)	BPH-NB 10/63 Scr 8/1964
	LEAZES	0-6-0ST	OC	HL	3830	1934	(m)	BPH-Bp 4/64 (14)
	DELTA ("W.D. No.2"until 1964)	0-6-0ST	IC	HE	3189	1944	(m)	BPH (4)
	GAMMA ("W.D. No.1"until 1964)	0-6-0ST	IC	WB	2779	1945	(m)	BPH (4)
	"STELLA No.2"	0-4-0ST	OC	RSH	7799	1954	(m)	BPH (15)
2505/79	ALPHA	0-6-0DH		NBL	27592	1957	(m)	BPH (4)
	B No.35	0-4-0ST	OC	HL	3254	1917	(m)	LP Scr 7/1965
	"LITTLEBURN"	0-4-0ST	OC	KS	4143	1919	(m)	LP-NB 9/63 Scr 8/1964
504		0-4-0ST	OC	RSH	7662	1950	(m)	LP-EH 4/65 Scr 9/1966
	POWERFUL	0-6-0ST	OC	MW	1602	1903	(q)	NB Scr 10/1963
	BETA	0-6-0DH		NBL	27717	1957	(r)	BPH (4)

(a) ex Dorman, Long & Co Ltd, 1/1/1947
(b) ex East Hetton Collieries Ltd, 1/1/1947
(c) ex Randolph Coal Co Ltd, 1/1/1947
(d) ex Henry Stobart & Co Ltd, 1/1/1947
(e) ex Weardale Steel, Coal & Coke Co Ltd, 1/1/1947

(1) to No.3 Area, 4/1959
(2) on loan to Derek Crouch (Contractors) Ltd from 18/3/1958; to Chilton Colliery, c5/1958. Scr 12/1962
(3) dismantled by 5/1954; remains at Bowburn and Area Central Workshops, Tursdale, scrapped in 1956

(f) ex WD, 75196, c11/1947
(g) ex No.8 (Central Northumberland)
    Area, Seaton Delaval Colliery,
    11/1949
(h) ex No.6 Area, Leadgate, loan,
    10/1956; purchased 1/1957
(j) ex RAF (Air Ministry), Cranwell,
    Lincs, 10/1957
(k) New to Dean & Chapter Colliery, but
    transferred to Mainsforth Colliery
    on same day
(m) ex No.5 Area, 1/1/1963
(n) ex No.5 Area, 1/1/1963, on loan
    from No.2 Area; purchased, 10/1963.
    Used as stationary boiler for
    heating colliery baths
(p) ex No.5 Area, 1/1/1963, on loan
    from No.2 Area
(q) ex No.5 Area, 1/1/1963; loco stored
    on site
(r) ex Andrew Barclay, Sons & Co Ltd,
    Kilmarnock, Ayrshire, Scotland,
    8/1963; previously NBL demonstrat-
    ion loco

(4) to South Durham Area, 26/3/1967
(5) to Derek Crouch (Contractors) Ltd,
    18/3/1958
(6) to Derek Crouch (Contractors) Ltd,
    Auckland Park D.P., c10/1958
(7) to Randolph Coke & Chemical Co Ltd,
    20/5/1957
(8) to No.5 Area, c/1950
(9) to No.5 Area, Brandon Colliery,
    1/1950; ret. to Chilton Colliery,
    23/6/1950; to Dean & Chapter
    Colliery, 26/6/1950; to No.2 Area,
    Philadelphia, 4/1952
(10) sold for scrap, 1/1966
(11) to North Northumberland Area,
    Ashington, 10/1966
(12) ordered by No.4 Area for Sherburn
    Hill Colliery, but not delivered
    before colliery was transferred to
    No.3 Area, 4/1959
(13) ret. to No.2 Area, Philadelphia,
    12/1963
(14) sold for scrap, 2/1966
(15) to Coal Products Division, Norwood
    Coking Plant, Gateshead, 5/1963

Gauge: 2' 6"

-		0-6-0DM	HE	4060	1950	(a)	PWG	(1)	
-		0-6-0DM	HE	4061	1950	(a)	PWG	(1)	

(a) ex No.5 Area, 1/1/1963; stored

(1) to No.2 Area, Lambton Engine Works,
    9/1964, for modification prior to
    being sent underground at Thris-
    lington Colliery

Gauge: 2' 3"

-		4wDM	HE	4175	1949			
		reb	TCW		1960	(a)	M	(1)
-		4wDM	HE	6628	1966	New	M	(1)

(a) ex Area Central Workshops, Tursdale, (1) to South Durham Area, 26/3/1967
    3/1960; previously 2' 0" gauge

Gauge: 2' 0"

-	4wDM	HE	3518	1948	New	A-Bs	/52-TCW	/60
							Scr	/1960
-	4wDM	HE	3655	1949	New	A-Bs	/52-D&C 3/58	
							(1)	
-	4wDM	HE	4175	1949	New	A-Bs	/52-TCW	/56
							(2)	
-	4wDM	HE	3496	1947	(a)	PWG	(3)	
-	4wDM	HE	4554	1954	(b)	BPH-EH	5/66	
							(1)	
-	4wDM	HE	4441	1952	(b)	HW	Scr 11/1964	
-	0-4-0DM	RH	392154	1956	(c)	TTC	(1)	

(a) ex No.5 Area, 1/1/1963; loco stored
(b) ex No.5 Area, 1/1/1963
(c) ex Fishburn Colliery, underground,
    1/1967, for use as demonstration
    loco in apprentice training

(1) to South Durham Area, 26/3/1967
(2) stored until /1959, when work begun
    to convert loco to 2' 3" gauge
    (q.v.)
(3) to Ayle Coal Co Ltd, Alston,
    Cumberland, 7/1963

No.5 (Mid-West Durham) Area

On 1st January 1963 this Area was divided between Nos.4 and 6 Areas, the latter then becoming No.5 Area (q.v.).

No numbering scheme was introduced by this Area for the 37 locomotives acquired from its constituent companies. New locomotives were numbered from 501 upwards, but this scheme was not completed.

This Area operated two railways :

Beamish Railway, with loco sheds at:

Bm	Beamish Engine Works
HH	Handen Hold Colliery, West Pelton

Sacriston Railway (closed 2/1955), with sheds at:

BFW	Bank Foot, Waldridge
Sa	Sacriston Colliery

Other locations

BFC	Bank Foot Coking Plant, Crook (locos administered by No.5 Area; closed 10/1960)
Be	Bearpark Colliery (rail traffic ceased, 9/1962)
Bp	Brancepeth Colliery, Willington
Br	Brandon 'C' Colliery, Brandon (merged with Brandon Pit House Colliery, 20/8/1960)
BPH	Brandon Pit House Colliery, near Meadowfield
EHH	East Hedley Hope Colliery (closed 31/1/1959)
HW	Hole-in-the-Wall Colliery, Crook
LEW	Lambton Engine Works, Philadelphia (repairs only)
LP	Langley Park Colliery
Ma	Malton Colliery, near Lanchester (NCB shunting ceased about 1956)
NB	New Brancepeth Colliery (closed 17/7/1953) and Coking Plant (locos administered by No.5 Area - closed 7/1957) New Brancepeth Coal Stocking Site
PWG	Pease's West Garage, Crook
Rd	Roddymoor Colliery, Crook (rail traffic ceased in 1962)
SoP	South Pelaw Colliery, near Chester-le-Street (NCB shunting ceased in 1954)
SGC	Stella Gill Coking Plant, Pelton Fell (locos administered by No.5 Area; plant closed, 4/1962)
TC	Tudhoe Coking Plant, Spennymoor (locos administered by No.5 Area; closed 8/1955)
UM	Ushaw Moor Colliery (NCB shunting ceased in 1948)
WB	West Brandon Drift, near Waterhouses (closed 22/8/1958)
WT	West Thornley Colliery, near Tow Law (no locos from 10/1957)

```
Gauge: 4' 8½"

(No.25)              0-6-0ST  OC  CF     1155  1898  (a)  Be-EHH c/48
                                                           Scr  c5/1949
      MOSTYN         0-4-0ST  OC  LG ⚡         1906  (a)  Be-Ma c/48
                                                         -Be c12/49
                                                           Scr   /1950
      FLORENCE       0-6-0ST  OC  HC      880  1910  (a)  Be   Scr  9/1961
      "LITTLEBURN"   0-4-0ST  OC  KS     4143  1919  (a)  Be-LP c8/51
                                                         -Be c/53-EHH 4/56
                                                         -Be 8/56-LP 11/61
                                                           (1)
      -              4wPM         Bearpark           (a)  EHH  Scr c12/1952
      MARGARET       0-6-0ST  IC  AB     1005  1904
                                 reb AB  8833  1924  (b)  BFW-Bm 11/55
                                                         -HH c1/58-Bm c12/58
                                                         -Br 8/59-Bp 1/60
                                                           Scr   5/1962
      CECIL          0-6-0T   IC  HC     1524  1924  (b)  BFW-Bm 5/55-Be 2/57
                                                         -Br 3/57-BFC 4/58
                                                         -Rd 11/60-Bp 10/61
                                                           (1)
1     SACRISTON      0-4-0ST  OC  CF     1210  1901  (b)  Sa   Scr   /1951
(2    CHARLAW)       0-4-0ST  OC  P      1180  1912  (b)  Sa-LP 12/55
                                                         -SGC 7/61
                                                           Scr   /1962
      B No.16        0-4-0ST  OC  RS     2725  1890
                                 reb HL  5809  1920  (c)  LP-EHH 3/50-LP /51
                                                           Scr   2/1962
      B No.35        0-4-0ST  OC  HL     3254  1917  (c)  LP   (1)
3     TWIZELL        0-6-0T   IC  RS     2730  1891  (d)  Bm-HH /51-Bm /52
                                                         -HH c/57-Bm /58
                                                         -HH c1/61-Bm c8/61
                                                           (2)
4     LINHOPE        0-6-0T   IC  RS     2822  1895  (d)  Bm-HH c/53-Bm /55
                                                         -HH /58-Bm /59
                                                         -HH c5/60-Bm c6/60
                                                           (2)
No.5  MAJOR          0-6-0T   IC  K      4294  1905
                                 reb HL  2812  1931  (d)  Bm   (2)
40                   0-6-0ST  IC  RS     1919  1869
                                 reb HL  1182  1930  (d)  HH-Bm c8/51
                                                         -HH by 2/52-Bm /54
                                                           Scr  11/1955
38                   0-6-0ST  IC  RWH    1478  1870  (d)  HH   Scr  10/1951
(2    STANLEY)       0-6-0ST  IC  RS     2014  1872  (d)  HH-Bm /51
                                                           Scr  12/1961
      STELLA No.1    0-4-0ST  OC  HL     3504  1923  (e)  SGC-Bp 3/52
                                                         -Br 1/53-BPH 9/60
                                                           Scr   7/1961
4                    0-6-0ST  OC  Joicey 210   1869
                                 reb HL  7409  1897
                                 reb Thornley  1924
                                 reb Thornley  1931  (f)  NB-Bp 1/53
                                                           Scr   3/1955
      POWERFUL       0-6-0ST  OC  MW     1602  1903  (f)  NB-LP c/54-NB c/54
                                                         Be by 3/56-NB 8/56
                                                           (3)
      THE ALLY       0-6-0ST  OC  HL     3185  1916  (f)  NB-Br 7/57-BPH 9/60
                                                           (1)
11                   0-4-0T   OC  HL     2685  1906
                                 reb RSH/NCB    1958  (g)  BFC-Rd 11/60
                                                         -Bp 3/62
                                                           (1)
12    PATRICIA       0-4-0ST  OC  HL     2993  1913  (g)  BFC  Scr   6/1960
```

14		0-4-0ST	OC	P	1467	1917	(g)	BFC-Rd c8/60 -BPH 3/62 (1)
16		0-4-0ST	OC	RS	2325	1894	(g)	UM-EHH /48-LP /51 -EHH /51 Scr 3/1957
	SILKSTONE	0-6-0ST	IC	MW	341	1871		
				reb		1903		
				reb		1925		
				reb		1935	(h)	Ma-Be 5/56-EHH 8/56 Scr 4/1959
	(HAMSTEELS)	0-6-0ST	IC	MW	569	1875		
				reb MW		1922	(h)	Ma-Bp 7/53 Scr c4/1954
	-	0-6-0ST	OC	BH	1034	1892		
				reb HL	3668	1904	(h)	Ma Scr /1948
	BRANDON	0-6-0ST	IC	MW	200	1867	(j)	Bp Scr c/1948
	(HELMINGTON)	0-4-0ST	OC	RWH	1882	1882	(j)	Bp Scr 6/1952
	HOWDEN DENE No.1	0-6-0T	OC	HL	2880	1911	(j)	Bp (1)
	STAGSHAW	0-6-0ST	OC	HL	3513	1927		
				reb HE/NCB		1961	(j)	Bp (1)
	HOWDEN DENE No.2	0-6-0ST	OC	RS	4113	1937	(j)	Bp (1)
	WILLINGTON	0-4-0ST	OC	AE	1509	1907		
				reb TJR		1920	(j)	Br Scr c11/1953
	JUPITER	0-4-0ST	OC	MW	1880	1915	(j)	Br Scr 2/1962
	LEAZES	0-6-0ST	OC	HL	3830	1934	(j)	Br-BPH 9/60 (1)
75256 : later "W.D.No.1"		0-6-0ST	IC	WB	2779	1945	(j)	Br-BPH 9/60 (1)
	-	4wPM		NCB (Bm)		1948	(k)	SoP Scr /1954
51		0-6-0ST	IC	RSH	7101	1943	(m)	Br (4)
5		0-6-0ST	OC	BH				
				reb HL		1910		
				reb Thornley		1925	(n)	TC Scr c3/1956
21		0-4-0ST	OC	KS	4028	1919	(n)	TC Scr c3/1956
501		0-4-0ST	OC	AB	2281	1950	New	Be (1)
502		0-4-0ST	OC	AB	2317	1950	New	SGC-LEW /61-SGC1/62 (5)
503	"SACRISTON"	0-4-0ST	OC	RSH	7605	1949	New	Sa-Bm /55-HH c9/59 -Bm c5/60-HH 6/60 (2)
504		0-4-0ST	OC	RSH	7662	1950	New	LP (1)
	DAVID	0-4-0ST	OC	RSH	6940	1938	(p)	SGC (2)
505		0-6-0ST	IC	HE	3819	1954	New	Bp (1)
	"STELLA No.2"	0-4-0ST	OC	RSH	7799	1954	New	Bp-Br 11/55-BFC 5/56 -Br 1/58-BPH 9/60 (1)
39	BURNHOPESIDE	0-6-0ST	OC	BH	888	1887		
				reb HL		1931	(q)	HH (6)
2505/78		4wDM		FH	3852	1957	New	Br-BPH 9/60
				reb NCB		1958		(7)
2505/79		0-6-0DH		NBL	27592	1957	New	Br-BPH 9/60 (1)
41		0-6-0T	OC	KS	3074	1917	(r)	Br (8)
	"W.D. No.2"	0-6-0ST	IC	HE	3189	1944	(s)	Bp-BPH 12/60 (1)
9		0-6-0	IC	ED		1877	(t)	Br (9)
	-	0-4-0BE		Booth			(u)	BFC Scr
	-	0-4-0DH		NBL	27414	1954	(v)	Br (10)

⨋ probably a rebuild of an older locomotive built by another firm.

(a) ex Bearpark Coal & Coke Co Ltd, 1/1/1947
(b) ex Charlaw & Sacriston Collieries Co Ltd, 1/1/1947

(1) to No.4 Area, 1/1/1963
(2) to No.5 Area, 1/1/1963
(3) from date of becoming coal stocking site loco stored in shed; to No.4

(c) ex Consett Iron Co Ltd, 1/1/1947
(d) ex Lambton, Hetton & Joicey Collieries Ltd, 1/1/1947
(e) ex Mid-Durham Carbonisation Co Ltd, 1/1/1947
(f) ex New Brancepeth Colliery Co Ltd, 1/1/1947
(g) ex Pease & Partners Ltd, 1/1/1947
(h) ex Sir S. A. Sadler Ltd, 1/1/1947
(j) ex Strakers & Love Ltd, 1/1/1947
(k) built from a Guy lorry
(m) ex No.2 Area, Philadelphia, /1949, loan
(n) ex No.4 Area, c/1950
(p) ex North Bitchburn Fireclay Co Ltd, Rough Lea Brickworks, 4/1954
(q) ex No.6 Area, Craghead Colliery, c/1955, loan
(r) ex No.2 Area, Philadelphia, 10/1959, loan
(s) ex Derek Crouch (Contractors) Ltd, NCBOE Auckland Park DP, 11/1960; delivered 12/1960
(t) ex No.2 Area, Philadelphia, for use as stationary boiler for heating colliery baths, 8/1961, loan
(u) ex Pease & Partners Ltd, OOU at Vesting Day
(v) ex NBL for trials, /1955

Area, 1/1/1963
(4) ret. to No.2 Area, Philadelphia, /1949; ex No.4 Area, Chilton Colliery, to Brandon Colliery, 1/1/1950; ret. to No.4 Area, Chilton Colliery, 6/1950
(5) to No.6 Area, Norwood Coking Plant, 11/1962
(6) ret. to No.6 Area, Craghead Colliery, by 1/1956
(7) to No.2 Area, Philadelphia, 2/1962
(8) ret. to No.2 Area, Philadelphia, 2/1961; ex No.2 Area, Philadelphia, to Brandon Pit House Colliery, loan, 11/1962; to No.4 Area, 1/1/1963
(9) ret. to No.2 Area, Philadelphia, 6/1962; ret. on loan to Brancepeth Colliery, 9/1962; loan transferred to No.4 Area, 1/1/1963
(10) ret. to NBL, 5/1955

Gauge: 3' 6"

15		0-4-0ST	OC	MW reb LG		c1900	(a)	BFC	Scr	c3/1948

(a) ex Pease & Partners Ltd; OOU at Vesting Day

Gauge: 2' 6"

-		0-6-0DM	HE	4060	1950	New	WB-PWG	12/59 (1)
-		0-6-0DM	HE	4061	1950	New	WB-PWG	12/59 (1)
-		0-6-0DM	HE	4062	1951	New	WB	(2)

(1) to No.4 Area, 1/1/1963
(2) to No.1 Area, Wearmouth Colliery, /1951, for underground

Gauge: 2' 0"

-	4wDM	HE	3496	1947	New(a)	HW-WT 4/56 -HW 10/57-PWG 7/60 (1)
-	4wDM	HE	4441	1952	New	HW (1)
-	4wDM	HE	4442	1952	New	HW-PWG 7/60 Scr /1962
-	4wDM	HE	4444	1953	New	HW Scr 5/1962
-	4wDM	HE	4554	1954	New	HW-BPH 9/60 (1)

(a) loaned to Crossley Sanitary Pipes Ltd, Crook, c/1955
(1) to No.4 Area, 1/1/1963

On 1st January 1963 this Area was combined with part of the original No.5 Area to form a new No.5 Area.

On 26th March 1967 this Area was combined with the former No.1 Area to form the new North Durham Area (q.v.).

In 1949 a numbering scheme was introduced for locomotives in this Area. With the exception of one loco scrapped in 1947 and a steam crane, all the locomotives taken over on Vesting Day were included, although some had already been scrapped. These were allocated Nos. 1 - 76 according to the Group in which the loco was in 1949, except that the former Consett Iron Co. locomotives were kept roughly as a group, and locomotives at Norwood Coking Plant (administered by the Area) were numbered at the end of the list. One locomotive on order at Vesting Day and two locomotives purchased second-hand in 1947 were also included in this section. The allocation was as follows:

'A' Group	:	1 - 17
'B' Group	:	18 - 33
'C' Group	:	34 - 40
'D' Group and Consett Iron Co	:	41 - 60
'E' Group	:	61 - 72
Norwood Coking Plant	:	73 - 76

Locomotives bought by the Area, with the exception of those above, were numbered from 77 upwards. With the purchase of two diesels in 1960, a new scheme was started, beginning at 101, but the locomotives acquired for the Bowes Railway in 1965 were not included, as they were purchased by the Division and included in a Divisional numbering scheme.

The locomotives taken over from the former No.5 Area on 1st January 1963 were not re-numbered.

The Area operated the following railways:

Bowes Railway, on which locos were kept at:

K	Kibblesworth Colliery (temporary)
MH	Marley Hill Loco Shed
SBF	Springwell Bank Foot Loco Shed, Leam Lane
SW	Springwell Workshops (repairs only)

Chopwell & Garesfield Railway, later known as the Derwenthaugh Railway, and including the Whittonstall line, with loco sheds at:

Ch	Chopwell Colliery (shed closed 2/1961)
D	Derwenthaugh Loco Shed, Swalwell

There was also a small shed at Garesfield Colliery, High Spen, but transfers involving it were too frequent to be recorded.

Pelaw Main Railway, with loco sheds at:

BF	Blackhouse Fell, near Birtley (closed 31/1/1959)
EB	Eighton Banks, Galloping Green (closed 1948)
OE	Ouston 'E' Colliery (closed 31/1/1959)
PMS	Pelaw Main Staithes, Bill Quay (closed 5/1964)
RA	Ravensworth Ann Colliery, near Birtley
SP	Shop Pit, near Lamesley
S	Starrs, Wrekenton

On the closure of part of this Railway in January 1959, the last three sheds were taken over by the Bowes Railway.

Stella Unit Railway ⚡, with loco sheds at:

G	Greenside Colliery (shed closed 8/1961)
St	Stargate Colliery, near Ryton (shed closed 8/1961)

⚡ no official title

On 1st January 1963 the Area also took over

Beamish Railway, with loco sheds at:

Bm	Beamish Engine Works (closed 7/8/1963)
HH	Handen Hold Colliery, West Pelton (shed closed, 24/12/1966)

Other locations

Ad	Addison Colliery, Ryton (closed 22/2/1963)
AxP	Axwell Park Colliery, Swalwell (closed 7/8/1954)
BB	Blaydon Burn Colliery, Blaydon (closed 3/11/1956)
CV	Clara Vale Colliery (closed 5/2/1966)
Con	Consett Iron Works (temporary)
CD	Clockburn Drift, Winlaton Mill (later included with Marley Hill Colliery)
Cr	Craghead Colliery (rail traffic ceased, 1/7/1966)
ET	East Tanfield Colliery (rail traffic ceased,1959)
Hm	Hamsterley Colliery (rail traffic ceased,6/1953)
Lg	Leadgate Loco Shed (closed 21/12/1965)
LD	Lilley Drift, Rowlands Gill (closed 5/1/1957)
MB	Morrison Busty Colliery, Annfield Plain
MTC	Morrison Area Apprentice Training Centre, Annfield Plain
NC	Norwood Coking Plant, Gateshead (locos administered by No.6 Area – to Coal Products Division, 1/1/1963)
SM	South Medomsley Colliery, near Dipton (merged with Eden Colliery, 30/12/1961)
SGC	Stella Gill Coking Plant, Pelton Fell (closed: locos on salvage work until 11/1963)
TL	Tanfield Lea Colliery (closed 25/8/1962)
VG	Victoria Garesfield Colliery, Rowlands Gill (closed 13/7/1962)
W	Watergate Colliery, near Sunniside (closed 20/8/1964)

Gauge: 4' 8½"

No.	Name								History	

1   (VICTORIA No.4)   0-6-0ST IC RS   2847 1896
                                   reb   1904 (g) VG   Scr 10/1962
2   (VICTORIA No.5)   0-6-0ST IC RS   2879 1900 (g) VG   Scr 10/1962
3   ASHINGTON   0-4-0ST OC B   303 1883
                                   reb RS 2987 1900 (g) LD-BB 3/57-D 4/58
                                                           Scr   3/1959
4   (BLAYDON BURN No.2) 0-4-0ST OC HC   1514 1923 (g) BB-Ch by 9/50
                                                           -D 11/50-BB /51
                                                           -D 2/52-Ch 3/52
                                                           -D 8/52-VG 4/55
                                                           -D 8/56-St 12/56
                                                           -Ad /59-G 5/60
                                                           -Ad c6/61-CV 11/62
                                                           -MH 12/64-MB 7/65
                                                           (1)
5   (ENERGY)   0-4-0ST OC HC   764 1906
                                   reb HL 8860 1934 (g) BB-D 6/58
                                                           Scr 12/1960
6   (INDUSTRY)   0-4-0ST OC HC   749 1906 (g) BB-D 11/59
                                                           Scr 11/1962
7   (BETTY)   0-4-0ST OC RS   3376 1909 (g) BB-Ad c/59
                                                           Scr   7/1963
8   (GEORGE)   0-4-0ST OC HC   1190 1916 (g) BB-D 11/58
                                                           Scr   3/1959
9   (GERALD)   0-4-0ST OC HL   2426 1899 (g) BB-Ad /57-BB c/57
                                                           -Ad /58-St /59
                                                           -Ad c/59-St c/60
                                                           -Ad c5/61-CV 6/61
                                                           Scr   5/1966
10 (WALDRIDGE No.2)   0-4-0ST OC HC   674 1903
                                   reb HL 4161 1925 (g) W-LD c/51-BB c/51
                                                           -CV c/59-Ad c6/61
                                                           Scr   1/1962
11 (AXWELL)   0-4-0ST OC HL   2330 1896 (g) AxP-BB c/48
                                                           -AxP c/51-LD c/54
                                                           -St c/56-Ad c/57
                                                           Scr   8/1960
12 (STELLA)   0-4-0ST OC HL   2583 1904
                                   reb HL   1931 (k) Ad-CV c/51-D c/53
                                                           -CV/54 Scr   7/1960
13 (EMMA)   0-4-0ST OC HL   2740 1908 (k) Ad-Lg 5/56
                                                           Scr   2/1959
14 (JOAN)   0-4-0ST OC HL   2617 1905 (k) St-Ad c/50-CV c5/60
                                                           Scr   7/1963
15 (MURIEL)   0-4-0ST OC HL   2694 1907 (k) St-Ad c/58-St c/59
                                                           -Ad c5/61
                                                           Scr   7/1963
16 (VICTORY)   0-4-0ST OC HL   3438 1920 (k) G-St c/51-Ad c/60
                                                           Scr 10/1961
17 CLARA   0-4-0ST OC HL   2281 1895 (k) CV   Scr c12/1960
-   3   0-6-2ST IC BH   938 1888
                                   reb HL 3045 1903 (a) SBF   Scr   9/1947
18 (4)   0-4-0ST OC KS   4030 1919 (a) MH-TL 4/48-MH 9/49
                                                           -ET 5/50-TL 10/50
                                                           -MH 4/51-TL 1/53
                                                           -ET 2/53-MH 3/53
                                                           -TL 11/54-MH 12/55
                                                           -TL 5/59-MH 8/62
                                                           -CV 6/64
                                                           Scr   5/1966
19 6   0-6-0ST OC HL   2515 1901
                                   reb LG   1930 (a) SBF   Scr   4/1964

20	9	0-6-0PT	IC	SS	4051	1894		MH-SBF 5/47	
				reb Caerphilly		1930	(a)		Scr 4/1964
(21)	10	0-6-0PT	IC	NBL	16628	1905			
				reb Sdn		1924	(a)	SBF Scr 2/1950	
22	(11)	0-6-0ST	OC	HL	3103	1915	(a)	SBF-MH (via reps at RSH) 9/50 (1)	
23	(12)	0-6-0ST	OC	HL	2719	1907			
				reb RS		1932	(a)	MH-D 12/50-MH 12/51 (1)	
24	13	0-6-0ST	IC	HL	2545	1902	(a)	SBF-D (loan)6/6/58 -SBF 20/6/58 -SW 10/65 (1)	
25	14	0-6-0ST	IC	HL	3569	1923	(a)	MH-SBF 6/47 -SW 10/65 (1)	
26	15	0-6-0T	IC	HE	1506	1930	(a)	MH-SBF 9/49 -SW 10/65 (1)	
27	16	0-6-0ST	IC	VF	5288	1945	(a)	SBF-D 6/65 (1)	
28	(17)	0-6-0ST	IC	VF	5298	1945	(a)	MH (1)	
29	18	0-6-0T	OC	HC	1255	1917	(n)	SBF-D 10/63 Scr 4/1966	
30	19	0-4-0ST	OC	AB	1883	1927	(p)	MH-BB 1/48-SBF 3/48 -Cr c1/49-MH 8/49 -SBF c10/49 -AxP 12/49-MH c1/50 -SBF 9/53-RA 5/63 -Lg 1/64 Scr 8/1965	
31	21 (EDEN until 5/1949)	0-4-0ST	OC	HL	2481	1900	(e)	TL-MH 5/49-TL 9/49 -MH 12/50-TL 4/51 -MH 11/51-TL 1/52 -MH 1/53-TL 2/53 -MH 11/54-TL 12/55 -MH 7/57-TL c1/58 -MH 5/59-TL 11/59 -MH 8/62-Lg 12/62 Scr 4/1964	
32	(STANLEY No.1) later (No.1)	0-4-0ST	OC	AB	1659	1920	(h)	ET-MH 5/50 -ET 10/50-MH 7/54 (1)	
(33)	STANLEY No.2	0-4-0ST	OC	HCR					
				reb LG		1914	(h)	ET Scr 6/1952	
34	HOLMSIDE	0-6-0ST	OC	RSH	6943	1938	(d)	MB-MH (reps) 7/65 -MB 1/66 (1)	
35	HOLMSIDE No.2	0-6-0ST	OC	CF	1204	1901	(d)	MB Scr 5/1962	
36	(HOLMSIDE No.3)	0-6-0ST	OC	HL	2956	1912	(d)	Cr-MB c/50-D 9/57 -Cr 12/57-SW(reps) 10/64 Scr 4/1966	
37	(HOLMSIDE No.4)	0-6-0ST	OC	HL	3528	1922	(d)	MB-Cr c/51-HH 8/66 (1)	
38	(CRAGHEAD)	0-6-0ST	OC	BH	971	1890			
				reb HL		1911	(d)	MB Scr 1/1966	
39	(BURNHOPESIDE)	0-6-0ST	OC	BH	888	1887			
				reb HL		1931	(d)	Cr-No.5 Area(loan) c/55-Cr by 1/57 Scr 9/1959	
(40)	37	0-6-0ST	IC	RWH	1430	1868	(e)	TL-MB c5/47 (2)	

41	(A No. 5)	0-6-0PT	IC	K	2509	1883		
				reb HC		1900	(b)	Ch-D 6/49-Ch /52
								-D 1/54(1)
42	(A No. 6)	0-6-0PT	IC	K	2510	1883		
				reb RS	2915	1899	(b)	Con-D 10/47-Ch 1/54
								-Lg c/55-D by 9/55
								-Ch /56-D 3/57
								-Ch 4/57-D 6/57
								-Ch 1/58-D 2/58
								(1)
43	(A No. 7)	0-6-0PT	IC	K	3905	1899	(b)	Con-Lg 1/49
								Scr 2/1964
44	(A No. 9)	0-6-0PT	IC	HL	3891	1936	(b)	Ch-D /49
								-Ch by 9/50-D /51
								-Ch by 6/52-D c/53
								-Ch 9/55-D c7/60
								-MB 11/60-D 3/61
								Scr 6/1964
45	(A No.10)	0-6-0PT	IC	K	4051	1901	(b)	Ch-D 8/48
								Scr 6/1964
46	(A No.11)	0-6-0PT	IC	HL	2641	1906	(b)	D-Lg 3/49
								Scr 6/1966
47	(A No.13)	0-6-0PT	IC	NLE	249	1908	(b)	Con-Lg 1/49
								Scr 6/1963
48	(A No.14)	0-6-0PT	IC	HL	3080	1914	(b)	D-Ch /57-D 6/9/57
								-Ch 23/9/57-D c7/60
								Scr 6/1964
(49)	A No.15	0-6-0PT	IC	K	5179	1917	(b)	Con-Lg 1/49
								Scr c/1953
50	(A No.16)	0-6-0PT	IC	HC	1448	1921	(b)	Con-D (reps) 12/48
								-Lg 2/49
								Scr 10/1964
51	(A No.18)	0-6-0PT	IC	HL	3905	1937	(b)	Con-Lg 1/49
								-MB 3/61-Lg 3/63
								Scr 6/1966
52	(B No. 7)	0-4-0ST	OC	HL	3474	1920	(b)	Con-Ch c/48
								-D 7/48-Con 9/48
								-Lg 1/49-SP 5/66
								(1)
53	(B No.11)	0-4-0ST	OC	HL	3391	1919	(b)	Ch-D c/50-Ch 6/2/52
								-D 20/2/52
								Scr 9/1962
54	(HAMSTERLEY No.1)	0-4-0ST	OC	HL	3467	1920	(c)	Hm-D (reps) 3/48
	(later D54)							-Hm 6/48-D 5/7/53
								-OE 7/53-BF c/59
								-OE 7/60-SBF 2/61
								-S 9/62-SBF c11/62
								-RA 5/63
								Scr 12/1965
55		0-4-0ST	OC	AB	1811	1923	(j)	SM-Lg /52-SM /53
								-Lg c/54
								Scr /1959
(56)	B No.21	0-4-0ST	OC	HL	2377	1897	(b)	D Scr 3/1951
57	(B No.22)	0-4-0ST	OC	CF	1163	1898	(b)	D-Ad 5/56
								-VG c12/56-D 4/62
								Scr 11/1962
58	(B No.26)	0-4-0ST	OC	HL	2639	1905	(b)	D-Hm 3/48-D 6/48
								-Lg 1/50-D c6/50
								-Lg 3/51-SM by 10/55
								-Lg c6/56
								(3)
59	(B No.28)	0-4-0ST	OC	HL	3003	1913	(b)	Con-Lg 1/49-D 3/51
								-VG 12/53-D 3/54
								-St 1/55-D 3/56
								Scr 9/1960

```
60   (B No.19)            0-4-0ST   OC  HL    3752  1930  (b)  D-Ch 8/52-D 10/52
                                                               -BB 9/57-D 12/57
                                                                        (4)
     E No.13 (ROSIE)      0-4-0VBCr OC  HL    2984  1913  (b)  D       Scr by 3/1957
61   DERWENT              0-6-0ST   OC  AB     970  1903
                                       reb RSH      1945  (f)  OE-SP c12/52
                                                               -OE c5/60-SP c9/60
                                                               -S 5/63-D 8/64
                                                               -CV 9/65
                                                                    Scr    4/1966

62   TYNE                 0-4-0ST   OC  AB     786  1896
                                       reb AB       1940  (f)  EB-RA c1/51
                                                               -OE c12/51-PMS c/54
                                                               -OE c7/55-PMS c/56
                                                                    Scr 10/1964

63   1308                 0-4-0T    IC  Ghd     27  1891  (f)  SP-RA by 6/51-EB
                                                               (for reps) c9/52
                                                               -RA c5/53-W c2/54
                                                               -RA c12/54-OE c1/57
                                                               -RA c2/58-OE c1/59
                                                               -RA c12/59
                                                                    Scr  10/1963

64   1310                 0-4-0T    IC  Ghd     38  1891  (f)  RA-EB by 6/51
                                                               -RA c/52-SP c1/53
                                                               -RA c5/53-OE(reps)
                                                                c/54-S c5/55
                                                               -RA c2/57-OE c1/58
                                                               -RA c1/59-W c12/59
                                                                        (5)

65   HENRY C.EMBLETON     0-6-0T    OC  HL    3766  1930  (f)  BF-OE c5/53-BF c/54
                                                               -OE 1/59-D 2/59
                                                                        (1)

66   CHARLES NELSON       0-4-0ST   OC  P     1748  1928  (f)  S-EB by 9/50-OE
                                                               (reps)c12/51-RA c/54
                                                               -S 1/55-RA c3/60
                                                               -SP c6/61-RA c1/63
                                                               -SP (reps) 4/64
                                                               -S 8/64-RA 6/9/65
                                                               -S 21/9/65-RA 4/66
                                                               -S 5/66-RA 5/3/67
                                                               -S 11/3/67
                                                                        (1)

67   NCB-PELAW            0-4-0ST   OC  P     2093  1947  (m)  SP-S 12/49-EB c5/50
                                                               -OE c1/51-EB c12/51
                                                               -S c/54-SP c1/60
                                                               -RA c/61-SP (reps)
                                                                5/63-RA 4/64-SP
                                                                6/9/65-RA 21/9/65
                                                               -S (reps) 4/66
                                                               -RA 5/66-S (reps)
                                                                5/3/67-RA 11/3/67
                                                                        (1)

68   CLAUDE               0-4-0ST   OC  HL    2347  1896  (g)  BB-W c/50
                                                               -OE c12/59-RA c/60
                                                                    Scr  10/1963

69   CHARLES PERKINS      0-4-0T    OC  HL    2986  1913  (f)  PMS    Scr  10/1964
(70) 900                  0-4-0T    IC  Ghd     35  1888  (f)  RA     Scr   /1947
(71) 26A                  4-4-0T    OC  BP     772  1867  (f)  EB     Scr  12/1948
(72) 44A                  4-4-0T    OC  BP     868  1869  (f)  BF-EB c/48
                                                                    Scr  12/1948

73   HASWELL              0-6-0T    IC  HC    1251  1917  (g)  NC-D 1/48-VG  /49
                                                               -D c/50
                                                                    Scr  10/1952

74   NELL                 0-4-0ST   OC  HC    1191  1916  (g)  NC     Scr   6/1962
75   ERNEST BURY          0-6-0ST   OC  HL    3282  1917  (g)  NC     (6)
```

No.	Name	Type	Cyl	Builder	Wks No	Date	Status	Disposal	Qty
76	VENTURE	0-4-0ST	OC	HL	2837	1910	(g)	NC	(6)
77	"NORWOOD"	0-6-0ST	OC	RSH	7412	1948	New	NC	(6)
78		0-4-0ST	OC	RSH	7538	1949	New	BB-G by c/51-Ad /54 -G by 10/55-D 1/60	(1)
79		0-6-0ST	OC	RSH	7545	1949	New	MB-MH (reps) 1/66 -MB 2/67	(1)
80		0-6-0ST	OC	RSH	7546	1949	New	Cr-MB 10/66	(1)
81		0-4-0ST	OC	RSH	7604	1949	New	S-SP c12/49-S c/53 -SBF 5/62-S (via SW reps) 10/65	(1)
82	(D1)	0-6-0ST	IC	HE	3689	1949	New	D	(1)
83	(20)	0-6-0ST	IC	HE	3688	1949	New	MH	(1)
84		0-6-0ST	OC	RSH	7641	1949	New	Lg-MB 3/63	(1)
85	(22)	0-4-0ST	OC	AB	2274	1949	New	SBF-ET 7/54 -TL 10/57-ET c11/57 -TL 4/58-MH 11/59	(1)
86	(23)	0-6-0ST	IC	RSH	7751	1953	New	SBF-D 9/65	(1)
87		4wVBT	VCG	S	9583	1955	New	D	Scr 1/1965
88		4wVBT	VCG	S	9584	1955	New	D	(7)
89	(86 till 10/1955)	4wVBT	VCG	S	9581	1955	New	D	Scr 1/1965
90	24	0-6-0ST	IC	HE	3833	1955	New	SBF-D 9/66	(1)
91		0-6-0PT	IC	HL	3952	1938	(q)	Lg	Scr 4/1964
101		4wDM		FH	3922	1959	New	S-SBF 11/62 -S by 9/63 -SBF 3/64-S c8/64 -SP 11/3/67, ret. to S same day	(1)
102		4wDM		FH	3923	1959	New	S-SBF 9/63-S 3/64 -SBF c6/64 -K 1/10/64 -SBF 9/10/64-S 9/65 -SW (reps) 12/65 -SBF 2/66	(1)
60		0-4-0ST	OC	NCB	(D)	1960	(r)	D	Scr 4/1966
41 ∅		0-6-0T	OC	KS	3074	1917	(s)	MB	(8)
60 ∅		0-6-0ST✄	IC	HE	3686	1948	(t)	SBF	(9)
No.92	502	0-4-0ST	OC	AB	2317	1950	(u)	NC	(6)
3	TWIZELL	0-6-0T	IC	RS	2730	1891	(v)	Bm-HH 7/63	(1)
4	LINHOPE	0-6-0T	IC	RS	2822	1895	(v)	Bm	Scr 7/1963
No.5	MAJOR	0-6-0T	IC	K	4294	1905	(v)	Bm-HH 7/63-D 4/66	(1)
503	"SACRISTON"	0-4-0ST	OC	RSH	7605	1949	(v)	HH	(1)
	DAVID	0-4-0ST	OC	RSH	6940	1938	(v)	SGC	Scr 11/1963
103		0-6-0DH		S	10157	1963	New	SBF	(1)
104		0-6-0DH		S	10158	1963	New	SBF	(1)
(88)		4wDH		TH	135C	1964	(w)	D	(1)
No.500		0-6-0DH		HE	6611	1965	New	SBF	(1)
No.502		0-6-0DH		HE	6613	1965	New	SBF	(1)
No.503		0-6-0DH		HE	6614	1965	New	SBF	(1)
No.504		0-6-0DH		HE	6615	1965	New	SBF	(1)

∅ No.2 Area's numbering   ✄ Fitted with mechanical stoker

(a) ex John Bowes & Partners Ltd,
1/1/1947
(b) ex Consett Iron Co Ltd, 1/1/1947
(c) ex Hamsterley Colliery Ltd, 1/1/1947
(d) ex Holmside & South Moor Collieries
Ltd, 1/1/1947
(e) ex Lambton, Hetton & Joicey Collieries Ltd, 1/1/1947
(f) ex Pelaw Main Collieries Ltd,
1/1/1947
(g) ex Priestman Collieries Ltd,1/1/1947
(h) ex South Derwent Coal Co Ltd,
1/1/1947
(j) ex South Medomsley Colliery Co Ltd,
1/1/1947
(k) ex Stella Coal Co Ltd, 1/1/1947
(m) ordered by Pelaw Main Collieries
Ltd; delivered to NCB 9/1947
(n) ex Port of London Authority, 61,
11/1947; delivered after reps at HC,
7/1948
(p) ex ICI, Ardeer Works, Ayrshire,
Scotland, LOCH RANNOCH, via Ridley
Shaw, 12/1947
(q) ex Consett Iron Co Ltd, 11/1957
(r) reb at Derwenthaugh of HL 3752/1930
with HC boiler and larger cab, /1960
(s) ex No.2 Area, Philadelphia, loan,
5/1961
(t) ex No.2 Area, Philadelphia, for
trials with mechanical stoker,9/1962
(u) ex No.5 Area, Stella Gill Coking
Plant, 10/1962
(v) ex No.5 Area, 1/1/1963
(w) reb of S 9584/1955

(1) to North Durham Area, 26/3/1967
(2) to No.2 Area, Philadelphia,10/1949
(3) to No.4 Area, West Auckland Coal
Preparation Plant, loan, 10/1956;
sold, 1/1957
(4) reb. at Derwenthaugh, /1960 (see(r))
(5) to Steam Power Trust, /1965, for
Middleton Railway, Leeds, Yorks,
W.R., 6/1965
(6) to Coal Products Division,1/1/1963
(7) to TH for conversion to diesel,
1/1964
(8) to No.2 Area, Philadelphia, 7/1961
(9) to No.3 Area, Sherburn Hill
Colliery, 10/1962

N.B. At Vesting Day A No. 17 0-6-0PT IC HC 1449/1921 was at
Derwenthaugh, and was transferred to Consett Iron Works
2/7/1947; as far as is known this locomotive did not
come on to NCB books.

Locomotives on trial, 1958

Gauge: 4' 8½"

	-	0-6-0D	NBL			(a)	SBF	(1)
	-	0-6-0DE	YE	2668	1958	(b)	SBF	(2)
	-	0-6-0DM	HE			(c)	SBF	(3)
No.5		0-6-0DM	WB	3123	1957	(d)	SBF	(4)
	-	0-4-0DE	BT			(e)	SBF	(5)

(a) ex NBL, 3/1958
(b) ex YE, 4/1958
(c) ex HE, 5/1958
(d) ex West Midlands No.2 (Cannock
Chase) Area, Littleton Colliery,
Staffs, 9/1958
(e) ex BT, 12/1958

(1) ret. to NBL, 4/1958
(2) to Northern (Northumberland &
Cumberland) Division, No.3 Area,
Ashington, for trials, 5/1958
(3) ret. to HE, 6/1958
(4) to West Midlands No.2 (Cannock
Chase) Area, Hilton Main Colliery,
Staffs, 10/1958
(5) ret. to BT, 12/1958

Gauge: 4' 0"

-		4wWE	M.Coulson & Co				
			Spennymoor c1901 (a) Ch	Scr	c/1951		

(a) ex Consett Iron Co Ltd, 1/1/1947;
    derelict at coke ovens (closed)

Gauge: 3' 6"

-	0-6-0DMF	HC	DM632	1947	(a)	CD	(1)
-	0-6-0DMF	HC	DM639	1947	(a)	CD	(1)
-	0-6-0DMF	HC	DM709	1955	New	CD	(1)
-	0-6-0DMF	HC	DM993	1956	New	CD	(1)
-	0-6-0DMF	HC	DM1063	1957	New	CD	(1)

(a) ex No.1 (Fife & Clackmannan) Area,   (1) to North Durham Area, 26/3/1967
    Scotland, Rothes Colliery,   /1950;
    installed, 3/1952

Gauge: 2' 0"

-	4wDM	RH	268873	1952	(a)	MTC	(1)
-	4wDM	RH	268874	1952	(a)	MTC	(1)

(a) ex Watergate Colliery, underground, (1) to North Durham Area, 26/3/1967
    10/1965

Durham Division, Coking Plants

    On 1st January 1963 these were transferred to the new Coal Products
Division (Northern Region) (q.v.).
    All the plants below were shunted by locomotives from the Areas in
which they were situated, but as part of the rebuilding of all these plants
a coke car loco was introduced where one was not already used.

Locations

BpC	Brancepeth Coking Plant, Willington
DC	Derwenthaugh Coking Plant, Winlaton Mill
FC	Fishburn Coking Plant, Fishburn
HC	Hawthorn Coking Plant, Murton
LC	Lambton Coking Plant, Fencehouses
MC	Monkton Coking Plant, Wardley
NC	Norwood Coking Plant, Gateshead

Gauge: 4' 8½"

-	0-4-0WE	HL	3859	1937	(a)	BpC	(1)
-	0-4-0WE	GB	2047	1946	(b)	NC	(1)
-	0-4-0WE	RSH	7692	1953	New	FC	(1)
-	0-4-0WE	RSH	7804	1954	New	LC	(1)
-	0-4-0WE	RSH	7882	1957	New	DC	(1)
-	0-4-0WE	RSH	7886	1958	New	HC	(1)
-	0-4-0WE	RSH	8059	1959	New	MC	(1)

(a) ex Strakers & Love Ltd, 1/1/1947   (1) to Coal Products Division, 1/1/1963
(b) ordered by Priestman Collieries
    Ltd, but not delivered until
    2/1947

Opencast Executive   (NCBOE)

The Ministry of Fuel & Power developed quite a number of coal disposal points in various parts of the country, and on 1st April 1952 these were transferred to the newly-formed Opencast Executive. Some the Executive operated itself; some were operated by the NCB Area in which they were located; all were eventually to be taken over by contractors operating for the Executive. There were two such points in Co. Durham:

Auckland Park Disposal Point (operated by No.4 Area; taken over by Derek Crouch (Contractors) Ltd, 18/3/1958 (q.v.); closed 11/9/1959)

Gauge: 4' 8½"

	HENRY CORT	0-4-0ST	OC	BH	607	1881	(a)	Scr	1/1949
	ACTIVE	0-4-0ST	OC	RS	3075	1901			
				reb R.Shaw		1931	(a)	(1)	
No.1	"CLARENCE"	0-4-0ST	OC	BH	985	1890	(b)	(2)	
108	HECTOR	0-6-0ST	OC	HL	2613	1905	(c)	(3)	
No.1		0-6-0ST	IC	HCR					
				reb HL	9294	1914	(d)	Scr	1/1949
113	PLUTO	0-6-0ST	OC	HL	2655	1906	(e)	(4)	
	ANGELA	0-4-0ST	OC	AE	1793	1918	(f)	(5)	
107	ATLAS	0-6-0ST	OC	HL	2612	1905	(g)	(6)	
	PATRIOT	0-6-0T	IC	BV		1920	(h)	(7)	

(a) ex Dorman, Long & Co Ltd, 1/1/1947
(b) ex Mainsforth Colliery, 6/1947
(c) ex Chilton Colliery, 6/1948
(d) ex Sherburn Hill Colliery, c7/1948
(e) ex Chilton Colliery, 11/1949
(f) ex Chilton Colliery, 2/1951
(g) ex Chilton Colliery, 12/1951
(h) ex Bowburn Colliery, 1/1954

(1) to Mainsforth Colliery, 2/1950
(2) to Mainsforth Colliery, c8/1948; ret. to Auckland Park, 4/1949; to Randolph Colliery, 6/1949; ret. to Auckland Park, c/1956; to Derek Crouch (Contractors) Ltd, 18/3/1958
(3) to Dean & Chapter Colliery, 9/1948
(4) to Chilton Colliery, 2/1951; ret. to Auckland Park, 3/1958; to Derek Crouch (Contractors) Ltd, loan, 18/3/1958
(5) to Mainsforth Colliery, 12/1951
(6) to Dean & Chapter Colliery, c1/1955
(7) to Mainsforth Colliery, c/1957

Swalwell Disposal Point (operated by NCBOE and its predecessors until 1/2/1954, when taken over by Mechanical Navvies Ltd q.v.)

Gauge: 4' 8½"

75169		0-6-0ST	IC	WB	2757	1944	(a)	(1)
75006		0-6-0ST	IC	HE	2855	1943	(b)	(2)
-		0-6-0T	IC	RWH	1645	1875		
				reb York		1901	(c)	(1)
75167		0-6-0ST	IC	WB	2755	1944	(d)	(1)
71495		0-6-0ST	IC	HC	1771	1944	(e)	(1)

(a) ex WD
(b) ex Talywain D.P., Monmouthshire, 7/1945
(c) ex Crofton Screens, Northumberland, /1951
(d) ex Broomhill D.P., Northumberland, 8/1951
(e) ex Northern (N&C) Division, No.8 Area, Northumberland, Seaton Delaval Colliery, c9/1951

(1) to Mechanical Navvies Ltd, 1/2/1954
(2) to Widdrington D.P., Chevington, Northumberland

North Durham Area

On 26th March 1967 this Area was formed by a combination of the former No.1 and No.5 Areas. It took over 116 surface locomotives, 14 being narrow gauge. 72 steam locomotives were included, of which only two survived at the end of March 1974.

The Area continued the former Divisional numbering scheme (which had begun at 500) for all locomotives acquired from 1968 onwards, but its application necessitated certain locos being re-numbered out of the scheme, nor was it applied to all the Area's diesel locomotives.

On 1st April 1974 this Area was combined with the Northumberland Area and South Durham Area to form the North-East Area (q.v.).

The Area took over the following railways:

Bowes Railway, on which locos were kept at:

MH	Marley Hill Loco Shed (closed 30/7/1971)
RA	Ravensworth Ann Colliery, near Birtley ⚹ (shed closed 8/3/1968)
SP	Shop Pit Loco Shed, near Lamesley ⚹ (closed 18/4/1973)
SBF	Springwell Bank Foot Loco Shed, Leam Lane
SW	Springwell Workshops (only locos under repair or awaiting scrap)
S	Starrs Loco Shed, Wrekenton ⚹ (closed 18/4/1973)

⚹ on Pelaw Main branch (closed 18/4/1973)

Harton Railway, on which locos were kept at:

Ha	Harton Colliery, South Shields (closed 25/7/1969)
We	Westoe Colliery, South Shields
Wh	Whitburn Colliery (closed 7/6/1968)

Lambton Railway, on which locos were kept at:

LS	Lambton Staithes, Sunderland (closed; loco awaiting disposal, 3/1967)
P	Lambton Railway Loco Sheds, Philadelphia

Other locations

UTC	Area Apprentice Training Centre, Usworth (no loco from 9/1970)
MTC	Area Engineering Training Centre, Annfield Plain (also known as North Durham Engineering Centre or Morrison Training Centre)
B	Boldon Colliery
CD	Clockburn Drift, Winlaton Mill (part of Marley Hill Colliery)
Da	Dawdon Colliery (South Durham Area - loco on loan)
D	Derwenthaugh Loco Shed, Swalwell
HH	Handen Hold Colliery, West Pelton (closed; locos awaiting disposal, 3/1967)
Hn	Herrington Colliery, New Herrington
Hy	Hylton Colliery, Castletown, Sunderland
LEW	Lambton Engine Works, Philadelphia (Workshops Division)
MB	Morrison Busty Colliery, Annfield Plain (closed 5/10/1973)
Sk	Silksworth Colliery, near Sunderland (closed 5/11/1971)
Wa/U	Wardley Colliery, White Mare Pool; re-named Usworth Colliery from 20/1/1969
WF	Washington 'F' Colliery Landsale Depot (closed 4/1969)
WG	Washington Glebe Colliery (loco stored, 4/1969-8/1970)
Wm	Wearmouth Colliery, Sunderland

Gauge: 4' 8½"

6		0-6-0ST	OC	RSH	7603	1949	(a)	B-D 7/68
								Scr 10/1972
7		0-6-0ST	OC	RSH	7695	1951	(a)	B Scr 7/1970
2120/210 (No.507 till		0-6-0DH		HE	6618	1965	(a)	B-We /68-B /68
c8/1969)								-We 5/68-P 2/69
								-B c5/69-P 1/71
								-B 3/71-D 6/72
								(1)
37		0-4-0ST	OC	RSH	7755	1953	(b)	Da (2)
	WILL	0-6-0T	IC	AB	999	1904	(a)	Hy Scr 2/1968
4		0-6-0ST	OC	RSH	7690	1951	(a)	Hy Scr 2/1968
8		0-4-0ST	OC	RSH	7807	1954	(a)	Hy Scr 2/1968
2505/78		4wDM		FH	3852	1957		
		reb	NCB			1958	(a)	Hy-Wm 12/68
								-Hy 1/69
								Scr c7/1970
32		0-4-0ST	OC	HL	2826	1910	(a)	LS Scr 8/1967
1		0-6-0DH		NBL	27410	1955	(a)	P-Wm 1/68
								(1)
2		0-6-0ST	OC	RSH	7599	1949	(a)	P-SDM 4/67-P 6/67
								Scr 2/1970
3		0-6-0ST	OC	RSH	7687	1951	(a)	P Scr 10/1968
4		0-6-0ST	OC	RSH	7688	1951	(a)	P Scr 12/1968
5		0-6-2T	IC	RS	3377	1909	(a)	P (3)
7		0-6-0ST	IC	HE	3820	1954	(a)	P-D 3/69
								Scr 10/1972
8		0-6-0ST	OC	RSH	7691	1952	(a)	P Scr 3/1970
10		0-6-2T	IC	RS	3378	1909	(a)	P Scr 1/1969
11		0-4-0ST	OC	HC	1412	1920		
		reb	HC			1948	(a)	P-Hy 3/69
								Scr 6/1972
27		0-6-0T	IC	RS	491	1846		
		reb	NER			1864		
		reb	NER			1873		
		reb	LEW			1904	(a)	P Scr 11/1968
28		0-4-0ST	OC	HL	2530	1902	(a)	P Scr 10/1968
29		0-6-2T	IC	K	4263	1904	(a)	P (4)
30		0-6-2T	IC	K	4532	1907	(a)	P Scr 1/1969
31		0-6-2T	IC	K	4533	1907	(a)	P Scr 11/1968
42		0-6-2T	IC	RS	3801	1920	(a)	P Scr 5/1970
45		0-6-0ST	IC	HL	2932	1912	(a)	P Scr 12/1970
47		0-4-0ST	OC	HL	3543	1923	(a)	P-Hy 12/68
								Scr 6/1972
51		0-6-0ST	IC	RSH	7101	1943	(a)	P-MB 8/69
								Scr 3/1971
52		0-6-2T	IC	NR	5408	1899	(a)	P (5)
58		0-6-0ST	IC	VF	5299	1945	(a)	P-D 3/69
								Scr 10/1972
59		0-6-0ST	IC	VF	5300	1945	(a)	P-D 3/69
								Scr 10/1972
63		0-6-0ST	OC	RSH	7600	1949	(a)	P Scr 5/1970
34		0-4-0ST	OC	HL	2954	1912	(a)	Sk Scr 2/1970
35		0-4-0ST	OC	HL	3024	1913	(a)	Sk Scr 2/1970
(3)		0-6-0ST	OC	RSH	7339	1947	(a)	WF-WG 4/69
								Scr 8/1970
9		0-6-0ST	OC	RSH	7749	1952	(a)	Wh Scr 4/1968
10		0-6-0ST	OC	RSH	7811	1954	(a)	Wh Scr 4/1968
2120/208 (No.505 till		0-6-0DH		HE	6616	1965	(a)	Wh-We 6/68-B c8/68
11/1970)								-We 10/68-B 11/70
								(1)
(209) (No.506 till		0-6-0DH		HE	6617	1965	(a)	Wh-B 6/68-SBF
8/1969)								(reps) 10/68-P 2/69

No.	Name	Type	Cyl	Builder	Works No	Year		Disposal
								-D 4/71-SBF (reps)
								11/72-D 1/73
								(1)
2120/211 (No.509 till 6/1972)		0-6-0DH		AB	514	1966	(a)	Wh-SBF (reps) 3/68
								-B 5/68
								-SBF (reps) 3/71
								-B 5/72
								(1)
	JEAN	0-6-0T	IC	HL	2769	1909	(a)	Wm Scr 2/1971
33		0-4-0ST	OC	HL	2827	1910	(a)	Wm-P 6/67
								Scr 10/1968
No.2		0-4-0ST	OC	HL	3493	1922	(a)	Wm Scr 3/1969
2	"2B"	0-6-0ST⟋	IC	HE	3191	1944	(a)	Wm Scr 3/1969
5		0-6-0ST	IC	RSH	7132	1944	(a)	Wm Scr 3/1969
10	(form. "10"; orig. (4))	0-6-0ST	IC	RSH	7294	1945	(a)	Wm-LEW 1/68-P 7/68
								-Wm 11/68-MB 2/70
								(1)
	DIANA	0-6-0T	IC	RSH	7304	1946	(a)	Wm Scr 3/1969
3		0-6-0ST	OC	RSH	7689	1951	(a)	Wm Scr 2/1968
No.39		0-4-0ST	OC	RSH	7757	1953	(a)	Wm-Hy c10/68
								Scr 12/1972
–		0-4-0DH		AB	478	1963	(a)	Wm-Hy 1/70
								-SBF 5/7/72
								-S 11/7/72
								-SW (reps) 9/72
								-S 11/72
								-SW 12/4/73
								-SBF 17/4/73
								(1)
No.501		0-6-0DH		HE	6612	1965	(a)	Wm-SBF (reps) 3/70
								-D 10/70
								(1)
1		4wWE		Siemens		1907	(a)	We (6)
2		4wWE		Siemens		1908	(a)	We (1)
E3		4w-4wWE		Siemens		1909	(a)	Ha-We 7/69
								(1)
4		4w-4wWE		Siemens		1909	(a)	We (1)
7		4w-4wWE		KS	1202	1911		
				reb NCB		1953	(a)	We (1)
8		4w-4wWE		KS	1203	1911	(a)	We (1)
9		4w-4wWE		AEG	1565	1913	(a)	We (1)
E10		4wWE		Siemens	862	1913	(a)	We (1)
11 (No.11 till c8/67)		4w-4wWE		EE	1795	1951		
				Bg	3351	1951	(a)	We (1)
12 (No.12 till c8/67)		4w-4wWE		EE	1794	1951		
				Bg	3350	1951	(a)	We (1)
13 (No.13 till c8/67)		4w-4wWE		EE	2308	1957		
				Bg	3469	1957	(a)	We (1)
14 (No.14 till c8/67)		4w-4wWE		EE	2599	1959		
				Bg	3519	1959	(a)	We (1)
15 (No.15 till c8/67)		4w-4wWE		EE	2600	1959		
				Bg	3520	1959	(a)	We (1)
–		4wDMTW		Bg	3585	1962	(a)	We (1)
41		0-6-0PT	IC	K	2509	1883	(c)	D (7)
42		0-6-0PT	IC	K	2510	1883		
				reb RS	2915	1899	(c)	D Scr 8/1968
No.5	MAJOR	0-6-0T	IC	K	4294	1905	(c)	D Scr 5/1970
65	HENRY C.EMBLETON	0-6-0T	IC	HL	3766	1930	(c)	D Scr 2/1970
27		0-6-0ST	IC	VF	5288	1945	(c)	D Scr 3/1971
78		0-4-0ST	OC	RSH	7538	1949	(c)	D Scr 3/1971
82		0-6-0ST	IC	HE	3689	1949	(c)	D Scr 3/1971
86	23	0-6-0ST	IC	RSH	7751	1953	(c)	D Scr 3/1968
90	24	0-6-0ST	IC	HE	3833	1955	(c)	D Scr 10/1970
(88)		4wDH		TH	135C	1964	(c)	D (1)

No.	Name	Type		Maker	Works No.	Built		History
3	(TWIZELL)	0-6-0T	IC	RS	2730	1891	(c)	HH-MB 2/68 (8)
37		0-6-0ST	OC	HL	3528	1922	(c)	HH Scr 4/1969
503	"SACRISTON"	0-4-0ST	OC	RSH	7605	1949	(c)	HH Scr 4/1969
4		0-4-0ST	OC	HC	1514	1923	(c)	MB Scr 9/1973
34	(HOLMSIDE)	0-6-0ST	IC	RSH	6943	1938	(c)	MB Scr 7/1968
79		0-6-0ST	OC	RSH	7545	1949	(c)	MB Scr 3/1971
80		0-6-0ST	OC	RSH	7546	1949	(c)	MB Scr 7/1968
84		0-6-0ST	OC	RSH	7641	1949	(c)	MB Scr 7/1968
23		0-6-0ST	OC	HL	2719	1907	(c)	MH Scr 1/1971
22		0-6-0ST	OC	HL	3103	1915	(c)	MH Scr 7/1970
32		0-4-0ST	OC	AB	1659	1920	(c)	MH-SBF 4/5/68 -S 18/5/68-SP 1/71 -SW 4/73 (9)
28		0-6-0ST	IC	VF	5298	1945	(c)	MH-MB 11/68 Scr 8/1971
83		0-6-0ST	IC	HE	3688	1949	(c)	MH-MB 11/70 (1)
85		0-4-0ST	OC	AB	2274	1949	(c)	MH (10)
67	NCB-PELAW	0-4-0ST	OC	P	2093	1947	(c)	RA-S 3/68-SW 5/68 Scr 12/1968
66	(CHARLES NELSON)	0-4-0ST	OC	P	1748	1928	(c)	S-SP 4/67-S 1/71 -SP 9/72-S 12/4/73 -SW 17/4/73 Scr 7/1973
81		0-4-0ST	OC	RSH	7604	1949	(c)	S-RA 4/3/68 -SP 8/3/68-SW 7/72 Scr 10/1972
101		4wDM		FH	3922	1959	(c)	S-SBF (reps) 12/67 -S 9/68-SBF (reps) 7/70-S 12/70 -SW (reps) 7/72 -S 9/72 -SBF(reps) 21/9/72 -SW (reps) 11/72 -SBF 1/73-S 12/4/73 -SW 25/4/73 (11)
102		4wDM		FH	3923	1959	(c)	SBF-S 12/67 -SBF (reps) 9/68 -S 7/69-SBF 1/71 -S 10/71-SBF c4/72 -SW (reps) 7/72 -SBF c8/72-S 9/72 -SBF (reps) 11/72 -S c12/72-SBF 1/73 -SW (reps) c10/73 (1)
103		0-6-0DH		S	10157	1963	(c)	SBF (1)
104		0-6-0DH		S	10158	1963	(c)	SBF (1)
No.500		0-6-0DH		HE	6611	1965	(c)	SBF (1)
No.502		0-6-0DH		HE	6613	1965	(c)	SBF (1)
No.503		0-6-0DH		HE	6614	1965	(c)	SBF (1)
No.504		0-6-0DH		HE	6615	1965	(c)	SBF (1)
52		0-4-0ST	OC	HL	3474	1920	(c)	SP-SW 5/68 Scr 12/1968
24	13	0-6-0ST	IC	HL	2545	1902	(c)	SW Scr 6/1968
25	14	0-6-0ST	IC	HL	3569	1923	(c)	SW Scr 6/1968
26	15	0-6-0T	IC	HE	1506	1930	(c)	SW Scr 6/1968
No.157		0-4-0DH		HE	6676	1967	New	Sk-D 4/72 (1)
14		0-4-0ST	OC	HL	3056	1914	(d)	P (12)

506	(D9504 till 8/69)	0-6-0DH	Sdn		1964	(e)	P-SDM 8/73-P 9/73 -B 2/74	(1)
507	(D9525 till 8/69)	0-6-0DH	Sdn		1965	(e)	P	(1)
508	(D9540 till 8/69)	0-6-0DH	Sdn		1965	(e)	P	(13)
509	(12119 till 8/69)	0-6-0DE	Dar		1952	(f)	P	(1)
510	(12120 till 8/69)	0-6-0DE	Dar		1952	(f)	P	(1)
D2102		0-6-0DM	Don		1960	(g)	P	(14)
12078		0-6-0DE	Derby		1950	(h)	P	(15)
D3140		0-6-0DE	Dar		1955	(j)	P	(16)
511	(12133 till 8/69)	0-6-0DE	Dar		1952	(k)	P	(1)
512	(12060 till 5/71)	0-6-0DE	Derby		1949	(m)	D-P4/71(1)	
513	(12098 till 6/71)	0-6-0DE	Derby		1952	(m)	D-P4/71(1)	
12050		0-6-0DE	Derby		1949	(n)	P	(17)
514	(12084 till 12/71)	0-6-0DE	Derby		1950	(p)	P-Sk 4/72-Hy 7/72	(1)
2516		0-6-0DM	HC	D1207	1961	(q)	B	(18)

∦ fitted with Giesl ejector

(a) ex No.1 Area, 26/3/1967
(b) on loan from No.1 Area to No.3 Area prior to 26/3/1967; from NDM to SDM after that date
(c) ex No.5 Area, 26/3/1967
(d) ex South Durham Area, Vane Tempest Colliery, 10/1968, to be stored awaiting preservation
(e) ex BR, Doncaster, Yorks, W.R., 11/1968
(f) ex BR, Hull, Yorks, E.R., 2/1969
(g) ex BR, Darlington, hire, 21/2/1969
(h) ex BR, Tyne Dock, hire, 28/2/1969
(j) ex BR, Thornaby, Teeside, hire, 10/3/1969
(k) ex BR, Immingham, Lincs, 5/1969
(m) ex BR, Newton Heath, Lancs, 3/1971
(n) ex BR, Longsight, Manchester, Lancs, 4/1971; purchased for spares only
(p) ex Northumberland Area, Burradon Colliery, 11/1971
(q) ex BR, Gateshead, hire, 16/4/1973

(1) to North-East Area, 1/4/1974
(2) Scr by South Durham Area, 12/1967
(3) to North Eastern Locomotive Preservation Group, for North Yorkshire Moors Rly, 7/1970; moved 8/1970
(4) to North Eastern Locomotive Preservation Group, for North Yorkshire Moors Rly, 6/1970; moved 7/1970
(5) to Keighley & Worth Valley Railway, Yorks, W.R., 2/1971
(6) to North of England Open-Air Museum, Marley Hill Loco Shed, 8/1973
(7) to North of England Open-Air Museum, Marley Hill Loco Shed, 4/1972
(8) to North of England Open-Air Museum, Marley Hill Loco Shed, 3/1972
(9) to North of England Open-Air Museum, Marley Hill Loco Shed, 7/1973 (owned by Stephenson & Hawthorn Locomotive Trust)
(10) to Thomas Ness Ltd, St.Anthony's Tar Works, Walker, Newcastle, 10/1970
(11) to South Durham Area, East Hetton Colliery, 9/1973
(12) to North of England Open-Air Museum, Marley Hill Loco Shed, 12/1972
(13) to Northumberland Area, Burradon Colliery, 11/1971
(14) ret. to BR, 28/2/1969
(15) ret. to BR, 10/3/1969
(16) ret. to BR, 21/3/1969
(17) remains scrapped c11/1971
(18) ret. to BR, 24/4/1973

Gauge: 3' 6" (underground locomotives working out to surface)

```
632              0-6-0DMF    HC   DM632   1947  (a)  MH(CD) (1)
639              0-6-0DMF    HC   DM639   1947  (a)  MH(CD) (1)
709              0-6-0DMF    HC   DM709   1955  (a)  MH(CD) (1)
993              0-6-0DMF    HC   DM993   1956  (a)  MH(CD) (1)
-                0-6-0DMF    HC   DM1063  1957  (a)  MH(CD) (1)
```

(a) ex No.5 Area, 26/3/1967   (1) to North-East Area, 1/4/1974

Gauge: 2' 8½"

```
-                0-4-0DMF    HE   2980    1944  (a)  UTC-MTC 9/70
                                                        Scr 10/1973
```

(a) ex No.1 Area, 26/3/1967 (static
    exhibit)

Gauge: 2' 6"

```
-                4wDM    RH   256314  1949  (a)  LEW    (1)
-                4wDM    RH   256323  1949  (a)  LEW    (1)
```

(a) ex Morrison Busty Colliery, under-   (1) to North-East Area, 1/4/1974
    ground, 1/1974; prev. 2' 2" gauge   (under conversion)

```
-                4wBE    GB   2573      1955  (a)  B      (1)
-                4wBE    WN   TJ189/2   1952  (b)  Wm     (1)
-                4wBE    GB   2572      1955  (c)  Wm     (2)
-                4wBE    WN   TJ189/1   1952  (d)  Wm     (1)
```

(a) ex No.1 Area, 26/3/1967   (1) to North-East Area, 1/4/1974
(b) ex Silksworth Colliery, under-   (2) to Stella Gill Machinery Stores,
    ground, 6/1968   2/1970 (see underground list)
(c) ex Harton Colliery, 1/1970;
    prev. 2' 0" gauge
(d) ex Wearmouth Colliery, underground,
    9/1971

Gauge: 2' 0"

```
-                4wDM    RH   268873  1952  (a)  MTC      (1)
-                4wDM    RH   268873  1952  (a)  MTC      (2)
No.1             4wDM    RH   371541  1954  (b)  LEW-Hn 11/67
                                                          (3)
(No.2)           4wDM    RH   371551  1954  (b)  Hn       (3)
B/L 92           4wDM    RH   398070  1957  (c)  Hn       (3)
```

(a) ex No.5 Area, 26/3/1967   (1) to South Durham Area, Seaham
(b) ex No.1 Area, 26/3/1967   Training Centre, 12/1973
(c) ex Scottish South Area, Arniston   (2) parts used to repair RH 268873;
    Machinery Stores, Gorebridge, Mid-   remainder scrapped /1969
    lothian, 9/1971; prev. 1' 10" gauge (3) to North-East Area, 1/4/1974

```
-                4wBE    GB   2378    1951  (a)  Wa/U    (1)
-                4wBE    GB   2572    1955  (a)  Ha      (2)
-                4wBE    EE   2519    1958
                 Bg      3500         1958  (b)  MTC     (1)
```

(a) ex No.1 Area, 26/3/1967   (1) to North-East Area, 1/4/1974
(b) ex No.5 Area, 26/3/1967   (2) converted to 2' 6" gauge, and
                                            transferred to Wearmouth Colliery,
                                            1/1970 (q.v.)

On 26th March 1967 this Area was formed by a combination of the former No.3 and No.4 Areas. It took over 80 surface locomotives, of which 14 were narrow gauge. 40 steam locomotives were included, of which eleven survived at the end of March 1974.

No numbering scheme was introduced for existing locomotives, nor for those acquired since 1967.

On 1st April 1974 this Area was combined with North Durham Area and Northumberland Area to form the North-East Area (q.v.).

Locations

TTC	Area Apprentice Training Centre, Tursdale (no loco from /1968)
STC	Area Training Centre, Seaham
Bl	Blackhall Colliery
Bo	Bowburn Colliery (closed 22/7/1967)
Bp	Brancepeth Colliery, Willington (closed 22/7/1967)
BPH	Brandon Pit House Colliery, near Meadowfield (closed 15/3/1968)
ACW	Central Workshops, Ashington, Northumberland (Workshops Division)
TCW	Central Workshops, Tursdale (Workshops Division)
Da	Dawdon Colliery
DH	Deaf Hill Colliery (closed; locos awaiting disposal, 3/1967)
D&C	Dean & Chapter Colliery, Ferryhill(closed; loco awaiting disposal, 3/1967)
E	Easington Colliery
EH	East Hetton Colliery, near Kelloe
Ep	Eppleton Colliery, Hetton-le-Hole
F	Fishburn Colliery (closed 30/11/1973, leaving locos on hire to Fishburn Coking Plant (National Smokeless Fuels Ltd)
H	Horden Colliery
LEW	Lambton Engine Works, Philadelphia (Workshops Division)
M	Mainsforth Colliery, Ferryhill Station (closed 6/12/1968)
Mu	Murton Colliery
Se	Seaham Colliery
SWW	Seaham Wagon Works, Dawdon
Sh	Shotton Colliery (closed 1/9/1972)
SH	South Hetton Loco Sheds
T	Thornley Colliery (closed 9/1/1970), leaving Thornley Coal Preparation Plant
Th	Thrislington Coal Preparation Plant, West Cornforth (closed 26/3/1970)
TG	Trimdon Grange Colliery (closed 16/2/1968)
VT	Vane Tempest Colliery, Seaham
WA	West Auckland Coal Preparation Plant (closed 18/8/1967)
WH	Wheatley Hill Colliery (closed 3/5/1968)

Gauge: 4' 8½"

-		0-6-0ST	IC	VF	5307	1945	(a)	Bl	Scr	4/1969
	HORDEN	0-6-0T	IC	RSH	7305	1946	(a)	Bl	Scr	4/1969
-		0-6-0DH		AB	498	1965	(a)	Bl	(1)	
12		0-4-0ST	OC	HL	2789	1912	(a)	Da	Scr	12/1967
49		0-4-0ST	OC	MW	2035	1924	(a)	Da	Scr	12/1967
60		0-6-0ST	IC	HE	3686	1948	(a)	Da-LEW 7/67-Da 2/68 (1)		
37		0-4-0ST	OC	RSH	7755	1953	(b)	Da	Scr	12/1967
-		6wDM		KS	4421	1929	(a)	DH	(2)	
-		0-6-0ST	IC	VF	5305	1945	(a)	E	Scr	11/1969
No.3	(6D till /72)	0-6-0DM		HE	5342	1958	(a)	E	(1)	
	EASINGTON No.1	0-6-0DH		AB	491	1964	(a)	E	(1)	
	HORDEN No.2	0-6-0ST	OC	HL	3440	1920	(a)	H	Scr	9/1970
	MONTY	0-6-0ST	IC	RSH	7146	1944	(a)	H	(1)	
	(HORDEN No.1)	0-6-0DH		AB	488	1964	(a)	H	(1)	

No.	Name	Type		Builder	Works No.	Year		Notes		
No.24		0-6-0ST	OC	AB	1321	1913				
		reb Thornley				1929	(a)	Se	Scr	4/1969
83	LONDONDERRY	0-4-0ST	OC	AB	1724	1922	(a)	Se	Scr	c3/1968
48		0-4-0ST	OC	HL	3544	1923	(a)	Se	Scr	5/1959
38		0-4-0ST	OC	RSH	7756	1953	(a)	Se	Scr	9/1968
10D		0-6-0DM		HE	5304	1959	(a)	Se-Da	4/67	
								(1)		
-		0-4-0DH		AB	523	1967	(a)	Se-Da 7/72-Se 1/73		
								(1)		
-		0-4-0DH		AB	524	1967	(a)	Se-Da 5/70-Se 5/70		
								(1)		
-		0-6-0ST	OC	AB	1015	1904	(a)	Sh-ACW 6/69		
								-Sh c10/69		
								(3)		
-		0-6-0ST	OC	P	1310	1914	(a)	Sh	Scr	11/1972
71		0-6-0ST	IC	VF	5308	1945	(a)	SH	(1)	
72		0-6-0ST	IC	VF	5309	1945	(a)	SH	(4)	
62		0-6-0ST	IC	HE	3687	1949	(a)	SH	(1)	
68		0-6-0ST	IC	HE	3784	1953	(a)	SH	(1)	
69		0-6-0ST⊬	IC	HE	3785	1953	(a)	SH	(1)	
61		0-6-0ST	IC	HE	3821	1954	(a)	SH	(1)	
64		0-6-0DH		NBL	27763	1959	(a)	SH-Bl	9/68	
								(1)		
65		0-6-0DH		NBL	27764	1959	(a)	SH	(1)	
66		0-6-0DH		NBL	27765	1959	(a)	SH	(1)	
-		4wPM		MH	L116	1939	(a)	SWW	Scr	2/1971
XL5		4wDM		LEW		c1955	(a)	SWW	Scr	9/1970
No.17		0-6-0T	OC	KS	3098	1918				
		reb Thornley				1938	(a)	T	Scr	4/1969
No.27		0-6-0T	OC	KS	3100	1918				
		reb Thornley				1942	(a)	T	Scr	4/1969
148	TAURUS	0-4-0ST	OC	HL	3384	1919	(a)	T	Scr	4/1969
14		0-4-0ST	OC	HL	3056	1914	(a)	VT	(5)	
84	CASTLEREAGH	0-4-0ST	OC	AB	1885	1926	(a)	VT	Scr	4/1968
50		0-4-0ST	OC	LEW		1957	(a)	VT-Bl	7/67	
									Scr	4/1968
No.2		0-6-0DM		AB	423	1958	(a)	WH-T 5/68-Da 10/72		
								(1)		
No.52		0-4-0ST	OC	AB	2275	1949	(c)	Bo-T 12/67		
									Scr	8/1970
8D		0-6-0DM		HE	5303	1958	(c)	Bo-Da 9/67		
								(1)		
	HOWDEN DENE No.1	0-6-0T	OC	HL	2880	1911	(c)	Bp	(6)	
	STAGSHAW	0-6-0ST	OC	HL	3513	1927				
		reb HE/NCB				1961	(c)	Bp-WH 5/67-Sh 7/68		
								(7)		
	HOWDEN DENE No.2	0-6-0ST	OC	RS	4113	1937	(c)	Bp	Scr	5/1967
505		0-6-0ST	IC	HE	3819	1954	(c)	Bp	Scr	5/1969
	DELTA	0-6-0ST	IC	HE	3189	1944	(c)	BPH-E 1/68-Bl 9/68		
								-LEW 9/69-Bl 12/69		
								(1)		
	GAMMA	0-6-0ST	IC	WB	2779	1945	(c)	BPH-VT 12/67		
								(1)		
	(ALPHA)	0-6-0DH		NBL	27592	1957	(c)	BPH-H 4/68		
								(1)		
67	BETA	0-6-0DH		NBL	27717	1957	(c)	BPH-SH 4/68		
								(1)		
504		0-4-0ST	OC	RSH	7662	1950	(c)	EH	Scr	4/1969
22		0-4-0ST	OC	AB	2320	1952	(c)	EH-TG 4/67-EH 8/69		
								-Bl 11/72-T 12/72		
								-EH 3/73-Bl 5/73		
								(1)		
1D		0-6-0DM		HE	4986	1956	(c)	EH-LEW 12/70		
								-EH 1/71		
								(1)		

7D	0-6-0DM		HE	5177	1958	(c)	EH-B1 4/72-EH 5/72	(1)
-	0-6-0DM		RH	408296	1957	(c)	F-TG 3/67-F 10/67 -T 9/70-EH 12/70 -B1 2/71-F 5/71 -T 10/71	(1)
5D	0-6-0DM		HE	5341	1958	(c)	F-B1 7/73	(1)
9D	0-6-0DM		HE	5382	1959	(c)	F	(8)
No.140	0-6-0T	OC	HC	1821	1948	(c)	M-Th 4/68	(9)
3D	0-6-0DM		HE	5302	1958	(c)	M-E 1/69	(1)
11D	0-6-0DM		HE	5305	1959	(c)	M-F 2/69	(8)
No.50	0-4-0ST	OC	AB	2277	1950	(c)	Th-T 4/70	Scr 9/1971
No.57	0-4-0ST	OC	AB	2341	1953	(c)	Th	Scr 9/1968
110 HERCULES	0-6-0ST	OC	HL	2654	1906	(c)	WA	Scr 5/1969
D2	0-6-0DM		RH	395303	1956	(c)	WA	(10)
-	0-4-0DH		AB	547	1967	New	VT	(1)
-	0-4-0DH		AB	548	1967	New	Da	(1)
2	0-6-0ST	OC	RSH	7599	1949	(d)	E	(11)
-	0-4-0DH		AB	550	1967	New	Se	(1)
-	4wDM		MR	5766	1963	(e)	SWW	(1)
No.61 (No.112 till 4/73)	0-6-0DH		AB	582	1973	New	SH	(1)
No.72 (No.113 till 4/73)	0-6-0DH		AB	583	1973	New	SH	(1)
No.69 (No.114 till 6/73)	0-6-0DH		AB	584	1973	New	SH	(1)
No.71 (No.115 till 8/73)	0-6-0DH		AB	585	1973	New	SH	(1)
506	0-6-0DH		Sdn		1964	(f)	H	(12)
101	4wDM		FH	3922	1959	(g)	EH-SH 10/73	(1)

✗ fitted with mechanical stoker (latterly disconnected)

(a) ex No.3 Area, 26/3/1967
(b) on loan from No.1 Area to No.3 Area prior to 26/3/1967; from NDM to 3DM after that date
(c) ex No.4 Area, 26/3/1967
(i) ex North Durham Area, Philadelphia, loan, 4/1967
(e) ex CWS Ltd, Southend Coal Concentration Depot, Essex, 4/1970
(f) ex North Durham Area, Philadelphia, loan, 8/1973
(g) ex North Durham Area, Springwell Workshops, 9/1973

(1) to North-East Area, 1/4/1974
(2) to Rom River Reinforcement Co Ltd, Lichfield, Staffs, 12/1967; moved 2/1968
(3) to Stephenson & Hawthorn Locomotive Trust, NCB Backworth Loco Sheds, Northumberland, 11/1972
(4) to Colne Valley Railway, near Castle Hedingham, Essex, 12/1973
(5) to North Durham Area, Philadelphia, for subsequent preservation, 10/1968
(6) hired to Coal Products Division for use at Brancepeth Coking Plant, 4/1967-12/1967; Scr 5/1968
(7) to North of England Open-Air Museum, Marley Hill Loco Shed, 7/1972 (owned by Stephenson & Hawthorn Locomotive Trust)
(8) hired to National Smokeless Fuels Ltd for Fishburn Coking Plant from 11/1973; to North-East Area, 1/4/1974
(9) to Horden Colliery, 3/1971, for use as stationary boiler for colliery baths; to North-East Area, 1/4/1974
(10) to T.J.Thomson & Son Ltd, Stockton, Teesside, 10/1969
(11) ret. to North Durham Area, Philadelphia, 6/1967
(12) ret. to North Durham Area, Philadelphia, 9/1973

Gauge: 2' 3"

–	4wDM	HE	4175	1949	(a)	M	(1)
–	4wDM	HE	6628	1966	(a)	M	(2)

(a) ex No.4 Area, 26/3/1967

(1) to East Hetton Colliery, 3/1969, and re-converted to 2' 0" gauge (q.v.)
(2) to East Hetton Colliery, 2/1970, and converted to 2' 0" gauge (q.v.)

Gauge: 2' 0"

–	4wDM	RH	211614	1941	(a)	H	Scr 6/1973
–	4wDM	RH	217986	1942	(a)	H	Scr 6/1973
–	4wDM	RH	223690	1944	(a)	SH	Scr 10/1971
–	0-4-0DM	RH	338425	1955	(a)	H-Bl	4/72(1)
–	0-4-0DM	RH	338426	1955	(a)	Bl	Scr 2/1973
–	0-4-0DM	RH	392154	1956	(a)	TTC	Scr 1/1969
–	0-4-0DM	RH	392157	1956	(a)	LEW-TTC	10/68 (2)
–	0-4-0DM	RH	393979	1956	(a)	DH	(3)
–	4wDM	HE	3655	1949	(b)	D&C	(4)
–	4wDM	HE	4554	1954	(b)	EH	Scr 2/1970
–	4wDM	HE	4175	1949	(c)	EH	(1)
–	4wDM	HE	6628	1966	(d)	EH	(1)
–	0-4-0DM	HE	4805	1956	(e)	Da	(1)
–	0-4-0DM	HE	4803	1956	(f)	H	Scr 6/1973
–	0-4-0DM	HE	4685	1955	(g)	Da	(1)
–	0-4-0DM	HE	4387	1954	(h)	H	(1)
–	0-4-0DM	HE	4109	1952	(j)	H	(1)
–	0-4-0DM	HC	DM692	1952	(k)	Bl	(1)
–	0-4-0DM	HE	4092	1952	(k)	Bl	(1)
–	0-4-0DM	HE	4502	1954	(k)	Bl	(1)
–	4wDM	RH	268873	1952	(m)	STC	(1)

(a) ex No.3 Area, 26/3/1967
(b) ex No.4 Area, 26/3/1967
(c) ex Mainsforth Colliery, 3/1969; converted from 2' 3" gauge (q.v.)
(d) ex Mainsforth Colliery, 2/1970; converted from 2' 3" gauge (q.v.)
(e) ex Scottish North Area, Blairhall Colliery, Fifeshire, 2/1970 ⚡
(f) ex Scottish North Area, Blairhall Colliery, Fifeshire, 4/1970 ⚡
(g) ex Scottish North Area, Blairhall Colliery, Fifeshire, 12/1970 ⚡
(h) ex Horden Colliery, underground, 10/1971
(j) ex Horden Colliery, underground, 11/1972
(k) ex Shotton Colliery, underground, 3/1973
(m) ex North Durham Area, Morrison Training Centre, 12/1973

(1) to North-East Area, 1/4/1974
(2) dism. from /1969; s/s c/1971
(3) to Northumberland Area, Havannah Colliery, 8/1967
(4) to Anston Plant Manufacturing Co Ltd, Sheffield, Yorks, W.R., 2/1968

⚡ commenced work /1973

–	4wBE	WN	TJ189/3	1952	(a)	Mu	(1)
–	4wBE	WN	BS199/2	1954	(a)	Ep	(1)

(a) ex No.3 Area, 26/3/1967

(1) to North-East Area, 1/4/1974

North-East Area

On 1st April 1974 this Area was formed by an amalgamation of the former Northumberland, North Durham and South Durham Areas, with its headquarters at Team Valley, Gateshead. It took over 160 surface locomotives, of which 34 were narrow gauge. 22 steam locomotives were included, but regular steam working continued only at Backworth and South Hetton, and as stand-by at Vane Tempest Colliery, Seaham.

Locomotives are kept or repaired at the following locations:

NORTHUMBERLAND

ACW	Central Workshops, Ashington (surface loco repairs ceased, 3/1975)
As	Ashington Colliery, Ashington
ATC ✗	Area Training Centre, Ashington
BD ✗	Bewick Drift, Lynemouth (part of Lynemouth Colliery)
Bt	Bates Colliery, Blyth
En ✗	Ellington Colliery, Ellington
Ly	Lynemouth Colliery, Lynemouth (locos exchanged with Ashington Colliery as required)
Nt	Netherton Colliery, Netherton (closed; locos awaiting disposal, 4/1974)
Sb	Shilbottle Colliery, Shilbottle
Wt	Whittle Colliery, Newton-on-the-Moor

TYNE & WEAR

B	Boldon Colliery, Boldon
Bd	Burradon Loco Shed, Burradon (served Burradon Colliery (closed 22/11/1975), Havannah and Brenkley Collieries and Weetslade Coal Preparation Plant and Coal Concentration Depot)
BF ✗	Black Fell Loco Shed, Eighton Banks (test track for underground locos: not regularly in use)
Bk	Backworth Colliery (Eccles Pit), Backworth
CD ✗	Clockburn Drift, Winlaton Mill (worked as part of Marley Hill Colliery)
D	Derwenthaugh Loco Shed, Swalwell (serves Clockburn Drift and Derwent-haugh Coking Plant (NSF)
Dy	Dudley Colliery, Dudley
Ep ✗	Eppleton Colliery, Hetton-le-Hole (part of Hawthorn Combined Mine)
Hn ✗	Herrington Colliery, New Herrington
Hv ✗	Havannah Colliery, Hazlerigg
Hy	Hylton Colliery, Castletown (rail traffic ceased 2/1975)
LEW	Lambton Engine Works, Philadelphia (repairs only)
P	Lambton Railway Loco Shed, Philadelphia (serves Herrington and Houghton Collieries, and Lambton Coal Preparation and Coking Plants, Fencehouses) (NSF)
SBF	Springwell Bank Foot Loco Shed, Leam Lane (Bowes Railway) (served Usworth Colliery at Wardley, Monkton Coal Preparation and Coking Plants (NSF) and Jarrow Staithes)
SW	Springwell Workshops, Springwell (Bowes Railway) (repairs only - closed 9/3/1975)
Wa/U ✗	Usworth Colliery (Wardley No.1 Shaft), Wardley (closed 8/8/1974)
Wa	Wardley Loco Shed, Wardley (Bowes Railway) (serves Monkton Coal Preparation and Coking Plants (NSF) and Jarrow Staithes)
We	Westoe Colliery, South Shields (Harton Railway) (also serves Harton High and Low Staithes, South Shields)
Wm	Wearmouth Colliery, Sunderland
Ws	Weetslade Loco Shed, near Burradon (serves Weetslade Coal Preparation Plant and Coal Concentration Plant, and Havannah and Brenkley Collieries)

COUNTY DURHAM

Bl	Blackhall Colliery, Blackhall
Da	Dawdon Colliery, Dawdon
E	Easington Colliery, Easington
EH	East Hetton Colliery, Quarrington Hill

```
F        Fishburn Coal Preparation Plant, Fishburn (closed 10/1974); locos
         also hired to Fishburn Coking Plant (NSF) until 25/2/1975)
H        Horden Colliery, Horden
MB       Morrison Busty Colliery, Annfield Plain (closed; locos awaiting
         disposal, 4/1974)
MTC    ∕ Morrison Loco Training Centre, Annfield Plain (closed; loco awaiting
         disposal, 4/1974)
Mu     ∕ Murton Colliery, Murton (part of Hawthorn Combined Mine)
Se       Seaham Colliery, New Seaham
SH       South Hetton Loco Sheds, South Hetton (serves South Hetton Colliery and
         Hawthorn Combined Mine,Coal Preparation Plant and Coking Plant (NSF)
STC    ∕ Seaham Loco Training Centre, Seaham (at Seaham Colliery)
SWW      Seaham Wagon Works, Dawdon
T        Thornley Coal Preparation Plant, Thornley
VT       Vane Tempest Colliery, Seaham
```

∕ narrow gauge locomotives only

Locomotives have also been repaired at:

```
SG       British Rail's South Gosforth Diesel Maintenance Depot, Newcastle-
         upon-Tyne
```

In May 1972 the former Northumberland Area began a re-numbering scheme, as follows: Ashington group - 1 to 20; Bates - 21 to 30; Backworth and Burradon group - 31 to 50; Shilbottle and Whittle - 51 to 60; additional stock - 61 upwards. This had not been fully implemented at the time of re-organisation.

The locomotive lists below were accurate to 31st December 1975.

Gauge: 4' 8½"

```
(No.55)              D4056   0-6-0DE    Dar            1961  (a)  ACW-Sb c6/74
38                   D1/9513 0-6-0DH    Sdn            1964  (a)  ACW-Bk c6/74
                                                                 -Bd 7/74
         9312/101            0-6-0DE    YE      2708   1959  (a)  As-Bt 12/74
                                                                 -H 1/75
         9312/102            0-6-0DH    NBL    27766   1959  (a)  As       Scr  8/1974
No.1     9312/92    (D9500)  0-6-0DH    Sdn            1964  (a)  As
No.4     9312/96    (D9514)  0-6-0DH    Sdn            1964  (a)  As-SG 10/75
                                                                 -As 11/75
No.5     9312/91    (D9536)  0-6-0DH    Sdn            1965  (a)  As
No.6     9312/94    (D9527)  0-6-0DH    Sdn            1965  (a)  As
No.7     9312/95    (D9518)  0-6-0DH    Sdn            1964  (a)  As-LEW 6/75
                                                                 -As 9/75
No.8     9312/93    (D9517)  0-6-0DH    Sdn            1965  (a)  As
No.9     9312/99    (D9508)  0-6-0DH    Sdn            1964  (a)  As
                    D2/9531  0-6-0DH    Sdn            1965  (a)  As
         9312/98    (D9511)  0-6-0DH    Sdn            1964  (b)  As
                    D9545    0-6-0DH    Sdn            1965  (b)  As
No.63                        0-4-0DE    RH    384141   1955
                                       (carries 384161)         (a)  Bd
16                           0-6-0ST OC RSH    7944    1957  (a)  Bd-Bk 7/74

41       (No.27 till 7/75)   0-6-0DE    RH    421438   1958  (a)  Bd
                    D9502    0-6-0DH    Sdn            1964  (a)  Bd
No.36    2233/508  (D9540)   0-6-0DH    Sdn            1965  (a)  Bd
37                 (D9535)   0-6-0DH    Sdn            1965  (a)  Bd
                    D9555    0-6-0DH    Sdn            1965  (a)  Bd-As 2/75
```

9			0-6-0ST	IC	RSH	7097	1943	(a)	Bk	
49			0-6-0ST	IC	RSH	7098	1943	(a)	Bk	
48			0-6-0ST	IC	HE	2864	1943	(a)	Bk	
48			0-6-0ST	IC	HE	3172	1944	(a)	Bk	
6			0-6-0ST	IC	WB	2749	1944	(a)	Bk	
44			0-6-0ST	OC	RSH	7760	1953	(a)	Bk	(2)
No.20			0-4-0DE		RH	312987	1952	(a)	Bt	
	2100/525	D3038	0-6-0DE		Derby		1953	(a)	Bt	
No.26			0-6-0DE		RH	420141	1958	(a)	Bt	
		D3638	0-6-0DE		Dar		1958	(a)	Bt-ACW 3/75 (4)	
		D3648	0-6-0DE		Dar		1959	(a)	Bt	
C21			0-6-0DE		RH	421440	1958	(a)	Bt	Scr 6/1975
No.65			0-6-0DH		EEV	D1121	1966	(a)	Bt-LEW 4/75-H 9/75 -Se 11/75-H 12/75	
No.66			0-6-0DH		HE	6662	1966	(a)	Bt-LEW 10/75	
No.67			0-6-0DH		AB	549	1967	(a)	Bt	
No.22			0-6-0DE		RH	425474	1958	(a)	Dy	
47			0-6-0ST	IC	HE	3166	1944	(a)	Nt	Scr 9/1974
No.2	9312/100	(D9528)	0-6-0DH		Sdn		1965	(a)	Ly-As 10/75-Ly 12/75	
No.3	9312/90	(D9521)	0-6-0DH		Sdn		1964	(a)	Ly	
No.50			0-4-0ST	OC	AB	2245	1947	(a)	Nt	Scr 9/1974
No.52		(D4070)	0-6-0DE		Dar		1961	(a)	Sb-ACW 9/74	
					reb LEW		1976		-LEW 10/75	
No.56		(D4068)	0-6-0DE		Dar		1961	(a)	Sb	
No.51		(D4069)	0-6-0DE		Dar		1961	(a)	Wt	
No.53		(D4072)	0-6-0DE		Dar		1961	(a)	Wt	
No.54		(D4074)	0-6-0DE		Dar		1961	(a)	Wt	
506		(D9504)	0-6-0DH		Sdn		1964	(c)	B-Bk 12/74-Bd 1/75	
	2120/208		0-6-0DH		HE	6616	1965	(c)	B	
	2120/211		0-6-0DH		AB	514	1966	(c)	B	
(88)			4wDH		TH	135C	1964	(c)	D	
No.501			0-6-0DH		HE	6612	1965	(c)	D	
(209)			0-6-0DH		HE	6617	1965	(c)	D	
	2120/210		0-6-0DH		HE	6618	1965	(c)	D	
No.157			0-4-0DH		HE	6676	1967	(c)	D	
514		(12084)	0-6-0DE		Derby		1950	(c)	Hy-P 3/75-E 12/75	
10			0-6-0ST	IC	RSH	7294	1945	(c)	MB	Scr 7/1974
83			0-6-0ST	IC	HE	3688	1949	(c)	MB	Scr 7/1974
512		(12060)	0-6-0DE		Derby		1949	(c)	P	
509		(12119)	0-6-0DE		Dar		1952	(c)	P	
510		(12120)	0-6-0DE		Dar		1952	(c)	P	
511		(12133)	0-6-0DE		Dar		1952	(c)	P	
513		(12098)	0-6-0DE		Derby		1952	(c)	P	
507		(D9525)	0-6-0DH		Sdn		1965	(c)	P-Bd 3/75-As 3/75 -Ly 10/75-Bk 12/75	
-			0-4-0DH		AB	478	1963	(c)	SBF	
103			0-6-0DH		S	10157	1963	(c)	SBF	
104			0-6-0DH		S	10158	1963	(c)	SBF	
No.500			0-6-0DH		HE	6611	1965	(c)	SBF	
No.502			0-6-0DH		HE	6613	1965	(c)	SBF	
No.503			0-6-0DH		HE	6614	1965	(c)	SBF	
No.504			0-6-0DH		HE	6615	1965	(c)	SBF	
102			4wDM		FH	3923	1959	(c)	SW	Scr 9/1975
1			0-6-0DH		NBL	27410	1955	(c)	Wm	
2			4wWE		Siemens		1908	(c)	We	
3			4w-4wWE		Siemens		1909	(c)	We	
4			4w-4wWE		Siemens		1909	(c)	We	
7			4w-4wWE		KS	1202	1911			
					reb NCB		1953	(c)	We	
8			4w-4wWE		KS	1203	1911	(c)	We	Scr 8/1974
9			4w-4wWE		AEG	1565	1913	(c)	We	Scr 8/1974
E10			4wWE		Siemens	862	1913	(c)	We	
11			4w-4wWE		EE	1795	1951			
					Bg	3351	1951	(c)	We	

No.	Name	Type		Builder	Works No	Year		Status
12		4w-4wWE		EE	1794	1951		
				Bg	3350	1951	(c)	We
13		4w-4wWE		EE	2308	1957		
				Bg	3469	1957	(c)	We
14		4w-4wWE		EE	2599	1959		
				Bg	3519	1959	(c)	We
15		4w-4wWE		EE	2600	1959		
				Bg	3520	1959	(c)	We
–		4wDMTW		Bg	3585	1962	(c)	We
	DELTA	0-6-0ST	IC	HE	3189	1944	(d)	Bl Scr 8/1975
No.22		0-4-0ST	OC	AB	2320	1952	(d)	Bl-F 5/74
5D		0-6-0DM		HE	5341	1958	(d)	Bl
64		0-6-0DH		NBL	27763	1959	(d)	Bl
–		0-6-0DH		AB	498	1965	(d)	Bl-AB (reps) 5/75 -E 9/10/75 -Bl 28/10/75
60		0-6-0ST	IC	HE	3686	1948	(d)	Da
No.2		0-6-0DM		AB	423	1958	(d)	Da
8D		0-6-0DM		HE	5303	1958	(d)	Da-LEW 11/74-Bt 2/75
10D		0-6-0DM		HE	5304	1959	(d)	Da
–		0-4-0DH		AB	548	1967	(d)	Da
3D		0-6-0DM		HE	5302	1958	(d)	E-LEW 10/75
No.3		0-6-0DM		HE	5342	1958	(d)	E-LEW 2/75 (3)
	EASINGTON No.1	0-6-0DH		AB	491	1964	(d)	E
1D		0-6-0DM		HE	4986	1956	(d)	EH-LEW 6/75 -EH 11/75
7D		0-6-0DM		HE	5177	1958	(d)	EH-LEW 2/75-EH 6/75
9D		0-6-0DM		HE	5382	1958	(e)	F (1)
11D		0-6-0DM		HE	5305	1959	(e)	F-LEW 5/74-Bt 1/75 -F 2/75 (1)
	MONTY	0-6-0ST	IC	RSH	7146	1944	(d)	H
No.140		0-6-0T	OC	HC	1821	1948	(d)	H
–		0-6-0DH		NBL	27592	1957	(d)	H-E 11/74-H 2/1/75 -LEW 14/1/75-H 9/75
–		0-6-0DH		AB	488	1964	(d)	H
–		0-4-0DH		AB	523	1967	(d)	Se-LEW 9/75
–		0-4-0DH		AB	524	1967	(d)	Se-LEW 6/74-Se 9/74
–		0-4-0DH		AB	550	1968	(d)	Se-LEW 9/74-Se 2/75
71		0-6-0ST	IC	VF	5308	1945	(d)	SH
62		0-6-0ST	IC	HE	3687	1948	(d)	SH
68		0-6-0ST	IC	HE	3784	1953	(d)	SH Scr 6/1974
69		0-6-0ST	IC	HE	3785	1953	(d)	SH
61		0-6-0ST	IC	HE	3821	1954	(d)	SH Scr 6/1974
67	BETA	0-6-0DH		NBL	27717	1957	(d)	SH
65		0-6-0DH		NBL	27764	1959	(d)	SH
66		0-6-0DH		NBL	27765	1959	(d)	SH
101		4wDM		FH	3922	1959	(d)	SH-T 10/74
No.61		0-6-0DH		AB	582	1973	(d)	SH
No.72		0-6-0DH		AB	583	1973	(d)	SH
No.69		0-6-0DH		AB	584	1973	(d)	SH
No.71		0-6-0DH		AB	585	1973	(d)	SH
–		4wDM		MR	5766	1963	(d)	SWW
–		0-6-0DM		RH	408296	1958	(d)	T
	2502/7 ≠ (GAMMA)	0-6-0ST	IC	WB	2779	1945	(d)	VT
–		0-4-0DH		AB	547	1967	(d)	VT
	D3088	0-6-0DE		Derby		1954	(f)	As-ACW 7/74 -Bt 12/74
No.594 20/104/997		0-6-0DH		AB	594	1974	New	Da
–		0-4-0DH		RR	10201	1964	(g)	Bl-E 10/75
	SAM	0-6-0DM		HE	5647	1960	(h)	LEW Scr 3/1975
20/110/701		0-6-0DH		NBL	27588	1957	(j)	LEW-Bl 8/75
20/110/702		0-6-0DH		NBL	27589	1957	(j)	LEW-Bl 10/75

/ NCB representative in celebrations of 150th anniversary
of Stockton & Darlington Railway, Shildon, August 1975

(a) ex Northumberland Area, 1/4/1974
(b) ex Northumberland Area, 1/4/1974;
    used only for spares
(c) ex North Durham Area, 1/4/1974
(d) ex South Durham Area, 1/4/1974
(e) ex South Durham Area, 1/4/1974,
    but hired to National Smokeless
    Fuels Ltd, Fishburn Coking Plant,
    Fishburn, until 25/2/1975
(f) ex British Railways, c5/1974
(g) ex British Steel Corporation,
    Harlaxton Quarries, Lincs, via
    reps at AB, 12/1974
(h) ex NCB Doncaster Area, Askern Main
    Colliery, Askern, Yorks, W.R.,
    12/1974
(j) ex British Steel Corporation,
    Appleby-Frodingham Works, Humber-
    side, per AB, 7/1975

(1) to National Smokeless Fuels Ltd,
    Fishburn Coking Plant, Fishburn,
    25/2/1975
(2) to Stephenson & Hawthorn Locomotive
    Trust, Marley Hill, for preser-
    vation, 3/1975; moved
(3) parts salvaged to repair other
    locos; remainder scrapped 5/1975
(4) parts salvaged to repair other
    locos; remainder scrapped 9/1975

Gauge: 3' 6" (underground locos working out to surface)

632	0-6-0DMF	HC	DM632	1947	(a)	CD
639	0-6-0DMF	HC	DM639	1947	(a)	CD
709	0-6-0DMF	HC	DM709	1955	(a)	CD
993	0-6-0DMF	HC	DM993	1956	(a)	CD
-	0-6-0DMF	HC	DM1063	1957	(a)	CD

(a) ex North Durham Area, 1/4/1974

Gauge: 3' 0"

C/H 1117	0-4-0DM	HE	4635	1954	(a)	En	
–	4w-4wDH	HE	7099	1973	(b)	BF	(1)

(a) ex Northumberland Area, 1/4/1974   (1) to Ellington Colliery, underground,
(b) ex Bates Colliery, Blyth, under-   c6/1975
    ground, 1/1975

–	4wBE	CE	5921	1972	(a)	BD

(a) ex Northumberland Area, 1/4/1974

Gauge: 2' 8¼"

–	0-4-0DMF	HE	6980	1968	(a)	ATC

(a) ex Northumberland Area, 1/4/1974

Gauge: 2' 6"

–	4wDM	RH	256314	1949	(a)	LEW-We 5/74
–	4wDM	RH	256323	1949	(a)	LEW-We 6/74 -ACW 12/75

(a) ex North Durham Area, 1/4/1974;
    under conversion from 2' 2" gauge

–	4wBE	WN	TJ189/1	1952	(a)	Wm	
–	4wBE	WN	TJ189/2	1952	(a)	Wm	
–	4wBE	GB	2573	1955	(a)	B	Scr 11/1975
–	4wBE	EE	2466	1957			
		Bg	3501	1957	(b)	B	
–	4wBE	WN	TJ189/3	1952	(c)	Wm	

(a) ex North Durham Area, 1/4/1974
(b) ex Lambton Engine Works, 2/1975;
    prev. Usworth Colliery, underground,
    2' 0" gauge
(c) ex Murton Colliery, 4/1975; prev.
    2' 0" gauge

303

Gauge: 2' 0"

-	4wDM	RH	268866	1949	(a)	Wt	Scr c12/1974
-	0-4-0DM	RH	393979	1955	(a)	Wt	Scr 9/1975
-	0-4-0DM	HE	6619	1968	(a)	Wt	
-	4wDM	RH	371541	1954	(b)	Hn	
-	4wDM	RH	371551	1954	(b)	Hn	(1)
B/L 92	0-4-0DM	RH	398070	1957	(b)	Hn	
-	4wDM	HE	4175	1949	(c)	EH	
-	4wDM	RH	268873	1952	(c)	STC	
-	0-4-0DM	HC	DM692	1952	(c)	Bl	
-	0-4-0DM	HE	4092	1952	(c)	Bl	
-	0-4-0DM	HE	4109	1953	(c)	H-ACW 12/75	
-	0-4-0DM	HE	4387	1953	(c)	H-ACW 9/74-H 12/75	
-	0-4-0DM	HE	4502	1954	(c)	Bl	
-	0-4-0DM	HE	4685	1955	(c)	Da	
-	0-4-0DM	RH	338425	1955	(c)	Bl	
-	0-4-0DM	HE	4803	1956	(c)	Da	
-	4wDM	HE	6628	1966	(c)	EH-ACW 12/75	
-	0-4-0DM	HE	5596	1961	(d)	STC	
-	0-6-0DM	HC	DM852	1954	(e)	STC	
20.180.4	4wDH	HE	6347	1974	New	Ep	
-	4wDH	HE	6348	1975	New	Mu	

(a) ex Northumberland Area, 1/4/1974
(b) ex North Durham Area, 1/4/1974
(c) ex South Durham Area, 1/4/1974
(d) ex Fishburn Colliery, underground,
    5/1974
(e) ex Ashington Central Workshops,
    7/1974 (see underground list)

(1) cannibalised during 1974 to provide
    parts for RH 371541

-	4wBE	CE	B0112	1973	(a)	Hv	
-	4wBE	GB	2378	1951	(b)	Wa/U	(1)
-	4wBE	EE	2519	1957			
		Bg	3500	1957	(b)	MTC-STC 10/74	
-	4wBE	WN	TJ189/3	1952	(c)	Mu	(2)
-	4wBE	WN	BS199/2	1954	(c)	Ep	Scr 6/1975
20.004.5	4wBE	CE	B0451	1975	New	Wt	

(a) ex Northumberland Area, 1/4/1974
(b) ex North Durham Area, 1/4/1974
(c) ex South Durham Area, 1/4/1974

(1) to Baye, Wilson & Co Ltd, L . \ouse,
    Wakefield, Yorks, 1/1975
(2) to Wearmouth Colliery, 4/1975,
    after conversion to 2' 6" gauge
    (q.v.)

NATIONAL SMOKELESS FUELS LTD
(subsidiary of the NCB; Coal Products Division until 1/4/1973)

When the Coal Products Division was created on 1st January 1963, all
the Co. Durham coking plants came under its Northern Region, together with the
Dumbreck Coking Plant at Kilsyth in Scotland. This was closed in January 1967.
On 1st January 1970 the Northern Region was abolished, and Co. Durham was
divided up into the West Durham Coking Management Unit and the East Durham
Coking Management Unit. On 1st January 1973 these were amalgamated to form the
Durham Coking Management Unit.

Locations

BpC   Brancepeth Coking Plant, Willington - shunted by locos from
      Brancepeth Colliery until 4/1967; closed 12/1967.
DC   Derwenthaugh Coking Plant, Winlaton Mill - shunted by locos from
      Derwenthaugh Loco Shed, Swalwell
FC   Fishburn Coking Plant, Fishburn - shunted by locos from
      Fishburn Colliery until 11/1973, after which they were hired from
      South Durham Area (North-East Area from 1/4/1974), though still
      working from the former colliery loco shed, until 17/2/1975, when
      the coking plant assumed responsibility
HC   Hawthorn Coking Plant, Murton - shunted by locos from
      South Hetton Loco Sheds
LC   Lambton Coking Plant, Fencehouses - shunted by locos from
      Lambton Railway Loco Sheds, Philadelphia
LEW   Lambton Engine Works, Philadelphia (repairs only)
MC   Monkton Coking Plant, Wardley - shunted by locos from
      Springwell Bank Foot Loco Shed, Leam Lane (Bowes Railway)
NC   Norwood Coking Plant, Gateshead

No numbering scheme has been introduced for shunting locomotives.

Shunting locomotives

Gauge: 4' 8½"

76	VENTURE	0-4-0ST	OC	HL	2837	1910	(a)	NC	Scr	12/1965
No.75	ERNEST BURY	0-6-0ST	OC	HL	3282	1917	(a)	NC	Scr	2/1963
No.77	"NORWOOD"	0-6-0ST	OC	RSH	7412	1948	(a)	NC-LEW 3/69 -NC 10/69		
No.92	502	0-4-0ST	OC	AB	2317	1950	(a)	NC	Scr	9/1971
	"STELLA No.2"	0-4-0ST	OC	RSH	7799	1954	(b)	NC	Scr	9/1971
No.12		0-6-0DH		HC	D1378	1966	(c)	NC	(1)	
	HOWDEN DENE No.1	0-6-0T	OC	HL	2880	1911	(d)	BpC	(2)	
-		0-4-0DH	EE V		D1125	1966	(e)	NC	(3)	
-		0-4-0DH		HE		1968	(f)	NC	(4)	
-		4wDH		TH	199V	1968	(g)	NC	(5)	
No.2		0-4-0DH		HE	6677	1968	New	NC		
No.1		0-4-0DH		HE	6688	1968	New	NC		
9D		0-6-0DM		HE	5382	1958	(h)	FC		
11D		0-6-0DM		HE	5305	1959	(h)	FC-LEW 6/74 -Bt 1/75-FC 2/75		
No.22		0-4-0ST	OC	AB	2320	1952	(j)	FC		

(a) ex No.5 Area, 1/1/1963
(b) ex No.4 Area, Brandon Pit House
    Colliery, 5/1963
(c) ex HC for trials, /1966
(d) ex South Durham Area, Brancepeth
    Colliery, hire, 4/1967
(e) ex EE V for trials /1967
(f) ex HE for trials, c5/1968
(g) ex TH for trials, 8/1968
(h) ex South Durham Area, Fishburn
    Colliery, hire, 11/1973 (hired from
    North-East Area from 1/4/1974);
    taken over, 17/2/1975
(j) ex North-East Area, Blackhall
    Colliery, 5/1974, hire

(1) ret. to HC, /1966
(2) ret. to South Durham Area, 12/1967
(3) ret. to EE V
(4) ret. to HE, c5/1968
(5) to Northumberland Area, Bates
    Colliery, Blyth, for trials, 9/1968

Coke Car locomotives

The diesel locomotives below were purchased to deputise for the electric loco during the rebuilding of coke ovens, though in the event some have been little used.

Gauge: 4' 8½"

-		0-4-0WE	HL	3859	1937	(a)	BpC	(1)
-		0-4-0WE	GB	2047	1946	(a)	NC	
-		0-4-0WE	RSH	7692	1953	(a)	FC	
-		0-4-0WE	RSH	7804	1954	(a)	LC	
-		0-4-0WE	RSH	7882	1957	(a)	DC	
-		0-4-0WE	RSH	7886	1958	(a)	HC	
-		0-4-0WE	RSH	8059	1959	(a)	MC	
No.18		0-4-0DM	RH	243081	1948	(b)	MC	Scr 5/1973
-		0-4-0DH	HE	6263	1964	(c)	DC-NC	9/72-HC 1/73
No. 1	D.P.WELLMAN	0-4-0DM	RH	319295	1953	(d)	MC	
No. 2		0-4-0DM	RH	313391	1952	(e)	MC	

(a) ex Durham Division, 1/1/1963
(b) ex River Wear Commissioners,
    Sunderland, 12/1970
(c) ex South Western Gas Board, Exeter
    Gas Works, Devon, 5/1971
(d) ex North Western Gas Board, Bradford
    Road Gas Works, Manchester, Lancs,
    2/1972
(e) ex North Western Gas Board, Warring-
    ton Gas Works, Lancs, 2/1972

(1) parts used to repair other locos
    after 1967; remains scrapped c/1969

To avoid unnecessary duplication, the underground locomotives have been grouped together into two main sections. The first section includes all Co. Durham locomotives up to the re-organisation of April 1974, and is based on the former North and South Durham Areas; which previous Area a locomotive was in at any particular time can be deduced from the history of the location. The second section lists all locomotives taken over by the North-East Area on 1st April 1974, and includes those in Northumberland.

Section 1 - Up to April 1974

<u>North Durham Area</u> (incorporating former Nos. 1 and 5 (originally No. 6) Areas, and part of No. 2 and old No. 5 Areas)

The loco numbering given below is that of the Area Plant Registry scheme, which all locos have to carry. Certain collieries also have their own numbering scheme, but to avoid confusion this is not given.

Locations

WMS	Area Machinery Stores, Whitburn (temporary)
B	Boldon Colliery
WCW	Central Workshops, Whitburn (Workshops Division)
Cr	Craghead Colliery (closed 11/4/1969)
Hn	Herrington Colliery, New Herrington
Hw	Heworth Colliery, Heworth (closed 29/6/1963)
LEW	Lambton Engine Works, Philadelphia (Workshops Division)
L	Louisa Colliery, Stanley (merged with Morrison Busty Colliery, 31/12/1955, but separate loco allocation maintained until loco haulage ceased in /1967)
MH	Marley Hill Colliery (locos originally allocated to Clockburn Drift, subsequently merged with Marley Hill)
MB	Morrison Busty Colliery, Annfield Plain (closed 5/10/1973)
R	Ryhope Colliery (to No.3 Area 28/6/1965)
Sa	Sacriston Colliery (loco haulage ceased in /1962)
Sk	Silksworth Colliery (closed 5/11/1971)
SGS	Stella Gill Withdrawn Machinery Stores, Pelton Fell (temporary)
U	Usworth Colliery (Wardley No.1 Shaft)(Wardley Colliery until 1/1969)
Wa	Wardley Colliery, White Mare Pool (name changed to Usworth Colliery, 1/1969)
WF	Washington 'F' Colliery (closed 21/6/1968)
W	Watergate Colliery, near Sunniside (closed 20/8/1964)
Wm	Wearmouth Colliery, Sunderland
We	Westoe Colliery, South Shields
Wh	Whitburn Colliery (closed 7/6/1968)

For other abbreviations see South Durham Area list.

Diesel locomotives

Gauge: 3' 6"

21		0-6-0DMF	HC	D632	1947	(a)	MH	(1)
22		0-6-0DMF	HC	D639	1947	(a)	MH	(1)
23		0-6-0DMF	HC	D709	1955	New	MH	(1)
24		0-6-0DMF	HC	D993	1956	New	MH	(1)
25		0-6-0DMF	HC	D1063	1957	New	MH	(1)

(a) ex No.1 (Fife & Clackmannan) Area, (1) to North-East Area, 1/4/1974
    Rothes Colliery, Scotland, /1950;
    installed 3/1952

Gauge: 2' 6"

No.	Type	Builder	Works No.	Year		Disposal
393	0-4-0DMF	NBL	26249	1947	New	Sk-WCW 4/62 -R 6/63 (1)
394	0-4-0DMF	NBL	26414	1947	New	Sk-R 9/62 (1)
113	0-4-0DMF	NBL	26687	1948	New	Wm Scr 2/1968
114	0-4-0DMF	NBL	26688	1948	New	Wm-R 6/64-Wm 11/64 Scr 2/1968
134	0-4-0DMF	NBL	26689	1948	New	Wh-R c/51 (1)
137	0-4-0DMF	NBL	26690	1948	New	Wh-R c/51 (1)
135	0-4-0DMF	NBL	26691	1948	New	Wh-R c/51 (1)
136	0-4-0DMF	NBL	26692	1948	New	Wh-R c/51 (1)
115	0-4-0DMF	NBL	26693	1948	New	Wm-R 1/64-Wm 11/64 Scr 5/1965
116	0-4-0DMF	NBL	26694	1948	New	Wm Scr 5/1968
112	0-6-0DMF	HE	4062	1951	(a)	Wm (2)
111	0-6-0DMF	HE	4071	1954	New	Wm (2)
118	0-6-0DMF	HE	4070	1958	New	Wm (2)
138	0-6-0DMF	HC	D1349	1964	New	R-No.3 Area 6/65 -Wm 4/66 (2)
124	0-6-0DMF	HC	D1350	1964	New	Wm (2)
126	0-6-0DMF	HE	6229	1965	New	Wm (2)
127	0-6-0DMF	HC	D1357	1966	New	Wm (2)
128	0-6-0DMF	HC	D1358	1966	New	Wm (2)
24	0-6-0DMF	HE	4060	1950	(b)	Wm (2)
25	0-6-0DMF	HE	4061	1950	(b)	Wm (2)

(a) ex No.5 Area, West Brandon Drift, /1951
(b) ex South Durham Area, Thrislington Colliery, 6/1967

(1) to No.3 Area, 28/6/1965
(2) to North-East Area, 1/4/1974

Gauge: 2' 2"

No.	Type	Builder	Works No.	Year		Disposal
1	4wDMF	RH	249536	1948	New	L Scr 2/1965
2	4wDMF	RH	249535	1948	New	L Scr 7/1967
3	4wDMF	RH	242469	1947	New	L Scr 12/1961
4	4wDMF	RH	256295	1948	New	Cr (1)
5	4wDMF	RH	256297	1948	New	Cr Scr 6/1969
6	4wDMF	RH	256299	1948	New	Cr Scr 6/1969
7	4wDMF	RH	256314	1949	New	MB (2)
8	4wDMF	RH	256323	1949	New	MB (2)
9	4wDMF	RH	268871✗	1951	New	L (3)
10	4wDMF	RH	268872	1952	New	L Scr 2/1965
11	4wDMF	RH	268877	1955	New	L Scr 2/1965
12	0-6-0DMF	HC	D891	1955	New	L Scr 2/1969
13	0-6-0DMF	HC	D892	1955	New	L Scr 2/1969
14	4wDMF	RH	268879	1957	New	Cr Scr 6/1969

✗ rebuilt with body from RH 242469

(1) to North of England Open-Air Museum, Beamish, for preservation, c11/1969
(2) to Lambton Engine Works, 1/1974, for conversion to 2' 6" gauge (see surface list)
(3) to East Wales Area, Britannia Mining School, Pengam, Monmouthshire, 6/1967

Gauge: 2' 0"

285	0-4-0DMF	HE	4078	1950	New	Mu-VT 4/52 -D&C 3/56-SoH 5/56 -LEW 10/57-Hn 3/58 Scr 5/1967
284	0-4-0DMF	HE	4079	1950	New	Mu-VT 4/51 -LEW 1/64-Hn 4/64 (1)
411	0-6-0DMF	HC	D825	1952	New	Hn (2)
412	0-6-0DMF	HC	D826	1952	New	Hn (3)
41	4wDMF	RH	268873	1952	New	W (4)
42	4wDMF	RH	268874	1952	New	W (4)
414	0-6-0DMF	HC	D872	1954	New	Hn (2)
419	0-6-0DMF	HC	D873	1955	New	Hn (2)
421	0-6-0DMF	HC	D874	1956	New	Hn (2)
420	0-6-0DMF	HC	D875	1956	New	Hn (2)
422	0-6-0DMF	HC	D1245	1961	New	Hn-VT 3/61 (5)
423	0-6-0DMF	HC	D1281	1963	New	Hn (2)
26	0-4-0DMF	HE	4093	1952	(a)	LEW-Hn 9/67 (2)
424	0-6-0DMF	HC	D1400	1967	New	Hn (2)

(a) ex No.4 Area, Dean & Chapter
    Colliery, 10/1966

(1) withdrawn from service c/1969 and
    scrapped
(2) to North-East Area, 1/4/1974
(3) withdrawn from service c/1969 and
    used as spares for other locos;
    remains scrapped, 7/1973
(4) to Morrison Training Centre,
    Annfield Plain, 10/1965 (see
    surface lists)
(5) to No.3 Area, 28/6/1965

Battery locomotives

Gauge: 2' 6"

62	4wBE	LMM	1101	1952	New	B-Wm 4/63 Scr 2/1968
117	4wBE	LMM	1104	1952	New	Wm Scr 9/1966
391	4wBE	WN	TJ189/2	1952	New	Sk (1)
392	4wBE	WN	BS199	1954	New	Sk (2)
66	4wBE	GB	2544	1955	New	B-Wm 11/68 (3)
51	4wBE	GB	2545	1955	New	Wm (4)
68	4wBE	EE	2076	1955		
		Bg	3427	1955	New	Wh-Sk 8/68 (5)
69	4wBE	EE	2077	1955		
		Bg	3428	1955	New	Wh-Wm 10/68 (6)
70	4wBE	EE	2078	1955		
		Bg	3429	1955	New	Wh-B 1/69 (7)
67	4wBE	EE	2080	1955		
		Bg	3439	1955	New	Wh-We 5/68 (7)
63	4wBE	EE	2227	1955		
		Bg	3444	1955	New	B (7)

No.	Note	Type	Builder	Works No.	Year		Disposal	Ref
64		4wBE	EE	2228	1955			
			Bg	3445	1955	New	B	(7)
65		4wBE	EE	2229	1955			
			Bg	3446	1955	New	B	(7)
52		4wBE	EE	2328	1956			
			Bg	3470	1956	New	We	(7)
53		4wBE	EE	2329	1957			
			Bg	3471	1957	New	We	(7)
71		4wBE	EE	2330	1956			
			Bg	3473	1956	New	Wh-Wm 6/68	(7)
181		4wBE	EE	2331	1956			
			Bg	3472	1956	New	B	(7)
54		4wBE	EE	2418	1958			
			Bg	3497	1958	New	We	(7)
55		4wBE	EE	2419	1958			
			Bg	3498	1958	New	We	(7)
56		4wBE	EE	2420	1958			
			Bg	3499	1958	New	We	(7)
182		4wBE	EE	2523	1957			
			Bg	3496	1957	New	B	(8)
57		4wBE	EE	2626	1958			
			Bg	3521	1958	New	We	(7)
119		4wBE	EE	2627	1958			
			Bg	3522	1958	New	Wm-B 4/63	(7)
120		4wBE	EE	2628	1958			
			Bg	3523	1958	New	Wm-We 1/67 -Sk 11/67-B 6/72 -Wm 9/72-WMS 10/72 -We 3/74	(7)
32		4wBE	GB	2572	1955	(a)	We-B 5/60	(9)
31		4wBE	GB	2573	1955	(a)	We	(10)
395		4wBE	EE	2661	1959			
			RSH		1959	New	Sk-We 10/71 -LEW 8/73	(7)
396		4wBE	EE	2662	1959			
			RSH		1959	New	Sk	(11)
415		4wBE	WN	TJ189/1	1952	(b)	Sk-We 5/69 -Wm 11/69	(12)
151	(58 till 8/1967)	4wBE	EE	2740	1959			
			Bg	3542	1959	New	We	(7)
183		4wBE	EE	2955	1960			
			Bg	3566	1960	New	B	
397		4wBE	EE	3149	1960			
			RSH		1960	New	Sk	(11)
152	(orig. 59)	4wBE	EE	3150	1960			
			Bg	3567	1960	New	We	(7)
398		4wBE	EE	3155	1961			
			RSH		1961	New	Sk-We 4/71	(7)
153		4wBE	EE	3173	1962			
			Bg	3583	1962	New	We	(7)
154		4wBE	EE	3336	1963			
			Bg	3595	1963	New	We-WMS 10/67 -Bg/D (reps) 11/67 -We c/69	(7)
155		4wBE	EE	3399	1963			
			Bg	3599	1963	New	We	(7)

No.	Name	Type	Builder	Works No.	Year		Disposal	Note
123		4wBE	EE	3404	1963			
			Bg	3603	1963	New	Wm	(7)
156		4wBE	EE	3820	1966			
			Bg	3642	1966	New	We	(7)
157		4wBE	EE	3842	1967			
			Bg	3645	1967	New	We	(7)
518		4wBE	EE V	3849	1967	New	Sk-We 6/72 -LEW 8/73	(7)
158		4wBE	EE	3871	1968			
			Bg	3649	1968	New	We	(7)
1		4wBE	EE	2027	1954			
			Bg	3414	1954	(c)	Sk-We 2/70	(7)
41		4wBE	EE	1809	1952			
			Bg	3353	1952	(d)	Wm	(7)
2		4wBE	EE	2028	1954			
			Bg	3415	1954	(e)	B	(7)
47		4wBE	EE	3174	1962			
			Bg	3584	1962	(f)	We	
32		4wBE	GB	2572	1955	(g)	B	Scr 3/1972

(a) ex Area Central Workshops, Whitburn, 2/1959; reb. from 2' 0" gauge (q.v.)
(b) ex Lambton Engine Works, Philadelphia, 8/1959; reb. from 2' 0" gauge (q.v.)
(c) ex Washington 'F' Colliery, 7/1968; prev. 2' 0" gauge (q.v.)
(d) ex Washington 'F' Colliery, 8/1968; prev. 2' 0" gauge (q.v.)
(e) ex Wardley Colliery, 12/1968; prev. 2' 0" gauge (q.v.)
(f) ex Usworth Colliery, 3/1969; prev. 2' 0" gauge (q.v.)
(g) ex Stella Gill Machinery Stores, 6/1971; prev. 2' 0" gauge surface loco at Harton Colliery (q.v.)

(1) to Wearmouth Colliery, 6/1968, for working on the surface (q.v.)
(2) taken out of service c/1965, and parts used to repair 391 and 415; remains scrapped 10/1970
(3) to Stella Gill Machinery Stores, 6/1970; scrapped 9/1972
(4) to Area Central Workshops, Whitburn, /1958, for rebuilding to 2' 0" gauge (q.v.)
(5) to Stella Gill Machinery Stores for spares, 3/1971; remains scrapped 3/1971
(6) parts sent to Westoe Colliery; remains scrapped 3/1973
(7) to North-East Area, 1/4/1974
(8) withdrawn from service, 7/1971, and parts used to repair other locos; to North-East Area, 1/4/1974
(9) to Area Central Workshops, Whitburn, 1/1961, for rebuilding to 2' 0" gauge (see also 'g')
(10) to Boldon Colliery, 5/1960, for working on the surface (q.v.)
(11) to South Durham Area, Murton Colliery, 6/1972
(12) transferred to working on the surface, 9/1971 (q.v.)

Gauge: 2' 0"

No.	Name	Type	Builder	Works No.	Year		Disposal	Note
415		4wBE	WN	TJ189/1	1952	New	Hn-LEW 11/56 -Mu 12/56 -Ep 7/11/58	(1)
416		4wBE	WN	TJ189/3	1952	New	Hn-LEW 10/56 -Ep 12/56-Mu 3/58 -LEW 6/63-Mu 12/63	(2)
41	RUSHFORD	4wBE	EE	1809	1952			
			Bg	3353	1952	New	Wa-WF 10/58	(3)

No.	Type	Builder	Works No.	Year	New	Location	Notes
33	4wBE	GB	2378	1951	(a)	Hw-Wa	3/57 (4)
43	4wBE	EE	2026	1954			
		Bg	3413	1954	New	Wa/U	(5)
1	4wBE	EE	2027	1954			
		Bg	3414	1954	New	WF	(6)
2	4wBE	EE	2028	1954			
		Bg	3415	1954	New	WF	(7)
?	4wBE	GB	2517	1954	New	Sa	Scr 10/1962
?	4wBE	GB	2518	1954	New	Sa	Scr 10/1962
32	4wBE	GB	2572	1955	New	Hw	(8)
31	4wBE	GB	2573	1955	New	Hw	(9)
42	4wBE	EE	2079	1955			
		Bg	3430	1955	New	Wa/U	(5)
44	4wBE	EE	2230	1955			
		Bg	3431	1955	New	Wa/U	(5)
46	4wBE	EE	2466	1957			
		Bg	3501	1957	New	Wa/U	(5)
34	4wBE	EE	2467	1957			
		Bg	3495	1957	(b)	Wa/U	(5)
35	4wBE	EE	2519	1958			
		Bg	3500	1958	New	Hw-WF	9/63 (10)
51	4wBE	GB	2545	1955	(c)	Wa-WF	9/62 Scr 4/1965
47	4wBE	EE	3174	1962			
		Bg	3584	1962	New	Wa/U	(11)

(a) ex No.3 Area, Shotton Colliery, 6/1954
(b) New to Heworth Colliery, but transferred to Wardley Colliery same day (30/8/1957)
(c) ex Area Central Workshops, Whitburn, 12/1958; reb. from 2' 6" gauge (q.v.)

(1) to Lambton Engine Works, Philadelphia, 8/11/1958, for reb. to 2' 6" gauge (q.v.)
(2) transferred to working on the surface, 3/1964 (q.v.)
(3) reb. to 2' 6" gauge, and transferred to Wearmouth Colliery, 3/1968
(4) transferred to working on the surface, 3/1959; ret. underground by 11/1961; ret. to working on the surface by 11/1964 (q.v.)
(5) to North-East Area, 1/4/1974
(6) reb. to 2' 6" gauge, and transferred to Silksworth Colliery, 7/1968
(7) reb. to 2' 6" gauge, and transferred to Boldon Colliery, 12/1968
(8) to Area Central Workshops, Whitburn, /1958, for rebuilding to 2' 6" gauge (q.v.); ret. to 2' 0" gauge /1961, and ret. to Heworth Colliery, 11/1961; to Area Central Workshops, Whitburn, 2/1964, prior to transfer to Harton Colliery for working on the surface (q.v.)
(9) to Area Central Workshops, Whitburn, /1958, for rebuilding to 2' 6" gauge
(10) to Morrison Training Centre, Annfield Plain, 7/1968 (see surface lists)
(11) reb. to 2' 6" gauge, and transferred to Westoe Colliery, 3/1969

∅

<u>South Durham Area</u>   (incorporating former Nos.3 and 4 Areas, and part of
No.2 and old No.5 Areas)

The loco numbering scheme given below is the Area Plant Registry
scheme, which all locos have to carry. Certain collieries also had their
own numbering scheme, but only the scheme for Murton and Eppleton locos working
to Hawthorn Combined Mine is given.

Locations

ACW	Central Workshops, Ashington, Northumberland (Workshops Div.)
TCW	Central Workshops, Tursdale (Workshops Division)
Bl	Blackhall Colliery, Blackhall
BMS	Blackhall Machinery Stores (closed /1968)
Bo	Bowburn Colliery (closed 22/7/1967)
C	Chilton Colliery (shed closed 15/1/1966)
Da	Dawdon Colliery, Dawdon
D&C	Dean & Chapter Colliery, Ferryhill (closed 15/1/1966)
E	Easington Colliery
El	Elemore Colliery, Easington Lane (closed 2/1/1974)
Ep	Eppleton Colliery, Hetton-le-Hole
F	Fishburn Colliery (closed 30/11/1973)
H	Horden Colliery, Horden
M	Mainsforth Colliery, Ferryhill Station (closed 7/12/1968)
Mu	Murton Colliery, Murton
LEW	Lambton Engine Works, Philadelphia (Workshops Division)
R	Ryhope Colliery (locos out of use; closed 25/11/1966)
SH	Sherburn Hill Colliery (closed 7/8/1965)
SoH	South Hetton Colliery (temporarily)
Th	Thrislington Colliery, West Cornforth (closed 4/3/1967)
VT	Vane Tempest Colliery Seaham

For other abbreviations see North Durham Area list.

Diesel locomotives

Gauge: 3' 0"

40	0-6-0DMF		HC	D830	1954	New	E	(1)
39	0-6-0DMF		HC	D831	1954	New	E	(1)
44	0-6-0DMF		HC	D966	1955	New	E	(1)
68	0-6-0DMF		HC	D1323	1965	New	E	(1)
89	0-6-0DMF	⁄	HC	D1402	1968	New	E	(1)
90	0-6-0DMF	⁄	HC	D1403	1968	New	E	(1)
91	0-6-0DMF		HC	D1407	1968	New	E	(1)
95	0-4-0DMF		HE	7116	1970	New	E	(1)
98	0-4-0DMF		HE	7117	1970	New	E	(1)
116	0-6-0DMF	⁄	HB	D1423	1972	New	E	(1)
121	4w-4wDHF		HE	7099	1973	New	E	(1)
124	4w-4wDHF		HE	7100	1974	New	E	(1)

⁄ Tandem unit

(1) to North-East Area, 1/4/1974

Gauge: 2' 8½"

22	0-4-0DMF	HE	2980	1944	(a)	Bl	(1)
11	0-4-0DMF	HE	3330	1946	(a)	H	(2)
20	0-6-0DMF	HE	3476	1947	New	Bl	(3)
21	0-6-0DMF	HE	4058	1950	New	Bl	(3)

(a) ex Horden Collieries Ltd, 1/1/1947   (1) to No.1 Area, Area Apprentice
                                              Training Centre, Usworth, 1/1961
                                              (see surface lists)
                                          (2) to TWW, Middlesbrough, Yorks, N.R.,

for scrap, 6/1960
(3) dismantled underground from /1962;
scrapped 8/1972

Gauge: 2' 6"

14	0-4-0DMF	HE	4100	1953	New	Th	(1)	
15	0-4-0DMF	HE	4101	1952	New	Th	(1)	
10	0-4-0DMF	HE	5424	1959	New	Th	(1)	
25	0-6-0DMF	HE	4061	1950	(a)	Th	(2)	
393	0-4-0DMF	NBL	26249	1947	(b)	R	Scr	5/1966
394	0-4-0DMF	NBL	26414	1947	(b)	R	Scr	5/1966
134	0-4-0DMF	NBL	26689	1948	(b)	R	Scr	5/1966
137	0-4-0DMF	NBL	26690	1948	(b)	R	Scr	5/1966
135	0-4-0DMF	NBL	26691	1948	(b)	R	Scr	5/1966
136	0-4-0DMF	NBL	26692	1948	(b)	R	Scr	5/1966
138	0-6-0DMF	HC	D1349	1964	(b)	R	(3)	
24	0-6-0DMF	HE	4060	1950	(c)	Th	(2)	

(a) ex Lambton Engine Works, Philadelphia, 6/1965; prev. at Pease's West Garage (see surface lists)
(b) ex No.1 Area, 28/6/1965; locos out of use
(c) ex Lambton Engine Works, Philadelphia, 9/1965; prev. at Pease's West Garage

(1) abandoned underground after closure of colliery, 3/1967
(2) to North Durham Area, Wearmouth Colliery, 6/1967
(3) to Lambton Engine Works, Philadelphia, 9/1965; to No.1 Area, Wearmouth Colliery, 4/1966

Gauge: 2' 3½"

341	0-4-0DMF	HE	3524	1947	New	El	(1)
342	0-4-0DMF	HE	4631	1953	New	El	(1)
343	0-4-0DMF	HE	4632	1953	New	El	(1)
344	4wDMF	RH	418805	1958	New	El	(2)

(1) believed not to have been converted when colliery changed to 2' 0" gauge, /1961; to Area Training Centre, Seaham, 7/1965 (see surface lists)
(2) converted to 2' 0" gauge, c/1961 (q.v.)

Gauge: 2' 0"

285	0-4-0DMF	HE	4078	1950	New	Mu-VT 4/52 -D&C 3/56-SoH 5/56 -LEW 10/57-Hn 3/58	(1)
284	0-4-0DMF	HE	4079	1950	New	Mu-VT 4/51 -LEW 1/64-Hn 4/64	(1)
282	0-6-0DMF	HC	D804	1951	New	VT	(2)
283	0-6-0DMF	HC	D805	1951	New	VT	Scr 4/1973
24	0-4-0DMF	HE	4091	1952	New	D&C-H 6/67-ACW 8/68	Scr 7/1970
25	0-4-0DMF	HE	4092	1952	New	D&C-F 12/65-Sh 4/68	(3)
26	0-4-0DMF	HE	4093	1952	New	D&C-LEW 10/66	(4)
9	0-4-0DMF	HE	4094	1952	New	H	(2)
49	0-4-0DMF	HE	4108	1952	New	C	(5)
50	0-4-0DMF	HE	4109	1952	New	C-D&C 7/64-H 6/67	(6)
51	0-4-0DMF	HE	4110	1952	New	C-D&C 7/63-H 6/67	(2)

38	0-4-0DMF		HC	D692	1952	New	E-Sh 1/57
							(3)
6	0-6-0DMF		HC	D818	1952	New	H (2)
7	0-6-0DMF		HC	D819	1952	New	H (2)
10	0-4-0DMF		HE	4387	1952	New	H (7)
286	0-6-0DMF		HC	D842	1954	New	VT (2)
262	0-6-0DMF		HC	D852	1954	New	Da-ACW 10/73
							(2)
413	0-6-0DMF		HC	D853	1954	New	Da-Hn 10/54
							-Da 2/56-VT 10/64
							-ACW 12/67-Da 5/68
							(2)
5	0-6-0DMF		HC	D893	1954	New	H (2)
8	0-4-0DMF		HE	4502	1954	New	H-DH(surface) 9/55
							-Sh 5/59
							(3)
27	0-4-0DMF		HE	4504	1955	New	D&C-F 8/56
							-D&C 1/57-C 10/64
							(5)
19	0-4-0DMF		RH	392154	1956	New	F (8)
20	0-4-0DMF		RH	392156	1956	New	F-D&C 4/62-C 6/63
							(5)
65	0-4-0DMF		RH	392157	1956	New	F (9)
66	0-4-0DMF		RH	392160	1956	New	F Scr 4/1967
263	0-6-0DMF		HC	D1015	1956	(a)	Da (2)
53	0-6-0DMF		HC	D1118	1958	New	Sh-Bl 9/67
							(2)
54	0-6-0DMF		HC	D1119	1958	New	Sh-F 5/68
							(2)
72	0-6-0DMF		HC	D1127	1958	New	D&C-F 11/65
							(2)
264	0-6-0DMF		HC	D1064	1959	New	Da (2)
345	0-6-0DMF	≠	HC	D1065	1959	New	El (2)
346	0-6-0DMF	≠	HC	D1066	1959	New	El (2)
347	0-6-0DMF	≠	HC	D1067	1959	New	El-Bl 4/72
							(2)
265	0-6-0DMF		HC	D1169	1960	New	Da (2)
266	0-6-0DMF		HC	D1170	1960	New	Da (2)
422	0-6-0DMF		HC	D1245	1961	New	Hn-VT 3/61
							(2)
348	0-6-0DMF	≠	HC	D1247	1961	New	El (2)
349	0-6-0DMF	≠	HC	D1248	1961	New	El (2)
344	4wDMF		RH	418805	1958	(b)	El-LEW 1/64
							s/s c/1966
80	0-4-0DMF		HE	5596	1961	New	F (2)
81	0-4-0DMF		HE	5600	1961	New	D&C-F 1/62
							Scr 12/1970
58	0-6-0DMF		HE	5609	1962	New	Bl (2)
82	0-4-0DMF		HE	6050	1962	New	F Scr 1/1973
60	0-6-0DMF		HC	D1325	1963	New	Sh-VT 9/72
							(2)
64	0-6-0DMF		HE	5610	1964	New	Bl (2)
66	0-6-0DMF		HC	D1322	1964	New	H (2)
67	0-6-0DMF		HC	D1366	1965	New	H (2)
86	0-6-0DMF		HC	D1399	1967	New	VT (2)
87	0-6-0DMF		HC	D1401	1968	New	H (2)
101	0-6-0DMF		HC	D1412	1970	New	H (2)
106	0-6-0DMF		HB	D1416	1971	New	F (2)

≠ fitted with 15-ton brake tender when working at Elemore Colliery

(a) apparently delivered new to No.5   (1) to No.1 Area, 28/6/1965
Area,Brandon Colliery, but diverted (2) to North-East Area, 1/4/1974
to Dawdon Colliery within a few days (3) to Blackhall Colliery, 3/1973, for

(b) converted from 2' 3¼" gauge (q.v.)

working on the surface (q.v.)
(4) to North Durham Area, Herrington
    Colliery, 9/1967
(5) abandoned underground after closure
    of Dean & Chapter Colliery, 1/1966
(6) transferred to working on the
    surface, 11/72 (q.v.)
(7) transferred to working on the
    surface, 10/1971, (q.v.)
(8) to Area Apprentice Training Centre,
    Tursdale, 1/1967 (see surface list)
(9) to Blackhall Colliery for working
    on the surface, 10/1962 (q.v.)

Mine ranger captive track system

93	UMM		1969	New	Da-UMM 3/71 -Da 3/73 (1)
96	UMM		1970	New	Da-UMM 3/71 -Da 3/73 (1)
105	UMM		1971	New	Da (2)
107	UMM		1971	New	Da (2)
122	UMM		1973	New	Da (2)
123	UMM		1973	New	Da (2)

(1) ret. to makers, 12/1973
(2) to North-East Area, 1/4/1974

Road-railer captive monorail system for high-speed man-riding trains

94	Becorit	DRL 25/1/201	1969	New	Da	(1)
102	Becorit	DRL 25/1/217	1970	New	Da	(1)
104	Becorit	DRL 25/2/209	1970	(a)	Da	(1)
108	Becorit	DRL 40/1/502	1971	New	Da-Mu 4/72	(1)
109	Becorit	DRL 40/1/501	1971	New	Mu	(1)
110	Becorit	DRL 40/1/503	1971	New	Mu-Da 5/72	(1)
111	Becorit	DRL 40/1/504	1972	New	Mu	(1)
117	Becorit	DRL 25/1/224	1972	New	Da	(1)
118	Becorit	DRL 40/4/509	1972	New	Da	(1)
119	Becorit	DRL 40/4/510	1972	New	Da	(1)
120	Becorit	DRL 40/4/508	1972	New	Mu	(1)

(a) ex North Derbyshire Area, High   (1) to North-East Area, 1/4/1974
    Moor Colliery, 1/1971

Battery locomotives

Gauge: 3' 0"

34	4wBE	GB	2395	1953	(a)	E	(1)
33	4wBE	GB	2403	1953	(a)	E	(1)
49	4wBE	EE	2342	1957			
		RSH		1957	New	E	(1)
50	4wBE	EE	2343	1957			
		RSH		1957	New	E	(1)
51	4wBE	EE	2344	1957			
		RSH		1957	New	E	(1)
88	4wBE	EE V	3845	1968	New	E	(1)

(a) prev. 2' 0" gauge (q.v.)   (1) to North-East Area, 1/4/1974

Gauge: 2' 3"

40		4wBE	GB ⚡ 2626	1955	New	M	(1)
41		4wBE	GB ⚡ 2627	1956	New	M	(1)
42		4wBE	GB ⚡ 2628	1955	New	M	(1)
28		4wBE	LMM 1075	1951	(a)	M	Scr 6/1966

⚡ built to LMM design

(a) ex Area Central Workshops, Tursdale, (1) abandoned underground after closure
    7/1964; prev. 2' 0" gauge   of colliery; written off 11/1969

Gauge: 2' 0"

261		4wBE	Atlas 2458	1946	(a)	VT-Da 5/55
						-LEW 11/55-Ep 7/56
						(1)
281		4wBE	Atlas 2456	1947	New	VT-Da 10/11/62
						-LEW 21/11/62
						-Sh 2/64
						(2)
13		4wBE	Atlas 2459	1948	New	H-TCW 5/64
						Scr 8/1968
14		4wBE	Atlas 2460	1948	New	H Scr 8/1968
16		4wBE	Atlas 2461	1948	New	E-H 2/55
						Scr 8/1968
15		4wBE	Atlas 2462	1948	New	H Scr 8/1968
7		4wBE	LMM 1074	1951	New	D&C-SH by /54
						Scr 5/1966
28		4wBE	LMM 1075	1951	New	D&C-TCW 4/62
						(3)
415		4wBE	WN TJ189/1	1952	New	Hn-LEW 11/56
						-Mu 12/56
						-Ep 7/11/58
						(4)
416		4wBE	WN TJ189/3	1952	New	Hn-LEW 10/56
						-Ep 12/56-Mu 3/58
						(5)
17		4wBE	GB 2378	1951	New	H-Sh c/53
						(6)
62		4wBE	GB 2382	1953	New	Sh-Bl ?/?-TCW 6/61
						-BMS 3/62
						(7)
?		4wBE	GB 2392	1953	New	Bl s/s
34		4wBE	GB 2395	1953	New	E (8)
43		4wBE	GB 2400	1953	New	Sh-E ?/?-Sh c/57
						-Bl 2/59-H 6/63
						-Bl 2/65-LEW c/67
						(9)
33		4wBE	GB 2403	1953	New	E (8)
18		4wBE	GB 2406	1953	New	H s/s c/1958
?		4wBE	GB 2436	1953	New	E-TCW 6/61
						s/s c/1962
35		4wBE	GB 2481	1954	New	E-Bl 7/56-TCW 5/61
						-BMS 5/62-H 3/64
						-Bl 8/66-BMS 11/67
						s/s c/1968
36		4wBE	GB 2482	1954	New	E s/s
301		4wBE	WN BS199/2	1954	New	Ep-LEW 10/61
						(10)
321		4wBE	WN BS1310/1	1955	New	Mu-Ep 12/59
						-LEW 12/63-Bl 8/65
						Scr 1/1967
322		4wBE	WN BS1310/2	1955	New	Mu (11)

302		4wBE	WN	BS1312/1	1956	New	Ep-LEW 1/63
							s/s

The Area Plant Control cards quoted the makers' numbers of 322 as BS 1312/1 and that of 301 as BS1310/1, the latter number also being quoted for 321; the above version is believed to be the correct one.

4		4wBE	GB	2787	1957	New	Bo Scr 12/1965
56		4wBE	WN	BS2063/1	1958	New	BMS-Bl 9/59
							-BMS /62-Bl 3/63
							-BMS 9/67
							s/s c/1968
441	1	4wBE ⟋	EE	2469	1958		
			RSH		1958	New	Mu (12)
442	2	4wBE ⟋	EE	2470	1958		
			RSH		1958	New	Mu (12)
443	5	4wBE ⟋	EE	2471	1958		
			RSH		1958	New	Mu (12)
457	11	4wBE ⟋	EE	2472	1958		
			RSH		1958	New	Mu (12)
449	10	4wBE ⟋	EE	2473	1958		
			RSH		1958	New	Mu (12)
458	12	4wBE ⟋	EE	2474	1958		
			RSH		1958	New	Mu (12)
451	13	4wBE ⟋	EE	2475	1958		
			RSH		1958	New	Ep-Mu 2/71
							Scr 6/1973
456	19	4wBE ⟋	EE	2476	1958		
			RSH		1958	New	Ep-Mu 2/71
							(12)
460	20	4wBE ⟋	EE	2477	1958		
			RSH		1958	New	Ep (12)
462	22	4wBE ⟋	EE	2478	1959		
			RSH		1959	New	Mu (12)
461	21	4wBE ⦸	EE	2479	1959		
			RSH		1959	New	Mu (12)
459	18	4wBE ⦸	EE	2480	1958		
			RSH		1958	New	Mu (12)
455	17	4wBE ⦸	EE	2481	1958		
			RSH		1958	New	Ep (12)
454	16	4wBE ⦸	EE	2482	1958		
			RSH		1958	New	Ep-Mu 8/67
							(12)
453	15	4wBE ⦸	EE	2483	1958		
			RSH		1958	New	Ep (12)
452	14	4wBE ⦸	EE	2484	1958		
			RSH		1958	New	Ep (12)
450	9	4wBE ⦸	EE	2485	1958		
			RSH		1958	New	Mu (12)
446	8	4wBE ⦸	EE	2486	1958		
			RSH		1958	New	Ep (12)
447	6	4wBE ⦸	EE	2487	1958		
			RSH		1958	New	Mu (12)
448	7	4wBE ⦸	EE	2488	1958		
			RSH		1958	New	Mu (12)
445	4	4wBE ⦸	EE	2489	1958		
			RSH		1958	New	Ep (12)
444	3	4wBE ⦸	EE	2490	1958		
			RSH		1958	New	Ep (12)
463	23	4wBE ⟋	EE	2736	1959		
			RSH		1959	New	Mu (12)
464	24	4wBE ⟋	EE	2737	1960		
			RSH		1960	New	Mu-Ep 7/67
							-Mu by 11/69
							(12)

465	25	4wBE ⚡	EE	2848	1960				
			RSH		1960	New	Mu	(12)	
466	26	4wBE ⚡	EE	2849	1960				
			RSH		1960	New	Mu-Ep 8/67		
							(12)		
287	28	4wBE	HC		1960	New	VT-Ep 3/61		
							(12)		
467	27	4wBE ⚡	EE	3167	1961				
			RSH		1961	New	Mu	(12)	
468	29	4wBE ø	EE	3401	1963				
			EES		1963	New	Ep	(12)	
469	30	4wBE ⚡	EE	1960	1954				
			Bg	3379	1954	(b)	Mu-Ep 10/70		
							Scr 12/1973		
470	31	4wBE ⚡	EE	1961	1954				
			Bg	3380	1954	(c)	LEW-Mu 8/67		
							(12)		
3	32	4wBE ø	EE	2637	1960				
			RSH		1960	(d)	Mu	(12)	
1	34	4wBE ø	EE	2635	1960				
			RSH		1960	(e)	Mu	(12)	
4	33	4wBE ø	EE	2638	1960				
			RSH		1960	(f)	Mu	(12)	
396		4wBE ø	EE	2662	1959				
			RSH		1959	(g)	Mu	(12)	
397		4wBE ø	EE	3149	1962				
			RSH		1962	(g)	Mu	(12)	

⚡ built as tandem units   ø converted to tandem units

(a) ex Londonderry Collieries Ltd, 1/1/1947
(b) ex North Western No.5 (North Wales) Area, Llay Main Colliery, Denbighs, 2/1964
(c) ex North Western No.5 (North Wales) Area, Llay Main Colliery, Denbighs, 2/1964; delivered to South Hetton Loco Shed (surface); to Lambton Engine Works, Philadelphia, 4/1965
(d) ex Northumberland Area, Rising Sun Colliery, Wallsend, 12/1969; put into service, 5/1970
(e) ex Northumberland Area, Whittle Colliery, Newton-on-the-Moor, 12/1969; put into service, 8/1970
(f) ex Northumberland Area, Whittle Colliery, Newton-on-the-Moor, 12/1969; put into service, 12/1970
(g) ex North Durham Area, Silksworth Colliery, 6/1972; prev. 2' 6" gauge

(1) transferred to working on the surface, 8/1959 (q.v.)
(2) to Easington Colliery to be used for spares, /1965; remains scrapped
(3) reb. to 2' 3" gauge, /1964 (q.v.)
(4) to Lambton Engine Works, Philadelphia, 8/11/1958; reb. to 2' 6" gauge, /1959 (see North Durham Area list)
(5) transferred to working on the surface, 3/1964 (q.v.)
(6) to No.1 Area, Heworth Colliery, 6/1954
(7) to J. Lister & Sons Ltd, Consett, 2/1968; re-sold to Ayle Colliery Co Ltd, Alston, Cumberland
(8) reb. to 3' 0" gauge (q.v.)
(9) used for spares; remains scrapped
(10) ret. to Eppleton Colliery, 3/1963, for working on the surface (q.v.)
(11) transferred to working on the surface, 12/1959 (q.v.)
(12) to North-East Area, 1/4/1974

ø

North-East Area

       This Area was formed on 1st April 1974 by an amalgamation of the former Northumberland, North Durham and South Durham Areas. It took over 197 underground locomotives, consisting of 91 diesel locomotives, 88 battery locomotives and 18 other types of haulage unit, loosely classed as locomotives.

       The numbering given is that of the Area Plant Control scheme, first introduced about 1958. The first number given below is the code of the location to which it was first delivered. Of the four figures, the first showed the number of the Division; Durham received numbers in the 2xxx series and Northumberland in the 9xxx series. The second figure was the number of the Area within the Division, and then the various locations were numbered in alphabetical order within the Area from 01 upwards to give the last two figures. This operated until 1967, when new location numbers in the 05xxx series were used. These in turn were replaced by a new system in 1974. Under this the North-East Area became 20, and then all plant, regardless of type, was numbered in the same series of numbers. These numbers are carried by all plant, including locomotives. During 1975-1976 underground locomotives were transferred to the responsibility of the central Plant Pool, but the numbering schemes of 1958, 1967 and 1974 remained unaltered.

       Quite a number of locomotives also carry an individual colliery number, e.g. 'No.1'. To avoid confusion this is not given.

Locomotives have been kept at the following locations:

NORTHUMBERLAND

ACW	Central Workshops, Ashington (repairs only)
Bt	Bates Colliery, Blyth
En	Ellington Colliery, Ellington)
Ly	Lynemouth Colliery, Lynemouth) one complex underground
SD	Seaton Delaval Yard, Seaton Delaval (locos stored; closed 31/3/1975)
Sb	Shilbottle Colliery, Shilbottle
Wt	Whittle Colliery, Newton-on-the-Moor

TYNE & WEAR

BF	Black Fell Loco Shed, Eighton Banks (underground loco testing track)
B	Boldon Colliery, Boldon
Ep	Eppleton Colliery, near Hetton-le-Hole
Hn	Herrington Colliery, New Herrington
LEW	Lambton Engine Works, Philadelphia (repairs only)
MH	Marley Hill Colliery, near Sunniside
U	Usworth Colliery (Wardley No.1 Shaft), White Mare Pool (closed 8/8/1974)
We	Westoe Colliery, South Shields
Wm	Wearmouth Colliery, Sunderland
WMS	Machinery Stores, Whitburn Central Workshops, Whitburn (locos stored)

Co. DURHAM

Bl	Blackhall Colliery, Blackhall
Da	Dawdon Colliery, Dawdon
E	Easington Colliery, Easington
El	Elemore Colliery, Easington Lane ✗
F	Fishburn Colliery, Fishburn ✗
H	Horden Colliery, Horden
Mu	Murton Colliery, Murton
TMS	Machinery Stores, Tursdale Central Workshops, Tursdale (locos stored)
VT	Vane Tempest Colliery, Seaham

       ✗ closed; locos awaiting disposal, 1/4/1974

ø

Diesel locomotives

Gauge: 3' 6"

2620/21	0-6-0DMF	HC	D632	1947	(a)	MH
2620/22	0-6-0DMF	HC	D639	1947	(a)	MH
2620/23	0-6-0DMF	HC	D709	1955	(a)	MH
2620/24	0-6-0DMF	HC	D993	1956	(a)	MH
2620/25	0-6-0DMF	HC	D1063	1957	(a)	MH

(a) ex North Durham Area, 1/4/1974

Gauge: 3' 0"   (⟋ tandem units)

9306/105	0-6-0DMF ⟋	HC	D1271	1962	(a)	ACW-Bt 5/74
9307/51	0-4-0DMF	HE	4139	1952	(a)	Bt
9215/13	0-6-0DMF	HC	D1058	1957	(a)	Bt-ACW 9/75
9307/56	0-4-0DMF	HE	5439	1959	(a)	Bt
9215/16	0-6-0DMF	HC	D1237	1961	(a)	Bt
9306/106	0-6-0DMF ⟋	HC	D1272	1962	(a)	Bt
9306/107	0-6-0DMF ⟋	HC	D1273	1962	(a)	Bt
9306/108	0-6-0DMF ⟋	HC	D1274	1962	(a)	Bt
9185/17	0-6-0DMF	HC	D1282	1962	(a)	Bt-ACW 9/74-Bt 3/75
9306/110	0-6-0DMF	HC	D1379	1966	(a)	Bt
9307/52	0-4-0DMF	HE	4140	1952	(a)	En
9306/94	0-6-0DMF	HC	D967	1955	(a)	En
9306/98	0-6-0DMF	HC	D1025	1957	(a)	En
9306/96	0-6-0DMF	HC	D1040	1957	(a)	En
9306/97	0-6-0DMF	HC	D1041	1957	(a)	En
9307/100	0-6-0DMF	HC	D1162	1959	(a)	En
9311/54	0-4-0DMF	HE	6603	1965	(a)	En
9307/87	4w-4wDHF	HE	7308	1974	(a)	En
9215/7	0-6-0DMF	HC	D661	1951	(a)	Ly
9215/8	0-6-0DMF	HC	D662	1951	(a)	Ly
9306/103	0-6-0DMF ⟋	HC	D1269	1961	(a)	Ly
9306/104	0-6-0DMF ⟋	HC	D1270	1961	(a)	Ly
9306/86	0-6-0DMF	HB	D1422	1972	(a)	Ly
9311/53	0-4-0DMF	HE	6602	1965	(a)	SD-ACW 12/74
2303/40	0-6-0DMF	HC	D830	1954	(b)	E
2303/39	0-6-0DMF	HC	D831	1954	(b)	E
2303/44	0-6-0DMF	HC	D966	1955	(b)	E
2303/68	0-6-0DMF	HC	D1323	1965	(b)	E
05100/89	0-6-0DMF ⟋	HC	D1402	1968	(b)	E
05100/90	0-6-0DMF ⟋	HC	D1403	1968	(b)	E
05100/91	0-6-0DMF ⟋	HC	D1407	1968	(b)	E
05100/95	0-4-0DMF	HE	7116	1970	(b)	E-HE (reps) 6/74 -E 5/75
05100/98	0-4-0DMF	HE	7117	1970	(b)	E
05100/116	0-6-0DMF ⟋	HB	D1423	1972	(b)	E
05100/121	4w-4wDHF	HE	7099	1973	(b)	E-Bt 12/74-BF 1/75 -En c6/75
05100/124	4w-4wDHF	HE	7100	1974	(b)	E
9307/88	4w-4wDHF	HE	7309	1974	New	En-E 3/75
-	0-6-0DMF	HE	6655	1969	(c)	E (1)

(a) ex Northumberland Area, 1/4/1974
(b) ex South Durham Area, 1/4/1974
(c) ex North Yorkshire Area, Rothwell
    Colliery, Rothwell, 1/1975

(1) ret. to North Yorkshire Area,
    Rothwell Colliery, 2/1975, without
    being installed

Gauge: 2' 6"

2549/24	0-6-0DMF	HE	4060	1950	(a)	Wm
2549/25	0-6-0DMF	HE	4061	1950	(a)	Wm
2111/112	0-6-0DMF	HE	4062	1951	(a)	Wm
2111/111	0-6-0DMF	HE	4071	1954	(a)	Wm
2111/118	0-6-0DMF	HE	4070	1958	(a)	Wm
2105/138	0-6-0DMF	HC	D1349	1964	(a)	Wm
2111/124	0-6-0DMF	HC	D1350	1964	(a)	Wm
2111/126	0-6-0DMF	HE	6229	1965	(a)	Wm
2111/127	0-6-0DMF	HC	D1357	1966	(a)	Wm
2111/128	0-6-0DMF	HC	D1358	1966	(a)	Wm

(a) ex North Durham Area, 1/4/1974

Gauge: 2' 0"

2201/262	0-6-0DMF	HC	D852	1954	(a)	ACW (3)
2404/26	0-4-0DMF	HE	4093	1952	(b)	Hn
2206/411	0-6-0DMF	HC	D825	1952	(b)	Hn-ACW 12/75
2206/414	0-6-0DMF	HC	D872	1954	(b)	Hn
2206/419	0-6-0DMF	HC	D873	1955	(b)	Hn
2206/421	0-6-0DMF	HC	D874	1956	(b)	Hn
2206/420	0-6-0DMF	HC	D875	1956	(b)	Hn
2206/423	0-6-0DMF	HC	D1281	1963	(b)	Hn
2126/424	0-6-0DMF	HC	D1400	1967	(b)	Hn
2305/53	0-6-0DMF	HC	D1118	1958	(c)	Bl-ACW 5/75-H 11/75
2203/347	0-6-0DMF	HC	D1067	1959	(c)	Bl
2301/58	0-6-0DMF	HE	5609	1962	(c)	Bl
2301/64	0-6-0DMF	HE	5610	1964	(c)	Bl
2206/413	0-6-0DMF	HC	D853	1954	(c)	Da
2201/263	0-6-0DMF	HC	D1015	1956	(c)	Da
2201/264	0-6-0DMF	HC	D1064	1959	(c)	Da
2201/265	0-6-0DMF	HC	D1169	1960	(c)	Da
2201/266	0-6-0DMF	HC	D1170	1960	(c)	Da
2203/345	0-6-0DMF	HC	D1065	1959	(c)	El-ACW 7/75
2203/346	0-6-0DMF	HC	D1066	1959	(c)	El-ACW 7/75 Scr 10/75
2203/348	0-6-0DMF	HC	D1247	1961	(c)	El-ACW 10/75
2203/349	0-6-0DMF	HC	D1248	1961	(c)	El-(2)-TMS 1/75
2305/54	0-6-0DMF	HC	D1119	1958	(c)	F-Bl 1/75-ACW 9/75
2404/72	0-6-0DMF	HC	D1127	1958	(c)	F-ACW 4/74-Da 1/75
2407/80	0-4-0DMF	HE	5596	1961	(c)	F (1)
05130/106	0-6-0DMF	HC	D1416	1971	(c)	F-VT 7/74
2304/9	0-4-0DMF	HE	4094	1952	(c)	H
2403/51	0-4-0DMF	HE	4110	1952	(c)	H
2304/6	0-6-0DMF	HC	D818	1952	(c)	H
2304/7	0-6-0DMF	HC	D819	1952	(c)	H
2304/5	0-6-0DMF	HC	D893	1954	(c)	H
2304/66	0-6-0DMF	HC	D1322	1964	(c)	H
2304/67	0-6-0DMF	HC	D1366	1965	(c)	H-ACW 11/75
05150/87	0-6-0DMF	HC	D1401	1968	(c)	H
05150/101	0-6-0DMF	HC	D1412	1970	(c)	H
2216/282	0-6-0DMF	HC	D804	1951	(c)	VT
2216/286	0-6-0DMF	HC	D842	1954	(c)	VT
2206/422	0-6-0DMF	HC	D1245	1961	(c)	VT
2305/60	0-6-0DMF	HC	D1325	1963	(c)	VT
05280/86	0-6-0DMF	HC	D1399	1967	(c)	VT

(a) ex South Durham Area, Dawdon (1) to Seaham Loco Training Centre,
  Colliery, under repair, 1/4/1974   5/1974 (see surface list)
(b) ex North Durham Area, 1/4/1974 (2) removed via Murton Colliery,
(c) ex South Durham Area, 1/4/1974   5/1974; part to Seaton Delaval
                Stores, 7/1974; both sections to
                Tursdale Machinery Stores, as
                shown, 1/1975
            (3) to Seaham Loco Training Centre,
             7/1974 (see surface list)

Mine ranger captive track system

9307/81	UMM	1968	(a)	SD-WMS 3/75	
				Scr	9/1975
9307/80	UMM	1969	(a)	SD-WMS 3/75	
9307/79	UMM	1970	(a)	SD-WMS 3/75	
				Scr	9/1975
05080/105	UMM	1971	(b)	Da	
05080/107	UMM	1971	(b)	Da	
05080/122	UMM	1973	(b)	Da	
05080/123	UMM	1973	(b)	Da	

(a) ex Northumberland Area, 1/4/1974
(b) ex South Durham Area, 1/4/1974

Road-railer captive monorail system for high-speed man-riding and materials trains

05080/94	Becorit	DRL 25/1/201	1969	(a)	Da
05080/102	Becorit	DRL 25/1/217	1970	(a)	Da
05080/104	Becorit	DRL 25/2/209	1970	(a)	Da
05350/110	Becorit	DRL 40/1/503	1971	(a)	Da
05080/117	Becorit	DRL 25/1/224	1972	(a)	Da
05080/118	Becorit	DRL 40/4/509	1972	(a)	Da
05080/119	Becorit	DRL 40/4/510	1972	(a)	Da
05350/109	Becorit	DRL 40/1/501	1971	(a)	Mu
05350/108	Becorit	DRL 40/1/502	1971	(a)	Mu
05350/111	Becorit	DRL 40/1/504	1972	(a)	Mu
05350/120	Becorit	DRL 40/4/508	1972	(a)	Mu
20/090/1	Becorit	DRL 40/3/518	1974	New	Da

(a) ex South Durham Area, 1/4/1974

Battery locomotives

Gauge: 3' 0"

9215/9	4wBE	GB	2360	1952	(a)	Bt-LEW 1/75
9215/10	4wBE	GB	2361	1952	(a)	Bt
9215/15	4wBE	GB	2938	1958	(a)	Bt
9311/23	4wBE	LMM	1076	1951	(a)	Sb
9311/24	4wBE	LMM	1077	1951	(a)	Sb
9185/18	4wBE	EE V	3655	1965	(a)	SD-LEW 3/75
2303/34	4wBE	GB	2395	1953	(b)	E

2303/33	4wBE	GB	2403	1953	(b)	E	
2303/49	4wBE	EE	2342	1957			
		RSH		1957	(b)	E	(1)
2303/50	4wBE	EE	2343	1957			
		RSH		1957	(b)	E	
2303/51	4wBE	EE	2344	1957			
		RSH		1957	(b)	E	
05100/88	4wBE	EE V	3845	1968	(b)	E	

(a) ex Northumberland Area, 1/4/1974   (1) cannibalised for spares, 2/1975;
(b) ex South Durham Area, 1/4/1974   frame scrapped, 7/1975

Gauge: 2' 6"

2107/2	4wBE	EE	2028	1954			
		Bg	3415	1954	(a)	B	
2112/70	4wBE	EE	2078	1955			
		Bg	3429	1955	(a)	B	
2101/63	4wBE	EE	2227	1955			
		Bg	3444	1955	(a)	B	
2101/64	4wBE	EE	2228	1955			
		Bg	3445	1955	(a)	B	
2101/65	4wBE	EE	2229	1955			
		Bg	3446	1955	(a)	B	
2101/181	4wBE	EE	2331	1956			
		Bg	3472	1956	(a)	B	
2101/182	4wBE	EE	2523	1957			
		Bg	3496	1957	(b)	B	
2111/119	4wBE	EE	2627	1958			
		Bg	3522	1958	(a)	B	
2101/183	4wBE	EE	2955	1960			
		Bg	3566	1960	(a)	B	
2214/395	4wBE	EE	2661	1959			
		RSH		1959	(a)	LEW—We 6/75	
2214/518	4wBE	EE V	3849	1967	(a)	LEW	
2107/1	4wBE	EE	2027	1954			
		Bg	3414	1954	(a)	We	
2112/67	4wBE	EE	2080	1955			
		Bg	3439	1955	(a)	We	Scr 7/1975
2110/52	4wBE	EE	2328	1956			
		Bg	3470	1956	(a)	We	
2110/53	4wBE	EE	2329	1957			
		Bg	3471	1957	(a)	We	
2110/54	4wBE	EE	2418	1958			
		Bg	3497	1958	(a)	We	
2110/55	4wBE	EE	2419	1958			
		Bg	3498	1958	(a)	We	
2110/56	4wBE	EE	2420	1958			
		Bg	3499	1958	(a)	We	
2110/57	4wBE	EE	2626	1958			
		Bg	3521	1958	(a)	We	
2111/120	4wBE	EE	2628	1958			
		Bg	3523	1958	(a)	We	
2110/151	4wBE	EE	2740	1959			
		Bg	3542	1959	(a)	We	
2110/152	4wBE	EE	3150	1960			
		Bg	3567	1960	(a)	We	
2214/398	4wBE	EE	3155	1961			
		RSH		1961	(a)	We	
2110/153	4wBE	EE	3173	1962			
		Bg	3583	1962	(a)	We	

2109/47	4wBE	EE	3174	1962		
		Bg	3584	1962	(a)	We
2110/154	4wBE	EE	3336	1963		
		Bg	3595	1963	(a)	We
2110/155	4wBE	EE	3399	1963		
		Bg	3599	1963	(a)	We
2110/156	4wBE	EE	3820	1966		
		Bg	3642	1966	(a)	We
2110/157	4wBE	EE	3842	1967		
		Bg	3645	1967	(a)	We
2110/158	4wBE	EE	3871	1968		
		Bg	3649	1968	(a)	We
2109/41	4wBE	EE	1809	1952		
		Bg	3353	1952	(a)	Wm
2112/71	4wBE	EE	2330	1956		
		Bg	3473	1956	(a)	Wm
2111/123	4wBE	EE	3404	1963		
		Bg	3603	1963	(a)	Wm

(a) ex North Durham Area, 1/4/1974
(b) ex North Durham Area, 1/4/1974;
    used as source of spares

Gauge: 2' 0"   (⫻ tandem unit)

9120/2	4wBE	EE	2636	1960		
		RSH		1960	(a)	SD-LEW 2/75
9120/5	4wBE	EE	2639	1960		
		RSH		1960	(a)	SD-LEW 2/75
9303/25	4wBE	EE	2527	1957		
		RSH		1957	(a)	Wt
9303/26	4wBE	EE	2696	1959		
		Bg		1959	(a)	Wt
2109/43	4wBE	EE	2026	1954		
		Bg	3413	1954	(b)	U-LEW 10/74
2109/42	4wBE	EE	2079	1955		
		Bg	3430	1955	(b)	U-LEW 10/74
2109/44	4wBE	EE	2230	1955		
		Bg	3431	1955	(b)	U-LEW 11/74
2109/46	4wBE	EE	2466	1957		
		Bg	3501	1957	(b)	U-LEW 11/74 (1)
2103/34	4wBE	EE	2467	1957		
		Bg	3495	1957	(b)	U-LEW 10/74
2207/460	4wBE ⫻	EE	2477	1959		
		RSH		1959	(c)	Ep
2207/455	4wBE ⫻	EE	2481	1958		
		RSH		1958	(c)	Ep
2207/453	4wBE ⫻	EE	2483	1958		
		RSH		1958	(c)	Ep
2207/452	4wBE ⫻	EE	2484	1958		
		RSH		1958	(c)	Ep
2207/446	4wBE ⫻	EE	2486	1958		
		RSH		1958	(c)	Ep
2207/445	4wBE ⫻	EE	2489	1958		
		RSH		1958	(c)	Ep

2207/444	4wBE ⚡	EE	2490	1958		
		RSH		1958	(c)	Ep
2220/466	4wBE ⚡	EE	2849	1960		
		RSH		1960	(c)	Ep
2216/287	4wBE	HC		1960	(c)	Ep
2220/468	4wBE ⚡	EE S	3401	1963	(c)	Ep
2220/470	4wBE	EE	1961	1954		
		Bg	3380	1954	(c)	Mu
2207/441	4wBE ⚡	EE	2469	1958		
		RSH		1958	(c)	Mu
2207/442	4wBE ⚡	EE	2470	1958		
		RSH		1958	(c)	Mu
2207/443	4wBE ⚡	EE	2471	1958		
		RSH		1958	(c)	Mu
2207/457	4wBE ⚡	EE	2472	1958		
		RSH		1958	(c)	Mu
2207/449	4wBE ⚡	EE	2473	1958		
		RSH		1958	(c)	Mu
2207/458	4wBE ⚡	EE	2474	1958		
		RSH		1958	(c)	Mu
2207/456	4wBE ⚡	EE	2476	1958		
		RSH		1958	(c)	Mu
2207/462	4wBE ⚡	EE	2478	1959		
		RSH		1959	(c)	Mu
2207/461	4wBE ⚡	EE	2479	1959		
		RSH		1959	(c)	Mu
2207/459	4wBE ⚡	EE	2480	1958		
		RSH		1958	(c)	Mu
2207/454	4wBE ⚡	EE	2482	1958		
		RSH		1958	(c)	Mu
2207/450	4wBE ⚡	EE	2485	1958		
		RSH		1958	(c)	Mu
2207/447	4wBE ⚡	EE	2487	1958		
		RSH		1958	(c)	Mu
2207/448	4wBE ⚡	EE	2488	1958		
		RSH		1958	(c)	Mu
9120/1	4wBE ⚡	EE	2635	1960		
		RSH		1960	(c)	Mu
9120/3	4wBE ⚡	EE	2637	1960		
		RSH		1960	(c)	Mu
9120/4	4wBE ⚡	EE	2638	1960		
		RSH		1960	(c)	Mu
2214/396	4wBE ⚡	EE	2662	1959		
		RSH		1959	(c)	Mu
2220/463	4wBE ⚡	EE	2736	1959		
		RSH		1959	(c)	Mu
2220/464	4wBE ⚡	EE	2737	1959		
		RSH		1959	(c)	Mu
2220/465	4wBE ⚡	EE	2848	1960		
		RSH		1960	(c)	Mu
2214/397	4wBE ⚡	EE	3149	1962		
		RSH		1962	(c)	Mu
2220/467	4wBE ⚡	EE	3167	1961		
		RSH		1961	(c)	Mu

(a) ex Northumberland Area, 1/4/1974
(b) ex North Durham Area, 1/4/1974
(c) ex South Durham Area, 1/4/1974

(1) to Boldon Colliery, 2/1975, for working on surface, after conversion to 2' 0" gauge (see surface list)

SECTION 4

CONTRACTORS' LOCOMOTIVES

used on contracts in Co. Durham

SIR WILLIAM ARROL & CO LTD
Contract at South Dock, Sunderland, for River Wear Commissioners, 1923-1924

Gauge: 4' 8½"

PRESTON	0-4-0ST	OC	AB	1800	1923	New	(1)
-	0-4-0ST	OC	AB	1818	1924	New	(2)

      (1) later at Casebourne & Co Ltd,
            Haverton Hill
      (2) later at British Fibrocement Works
            Ltd, Erith, Kent

R. BLACKETT & SON
Road widening contract, Darlington, 1905

Gauge: 2' 0"

-	0-4-0WT	OK		(a)	s/s

(a) ex ?

COX & DANKS LTD
Contract for dismantling British Railways Blackhill Branch, 1965

Gauge: 4' 8½"

-	4wDM	FH	3374	1950	(a)	(1)	

(a) hired from Robinson & Hannon Ltd,   (1) ret. to Robinson & Hannon Ltd,
    Blaydon   Blaydon, 7/1965

JOHN CRAVEN & SONS
Contract at Sunderland, possibly the construction of the South Docks for the
Sunderland Dock Co, 1848-1850

    An auction sale of plant belonging to these contractors, including
    a locomotive and tender, was held at the Docks from 18th-20th
    February 1850.

EASTON, GIBB & SON LTD
Construction of Dunston-Gateshead extension for North Eastern Railway,
1903-1906

Gauge: 4' 8½"

50	0-6-0ST	IC	MW	1599	1903	New	(1)
51	0-6-0ST	IC	MW	1604	1903	New	(1)
59	0-6-0ST	IC	MW	1669	1905	New	(1)

      (1) to Newport Docks extension contract,
            Monmouthshire

J. T. FIRBANK
Construction of Wear Valley Extension Railway from Stanhope to Wearhead for North Eastern Railway, opened in October 1895.

Gauge: 4' 8½"

PORTSMOUTH	0-6-0ST	IC	HE	4	1865	(a)	(1)

(a) ex ? (an earlier contract)   (1) to Caterham contract, Surrey

      May have used other locomotives unknown

FORSTER & LAWTON
1. Construction of Pensher (Penshaw) to Sunderland line for York, Newcastle & Berwick Railway, 1851-1853
2. Construction of Seaham to Sunderland section of the Londonderry Railway for Marquis of Londonderry, 1853-1854

Gauge: 4' 8½"

-	0-4-0	OC	RS	753	1849	(a) 1-2	(1)

(a) ex contract at Berwick,   (1) to Marquis of Londonderry,
     Northumberland   Londonderry Railway, c/1854

W. J. FOSTER
Construction of Crookfoot Reservoir, near Elwick, for Hartlepools Corporation

Gauge: 3' 0"

CROOKFOOT	0-4-0ST	OC	AB	719	1892	New	(1)

                                   (1) later at Haslingden contract,
                                        Lancs

GOLIGHTLY
Contract at Spennymoor (?)

Gauge: 2' 0"

-	4wPM	MR	✗	1930	(a) s/s

        ✗ either MR 5067 or 5130

(a) ex Durham County Water Board,
     Burnhope Reservoir construction

HIRST & SONS
Dock extension works and construction of graving dock at West Hartlepool,
? - 1884

       Three four-coupled locomotives were advertised for sale in July 1884
       after the completion of the above contract

HOLLOWAY BROTHERS (LONDON) LTD
Construction of Seaton Carew Breakwater, 1919- ?

Gauge: 4' 8½"

YORKSHIRE 2		0-6-0T	IC	HC	1070	1914	(a) (1)
-		0-6-0ST	IC	MW	1665	1905	(b) (2)
JEANIE		0-6-0ST	IC	MW			
				reb.		1904	(c) s/s
62		0-6-0ST	IC	MW			(c) s/s
64		0-6-0ST	IC	MW	1144	1890	(d) s/s
65	IRENE	0-6-0ST	IC	MW			(c) s/s
-		0-4-0ST	OC	AE			
				reb.		1907	(c) s/s

(a) form. Sir John Jackson Ltd,
    Amesbury, Wilts
(b) form. Easton, Gibb & Son Ltd,
    Rosyth Dockyard contract, Fife
(c) ex ?
(d) ex South Metropolitan Gas Co,
    East Greenwich, London, /1920

(1) later at E.R.Cole, Shepherds Bush,
    London
(2) later at Holland, Hannan & Cubitts
    Ltd, Downham Estate contract, Kent

JACKSON, BEAN & GOW
Contract at Jarrow Docks (for Jarrow Iron Co ?), c1858-1859

An auction took place on 27th-28th April 1859 of plant used
on the above contract, including a "locomotive engine".

SIR JOHN JACKSON LTD
Hudson Dock Extension Works, South Docks, Sunderland, ?-1904 (for River Wear
Commissioners)

Gauge: 4' 8½"

-	0-6-0ST			(a) (1)

(a) ex ?

(1) advertised for sale, 7/1904

B. C. LAWTON
Construction of Team Valley line, Gateshead to Newton Hall Junction, Durham,
for North Eastern Railway, 1865-1868

Gauge: 4' 8½"

-		0-4-0ST	OC	John Harris			New? (1)
-		0-4-0ST	OC	John Harris			New? (1)
-		0-4-0ST	OC	John Harris			New? (1)
FAT NELLY		0-6-0ST	IC	MW	179	1866	New (2)
ALEXANDRA		0-6-0ST	IC	HE	13	1867	New s/s

(1) to Birtley Iron Co,/1869
(2) to W.Scott, Burntisland, Fife

T. A. MATTHEWS
Contract at Hartlepool, c1886 (?)

Gauge: 4' 8½"

MERCURY	0-6-0ST	IC	MW	995	1886	New (1)

(1) later at Lilleshall Co Ltd,
    Oakengates, Shropshire

MITCHELL BROS LTD
Construction of West Dunston line and West Dunston Staithes for North Eastern Railway,   -1913

Gauge: 4' 8½"

        Five locomotives were advertised for sale on 30th May 1913
        following the above contract.

JOHN MOFFAT
Construction of new road from Port Clarence to Hartlepool,   c1918

Gauge: 4' 8½"

        -              0-6-0ST   SS   (a) (1)

(a) ex ?   (1) advertised for sale, 11/1918

Gauge: 3' 0"

    MAC   0-4-0ST   OC   WB   1516 1898 (a) (1)

(a) ex contract in Manchester   (1) to Great West Road contract,
                                         Brentford, Middlesex

MORKILL & PRODHAM
Construction of Blackhill Branch (Blaydon-Consett) for North Eastern Railway, 1865-1867

Gauge: 4' 8½"

    MUDLARK   0-6-0ST   IC   MW   171 1865 New (1)

                          (1) repaired by Hopper, Radcliffe & Co,
                              Fencehouses, c/1872 (?); later at
                              T.Nelson & Co, Bangor

JOHN NELSON
Construction of Redheugh Deviation and branch for North Eastern Railway, 1899

Gauge: 4' 8½"

    WIGAN   0-4-0ST   OC   HE   361 1885 (a) (1)
    BRADFORD   0-6-0ST   IC   MW   181 1865 (b) (2)

(a) form. T.A.Walker, Manchester Ship   (1) to Barmoor Coal Co Ltd, Morpeth,
    Canal contract, Lancs   Northumberland
(b) form. Walter Byrom   (2) later W.Ratcliffe & Co, Uppingham,
                                            Rutland

        N.B.   Contract completed by D. Shanks (q.v.)

H. M. NOWELL
Construction of Dunston Staithes for North Eastern Railway,   -1903

Gauge: 4' 8½"

    DUNSTON   0-6-0ST   IC   MW   1446 1899 New (1)
    REDHEUGH   0-6-0ST   IC   MW   1455 1899 New (2)
    -                0-6-0T   HE   (a) (3)

(a) ex ?   (1) to David Shanks, Penshaw contract
                                      (2) later W.E.Chivers, Yapton
                                      (3) advertised for sale, together with
                                          a MW six-coupled tank engine
                                          (?REDHEUGH), 5/1903

SIR LINDSAY PARKINSON & CO LTD
Contract at Seaton Carew for Ministry of Mines, 1943-1945 (see main text)

Gauge: 4' 8½"

	JEANETTE	0-6-0ST	IC	HC	1699	1938	(a)	(1)

(a) ex Dale contract, Pembrokeshire,   (1) to Egypt, c/1945
    c/1943

S. PEARSON & SON LTD
Construction of Seaham South Dock for Seaham Harbour Dock Co Ltd, 1899-1907

Gauge: 4' 8½"

	REX	0-4-0ST	OC	MW	838	1885	(a)	(1)
	DICK	0-4-0ST	OC	HE	628	1895	(b)	(1)
	URMSTON	0-6-0ST	IC	HE	450	1888	(c)	(2)
	STANLEY						(c)	(3)
	-	0-4-0ST	OC	MW	329	1870	(d)	(4)
88	CHARLES STEWART	0-4-0ST	OC	P	773	1899	New	(5)
	HOWARD						(e)	s/s
99	LONDONDERRY	0-4-0ST	OC	P	806	1900	New	(6)
	SANKEY	0-4-0ST	OC	MW	1088	1888	(f)	(4)

(a) ex A.Robbins, contr, Warrington,   (1) to Seaham Harbour Dock Co Ltd,
    Lancs, c/1899   /1905
(b) ex Wootton Bassett contract,   (2) later on Gretna contract, Dumfries-
    Gloucs   shire
(c) ex ?   (3) to Topham, Jones & Railton, contrs
(d) form. Monk & Newall, contrs,   (4) later on Dover Breakwater contract,
    FREDERICK WILLIAM   Kent
(e) ex ?, by /1901   (5) to Lord Leconfield, Crowgarth Iron
(f) form. T.A.Walker, contr   Ore Mines, Cleator Moor, Cumbs
                                          (6) to King George V Dock contract,
                                              Hull, Yorks, E.R.

T. D. RIDLEY & SONS
Construction of railway for Harton Coal Co Ltd, South Shields,   ?-1903

Gauge: 4' 8½"

	-	0-4-0ST	BH				(a)	(1)
	-	0-6-0ST	BH				(a)	(1)

(a) ex ?   (1) advertised for sale, 7/1903

It seems likely that the following locomotives were also used on contracts in
Co. Durham

Gauge: 4' 8½"

	MIDGE	0-4-0ST	OC	BH	231	1872	(a)	(1)
	TEAM VALLEY	0-4-0ST	OC	HL	2489	1901	New	(1)

(a) form. John Nelson, contr   (1) to Palmers Shipbuilding & Iron Co

WALTER SCOTT & CO
1. Haswell Curve Improvement for North Eastern Railway, 1892

Gauge: 4' 8½"

LULI	0-4-0ST	OC	MW	892	1884	(a)	(1)

(a) ex C.Brand & Sons, contrs   (1) to Charwelton-Quainton Road
                                  contract, Northants/Bucks

2. Construction of Winston Reservoir, 1893

Gauge: 3' 0"

COTHERSTONE	0-4-0ST	OC	HE	102	1873	(a)	s/s
LANCASHIRE WITCH	0-4-0ST	OC	MW	614	1876	(b)	(1)
BALDERSDALE	0-4-0ST	OC	HE	92	1872	(c)	(2)

(a) ex Newcastle Central-Manors widen- (1) to Charwelton-Quainton Road
    ing contract, Northumberland   contract, Northants/Bucks
(b) ex Gossdoney-Killeshemdra contract, (2) to Enoch Tempest, contr, by /1902
    Ireland
(c) form. Huddersfield Corporation

3. Felling to Heworth widening for North Eastern Railway, c/1895

Gauge: 4' 8½"

-	GR	(a)	s/s

(a) ex ?

WALTER SCOTT & MIDDLETON
1. Construction of Hart to Seaham line for North Eastern Railway, 1900-1905

Gauge: 4' 8½"

ALEXANDRA	0-6-0ST	IC	MW	1484	1901	New	(1)
BRADFORD	0-6-0ST	IC	MW	899	1885	(a)	
			reb. MW		1899		(2)
BERTHA	0-6-0ST	IC	MW	1059	1888	(b)	s/s
HILDA	0-6-0ST	IC	MW			(c)	(3)
BRACKLEY	0-6-0ST	IC	HE	164	1876	(d)	(3)

(a) form. Chas. Baker & Sons, Bradford, (1) later on Whitemoor Sidings contract,
    contrs   Cambs
(b) orig. T.A.Walker, Manchester Ship   (2) to Chapman & Furneaux Ltd,
    Canal contract, Lancs   Gateshead, c/1902
(c) ex ?   (3) later on Ashendon-Aynho contract,
(d) ex Pallion contract   Bucks/Oxon

2. Contract at Pallion, Sunderland, 1902-1903

Gauge: 4' 8½"

BRACKLEY	0-6-0ST	IC	HE	164	1876	(a)	(1)
PALLION	0-6-0ST	IC	MW	1525	1902	New	(2)

(a) ex Charwelton-Quainton Road   (1) to Hart-Seaham contract
    contract, Northants/Bucks   (2) to Geo. Cohen, Pembrey, Carmarthen,
                                             by /1915

DAVID SHANKS
Pelaw Main to Felling widening for North Eastern Railway, 1894-1895

Gauge: 4' 8½"

| AIRDRIE | 0-4-0ST | OC | BH | 1074 | 1893 | New | (1) |
| - | 0-6-0ST | OC | BH | 1078 | 1893 | New | (1) |

(1) for sale at contractors' yard,
Felling, 6/1895

EXECUTORS OF DAVID SHANKS
1. Penshaw to Wapping Branch widening for North Eastern Railway, 1900-1902
2. Completion of Redheugh Deviation and Dunston extension for North Eastern
   Railway, 1902-1904 (see also John Nelson)

Gauge: 4' 8½"

VICTORIA	0-6-0ST	OC	BH	1078	1893	(a)	1-2	(1)
ACKLINGTON	0-6-0ST	OC	FW	371	1878	(b)	1	s/s
PEGGY	0-6-0ST	IC	HC	540	1900	(c)	1-2	(2)
DUNSTON	0-6-0ST	IC	MW	1446	1899	(d)	1-2	(3)
CORONATION	0-6-0ST	IC	MW	1561	1902	New	2	(4)

(a) ex Felling contract (?)
(b) ex Broomhill Coal Co Ltd, North-
    umberland, c/1900
(c) ex Northallerton widening contract,
    Yorks, N.R.
(d) ex H.M.Nowell, Dunston contract

(1) to Henry Heys Ltd, Bacup, Lancs
(2) to Newbiggin Colliery Co Ltd,
    Northumberland, c/1907
(3) to C.J.Wills, contr (?), c/1904
(4) to Doncaster contract, Yorks, W.R.

I.C.TONE
1. Construction of Pelaw to South Shields line for North Eastern Railway,
   c1869-1872

Gauge: 4' 8½"

| BRITANNIA | 0-4-0T | | Hopper | | 1869 | New? | (1) |
| PELAW | 0-6-0T | OC | BH | 60 | 1868 | New | (2) |

(1) for sale, 5/1872
(2) to Birtley Iron Co, c/1873

2. Construction of Queen Alexandra Bridge, Sunderland, 1903

Gauge: 4' 8½"

| - | 0-4-0ST | OC | BH | 188 | 1872 | (a) | (1) |

(a) ex ?

(1) to Ford Paper Works Ltd, Sunderland

J. TORBUCK
Details unknown. Depot was at Hartlepool.

Gauge: 4' 8½"

| - | 0-4-0ST | OC | AB | | 1883 | (a) | (1) |

(a) ex ?

(1) to Richardsons, Westgarth & Co Ltd,
    West Hartlepool

THOMAS W. WARD LTD
Dismantling of part of Palmers Shipbuilding & Iron Co Ltd's steelworks and
shipyard, Jarrow, 1937

Gauge: 4' 8½"

KING GEORGE	0-6-0ST	IC	HC	1040	1913	(a)	(1)

(a) form. Darwen & Mostyn Iron Co Ltd,   (1) to ?
    Darwen, Lancs

WHITAKER BROS LTD
Construction of new line from Annfield Plain to Pelton for North Eastern
Railway, 1891-1893

Gauge: 4' 8½"

11	0-4-0ST	OC	BH	1018	1890	New (1)

                              (1) later James Laycock & Co, Seghill
                                  Colliery, Northumberland

There is a possibility that 0-4-0ST   OC   MW 1074/1888 was also used on this
contract. It was at Seghill Colliery with BH 1018 and had been delivered to
Whitaker Bros Ltd for the construction of the East & West Yorkshire Union
Railway, Yorks, W.R.

UNKNOWN CONTRACTOR
Road widening contract, Ferryhill, c/1920

Gauge: Narrow

39	NORWICH	0-4-0T	OC	OK		(a) s/s

(a) ex ?

UNKNOWN CONTRACTOR
Construction of Newcastle & Darlington Junction Railway, 1842-1844

Gauge: 4' 8½"

HAWK	2-2-0	Stark & Fulton		(a)	(1)
VULTURE	2-2-0	Stark & Fulton		(a)	(1)
EAGLE	2-2-0	Stark & Fulton		(a)	(1)
-	2-2-0	Jones, Turner & Evans	1839	(a)	(1)
-	2-2-0	Jones, Turner & Evans	1839	(a)	(1)
-	2-2-0	Jones, Turner & Evans	1839	(a)	(1)
-	2-2-0	Bury	1839	(a)	(1)
-	2-2-0 (?)	Nasmyth Gaskell	1840?	(a)	(1)

(a) ex Midland Counties Railway, c/1842 (1) to Newcastle & Darlington Junction
    (? on loan)   Railway, /1844

SECTION 5

PRESERVED LOCOMOTIVES

(a) in the county

(b) Co. Durham locomotives preserved outside the county

PRESERVED LOCOMOTIVES

(as at 31/12/1975)

(a) Locomotives preserved in the county

A4 PRESERVATION SOCIETY LTD, N.C.B. Lambton Railway Loco Sheds, Philadelphia

Gauge: 4' 8½"

4498   SIR NIGEL GRESLEY 4-6-2   3C Don   1863 1937 (a)

(a) LNER Gresley A4 class. Wdn as BR 60007, 2/1966. Ex BR, 3/1967, after
    restoration to LNER blue livery at Crewe Works, 2/1966-3/1967, and stored
    at Crewe until moved here, 7/1968. Used on enthusiasts' special trains.

DARLINGTON (NORTH ROAD) RAILWAY MUSEUM SOCIETY, Darlington (North Road)
Station, Darlington

Gauge: 4' 8½" (static exhibits)

1275		0-6-0	IC	D	708	1874	(a)
1463		2-4-0	IC	Dar		1885	(b)
17		0-4-0VBT	OC	HW	33	1873	(c)
25	DERWENT	0-6-0	OC	Kitching		1845	(d)
1	LOCOMOTION	0-4-0	VC	RS	3	1825	(e)

(a) ex York Railway Museum, 6/1975. Bouch 1001 class. Wdn as LNER 1275,
    2/1925. Restored to original condition and livery for Railway Centenary
    Celebrations, 1925, and later placed on display at York. Appeared at
    150th anniversary of Stockton & Darlington Railway at Shildon, 8/1975.
(b) ex York Railway Museum, 6/1975. T.W.Worsdell 1463 class, LNER E5 class.
    Appeared at Railway Centenary Celebrations, 1925. Wdn as LNER 1463,
    8/1927, restored to original condition and livery and placed on display
    at York. Removed with other locos for storage during Second World War,
    but not returned to York until 1957.
(c) ex Head, Wrightson & Co Ltd, Thornaby, Co. Cleveland, 9/1975, after
    exhibition at 150th anniversary celebrations of Stockton & Darlington
    Railway at Shildon, 8/1975; Seaham Harbour Dock Co Ltd until 6/1962.
(d) Originally Stockton & Darlington Railway. Wdn and sold by NER to J.Pease
    & Co, c/1865. Presented to NER by Pease & Partners, 3/1898, and placed on
    display at Bank Top Station, Darlington, until moved to this museum, 9/1975.
(e) Originally Stockton & Darlington Railway. Wdn from service in 1846 but
    worked occasionally afterwards. Sold for scrap, 1850, but instead
    installed as pumping engine at J. Pease & Co's Lucy Pit, Billy Row, Crook.
    Returned to Stockton & Darlington Railway, restored and placed on display
    near North Road Station, Darlington, 6/1857. Later removed, and displayed
    at several exhibitions. Placed on display at Bank Top Station, Darlington,
    in 1890. Moved to North Road Museum, 9/1975.

<u>DURHAM COUNTY COUNCIL</u>, Dinsdale Residential School, near Darlington

Gauge: 4' 8½" (static exhibit)

No.4   0-4-0DM   JF 4210087 1953 (a)

(a) ex British Steel Corporation, Stockton Malleable Works, Teesside, 11/1971

<u>NORTH OF ENGLAND OPEN-AIR MUSEUM</u>

The Museum's Headquarters is at Beamish Hall, near Stanley. In 1971 the Museum
took over the former Bowes Railway Loco Shed at Marley Hill in conjunction with
the Stephenson & Hawthorn Locomotive Trust, but new facilities constructed at
Beamish in 1974 made it possible to move locomotives to the main Museum area.

In December 1975 the Museum's locomotives were at the following locations:

1. <u>Beamish Hall</u>, near Stanley

Gauge: 4' 8½"

18	-	0-4-0	VC	G.Stephenson	c1822	(a)
		0-4-0ST	OC	Lewin	c1875	(b)
	MALLEABLE No.5	0-4-0ST	OC			(c)
	-	0-4-0VBT	OC	HW	1871	(d)
	W.D. 10756	4wPM		MR 1364	1918	(e)
	-	4wDM		RH 476140	1963	(f)
	LOCOMOTION	0-4-0	VC	Beamish	1975	(g)
65033		0-6-0	IC	Ghd	1889	(h)

(a) ex British Railways Board, York Railway Museum, 6/1974; Lambton, Hetton &
    Joicey Collieries Ltd until 7/1926
(b) ex Seaham Harbour Dock Co Ltd, 1/1975
(c) stored at Marley Hill until 3/1975; ex British Steel Corporation, Stockton
    Malleable Works, Teesside, 8/1971 (originally South Durham Steel & Iron Co
    Ltd)
(d) stored at Marley Hill until 3/1975; stored at British Steel Corporation,
    Consett Works, until 9/1971; preserved at Head, Wrightson & Co Ltd,
    Thornaby, Teesside, until 7/1970; originally at Dorking Lime Co Ltd,
    Betchworth, Surrey, until /1961
(e) stored at Marley Hill until 3/1975; stored at Beamish Hall until 9/1971;
    ex Newalls Insulation & Chemical Co Ltd, Sandyford Works, Renfrewshire,
    Scotland, via restoration at the firm's Washington Works, 4/1971
(f) stored at Marley Hill until 3/1975; ex British Gas Corporation, Northern
    Division, Redheugh Gas Works, Gateshead, 3/1973 (on permanent loan)
(g) Full-size working replica of LOCOMOTION, RS 3/1825, built at Beamish
    between 1973 and 1975 for 150th anniversary of Stockton & Darlington
    Railway, 1975. Hired out to other organisations as arranged
(h) stored at Marley Hill until 8/1975; stored at British Steel Corporation,
    Consett Works, until 12/1973. NER Worsdell C1 class, originally built as
    C class Worsdell-Von Borries 2-cylinder compound. Originally NER 876.
    LNER J21 class. Wdn as BR 65033, 4/1962, and stored at Darlington until
    presented by BRB and moved to Consett, 7/1970

Gauge: 2' 2"

-	4wDM	RH	256295	1948	(a)

(a) ex NCB North Durham Area, Craghead Colliery, c11/1969

Gauge: 2' 0"

-	4wDM	RH	189963	1939	(a)

(a) ex Slater & Co (Limestone) Ltd, Marsden Quarries, c/1967, and taken to
Museum's store at Brancepeth Castle (now closed); present location
uncertain

2. **Marley Hill Loco Shed**, near Sunniside

Gauge: 4' 8½"

3	TWIZELL	0-6-0T	IC	RS	2730	1891	(a)
41		0-6-0PT	IC	K	2509	1883	(b)
14		0-4-0ST	OC	HL	3056	1914	(c)
1		4wWE		Siemens		1907	(d)

(a) ex NCB North Durham Area, Morrison Busty Colliery, 3/1972 (originally
Lambton, Hetton & Joicey Collieries Ltd, Beamish Railway)
(b) ex NCB North Durham Area, Derwenthaugh, 4/1972 (originally Consett Iron
Co Ltd)
(c) ex NCB North Durham Area, Philadelphia, 12/1972 (originally Lambton,
Hetton & Joicey Collieries Ltd, Lambton Railway)
(d) ex NCB North Durham Area, Westoe Loco Shed, South Shields, 8/1973
(originally Harton Coal Co Ltd)

3. **Dinting Railway Centre Ltd**, near Glossop, Derbyshire

Gauge: 4' 8½"

JACOB	0-4-0PM	Bg	680	1916	(a)

(a) ex W. & R. Jacob (Liverpool) Ltd, Fazakerley, Lancs, 9/1968; stored
pending removal

SEDGEFIELD DISTRICT COUNCIL, Burke Street Depot, Shildon
(Shildon Urban District Council until 1/4/1974)

Gauge: 4' 8½"

(BRADYLL)	0-6-0	OC	Hackworth	(a)

(a) Wdn from service by South Hetton Coal Co c/1875 but converted for use as a
snow plough. To NCB No.2 Area, 1/1/1947; renovated and erected at Lambton
Engine Works, Philadelphia,/1948. Transferred to this site 6/1973, pending
removal to proposed museum at Soho Works, Shildon, in memorial to Hackworth

STEPHENSON & HAWTHORN LOCOMOTIVE TRUST/TANFIELD RAILWAY CO, Marley Hill Loco Shed, near Sunniside

The Trust occupies the Marley Hill Loco Shed in conjunction with the North of England Open-Air Museum, Beamish. In 1975 the Trust set up the Tanfield Railway Co, through which it intends to re-open part of the former BR Tanfield Branch southwards from Marley Hill.

Gauge: 4' 8½"

	STAGSHAW	0-6-0ST	OC	HL	3513	1927	(a)
21		0-4-0ST	OC	RSH	7796	1954	(b)
32		0-4-0ST	OC	AB	1659	1920	(c)
38		0-6-0T	OC	HC	1823	1949	(d)
38		0-6-0ST	OC	RSH	7763	1954	(e)
	(HENDON)	0-4-0CT	OC	RSH	7007	1940	(f)
SIR CECIL A. COCHRANE		0-4-0ST	OC	RSH	7409	1948	(g)
	(CYCLOPS)	0-4-0ST	OC	HL	2711	1907	
				reb.DL		1956	(h)

(a) ex NCB South Durham Area, Shotton Colliery, 7/1972 (originally Strakers & Love Ltd)
(b) ex Central Electricity Generating Board, Stella South G.S., Blaydon, 5/1973
(c) ex NCB North Durham Area, Springwell Shops, 7/1973 (originally South Derwent Coal Co Ltd, and later NCB Bowes Railway)
(d) ex NCB Northumberland Area, Shilbottle Colliery, 10/1973
(e) ex NCB Northumberland Area, Shilbottle Colliery, 11/1973
(f) cx Blaydon Metals Ltd, Blaydon, 1/1974 (Doxford & Sunderland Ltd until 5/1971
(g) stored at NCB Backworth Loco Shed, Tyne & Wear, until 8/1975; Northern Gas Board, Redheugh Gas Works, Gateshead, until 5/1971
(h) ex British Steel Corporation, Lackenby Works, Middlesbrough, Co. Cleveland, 12/1975

The Trust also has locomotives at NCB Backworth Loco Shed, Tyne & Wear (see page 344)

TYNE & WEAR INDUSTRIAL MONUMENTS TRUST, Springwell, near Gateshead

During 1976 the Trust will assume responsibility for the Bowes Railway preservation scheme, whose headquarters will be at Springwell.

Gauge: 4' 8½"

-		0-6-0ST	IC	HE	2879	1943	(a)

(a) ex NCB North Yorkshire Area, Newmarket Colliery, Stanley, Yorks, 1/1975 (owned by W. Maxwell)

J.M.BALDOCK, Hollycombe Steam Fair and Railway, Liphook, Sussex

Gauge: 1' 10¼"

No.1 CALEDONIA   0-4-0WT OC AB   1995 1931 (a)

(a) ex Hampshire Light Railway & Museum Co Ltd, near Eastleigh, Hants, c7/1967;
    Dinorwic Slate Quarries Co Ltd, Caernarvonshire, until 8/1962; Raisby
    Quarries Ltd, Coxhoe, until/1948; orig. Durham County Water Board,
    Burnhope Reservoir, near Wearhead

M.BAMFORD, JCB Excavators Ltd, near Rocester, Staffs

Gauge: 4' 8½"

      ROKER   0-4-0CT OC RSH   7006 1940 (a)

(a) ex J.W.Hardwick, Sons & Co Ltd, West Ewell, Surrey, 2/1974; J.I.Blackburn
    & Co, Godalming, Surrey, until 1/1974; Dalescroft Railfans Club, (stored
    at British Steel Corporation, Britannia Works, Middlesbrough, Teesside)
    until 9/1973; orig. Doxford & Sunderland Ltd until 3/1971

J.I.BLACKBURN & CO, Godalming, Surrey

Gauge: 4' 8½"

      PALLION   0-4-0CT OC HL   2517 1902 (a)

(a) ex Dalescroft Railfans Club (stored at British Steel Corporation, Britannia
    Works, Middlesbrough, Teesside), 10/1973; orig. Doxford & Sunderland Ltd
    until 5/1971

ALAN BLOOM, Bressingham Hall, near Diss, Norfolk

Gauge: 4' 8½"

      MILLFIELD   0-4-0CT OC RSH   7070 1942 (a)

(a) ex Doxford & Sunderland Ltd, Sunderland, 1/1971

CAERPHILLY RAILWAY SOCIETY, Caerphilly, Glamorgan

Gauge: 4' 8½"

      -               0-6-2T   IC Cdf   306   1897 (a)

(a) ex British Railways Board, 7/1967, and moved to present site; NCB Durham
    No.2 Area, South Hetton Loco Sheds, until 2/1962; orig. Taff Vale Railway

CLEVELAND COUNTY COUNCIL, Preston Park & Museum, near Eaglescliffe
(County Borough of Teesside until 1/4/1974)

Gauge: 4' 8½"

16   0-4-0VBT VC HW   21 1870 (a)

(a) ex Head, Wrightson & Co Ltd, Thornaby, Teesside, 10/1970 (preserved);
    Seaham Harbour Dock Co Ltd, Seaham, until 6/1959

COLNE VALLEY RAILWAY, near Castle Hedingham, Essex

Gauge: 4' 8½"

72	0-6-0ST	IC	VF	5309	1945	(a)

(a) ex NCB South Durham Area, South Hetton Loco Sheds, 12/1973; orig. South
    Hetton Coal Co Ltd

DINTING RAILWAY CENTRE LTD, near Glossop, Derbyshire

Gauge: 4' 8½"

(SOUTHWICK)	0-4-0CT	OC	RSH	7069	1942	(a)

(a) ex Doxford & Sunderland Ltd, Sunderland, 4/1971

also

JACOB	0-4-0PM		Bg	680	1916	(b)

(b) stored for North of England Open-Air Museum, Co. Durham (see page 340)

EAST SOMERSET RAILWAY, Cranmore, near Shepton Mallet, Somerset

Gauge: 4' 8½"

68005 (71515 till 1/74)	0-6-0ST	IC	RSH	7169	1944	(a)

(a) ex Johnsons (Chopwell) Ltd, Swalwell, 8/1973 (property of R.P.Weisham
    and N.J.Smith)

KEIGHLEY & WORTH VALLEY RAILWAY LTD, Haworth, Yorks, W.R.

Gauge: 4' 8½"

52	0-6-2T	IC	NR	5408	1899	(a)

(a) ex NCB North Durham Area, Philadelphia, 2/1971; orig. Lambton, Hetton &
    Joicey Collieries Ltd, Lambton Railway

LYTHAM MOTIVE POWER MUSEUM, Lytham St. Annes, Lancs

Gauge: 4' 8½"

HOTTO	4wPM		H	965	1930	(a)

(a) ex Wiggins Teape Ltd, Sunderland, /1972

MIDDLETON RAILWAY TRUST, Hunslet, Leeds, Yorks, W.R.

Gauge: 4' 8½"

1310	0-4-0T	IC	Ghd	38	1891	(a)

(a) ex NCB Durham No.5 Area, Watergate Colliery, 6/1965 (property of Steam
    Power Trust '65); prev. Pelaw Main Collieries Ltd; orig. NER 1310 (Y7 class)

NORTH YORKSHIRE MOORS RAILWAY PRESERVATION SOCIETY LTD, Goathland, Cleveland

Gauge: 4' 8½"

29		0-6-2T	IC	K	4263	1904	(a)
5		0-6-2T	IC	RS	3377	1909	(b)
21		0-4-0DM		JF	4210094	1954	
			reb.	JF		1966	(c)
	EUSTACE FORTH	0-4-0ST	OC	RSH	7063	1942	(d)

(a) ex NCB North Durham Area, Philadelphia, 6/1970; arr. 7/1970; orig.
    Lambton, Hetton & Joicey Collieries Ltd, Lambton Railway
(b) ex NCB North Durham Area, Philadelphia, 6/1970; arr. 8/1970; orig.
    Lambton, Hetton & Joicey Collieries Ltd, Lambton Railway
(c) ex British Steel Corporation, Hartlepool Works, 5/1972 (permanent loan)
(d) ex Central Electricity Generating Board, Dunston G.S., 6/1972

ROYAL SCOTTISH MUSEUM, Edinburgh, Scotland

Gauge: 5' 0"

"WYLAM DILLY"	2-2-0	VCG	Wm.Hedley	1813	(a)

(a) ex T.Hedley & Bros, Craghead Colliery, 10/1882

SCIENCE MUSEUM, South Kensington, London, S.W.7

Gauge: 4' 8½"

BAUXITE No.2	0-4-0ST	OC	BH	305	1874	(a)

(a) presented by North Eastern Historical Engineering & Industrial Locomotive
    Society, 10/1953; presented to Society by Cohen, from International
    Aluminium Co Ltd, Hebburn

SOUTH TYNEDALE RAILWAY PRESERVATION SOCIETY, Slaggyford Station, near Alston, Cumbria

Gauge: 4' 8½"

No.13		0-4-0ST	OC	HL	3732	1928	(a)
	MC156	0-4-0DM		JF	22900	1941	(b)

(a) ex Central Electricity Generating Board, Dunston G.S., 12/1973
(b) ex Caterpillar Tractor Co Ltd, Birtley, 8/1974

STEPHENSON & HAWTHORN LOCOMOTIVE TRUST, NCB Backworth Colliery, Tyne & Wear

Gauge: 4' 8½" (locos stored)

	-	0-6-0ST	OC	AB	1015	1904	(a)
44		0-6-0ST	OC	RSH	7760	1953	(b)

(a) ex NCB South Durham Area, Shotton Colliery, 11/1972; orig. Horden
    Collieries Ltd
(b) ex NCB North-East Area, Backworth Colliery, 3/1975

The Trust also has locomotives at Marley Hill, Tyne & Wear (see section 'a')

SECTION 6

OWNER INDEX

In this index will be found an alphabetical list of all the owners of locomotive-worked locations in this book, with both latest and former titles given. Companies which are main entries are marked thus ⨍, and those still possessing locomotives on 1st January 1976 are underlined.

OWNER INDEX (CONTRACTORS)

OWNER INDEX (PRESERVED LOCOMOTIVES)

In County Durham

Outside County Durham

SECTION 7

LOCATION INDEX

LOCATION INDEX

In the index below the main industries in Co. Durham are listed in alphabetical order, and each locomotive-worked location in that industry then listed, again in alphabetical order.

(a)   Brickworks

Barnsdon Works, Washington	139	Newfield	86
Blaydon Burn	167	Newton Cap	142
Coatham Stob, Eaglescliffe	91	North Bitchburn	141/143
Cornsay	94	Page Bank	99/148
Eaglescliffe	91	Pelton	163
Eclipse Works, Crook	164	Rough Lea	141/143
Eldon	93	Shotton	109/183
Lilley, Rowlands Gill	168	Union Works, Birtley	33
Lumley	94	West Hunwick	217

(b)   Collieries

In this first list are included all Co. Durham collieries which were served by private railways and sidings, except some early pits on the railways of the Earl of Durham and Marquis of Londonderry. Collieries which were only worked, or used locomotives, under the National Coal Board are marked thus (∅). In a number of cases one colliery name is collectively given to a number of separately-named pits in the same area; these are marked thus (↗). In cases where a colliery had more than one name, all names have been included. Where names have changed slightly, the former section of the name is given in brackets.

	Abbey Wood Drift	28	Andrews House	38/39
	Addison	195/225	Anna	182/189
	Adventure	127/131/171/254	∅↗ Arnghyll	226
	Alexandrina	127/131	Auckland Park	34/79/226
	Alma	124	Axwell Garesfield	167
∅	Alma Drift	251	Axwell Park	167/226
	Beamish Air	123	Bowburn	79/228
	Beamish Mary	123/226	Bowburn (West Hetton)	216
	Beamish Second	123/227	Bowden Close	152
	Bearpark	31/227	Bradley	59
	Belmont	128	∅ Bradley Drift	229
	Bewicke Main	157/161	Brancepeth	200/229
∅	Bildershaw	227	Brandon	201/229
	Billingside Drift	59	Brandon Pit House	201/229
	Binchester	35/216	Brasside	114/116
	Black Boy	34/36/222	Brass Thill Drift	126
	Blackburn Fell Drift	39/227	Brooms Drift	59
	Blackhall	109/227	Broomside	127
	Blackhill/Blackhill Drift	61	Browney	80
	Blackhouse 'H'	161	Burnhope	176/230
	Black Prince	213	Burnopfield	38/230
↗	Blaydon Burn	167/228	Byermoor	39/230
	Blaydon Main	168/195	Byers Green	36/216
	Boldon	99/228	Byron	57

Carterthorne 172
Cassop 52
Cassop Moor 52
Cassop Vale 52
Castle Eden 53/109
Charlaw 57
Chilton 82/152/198/231
≠ Chopwell 62/231
Clara Vale 195/231
∅ Clockburn Drift 231

≠ Cocken 114/116
Cornsay 94
Coxhoe 105/216
Craghead 107/232
Crake Scar 222
Crane Row 222
Crookbank 38
Crookhall 59/222
Crowtrees 52/105/216
Croxdale 213

Dawdon 131/133/232
∅ Deaf Hill 232
Dean & Chapter 36/83/232
Delves 61

≠ Derwent 61/233
≠ Dipton 39
Dorothea 114/233
Dunwell 127

Easington 92/133/233
East Hedley Hope 32/233
East Hetton 92/233
East Howle 52
East Stanley 123
East Tanfield 123/185/234
Eden 61/234

Eldon 153
Elemore 107/234
Emma 195/234
Eppleton 107/234
Esther 189
≠ Etherley 198

Felling 44
Finchale 28
Fishburn 198/235

Follonsby 39/251
Framwellgate (Moor) 96/114/116/128/131
Frankland 114/116

Garesfield 51/62/235
Gordon House 140

Greenside 195/235
Greenwell Wood Drift 125

Hamsteels 179/254
Hamsterley 98/235
Handen Hold 123/235
Harraton 116/235
Harton 99/235
Haswell 103/190
∅ Hawthorn 237
Hazard 121/127
≠ Hebburn 207
Hedley Hill 213
(New) Herrington 116/237
Hetton 107/237

Heworth 159/238
∅ High Marley Hill Drift 238
∅≠ Hole-in-the-Wall 238
Hollymoor 218
Holmside 107
Horden 109/238
Houghton 114/239
Humber Hill Drift 61/232
Hunwick 37
Hutton Henry 109
Hylton 215/239

Inkerman 111

Iveston 61

Kibblesworth 39/173/239

Kibblesworth Grange Drift 39

Lady Park Drift 161
Lady Seaham 127
Lambton 'A' 112
Lambton 'D' 114/239
Lambton Main 112
Langley Park 73/240
Latter Day Saints 61
Leasingthorne 37/83/222/241
Letch 127
Lilley Drift 168/241
Lintz 126/182/189

Littleburn 32/143/254
Littletown 112/118
Londonderry 127
Louisa 108/241
Low Beechburn 134
Ludworth 147/213
Lumley Second 116
Lumley Third 116
Lumley Sixth 116/241
Lumley Seventh 116

Urpeth 'B'	159/161	Ushaw Moor	156/251
Urpeth Busty	157/159	Usworth	208/251
Urpeth 'C'	157/251		

Vane Tempest	133/251	Victory	61/232
Victoria Garesfield	169/251		

✗	Waldridge	57/169	West Lucy	150
∅	Wardley No.1	251/252	West Pelton	124
	Wardley (No.2)	39/251/252	West Stanley	185
	Wash Houses	161	∅ West Thornley	213/253
∅	Washington 'F'	252	Westoe	100/253
∅	Washington Glebe	252	Westerton	35/222/254
	Watergate	170/252	Wheatley Hill	147/213/253
	(Monk) Wearmouth	215/252	Whitburn	99/253
∅	West Brandon Drift	252	Whittonstall Drift	62/253
	West Edmonsley	57	Willington	202
	West Edward	150	Windlestone	198
	West Ellimore	59	Wingate Grange	220/253
	West Emma	150	Witton	56/253
	West Hetton	105/216	Woodland	51/222
	West Hunwick	37/217	Woodside Winnings	61
	West Lintz Drift	126	Wooley	156/254

(c)   **Collieries** - mentioned in text, but not served by private railways, etc:

1. **Pre-1947**

Copley	139	South Garesfield	189/254
Fir Tree Drift	74	South Kelloe	216
Heugh Hall	216	Westwood	59
Little Chilton	152/216	Whitwell	53
Merrington	216	Whitworth	216
Shotley	139		

2. **Post-1947** - see list on p.254

(d)   **Collieries in Northumberland**, served by private railway systems, etc., and incorporated into NCB North-East Area on 1st April 1974:

Ashington	255	Ellington	255
Backworth (Eccles)	255	Havannah Drift	256
Bates	255	Lynemouth	256
Bewick Drift, Lynemouth Colliery	256	Netherton	256
Brenkley Drift	255	Shilbottle	256
Burradon	255	Woodhorn	255
Dudley	255	Whittle	256

SECTION 8

LOCOMOTIVE BUILDERS

LOCOMOTIVE BUILDERS

(1) (excluding firms who built locos for themselves)

AB	Andrew Barclay, Sons & Co Ltd, Kilmarnock, Ayrshire
AE	Avonside Engine Co Ltd, Bristol
AEG	Allgemeine Elektricitaats Gesellschaft, Berlin, Germany
Atlas	Atlas Loco & Manufacturing Co Ltd, Ohio, U.S.A.
AW	Sir W.G. Armstrong, Whitworth & Co (Engineers) Ltd, Newcastle-upon-Tyne

B	Barclays & Co, Kilmarnock, Ayrshire
Becorit	Becorit (G.B.) Ltd, Nottingham (power pack supplied by HE)
Bg	E.E. Baguley Ltd, Burton-on-Trent, Staffs
BH	Black, Hawthorn & Co Ltd, Gateshead, Co. Durham (later CF)
Blair	Blair & Co Ltd, Stockton-on-Tees, Co. Durham
Blyth & Tyne	Blyth & Tyne Railway (works at Percy Main, Northumberland)
Bond	J. Bond, Tow Law, Co. Durham
Booth	Joseph Booth, Rodley, Yorks, W.R.
I.W. Boulton	I.W. Boulton, Ashton-under-Lyne, Lancs
BP	Beyer, Peacock & Co Ltd, Manchester
BP/BT	locos built jointly by BP and BT
BT	Brush Electrical Engineering Co Ltd, Loughborough, Leics
BTH	British Thomson-Houston Co Ltd, Rugby, Warwickshire
Bury	Bury, Curtis & Kennedy, Liverpool
Butterley	Butterley Co Ltd, Butterley, Derbyshire
Bwn	Baldwin Locomotive Works, Philadelphia, U.S.A.

Caerphilly	Caerphilly Works, Glamorgan, Great Western Railway
CC	Clarke, Chapman & Co Ltd, Gateshead, Co. Durham
Cdf	Cardiff Works, Glamorgan, Taff Vale Railway
CE	International Combustion Ltd, Clayton Works, Hatton, Derbyshire
CF	Chapman & Furneaux Ltd, Gateshead, Co. Durham (successors to BH)
CoS	Cowans, Sheldon & Co Ltd, Carlisle, Cumberland
Coulson	M. Coulson & Co, Spennymoor, Co. Durham
Coulthard	John (later Ralph) Coulthard, Gateshead, Co. Durham

D	Dubs & Co, Glasgow (later part of NBL)
Dar	Darlington Works, Co.Durham, British Railways (and predecessors)
Davenport	Davenport Locomotive Works, Iowa, U.S.A.
DC	Drewry Car Co Ltd, London
DC/Bg	built by Bg for DC
DC/VF	built by VF for DC
Derby	Derby Works, British Railways
DK	Dick, Kerr & Co, Kilmarnock, Ayrshire
Don	Doncaster Works, Yorks, W.R.,British Railways (and predecessors)

EB	E. Borrows & Sons, St. Helens, Lancs
EE	English Electric Co Ltd (locos also subcontracted to Bg and RSH)
EE S	English Electric Co Ltd, Stephenson Works, Darlington,Co.Durham
EE V	English Electric Co Ltd, Vulcan Works, Newton-le-Willows, Lancs
EV	Ebbw Vale Steel & Iron Co Ltd, Ebbw Vale, Glamorgan

Fairbairn	W. Fairbairn & Sons, Manchester
F&H	Fossick & Hackworth, Stockton-on-Tees, Co. Durham
FH	F.C. Hibberd & Co Ltd, Park Royal, London (later at Butterley Works, Derbyshire

FJ	Fletcher, Jennings & Co Ltd, Whitehaven, Cumberland (later LE)
FW	Fox, Walker & Co Ltd, Bristol (later P)
GB	Greenbat Ltd, Albion Works, Leeds (form. Greenwood & Batley Ltd)
GEC	General Electric Co Ltd, Witton, Birmingham
GH	Gibb & Hogg Ltd, Airdrie, Lanarkshire
Ghd	Gateshead Works, Co. Durham, North Eastern Railway
Goodman	Goodman Bros., Chicago, U.S.A.
GR	Grant, Ritchie & Co Ltd, Kilmarnock, Ayrshire
Grange Iron Wks	Grange Iron Works, Belmont, near Durham City, Co. Durham
GW	Gilkes, Wilson & Co, Middlesbrough, Yorks, N.R. (later HG)
H	J.& F. Howard Ltd, Bedford
Hackworth	Timothy Hackworth, Shildon, Co. Durham
Haigh	Haigh Foundry, Wigan, Lancs
Hanomag	Hannoversche-Maschienenbau-AG, Hannover-Linden, Germany
Harris	John Harris, Darlington, Co. Durham
W. Hedley	William Hedley, Wylam Colliery, Wylam, Northumberland
H&C	Hudswell & Clarke, Leeds
HB	Hudswell Badger Ltd, Leeds
HC	Hudswell, Clarke & Co Ltd, Leeds
HCR	Hudswell, Clarke & Rodgers, Leeds
HE	Hunslet Engine Co Ltd, Leeds
HG	Hopkins, Gilkes & Co, Middlesbrough, Yorks, N.R. (prev. GW)
HH	Henry Hughes & Co Ltd, Loughborough, Leics
HL	R. & W. Hawthorn, Leslie & Co Ltd, Newcastle-upon-Tyne (prev. RWH; became part of RSH)
H(L)	Hawthorns & Co Ltd, Leith, Midlothian
Hopper	George Hopper, Britannia Ironworks, Fencehouses, Co. Durham
HR	Hardy Railmotors Ltd, Slough, Bucks
HW	Head, Wrightson & Co Ltd, Thornaby, Yorks, N.R.
I'Anson	Charles I'Anson & Co, Darlington, Co. Durham
JF	John Fowler & Co (Leeds) Ltd, Leeds
Joicey	J. & G. Joicey & Co Ltd, Newcastle-upon-Tyne
Jones, Turner & Evans	Jones, Turner & Evans, Newton-le-Willows, Lancs
K	Kitson & Co Ltd, Leeds
KC	Kent Construction & Engineering Co Ltd, Ashford, Kent
KE	Kilmarnock Engineering Co Ltd, Kilmarnock, Ayrshire
Kitching	W. & A. Kitching, Darlington, Co. Durham
KS	Kerr, Stuart & Co Ltd, Stoke-on-Trent, Staffs
L	R. A. Lister & Co Ltd, Dursley, Gloucestershire
LE	Lowca Engineering Co Ltd, Whitehaven, Cumberland (prev. FJ; later NLE)
Lewin	Stephen Lewin, Poole, Dorset
LG	Lingford, Gardiner & Co Ltd, Bishop Auckland, Co. Durham
LMM	Logan Mining & Machinery Co Ltd, Dundee, Angus
MF	Marshall, Fleming & Co, Motherwell, Lanarkshire
MH	Muir Hill Engineering Ltd, Manchester
Miller	Miller & Co Ltd, Coatbridge, Lanarkshire (? dealers only)
MR	Motor Rail Ltd, Bedford
MW	Manning, Wardle & Co Ltd, Leeds

N	Neilson & Co, Glasgow (later NR)
Nasmyth Gaskell	Nasmyth, Gaskell & Co, Bridgwater Foundry, Patricroft, Manchester
NBL	North British Locomotive Co Ltd, Glasgow (formed from D, NR & SS)
Neasden	Neasden Works, London, Metropolitan Railway
NLE	New Lowca Engineering Co Ltd, Whitehaven, Cumberland (prev. LE)
NR	Neilson, Reid & Co Ltd, Glasgow (prev. N; later part of NBL)
OK	Orenstein & Koppel A.G., Berlin, Germany
P	Peckett & Sons Ltd, Bristol (prev. FW)
Priestman	Priestman Bros, Wolverhampton, Staffs
RH	Ruston & Hornsby Ltd, Lincoln
Ridley	Thomas D. Ridley & Sons, Middlesbrough, Yorks, N.R.
Ridley Shaw	Ridley, Shaw & Co Ltd, Middlesbrough, Yorks, N.R.
RR	Rolls Royce Ltd, Shrewsbury, Shropshire
RS	Robert Stephenson & Co Ltd, Newcastle-upon-Tyne (Darlington, Co. Durham, after 1901) (became part of RSH)
RSH	Robert Stephenson & Hawthorns Ltd, Newcastle-upon-Tyne and Darlington, Co. Durham (formed from HL & RS)
RWH	R. & W. Hawthorn & Co, Newcastle-upon-Tyne (later HL)
S	Sentinel (Shrewsbury) Ltd, Shrewsbury, Shropshire (and predecessors)
Sdn	Swindon Works, Wiltshire, Great Western Railway
Siemens	Siemens Bros Ltd, London
SS	Sharp, Stewart & Co Ltd, Manchester (Glasgow from 1888) (later part of NBL)
Stark & Fulton	Stark & Fulton, Glasgow
Tayleur	Charles Tayleur & Co, Newton-le-Willows, Lancs (later VF)
TH	Thomas Hill (Rotherham) Ltd, Kilnhurst, Yorks, W.R.
TR	Thomas Richardson & Sons, West Hartlepool, Co. Durham
TS	Thomas Smith & Sons (Rodley) Ltd, Rodley, Yorks, W.R.
TW	Thornewill & Warham, Burton-on-Trent, Staffs
UMM	Underground Mining Machinery Ltd, Newton Aycliffe, Co. Durham
VF	Vulcan Foundry Ltd, Newton-le-Willows, Lancs (prev. Tayleur)
WB	W. G. Bagnall Ltd, Stafford
WB/BT	built jointly by WB and BT
West Hartlepool	West Hartlepool Works, West Hartlepool Harbour & Railway Co
WN	W. Neill & Son (St. Helens) Ltd, St. Helens, Lancs
WR	Wingrove & Rogers Ltd, Southport, Lancs; later at Kirkby, Liverpool
YE	Yorkshire Engine Co Ltd, Sheffield, Yorks, W.R.
York	York Works, North Eastern Railway (later LNER)

(11) firms who built locomotives for themselves

Aycliffe   Aycliffe Lime & Limestone Co Ltd, Co Durham

Barningham   William Barningham, Darlington, Co. Durham
Bearpark   Bearpark Coal & Coke Co Ltd, and Bearpark Colliery under NCB
Birtley   Birtley Iron Co Ltd, Co. Durham
Blacklock   F.Blacklock, Old Durham Road Scrapyard, Gateshead, Co. Durham
Brancepeth   Strakers & Love, Brancepeth Colliery, Co. Durham
BV   Bolckow, Vaughan & Co Ltd, Cleveland Works, Middlesbrough,
                   Yorks, N.R.

Cochrane   Cochrane & Co Ltd, Ormesby Ironworks, Middlesbrough, Yorks, N.R.
Coles   Steels Engineering Products Ltd, Sunderland, Co. Durham
                   (manufacturers of Coles cranes)
Consett   Consett Iron Co Ltd, Consett Works, Co. Durham

Earl of Durham   Earl of Durham, Lambton Engine Works, Philadelphia, Co. Durham
DL   Dorman, Long & Co Ltd, Britannia Works, Middlesbrough, Co.Durham

Hetton Colly   Hetton Coal Co Ltd, Hetton Engine works, Hetton, Co. Durham

LEW   Lambton, Hetton & Joicey Collieries Ltd, Lambton Engine Works,
                   Philadelphia, Co. Durham (later NCB)

Marley Hill   John Bowes, Esq., & Partners, Marley Hill Loco Shed, Pontop &
                   Jarrow Railway, Co. Durham

Seaham   Marquis of Londonderry, Seaham Engine Works, Seaham Harbour,
                   Co. Durham

J. Tait   James Tait Jnr, Middlesbrough, Yorks, N.R.
Thornley   Weardale Steel, Coal & Coke Co Ltd,Thornley Colliery, Co.Durham
TIW   Pease & Partners, Tees Ironworks, Middlesbrough, Yorks, N.R.
Tow Law   Weardale Iron & Coal Co Ltd, Tow Law Ironworks, Co. Durham
Tudhoe   Weardale Steel Coal & Coke Co Ltd, Tudhoe Ironworks, Co. Durham

Wake   J.F. Wake, Geneva Works, Darlington, Co. Durham

SECTION 9

Notes on lesser known locomotive builders of North-East England

Sir W.G. Armstrong, Whitworth & Co (Engineers) Ltd, Newcastle-upon-Tyne

This famous munitions firm commenced building locomotives at its Scotswood
Works in 1919, and gradually turned to diesel types, which continued up to
1939. After the Second World War the locomotive side of the business was
employed on the overhaul of Ministry of Supply locos, and when this
finished the department closed down.

Joseph Bond, Castle Foundry, Tow Law, Co. Durham

Had a general engineering business, and is believed to have built only a
small number of locomotives, finishing in the 1870's. The firm continues,
still in the Bond family.

M. Coulson & Co, Spennymoor, Co. Durham

Had a general engineering business, and although the firm undertook a
number of locomotive repairs before and after the Second World War, it is
doubtful whether the firm actually built any locomotives.

John & Ralph Coulthard, Quarry Field Works, Gateshead, Co. Durham

These two brothers entered business in 1840, building, repairing and
dealing in engines, boilers, pumps and locomotives. John Coulthard left the
partnership in April 1853, leaving his brother to continue alone. Considerable doubt now exists as to the authenticity of locomotives credited to
Coulthard, some of which may well have been built by other manufacturers
with Coulthard acting as agent. Ralph Coulthard retired from business in
1865, advertising his stock in June of that year, and in August 1865 the
works was taken over by the newly-formed firm of Black, Hawthorn & Co
(q.v.)

Gilkes, Wilson & Co, Tees Engine Works, Middlesbrough, Yorks, N.R.

This engine works was originally the locomotive works of the Stockton &
Darlington Railway, Gilkes being manager. In 1844 he joined Wilson, and
took over the works. They were subsequently joined by Leatham, who died in
1858. His place was then taken by J.B.Pease, the firm then becoming Gilkes,
Wilson & Pease.

Hopkins, Gilkes & Co, Middlesbrough, Yorks, N.R.

Hopkins, Snowden & Co was formed in 1853, and owned the Teesside Iron Works
at Middlesbrough. In 1861 Snowden retired, the business then becoming
Hopkins & Co. In 1865 this firm amalgamated with Gilkes, Wilson & Pease to
become Hopkins, Gilkes & Co. In February 1880 the firm was re-constituted
as Teesside Iron & Engine Works Co Ltd, and thereafter the locomotive side
of the business was discontinued.

Grange Iron Works, Belmont, near Durham City, Co. Durham

This rather obscure firm was mainly concerned with foundry work, and
structural and general engineering. In the 1860's and 1870's it is known to
have built a small number of locomotives, some estimate not more than six.
The works closed about 1920.

Timothy Hackworth, Soho Works, Shildon, Co. Durham

He was responsible for the maintainance of the locomotives of the Stockton
& Darlington Railway, with a works at Shildon. Under his contract he did
both this and built locomotives in a new works which he set up with Downing.
Thomas, a brother of Timothy, was appointed manager, and remained thus until 1840.

Fossick & Hackworth, Stockton-on-Tees, Co. Durham

In 1840 Thomas Hackworth opened a works in Stockton in partnership with
George Fossick. In 1865 Hackworth retired, and the firm became
Fossick & Blair, George Blair having previously been works manager. In 1866

Fossick died, and the firm became

Blair & Co Ltd, under which title the business was carried on until it closed about 1920. From about 1870 the firm gave up locomotive building, and concentrated more on marine work.

John Harris, Hopetown Foundry, Darlington, Co. Durham

Took over the business of W. & A. Kitching (q.v.) about 1860. He is believed to have built only a small number of locomotives, concentrating mainly on foundry and general engineering work.

Head, Wrightson & Co Ltd, Thornaby, Yorks, N.R.

About 1855 the Teesdale Iron Works was opened by Head and Wright. Shortly afterwards Wright was replaced by Ashley, who in turn gave way to Wrightson in 1860. It is not known how many locomotives the firm built, but all appear to have been vertical-boilered and to date from 1865-1875. The firm continues.

George Hopper, Britannia Iron Works, Fencehouses, Co. Durham

This business is believed to have started in the early 1840's, and closed in 1883. He is believed to have built about six locomotives.

I'Anson & Co Ltd, Darlington, Co. Durham

For the history of this firm see the main section. It is believed to have built only a few small locomotives, apparently only in the 1870's.

J. & G. Joicey & Co Ltd, Pottery Lane, Newcastle-upon-Tyne

This firm of general engineers began in 1855, and concentrated on various types of steam engine, mainly for winding, hauling and pumping. Locomotives were numbered into a general list of products, but it is not known how many were built. The firm closed in 1926. N.B. One of the firm's winding engines, from Beamish Second Pit (q.v.), is preserved at the North of England Open-Air Museum at Beamish.

W. & A. Kitching, Hopetown Foundry, Darlington, Co. Durham

This works opened in 1832, and built locomotives until about 1860, when it passed to John Harris (see above).

Lingford, Gardiner & Co Ltd, Auckland Engine Works, Bishop Auckland, Co. Durham

This firm was established in the 1850's, and built various types of steam engine, together with general engineering repairs for collieries. Although their advertisements described them as "Builders, Hirers and Repairers of Locomotives", they are believed to have built only two or three new locomotives; many of the engines reputedly built by them and carrying their plates were actually reconstructions of engines purchased by them and then offered for sale or hire. The firm went into liquidation in 1931.

T. Richardson & Sons, Hartlepool Iron Works, Hartlepool, Co. Durham

This firm built and repaired a considerable quantity of locomotives from 1847 onwards, numbering them into the general list of products. From about 1870 the firm concentrated on marine engine work. For subsequent history see main section.

T. D. Ridley, Middlesbrough, Yorks, N.R.

This man was basically a public works contractor, beginning in 1875. In 1896 he retired, and the firm became known as

T. D. Ridley & Sons, and later

Ridley, Shaw & Co Ltd. They are believed to have built no more than three locomotives, though a considerable amount of locomotive repair work was undertaken right up to the 1950's. The firm closed down in 1958.

SECTION 10

LOCOMOTIVE INDEX

LOCOMOTIVE INDEX

This index is intended to provide a quick source of reference to the principal details of the majority of the locomotives listed in this book. The inclusion of page numbers enables the ownership of any loco to be established.

The details quoted are always those of the loco when new, and have been extracted where possible from the records kept by the locomotive builders. We are grateful to Andrew Barclay, Sons & Co Ltd for kindly checking the details of their own locomotives, the North British Locomotive Co Ltd and John Fowler & Co (Leeds) Ltd, and to various friends who have had direct access to builders' records and have willingly given every help they could.

We also thought it appropriate in a book on Co. Durham to give brief historical details of the locomotive builders in North-East England, the major builders in this section and the minor builders in a note at the end.

Dates : Where possible, the full date given is that of dispatch from the builder's works; but where these are not available, delivery dates taken from customers' records have been given. It must, however, be noted that the year quoted in these lists may well not be the year on the works' plate; quite a number of discrepancies are known when delivery has been close to the New Year. As far as is known, the year given in the main section of the book is that which was carried on the plate.

Products of the following builders, not covered by the detailed tables below, will be found on the page numbers quoted:

AEG	102/260/290/300	D	67/214/338
Atlas	134/317	Dar	51/101/179/217/222
AW	55/174		258/292/299/300/338
		Davenport	137
		DC	31/182
B	168/193/222/280	DC/Bg	135
Becorit	316/323	DC/VF	136
Bg ⚡	110/260/290/301/340/343	Derby	112/292/300/301
Blair	118/132	DK	55/120/122/165
Blyth & Tyne	101/180	Don	162/292/338
Bond	214		
Booth	67/151/277		
I.W.Boulton	215	EB	208
BT	285		
BTH	54		
Bury	156/335	Fairbairn	214
Butterley	183	F.& H.	53/132
Bwn	58/198		
		GEC	57
⚡ see also EE list		GH	34/39/79/83/84
		Ghd	42/101/102/162/180
CC	69		257/258/283/339/343
Cdf	120/259/264/342	Goodman	48/70
CE	47/209/303/304	GR	119/263/268/333
CoS	68/69	Grange I.W.	140/141/172/187
Coulson	71/285	GW	214
Coulthard(?)	41		

AB - <u>ANDREW BARCLAY, SONS & CO LTD</u>, Caledonia Works, Kilmarnock, Ayrshire.
(member of Hunslet group from 21/8/1972)

⌿ date of order number ø date of boiler test

WORKS No.	DATE EX-WORKS	GAUGE AS BUILT ft.ins.	TYPE	CYLS.(bore x stroke) ins.ins.	DRIVING WH.DIAM. ft.ins.	NOTES	SEE PAGE
3	1859⌿	4 8½	0-4-0ST	OC 10 x 18	3 0	reb. to AB 277	162/193
52	10.1866⌿	4 8½	0-4-0ST	OC 8 x 17	3 0		164
70	3. 2.1868⌿	4 8½	0-4-0ST	OC 9 x 18	3 0		197
233	14. 7.1881⌿	4 8½	0-4-0ST	OC 13 x 20	3 2		193
266	21. 3.1884⌿	4 8½	0-4-0ST	OC 11 x 18	3 0		45
277	24. 6.1884⌿	4 8½	0-4-0ST	OC 11 x 18	3 0	reb. of AB 3/1859	162/193
299	10. 1.1888⌿	4 8½	0-4-0ST	OC 13 x 20	3 2		182
305	14. 1.1888⌿	4 8½	0-4-0ST	OC 13 x 20	3 2		214
641	15. 4.1889⌿	4 8½	0-4-0ST	OC 15 x 20	3 7		208
656	7. 2.1890⌿	4 8½	0-4-0ST	OC 13 x 20	3 2		39/83/84
688	1. 5.1891⌿	4 8½	0-4-0ST	OC 13 x 20	3 4		193
693	2. 5.1891⌿	4 8½	0-4-0ST	OC 12 x 18	3 0		28
694	22. 4.1891⌿	4 8½	0-6-0ST	OC 14 x 22	3 5		222
698	1891⌿	4 8½	0-6-0T	OC 14 x 22	3 5		93
719	27. 6.1892⌿	3 0	0-4-0ST	OC 8 x 17	2 6		329
730	18. 4.1893⌿	4 8½	0-4-0ST	OC 10 x 18	2 10		134
733	9.11.1893⌿	4 8½	0-4-0ST	OC 10 x 18	3 0		137
773	5. 3.1897⌿	4 8½	0-4-0ST	OC 12 x 20	2 10		56
786	1896	4 8½	0-4-0ST	OC 12 x 20	3 2		162/283
803	26. 8.1897	4 8½	0-6-0ST	IC 16 x 24	3 9		169
805	21.10.1897	4 8½	0-4-0ST	OC 14 x 22	3 5		164
823	18. 6.1898	4 8½	0-4-0ST	OC 13 x 20	3 8		176
833	4. 7.1899	4 8½	0-6-0ST	IC 16 x 24	3 8		215/258
895	10. 5.1901	4 8½	0-4-0ST	OC 13 x 19	3 4½		66/73
909	17. 7.1901	4 8½	0-6-0ST	IC 16 x 24	3 9		215
911	1901	4 8½	0-6-0T	IC 16 x 24	4 0		215/258
912	23. 7.1901	4 8½	0-6-0ST	OC 12 x 20	3 2		92/267
961	26. 4.1903ø	4 8½	0-6-0ST	OC 15 x 22	3 5		198/199
969	23. 3.1903	4 8½	0-4-0ST	OC 10 x 18	2 8½		93
970	1. 4.1903	4 8½	0-6-0ST	OC 14 x 22	3 5		162/283
973	30.12.1903ø	4 8½	0-4-0ST	OC 14 x 22	3 5		185
999	30.12.1903ø	4 8½	0-6-0T	IC 17 x 24	4 0		215/258/289
1005	13. 4.1904	4 8½	0-6-0ST	IC 16 x 24	3 9		57/169/275
1015	8. 7.1904	4 8½	0-6-0ST	OC 15 x 22	3 5		109/267/295/344
1066	21. 8.1906	4 8½	0-4-0ST	OC 14 x 22	3 5		214
1082	21.11.1907	4 8½	0-4-0ST	OC 14 x 22	3 5		179
1085	30.10.1907	4 8½	0-4-0ST	OC 12 x 20	3 2		142/152/153/198 199/200/271
1097	27. 5.1907	4 8½	0-6-0ST	OC 15 x 22	3 5		198/199
1127	25.11.1907	4 8½	0-4-0ST	OC 14 x 22	3 5		162
1223	14. 3.1911	4 8½	0-4-0ST	OC 10 x 18	3 0		206
1256	26. 2.1912	4 8½	0-4-0ST	OC 10 x 18	3 0		184
1287	17. 6.1914	4 8½	0-4-0ST	OC 10 x 18	3 0		145
1289	26.12.1912	4 8½	0-4-0ST	OC 14 x 22	3 5		171
1305	26.11.1912	4 8½	0-4-0CT	OC 14 x 22	3 5		87
1321	23. 7.1913	4 8½	0-6-0ST	OC 15 x 22	3 5		214/267/295
1337	22. 9.1913	4 8½	0-4-0ST	OC 13 x 20	3 2		170
1363	19. 1.1914	4 8½	0-4-0ST	OC 16 x 22	3 7		182/187
1404	27. 3.1915	4 8½	0-6-0ST	OC 16 x 22	3 7		52/80
1453	4. 4.1918	2 0	0-4-0WT	OC 6¾ x 10¾	1 10		89
1497	11.12.1916	4 8½	0-6-0ST	OC 14 x 22	3 5		94
1501	30. 4.1917	4 8½	0-4-0ST	OC 16 x 22	3 7		182/187
1609	30. 9.1918	4 8½	0-4-0ST	OC 16 x 22	3 7		182/187
1639	29.12.1922	4 8½	0-6-0ST	OC 14 x 22	3 5		101/102/258
1659	3. 3.1920	4 8½	0-4-0ST	OC 14 x 22	3 5		185/281/291/341
1665	29. 5.1920	4 8½	0-4-0CT	OC 14 x 22	3 5		68/72
1715	20.12.1920	4 8½	0-4-0CT	OC 14 x 22	3 5		68

1724	7. 3.1922	4 8½	0-4-0ST	OC	14 x 22	3 5	133/264/268/295
1768	1. 8.1922	4 8½	0-4-0ST	OC	12 x 20	3 2	56
1770	7.10.1921	4 8½	0-6-0ST	OC	12 x 20	3 2	136
1800	4.12.1923	4 8½	0-4-0ST	OC	12 x 20	3 2	328
1811	22.12.1923	4 8½	0-4-0ST	OC	14 x 22	3 5	193/282
1818	4. 1.1924	4 8½	0-4-0ST	OC	12 x 20	3 2	328
1855	30. 3.1931	2 0	0-4-0WT	OC	7 x 11	1 10	89
1883	7.10.1927	4 8½	0-4-0ST	OC	16 x 24	3 7	281
1885	12. 1.1926	4 8½	0-4-0ST	OC	14 x 22	3 5	133/264/268/295
1988	31. 3.1931	4 8½	0-4-0ST	OC	12 x 20	3 2	89
1991	14. 7.1931	2 0	0-4-0WT	OC	7 x 11	1 10	89
1994	8.10.1931	2 0	0-4-0WT	OC	7 x 11	1 10	89
1995	30.11.1931	2 0	0-4-0WT	OC	7 x 11	1 10	89/172/342
2029	9. 3.1937	4 8½	0-6-0T	OC	16 x 24	3 8	164
2078	24.11.1939	4 8½	0-4-0ST	OC	16 x 24	3 8	65
2091	18. 4.1940	4 8½	0-4-0ST	OC	16 x 24	3 8	67/72
2105	27. 8.1940	4 8½	0-4-0ST	OC	16 x 24	3 7	187
2111	2. 7.1941	4 8½	0-4-0CT	OC	12 x 22	3 6	68
2118	23. 6.1941	4 8½	0-4-0ST	OC	14 x 22	3 5	170
2119	25. 7.1941	4 8½	0-4-0ST	OC	14 x 22	3 5	172
2160	10. 3.1943	4 8½	0-4-0ST	OC	14 x 22	3 5	133/264/268
2165	11.12.1944	4 8½	0-4-0ST	OC	14 x 22	3 5	133/264
2245	17.12.1947	4 8½	0-4-0ST	OC	16 x 24	3 9	300
2274	20.10.1949	4 8½	0-4-0ST	OC	14 x 22	3 5	284/291
2275	27.10.1949	4 8½	0-4-0ST	OC	14 x 22	3 5	271/295
2276	16.11.1949	4 8½	0-4-0ST	OC	14 x 22	3 5	271
2277	19. 1.1950	4 8½	0-4-0ST	OC	14 x 22	3 5	271/296
2281	4. 9.1950	4 8½	0-4-0ST	OC	16 x 24	3 7	272/276
2317	20. 3.1950	4 8½	0-4-0ST	OC	14 x 22	3 5	276/284/305
2320	10. 1.1952	4 8½	0-4-0ST	OC	14 x 22	3 5	271/295/301/305
2321	24. 1.1952	4 8½	0-4-0ST	OC	14 x 22	3 5	271
2322	17. 3.1952	4 8½	0-4-0ST	OC	14 x 22	3 5	271
2341	8. 5.1953	4 8½	0-4-0ST	OC	14 x 22	3 5	272/296

Diesel locomotives

WORKS No.	DATE EX-WORKS	GAUGE AS BUILT ft.ins.	TYPE	HORSE POWER	DRIVING WH.DIAM. ft.ins.	NOTES	SEE PAGE
352	17. 3.1941	4 8½	0-4-0DM	153	3 5		135/144
380	5. 9.1950	4 8½	0-6-0DM	330	4 0		166
381	16. 4.1951	4 8½	0-6-0DM	330	4 0		166
382	17. 4.1951	4 8½	0-6-0DM	330	4 0		166
384	19.11.1951	4 8½	0-4-0DM	204	3 4½		170
423	29. 7.1958	4 8½	0-6-0DM	310	3 2		267/295/301
478	14.12.1963	4 8½	0-4-0DH	233	3 5		259/290/300
488	3. 2.1964	4 8½	0-6-0DH	380	3 5		268/294/301
491	13. 4.1964	4 8½	0-6-0DH	380	3 5		268/294/301
498	21. 1.1965	4 8½	0-6-0DH	380	3 5		268/294/301
514	16. 5.1966	4 8½	0-6-0DH	311	3 9		259/290/300
523	30. 1.1967	4 8½	0-4-0DH	233	3 9		268/295/301
524	7. 2.1967	4 8½	0-4-0DH	233	3 9		268/295/301
547	30. 3.1967	4 8½	0-4-0DH	233	3 9		268/296/301
548	26. 6.1967	4 8½	0-4-0DH	233	3 9		268/296
549	14.10.1967	4 8½	0-6-0DH	311	3 9		300
550	30. 8.1968	4 8½	0-4-0DH	233	3 9		296/301
582	23. 3.1973	4 8½	0-6-0DH	400	3 9		296/301
583	28. 3.1973	4 8½	0-6-0DH	400	3 9		296/301
584	18. 6.1973	4 8½	0-6-0DH	400	3 9		296/301
585	25. 7.1973	4 8½	0-6-0DH	400	3 9		296/301
594	10.12.1974	4 8½	0-6-0DH	400	3 9		301

AE - AVONSIDE ENGINE CO LTD, Bristol
(no dispatch dates known before 1924)

WORKS No.	DATE EX-WORKS	GAUGE AS BUILT ft.ins.	TYPE	CYLS.(bore x stroke) ins.ins	DRIVING WH.DIAM. ft.ins.	MAKERS CLASS	SEE PAGE
1054	1874	4 8½	0-4-0ST	OC 14 x 18	3 0		136
1055	1874	4 8½	0-4-0ST	OC 14 x 18	3 0		93/136
1387	1898	4 8½	0-4-0ST	OC 14 x 20	3 3	SS	123
1509	1907	4 8½	0-4-0ST	OC 12 x 18	2 11	1232	200/201/276
1613	1911	4 8½	0-4-0ST	OC 8½ x 12	2 1	Std	219
1618	1912	4 8½	0-6-0ST	OC 14 x 20	3 3	B3	166
1631	1912	4 8½	0-4-0ST	OC 12 x 18	3 0		153
1701	1915	4 8½	0-4-0T	OC 10 x 16	2 9	Special	195
1769	1917	4 8½	0-4-0ST	OC 12 x 18	2 11	Std	86
1793	1918	4 8½	0-4-0ST	OC 14 x 20	3 3	SS3	82/270/287
1801	1918	4 8½	0-4-0ST	OC 14 x 20	3 3	SS3	187
1932	15. 7.1924	4 8½	0-4-0ST	OC 12 x 18	2 11	5160	170
2000	6. 8.1930	4 8½	0-6-0ST	OC 14 x 22	3 6	B6	89
2066	7. 4.1933	2 0	0-4-0T	OC 7 x 12	2 0		89
2067	7. 4.1933	2 0	0-4-0T	OC 7 x 12	2 0		89
2071	28. 6.1933	2 0	0-4-0T	OC 7½ x 12	2 0		33/89
2072	30. 6.1933	2 0	0-4-0T	OC 7½ x 12	2 0		89
2073	6. 7.1933	2 0	0-4-0T	OC 7½ x 12	2 0		89

BH - BLACK, HAWTHORN & CO LTD, Gateshead, Co. Durham
This company was formed in 1865 to take over the engine works in Quarry
Lane formerly operated by Ralph Coulthard (see notes on local builders).
The firm's main output was to industrial customers, though they also supplied
main line railways and customers abroad. Besides locomotives, the firm also
built other types of steam engine, such as colliery pumping engines, and these
were also allocated numbers in the makers' serial list. Although serial
numbers were issued up to No. 1143, the last locomotive built was No. 1138.
The company went into voluntary liquidation in January 1897, and the business
was subsequently taken over by Chapman & Furneaux Ltd (q.v.).

Perhaps more than many firms, Black, Hawthorn frequently built locomotives for stock, and the actual customer's order might come as much as three
years later. To try to avoid too much confusion, the date of first ordering is
given in the list below, with customers' order dates (if different) shown in a
footnote. Very few delivery dates are recorded, but those known are also given.
The same problem also gives rise to uncertainty about many dates carried on
the maker's plate; the date given in the main text is that believed to have
been carried.

WORKS No.	DATE OF FIRST ORDERING	GAUGE AS BUILT ft.ins.	TYPE	CYLS.(bore x stroke) ins.ins.	DRIVING WH.DIAM. ft.ins.	NOTES	SEE PAGE
13	31.10.1866	4 8½	0-4-0ST	OC 10 x 17	3 0		28
17	16. 3.1866	4 8½	0-6-0	IC 16 x 24	4 6	%	119/262
22	26. 1.1867	4 8½	0-4-0ST	OC 10 x 17	3 0		177
31	12. 3.1867	4 8½	0-6-0ST	OC 14 x 20	3 4		147/214
32	12. 3.1867	4 8½	0-6-0ST	OC 15 x 20	4 0	@	119/180/262
34	23. 5.1867	4 8½	0-6-0	IC 16 x 24	4 8		132
37	26. 7.1867	4 8½	0-4-0ST	OC 12 x 19	3 3		155
38	26. 7.1867	4 8½	0-4-0ST	OC 12 x 18	3 3		208
48	8. 1.1868	4 8½	0-6-0T	OC 14 x 20	3 6		162
52	8. 1.1868	4 8½	0-6-0ST	OC 14 x 20	3 6		162
57	6. 4.1868	4 8½	0-6-0T	OC 16 x 24	3 6		214
60	11. 6.1868	4 8½	0-6-0T	OC 14 x 20	3 6		162/334
62	20. 6.1868	4 8½	0-4-0ST	OC 9 x 16	2 9		149
95	1. 1.1869	4 8½	0-4-0ST	OC 11 x 17	2 8½		177
120	16. 1.1871	4 8½	0-4-0ST	OC 12 x 19	3 2		148

128	1. 2.1869	4	8½	0-4-0ST	OC	9 x 16	2	9	149
166	28.10.1870/	4	8½	0-6-0ST	OC	14 x 20	3	6	52
173	29. 8.1871	4	8½	0-4-0ST	OC	12 x 19	3	2	164
174	17. 1.1871/	4	8½	0-4-0ST	OC	12 x 19	3	2	148
176	17. 1.1871/	4	8½	0-4-0ST	OC	12 x 19	3	2	149
188	29. 1.1872/	4	8½	0-4-0ST	OC	10 x 17	3	0	218/334
191	20. 4.1871	4	8½	0-4-0ST	OC	9 x 16	2	10	67
192	20. 4.1871	4	8½	0-4-0ST	OC	9 x 16	2	10	67
202	24. 3.1871	4	8½	0-4-0ST	OC	9 x 16	2	9	104
203	20. 4.1871/	4	8½	0-4-0ST	OC	9 x 16	2	9	44/132/171/180
204	20. 4.1871/	4	8½	0-4-0ST	OC	9 x 16	2	9	111
216	9.12.1871	4	8½	0-4-0ST	OC	14 x 20	3	6	149
223	16.10.1871	4	8½	0-4-0ST	OC	14 x 20	3	6	44
231	7. 5.1872/	4	8½	0-4-0ST	OC	10 x 17	2	9	149/332
237	24. 3.1873	4	8½	0-4-0ST	OC	12 x 19	3	2	208
244	11. 6.1873	4	8½	0-6-0ST	OC	14¾ x 22	4	2⅜	95
247	30. 7.1872/	4	8½	0-4-0ST	OC	9 x 16	2	10	67
248	30. 7.1872/	4	8½	0-4-0ST	OC	9 x 16	2	10	67
252	16.11.1872	3	0	0-4-0T	OC	6 x 12	2	0	139
258	3. 2.1873ø	2	0	0-4-2ST	OC	6 x 12	2	0	126
264	18. 4.1873	4	8½	0-4-0ST	OC	12 x 19	3	2	139
267	12. 8.1873ø	4	8½	0-4-0ST	OC	12 x 19	3	2	92
288	16. 8.1873/	4	8½	0-4-0ST	OC	12 x 19	3	2	165
289	12.11.1873	4	8½	0-4-0ST	OC	12 x 19	3	2	65
298	23. 9.1873/	4	8½	0-4-0ST	OC	12 x 19	3	2	88
304	9.10.1873	4	8½	0-6-0ST	IC	14 x 20	3	6	42
305	17.10.1873/	4	8½	0-4-0ST	OC	9 x 16	2	9	111/112/344
306	17.10.1873/	4	8½	0-4-0ST	OC	9 x 16	2	9	145
315	1. 1.1874/	4	8½	0-4-0ST	OC	12 x 19	3	2	149
316	1. 1.1874/	4	8½	0-4-0ST	OC	12 x 19	3	2	32
317	1. 1.1874/	4	8½	0-4-0ST	OC	12 x 19	3	2	44
318	1. 1.1874/	4	8½	0-4-0ST	OC	12 x 19	3	2	92
324	1. 1.1874/	4	8½	0-4-0ST	OC	9 x 16	2	9	145
326	3. 2.1874	4	8½	0-4-0ST	OC	12 x 19	3	2	65/70
327	3. 2.1874	4	8½	0-4-0ST	OC	12 x 19	3	2	65
328	25. 4.1875	4	8½	0-4-0ST	OC	12 x 19	3	2	65
354	25. 2.1875	4	8½	0-6-0ST	OC	14 x 20	3	6	177
355	25. 2.1875/	4	8½	0-6-0ST	OC	14 x 20	3	6	192/264
365	5. 7.1875/	4	8½	0-4-0ST	OC	12 x 19	3	2	39/83/84
367	5. 7.1875/	4	8½	0-4-0ST	OC	12 x 19	3	2	39/83/84
368	5. 7.1875ø	4	8½	0-4-0ST	OC	12 x 19	3	2	39/104
369	5. 7.1875ø	4	8½	0-4-0ST	OC	9 x 16	2	9	165
373	1. 9.1875/	4	8½	0-6-0ST	OC	14 x 20	3	6	166
387	1. 3.1876/	4	8½	0-4-0ST	OC	10 x 17	2	10	75
391	13. 3.1876/	4	8½	0-6-0ST	OC	14 x 20	3	6	36
395	31. 5.1876/	4	8½	0-4-0ST	OC	13 x 19	3	2	215
402	12. 9.1876	3	0	0-4-0ST	OC	5 x 10	1	8	36
403	12. 9.1876	3	0	0-4-0ST	OC	5 x 10	1	8	36
418	12. 2.1877/	4	8½	0-4-0ST	OC	10 x 17	2	10	104
424	10. 4.1877/	4	8½	0-4-0ST	OC	12 x 19	3	2	87
427	5 7.1877	4	8½	0-4-0ST	OC	12 x 19	3	2	34
435	1. 9.1877	3	0	0-4-0ST	OC	5 x 10	1	8	36
436	1. 9.1877	3	0	0-4-0ST	OC	5 x 10	1	8	36
439	19. 9.1877	2	10	0-4-0ST	OC	5 x 10	1	8	179
442	15.10.1877	3	0	0-4-0ST	OC	5 x 10	1	8	36
446	4. 1.1878	3	0	0-4-0ST	OC	5 x 10	1	8	36
447	4. 1.1878	3	0	0-4-0ST	OC	5 x 10	1	8	36/151
459	15. 4.1878	3	0	0-4-0ST	OC	5 x 10	1	8	36/38
476	3. 9.1878/	4	8½	0-4-0ST	OC	12 x 19	3	2	149
494	3. 5.1879ø	3	0	0-4-0ST	OC	5 x 10	1	8	36
495	3. 5.1879ø	3	0	0-4-0ST	OC	5 x 10	1	8	36
504	11. 6.1879	4	8½	0-6-0ST	OC	14 x 20	3	6	101
515	12. 9.1879	4	8½	0-4-0ST	OC	9 x 18	2	8	100/206
516	12. 9.1879	4	8½	0-4-0ST	OC	9 x 18	2	8	100/206
519	/ø	4	8½	0-4-0ST	OC	12 x 19	3	2	39

524	6.12.1879∅	4	8½	0-4-0ST OC	12 x 19	3	2	76
526	6.12.1879∅	4	8½	0-4-0ST OC	12 x 19	3	2	38
529	31.10.1879⁄	4	8½	0-4-0ST OC	10 x 17	2	10	206
544	14. 1.1881	4	8½	0-4-0ST OC	12 x 19	3	2	36/39
546	23. 3.1879⁄	4	8½	0-4-0ST OC	12 x 19	3	2	169
551	17.10.1879∅	4	8½	0-4-0ST OC	12 x 19	3	2	65/219
552	17.10.1879∅	4	8½	0-4-0ST OC	12 x 19	3	2	65/70
553	17.10.1879∅	4	8½	0-4-0ST OC	12 x 19	3	2	65
557	21. 1.1880	3	0	0-4-0ST OC	5 x 10	1	8	36
558	21. 1.1880	3	0	0-4-0ST OC	5 x 10	1	8	36
559	21. 1.1880	3	0	0-4-0ST OC	5 x 10	1	8	110
567	13. 4.1880	3	0	0-4-0ST OC	6 x 10	1	8	108
569	16. 4.1880⁄	4	8½	0-4-0ST OC	10 x 17	2	10	104
595	25.11.1880	3	0	0-4-0ST OC	6 x 10	1	10	36
596	25.11.1880	3	0	0-4-0ST OC	6 x 10	1	10	36
597	25.11.1880	3	0	0-4-0ST OC	6 x 10	1	10	36
598	25.11.1880	3	0	0-4-0ST OC	6 x 10	1	10	36
599	25.11.1880	3	0	0-4-0ST OC	6 x 10	1	10	36
601	25.11.1880	3	0	0-4-0ST OC	6 x 10	1	10	36
602	3. 8.1880	4	8½	0-6-0ST OC	17 x 26	4	6	162
606	20.12.1880	4	8½	0-4-0ST OC	14 x 19	3	2	76/97/183
607	20.12.1880	4	8½	0-4-0ST OC	14 x 19	3	2	34/37/79/270/287
613	4. 1.1881⁄	4	8½	0-4-0ST OC	12 x 19	3	2	53/110/187
645	8. 7.1881	4	8½	0-6-0ST OC	14 x 20	3	6	166
666	18.11.1881	4	8½	0-6-0ST OC	14 x 20	3	6	166
682	26. 1.1882⁄	4	8½	0-4-0ST OC	12 x 19	3	2	28/104
688	9. 3.1882	4	8½	0-4-0ST OC	15 x 20	3	7	119/262
692	17. 4.1882	4	8½	0-6-0ST IC	14 x 20	3	6	42
698	22. 6.1882	4	8½	0-4-0ST OC	12 x 19	3	2	65/70
704	24. 8.1882⁄	4	8½	0-6-0ST OC	14 x 20	3	6	92/214/267
716	15. 9.1882	4	8½	0-6-0ST IC	15 x 22	3	9½	93/101/179/208
762	27. 8.1883⁄	4	8½	0-4-0ST OC	12 x 19	3	2	208
763	19. 1.1883	4	8½	0-4-0ST OC	12 x 19	3	2	208
826	27. 5.1884	4	8½	0-6-0ST IC	15 x 22	3	9½	101/257
831	15.10.1884	4	8½	0-4-0VBCr OC	8 x 12	2	9	67
832	20.11.1884	4	8½	0-4-0ST OC	15 x 20	3	7	119/262
852	17. 5.1885⁄	4	8½	0-4-0ST OC	12 x 19	3	2	170
854	17. 5.1885⁄	4	8½	0-4-0ST OC	12 x 19	3	2	51/66/70
856	4. 8.1885	2	10	0-4-0ST OC	6 x 10	1	10	179
881	9.11.1886⁄	4	8½	0-4-0ST OC	10 x 17	2	11	111/112
888	9.11.1886⁄	4	8½	0-6-0ST OC	14 x 20	3	7	108/276/281
891	9.11.1886⁄	4	8½	0-6-0ST OC	12 x 19	3	2	42
897	6. 1.1887	4	8½	2-4-0VBCr OC	13½ x 21½	3	0	48/67
898	6. 1.1887	4	8½	2-4-0VBCr OC	13½ x 21½	3	0	67
908	7. 4.1887	4	8½	0-4-0ST OC	9 x 16	2	9	97
931	27. 1.1888	4	8½	0-4-0VBCr OC	12 x 21	3	0	67
935	11. 2.1888⁄	4	8½	0-4-0ST OC	12 x 19	3	2	111
937	7. 3.1888	4	8½	0-6-2ST IC	16 x 24	4	6⅞	42
938	4.1888∅	4	8½	0-6-2ST IC	16 x 24	4	6⅞	42/280
971	1889⁄	4	8½	0-6-0ST OC	14 x 20	3	7	108/281
976	12. 7.1889	4	8½	0-4-0ST OC	12 x 19	3	2	142
981	3. 8.1889	2	6	0-4-0ST OC	5 x 10	1	8½	209/210
985	13.11.1889	4	8½	0-4-0ST OC	12 x 19	3	2	75/83/271/287
991	12.11.1889	4	8½	0-4-0ST OC	12 x 19	3	3	141
992	12.11.1889⁄	4	8½	0-4-0ST OC	12 x 19	3	3	84/86/271
998	28.11.1889⁄	4	8½	0-4-0ST OC	12 x 19	3	3	151/156
1018	22. 7.1890⁄	4	8½	0-4-0ST OC	10 x 17	2	11	335
1019	?	4	8½	0-4-0ST OC	10 x 17	2	11	75
1025	3. 6.1891	4	8½	0-4-0ST OC	12 x 19	3	3	145
1026	8.10.1890	4	8½	0-4-0ST OC	12 x 19	3	3	219
1032	22. 1.1891⁄	4	8½	0-4-0ST OC	10 x 17	2	11	185
1034	22. 8.1892	4	8½	0-6-0ST OC	14 x 20	3	7	108/179/276
1037	9. 6.1891⁄	4	8½	0-4-0ST OC	12 x 19	3	3	57
1038	9. 6.1891⁄	4	8½	0-4-0ST OC	12 x 19	3	3	193
1048	18. 8.1891	4	8½	0-4-0VBCr OC	12 x 21½	3	0	67

1049	18. 8.1891ø	4 8½	0-4-0VBCr	OC	12 x 21½	3 0	48/67
1051	18. 8.1891ø	4 8½	0-4-0VBCr	OC	12 x 21½	3 0	67
1065	7. 4.1892	2 3½	0-4-0ST	OC	6 x 10	1 9	203
1071	21 7.1892	4 8½	0-6-2ST	IC	16 x 24	4 6⅞	43
1074	15. 8.1892	4 8½	0-4-0ST	OC	12 x 19	3 3	334
1078	23.11.1892	4 8½	0-6-0ST	OC	12 x 19	3 3	334
1095	20. 6.1894✓	4 8½	0-4-0ST	OC	14 x 19	3 2	82/85/271
1096	20. 6.1894✓	4 8½	0-4-0ST	OC	12 x 19	3 3	143
1098	21. 7.1894✓	4 8½	0-4-0ST	OC	10 x 17	2 11	206
1113	5. 4.1894✓	4 8½	0-4-0ST	OC	12 x 19	3 3	66
1114	24. 4.1895	4 8½	0-4-0ST	OC	6½x 12	2 0½	218
1121	8. 8.1895	4 8½	0-4-0ST	OC	6½x 12	2 0½	218
1122	8. 8.1895	4 8½	0-4-0ST	OC	6½x 12	2 0½	218

✓ Date of order for stock; dates of customers' orders are as follows:

62	-	20.10.1868;	166	-	11.12.1872;	174	-	8. 1.1872;
176	-	27. 1.1872;	188	-	23. 7.1872;	203	-	10.10.1871;
204	-	30. 3.1872;	231	-	17. 2.1874, delivered -			1. 5.1874;
247	-	30. 9.1873, delivered -	11.11.1873;			248	-	30. 9.1873,
delivered -		29.12.1873;	288	-	3.1874;	298	-	26. 4.1875;
305	-	27.10.1874;	306	-	19. 2.1875;	315	-	19. 3.1874;
316	-	29. 7.1874;	317	-	21. 6.1875;	318	-	1. 1.1874;
324	-	24. 4.1875;	355	-	31. 8.1875, delivered -			5.10.1875;
365	-	31.10.1876;	367	-	30. 3.1877;	373	-	8.10.1875;
387	-	18. 5.1876;	391	-	17. 1.1877;	395	-	19.10.1879,
delivered -		19.10.1879;	418	-	7. 3.1877;	424	-	? ;
476	-	8.11.1879;	519	-	12.1879, delivered -			19.12.1879;
529	-	16. 2.1880;	546	-	23. 3.1881;	569	-	26. 1.1881;
613	-	21.12.1881;	682	-	13.11.1883;	704	-	18.10.1882;
762	-	12.1883;	852	-	22. 7.1886;	854	-	17. 5.1885;
881	-	? ;	888	-	? ;	891	-	? ;
935	-	? ;	971	-	7. 9.1890;	992	-	25. 4.1890;
998	-	? ;	1018	-	? ;	1037	-	? ;
1038	-	? ;	1095	-	28. 2.1896;	1096	-	30. 3.1895;
1098	-	20.10.1896;	1113	-	4. 4.1895.			

ø Delivery dates:

258	-	1874;	267	-	7.11.1873;	368	-	25. 5.1877;	369	-	17. 3.1876;
494	-	19. 7.1879;	495	-	22. 7.1879;	524	-	7. 3.1880;	526	-	30. 4.1880;
551	-	24. 8.1880;	552	-	24. 8.1880;	553	-	24. 8.1880;	938	-	26.10.1888;
1049	-	11.1892;	1051	-	6.1892.						

% built from material supplied by the Earl of Durham.
@ "Reconstruction of loco engine".

BP - BEYER, PEACOCK & CO LTD, Gorton, Manchester.

WORKS No.	BUILT	GAUGE AS BUILT ft.ins.	TYPE	CYLS.(bore x stroke) ins.ins.	DRIVING WH.DIAM. ft.ins.	NOTES	SEE PAGE
190	1860	4 8½	0-4-2ST	OC 16 x 24	5 0		192
417	1864	4 8½	4-4-0T	OC 17 x 24	5 9		162/192
425	1864	4 8½	4-4-0T	OC 17 x 24	5 9		192/264
550	1865	4 8½	0-6-0	IC 17 x 24	4 6		119/262
770	1867	4 8½	4-4-0T	OC 17 x 24	5 9		162
772	1867	4 8½	4-4-0T	OC 17 x 24	5 9		162/283
868	1868	4 8½	4-4-0T	OC 17 x 24	5 9		162/283

Diesel locomotives

WORKS No.	DATE EX-WORKS	GAUGE AS BUILT ft.ins.	TYPE	HORSE POWER	DRIVING WH.DIAM. ft.ins.	NOTES	SEE PAGE
7873/BT 443	1962	4 8½	0-4-0DE	230	3 4		170
7946/BT 339	1961	4 8½	0-4-0DE	230	3 4		170
7947/BT 340	1961	4 8½	0-4-0DE	230	3 4		170

CF - <u>CHAPMAN & FURNEAUX LTD</u>, Gateshead, Co. Durham.

This firm was formed in 1897 to take over the business of Black, Hawthorn & Co Ltd (q.v.), which had gone into voluntary liquidation. They continued the Black Hawthorn serial numbers, their first locomotive being No. 1144. The firm closed down in 1902, the last locomotive to be built at Gateshead being No. 1212, though Nos. 1213-1215 were built by Hudswell, Clarke & Co Ltd, Leeds, as their Nos. 617,618 and 631. The goodwill of the firm was taken over by R. & W. Hawthorn, Leslie & Co Ltd (q.v.) of Newcastle-upon-Tyne.

WORKS No.	DATE OF FIRST ORDERING	GAUGE AS BUILT ft.ins.	TYPE	CYLS.(bore x stroke) ins.ins.	DRIVING WH.DIAM. ft.ins.	NOTES	SEE PAGE
1155	4.12.1897ø	4 8½	0-6-OST OC	14 x 20	3 7		31/275
1158	4. 3.1898ø	4 8½	0-6-2T IC	17 x 24	4 3		43/101
1163	16. 5.1898ø	4 8½	0-4-OST OC	13 x 19	3 4		66/73/282
1183	25. 4.1899✗	4 8½	0-4-OST OC	12 x 19	3 3		217
1187	1. 7.1899✗	4 8½	0-4-OST OC	12 x 19	3 3		142
1189	1. 8.1899	4 8½	0-4-OST OC	14 x 19	3 2		30
1190	9. 8.1899✗	4 8½	0-4-OST OC	14 x 19	3 3		167
1193	21.11.1899✗	4 8½	0-4-OST OC	12 x 19	3 3		185/190
1196	15.12.1899✗	4 8½	0-4-OST OC	14 x 19	3 2		214
1198	3. 4.1900✗	4 8½	0-4-OST OC	12 x 19	3 3		167
1199	26. 3.1900✗	4 8½	0-4-OST OC	14 x 19	3 2		80
1202	10. 7.1900	4 8½	0-4-OST OC	14 x 19	3 2		105
1203	16.10.1900	4 8½	0-4-OST OC	15 x 22	3 8		42/44
1204	31.10.1900	4 8½	0-6-OST OC	16 x 24	3 8		108/281
1205	12.11.1900ø	4 8½	0-4-OST OC	13 x 19	3 4½		65/73
1206	12.11.1900	4 8½	0-4-OVBCr OC	12 x 21½	3 0		48/69
1210	18. 4.1901✗	4 8½	0-4-OST OC	14 x 19	3 2		57/275

✗ Date of order for stock; dates of customers' orders are as follows:
1183 - 30. 6.1899; 1187 - 30.11.1899; 1190 - 15.12.1899; 1193 - 30. 4.1900;
1196 - 11. 6.1900; 1198 - 29.10.1901; 1199 - 23. 7.1900; 1210 - 15. 1.1902.

ø Delivery dates:
1155 - 2.1898; 1158 - 29.12.1898; 1163 - 16.12.1898; 1205 - 30. 7.1901.

EE - <u>ENGLISH ELECTRIC CO LTD</u>

In the list below sub-contracted locomotives were built either by E.E.Baguley Ltd of Burton-on-Trent, Staffs, or by Robert Stephenson & Hawthorns Ltd (q.v.).

N.B. In the list below the dates given up to 1942 are ex-works; from 1951 they are the date of arrival at the customer's location.

WORKS Nos.	DATE BUILT (see above)	GAUGE AS BUILT ft.ins.	TYPE	HORSE-POWER	NOTES	SEE PAGE
512	1920	4 8½	4wBE	60 b.h.p.		174
518	1921	4 8½	4wBE	60 b.h.p.		208
519	1921	4 8½	4wBE	60 b.h.p.		208
570	1923	4 8½	4wBE	60 b.h.p.		208
1214	1942	4 8½	4wWE	400 b.h.p.		54
1794/Bg 3350	1951	4 8½	4w-4wWE	400 b.h.p.		260/290/301
1795/Bg 3351	1951	4 8½	4w-4wWE	400 b.h.p.		260/290/300
1809/Bg 3353	30. 5.1952	2 0	4wBE	64 h.p.		311/325
1960/Bg 3379	1954	2 0	4wBE	64 h.p.		319
1961/Bg 3380	1954	2 0	4wBE	64 h.p.		319/326
2026/Bg 3413	2. 7.1954	2 0	4wBE	64 h.p.		312/325
2027/Bg 3414	22.10.1954	2 0	4wBE	64 h.p.		311/312/325
2028/Bg 3415	19.10.1954	2 0	4wBE	64 h.p.		311/312/324
2076/Bg 3427	14. 2.1955	2 6	4wBE	64 h.p.		309
2077/Bg 3428	16. 2.1955	2 6	4wBE	64 h.p.		309
2078/Bg 3429	26. 2.1955	2 6	4wBE	64 h.p.		309/324

2079/Bg 3430	28. 9.1955	2 0	4wBE	64 h.p.	312/325
2080/Bg 3439	7. 5.1955	2 6	4wBE	64 h.p.	309/324
2227/Bg 3444	3.1955	2 6	4wBE	64 h.p.	309/324
2228/Bg 3445	30. 3.1955	2 6	4wBE	64 h.p.	310/324
2229/Bg 3446	4.1955	2 6	4wBE	64 h.p.	310/324
2230/Bg 3431	5.11.1955	2 0	4wBE	64 h.p.	312/325
2308/Bg 3469	15. 6.1957	4 8½	4w-4wWE	400 b.h.p.	260/290/301
2328/Bg 3470	19. 9.1956	2 6	4wBE	64 h.p.	310/324
2329/Bg 3471	7. 5.1957	2 6	4wBE	64 h.p.	310/324
2330/Bg 3473	12.12.1956	2 6	4wBE	64 h.p.	310/325
2331/Bg 3472	20.11.1956	2 6	4wBE	64 h.p.	310/324
2342/RSH	6.1957	3 0	4wBE	64 h.p.	316/324
2343/RSH	8.1957	3 0	4wBE	64 h.p.	316/324
2344/RSH	29.11.1957	3 0	4wBE	64 h.p.	316/324
2418/Bg 3497	10. 1.1958	2 6	4wBE	64 h.p.	310/324
2419/Bg 3498	20. 1.1958	2 6	4wBE	64 h.p.	310/324
2420/Bg 3499	6. 2.1958	2 6	4wBE	64 h.p.	310/324
2466/Bg 3501	14. 9.1957	2 0	4wBE	64 h.p.	303/312/325
2467/Bg 3495	30. 8.1957	2 0	4wBE	64 h.p.	312/325
2469/RSH	26. 3.1958	2 0	4wBE	64 h.p.	318/326
2470/RSH	27. 3.1958	2 0	4wBE	64 h.p.	318/326
2471/RSH	2. 7.1958	2 0	4wBE	64 h.p.	318/326
2472/RSH	8.10.1958	2 0	4wBE	64 h.p.	318/326
2473/RSH	3.10.1958	2 0	4wBE	64 h.p.	318/326
2474/RSH	29.10.1958	2 0	4wBE	64 h.p.	318
2475/RSH	4.11.1958	2 0	4wBE	64 h.p.	318/326
2476/RSH	24.12.1958	2 0	4wBE	64 h.p.	318/325
2477/RSH	6. 2.1959	2 0	4wBE	64 h.p.	318/326
2478/RSH	2. 4.1959	2 0	4wBE	64 h.p.	318/326
2479/RSH	16. 2.1959	2 0	4wBE	64 h.p.	318/326
2480/RSH	18.12.1958	2 0	4wBE	64 h.p.	318/325
2481/RSH	10.12.1958	2 0	4wBE	64 h.p.	318/326
2482/RSH	2.12.1958	2 0	4wBE	64 h.p.	318/325
2483/RSH	19.11.1958	2 0	4wBE	64 h.p.	318/325
2484/RSH	14.11.1958	2 0	4wBE	64 h.p.	318/326
2485/RSH	3.10.1958	2 0	4wBE	64 h.p.	318/325
2486/RSH	2.10.1958	2 0	4wBE	64 h.p.	318/326
2487/RSH	22. 8.1958	2 0	4wBE	64 h.p.	318/326
2488/RSH	22. 8.1958	2 0	4wBE	64 h.p.	318/325
2489/RSH	16. 6.1958	2 0	4wBE	64 h.p.	318/326
2490/RSH	16. 6.1958	2 0	4wBE	64 h.p.	293/304/312
2519/Bg 3500	7.1958	2 0	4wBE	64 h.p.	310/324
2523/Bg 3496	21.10.1957	2 6	4wBE	64 h.p.	325
2527/RSH	.1959	2 0	4wBE	64 h.p.	260/290/301
2599/Bg 3519	8. 4.1959	4 8½	4w-4wWE	400 b.h.p.	260/290/301
2600/Bg 3520	29. 4.1959	4 8½	4w-4wWE	400 b.h.p.	310/324
2626/Bg 3521	22.10.1958	2 6	4wBE	64 h.p.	310/324
2627/Bg 3522	12.1958	2 6	4wBE	64 h.p.	310/324
2628/Bg 3523	12.1958	2 6	4wBE	64 h.p.	319/326
2635/RSH	.1960	2 0	4wBE	64 h.p.	325
2636/RSH	.1960	2 0	4wBE	64 h.p.	319/326
2637/RSH	.1960	2 0	4wBE	64 h.p.	319/326
2638/RSH	.1960	2 0	4wBE	64 h.p.	325
2639/RSH	.1960	2 0	4wBE	64 h.p.	310/324
2661/RSH	10. 6.1959	2 6	4wBE	64 h.p.	310/319/326
2662/RSH	6. 7.1959	2 6	4wBE	64 h.p.	325
2696/RSH	1959	2 0	4wBE	64 h.p.	318/326
2736/RSH	14.12.1959	2 0	4wBE	64 h.p.	318/326
2737/RSH	11. 1.1960	2 0	4wBE	64 h.p.	310/324
2740/Bg 3542	26.11.1959	2 6	4wBE	64 h.p.	319/326
2848/RSH	11. 3.1960	2 0	4wBE	64 h.p.	319/326
2849/RSH	11. 3.1960	2 0	4wBE	64 h.p.	310/324
2955/Bg 3566	26.11.1960	2 6	4wBE	64 h.p.	310/319/326
3149/RSH	23.12.1960	2 6	4wBE	64 h.p.	310/324
3150/Bg 3567	22.12.1960	2 6	4wBE	64 h.p.	

3155/RSH	19. 5.1961	2 6	4wBE	64 h.p.	310/324
3167/RSH	14.11.1961	2 0	4wBE	64 h.p.	319/326
3173/Bg 3583	22. 3.1962	2 6	4wBE	64 h.p.	310/324
3174/Bg 3584	27. 4.1962	2 0	4wBE	64 h.p.	311/312/325
3336/Bg 3595	31. 3.1963	2 6	4wBE	64 h.p.	310/325
3399/Bg 3599	29. 3.1963	2 6	4wBE	64 h.p.	310/325
3401/EE(S)	16. 5.1963	2 0	4wBE	64 h.p.	319/326
3404/Bg 3603	13. 9.1963	2 6	4wBE	64 h.p.	311/325
3655/EE(V)	1965	3 0	4wBE	64 h.p.	323
3820/Bg 3642	16.12.1966	2 6	4wBE	64 h.p.	311/325
3842/Bg 3645	21.11.1967	2 6	4wBE	64 h.p.	311/325
3845/EE(V)	8. 2.1968	3 0	4wBE	64 h.p.	316/324
3849	1967	2 6	4wBE	64 h.p.	311/324
3871/Bg 3649	28. 3.1968	2 6	4wBE	64 h.p.	311/325

Diesel locomotives (built at Vulcan Works, Newton-le-Willows, Lancs)

WORKS No.	DATE EX-WORKS	GAUGE AS BUILT ft.ins.	TYPE	HORSE-POWER	DRIVING WH.DIAM. ft.ins.	SEE PAGE
D227/EE 2346	1956	4 8½	0-6-0DH			94/197
D1121	1966	4 8½	0-6-0DH	305 h.p.		300
D1123	1966	4 8½	0-4-0DH	305 h.p.		140
D1125	1966	4 8½	0-4-0DH	305 h.p.		305
D1126	1966	4 8½	0-4-0DH	305 h.p.		140
D1191	1967	4 8½	0-6-0DH	305 h.p.		181
D1192	1967	4 8½	0-6-0DH	305 h.p.		181
D1193	1967	4 8½	0-6-0DH	305 h.p.		181
D1194	1967	4 8½	0-6-0DH	305 h.p.		181
D1195	1967	4 8½	0-6-0DH	305 h.p.		181

KC - KENT CONSTRUCTION & ENGINEERING CO LTD, Ashford, Kent (to FH, 1930)
FH - F.C. HIBBERD & CO LTD, Park Royal, London; from 1964, Butterley Works, Derbyshire. (Trademark : "Planet").

@ Built by KC
ø later rebuilt to 2'8½" gauge
≁ rebuilt to 4wDM

WORKS No.	DATE EX-WORKS	GAUGE AS BUILT ft.ins.	TYPE	HORSE-POWER	WEIGHT (tons)	SEE PAGE
1470 @	1926(?)	4 8½	4wPM			56
1652 @	1.1930	2 0	4wPM	20 h.p.		89
1655 @	1.1930	2 0	4wPM	20 h.p.		89
1782	23.12.1931	2 4 ø	4wPM	16/25 h.p.	4	99/148
1829	8.1933	4 8½	4wPM	40 h.p.	8	164
1892	12.11.1934	2 8½	4wPM	24 h.p.	4	99/148
1893	10.1934	2 8½	4wPM ≁	20 h.p.	2½	99
2064	7.1937	2 6	4wPM	20 h.p.		174
3374	2.1950	4 8½	4wDM		11	94/176/184/328
3492	6.1951	4 8½	4wDM		18¼	45
3572	8.1952	4 8½	4wDM		11	97/98
3808	4.1956	4 8½	4wDM	117 h.p.	23	45
3852	8. 4.1957	4 8½	4wDM	75 h.p.	20¼	259/264/276/289
3865	10. 2.1958	4 8½	4wDM	117 h.p.	23	184
3890	10.1958	4 8½	4wDM	170 h.p.	24½	207
3891	11.1958	4 8½	4wDM	170 h.p.	24½	207
3922	31.12.1959	4 8½	4wDM	134 h.p.	20	284/291/296/301
3923	31.12.1959	4 8½	4wDM	134 h.p.	20	284/291/300
3967	8.1961	4 8½	4wDH		16	218
Unidentified						54

FJ - FLETCHER, JENNINGS & CO LTD, Whitehaven, Cumberland.

WORKS No.	BUILT	GAUGE AS BUILT ft.ins.	TYPE	CYLS.(bore x stroke) ins.ins.	DRIVING WH.DIAM. ft.ins.	SEE PAGE
31	1864	4 8½	0-4-0ST	OC 10 x 20	4 0	36/37/39
47	1865	4 8½	0-4-0T	OC 10 x 20		37
72	1867	4 8½	0-4-0T	OC 12 x 20		38/217
87	1871	4 8½	0-4-0ST	OC 12 x 20		63
112	1873	4 8½	0-4-0T	OC 12 x 20	3 5	141/143
125	1874	4 8½	0-4-0WT	OC 12 x 20		42/44/148
167	1879	4 8½	0-6-0ST	IC 14 x 20	3 6	169
187	1882	4 8½	0-4-0T	OC 14 x 20	3 6	185

FW - FOX, WALKER & CO LTD, Bristol.

WORKS No.	DATE EX-WORKS	GAUGE AS BUILT ft.ins.	TYPE	CYLS.(bore x stroke) ins.ins	DRIVING WH.DIAM. ft.ins.	MAKERS CLASS	SEE PAGE
140	1872	4 8½	0-6-0ST	OC 13 x 20			164
169	11.12.1872	4 8½	0-6-0ST	OC 13 x 20			31/75
170	14. 1.1873	4 8½	0-6-0ST	OC 13 x 20			31
171	6. 1.1873	4 8½	0-6-0ST	OC 13 x 20	3 6½	B	94
265	c12. 1.1875	4 8½	0-6-0ST	OC 13 x 20		B	31
289	11. 4.1876	4 8½	0-6-0ST	OC 13 x 20		B1	200/201
371	.1878	4 8½	0-6-0ST	OC 13 x 20	3 7	B1	334
375	.1878	4 8½	0-4-0ST	OC 12 x 18		W1	140

Unidentified | | | | | | | 31

GB - GREENBAT LTD, Leeds, Yorkshire (formerly Greenwood & Batley Ltd)

WORKS No.	DATE EX-WORKS	GAUGE AS BUILT ft.ins.	TYPE	HORSE POWER	MAKERS CLASS	SEE PAGE
1448	19. 6.1936	4 8½	4wWE	50	Coke Car Loco	50/188
2047	19. 2.1947	4 8½	0-4-0WE	80	Coke Car Loco	286/306
2130	1. 9.1948	2 0	4wBE	6		194
2319	1950	3 5½	4wWE	12	Trolley Loco	194
2360	1. 9.1952	3 0	4wBE	20	GB 5	323
2361	1. 9.1952	3 0	4wBE	20	GB 5	323
2368	25. 3.1952	4 8½	0-4-0WE	80	Coke Car Loco	48/70
2378	21. 1.1953	2 0	4wBE	5	GB 2	261/293/304/312/317
2382	21. 1.1953	2 0	4wBE	5	GB 2	317
2392	23. 1.1953	2 0	4wBE	5	GB 2	317
2395	10. 4.1953	2 0	4wBE	40	GB 7	316/317/323
2400	2. 7.1953	2 0	4wBE	40	GB 7	317
2403	2. 7.1953	2 0	4wBE	40	GB 7	316/317/324
2406	23. 1.1953	2 0	4wBE	5	GB 2	317
2436	26. 1.1953	2 0	4wBE	5	GB 2	317
2481	17. 5.1954	2 0	4wBE	40	GB 7	317
2482	17. 5.1954	2 0	4wBE	40	GB 7	317
2517	20.10.1954	2 0	4wBE	50	GB 9	312
2518	20.10.1954	2 0	4wBE	50	GB 9	312
2544	4. 2.1955	2 6	4wBE	50	GB 9	309
2545	3. 2.1955	2 6	4wBE	50	GB 9	309/312
2572	18. 1.1955	2 0	4wBE	15	GB 4	261/293/310/311/312
2573	18. 1.1955	2 0	4wBE	15	GB 4	260/293/303/310/312
2626	6.1955	2 3	4wBE	52	⚡	317
2627	6.1955	2 3	4wBE	52	⚡	317
2628	7.1955	2 3	4wBE	52	⚡	318
2787	19. 7.1957	2 0	4wBE	52	⚡	58
2848	7.11.1957	2 0	4wBE	5	GB 2	317
2937	30. 3.1960	4 8½	0-4-0WE	80	Coke Car Loco	50/189

2938	14.10.1958	3 0	4wBE	30	GB 6	323
2996	30. 3.1960	2 6	4wBE	14	GB 4	47
6017	28.11.1960	2 6	4wBE	14	GB 4	47
6018	21.11.1960	2 6	4wBE	14	GB 4	47
420167	2.1969	2 0	4wBE	26	ø	210
420253	6.1970	2 0	4wBE	40		210
420288	5.1971	2 0	4wBE	5	GB 2	204/205
420306	1972	4 8½	4wWE	90	Coke Car Loco	48

≠ built by GB to LMM design
ø returned to GB and parts used in construction of other locos

HC - <u>HUDSWELL, CLARKE & CO LTD</u>, Leeds, Yorkshire.
HCR <u>Hudswell, Clarke & Rodgers</u>
H&C <u>Hudswell & Clarke</u>
HB <u>Hudswell Badger Ltd</u> (from /1972)

WORKS No.	DATE EX-WORKS	GAUGE AS BUILT ft.ins.	TYPE	CYLS.(bore x stroke) ins.ins	DRIVING WH.DIAM. ft.ins.	NOTES	SEE PAGE
21	3. 4.1865	4 8½	0-6-0ST	IC 13 x 18	3 6		118
30	30. 9.1864	4 8½	0-6-0	IC 17 x 24	5 0		119
31	1864	4 8½	tender to	No. 30			
32	10. 6.1864	4 8½	0-4-0ST	OC 8½ x 13	2 6		149
45	26. 5.1865	4 8½	0-6-0ST	IC 13 x 18	3 6		202
71	9. 8.1866	4 8½	0-6-0	IC 17 x 24	4 0		119/262
72	30.10.1866	4 8½	0-6-0	IC 17 x 24	4 0		85/119
73	1866	4 8½	tender to	No. 71			
74	1866	4 8½	tender to	No. 72			
76	7. 5.1866	4 8½	0-6-0ST	IC 13 x 18	3 0		118
78	8. 8.1866	4 8½	0-6-0ST	IC 13 x 18	3 0		118
79	7. 2.1868	4 8½	0-4-0ST	OC 14 x 20	3 6		85/119
96	28. 6.1870	4 8½	0-4-0ST	OC 15 x 20	3 6		119/262
98	9. 9.1870	4 8½	0-6-0ST	IC 17 x 24	4 0	reb.from 0-6-0	118
101	14.11.1870	4 8½	0-4-0ST	OC 9 x 15	2 9		148
103	23. 2.1871	4 8½	0-4-0ST	OC 10 x 16	2 9		185
107	4. 9.1871	4 8½	0-4-0ST	OC 10 x 16	2 9		139
124	29.10.1872	4 8½	0-4-0ST	OC 13 x 20	3 6		200/202
129	30. 9.1873	4 8½	0-4-0ST	OC 10 x 16	2 9		198
130	28. 6.1873	4 8½	0-4-0ST	OC 15 x 20	3 6½		119
139	17. 9.1874	4 8½	0-4-0ST	OC 10 x 16	2 9		45
169	26.10.1875	4 8½	0-4-0ST	OC 15 x 20	3 6½		119/262
176	15. 3.1876	4 8½	0-4-0ST	OC 11 x 17	2 9		179
203	20.12.1878	4 8½	0-4-0ST	OC 10 x 16	2 9		97
221	12. 1.1882	4 8½	0-4-0ST	OC 13 x 20	3 3		164/208
230	8. 8.1881	4 8½	0-4-0ST	OC 15 x 20	3 6		119/262
266	31.12.1883	4 8½	0-6-0ST	OC 14 x 20	3 5½		164
324	5. 3.1889	4 8½	0-4-0ST	OC 13 x 18	3 0		80
332	23. 9.1889	4 8½	0-6-0T	IC 14 x 20	3 3		102/257
439	2. 3.1896	4 8½	0-6-0ST	IC 13 x 20	3 3		168
485	18. 6.1897	3 0	0-4-0ST	OC 8 x 12	2 0		71
535	9. 4.1900	4 8½	0-4-0ST	OC 10 x 16	2 9		218
540	6. 2.1900	4 8½	0-6-0ST	IC 12 x 18	3 1		334
673	9. 3.1906	4 8½	0-6-0ST	IC 12 x 18	3 1		156
674	14. 8.1903	4 8½	0-4-0ST	OC 12 x 18	3 1½		169/170/280
683	28.11.1903	4 8½	0-4-0ST	OC 12 x 18	3 1½		219
694	22. 3.1904	4 8½	0-6-0T	IC 15½ x 20	3 7		203
702	23. 6.1904	4 8½	0-4-0ST	OC 13 x 19	3 4½		66/72/73
749	31. 1.1906	4 8½	0-4-0ST	OC 16 x 24	3 8		167/280
764	23. 4.1906	4 8½	0-4-0ST	OC 16 x 24	3 8		167/280
809	29. 6.1907	4 8½	0-6-0PT	IC 18 x 26	4 2⅞		64

880	15. 4.1910	4 8½	0-6-0ST	OC 14 x 20	3 7		31/275
1039	18. 9.1913	4 8½	0-6-0T	OC 16 x 24	4 0		164
1040	28. 8.1913	4 8½	0-6-0ST	IC 13 x 20	3 3		149/335
1070	25.11.1914	4 8½	0-6-0T	IC 15½x 20	3 4		330
1190	13. 1.1916	4 8½	0-4-0ST	OC 14 x 20	3 3½		167/280
1191	25. 1.1916	4 8½	0-4-0ST	OC 14 x 20	3 3½		167/168/283
1199	24. 1.1916	4 8½	0-4-0ST	OC 14 x 20	3 3½		76
1201	25. 8.1916	4 8½	0-4-0ST	OC 14 x 20	3 3½		169
1207	29. 2.1916	4 8½	0-4-0ST	OC 10 x 16	2 9½		218
1251	15. 2.1917	4 8½	0-6-0T	IC 15½x 20	3 4		169/283
1255	27. 7.1917	4 8½	0-6-0T	OC 16 x 24	3 9	reb.HC 1948	281
1335	5. 6.1918	4 8½	0-6-0T	IC 16 x 24	3 9		85/271
1402	23.10.1922	4 8½	0-4-0ST	OC 14 x 20	3 3½		83/86/271
1412	20. 8.1920	4 8½	0-4-0ST	OC 16 x 24	3 9		119/259/262/268/289
1448	26. 5.1921	4 8½	0-6-0PT	IC 18 x 26	4 2⅝		64/282
1449	26. 5.1921	4 8½	0-6-0PT	IC 18 x 26	4 2⅝		64/285
1484	4. 9.1922	4 8½	0-4-0ST	OC 12 x 18	3 1½		219
1493	28.12.1923	4 8½	0-4-0ST	OC 12 x 18	3 1½		219
1507	30. 6.1923	4 8½	0-4-0ST	OC 9 x 15	2 9½		178
1513	20. 3.1924	4 8½	0-6-0ST	IC 13 x 20	3 3½		258
1514	19.12.1924	4 8½	0-4-0ST	OC 16 x 24	3 8		167/280/291
1524	30. 6.1924	4 8½	0-6-0T	IC 18 x 24	4 0		57/272/275
1541	10.11.1924	4 8½	0-6-0T	OC 17 x 24	3 9		272
1599	25. 8.1927	4 8½	0-4-0ST	OC 13 x 18	3 1½		218
1606	27. 6.1929	4 8½	0-6-0ST	IC 13 x 20	3 3½		136
1609	29. 7.1934	4 8½	0-6-0ST	IC 13 x 20	3 3½		55
1674	17. 3.1937	4 8½	0-6-0ST	IC 13 x 20	3 3½		55
1688	29.12.1937	4 8½	0-4-0ST	OC 14 x 22	3 3½		76
1699	9. 2.1938	4 8½	0-6-0ST	IC 13 x 20	3 3½		136/332
1722	30. 8.1941	4 8½	0-4-0ST	OC 14 x 22	3 3½		178
1733	10. 2.1943	4 8½	0-4-0ST	OC 14 x 22	3 3½		194
1734	28.12.1942	4 8½	0-4-0ST	OC 14 x 22	3 3½		194
1735	11.12.1942	4 8½	0-4-0ST	OC 14 x 22	3 3½		194/195
1771	29. 9.1944	4 8½	0-6-0ST	IC 18 x 26	4 3		112/287
1821	3. 1.1949	4 8½	0-6-0T	OC 16 x 24	3 9		271/296/301
1823	8. 6.1949	4 8½	0-6-0T	OC 17 x 24	3 9		341

Battery electric locomotive

ø	17. 4.1960⁄	2 0	4wBE	64 h.p.	319/326

ø prototype loco produced in conjunction with Hugh Wood & Co Ltd and English Electric Co Ltd. Believed not to have been given a works number.

⁄ Date of arrival at customer's location.

Diesel locomotives (works numbers prefixed by DM or D)

WORKS No.	DATE EX-WORKS	GAUGE AS BUILT ft.ins.	TYPE	HORSE POWER	DRIVING WH.DIAM. ft.ins.	SEE PAGE
607	14. 4.1938	4 8½	0-4-0DM	120	2 9½	32
624	10.1942	4 8½	0-6-0DM	150	3 0	170
632	30. 5.1947	3 6	0-6-0DMF	100	2 2½	286/293/302/307/321
639	18.12.1947	3 6	0-6-0DMF	100	2 2½	286/293/302/307/321
661	27. 9.1951	3 0	0-6-0DMF	100	2 2½	321
662	?	3 0	0-6-0DMF	100	2 2½	321
692	30. 5.1952	2 0	0-4-0DMF	68	2 2½	297/304/315
709	4. 2.1955	3 6	0-6-0DMF	100	2 2½	286/293/302/307/321
804	14.12.1951	2 0	0-6-0DMF	100	2 2½	314/322
805	4. 1.1952	2 0	0-6-0DMF	100	2 2½	314
818	31. 7.1952	2 0	0-6-0DMF	100	2 2½	315/322
819	1. 8.1952	2 0	0-6-0DMF	100	2 2½	315/322
825	30. 8.1952	2 0	0-6-0DMF	100	2 2½	309/322
826	30.10.1952	2 0	0-6-0DMF	100	2 2½	309
830	2. 7.1954	3 0	0-6-0DMF	100	2 2½	313/321
831	5. 7.1954	3 0	0-6-0DMF	100	2 2½	313/321
835	2.12.1954	4 8½	0-6-0DM	300		55

842	21.12.1954	2	0	0-6-0DMF	100	2	2½	315/342
852	3. 5.1954	2	0	0-6-0DMF	100	2	2½	304/315/322
853	11. 5.1954	2	0	0-6-0DMF	100	2	2½	315/322
872	1.12.1954	2	0	0-6-0DMF	100	2	2½	309/322
873	30.10.1955	2	0	0-6-0DMF	100	2	2½	309/322
874	19. 9.1956	2	0	0-6-0DMF	100	2	2½	309/322
875	3. 9.1956	2	0	0-6-0DMF	100	2	2½	309/322
891	23. 5.1955	2	2	0-6-0DMF	100	2	2½	308
892	27. 5.1955	2	2	0-6-0DMF	100	2	2½	308
893	29.12.1954	2	0	0-6-0DMF	100	2	2½	315/322
966	29. 7.1955	3	0	0-6-0DMF	100	2	2½	313/321
967	25.11.1955	3	0	0-6-0DMF	100	2	2½	321
978	28.12.1957	4	8½	0-4-0DM	260	3	9	50/187/189
993	29.10.1956	3	6	0-6-0DMF	100	2	2½	286/293/302/307/321
1013	1.12.1957	4	8½	0-4-0DM	260	3	9	50/189
1015	28. 6.1956	2	0	0-6-0DMF	100	2	2½	315/322
1025	27. 5.1957	3	0	0-6-0DMF	100	2	2½	321
1032	23.12.1957	4	8½	0-4-0DM	260	3	9	50/189
1040	29. 3.1957	3	0	0-6-0DMF	100	2	2½	321
1041	30. 4.1957	3	0	0-6-0DMF	100	2	2½	321
1052	3. 4.1958	4	8½	0-4-0DM	260	3	9	50/187/189
1058	29. 6.1957	3	0	0-6-0DMF	100	2	2½	321
1063	8.1957	3	6	0-6-0DMF	100	2	2½	286/293/302/307/321
1064	30. 1.1959	2	0	0-6-0DMF	100	2	2½	315/322
1065	30. 5.1959	2	0	0-6-0DMF	100	2	2½	315/322
1066	25. 6.1959	2	0	0-6-0DMF	100	2	2½	315/322
1067	30. 7.1959	2	0	0-6-0DMF	100	2	2½	315/322
1081	3. 1.1958	4	8½	0-4-0DM	260	3	9	50/189
1118	31. 3.1958	2	0	0-6-0DMF	100	2	2½	315/322
1119	29. 5.1958	2	0	0-6-0DMF	100	2	2½	315/322
1127	29. 6.1958	2	0	0-6-0DMF	100	2	2½	315/322
1141	22. 7.1959	4	8½	0-4-0DM	260	3	9	50/187/189
1159	30. 9.1959	4	8½	0-4-0DM	200			49/76
1161	30. 9.1959	4	8½	0-4-0DM	200			49/76
1162	27. 2.1959	3	0	0-6-0DMF	100	2	2½	321
1169	29. 2.1960	2	0	0-6-0DMF	100	2	2½	315/322
1170	7. 3.1960	2	0	0-6-0DMF	100	2	2½	315/322
1207	30. 9.1961	4	8½	0-6-0DM	204	3	6	292
1237	14. 3.1961	3	0	0-6-0DMF	100	2	2½	321
1245	30. 1.1961	2	0	0-6-0DMF	100	2	2½	309/315/322
1247	31. 5.1961	2	0	0-6-0DMF	100	2	2½	315/322
1248	8. 6.1961	2	0	0-6-0DMF	100	2	2½	315/322
1269	28.12.1961	3	0	0-6-0DMF	100	2	2½	321
1270	29.12.1961	3	0	0-6-0DMF	100	2	2½	321
1271	12. 2.1962	3	0	0-6-0DMF	100	2	2½	321
1272	12. 2.1962	3	0	0-6-0DMF	100	2	2½	321
1273	28. 2.1962	3	0	0-6-0DMF	100	2	2½	321
1274	28. 2.1962	3	0	0-6-0DMF	100	2	2½	321
1281	25. 2.1963	2	0	0-6-0DMF	100	2	2½	309/321
1282	12.11.1962	3	0	0-6-0DMF	100	2	2½	321
1322	30.10.1964	2	0	0-6-0DMF	100	2	2½	315/322
1323	1. 4.1965	3	0	0-6-0DMF	100	2	2½	313/321
1325	2. 1.1964	2	0	0-6-0DMF	100	2	2½	315/322
1346	6. 7.1965	4	8½	0-6-0DH	191			195
1349	31. 8.1964	2	6	0-6-0DMF	100	2	2½	308/314/322
1350	30. 9.1964	2	6	0-6-0DMF	100	2	2½	308/322
1357	15.11.1966	2	6	0-6-0DMF	100	2	2½	308/322
1358	30.11.1966	2	6	0-6-0DMF	100	2	2½	308/322
1366	30. 6.1965	2	0	0-6-0DMF	100	2	2½	315/322
1378	31. 5.1966	4	8½	0-6-0DH	307			305
1379	3. 8.1966	3	0	0-6-0DMF	100	2	2½	321
1399	2.10.1967	2	0	0-6-0DMF	100	2	2½	315/322
1400	30. 8.1967	2	0	0-6-0DMF	100	2	2½	309/322
1401	4. 1.1968	2	0	0-6-0DMF	100	2	2½	315/322
1402	29. 3.1968	3	0	0-6-0DMF	100	2	2½	313/321

WORKS No.	DATE	GAUGE	TYPE	CYLS.	BORE	DRIVING WH.		SEE PAGE
1403	29. 3.1968	3 0	0-6-0DMF	100	2 2½			313/321
1407	1. 7.1968	3 0	0-6-0DMF	100	2 2½			313/321
1412	4. 5.1970	2 0	0-6-0DMF	100	2 2½			315/322
1416	27. 2.1971	2 0	0-6-0DMF	100	2 2½			315/322
1422	20. 6.1972	3 0	0-6-0DMF	100	2 2½			321
1423	11.10.1972	3 0	0-6-0DMF	100	2 2½			313/321

HE — HUNSLET ENGINE CO LTD, Leeds, Yorkshire.

WORKS No.	DATE EX-WORKS	GAUGE AS BUILT ft.ins.	TYPE	CYLS.(bore x stroke) ins.ins.	DRIVING WH.DIAM. ft.ins.	NOTES	SEE PAGE
4	13.12.1865	4 8½	0-6-0ST IC	12 x 18	3 1		329
13	28. 2.1867	4 8½	0-6-0ST IC	12 x 18	3 1		330
14	31.10.1866	4 8½	0-4-0ST OC	10 x 15	2 9		164
18	18.10.1867	4 8½	0-4-0ST OC	10 x 15	2 9		184
30	3. 6.1869	4 8½	0-4-0ST OC	10 x 15	2 9		174
60	14. 8.1871	4 8½	0-4-0ST OC	12 x 18	3 1		174
78	10. 7.1872	4 8½	0-4-0ST OC	12 x 18	3 1		174
80	20. 5.1873	4 8½	0-4-0ST OC	10 x 15	2 9		174
92	24.10.1872	4 8½	0-4-0ST OC	8 x 14	2 4		333
102	10. 7.1873	4 8½	0-4-0ST OC	8 x 14	2 4		333
164	31. 5.1876	4 8½	0-6-0ST OC	12 x 18	3 1	(reb.13 x 18 cyls. c1886)	333
177	28. 5.1877	4 8½	0-4-0ST OC	12 x 18	3 1		187
205	12. 8.1878	4 8½	0-4-0ST OC	12 x 18	3 1		56/193
240	9. 3.1880	4 8½	0-4-0ST OC	12 x 18	3 1		171
286	7. 5.1883	4 8½	0-4-0ST OC	10 x 15	2 9		101/102
361	8. 1.1885	4 8½	0-4-0ST OC	9 x 14	2 8½		331
396	9. 4.1886	4 8½	0-6-0T IC	15 x 20	3 4		192/264
413	2. 3.1887	4 8½	0-4-0ST OC	13 x 18	3 1		187
450	24. 4.1888	4 8½	0-6-0ST IC	12 x 18	3 1		332
484	16.10.1889	4 8½	0-6-0ST IC	13 x 18	3 1		85
567	21. 7.1892	2 3½	0-4-0ST OC	8 x 10	1 9		203
580	6. 3.1893	4 8½	0-6-0ST OC	11 x 15	2 6		134
608	24.10.1895	4 8½	0-4-0ST OC	14 x 20	3 4		187
628	30. 5.1895	4 8½	0-4-0ST OC	10 x 15	2 10		180/332
894	22.12.1905	4 8½	0-4-0ST OC	14 x 20	3 4		187
951	4.12.1907	4 8½	0-4-0ST OC	16 x 22	3 7		187
1086	20.12.1911	4 8½	0-4-0ST OC	16 x 22	3 7		187
1087	20.12.1911	4 8½	0-4-0ST OC	16 x 22	3 7		187
1108	30. 9.1912	4 8½	0-4-0ST OC	16 x 22	3 7		187
1405	27. 4.1920	4 8½	0-4-0ST OC	16 x 22	3 7		187
1506	6. 6.1930	4 8½	0-6-0T IC	18 x 26	4 0		43/281/291
2855	21. 5.1943	4 8½	0-6-0ST IC	18 x 26	4 3		287
2864	27. 7.1943	4 8½	0-6-0ST IC	18 x 26	4 3		300
2879	23.10.1943	4 8½	0-6-0ST IC	18 x 26	4 3		341
3166	12. 5.1944	4 8½	0-6-0ST IC	18 x 26	4 3		300
3172	15. 6.1944	4 8½	0-6-0ST IC	18 x 26	4 3		300
3189	12.10.1944	4 8½	0-6-0ST IC	18 x 26	4 3		75/272/276 295/301
3191	28.10.1944	4 8½	0-6-0ST IC	18 x 26	4 3		258/290
3686	18. 1.1949	4 8½	0-6-0ST IC	18 x 26	4 3		259/264/268 284/294/301
3687	3. 1.1949	4 8½	0-6-0ST IC	18 x 26	4 3		264/268/295/301
3688	8. 2.1949	4 8½	0-6-0ST IC	18 x 26	4 3		284/291/300
3689	17. 2.1949	4 8½	0-6-0ST IC	18 x 26	4 3		284/290
3784	30. 6.1953	4 8½	0-6-0ST IC	18 x 26	4 3		264/267/295/301
3785	30. 6.1953	4 8½	0-6-0ST IC	18 x 26	4 3		264/267/295/301
3819	16. 6.1954	4 8½	0-6-0ST IC	18 x 26	4 3		272/276/295
3820	1. 7.1954	4 8½	0-6-0ST IC	18 x 26	4 3		259/262/289
3821	16. 7.1954	4 8½	0-6-0ST IC	18 x 26	4 3		264/267/295/301
3833	30. 9.1955	4 8½	0-6-0ST IC	18 x 26	4 3		284/290

Diesel locomotives

WORKS No.	DATE EX-WORKS	GAUGE AS BUILT ft.ins.	TYPE	HORSE POWER	DRIVING WH.DIAM. ft.ins.	SEE PAGE
1737	25. 7.1935	4 8½	4wDM	20	2 9	93/144
1929	10. 3.1938	2 6	4wDM	20	1 6	91
2652	11. 3.1943	4 8½	0-4-0DM	40/44	2 9	187/189
2839	1.10.1943	4 8½	0-4-0DM	40/44	2 9	99/218
2842	13.10.1942	2 0	4wDM	25	1 6	135
2843	13.10.1942	2 0	4wDM	25	1 6	135
2844	13.10.1942	2 0	4wDM	25	1 6	135
2980	26. 5.1944	2 8½	0-4-0DMF	50	2 0	109/260/293/313
2982	17. 5.1943	2 0	4wDM	25	1 6	140
3098	7.11.1944	2 0	4wDM	25	1 6	140
3308	12. 3.1946	2 6	4wDM	25	1 6	188
3330	2.12.1946	2 8½	0-4-0DMF	50	2 0	109/313
3476	24. 4.1947	2 8½	0-6-0DMF	100	2 0	313
3496	21.11.1947	2 0	4wDM	16	1 4	74/273/277
3504	18.11.1947	4 8½	0-6-0DM	186/204	3 4	47/69
3518	13.10.1948	2 0	4wDM	16	1 4	273
3524	3. 9.1947	2 4	0-4-0DMF	65	2 0	269/314
3580	27. 4.1949	4 8½	0-6-0DM	186/204	3 4	47/69
3655	9. 2.1952	2 0	4wDM	16	1 4	273/297
4010	1.12.1950	4 8½	0-4-0DM	300	4 0	47/69
4011	30.11.1950	4 8½	0-4-0DM	300	4 0	47/69
4058	3. 1.1950	2 8½	0-6-0DMF	100	2 0	313
4060	28. 9.1950	2 6	0-6-0DMF	100	2 0	273/277/308/314/322
4061	28. 9.1950	2 6	0-6-0DMF	100	2 0	273/277/308/314/322
4062	20.12.1951	2 6	0-6-0DMF	100	2 0	277/308/322
4070	19.12.1958	2 6	0-6-0DMF	100	2 0	308/322
4071	26. 2.1954	2 6	0-6-0DMF	100	2 0	308/322
4078	28. 6.1950	2 0	0-4-0DMF	70	2 0	309/314
4079	18. 8.1950	2 0	0-4-0DMF	70	2 0	309/314
4091	25. 1.1952	2 0	0-4-0DMF	70	2 0	314
4092	31. 3.1952	2 0	0-4-0DMF	70	2 0	297/304/314
4093	30. 4.1952	2 0	0-4-0DMF	70	2 0	309/314/322
4094	18. 6.1952	2 0	0-4-0DMF	70	2 0	314/322
4100	31. 3.1953	2 6	0-4-0DMF	70	2 0	314
4101	30. 4.1952	2 6	0-4-0DMF	70	2 0	314
4108	26. 6.1952	2 0	0-4-0DMF	70	2 0	314
4109	27. 6.1952	2 0	0-4-0DMF	70	2 0	297/304/314
4110	29. 9.1952	2 0	0-4-0DMF	70	2 0	314/322
4139	31.10.1949	3 0	0-4-0DMF	65	2 0	321
4140	23.11.1949	3 0	0-4-0DMF	65	2 0	321
4175	28.10.1954	2 0	4wDM	16	1 4	273/297/304
4387	31.12.1952	2 0	0-4-0DMF	65	2 0	297/304/315
4400	30.11.1954	2 6	4wDM	35	1 6	183
4431	30.11.1953	4 8½	0-4-0DM	300	4 0	47/69
4432	22.12.1953	4 8½	0-4-0DM	300	4 0	47/69
4441	30. 9.1952	2 0	4wDM	21	1 6	272/277
4442	15. 9.1952	2 0	4wDM	21	1 6	277
4444	30. 6.1953	2 0	4wDM	21	1 6	277
4502	31.12.1954	2 0	0-4-0DMF	70	2 0	269/297/304/315
4504	29. 7.1955	2 0	0-4-0DMF	70	2 0	315
4554	28. 4.1954	2 0	4wDM	21	1 6	273/277/297
4631	21. 5.1953	2 3½	0-4-0DMF	65	2 0	269/314
4632	1. 7.1954	2 3½	0-4-0DMF	65	2 0	269/314
4635	27. 9.1954	3 0	0-4-0DMF	65	2 0	303
4685	28.10.1955	2 0	0-4-0DMF	65	2 0	297/304
4803	21. 2.1956	3 0	0-4-0DMF	65	2 0	297/304
4805	23. 4.1956	2 0	0-4-0DMF	65	2 0	297
4979	17. 2.1955	2 0	0-4-0DM	15	1 5	125/210
4986	30. 4.1956	4 8½	0-6-0DM	204	3 4	272/295/301
4987	1. 8.1956	4 8½	0-6-0DM	204	3 4	47/69
4988	24. 1.1957	4 8½	0-6-0DM	204	3 4	47/69

4989	6. 5.1957	4 8½	0-6-0DM	204	3 4	47/69/72
4991	26. 4.1955	2 0	0-4-0DMF	15	1 5	125
5173	12. 8.1957	4 8½	0-6-0DM	204	3 4	47/69
5174	28.10.1957	4 8½	0-6-0DM	204	3 4	47/69
5175	18.11.1957	4 8½	0-6-0DM	204	3 4	47/69/72
5177	29. 2.1958	4 8½	0-6-0DM	204	3 4	271/296/301
5282	20.12.1957	2 6	4wDM	38	1 6	183
5302	13.10.1958	4 8½	0-6-0DM	204	3 4	272/296/301
5303	18.12.1958	4 8½	0-6-0DM	204	3 4	272/295/301
5304	29. 5.1959	4 8½	0-6-0DM	270	3 4	267/272/295/301
5305	29. 5.1959	4 8½	0-6-0DM	204	3 4	272/296/301/305
5341	22.12.1958	4 8½	0-6-0DM	270	3 4	271/296/301
5342	29.12.1958	4 8½	0-6-0DM	270	3 4	267/271/294/301
5375	1. 4.1958	4 8½	0-6-0DM	204	3 4	48/69/72
5376	30. 4.1958	4 8½	0-6-0DM	204	3 4	48/69
5377	9. 5.1958	4 8½	0-6-0DM	204	3 4	48/50/69
5378	30. 7.1958	4 8½	0-6-0DM	204	3 4	48/50/69
5379	27. 8.1958	4 8½	0-6-0DM	204	3 4	48/50/69/72
5380	29. 8.1958	4 8½	0-6-0DM	204	3 4	48/50/69
5381	15. 9.1958	4 8½	0-6-0DM	204	3 4	48/69
5382	29.12.1958	4 8½	0-6-0DM	204	3 4	272/296/301/305
5384	16. 2.1959	4 8½	0-4-0DM	204	3 9	48/69
5385	23. 2.1959	4 8½	0-4-0DM	204	3 9	48/50/69
5386	20. 3.1959	4 8½	0-4-0DM	204	3 9	48/50/69/72
5387	25. 3.1959	4 8½	0-4-0DM	204	3 9	69/72/170
5392	31. 3.1959	4 8½	0-6-0DH	204	3 4	48/69
5393	30. 4.1959	4 8½	0-6-0DH	204	3 4	48/69
5394	27. 5.1959	4 8½	0-6-0DH	204	3 4	48/70
5424	30. 7.1959	2 6	0-4-0DMF	76	2 0	314
5439	24. 6.1959	3 0	0-4-0DMF	65	2 0	321
5596	30. 6.1961	2 0	0-4-0DMF	76	2 0	304/315/322
5600	31. 7.1961	2 0	0-4-0DMF	76	2 0	315
5609	30.10.1962	2 0	0-6-0DMF	100	2 0	315/322
5610	25. 6.1964	2 0	0-6-0DMF	100	2 0	315/322
5647	30. 6.1960	4 8½	0-6-0DM	204	3 9	301
6050	31. 7.1962	2 0	0-4-0DMF	76	2 0	315
6229	26. 3.1965	2 6	0-6-0DMF	100	2 0	308/322
6263	30.12.1964	4 8½	0-4-0DH	195	3 4	306
6347	13. 1.1975	2 0	4wDH	60	2 0	304
6348	21. 2.1975	2 0	4wDH	60	2 0	304
6602	30. 7.1965	3 0	0-4-0DMF	66	2 0	321
6603	5.10.1965	3 0	0-4-0DMF	66	2 0	321
6611	5. 4.1965	4 8½	0-6-0DH	311	3 9	284/291/300
6612	8. 4.1965	4 8½	0-6-0DH	311	3 9	259/290/300
6613	9. 6.1965	4 8½	0-6-0DH	311	3 9	284/291/300
6614	21. 6.1965	4 8½	0-6-0DH	311	3 9	284/291/300
6615	29. 7.1965	4 8½	0-6-0DH	311	3 9	284/291/300
6616	31. 8.1965	4 8½	0-6-0DH	311	3 9	259/289/300
6617	30. 9.1965	4 8½	0-6-0DH	311	3 9	259/289/300
6618	5.11.1965	4 8½	0-6-0DH	311	3 9	259/289/300
6619	30. 6.1966	2 1½	0-4-0DMF	66	2 0	304
6628	30.11.1966	2 3½	4wDM	29	1 6	273/297/304
6655	17. 3.1969	3 0	0-6-0DMF	100	2 0	321
6662	6.12.1966	4 8½	0-6-0DH	311	3 9	300
6676	26. 6.1967	4 8½	0-4-0DH	233	3 9	291/300
6677	10. 1.1969	4 8½	0-4-0DH	252	3 9	305
6688	5.12.1968	4 8½	0-4-0DH	252	3 9	305
6980	28. 2.1968	2 8¼	0-4-0DMF	65	2 0	303
7099	9.1973	3 0	4w-4wDHF	216	2 0	303/313/321
7100	3.1974	3 0	4w-4wDHF	216	2 0	313/321
7116	16. 1.1970	3 0	0-4-0DMF	40	1 6	313/321
7117	10. 3.1970	3 0	0-4-0DMF	40	1 6	313/321
7308	27. 3.1974	3 0	4w-4wDHF	216	2 0	321
7309	23. 5.1974	3 0	4w-4wDHF	216	2 0	321

- **R.& W.HAWTHORN, LESLIE & CO LTD**, Forth Banks Works,Newcastle-upon-Tyne.

This company was formed in March 1886 by the amalgamation of R. & W. Hawthorn Ltd (q.v.) and Andrew Leslie & Co Ltd, shipbuilders, of Hebburn, Co. Durham. Whereas R. & W. Hawthorn had built chiefly main-line locomotives, the new firm concentrated more on industrial customers, and soon became the main suppliers of industrial locomotives in North-East England. In 1902 it also took over the goodwill of Chapman & Furneaux Ltd of Gateshead (q.v.), successors to Black, Hawthorn & Co Ltd (q.v.). The numbering scheme of R.& W.Hawthorn was continued, but which locomotive was the first to carry a HL plate is uncertain. No.2039 is known to have been supplied by HL, despite its building date of 1885.

The locomotive business was sold in May 1937 to Robert Stephenson & Co Ltd (q.v.), which changed its name in the following month to Robert Stephenson & Hawthorns Ltd (q.v.). Despite this, locomotives continued for a time to be turned out with HL plates, the last being No.3953 in March 1938.

Complete details of all Hawthorn Leslie locomotives are not yet available. The lists below are based on work done on HL records while they were still held by RSH at Newcastle. A different version of the works list gives the 0-4-0ST built with 12"x18" cylinders as having 3' 0½" driving wheels.

WORKS No.	DATE NEW TO CUSTOMER	GAUGE AS BUILT ft.ins.	TYPE	CYLS.(bore x stroke) ins.ins.	DRIVING WH.DIAM. ft.ins.	SEE PAGE
2039	1885	4 8½	0-4-0ST OC	12 x 18	3 0	76/104
2073	1886	4 8½	0-4-0ST OC	12 x 18	3 0	148
2110	1888	4 8½	0-4-0ST OC	14 x 20	3 6	52/80
2113	1888∅	4 8½	2-2-2CT IC	14 x 18		149
2134	1889	4 8½	0-4-0ST OC	14 x 20	3 6	185
2135	1889	4 8½	0-4-0ST OC	12 x 18	3 0	149
2139	1889	4 8½	0-4-0ST OC	12 x 18	3 0	143
2152	1889	4 8½	0-4-0ST OC	14 x 20	3 6	32/44
2169	1889	4 8½	0-4-0ST OC	12 x 18	3 0	149
2173	1890	4 8½	0-4-0CT OC	11 x 15	2 9	150/197
2176	1890	4 8½	0-4-0ST OC	12 x 19	3 4	65/193
2177	1890	4 8½	0-4-0ST OC	12 x 19	3 4	65/220
2185	1890	4 8½	0-4-0ST OC	14 x 20	3 6	153
2199	1891	4 8½	0-4-0ST OC	12 x 18	3 0	197
2235	7. 6.1892	4 8½	0-4-0ST OC	12 x 19	3 4	65
2236	1892	4 8½	0-4-0ST OC	12 x 19	3 4	66
2247	1892	4 8½	0-4-0ST OC	12 x 18	3 0	140/142/151/200
2249	1892	4 8½	0-4-0CT OC	12 x 15	2 10	58
2272	1893	4 8½	0-4-0CT OC	12 x 15	2 10	104
2273	1893	4 8½	0-4-0CT OC	12 x 15	2 10	104
2279	1893	4 8½	0-4-0ST OC	12 x 18	3 0	92/271
2281	3.1895	4 8½	0-4-0ST OC	12 x 18	3 0	197/280
2330	1896	4 8½	0-4-0ST OC	12 x 18	3 0	167/280
2334	1896	4 8½	0-4-0CT OC	12 x 15	2 10	98
2349	1896	4 8½	0-4-0ST OC	12 x 18	3 0	167/168/169/197/283
2357	1896	4 8½	0-4-0ST OC	14 x 20	3 6	29
2358	1896	4 8½	0-4-0ST OC	14 x 20	3 6	143
2377	2. 7.1897	4 8½	0-4-0ST OC	13 x 19	3 4½	66/73/282
2378	1898	4 8½	0-4-0ST OC	14 x 20	3 6	182/187
2387	1897	4 8½	0-4-0ST OC	12 x 18	2 10	145
2404	1899	4 8½	0-4-0ST OC	13 x 19	3 4½	66
2412	1899	4 8½	0-4-0ST OC	14 x 20	3 6	51/187/214
2425	1899	4 8½	0-4-0ST OC	14 x 20	3 6	28
2426	1899	4 8½	0-4-0ST OC	14 x 20	3 6	167/168/197/280
2429	1899	4 8½	0-6-0T IC	15 x 20	3 8	34
2431	1899	4 8½	0-4-0ST OC	12 x 18	3 0	219
2445	1899	4 8½	0-4-0ST OC	14 x 20	3 6	178/187

2447	1900	4	8½	0-4-0CT	OC	12 x 15	2	10	149/150
2449	1900	4	8½	0-4-0ST	OC	14 x 20	3	6	38/82
2453	1900	4	8½	0-4-0ST	OC	14 x 20	3	6	79/104/151/153
2456	1900	4	8½	0-4-0ST	OC	14 x 20	3	6	153/199/271
2468	1900	4	8½	0-4-0CT	OC	12 x 15	2	10	203
2478	1901	4	8½	0-4-0ST	OC	12 x 18	3	0	94/104
2479	1900	4	8½	0-4-0ST	OC	12 x 18	3	0	88
2481	1900	4	8½	0-4-0ST	OC	14 x 20	3	6	124/281
2484	1900	4	8½	0-6-0T	IC	16 x 24	4	1	92/271
2489	1901	4	8½	0-4-0ST	OC	14 x 20	3	6	149/332
2496	1901	4	8½	0-4-0ST	OC	12 x 18	3	0	183/219
2499	1901	4	8½	0-4-0CT	OC	12 x 15	2	10	58/96
2514	1901	4	8½	0-4-0ST	OC	12 x 18	2	10	145
2515	23.12.1901	4	8½	0-6-0ST	OC	15 x 22	3	9	42/280
2516	1902	4	8½	0-4-0CT	OC	12 x 15	2	10	187
2517	1902	4	8½	0-4-0CT	OC	12 x 15	2	10	87/342
2530	1902	4	8½	0-4-0ST	OC	14 x 20	3	6	85/119/259/262/289
2533	1902	4	8½	0-4-0ST	OC	12 x 18	3	0	177/206
2535	1902	4	8½	0-4-0CT	OC	12 x 15	2	10	87
2545	24.12.1902	4	8½	0-6-0ST	IC	17 x 26	4	6	43/281/291
2550	1903	4	8½	0-4-0CT	OC	12 x 15	2	10	87/104
2551	1903	4	8½	0-4-0CT	OC	12 x 15	2	10	87
2559	1903	4	8½	0-4-0ST	OC	14 x 20	3	6	151/152/200
2563	1903	4	8½	0-4-0ST	OC	12 x 18	3	0	88/153/154
2583	1904	4	8½	0-4-0ST	OC	14 x 20	3	6	197/280
2589	1904	4	8½	0-4-0ST	OC	14 x 20	3	6	164
2594	1905	4	8½	0-4-0CT	OC	12 x 15	2	10	87
2595	1904	4	8½	0-6-0ST	OC	16 x 24	3	10	37/82/270
2606	1905	4	8½	0-4-0CT	OC	12 x 15	2	10	93
2607	6.1905	4	8½	0-6-0ST	OC	15 x 22	3	9	52/80/82/85/270
2612	1905	4	8½	0-6-0ST	OC	14 x 22	3	4	38/82/270/287
2613	1905	4	8½	0-6-0ST	OC	14 x 22	3	4	34/79/82/83/270/287
2617	1905	4	8½	0-4-0ST	OC	14 x 22	3	6	197/280
2632	1906	4	8½	0-4-0CT	OC	12 x 15	2	10	87
2639	20. 2.1906	4	8½	0-4-0ST	OC	13 x 19	3	4	66/272/282
2640	26. 2.1906	4	8½	0-4-0ST	OC	13 x 19	3	4	66/73
2641	11. 4.1906	4	8½	0-6-0PT	IC	18 x 26	4	2⅜	64/282
2645	1906	4	8½	0-4-0ST	OC	14 x 22	3	6	140
2654	1906	4	8½	0-6-0ST	OC	14 x 22	3	4	37/38/82/270/296
2655	1906	4	8½	0-6-0ST	OC	14 x 22	3	4	34/75/79/85/270/287
2666	1906	4	8½	0-4-0ST	OC	14 x 22	3	4	149/207
2667	1907	4	8½	0-4-0ST	OC	14 x 22	3	4	149/207
2684	1907	4	8½	0-4-0ST	OC	13 x 19	3	4	104
2685	1906	4	8½	0-4-0T	OC	15 x 22	3	9	151/152/272/275
2694	7.1907	4	8½	0-4-0ST	OC	15 x 22	3	9	197/280
2701	1907	4	8½	0-4-0ST	OC	14 x 22	3	6	133/264
2702	1907	4	8½	0-4-0ST	OC	14 x 22	3	6	197
2711	1907	4	8½	0-4-0ST	OC	14 x 22	3	6	341
2713	1907	4	8½	0-4-0ST	OC	14 x 22	3	6	151/199/271
2719	7.11.1907	4	8½	0-6-0ST	OC	15 x 22	3	9	43/281/291
2732	1907	4	8½	0-6-0ST	OC	14 x 22	3	7	52/79/80/82/270
2737	1907	4	8½	0-6-0ST	OC	16 x 24	3	8	93/109/267
2740	1908	4	8½	0-4-0ST	OC	14 x 22	3	6	197/280
2769	1909	4	8½	0-6-0T	IC	17 x 26	4	1	215/258/290
2774	1909	4	8½	0-4-0T	OC	15 x 22	3	9	151
2780	1909	4	8½	0-4-0ST	OC	14 x 22	3	6	140
2784	1909	4	8½	0-4-0ST	OC	14 x 22	3	6	215
2789	1909	4	8½	0-4-0ST	OC	16 x 24	3	10	119/262/268/294
2798	1909	4	8½	0-4-0ST	OC	12 x 18	3	0	142/155/200/271
2799	1909	4	8½	0-4-0ST	OC	12 x 18	3	0	152/154/155
2823	1910	4	8½	0-4-0ST	OC	14 x 22	3	6	151/152/200/271
2824	1910	4	8½	0-4-0ST	OC	14 x 22	3	6	216/258
2826	1910	4	8½	0-4-0ST	OC	15 x 22	3	8	119/259/262/289
2827	1910	4	8½	0-4-0ST	OC	15 x 22	3	8	119/259/263/290
2833	1910	4	8½	0-6-0ST	OC	16 x 24	3	10	37/82/270

2837	1910	4 8½	0-4-0ST	OC	14 x 22	3 6	169/284/305
2839	1910	4 8½	0-4-0ST	OC	14 x 22	3 6	76
2871	1911	4 8½	0-4-0ST	OC	14 x 22	3 6	217
2880	1911	4 8½	0-6-0T	OC	17 x 24	3 8	200/202/271/276/295/305
2890	1911	4 8½	0-4-0ST	OC	14 x 22	3 6	75
2916	1912	4 8½	0-4-0ST	OC	14 x 22	3 6	38
2917	1912	4 8½	0-4-0ST	OC	14 x 22	3 6	104
2932	1912	4 8½	0-6-0ST	IC	15 x 22	3 9	119/122/134/259/263/289
2941	1912	4 8½	0-4-0ST	OC	12 x 18	3 0	84
2954	1912	4 8½	0-4-0ST	OC	15 x 22	3 8	119/259/263/289
2956	1912	4 8½	0-6-0ST	OC	16 x 24	3 8	108/281
2984	19. 1.1914	4 8½	0-4-0VBCr	OC	12 x 21½	3 0	69/283
2986	1913	4 8½	0-4-0T	OC	14 x 22	3 6	162/283
2989	1913	4 8½	0-4-0ST	OC	14 x 22	3 6	87
2993	1913	4 8½	0-4-0ST	OC	16 x 24	3 10	151/275
3003	19. 9.1913	4 8½	0-4-0ST	OC	13 x 19	3 4½	66/73/76/282
3004	23. 9.1913	4 8½	0-4-0ST	OC	13 x 19	3 4½	66/72/73
3022	3.11.1913	4 8½	0-4-0ST	OC	12 x 19	3 4½	66/72
3023	17.11.1913	4 8½	0-4-0ST	OC	12 x 19	3 4½	66/72/73
3024	1913	4 8½	0-4-0ST	OC	15 x 22	3 8	119/259/289
3029	1913	1 10	0-4-0ST	OC	5 x 10	1 8½	209
3053	1914	4 8½	0-4-0ST	OC	14 x 22	3 6	155
3055	1914	4 8½	0-4-0ST	OC	16 x 24	3 10	119/262/268
3056	1914	4 8½	0-4-0ST	OC	16 x 24	3 10	119/262/268/291/295/340
3080	19.12.1914	4 8½	0-6-0PT	IC	18 x 26	4 2⅜	64/282
3090	1914	4 8½	0-4-0ST	OC	14 x 22	3 6	55
3103	9. 4.1915	4 8½	0-6-0ST	OC	17 x 24	3 10	43/281/291
3104	1915	4 8½	0-6-0T	OC	17 x 24	3 10	152/199/271
3139	1915	4 8½	0-4-0ST	OC	12 x 18	3 0	84
3140	1915	4 8½	0-4-0ST	OC	12 x 18	3 0	83/84
3169	1916	4 8½	0-4-0ST	OC	14 x 22	3 4⅜	80
3185	1916	4 8½	0-6-0ST	OC	16 x 24	3 10	138/272/275
3237	1917	4 8½	0-4-0ST	OC	15 x 22	3 8	76/149
3248	1917	4 8½	0-4-0ST	OC	16 x 24	3 8	82
3251	1.10.1917	4 8½	0-4-0ST	OC	13 x 19	3 4½	66/73
3252	13.10.1917	4 8½	0-4-0ST	OC	13 x 19	3 4½	66/72/73
3253	29.10.1917	4 8½	0-4-0ST	OC	13 x 19	3 4½	66
3254	7.12.1917	4 8½	0-4-0ST	OC	13 x 19	3 4½	66/73/272/275
3282	1917	4 8½	0-6-0ST	OC	14 x 22	3 6	167/283/305
3300	1917	4 8½	0-4-0ST	OC	14 x 22	3 6	75
3319	1918	4 8½	0-4-0ST	OC	14 x 22	3 6	104
3349	1918	4 8½	0-4-0ST	OC	14 x 22	3 6	140
3352	1918	4 8½	0-4-0ST	OC	16 x 24	3 8	181
3354	1918	4 8½	0-4-0ST	OC	16 x 24	3 10	181/187
3355	1918	4 8½	0-4-0ST	OC	16 x 24	3 10	181/187
3384	1919	4 8½	0-4-0ST	OC	14 x 22	3 6	37/82/83/267/271/295
3390	22.10.1919	4 8½	0-4-0ST	OC	14 x 22	3 6	65
3391	24.11.1919	4 8½	0-4-0ST	OC	14 x 22	3 6	65/282
3418	1919	4 8½	0-4-0ST	OC	14 x 22	3 6	97
3426	1919	4 8½	0-4-0ST	OC	14 x 22	3 6	80/84
3438	10.1920	4 8½	0-4-0ST	OC	15 x 22	3 9	197/280
3440	1920	4 8½	0-6-0ST	OC	16 x 24	3 10	109/267/294
3467	1920	4 8½	0-4-0ST	OC	14 x 22	3 6	97/282
3471	1. 6.1921	4 8½	0-4-0ST	OC	16 x 24	3 10	67
3472	8. 6.1921	4 8½	0-4-0ST	OC	16 x 24	3 10	67
3473	16.11.1920	4 8½	0-4-0ST	OC	14 x 22	3 6	65
3474	15.11.1920	4 8½	0-4-0ST	OC	14 x 22	3 6	65/72/282/291
3475	13.12.1920	4 8½	0-4-0ST	OC	14 x 22	3 6	65
3476	29.12.1920	4 8½	0-4-0ST	OC	14 x 22	3 6	65/180
3492	1921	4 8½	0-4-0ST	OC	14 x 22	3 6	133/264
3493	1922	4 8½	0-4-0ST	OC	14 x 22	3 6	216/258/290
3494	1922	4 8½	0-4-0ST	OC	14 x 22	3 6	216/258
3495	24.12.1920	4 8½	0-4-0T	OC	14 x 22	3 6	65/70
3496	22. 7.1921	4 8½	0-4-0ST	OC	16 x 24	3 10	67/72/180
3497	11. 8.1921	4 8½	0-4-0ST	OC	16 x 24	3 10	67

WORKS No.	DATE	GAUGE	TYPE	CYLS.		DRIVING WH.	
3504	1923	4 8½	0-4-OST OC	14 x 22		3 6	135/275
3513	1927@	4 8½	0-6-OST OC	14 x 22		3 6	200/272/276/295/341
3527	1922	4 8½	0-6-OST OC	16 x 24		3 10	180
3528	1922	4 8½	0-6-OST OC	16 x 24		3 8	108/281/291
3543	1923	4 8½	0-4-OST OC	15 x 22		3 8	119/259/263/289
3544	1923	4 8½	0-4-OST OC	15 x 22		3 8	119/263/268/295
3568	1923	4 8½	0-6-OST OC	16 x 24		3 10	109/267
3569	6.11.1923	4 8½	0-6-OST IC	18 x 26		4 6	43/281/291
3572	1923	4 8½	0-4-OST OC	12 x 18		3 0	84
3573	1923	4 8½	0-4-OST OC	12 x 18		2 10	145
3576	1923	4 8½	0-4-OST OC	12 x 18		2 10	145
3577	1923	4 8½	0-4-OST OC	12 x 18		3 0	184
3584	1924∮	4 8½	0-4-OBE			3 3	139
3586	1924	4 8½	0-4-OST OC	12 x 18		3 0	55
3641	1926	4 8½	0-4-OST OC	14 x 22		3 6	54/55
3651	1926	4 8½	0-4-OST OC	14 x 22		3 6	55
3654	1927	4 8½	0-4-OST OC	14 x 22		3 6	32
3732	1928	4 8½	0-4-OST OC	14 x 22		3 6	55/344
3744	29. 4.1929	4 8½	0-4-OST OC	16 x 24		3 10	66/180
3745	12. 7.1929	4 8½	0-4-OST OC	16 x 24		3 10	66/170
3752	21. 2.1930	4 8½	0-4-OST OC	16 x 24		3 10	66/283
3753	21. 2.1930	4 8½	0-4-OST OC	16 x 24		3 10	66
3766	1930	4 8½	0-6-OT OC	18 x 24		4 0	162/283/290
3772	1930	4 8½	0-4-OST OC	14 x 22		3 6	55
3806	1934	4 8½	0-4-OST OC	12 x 20		3 1	219
3830	1934	4 8½	0-6-OST OC	18 x 24		4 0	202/272/276
3834	1934	4 8½	0-6-2T IC	18½x 26		4 6	120/264
3859	1937	4 8½	0-4-OWE Coke Car loco	2 9	80 h.p.		201/286/306
3861	1936	4 8½	0-4-OWE Coke Car loco	2 9	80 h.p.		(50)
3862	1936	4 8½	0-4-OWE Coke Car loco	2 9	80 h.p.		(50)
3873	27. 4.1936	4 8½	0-4-OST OC	16 x 24		3 8	65/180
3887	1936	4 8½	0-4-OST OC	12 x 20		3 1	219
3891	14.10.1936	4 8½	0-6-OPT IC	18 x 26		4 2⅝	64/282
3894	1936	4 8½	0-4-OST OC	12 x 20		3 1	93
3895	1937	4 8½	0-4-OST OC	12 x 20		3 1	30
3898	1936	4 8½	0-6-OST OC	16 x 24		3 8	180
3905	30. 4.1937	4 8½	0-6-OPT IC	18 x 26		4 2⅝	64/282
3906	26. 2.1937	4 8½	0-4-OST OC	16 x 24		3 8	65
3919	1937	4 8½	0-4-OST OC	16 x 24		3 8	181
3934	1937	4 8½	0-6-OST OC	14 x 22		3 6	144
3935	1937	4 8½	0-4-OST OC	16 x 24		3 8	187
3951	21. 2.1938	4 8½	0-6-OPT IC	18 x 26		4 2⅝	63
3952	11. 3.1938	4 8½	0-6-OPT IC	18 x 26		4 2⅝	63/284
3953	8. 3.1938	4 8½	0-4-OST OC	16 x 24		3 8	47/65/72

∮ Built to Cross' Patent
@ Originally built in 1923 as an experimental compressed steam loco.
   Rebuilt to standard 0-6-OST in 1927
∮ Built to Durtnall's Patent. Sold by RSH in 1939, with new (HL)
   plate dated 1939.

JF - JOHN FOWLER & CO (LEEDS) LTD, Leeds, Yorkshire.

WORKS No.	DATE EX-WORKS	GAUGE AS BUILT ft.ins.	TYPE	CYLS.(bore x stroke) ins.ins.	DRIVING WH.DIAM. ft.ins.	SEE PAGE
1539	25. 5.1871	4 8½	0-6-OT IC	8 x 14	2 6	152
1541	17. 7.1871	4 8½	0-6-OT IC	8 x 14	2 6	143
1542	1. 8.1871	4 8½	0-6-OT IC	8 x 14	2 6	208
1568	12.12.1871	4 8½	0-4-OST IC	8½ x 14	2 8	206
1572	1872	4 8½	0-4-OST OC			140
2078	3. 2.1874	4 8½	0-4-OST OC	12 x		151
2079	9. 3.1874	4 8½	0-4-OST OC	12 x		143

WORKS No.	DATE EX-WORKS	GAUGE AS BUILT ft.ins.	TYPE				SEE PAGE
2820	9. 9.1876	3 0	0-4-OTG	OC	5 x		32
2821	13.12.1876	3 0	0-4-OTG	OC	5 x		32
2834	22. 6.1876	4 8½	0-4-OST	OC	12 x		215
2849	15. 7.1876	4 8½	0-4-OST	OC	8½ x 12	2 6	126
5006	1885	3 0	0-4-OTG	OC	∤		32
5653	31. 3.1888	3 0	0-4-OTG	OC			32
5661	16. 4.1888	3 0	0-4-OTG	OC	5 x		138
5822	30.11.1888	3 0	0-4-OST	OC	5 x 10		151
5883	4. 3.1889	3 0	0-4-OTG	OC	5 x		138
16991	4.10.1926	2 0	0-6-OT	OC	8 x 12	2 0	89
unidentified							215

∤ compound locomotive, with cylinders 5½" x 9" and 5½" x 12".

Diesel locomotives

WORKS No.	DATE EX-WORKS	GAUGE AS BUILT ft.ins.	TYPE	HORSE POWER	DRIVING WH.DIAM. ft.ins.	SEE PAGE
22137	12.1937	4 8½	0-4-ODM	150	3 3	135/178
22488	1.1939	4 8½	0-4-ODM	80	3 0	31
22900	3.1941	4 8½	0-4-ODM	40	2 6	53/344
22934	1.1941	4 8½	0-4-ODM	150	3 3	178
22938	3.1941	4 8½	0-4-ODM	150	3 3	136
22943	6.1941	4 8½	0-4-ODM	150	3 3	178
22945	9.1941	4 8½	0-4-ODM	150	3 3	136
22948	11.1941	4 8½	0-4-ODM	150	3 3	178
22976	5.1942	4 8½	0-4-ODM	150	3 3	135
4000013	12.1947	4 8½	0-4-ODM	60	3 0	142/143
4100012	9.1948	4 8½	0-4-ODM	80	3 0	31/56
4110001	11.1949	4 8½	0-4-ODM	80	3 0	142/143
4110002	1.1950	4 8½	0-4-ODM	80	3 0	142
4110006	8.1950	4 8½	0-4-ODM	80	3 0	29/30/77
4110008	9.1950	4 8½	0-4-ODM	80	3 0	203
4160009	2.1953	4 8½	0-4-ODM	100	3 0	187
4200020	11.1947	4 8½	0-4-ODM	150	3 3	45
4210086	27. 7.1953∤	4 8½	0-4-ODM	150	3 3	187
4210087	9.1953	4 8½	0-4-ODM	150	3 3	339
4210089	5. 1.1954∤	4 8½	0-4-ODM	150	3 3	49/187/189
4210091	31. 3.1954∤	4 8½	0-4-ODM	150	3 3	49/187/189
4210094	2. 9.1954∤	4 8½	0-4-ODM	150	3 3	49/187/189/344
4210099	28. 3.1955	4 8½	0-4-ODM	150	3 3	49/187/189
4210102	30. 6.1955	4 8½	0-4-ODM	150	3 3	49/187/189
4210107	28.11.1955	4 8½	0-4-ODM	150	3 3	49/187/189
4210110	11. 4.1956	4 8½	0-4-ODM	150	3 3	49/187/189
4210128	16. 5.1957	4 8½	0-4-ODM	150	3 3	50/187/189
4210146	30. 5.1958	4 8½	0-4-ODM	150	3 3	49/187/188
4210147	26. 1.1959	4 8½	0-4-ODM	150	3 3	187/188
4210148	15. 1.1959	4 8½	0-4-ODM	150	3 3	50/187/188/189
4220027	10. 3.1964∤	4 8½	0-4-ODH	203	3 6	49/189
4220028	14. 4.1964∤	4 8½	0-4-ODH	203	3 6	49/189
4240001	15. 9.1959	4 8½	0-6-ODH	230	3 6	49/188
4240002	17.11.1959	4 8½	0-6-ODH	230	3 6	49/188
4240003	24.11.1959	4 8½	0-6-ODH	230	3 6	49/188
4240004	29.12.1959	4 8½	0-6-ODH	230	3 6	49/188
4240005	25. 1.1960	4 8½	0-6-ODH	230	3 6	49/188
4240006	25. 4.1960	4 8½	0-6-ODH	230	3 6	49/188
4240007	12. 4.1960	4 8½	0-6-ODH	230	3 6	49/188
4240008	27. 6.1960	4 8½	0-6-ODH	230	3 6	49/188
4240009	20.10.1960	4 8½	0-6-ODH	230	3 6	49/188
4240011	28. 3.1961	4 8½	0-6-ODH	230	3 6	49/189
4240013	4. 6.1962	4 8½	0-4-ODH	275	3 6	55
4240020	1964	4 8½	0-6-ODH	275	3 6	55

∤ date of arrival at customer's location.

K - KITSON & CO LTD, Leeds, Yorkshire.

WORKS No.	DATE NEW TO CUSTOMER	GAUGE AS BUILT ft.ins.	TYPE	CYLS. (bore x stroke) ins.ins.	DRIVING WH.DIAM. ft.ins.	SEE PAGE
1508	1868	4 8½	0-4-0ST	OC 10 x 18	3 0½	198
1705	1871	4 8½	0-4-0ST	OC 12 x 18	3 0½	153/156
1786	1871	4 8½	0-6-0ST	OC 13 x 20	3 6	222
1843	1872	4 8½	0-6-0ST	IC 16 x 24	3 10	63
1844	1872	4 8½	0-6-0ST	IC 16 x 24	3 10	63
1845	1872	4 8½	0-6-0ST	IC 16 x 24	3 10	63
1998	1874	4 8½	0-6-0ST	IC 16 x 24	4 0	63
2509	1883	4 8½	0-6-0PT	IC 17½x 26	4 2	63/282/290/340
2510	1883	4 8½	0-6-0PT	IC 17½x 26	4 2	63/282/290
3069	1887	4 8½	0-6-2T	IC 17½x 26	4 6	120/264
3580	1894	4 8½	0-6-2T	IC 17½x 26	4 6	120/264
3905	13.10.1899	4 8½	0-6-0PT	IC 18 x 26	4 2⅝	64/282
3906	6.11.1899	4 8½	0-6-0PT	IC 18 x 26	4 2⅝	64
4051	26. 6.1901	4 8½	0-6-0PT	IC 18 x 26	4 2⅝	64/282
4263	1904	4 8½	0-6-2T	IC 19 x 26	4 6	119/259/262/289/344
4294	1905	4 8½	0-6-0T	IC 17½x 26	4 6	123/275/284/290
4532	1907	4 8½	0-6-2T	IC 19 x 26	4 6	119/259/262/289
4533	1907	4 8½	0-6-2T	IC 19 x 26	4 6	119/259/262/289
5179	3. 7.1917	4 8½	0-6-0PT	IC 18 x 26	4 2⅝	64/282

KS - KERR, STUART & CO LTD, Stoke-on-Trent, Staffs.

WORKS No.	DATE EX-WORKS	GAUGE AS BUILT ft.ins.	TYPE	CYLS. (bore x stroke) ins.ins.	DRIVING WH.DIAM. ft.ins.	MAKER'S CLASS	SEE PAGE
1047	25. 2.1908	2 0	0-4-2ST	OC 7 x 12	2 0 ≁	TATTOO	89
1142	7. 2.1911	2 0	0-4-2ST	OC 7 x 12	2 0 ≁	TATTOO	89
1144	30. 9.1911	2 0	0-4-2ST	OC 7 x 12	2 0 ≁	TATTOO	89
1145	27. 1.1912	2 0	0-4-2ST	OC 7 x 12	2 0 ≁	TATTOO	89
1202	18. 5.1911	4 8½	4w-4wWE	4x70hp motors	2 9½	-	102/260/290/300
1203	30. 6.1911	4 8½	4w-4wWE	4x70hp motors	2 9½	-	102/260/290/300
1291	8. 2.1915	2 0	0-4-2ST	OC 7 x 12	2 0 ≁	TATTOO	89
2395	23. 2.1917	2 0	0-4-2ST	OC 7 x 12	2 0 ≁	TATTOO	89
2399	19. 9.1917	4 8½	0-4-0ST	OC 10 x 16	2 3	-	221
3074	14. 9.1917	4 8½	0-6-0T	OC 17 x 24	4 0	VICTORY	119/263/267 272/276/284
3095	4. 3.1918	4 8½	0-4-0ST	OC 15 x 20	3 3	MOSS BAY	187
3097	14. 3.1918	4 8½	0-4-0ST	OC 15 x 20	3 3	MOSS BAY	149
3098	26. 3.1918	4 8½	0-6-0T	OC 15 x 20	3 6	ARGENTINA	214/267/295
3100	8. 4.1918	4 8½	0-6-0T	OC 15 x 20	3 6	ARGENTINA	214/267/295
3126	22.10.1918	4 8½	0-4-0ST	OC 15 x 20	3 3	MOSS BAY	97/98/137
4001	20.12.1918	2 0	0-4-0ST	OC 6 x 9	1 8	WREN	89
4027	9. 5.1919	4 8½	0-4-0ST	OC 15 x 20	3 3	MOSS BAY	92/214/267
4028	9. 5.1919	4 8½	0-4-0ST	OC 15 x 20	3 3	MOSS BAY	214/271/276
4029	20. 5.1919	4 8½	0-4-0ST	OC 15 x 20	3 3	MOSS BAY	149
4030	23. 5.1919	4 8½	0-4-0ST	OC 15 x 20	3 3	MOSS BAY	42/44/280
4143	8.12.1919	4 8½	0-4-0ST	OC 15 x 20	3 3	MOSS BAY	31/32/143 272/275
4246	31. 1.1922	2 0	0-4-0ST	OC 6 x 9	1 8	WREN	221
4290	7. 2.1923	2 0	0-4-0ST	OC 6 x 9	1 8	WREN	89
4291	6. 4.1923	2 0	0-4-0ST	OC 6 x 9	1 8	WREN	89
4421	2.12.1929	4 8½	6wDM	90 h.p.	3 0	-	267/294

≁ radial wheels 1' 4½" diameter.

MW - MANNING, WARDLE & CO LTD, Leeds, Yorkshire.

The only dimensions given below are those confirmed by Manning Wardle individual engine records, but (except where otherwise stated) dimensions are:

Class		Dimensions		
D	8" x14"	2' 8"		
E	9½"x14"	2' 9"	or 9"x14"	2' 8½"
F	10" x16"	3' 0"	before 619	
		2' 9"	after 619	(some 10½"x16")
H	12" x18"	3' 0"		
old I	11" x17"	3' 1"	(some 12"x17")	
I altered	13½"x18"	3' 0"		
K	12" x17"	3' 1"	before 1000	
		3' 0"	after 1000	
L	12" x18"	3' 0"		
M	13" x18"	3' 0"	(some 14"x18")	

WORKS No.	DATE EX-WORKS	GAUGE AS BUILT ft.ins.	TYPE	CYLS.(bore x stroke) ins.ins.	DRIVING WH.DIAM. ft.ins.	MAKER'S CLASS	SEE PAGE
14	6. 8.1860	4 8½	0-4-0ST OC	9½ x 14		E	185
17	30.11.1860	4 8½	0-6-0ST IC	11 x 17		old I	164
23	21. 3.1861	4 8½	0-6-0ST IC	11 x 17		old I	103
49	27. 5.1862	4 8½	0-6-0ST IC	12 x 17		old I	156
57	5.11.1862	4 8½	0-6-0ST IC	11 x 17		old I	164
60	28. 3.1862	4 8½	0-4-0ST OC	9 x 14		E	52
87	27. 6.1864	4 8½	0-4-0ST OC	9 x 14		E	207
97	3.11.1863	4 8½	0-4-0ST OC	6 x 12	2 6	B	151
98	11.11.1863	4 8½	0-4-0ST OC	6 x 12	2 6	B	151
104	27. 1.1864	4 8½	0-6-0ST IC	13 x 18	3 0	M	200/201
112	15. 4.1864	4 8½	0-4-0ST OC	6 x 12	2 6	B	63/183
113	22. 4.1864	4 8½	0-4-0ST OC	6 x 12	2 6	B	151
144	27. 2.1865	4 8½	0-4-0ST OC	9½ x 14	2 6	E	155
148	14. 3.1865	4 8½	0-6-0ST IC	13 x 18	3 0	M	95
152	9. 5.1865	4 8½	0-6-0ST IC	13 x 18	3 0	M	118
171	2.10.1865	4 8½	0-6-0ST IC	12 x 17	3 1⅛	K	331
179	15. 1.1866	4 8½	0-6-0ST IC	12 x 17	3 1⅛	K	330
181	16.12.1865	4 8½	0-6-0ST IC	12 x 17	3 1⅛	K	331
194	13. 6.1866	4 8½	0-6-0ST IC	13 x 18	3 0	M	34/37
199	7. 8.1866	4 8½	0-4-0ST OC	9½ x 14		E	177
200	6. 2.1867	4 8½	0-6-0ST IC	13 x 18	3 0	M	200/276
241	4. 1.1868	4 8½	0-6-0ST IC	11 x 17		old I	94
242	30. 8.1867	4 8½	0-6-0ST IC	14 x 18		M	103
270	1.12.1869	4 8½	0-4-0ST OC	6 x 12		A	207
274	2. 4.1870	4 8½	0-6-0ST IC	12 x 17		K	178
320	13. 9.1870	4 8½	0-4-0ST OC	12 x 18	3 6	H	200/201/202
324	9. 1.1871	4 8½	0-6-0ST IC	13 x 18		M	198
329	2.12.1870	4 8½	0-4-0ST OC	12 x 18	3 0	H	332
341	24. 5.1871	4 8½	0-6-0ST IC	13 x 18		M	179/276
344	21. 4.1871	4 8½	0-4-0ST OC	12 x 18	3 0	H	119/262
416	2. 1.1873	4 8½	0-4-0ST OC	12 x 18		H	39
447	10. 7.1873	4 8½	0-4-0ST OC	12 x 18		H	185
455	20. 8.1874	4 8½	0-4-0ST OC	10 x 16		F	57/170
465	15. 8.1873	4 8½	0-4-0ST OC	12 x 18		H	53
466	8. 9.1873	4 8½	0-4-0ST OC	12 x 18		H	147/214
467	22. 9.1873	4 8½	0-4-0ST OC	12 x 18	3 0	H	142/199
479	3. 2.1874	4 8½	0-6-0ST IC	15 x 22	3 9	O	103
480	30. 1.1874	4 8½	0-6-0ST IC	15 x 22	3 9	O	179
492	20. 4.1874	4 8½	0-4-0ST OC	12 x 18		H	147/214
498	18. 5.1874	4 8½	0-4-0ST OC	12 x 18		H	141/156
540	29. 9.1875	4 8½	0-4-0ST OC	12 x 18		H	141/219
569	28. 9.1875	4 8½	0-6-0ST IC	15 x 22	3 9	O	179/276
573	25.11.1875	4 8½	0-4-0ST OC	12 x 18		H	156
575	9. 8.1876	4 8½	0-4-0ST OC	12 x 18	3 0	H	217
614	30. 6.1876	3 0	0-4-0ST OC	7 x 12	∅	C alt	332

693	2. 4.1878	4 8½	0-6-0ST	IC	15 x 22	4 0	O	198
697	7. 5.1878	4 8½	0-6-0ST	IC	15 x 22	3 9	O	192/264
744	25. 3.1880	4 8½	0-4-0ST	OC	12 x 18		H	156
756	5.10.1880	4 8½	0-4-0ST	OC	12 x 18		H	84/125
758	7. 3.1881	4 8½	0-6-0ST	IC	15 x 22		O	192/264
775	6. 2.1882	4 8½	0-6-0ST	IC	13 x 18		M	200
777	4. 2.1881	4 8½	0-4-0ST	OC	12 x 18	3 6	H	30
813	22.12.1881	4 8½	0-4-0ST	OC	8 x 14		D	84
838	10. 7.1885	4 8½	0-4-0ST	OC	10 x 18	3 1	Special	180/332
892	2. 7.1884	4 8½	0-4-0ST	OC	8 x 14	2 8	D	333
899	31. 5.1884	4 8½	0-6-0ST	IC	13 x 18	3 0	M	333
926	25.10.1884	4 8½	0-6-0ST	IC	13 x 18		M	153
942	9. 4.1885	4 8½	0-4-0ST	OC	8 x 14		D	184
995	30. 9.1886	4 8½	0-6-0ST	IC	12 x 17	3 1⅛	Special K	330
1020	8. 6.1887	4 8½	0-4-0ST	OC	10 x 16		F	98
1037	8.11.1887	4 8½	0-4-0ST	OC	10 x 16	2 7	F	148
1042	25. 1.1888	4 8½	0-4-0ST	OC	12 x 18		H	165
1059	30. 3.1888	4 8½	0-6-0ST	IC	12 x 17	3 1⅛	K	333
1072	23. 4.1888	4 8½	0-4-0ST	OC	12 x 18		H	176
1088	19.12.1888	4 8½	0-4-0ST	OC	10 x 16	2 9	F	332
1138	2. 8.1889	4 8½	0-6-0ST	IC	15 x 22	3 6	Special	38
1144	21. 5.1890	4 8½	0-6-0ST	IC	12 x 17	3 0	K	330
1150	16. 3.1891	4 8½	0-4-0ST	OC	10½x 16		F	146
1323	22. 9.1896	4 8½	0-4-0ST	OC	10 x 16		F	218
1327	19. 3.1897	4 8½	0-4-0ST	OC	12 x 18	3 0	H	56/184
1328	29. 3.1898	4 8½	0-4-0ST	OC	12 x 18	3 0	H	80/83/84
1365	30. 3.1898	4 8½	0-6-0ST	IC	12 x 18		L	137
1422	9. 1.1899	4 8½	0-4-0ST	OC	12 x 18		H	79/83/84/86/271
1446	29. 3.1899	4 8½	0-6-0ST	IC	12 x 18	3 0	L	331/334
1455	3. 8.1899	4 8½	0-6-0ST	IC	12 x 18	3 0	L	331
1469	8. 1.1900	4 8½	0-6-0ST	IC	16 x 22	3 6	Special	83
1484	1. 3.1901	4 8½	0-6-0ST	IC	13 x 18	3 0	M	333
1513	2. 9.1901	4 8½	0-6-0ST	IC	12 x 18		L	203
1517	19.12.1900	4 8½	0-4-0ST	OC	12 x 18	3 0	H	79/80/83/84
1525	15. 4.1902	4 8½	0-6-0ST	IC	13 x 18	3 0	M	333
1557	5. 9.1902	4 8½	0-4-0ST	OC	12 x 18	3 0	H	99
1561	2. 6.1902	4 8½	0-6-0ST	IC	12 x 17	3 0	K	334
1566	24. 6.1902	4 8½	0-6-0ST	IC	13 x 18		M	153
1599	8.10.1903	4 8½	0-6-0ST	IC	12 x 18	3 0	L	328
1602	30. 4.1903	4 8½	0-6-0ST	OC	15 x 22	3 6	Special	138/272/275
1604	28. 8.1903	4 8½	0-6-0ST	IC	12 x 17	3 0	K	328
1658	30. 6.1905	4 8½	0-4-0ST	OC	12 x 18		H	80
1659	17. 7.1905	4 8½	0-4-0ST	OC	13½x 18		I alt	97
1664	25. 8.1905	4 8½	0-6-0ST	IC	13 x 18		M	97
1665	29. 8.1905	4 8½	0-6-0ST	IC	13 x 18	3 0	M	330
1669	30.10.1905	4 8½	0-6-0ST	IC	13 x 18	3 0	M	170/328
1691	10. 7.1907	4 8½	0-6-0ST	IC	12 x 18		L	104
1697	10. 9.1906	4 8½	0-4-0ST	OC	12 x 18		H	79/80/84/86/270
1813	7. 4.1913	4 8½	0-6-0T	IC	18 x 24	4 2	Special	119/263
1880	13. 4.1915	4 8½	0-4-0ST	OC	16 x 24	3 8	Special	200/201/221/276
1887	22. 9.1915	4 8½	0-4-0ST	OC	14 x 18	3 1	Special	220
1903	25. 7.1916	4 8½	0-4-0ST	OC	14 x 18	3 6	P alt	30
1911	25. 1.1917	4 8½	0-4-0ST	OC	14 x 18	3 1	Special	220
1934	29. 9.1917	4 8½	0-6-0ST	OC	17 x 24	3 9	–	119/180/263
1967	14.11.1918	4 8½	0-4-0ST	OC	16 x 24	3 8	–	187
2023	9. 4.1923	4 8½	0-4-0ST	OC	15 x 22	3 9	–	119/262
2025	28. 6.1923	4 8½	0-6-0ST	IC	12 x 18	3 0½	–	197
2035	19. 5.1924	4 8½	0-4-0ST	OC	15 x 22	3 9	–	120/263/267/294
2036	28. 5.1924	4 8½	0-4-0ST	OC	15 x 22	3 9	–	120/263/267

⨍ rebuilt as MW 966/1888 for T.A. Walker, contr.
ø 2' 3" wheels fitted in 1889; may have had 2' 6" wheels originally.

NBL - NORTH BRITISH LOCOMOTIVE CO LTD, Glasgow.

WORKS No.	DATE NEW TO CUSTOMER	GAUGE AS BUILT ft.ins.	TYPE	CYLS.(bore x stroke) ins.ins.	DRIVING WH.DIAM. ft.ins.	SEE PAGE
16628	2.1905	4 8½	0-6-0ST IC	18 x 26	4 3	43/281
21522	7. 5.1917	4 8½	0-4-0CT OC	12 x 22	3 6	68

Diesel locomotives

WORKS No.	DATE NEW TO CUSTOMER	GAUGE AS BUILT ft.ins.	TYPE	HORSE POWER	DRIVING WH.DIAM. ft.ins.	SEE PAGE
26249	1947	2 6	0-4-0DMF	100	2 0	308/314
26414	1947	2 6	0-4-0DMF	100	2 0	308/314
26687	1948	2 6	0-4-0DMF	100	2 0	308
26688	1948	2 6	0-4-0DMF	100	2 0	308
26689	1948	2 6	0-4-0DMF	100	2 0	308/314
26690	1948	2 6	0-4-0DMF	100	2 0	308/314
26691	1948	2 6	0-4-0DMF	100	2 0	308/314
26692	1948	2 6	0-4-0DMF	100	2 0	308/314
26693	1948	2 6	0-4-0DMF	100	2 0	308
26694	1948	2 6	0-4-0DMF	100	2 0	308
27410	20. 7.1956	4 8½	0-6-0DH	400	3 6	259/262/289/300
27414	7.1954⨍	4 8½	0-6-0DH	312	3 6	276
27588	1957	4 8½	0-6-0DH	440	3 6	301
27589	1957	4 8½	0-6-0DH	440	3 6	301
27592	6.11.1957	4 8½	0-6-0DH	440	3 6	272/276/295/301
27717	1957⨍	4 8½	0-6-0DH	520	3 9	272/295/301
27763	2. 3.1959	4 8½	0-6-0DH	440	3 9	264/268/295/301
27764	13. 3.1959	4 8½	0-6-0DH	440	3 9	264/268/295/301
27765	29. 4.1959	4 8½	0-6-0DH	440	3 9	264/268/295/301
27766	5.1959	4 8½	0-6-0DH	440	3 9	299

⨍ Demonstration locomotive

P - PECKETT & SONS LTD, Bristol

WORKS No.	DATE EX-WORKS	GAUGE AS BUILT ft.ins.	TYPE	CYLS.(bore x stroke) ins.ins.	DRIVING WH.DIAM. ft.ins.	MAKER'S CLASS	SEE PAGE
452	5. 3.1889	4 8½	0-4-0ST OC	10 x 14	2 9	M3	111
467	28. 2.1888	4 8½	0-4-0ST OC	14 x 20	3 2	W4	182/187
521	28. 7.1891	4 8½	0-4-0ST OC	14 x 20	3 2	W4	214
525	18.10.1892	4 8½	0-6-0ST OC	14 x 20	3 7	B1	92
560	1. 2.1893	4 8½	0-4-0ST OC	14 x 20	3 2	W4	92/93/271
583	13.12.1894	4 8½	0-4-0ST OC	14 x 20	3 2	W4	153
615	20. 5.1896	4 8½	0-4-0ST OC	14 x 20	3 3¼	W4	119/122/263
629	29. 4.1896	4 8½	0-6-0ST IC	16 x 22	3 10	X	37/82/85/271
634	24. 2.1897	4 8½	0-4-0ST OC	12 x 18	3 0½	R1	45/125
644	9.11.1896	4 8½	0-4-0ST OC	10 x 14	2 6½	M4	134
657	1. 4.1897	4 8½	0-4-0ST OC	14 x 20	3 2	W4	182/187
669	28. 7.1897	4 8½	0-4-0ST OC	14 x 20	3 2	W4	79/83/85/86/271
677	24. 8.1897	4 8½	0-4-0ST OC	12 x 18	3 0½	R1	141/200/271
703	25. 1.1899	4 8½	0-4-0ST OC	14 x 20	3 2	W4	87
773	13. 6.1899	4 8½	0-4-0ST OC	10 x 15	2 6½	M4	332
774	23. 2.1899	4 8½	0-6-0ST IC	16 x 22	3 10	X	162
806	28.12.1899	4 8½	0-4-0ST OC	14 x 20	3 7	B1	332
845	13. 9.1900	4 8½	0-4-0ST OC	14 x 20	3 2	W4	125
880	14. 5.1901	4 8½	0-4-0ST OC	14 x 20	3 2	W4	125
916	16.10.1901	4 8½	0-4-0ST OC	12 x 18	3 0½	R1	38/86/171
971	9. 9.1903	4 8½	0-4-0ST OC	14 x 20	3 2	W4	183
1040	28.12.1905	4 8½	0-6-0ST IC	16 x 22	3 10	X	156

1052	4. 9.1905	4 8½	0-6-0ST OC 14 x 20	3 7		B2		180
1058	30. 7.1906	4 8½	0-4-0ST OC 14 x 20	3 2		W4		125
1083	12. 2.1906	4 8½	0-6-0ST OC 15 x 21	3 7		F		180
1092	13. 7.1906	4 8½	0-6-0ST OC 14 x 20	3 7		B2		153/154
1099	21.10.1907	4 8½	0-4-0ST OC 12 x 18	3 0½		R1		165
1180	3. 5.1912∅	4 8½	0-4-0ST OC 15 x 21	3 7		E		57/275
1194	19. 2.1912	4 8½	0-4-0ST OC 14 x 20	3 2½		W5		199/271
1210	25. 8.1910	4 8½	0-4-0ST OC 12 x 18	3 0½		R2		217
1219	20. 6.1910	4 8½	0-6-0ST IC 16 x 22	3 10		X2		152/198
1310	6. 5.1914	4 8½	0-6-0ST OC 14 x 20	3 7		B2		109/267/295
1337	27.10.1913	4 8½	0-4-0ST OC 12 x 18	3 0½		R2		141/171/271
1392	12. 4.1915	4 8½	0-4-0ST OC 15 x 21	3 7		E		149
1403	28. 1.1916	4 8½	0-6-0ST OC 14 x 20	3 7		B2		179/258/268
1413	2.12.1915	4 8½	0-4-0ST OC 15 x 21	3 7		E		149
1423	10. 1.1916	4 8½	0-6-0ST IC 16 x 22	3 10		X2		198/271
1430	26. 7.1916	4 8½	0-4-0ST OC 12 x 18	3 0½		R2		58
1455	22. 7.1918	4 8½	0-6-0ST OC 14 x 20	3 7		B2		179/258/268
1460	15.12.1916	4 8½	0-4-0ST OC 12 x 18	3 0½		R2		135/177/208/258
1467	9. 7.1917	4 8½	0-4-0ST OC 14 x 20	3 2½		W5		151/272/276
1468	18. 7.1917	4 8½	0-4-0ST OC 14 x 20	3 2½		W5		111
1508	4. 9.1918	4 8½	0-4-0ST OC 14 x 20	3 2½		W5		96
1510	27. 2.1919	4 8½	0-4-0ST OC 14 x 20	3 2½		W5		176
1544	7.10.1919	4 8½	0-4-0ST OC 12 x 18	3 0½		R2		171
1589	29. 3.1928⟋	4 8½	0-4-0ST OC 15 x 21	3 7		E		164
1616	27. 4.1923	4 8½	0-6-0ST OC 14 x 20	3 7		B2		166
1637	10. 9.1923	4 8½	0-4-0ST OC 12 x 18	3 0½		R2		171
1648	29.11.1923	4 8½	0-4-0ST OC 12 x 18	3 0½		R2		172
1671	20. 8.1924	3 0	0-4-0T OC 8 x 12	2 3		"1287"		71
1748	7. 6.1928	4 8½	0-4-0ST OC 14 x 22	3 2½		W6		162/283/291
1761	17. 4.1929	4 8½	0-4-0ST OC 14 x 22	3 2½		W6		164
1952	18. 7.1938	4 8½	0-6-0ST OC 16 x 24	3 10		OX2		166
1953	7. 9.1938	4 8½	0-6-0ST OC 16 x 24	3 10		OX2		166
1954	19.10.1938	4 8½	0-6-0ST OC 16 x 24	3 10		OX2		166
1955	15.12.1938	4 8½	0-6-0ST OC 16 x 24	3 10		OX2		166
2016	15.10.1941	4 8½	0-4-0ST OC 14 x 22	3 2½		W7		144/178
2032	12.11.1942	4 8½	0-4-0ST OC 14 x 22	3 2½		W7		194
2042	29. 3.1943	4 8½	0-4-0ST OC 14 x 22	3 2½		W7		144/178
2046	6. 9.1943	4 8½	0-4-0ST OC 12 x 20	3 0½		R4		137
2047	21. 9.1943	4 8½	0-4-0ST OC 12 x 20	3 0½		R4		137
2048	14. 2.1944	4 8½	0-4-0ST OC 12 x 20	3 0½		R4		136/137
2049	28. 8.1944	4 8½	0-4-0ST OC 12 x 20	3 0½		R4		87/137
2093	22. 9.1947	4 8½	0-4-0ST OC 14 x 22	3 2½		W7		283/291
2142	1953	4 8½	0-4-0ST OC 14 x 22	3 2½		Spl W7		145

∅ Peckett records suggest this loco was built in 1909.
⟋ Peckett records suggest this loco was built in 1922.

RH - RUSTON & HORNSBY LTD, Lincoln.

WORKS No.	DATE EX-WORKS	GAUGE AS BUILT ft.ins.	TYPE	HORSE POWER	DRIVING WH.DIAM. ft.ins.	MAKER'S CLASS		SEE PAGE
166012	11.1932	2 0	4wDM	16		16	HP	91
175121	5.1935	2 0	4wDM	21		18/21	HP	201
175399	10.1935	2 0	4wDM	21		18/21	HP	201
175420	3.1936	2 4	4wDM	21		18/21	HP	88/203/205
177535	3.1936	2 0	4wDM	42		36/42	HP	184/260
177640	7.1936	2 0	4wDM	10		10	HP	91
186322	8.1937	2 0	4wDM	20	1 3	16/20	HP	89
186342	8.1937	2 0	4wDM	20	1 3	16/20	HP	89
187059	10.1937	2 0	4wDM	40	1 8¼	33/40	HP	103/184/260
187071	11.1937	4 8½	4wDM	48	2 6	44/48	HP	144

189959	3.1938	2 0	4wDM	40	1 8¾	33/40	HP	103/184/260
189963	3.1939	2 0	4wDM	40	1 8¾	33/40	HP	103/184/260/340
198245	7.1939	2 6	4wDM	48	2 6	44/48	HP	91
198325	12.1940	4 8½	4wDM	88	3 0	80/88	HP	145/221
207102	3.1941	4 8½	4wDM	48	2 6	44/48	HP	164
210479	12.1942	4 8½	4wDM	88	3 0	80/88	HP	98
211614	6.1941	2 0	4wDM	20	1 4/	20DL		269/297
211641	1.1942	2 0	4wDM	20	1 4/	20DL		135
211683	10.1941	2 0	4wDM	20	1 4/	20DL		194
213836	7.1942	2 0	4wDM	20	1 4/	20DL		163
217986	12.1942	2 0	4wDM	20	1 4/	20DL		269/297
221642	3.1944	4 8½	4wDM	48	2 6	48DS		58
223690	1.1944	2 0	4wDM	20	1 4/	20DL		269/297
223716	1.1944	2 0	4wDM	20	1 4/	20DL		94
223747	4.1944	2 0	4wDM	20	1 4/	20DL		266/269
224352	3.1945	4 8½	4wDM	88	3 0	88DS		136
226268	6.1944	2 0	4wDM	20	1 4/	20DL		111
226278	7.1944	2 0	4wDM	20	1 4/	20DL		135
235512	8.1945	4 8½	4wDM	48	2 6	48DS		145
236362	4.1946	4 8½	4wDM	88	3 0	88DS		74/79
242469	4.1947	2 2	4wDMF	44	1 6	48DLZ		308
242914	7.1946	2 6	4wDM	48	1 6	48DL		91
243081	2.1948	4 8½	0-4-0DM	165	3 2½	165DS		164/306
247174	6.1947	2 0	4wDM	13	1 4	13DL		74
249535	1.1948	2 2	4wDMF	44	1 6	48DLZ		308
249536	1.1948	2 2	4wDMF	44	1 6	48DLZ		308
256295	9.1948	2 2	4wDMF	44	1 6	48DLZ		308/340
256297	9.1948	2 2	4wDMF	44	1 6	48DLZ		308
256299	11.1948	2 2	4wDMF	44	1 6	48DLZ		308
256314	1.1949	2 2	4wDMF	44	1 6	48DLZ		293/303/308
256323	1.1949	2 2	4wDMF	44	1 6	48DLZ		293/303/308
262996	1.1949	4 8½	4wDM	88	3 0	88DS		74
265615	8.1948	4 8½	4wDM	48	2 6	48DS		30
268866	12.1949	2 0	4wDM	44	1 6	48DLZ		304
268871	7.1951	2 2	4wDMF	44	1 6	48DLZ		308
268872	9.1952	2 2	4wDMF	44	1 6	48DLZ		308
268873	11.1952	2 0	4wDMF	44	1 6	48DLZ		286/293/297/304
268874	12.1952	2 0	4wDMF	44	1 6	48DLZ		286/293
268877	4.1955	2 2	4wDMF	44	1 6	48DLZ		308
268879	4.1957	2 2	4wDMF	44	1 6	48DLZ		309
275881	6.1949	4 8½	4wDM	88	3 0	88DS		173
279593	9.1949	4 8½	4wDM	44	2 6	48DS		144
280865	6.1949	2 0	4wDM	20	1 4/	20DLU		110
280866	6.1949	2 0	4wDM	20	1 4/	20DLU		110
281270	2.1951	4 8½	0-4-0DM	165	3 2½	165DS		44/104
287662	6.1950	2 0	4wDM	40	1 8¾	40DL		184/260
294263	3.1950	4 8½	4wDM	48	2 6	48DS		165/166
304471	4.1951	4 8½	0-4-0DM	165	3 2½	165DS		164
304472	4.1951	4 8½	0-4-0DM	165	3 2½	165DS		104/204
305302	8.1951	4 8½	4wDM	48	2 6	48DS		173
305303	12.1951	4 8½	4wDM	48	2 6	48DS		177
305320	2.1951	4 8½	4wDM	88	3 0	88DS		145
305323	6.1951	4 8½	4wDM	88	3 0	88DS		93/110
306087	12.1949	4 8½	4wDM	88	3 0	88DS		74
312427	8.1951	4 8½	4wDM	88	3 0	88DS		144
312987	6.1952	4 8½	0-4-0DE	155	3 2½	165DE		300
312988	9.1952	4 8½	0-4-0DE	155	3 2½	165DE		217
313391	6.1952	4 8½	0-4-0DM	165	3 2½	165DS		306
319288	2.1953	4 8½	0-4-0DM	165	3 2½	165DS		104/204
319295	12.1953	4 8½	0-4-0DM	165	3 2½	165DS		306
323600	3.1953	4 8½	0-4-0DE	155	3 2½	165DE		166
326062	11.1952	4 8½	4wDM	88	3 0	88DS		104
326071	9.1954	4 8½	4wDM	88	3 0	88DS		74/104
327966	3.1954	4 8½	0-4-0DM	165	3 2½	165DS		195
327969	8.1954	4 8½	0-4-0DM	165	3 2½	165DS		58/164

338424	2.1955	4	8½	4wDM	88	3	0	88DS	46
338425	5.1955	2	0	0-4-0DM	75	1	7	LHT	269/297/304
338426	6.1955	2	0	0-4-0DM	75	1	7	LHT	269/297
349087	10.1954	4	8½	0-4-0DE	155	3	2½	165DE	166
371541	3.1954	2	0	4wDM	20	1	4⟋	LAU	261/266/293/304
371551	6.1954	2	0	4wDM	20	1	4⟋	LAU	261/266/293/304
375360	1.1955	1	8	4wDM	20	1	4⟋	LAT	58
375696	7.1954	2	0	4wDM	20	1	4⟋	LBT	163
375717	5.1955	4	8½	0-4-0DM	165	3	2½	165DS	136
381751	2.1955	4	8½	0-4-0DE	155	3	2½	165DE	55/166
381752	2.1955	4	8½	0-4-0DE	155	3	2½	165DE	166
381753	6.1955	4	8½	0-4-0DE	155	3	2½	165DE	166
381755	8.1955	4	8½	0-4-0DE	155	3	2½	165DE	166
381757	9.1955	4	8½	0-4-0DE	155	3	2½	165DE	50/189
384141	11.1955	4	8½	0-4-0DE	155	3	2½	165DE	299
392154	5.1956	2	0	0-4-0DMF	75	1	7	LHG	273/297/315
392156	6.1956	2	0	0-4-0DMF	75	1	7	LHG	315
392157	7.1956	2	0	0-4-0DMF	75	1	7	LHG	269/297/315
392160	12.1956	2	0	0-4-0DMF	75	1	7	LHG	315
393979	5.1956	2	0	0-4-0DM	75	1	7	LHT	269/297/304
395294	4.1956	4	8½	0-4-0DE	155	3	2½	165DE	164
395303	9.1956	4	8½	0-6-0DM	165	3	2½	165DS	272/296
398070	3.1957	1	10	4wDMF	48	2	6	48DLG	293/304
402428	2.1956	1	8	4wDM	20	1	4⟋	LAT	58
408296	1.1957	4	8½	0-6-0DM	165	3	2½	165DS	272/296/301
408309	4.1957	4	8½	0-4-0DE	155	3	2½	165DE	50/189
412707	4.1957	4	8½	0-4-0DE	155	3	2½	165DE	55
412714	7.1957	4	8½	0-4-0DE	155	3	2½	165DE	55
416210	10.1957	4	8½	0-4-0DE	155	3	2½	165DE	164
418805	7.1958	2	3½	4wDMF	48	1	6	48DLG	314/315
420141	4.1958	4	8½	0-6-0DE	155	3	2½	165DE	300
421417	4.1958	4	8½	4wDM	88	3	0	88DS	217
421438	5.1958	4	8½	0-6-0DE	155	3	2½	165DE	299
421440	6.1958	4	8½	0-6-0DE	155	3	2½	165DE	300
425474	12.1958	4	8½	0-6-0DE	155	3	2½	165DE	300
425485	12.1958	4	8½	4wDM	88	3	0	88DS	46
432477	1.1959	4	8½	4wDM	88	3	0	88DS	46
432480	3.1959	4	8½	4wDM	88	3	0	88DS	221
443644	2.1961	4	8½	4wDM	48	2	6	48DS	164
463152	5.1961	4	8½	4wDM	88	3	0	88DS	46
476124	10.1962	1	8	4wDM	31½	1	4⟋	LBT	58
476140	6.1963	4	8½	4wDM	88	3	0	88DS	45/145/338

⟋ Driving wheel diameter 1' 4$\frac{5}{16}$".

RS — ROBERT STEPHENSON & CO LTD

This firm was founded in June 1823 with Robert Stephenson, the son of George Stephenson, as managing partner. At first its works was at South Street, Newcastle-upon-Tyne, but this was soon extended to Forth Banks. The company's reputation was always firmly based as a manufacturer of main line stock, and the majority of its products in industrial service were ordered new by the chief colliery railways or obtained second-hand from the North Eastern Railway. In 1901 the firm removed from Newcastle to a large new works at Darlington, and thereafter industrial orders were few. The firm also operated a shipyard at Hebburn-on-Tyne, Co. Durham, which it disposed of in 1912.

In May 1937 the company purchased the locomotive business of R. & W. Hawthorn, Leslie & Co Ltd (q.v.), and in the following month changed its title to Robert Stephenson & Hawthorns Ltd (q.v.). The firm had built 4155 locomotives.

N.B. Considerable dispute surrounds the authenticity of early works numbers.

WORKS No.	DATE NEW TO CUSTOMER	GAUGE AS BUILT ft.ins.	TYPE	CYLS.(bore x stroke) ins.ins.	DRIVING WH.DIAM. ft.ins.	SEE PAGE
1	12. 4.1826/	4 8½	0-4-0	VC 10 x 24	4 0	42/173
2	26. 4.1826/	4 8½	0-4-0	VC 10 x 24	4 0	42/173
3	9.1825	4 8½	0-4-0	VC 10 x 24	4 0	154/338
6	1826	4 8½	0-4-0	VC 10 x 24	4 0	192
15	1829	4 8½	0-6-0	OC 11 x 15	5 0	36
491	1846	4 8½	2-4-0	IC 14 x 22	5 8	119/259/262/289
624	1848	4 8½	0-6-0	IC 18 x 24	5 0	192/264
625	1848	4 8½	0-6-0	IC 18 x 24	5 0	192/264
753	1849	4 8½	0-4-0	OC 14 x 22	4 5	132/329
795	4. 7.1851	4 8½	0-4-0	OC 14 x 22	4 4½	42
816	5.12.1851	4 8½	0-4-0	OC 14 x 22	5 0¾	42
1073	1856	4 8½	0-6-0	IC 16¾x 24	4 6	132
1074	11. 9.1856	4 8½	0-6-0	IC 16 x 24	4 7½	42
1075	1856	4 8½	0-6-0	IC 15½x 22	5 0	132
1085	1857	4 8½	2-4-0T	OC		63
1096	1856	4 8½	0-6-0	IC 15½x 22	5 0	132
1100	1857	4 8½	2-4-0	IC 15 x 24	4 7½	107/121
1206	1860	4 8½	4-4-0	OC 16 x 22	5 0	132
1217	11.1859	4 8½	0-6-0	IC 16¾x 24	4 6	132
1313	17. 8.1860	4 8½	0-6-0	IC 16 x 24	4 6	43
1326	18. 5.1860	4 8½	0-6-0	IC 16¾x 24	4 6	132
1327	9.11.1860	4 8½	0-6-0	IC 16¾x 24	4 6	132
1416	2. 4.1862	4 8½	0-6-0	IC 16¾x 24	5 0	132
1417	4. 4.1862	4 8½	0-6-0	IC 16¾x 24	5 0	132
1516	13. 5.1864	4 8½	0-6-0	IC 16 x 24	4 6	42
1611	1. 9.1864	4 8½	0-6-0	IC 16 x 24	4 6	43
1612	10. 6.1864	4 8½	0-6-0ST	IC 13 x 18	3 6	43
1619	1865	4 8½	0-4-0T	9 x 16	2 9	149
1649	1865	4 8½	0-6-0	IC 13 x 18	3 6	107/121
1800	21. 7.1866	4 8½	0-6-0ST	IC 14 x 22	3 7	43
1801	1866	4 8½	0-4-0T	9 x 16	2 9	149
1913	1869	4 8½	0-6-0	17 x 24	4 7	192
1919	1869	4 8½	0-6-0ST	IC 14 x 20	3 3	107/119/121/123/275
1973	1870	4 8½	0-6-0	IC 17 x 24	5 0	101
2013	1872	4 8½	0-6-0ST	IC 14 x 20	3 7	123
2014	1872	4 8½	0-6-0ST	IC 14 x 20	3 7	123/275
2017	1873	4 8½	0-4-0ST	OC 13 x 18	3 6	111
2056	1872	4 8½	0-6-0	IC 17 x 24	5 0	101
2124	1873	4 8½	0-4-0ST	OC 9 x 18	2 9	111
2139	1873	4 8½	0-6-0ST	IC 14¾x 22	4 0	162
2160	1874	4 8½	0-6-0	IC 17 x 24	5 0	101
2238	1875	4 8½	0-6-0ST	IC 14¾x 22	4 0	180
2239	1875	4 8½	0-6-0ST	IC 14¾x 22	4 0	162
2240	1875	4 8½	0-6-0ST	IC 14¾x 22	4 0	162
2241	1875	4 8½	0-6-0ST	IC 14¾x 22	4 0	180
2244	1875	4 8½	0-6-0ST	IC 14¾x 22	4 0	162
2260	1876	4 8½	0-6-0	IC 17 x 24	4 6	119/262
2308	1876	4 8½	0-4-0ST	OC 15 x 20	3 8	119/262
2325	1894	4 8½	0-4-0ST	OC 13 x 18	3 6½	151/152/156/276
2326	1888	4 8½	0-4-0ST	OC 13 x 18	3 6½	150
2381	1880	4 8½	0-6-0ST	OC 15 x 18	3 6	111
2554	1885	4 8½	0-6-0ST	OC 13 x 18	3 6	111
2587	1884	4 8½	0-6-0	IC 17 x 26	5 1	101
2620	1887	4 8½	0-6-0ST	IC 14 x 20	3 7	169
2629	1887	4 8½	0-6-0ST	IC 15 x 22		101
2637	1888	4 8½	0-4-0ST	OC 13 x 18	3 6	111
2654	1888	4 8½	0-4-0ST	OC 12 x 19	3 4	65
2655	1888	4 8½	0-4-0ST	OC 12 x 19	3 4	65
2668	1889	4 8½	0-4-0ST	OC 13 x 18	3 6	111
2724	1890	4 8½	0-4-0ST	OC 12 x 19	3 4	65/193
2725	19. 7.1890	4 8½	0-4-0ST	OC 12 x 19	3 4	66/73/275
2730	1891	4 8½	0-6-0T	IC 17 x 24	4 0	123/275/284/291/340

2811	1893	4 8½	0-4-OST	OC reb.of BH 328		65
2821	1895	4 8½	0-6-OST	IC reb.of P.& J.Rly No.9		43
2822	1895	4 8½	0-6-0T	IC 17 x 24	4 0	123/275/284
2840	1896	4 8½	0-4-OST	OC 15 x 20	3 4	167
2847	1896	4 8½	0-6-OST	IC 15 x 20	3 7	169/280
2852	1897	4 8½	0-4-OST	OC 12 x 19	3 4½	66
2853	22. 8.1897	4 8½	0-4-OVBCr	OC 13½x 21½	3 0	69
2854	6. 2.1898	4 8½	0-4-OVBCr	OC 13½x 21½	3 0	48/69
2875	1897	4 8½	0-4-OST	OC 12 x 19	3 4	156
2879	1900	4 8½	0-6-OST	IC 15 x 20	3 7	169/280
2902	1898	4 8½	0-6-OST	IC reb.of RS 1516		42
2915	1899	4 8½	0-6-OPT	IC reb.of K 2510		63/282/290
2987	1900	4 8½	0-4-OST	OC reb.of B 303		168/280
2993	1901	4 8½	0-6-OST	IC 15 x 20	3 7	123
3057	1904	4 8½	0-4-OST	OC 14 x 20	3 3	162/176/187
3072	1901	4 8½	0-6-OST	OC 16 x 24	4 0	166
3075	1901	4 8½	0-4-OST	OC 12 x 18	3 1	34/79/167/267/270/287
3376	1909	4 8½	0-4-OST	OC 15 x 22	3 6	167/280
3377	1909	4 8½	0-6-2T	IC 18½x 26	4 6	119/259/262/289/344
3378	1909	4 8½	0-6-2T	IC 18½x 26	4 6	119/259/262/289
3801	1920	4 8½	0-6-2T	IC 18½x 26	4 6	119/259/263/289
4112	1935	4 8½	0-6-OST	OC 16 x 24	3 10	133/264
4113	1937	4 8½	0-6-OST	OC 16 x 24	3 10	200/272/276/295

∤ date ex-works

RSH - <u>ROBERT STEPHENSON & HAWTHORNS LTD</u>
    This company was formed in June 1937 after the purchase during the
previous month by Robert Stephenson & Co Ltd of the locomotive business of
R. & W. Hawthorn, Leslie & Co Ltd, which gave the firm works at both
Darlington and Newcastle-upon-Tyne.

    In 1938 the company took over the goodwill of Kitson & Co Ltd of Leeds,
and through them, of Manning, Wardle & Co Ltd, also of Leeds. In 1944 the
company became a subsidiary of Vulcan Foundry Ltd of Newton-le-Willows,
Lancashire, itself a subsidiary of the English Electric Co Ltd. In general the
firm concentrated on a standard range of products based on Hawthorn Leslie
designs. At first much of the locomotive building was done at Darlington,
while the Newcastle Works handled repair work; but in later years Newcastle
concentrated on steam locomotive work, while the Darlington Works handled
mainly diesel and battery-electric locomotives sub-contracted from English
Electric. The Newcastle Works closed in 1961, and in 1962 the parent company
took over full control of the Darlington Works, which closed in March 1964,
marking the end of industrial locomotive building in North-East England.

    The 4155 locomotives built by Robert Stephenson & Co Ltd were added
to the 2983 locomotives built by R. & W. Hawthorn, Leslie & Co Ltd and their
predecessors, R. & W. Hawthorn & Co, making the first RSH locomotive Works No.
6939. Full information about the locomotives built by the companies vested
in the English Electric group is not at present available.

WORKS No.	DATE EX-WORKS	GAUGE AS BUILT ft.ins.	TYPE	CYLS.(bore x stroke) ins.ins.	DRIVING WH.DIAM. ft.ins.	SEE PAGE
6939	29.12.1937	4 8½	0-4-OST	OC 12 x 20	3 1	193
6940	27. 1.1938	4 8½	0-4-OST	OC 12 x 20	3 1	143/276/284
6943	24. 4.1938	4 8½	0-6-OST	OC 16 x 24	3 8	108/281/291
6945	14.10.1938	4 8½	0-4-OST	OC 14 x 22	3 6	216/258
6963	28. 8.1939	4 8½	0-4-OST	OC 12 x 20	3 1	193
7006	28. 6.1940	4 8½	0-4-OCT	OC 12 x 15	2 10	87/342
7007	10. 7.1940	4 8½	0-4-OCT	OC 12 x 15	2 10	87/341
7011	19. 9.1940	4 8½	0-4-OST	OC 16 x 24	3 8	67
7013	1. 2.1941	4 8½	0-4-OST	OC 14 x 22	3 6	49/76
7016	24.12.1940	4 8½	0-4-OST	OC 16 x 24	3 8	67/181
7022	23. 3.1941	4 8½	0-4-OST	OC 16 x 24	3 8	67
7027	6. 3.1941	4 8½	0-6-OPT	IC 18 x 26	4 2⅞	63
7028	24. 3.1941	4 8½	0-6-OPT	IC 18 x 26	4 2⅞	63

7029	20. 6.1941	4 8½	0-6-0PT	IC	18 x 26	4 2⅜	64
7036	1940	4 8½	0-4-0ST	OC	16 x 24	3 8	181
7043	30. 1.1942	4 8½	0-4-0ST	OC	12 x 20	3 1	172/173/271
7045	20. 3.1942	4 8½	0-4-0ST	OC	16 x 24	3 8	187
7046	27.10.1941	4 8½	0-4-0ST	OC	14 x 22	3 6	178
7063	29.10.1942	4 8½	0-4-0ST	OC	14 x 22	3 6	55/344
7066	30. 9.1942	4 8½	0-4-0ST	OC	12 x 20	3 1	54
7068	4. 2.1943	4 8½	0-4-0ST	OC	16 x 24	3 8	140
7069	23.10.1942	4 8½	0-4-0CT	OC	12 x 15	2 10	87/343
7070	30.10.1942	4 8½	0-4-0CT	OC	12 x 15	2 10	87/342
7073	1943	4 8½	0-4-0ST	OC	16 x 24	3 8	76
7097	1943	4 8½	0-6-0ST	IC	18 x 26	4 3	300
7098	1943	4 8½	0-6-0ST	IC	18 x 26	4 3	300
7101	1943	4 8½	0-6-0ST	IC	18 x 26	4 3	259/263/271/276/289
7117	1943	4 8½	0-4-0ST	OC	16 x 24	3 8	140
7126	1943	4 8½	0-4-0CT	OC	12 x 15	2 10	104
7132	1944	4 8½	0-6-0ST	IC	18 x 26	4 3	258/290
7138	1944	4 8½	0-6-0ST	OC	16 x 24	3 8	166
7146	1944	4 8½	0-6-0ST	IC	18 x 26	4 3	267/271/294/301
7159	1945	4 8½	0-4-0ST	OC	12 x 20	3 1	172/173/271
7160	1945	4 8½	0-4-0ST	OC	16 x 24	3 8	76
7165	1944	4 8½	0-6-0ST	IC	18 x 26	4 3	112
7169	1944	4 8½	0-6-0ST	IC	18 x 26	4 3	112/343
7212	1945	4 8½	0-6-0ST	OC	16 x 24	3 8	166
7294	1945	4 8½	0-6-0ST	IC	18 x 26	4 3	258/290/300
7297	1945	4 8½	0-4-0ST	OC	14 x 22	3 6	30
7304	1946	4 8½	0-6-0T	IC	18 x 26	4 6	216/258/290
7305	1946	4 8½	0-6-0T	IC	18 x 26	4 6	109/267/294
7307	5. 7.1946	4 8½	0-4-0ST	OC	14 x 22	3 6	216/258
7308	1946	4 8½	0-4-0ST	OC	12 x 20	3 1	104
7339	8.10.1947	4 8½	0-6-0ST	OC	16 x 24	3 8	258/289
7340	1946	4 8½	0-4-0ST	OC	16 x 24	3 8	181
7342	1947	4 8½	0-4-0ST	OC	16 x 24	3 8	181
7345	1947	4 8½	0-4-0ST	OC	16 x 24	3 8	181
7346	1947	4 8½	0-4-0ST	OC	16 x 24	3 8	181
7347	1947	4 8½	0-4-0ST	OC	16 x 24	3 8	181
7359	1947	4 8½	0-4-0ST	OC	14 x 22	3 6	55
7409	1948	4 8½	0-4-0ST	OC	12 x 20	3 1	145/341
7412	18. 8.1948	4 8½	0-6-0ST	OC	16 x 24	3 8	284/305
7414	9.1948	4 8½	0-4-0ST	OC	14 x 22	3 6	258
7535	4. 4.1949	4 8½	0-4-0ST	OC	14 x 22	3 6	258
7538	1949	4 8½	0-4-0ST	OC	16 x 24	3 8	284/290
7539	22. 4.1949	4 8½	0-4-0ST	OC	16 x 24	3 8	271
7545	6.1949	4 8½	0-6-0ST	OC	16 x 24	3 8	284/291
7546	6.1949	4 8½	0-6-0ST	OC	16 x 24	3 8	284/291
7599	8.1949	4 8½	0-6-0ST	OC	16 x 24	3 8	258/259/262/289/296
7600	24. 8.1949	4 8½	0-6-0ST	OC	16 x 24	3 8	259/264/289
7603	13.12.1949	4 8½	0-6-0ST	OC	18 x 24	4 0	258/289
7604	1.11.1949	4 8½	0-4-0ST	OC	16 x 24	3 8	284/291
7605	1949	4 8½	0-4-0ST	OC	16 x 24	3 8	276/284/291
7641	1949	4 8½	0-6-0ST	OC	16 x 24	3 8	284/291
7660	1950	4 8½	0-4-0ST	OC	16 x 24	3 8	76
7662	19. 4.1950	4 8½	0-4-0ST	OC	16 x 24	3 8	272/276/295
7674	1951	4 8½	0-4-0ST	OC	16 x 24	3 8	170
7675	1951	4 8½	0-4-0ST	OC	16 x 24	3 8	197
7679	1951	4 8½	0-4-0ST	OC	14 x 22	3 6	55
7687	1951	4 8½	0-6-0ST	OC	18 x 24	4 0	259/262/289
7688	1951	4 8½	0-6-0ST	OC	18 x 24	4 0	259/262/289
7689	1951	4 8½	0-6-0ST	OC	18 x 24	4 0	259/290
7690	1951	4 8½	0-6-0ST	OC	18 x 24	4 0	259/289
7691	1952	4 8½	0-6-0ST	OC	18 x 24	4 0	259/262/289
7692	1953	4 8½	0-4-0WE		80 h.p.	2 9	286/306
7695	20.12.1951	4 8½	0-6-0ST	OC	18 x 24	4 0	258/289
7743	1953	4 8½	0-4-0ST	OC	14 x 22	3 6	55
7744	1953	4 8½	0-4-0ST	OC	14 x 22	3 6	55

7749	17.12.1952	4 8½	0-6-0ST	OC	18 x 24	4 0	258/289
7751	23. 7.1953	4 8½	0-6-0ST	IC	18 x 26	4 3	284/290
7755	4.1953	4 8½	0-4-0ST	OC	15 x 22	3 8	259/263/268/289/294
7756	4.1953	4 8½	0-4-0ST	OC	15 x 22	3 8	259/263/268/295
7757	4.1953	4 8½	0-4-0ST	OC	15 x 22	3 8	259/263/290
7760	1953	4 8½	0-6-0ST	OC	18 x 24	4 0	300/344
7763	1954	4 8½	0-6-0ST	OC	18 x 24	4 0	341
7796	1954	4 8½	0-4-0ST	OC	14 x 22	3 6	55/341
7798	1954	4 8½	0-4-0ST	OC	14 x 22	3 6	55
7799	10. 9.1954	4 8½	0-4-0ST	OC	14 x 22	3 6	272/276/305
7804	1954	4 8½	0-4-0WE		80 h.p.	2 9	286/306
7807	19.10.1954	4 8½	0-4-0ST	OC	14 x 22	3 6	258/289
7811	1.11.1954	4 8½	0-6-0ST	OC	18 x 24	4 0	258/289
7819	1954	4 8½	0-4-0ST	OC	16 x 24	3 8	194
7869	1956	4 8½	0-4-0DM				145/197
7882	4.11.1957	4 8½	0-4-0WE		80 h.p.	2 9	286/306
7886	1958	4 8½	0-4-0WE		80 h.p.	2 9	286/306
7899	1958	4 8½	0-4-0DM				145
7944	1957	4 8½	0-6-0ST	OC	18 x 24	4 0	299
8093	15.10.1959	4 8½	0-4-0WE		80 h.p.	2 9	286/306

RWH - **R. & W. HAWTHORN LTD**, Newcastle-upon-Tyne
This firm was founded in 1817 at Forth Banks, Newcastle, and soon entered locomotive building as the railway age developed, though they continued to produce other types of steam engine. Like their near-neighbours, Robert Stephenson & Co, they concentrated on main line locomotives. In 1886 the firm amalgamated with Andrew Leslie & Co Ltd, shipbuilders, of Hebburn-on-Tyne, Co. Durham, to form R. & W. Hawthorn, Leslie & Co Ltd (q.v.).

Complete details of all the company's products are not known.

WORKS No.	DATE BUILT	GAUGE AS BUILT ft.ins.	TYPE		CYLS.(bore x stroke) ins.ins.	DRIVING WH.DIAM. ft.ins.	SEE PAGE
297	1839	4 8½	0-6-0		14 x 18	4 0	220
308	1839	4 8½	0-6-0		14 x 18	4 0	118/220
476	1846	4 8½	0-6-0	IC	15 x 24/	4 3	42
479	1846	4 8½	0-6-0	IC	15 x 24/	4 3	132
1019	1857	4 8½	0-4-0ST	OC	13 x 19	4 0	138
1422	1867	4 8½	0-6-0ST	IC	15 x 22	3 9	43/107/119/121/263
1430	1868	4 8½	0-6-0ST	IC	15 x 22	3 6	107/119/121/124/263/281
1478	1870	4 8½	0-6-0ST	IC	15 x 22	4 6	107/119/121/123/124/275
1554	1872	4 8½	0-6-0	OC	16 x 24	4 6	214
1564	1873	4 8½	0-6-0	IC	17 x 24	5 0	101
1622	1874	4 8½	0-6-0ST	OC	16 x 24	4 6(?)	138/214/267
1635	1873	4 8½	0-4-0ST	OC	13 x 19	3 6	138
1645	1875	4 8½	0-6-0ST	IC	16 x 24	5 0½	112/287
1657	1875	4 8½	0-6-0ST	IC	15 x 22	4 0	162
1662	1875	4 8½	0-6-0ST	IC	15 x 22	4 0	162
1666	1875	4 8½	0-6-0ST	IC	15 x 22	4 0	162
1669	1875	4 8½	0-6-0ST	IC	15 x 22	4 0	162
1726	1875	4 8½	0-4-0ST	OC	11 x 18	3 0	197
1789	1879	4 8½	0-4-0ST	OC	10 x 15		97
1817	1880	4 8½	0-4-0ST	OC	11 x 18	3 0	197
1821	1880	4 8½	0-4-0ST	OC	15 x 20	3 6	201
1847	1881	4 8½	0-4-0ST	OC	12 x 18	3 0½	56/179
1877	1880	4 8½	0-4-0CT/WT	OC			149
1882	1882	4 8½	0-6-0ST	OC	12 x 18	3 0	200/276
1969	1883	4 8½	0-6-0ST	IC	16 x 24	4 6	106/119/121
1986	1884	4 8½	0-6-0ST	OC	15 x 20	3 6	42
2026	1885	4 8½	0-4-0ST	OC	10 x 15	2 9	149
2029	1885	4 8½	0-4-0ST	OC	12 x 18	3 0	164

/ another version gives 14" x 21".

S - SENTINEL (SHREWSBURY) LTD, Shrewsbury, Shropshire.
(form. Sentinel Wagon Works (1936) Ltd; orig. Sentinel Wagon Works Ltd)

N.B. CH indicates built at Chester Works (letters on works plate)

WORKS No.	DATE EX-WORKS	GAUGE AS BUILT ft.ins.	TYPE	CYLS.(b.x s.) or HORSEPOWER ins.ins.	DRIVING WH.DIAM. ft.ins.	NOTES	SEE PAGE
5988CH	1925	4 8½	4wVBT HC			reb.of LE 230	219
6076	4.1925	4 8½	4wVBT VCG	6¾ x 9	2 6		126/203
6218CH	5.1925	4 8½	4wVBT VCG			reb.of HC 683	219
6310CH	1926	4 8½	4wVBT VCG				218
6770CH	1926	2 0	4wVBT VCG				218
6902	1927	2 0	4wVBT VCG	6¾ x 9	1 8		89
6936	1927	4 8½	4wVBT VCG	6¾ x 9	2 6		162
7062	1927	4 8½	4wVBT VCG	6¾ x 9	2 6		184
7669	1928	4 8½	4wVBT VCG	6¾ x 9	2 6		193
7852	3.1929	4 8½	4wVBT VCG	6¾ x 9	2 6		93
9558	1953	4 8½	4wVBT VCG	100 h.p.	2 6		29/30/55
9563	5.1954	4 8½	4wVBT VCG	100 h.p.	2 6		183
9575	1954	4 8½	4wVBT VCG	200 h.p.	3 2		180
9581	2. 3.1955	4 8½	4wVBT VCG	200 h.p.	3 2		284
9583	24. 3.1955	4 8½	4wVBT VCG	200 h.p.	3 2		284
9584	31. 3.1955	4 8½	4wVBT VCG	200 h.p.	3 2		284
9597	9.11.1955	4 8½	4wVBT VCG	100 h.p.	2 6		55
9618	24. 1.1957	4 8½	4wVBT VCG	200 h.p.	3 2		180
9619	1957	4 8½	4wVBT VCG	200 h.p.	3 2		180

Diesel locomotives

WORKS No.	DATE EX-WORKS	GAUGE AS BUILT ft.ins.	TYPE	HORSE POWER	DRIVING WH.DIAM. ft.ins.	SEE PAGE
10003	11. 6.1959	4 8½	4wDH	200	3 2	55
10018	29. 1.1960	4 8½	4wDH	200	3 2	50
10025	3. 3.1960	4 8½	4wDH	200	3 2	50
10031	15. 3.1960	4 8½	4wDH	200	3 2	171
10077	12. 7.1961	4 8½	4wDH	200	3 2	171
10157	23. 3.1963	4 8½	0-6-0DH	325	3 6	284/291/300
10158	19. 4.1963	4 8½	0-6-0DH	325	3 6	284/291/300

RR - ROLLS ROYCE LTD, Shrewsbury, Shropshire.
(prev. Sentinel (Shrewsbury) Ltd).

WORKS No.	DATE EX-WORKS	GAUGE AS BUILT ft.ins.	TYPE	HORSE POWER	DRIVING WH.DIAM. ft.ins.	SEE PAGE
10201	30.11.1964	4 8½	0-4-0DH	325	3 6	301
10278	14. 3.1968	4 8½	0-6-0DH	375	3 6	48
10285	4. 7.1969	4 8½	0-6-0DH	375	3 6	48
10286	16. 7.1969	4 8½	0-6-0DH	375	3 6	48
10287	24. 7.1969	4 8½	0-6-0DH	375	3 6	48
10288	31. 8.1969	4 8½	0-6-0DH	375	3 6	48
10289	7. 9.1970	4 8½	0-6-0DH	375	3 6	48
10290	23.10.1970	4 8½	0-6-0DH	375	3 6	48

TH - THOMAS HILL (ROTHERHAM) LTD, Kilnhurst, Yorks.

WORKS No.	DATE EX-WORKS	GAUGE AS BUILT ft.ins.	TYPE	HORSE POWER	DRIVING WH.DIAM. ft.ins.	NOTES	SEE PAGE
104C	6.10.1960	4 8½	4wDH	308	3 2	reb.of S 9618	181
105V	22. 1.1961	4 8½	4wDH	178	2 8	reb.of S	264
111C	22. 9.1961	4 8½	4wDH	176	2 6		58
129V	30. 7.1963	4 8½	4wDH	179	3 2		76
131V	29.11.1963≠	4 8½	4wDH	179	3 2		76
135C	31. 1.1964	4 8½	4wDH	308	3 2	reb.of S 9584	284/290/300
148V	6. 5.1965	4 8½	4wDH	175	3 2		30
199V	19. 8.1968	4 8½	4wDH	210	3 2		305
221V	16. 6.1970	4 8½	4wDH	275	3 6		48
222V	24. 7.1970	4 8½	4wDH	275	3 6		48
223V	31. 8.1970	4 8½	4wDH	275	3 6		48
224V	10. 9.1970	4 8½	4wDH	275	3 6		48
231V	15. 4.1971	4 8½	4wDH	275	3 6		50
232V	13. 5.1971	4 8½	4wDH	272	3 6		50
233V	10. 5.1971	4 8½	4wDH	272	3 6		50

≠ delivery date; prev. demonstration loco.

VF - VULCAN FOUNDRY LTD, Newton-le-Willows, Lancs.

WORKS No.	DATE EX-WORKS	GAUGE AS BUILT ft.ins.	TYPE	CYLS.(bore x stroke) ins.ins.	DRIVING WH.DIAM. ft.ins.	SEE PAGE
422	1858	4 8½	0-6-0ST	OC 16 x 24		52/80
5288	1945	4 8½	0-6-0ST	IC 18 x 26	4 3	43/281/290
5298	1945	4 8½	0-6-0ST	IC 18 x 26	4 3	43/281/291
5299	1945	4 8½	0-6-0ST	IC 18 x 26	4 3	120/259/264/289
5300	1945	4 8½	0-6-0ST	IC 18 x 26	4 3	120/259/264/289
5305	1945	4 8½	0-6-0ST	IC 18 x 26	4 3	92/267/294
5307	1945	4 8½	0-6-0ST	IC 18 x 26	4 3	214/267/294
5308	1945	4 8½	0-6-0ST	IC 18 x 26	4 3	192/264/295/301
5309	1945	4 8½	0-6-0ST	IC 18 x 26	4 3	192/264/295/342
D227	1956	4 8½	0-6-0DH (see also entry for EE)			94/197

WB - W. G. BAGNALL LTD, Stafford.

WORKS No.	DATE EX-WORKS	GAUGE AS BUILT ft.ins.	TYPE	CYLS.(bore x stroke) ins.ins.	DRIVING WH.DIAM. ft.ins.	SEE PAGE
1381	11.1891	3 0	0-4-0ST	OC 5½x 10	1 8	150
1516	7.1898	3 0	0-4-0ST	OC 6 x 9	1 8	331
1877	5.1911	2 6	0-4-0ST	OC 6 x 9	1 7	91
1917	1910	2 6	0-4-0T	OC 8½x 12	2 0½	91
2058	1917	3 0	0-4-0ST	OC 7 x 12	1 9½	71
2084	1918	3 0	0-4-0ST	OC 7 x 12	1 9½	71
2169	23. 2.1922	4 8½	0-6-0ST	OC 13 x 18	2 9¼	58
2664	1942	4 8½	0-4-0ST	OC 12 x 18	3 0½	170
2749	9.1944	4 8½	0-6-0ST	IC 18 x 26	4 3	300
2755	10.1944	4 8½	0-6-0ST	IC 18 x 26	4 3	112/287
2757	10.1944	4 8½	0-6-0ST	IC 18 x 26	4 3	112/287
2779	29. 6.1945	4 8½	0-6-0ST	IC 18 x 26	4 3	202/272/276/295/301
2898	1948	4 8½	0-4-0F	OC 18½x 18	3 0½	150
3020	1951	4 8½	0-6-0DE	480 h.p.	4 0	47/69
3021	15. 6.1952	4 8½	0-6-0DE	480 h.p.	4 0	47/69
3123	6.12.1957	4 8½	0-6-0DE	304 h.p.	3 4	285

NOTES

1.   <u>Armstrong Whitworth (Metal Industries) Ltd</u>, Jarrow.   No.1
S 9558/1953, taken in April 1965, was the last survivor of
a number of Sentinel locomotives purchased by Durham
companies in the mid-1950's.

2.   <u>Associated Portland Cement Manufacturers Ltd</u>, Eastgate.
TH 148V/1965 shunts hopper wagons under the loading plant
in October 1971.

3. Aycliffe Lime & Limestone Co Ltd. A Foden steam lorry, converted at Aycliffe into a "locomotive". August 1948.

4. Aycliffe Lime & Limestone Co Ltd. AYRESOME No.12, MW 1903/1916, an "altered 'P' class" loco, at Aycliffe in April 1957.

5.   Bearpark Coal & Coke Co Ltd, Bearpark. Between 1875 and 1890
a number of companies replaced hand-tramming of tubs along the
tops of beehive coke ovens by 3' 0" gauge locomotives, built
either by Black Hawthorn or Fowler (as here).

6.   Birtley Brick Co Ltd, Birtley. This company was one of the few
which introduced locomotive haulage in clay pits, with 2' 0"
gauge AE 2071/1933, purchased from Durham County Water Board.

7.   <u>Bolckow, Vaughan & Co Ltd</u>. 153 PATRIOT, reputedly begun by two BV
employees in 1914 and completed in 1920. At Bowburn Colliery in
1952.

8.   <u>John Bowes & Partners Ltd</u> : <u>Pontop & Jarrow Railway</u>. 9, allegedly
built by Coulthard in 1848 and rebuilt by RS in 1860 to 0-6-0ST.

9. <u>John Bowes & Partners Ltd</u> : <u>Pontop & Jarrow Railway.</u> No.7,
BH 304/1874, at Jarrow about 1898.

10. <u>John Bowes & Partners Ltd</u> : <u>Pontop & Jarrow Railway.</u> No.3,
BH 938/1888, used for main line work between Springwell Bank Foot
and Jarrow Staithes, at Jarrow about 1898.

11. <u>John Bowes & Partners Ltd</u> : <u>Bowes Railway</u>. No.9, SS 4051/1894, an ex-Barry Railway loco rebuilt as a pannier tank by the GWR - one of a number of second-hand locos bought in the 1930's.

12. <u>John Bowes & Partners Ltd</u>, Felling Colliery. FELLING No.1, CF 1203/1901 - one of the last of the handful of locomotives built by Chapman & Furneaux Ltd (successors to Black Hawthorn) between 1898 and 1901.

13.   <u>Central Electricity Generating Board</u>. Before the 1914-1918 War
there was considerable interest on Tyneside with electrification
(cf. NER and Harton Coal Co Ltd). No.3, at Dunston G.S., was
built by Dick, Kerr & Co Ltd in 1908.

14.   <u>Central Electricity Generating Board</u>. One of the early pioneers
of diesel locomotives was Armstrong Whitworth at their Scotswood
Works in Newcastle. One of the few survivors is AW D21/1933, at
Dunston in June 1972.

15. Coatham Stob Estates Ltd/Eaglescliffe Bricks Ltd, Eaglescliffe.
2' 6" gauge ZURIEL, WB 1917/1910, in October 1938.

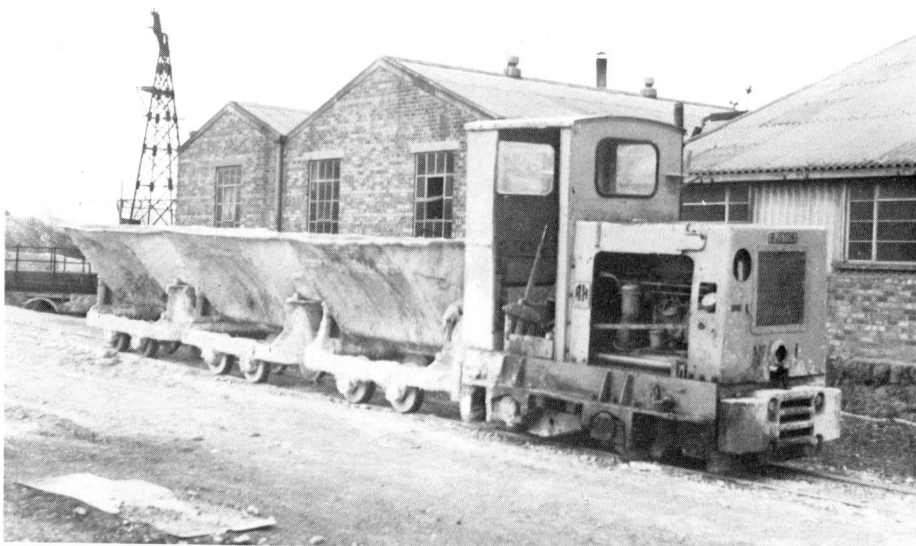

16. Chemical & Insulating Co Ltd, Darlington. This company has for
many years operated three different gauges, with three different
types of locomotive. One of the three diesels on the extensive
1' 8" gauge system is No.1, RH 375360/1955, taken in May 1973.

17.   Consett Iron Co Ltd.   A No.2, K 1844/1872, at Consett in 1935.

18.   Consett Iron Co Ltd.   A No.13,   NLE 249/1908, with water softener
apparatus, at Consett in 1935.

19. **Consett Iron Co Ltd**. A No.1, RSH 7027/1941, one of the last three 'A' class locomotives to be built, at Consett in June 1955.

20. **Consett Iron Co Ltd**. B No.24, AB 895/1901, at Consett in June 1955 - a Barclay loco built to Hawthorn Leslie design.

21.	**Consett Iron Co Ltd.**	52, HL 3474/1920, formerly B No.7, at
Allerdene Shop Pit on the Pelaw Main Railway,	February 1967
(note tank ladder).

22.	**Consett Iron Co Ltd.**	D 17, AB 1715/1920, at Consett in April 1953.

23.   Consett Iron Co Ltd. E No.13,   HL 2984/1913, at Derwenthaugh in 1953.

24.   Consett Iron Co Ltd. FYLDE,   P 1671/1924, one of four 3' 0" gauge
locomotives used at Butsfield Quarry, in June 1946.

25. <u>Darlington & Simpson Rolling Mills Ltd</u>, Darlington. RISE CARR, built in 1875 by Charles I'Anson & Co Ltd of Darlington.

26. <u>Dorman, Long & Co Ltd,</u> Parson Byers Quarry, Stanhope. HAWK, a four-coupled saddletank with outside valve gear, built by Hawthorn & Co Ltd of Leith about 1890, working at Parson Byers about 1922.

27. Dorman, Long & Co Ltd. ANGELA, AE 1793/1918, which came to Dean & Chapter Colliery, Ferryhill, from Burley Ironstone Quarry in Rutland, awaits scrap outside the Tursdale Central Workshops of NCB No.4 Area in August 1962.

28. Dorman, Long & Co Ltd. A Lambton Railway locomotive until 1914, H&C 72/1866 spent its last 25 years working the Sherburn Hill branch, first for Samuelsons and then for Dorman Long.

29.   Dorman Long (Steel) Ltd, Newfield Firebrick Works. P 916/1901, a Rl class locomotive, at Newfield in September 1958.

30.   Harton Coal Co Ltd : South Shields, Marsden & Whitburn Colliery Rly. Whitburn Colliery about 1900, with a former Blyth & Tyne Rly tender engine on a train for Harton Staithes, and 2, BH 504/1880, on a train in the original passenger station.

31.   **Harton Coal Co Ltd** : **Harton Railway**. This was the only colliery system to be electrified. 1, built by Siemens in 1907, crosses an ungated road with a train from Harton High Staithes to Westoe in March 1966.

32.   **Harton Coal Co Ltd** : **Harton Railway**. No.9, built by Allgemeine Elektricitaats Gesellschaft of Berlin, 1565/1913, stands at the Mowbray Road signal box, South Shields, in June 1964.

33. **R. & W. Hawthorn, Leslie & Co (Shipbuilders) Ltd**, Hebburn.
SANDOW, HL 2273/1893, an early example of the standard HL
crane tank design, at the firm's Hebburn Shipyard in June 1960.

34. **Horden Collieries Ltd.** Taken in August 1972, AB 1015/1904
spent most of its life at Shotton Colliery, and is now preserved.

35. <u>Hetton Coal Co Ltd</u> : <u>Hetton Railway</u>. One of George Stephenson's
locomotives of 1822, later rebuilt, working at Hetton about 1903.
It is now at the North of England Open-Air Museum, Beamish.

36. <u>Hetton Coal Co Ltd</u> : <u>Hetton Railway</u>. Copt Hill Engine House, with
the Warden Law Engine House chimney in the distance, in August 1959.

37. Holmside & South Moor Collieries Ltd. HOLMSIDE No.2, Chapman & Furneaux 1204/1901, at Morrison Busty Colliery, Annfield Plain, in 1953.

38. Holmside & South Moor Collieries Ltd. Craghead Bank Foot at Grange Villa (with set-rider climbing on to the set) in May 1957.

39.   Johnsons (Chopwell) Ltd.   71515, an ex-War Department 'Austerity'
locomotive, RSH 7169/1944, shunts at the NCB Opencast Executive's
Swalwell Disposal Point (operated by Johnsons) in May 1972.

40.   Johnsons (Chopwell) Ltd.   As in many other places, cheap second-hand
diesels from British Rail ousted steam.   Ex-BR 12088, built at Derby
in 1951, at Swalwell in September 1972.

41.   Lambton, Hetton & Joicey Collieries Ltd : Lambton Railway. For many years the main line work was handled by tender engines. 1, H&C 71/1866 stands at the coaling stage at the Philadelphia Sheds in 1952.

42.   Lambton, Hetton & Joicey Collieries Ltd : Lambton Railway.   20, RS 2260/1876, in full Philadelphia livery, stands outside the washing-out shed at Philadelphia in 1952.

43. Lambton, Hetton & Joicey Collieries Ltd : Lambton Railway. 21,
RS 2308/1876, shunts at Philadelphia in 1952, still carrying the
brass letters and numerals used by the Earl of Durham and Lambton
Collieries Ltd.

44. Lambton, Hetton & Joicey Collieries Ltd : Lambton Railway 24,
BH 832/1885, in the later Philadelphia livery of unlined black with
yellow lettering, stands at the Dorothea Pit, Philadelphia, in 1954.

45. <u>Lambton, Hetton & Joicey Collieries Ltd</u> : <u>Lambton Railway.</u> 27,
originally a 2-4-0 tender engine built RS 491/1846 for the York &
Newcastle Railway, underwent extensive alterations before becoming
the loco seen here at Philadelphia Sheds in February 1962.

46. <u>Lambton, Hetton & Joicey Collieries Ltd</u> : <u>Hetton Railway.</u> 37,
formerly Hetton Railway No.6, RWH 1430/1868, outside Hetton Shed
between the Wars.

47.   Lambton, Hetton & Joicey Collieries Ltd : Hetton Railway.   55,
K 3069/1887, one of the O-6-2T's later used on both railways for
main line work, crosses BR in Sunderland with a train from North
Moor to Lambton Staithes in 1957.

48.   Lambton, Hetton & Joicey Collieries Ltd : Lambton Railway. Using NCB
running powers over BR, 5, RS 3377/1909 passes Penshaw North signal
box with coal from Harraton Colliery to Sunderland in August 1964.

49.　Lambton, Hetton & Joicey Collieries Ltd : Beamish Railway. Locomotives from the Joicey Unit always remained separate. No.5 MAJOR, K 4294/1904, at Beamish in 1953.

50.　Lambton, Hetton & Joicey Collieries Ltd : Beamish Railway. A "rebuilding" which took many years and was never finished : STANLEY, RS 2014/1872, at Beamish Engine Works in March 1961.

51.   Londonderry Collieries Ltd. WYNYARD, AB 2165/1944, the last of
four similar locos owned by the firm, at Dawdon Colliery in April
1959.

52.   Mawson, Clark & Co Ltd, Dunston. FRED, HE 580/1893, with
driving wheels of only 2' 6" diameter.

53.   **North Bitchburn Coal Co Ltd**. CARBON, a rare photograph of a locomotive built by the Grange Iron Works, Belmont, near Durham.

54.   **River Wear Commissioners**, later Port of Sunderland Authority. 10, HC 221/1881.

55.   Northern Gas Board. One of the few RSH diesels - RSH 7899/1958,
       at the Redheugh Gas Works, Gateshead, in July 1959.

56.   Patons & Baldwins Ltd, Darlington. WB 2898/1948 (with a home-made
       chimney), one of only two fireless locomotives in Co. Durham,
       outside its shed in May 1967.

57.   Palmers Shipbuilding & Iron Co Ltd. No.12, HL 2135/1889 - the stan-
      dard early HL 0-4-0ST with 12"x18" cylinders (compare with photo No.81

58.   Palmers Shipbuilding & Iron Co Ltd. HL 2113/1888, the unusual 2-2-2CT
      built to Cross' Patent for Palmers.

59.　<u>Pelaw Main Collieries Ltd</u> : <u>Pelaw Main Railway</u>.　The only known photograph of a locomotive built by John Harris of Darlington - VICTORY, built (and photographed?) in 1863.

60.　<u>Pelaw Main Collieries Ltd</u> : <u>Pelaw Main Railway</u>.　BIRTLEY, built by Hawthorn & Co of Leith 221/1859,　as a 2-4-0WT for the Caledonian Railway.

61.   **Pelaw Main Collieries Ltd** : **Pelaw Main Railway**. Because of a narrow bridge, only locomotives with cut-down mountings could be used at Pelaw Main Staithes, Bill Quay. TYNE, AB 786/1896, at Bill Quay in 1963.

62.   **Pelaw Main Collieries Ltd** : **Pelaw Main Railway**. DERWENT, AB 970/1903, rebuilt by RSH in 1945, in the unlined green livery used in the 1950's, on the Team Valley section in April 1957.

63.   <u>Pelaw Main Collieries Ltd</u> : <u>Pelaw Main Railway</u>. This Railway too used many ex-main line locomotives.   One was MOSELEY, built at the Great Northern Railway's Doncaster Works in 1876.

64.   <u>Pelaw Main Collieries Ltd</u> : <u>Pelaw Main Railway</u>. An unusual choice for colliery work - ex-Metropolitan Railway 26A,   BP 772/1867, outside Eighton Banks Shed (see text for purpose of chain)

65.   <u>Pease & Partners Ltd</u>. 11, HL 2685/1906, at East Hetton Colliery, Kelloe, in June 1963.

66.   <u>Pease & Partners Ltd</u>. 16, RS 2325/1894, at East Hedley Hope Colliery in 1953.

67.   Priestman Collieries Ltd. RS 3376/1909, originally BETTY, later 7
of NCB No.6 Area, at Addison Colliery, Ryton, in May 1963.

68.   Priestman Collieries Ltd. RS 2879/1900, originally VICTORIA No.5,
later 2 of NCB No.6 Area, outside the shed at Victoria Garesfield
Colliery, Rowlands Gill.

69. <u>Priestman Collieries Ltd</u>. ASHINGTON, B 303/1883, rebuilt RS 2987/1900, at Lilley Drift, near Rowlands Gill, in 1953.

70. <u>Priestman Collieries Ltd</u>. ERNEST BURY, HL 3282/1917, at Norwood Coking Plant, Gateshead, in August 1962 - a standard HL 0-6-0ST with 14"x22" cylinders and 3' 6" wheels.

71.   Randolph Coke & Chemical Co Ltd. RSH 7159/1944 at the rear of
       the engine house at the top of the Randolph Incline, Evenwood,
       in August 1966.

72.   Ryhope Coal Co Ltd. Ex-LNER 1144 (J71 class), built at the NER
       Darlington Works in 1892, at Ryhope Colliery in 1954.

73. <u>Sir S.A. Sadler Ltd</u>. SILKSTONE, MW 341/1871, a much-travelled Manning Wardle 'M' class loco, at East Hedley Hope Colliery in 1953.

74. <u>Sir S.A. Sadler Ltd</u>. MW 569/1876, formerly named WHITWORTH and an 'O' class engine, at Malton Colliery, near Lanchester, in 1953.

75.   Seaham Harbour Dock Co Ltd. Ex-Londonderry Railway No.17, HW 33/1873,
      one of the few vertical-boilered locomotives in Co. Durham, stands
      amidst the chaldron wagons in May 1960.

76.   Seaham Harbour Dock Co Ltd. SEATON, begun at Seaham Engine Works as
      an 0-4-4T for the Londonderry Railway, but completed in 1901 as an
      0-6-0T, at Seaham in May 1957.

77.   Seaham Harbour Dock Co Ltd. SEAHAM, P 1052/1905, a Peckett 'B2' class loco, at Seaham in May 1960.

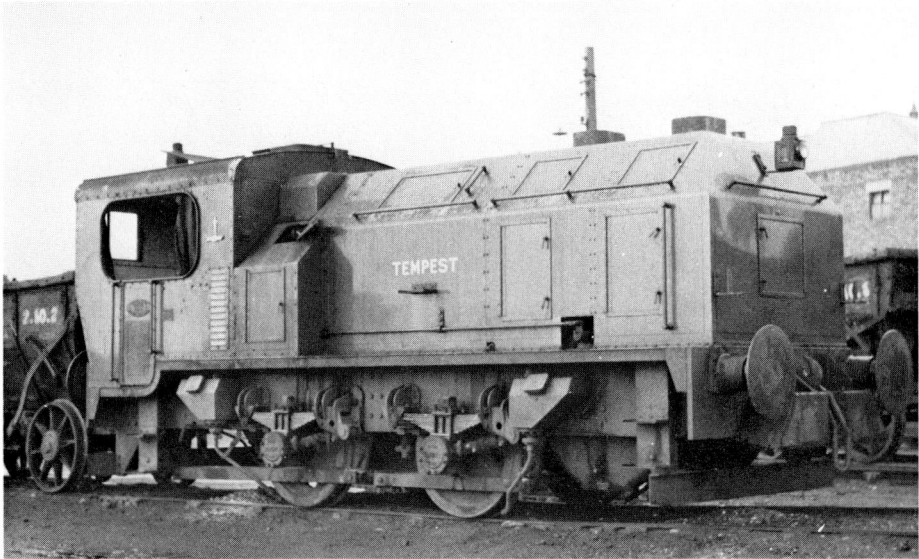

78.   Seaham Harbour Dock Co Ltd. The Dock Company was another firm to invest in Sentinel locomotives. 200hp S 9618/1957 in April 1957.

79. **Seaham Harbour Dock Co Ltd.**   25, RSH 7345/1947, one of the numerous second-hand locos purchased in the early 1960's, taken in July 1966, not long before the arrival of five new diesels.

80.   **Shell-Mex & B.P. Ltd**, Jarrow. No.16, DC 2164/1940, in May 1961.

81. <u>Smith, Patterson & Co Ltd</u>, Blaydon. JUBILEE, HL 3577/1923, the later standard HL 0-4-0ST with 12" cylinders (compare with photo No.57).

82. <u>South Derwent Coal Co Ltd</u>. SHIELD ROW, a 1914 rebuild by Lingford Gardiner, believed to be a Hudswell, Clarke & Rodgers loco.

83. <u>South Hetton Coal Co Ltd</u>. 1, BH 355/1875.

84. <u>South Hetton Coal Co Ltd</u>. 2, HAVERHILL, SS 2358/1873, a loco
originally built for the Cornwall Minerals Railway.

85.   South Hetton Coal Co Ltd.   No.6, rebuilt at South Hetton in 1909
        from a Metropolitan Railway 4-4-0T (compare photo No.64)

86.   South Hetton Coal Co Ltd.   No.7, Joicey 305/1883, another
        engine much rebuilt.

87. <u>South Hetton Coal Co Ltd</u>. No.8, later 68 of NCB No.2 Area, originally built RS 625/1848 as a 0-6-0 tender engine for LNWR, at South Hetton in 1949.

88. <u>South Hetton Coal Co Ltd</u>. No.9, SIR GEORGE, RS 624/1848, originally a sister loco to No.8, but rebuilt rather differently.

89.   Steetley Dolomite (Quarries) Ltd. No.15, AB 688/1891, rebuilt
by the makers in 1946, at Coxhoe in May 1957.

90.   Steetley Dolomite (Quarries) Ltd. HC 1735/1942, formerly
COXHOE No.4, working at Coxhoe in July 1961.

91. South Durham Steel & Iron Co Ltd, West Hartlepool. No.8,
HE 1108/1912, in August 1947. This firm owned nearly all the
Hunslet locomotives in Co. Durham in 1939.

92. Strakers & Love Ltd. HELMINGTON, RWH 1882/1882, rebuilt from
0-6-OST at Brancepeth in 1897, at Sunnybrow Colliery, Willington,
about 1905.

93. **Strakers & Love Ltd**. AE 1509/1907, formerly named WILLINGTON, at Brandon Colliery in August 1952.

94. **Strakers & Love Ltd**. JUPITER, MW 1880/1915, at Brandon Colliery in 1958.

95. <u>Strakers & Love Ltd</u>. HOWDEN DENE No.2, RS 4113/1937, at Brancepeth Coking Plant in June 1964.

96. <u>Strakers & Love Ltd</u>. All modern coking plants use electric locomotives to operate the coke car between the ovens and the quenching tower. HL 3859/1937 at Brancepeth Coking Plant, June 1964.

97.   **Tyne Improvment Commission**, later **Port of Tyne Authority**.
PEREYRA, MW 1042/1888, a Manning Wardle 'H' class loco,
at the South Pier Works, South Shields, in July 1933.

98.   **Washington Chemical Co Ltd**, later **Newalls Insulation & Chemical
Co Ltd**. One of the experimental HL designs of the 1920's –
No.2, HL 3584/1923, built to Durnell's Patent, at Washington in
October 1964.

99. Wallsend & Hebburn Coal Co Ltd. An earlier battery electric loco - No.2, EE 519/1921, on delivery to Hebburn Colliery.

100. Weardale Lead Co Ltd. A 2' 0" gauge battery-electric loco built by WR, at Redburn Mine, Rookhope, in May 1965 - a type of loco increasingly used underground in the expanding Weardale fluorspar industry.

101.   Weardale Steel, Coal & Coke Co Ltd. 4, formerly named WEARDALE,
        Joicey 210/1869, at Bolts Law on the Weatherhill & Rookhope Railway.

102.   Weardale Steel, Coal & Coke Co Ltd. 5, CHARLES ATTWOOD,
        GW 172/1863, at Tow Law Iron Works.

103.   Weardale Steel, Coal & Coke Co Ltd. 12, formerly named STAR, built at Tow Law Iron Works, and rebuilt at Tudhoe Colliery in 1909.

104.   Weardale Steel, Coal & Coke Co Ltd. 15, formerly named WOLSINGHAM, built at Tudhoe Iron Works in 1873, and rebuilt at Tudhoe Colliery in 1905.

105. <u>Weardale Steel, Coal & Coke Co Ltd</u>. 18, formerly named SUNDERLAND BRIDGE, RWH 1622/1874, at Thornley Colliery in 1949.

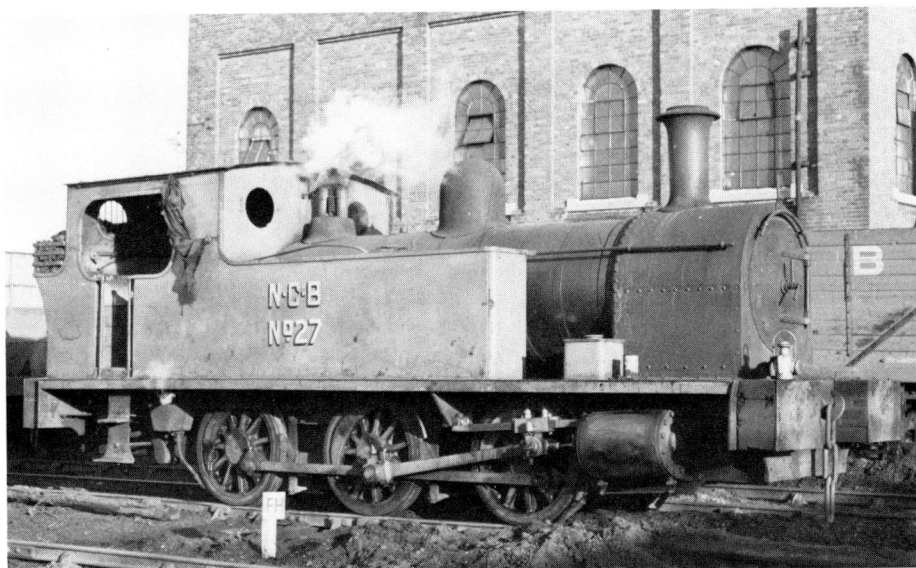

106. <u>Weardale Steel, Coal & Coke Co Ltd</u>. No.27, KS 3100/1918, at Thornley Colliery in 1958.

107. <u>Wearmouth Coal Co Ltd</u>. All six-coupled Wearmouth Coal Co engines were named after directors' children. BUNNY, AB 911/1901, at Wearmouth Colliery, Sunderland, in June 1952.

108. <u>Wearmouth Coal Co Ltd</u>. JEAN, HL 2769/1909, at Wearmouth Colliery in July 1956.

109. Wearmouth Coal Co Ltd. DIANA, RSH 7304/1946, at Wearmouth
Colliery in July 1956.

110. Wiggins Teape Ltd, Sunderland. One of the few 4' 8½" gauge petrol
locomotives to work in Co. Durham - H 965/1930 in June 1971.

111. **Sir Hedworth Williamsons Limeworks Ltd**, Sunderland. SYLVIA,
HC 1599/1927, outside the shed in September 1955.

112. **Woodland Collieries Co Ltd**. NELSON, K 1786/1871, believed to
be at Woodlands Junction **near** Evenwood.

113.   National Coal Board. In 1947 the NCB soon found a need for new
        locomotives, which came mainly from RSH and AB. 503 (No.5 Area),
        RSH 7605/1949, being coaled at Handen Hold Colliery loco shed in
        June 1965.

114.   National Coal Board. 501 (old No.5 Area), AB 2281/1950, at
        Langley Park Colliery in October 1963.

115.   National Coal Board : Lambton Railway. 63, RSH 7600/1949, at
        Philadelphia Sheds in August 1966 - a standard RSH 0-6-0ST with
        16"x24" cylinders.

116.   National Coal Board : S.S.M.& W.C.R. - RSH 7695/1951, fitted with
        Westinghouse brake, on a train of ex-Great North of Scotland
        Railway coaches at Westoe Lane Station, South Shields, in July 1952.

117.   <u>National Coal Board</u> : <u>Pelaw Main Railway</u>. 67, NCB-PELAW, P 2093/1947, so-called because it was on order at Vesting Day, at Ravensworth Ann Colliery, near Birtley, in October 1967.

118.   <u>National Coal Board</u> : <u>Harton Railway</u>. The NCB also purchased five new electric locos. 15, EE 2600/1959, with 3, built by Siemens in 1909, outside Westoe Shed in July 1970. Both locos are painted in the white livery then in use.

119.   National Coal Board. Under the NCB quite a number of locomotives
left their traditional haunts. Lambton Railway 48, HL 3544/1923,
at Seaham in July 1966, with the Seaham Incline on the left.

120.   National Coal Board. Ex-Pelaw Main Railway HENRY C. EMBLETON,
HL 3766/1930, at Derwenthaugh in February 1967.

121.   <u>National Coal Board</u>. Lambton Engine Works continued heavy steam loco work until 1969, including 0-6-0PT 6, completed for the Lambton Railway in 1958 from parts of locos 6, 7, 8 and 39, and taken here in May 1959.

122.   <u>National Coal Board</u>. Another Lambton Engine Works "loco" - XL5, converted from an Aveling-Barford dumper about 1955, at Seaham Wagon Works in May 1970.

123. <u>National Coal Board</u>. Another new feature was the introduction of narrow gauge diesel locos for surface work. RH 393979/1956 on the truncated remnant of the 2' 0" gauge line between Deaf Hill and Wingate Grange Collieries in June 1966.

124. <u>National Coal Board</u>. Double-ended 3' 6" gauge HC D1063/1957, in September 1957, on a man-riding train at Clockburn Drift (No.6 Area).

125. National Coal Board. The first Co. Durham NCB diesel
(4' 8½" gauge) came from the Ravenglass & Eskdale Railway - the
pioneer KS 4421/1929, here at Deaf Hill Colliery in June 1966.

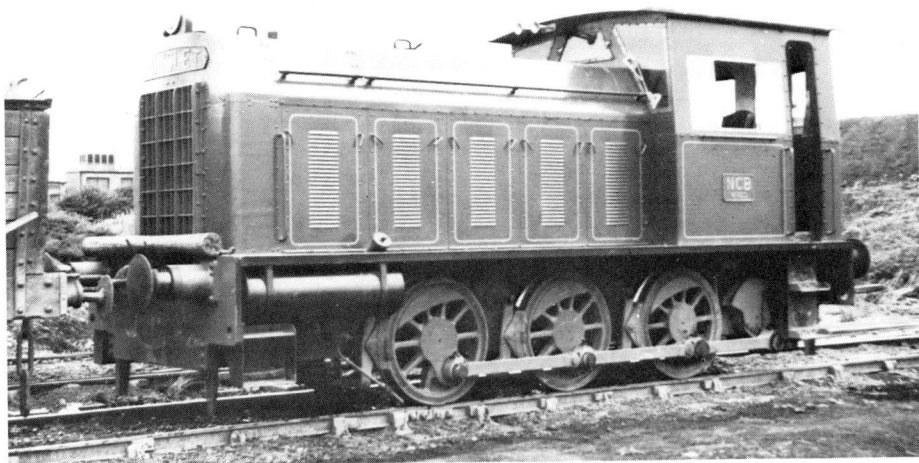

126. National Coal Board. The first large influx of diesels came in
No.4 Area, who, like the Consett Iron Co Ltd, adopted the standard
Hunslet design. 10D, HE 5304/1959, at Sherburn Hill Colliery in
September 1959.

127. National Coal Board : Pelaw Main Railway. The only small NCB diesels
in the late 1950's were "Planet" locos. 101, FH 3922/1959, leaves
Starrs at Wrekenton with a train for Springwell in October 1967.

128. National Coal Board. For very large diesels the NCB went to the
North British Company. BETA, NBL 27717/1957, at the end of the
branch from Brandon Pit House Colliery, at Meadowfield, in June 1965.

129.   National Coal Board : Pelaw Main Railway. Diesels, colliery closures and road transport made an increasing impact, especially on pre-1947 locos. 1308, NER Gateshead 27/1891, and 68, HL 2349/1896, await scrap at Ravensworth Ann Colliery, near Birtley, in June 1962.

130.   National Coal Board : Lambton Railway. Even so, five ex-Dorman Long locos were purchased in 1962-1963. 3, RSH 7687/1951, at Philadelphia Sheds in July 1963, the large RSH design with 18"x 24" cylinders.

131. National Coal Board. Later NCB policy has concentrated on standard HE and AB designs. No.157, HE 6676/1967, passes Seaburn Station on BR Sunderland-Gateshead line en route from Silksworth Colliery to Derwenthaugh in April 1972.

132. National Coal Board : Bowes Railway. No.504, HE 6615/1965, approaching Monkton with empties from Jarrow, April 1966.

133.   National Coal Board. AB 547/1967 at Vane Tempest Colliery,
         Seaham, in May 1970.

134.   National Coal Board. AB 585/1973 at South Hetton in October 1973.

135.   National Coal Board : Bowes Railway. Springwell Bank Foot Shed in
July 1963. Outside the shed are (left to right) RSH 7751/1953,
RSH 7604/1949,   HL 2545/1902 and HC 1255/1917.

136.   National Coal Board : Lambton Railway. The last week of steam
working in February 1969, with (left to right) D9504, BR Swindon
1964;   29, K 4263/1904 and 58, VF 5299/1945 outside the shed
during the lunch break.

137. **National Coal Board**. Yet, curiously, rope-haulage has outlived
the steam era which succeeded it. Hesledon Bank Head, on the line
from South Hetton to Seaham, with a full set coming over the kip,
in October 1973.

138. **National Coal Board : Bowes Railway**. Blackham's Hill Engine House,
with the ropes attached to the sets waiting to descend the Blackham's Hill East and West Inclines, in October 1973.

139.   National Coal Board. Locomotive haulage, both battery and
        electric, is extensively used underground. Two 64hp EE battery
        locos in tandem on the huge Murton/Eppleton/Hawthorn system at
        Eppleton Colliery in November 1969.

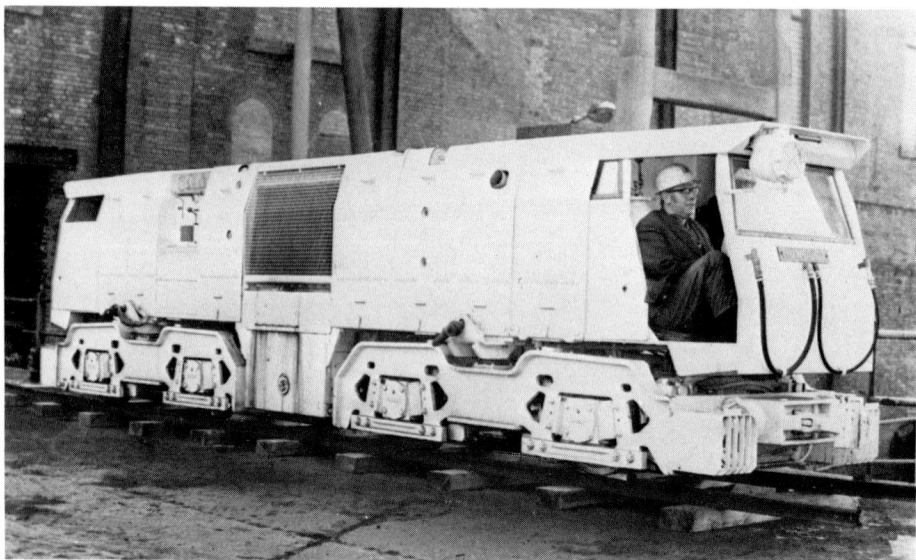

140.   National Coal Board. With collieries working over six miles out
        under the North Sea, new designs have been needed. 3' 0" gauge,
        HE 7099/1973, a 216hp 4w-4wDHF, at Easington Colliery in November
        1973.

141.   <u>National Coal Board</u>. Some early battery and diesel locomotives
        are now used in surface stockyards. 2' 6" gauge WN TJ 189/2,
        built in 1952, at Wearmouth Colliery, Sunderland, in October 1971.

142.   <u>National Coal Board</u>. The last regularly-working steam locomotive
        in industrial service in Co. Durham was 62, HE 3687/1948, here at
        South Hetton in October 1973.

143. <u>Preserved locomotives</u>. The main impetus for locomotive preservation in the county began with the North of England Open-Air Museum, Beamish. One of their first acquisitions was TWIZELL, RS 2730/1891, here at Morrison Busty Colliery in April 1966.

144. <u>Preserved locomotives</u>. The main centre has become the former Bowes Railway shed at Marley Hill, now leased to Tanfield Railway Company. Here the unidentified MALLEABLE No.5 and 21, RSH 7796/1954, await visitors on the shed's first open day in May 1973.